35 The colon 432
36 The apostrophe 434
37 Quotation marks 439
38 End punctuation 447
39 Other punctuation marks 449

PART VIII Mechanics 455

40 Abbreviations 457
41 Numbers 461
42 Italics 463
43 Spelling 466
44 The hyphen 475
45 Capitalization 479

PART IX Grammar Basics 485

46 Parts of speech 487
47 Sentence patterns 499
48 Subordinate word groups 508
49 Sentence types 519

PART X Researched Writing 523

50 Thinking like a researcher; gathering sources 525
51 Managing information; taking notes responsibly 543
52 Evaluating sources 552

WRITING MLA PAPERS 569

53 Supporting a thesis 570
54 Citing sources; avoiding plagiarism 577
55 Integrating sources 585
56 MLA documentation style 598
▶ MLA DIRECTORY: WORKS CITED MODELS 611
57 MLA manuscript format; sample research paper 662

WRITING APA PAPERS 674

58 Supporting a thesis 674
59 Citing sources; avoiding plagiarism 678
60 Integrating sources 683
61 APA documentation style 693
▶ APA DIRECTORY: REFERENCE LIST MODELS 702
62 APA manuscript format; sample research paper 735

WRITING *CHICAGO* PAPERS 754

63 *Chicago* papers 754
▶ *CHICAGO* DIRECTORY: NOTES AND BIBLIOGRAPHY MODELS 769

PART XI Writing in the Disciplines 805

64 Learning to write in a discipline 807
65 Approaching writing assignments in the disciplines 814

APPENDIX: A DOCUMENT DESIGN GALLERY 822 • GLOSSARY OF
USAGE 834 • ANSWERS TO EXERCISES 853 • INDEX Index–1

P9-DGF-168

tenth edition

The Bedford Handbook

Diana Hacker

Nancy Sommers
Harvard University

bedford/st.martin's
Macmillan Learning

Boston | New York

For Bedford/St. Martin's

Vice President, Editorial, Macmillan Learning Humanities: Edwin Hill
Editorial Director, English: Karen S. Henry
*Senior Publisher for Composition, Business and Technical Writing, Developmental
    Writing:* Leasa Burton
Executive Editor: Michelle M. Clark
Senior Editor: Mara Weible
Senior Media Editor: Barbara G. Flanagan
Senior Production Editor: Gregory Erb
Senior Media Producer: Allison Hart
Production Manager: Joe Ford
Marketing Manager: Emily Rowin
Assistant Editor: Stephanie Thomas
Copy Editor: Linda B. McLatchie
Indexer: Ellen Kuhl Repetto
Photo Editor: Martha Friedman
Permissions Manager: Kalina Ingham
Senior Art Director: Anna Palchik
Text Design: Claire Seng-Niemoeller
Cover Design: John Callahan
Composition: Cenveo Publisher Services
Printing and Binding: LSC Communications

Manufactured in the United States of America.

1   0   9   8   7   6
f   e   d   c   b   a

For information, write: Bedford/St. Martin's, 75 Arlington Street,
Boston, MA 02116   (617-399-4000)

ISBN 978-1-4576-8303-9 (Student Edition)
ISBN 978-1-319-09525-3 (Student Edition + LaunchPad Solo for Hacker Handbooks)
ISBN 978-1-319-11228-8 (Student Edition + *Writer's Help 2.0, Hacker Version*)
ISBN 978-1-319-07143-1 (Instructor's Annotated Edition)

Acknowledgments

Preface for Instructors

Dear Colleagues:

Welcome to the tenth edition of *The Bedford Handbook*. When you assign *The Bedford Handbook*, you send an important message to students: Writing is worth studying and practicing. And you give students the resource to answer their writing questions and to learn from the answers. College writing is high stakes, after all. Students learn to become nurses and teachers, psychologists and criminal justice professionals through writing. For academic success, no skill is more critical than effective writing.

As I worked on the new edition, I had the pleasure of finding answers to my own writing questions in a gracious and thoughtful group of editorial advisers (see p. xii), teachers of writing with many years of experience at two- and four-year schools and with many suggestions for smart ways to address the problems student writers have. I wanted each new feature in the tenth edition to address the specific challenges our students face as college writers—drafting and revising a thesis statement;

Nancy Sommers with student writer Michelle Nguyen

reading critically; locating, evaluating, and citing sources; making sentence-level decisions about grammar and punctuation — and to give students practice in building these core skills to become confident college writers.

As you page through the tenth edition, you'll discover many new features inspired by my thirty years as a writing teacher and by the expert advice of our talented team of reviewers, teachers who use *The Bedford Handbook* in their classrooms and who urged us to make the handbook even more practical, "more handy." We listened to our reviewers who asked for more hands-on practice around transferable skills, such as writing a thesis, making an argument, conducting research, and more. In the tenth edition, you'll find 20 new writing exercises to give students practice in developing core academic skills and applying handbook lessons; you'll also find more than 350 assignable exercises and activities in LaunchPad Solo for Hacker Handbooks and in *Writer's Help 2.0, Hacker Version*, the companion media. I am especially excited about our new "How to" boxes that offer students step-by-step, practical instruction on essential skills such as drafting an argumentative thesis, deciding when to paraphrase or summarize sources, and avoiding plagiarizing from the Web.

These new "How to" boxes offer students straightforward solutions to some of the biggest challenges they face as academic writers. My students report, for instance, that one of their major research challenges is locating authoritative sources beyond a quick Google search. Google is fast, but it's not efficient for academic research. So in the tenth edition, we respond with the new "How to go beyond a Google search" box (see p. 536) to give students a practical method for becoming more efficient and effective researchers.

Just as we want our students to go beyond an unreliable, superficial online search to conduct academic research, we want their writing instruction to be reliable and comprehensive. A search of free online materials might provide millions of results to students' questions about thesis or citation practices, but we know that these results are often more confusing than illuminating and that this method is neither an efficient nor an effective way to learn how to develop a thesis or cite sources.

In the tenth edition, you and your students will find new instruction on paraphrasing, guidelines for accurate citation of online sources (including **MLA's 2016 guidelines**), and step-by-step guidance on giving peer review comments. You'll also find practical "Writing guides" to help students write common assignments, such as an annotated bibliography, which many of you told me you assign. And you'll find new "Writer's choice" boxes, which offer a more rhetorical approach to sentence-level concerns. All the features in the new edition are designed to answer your students' questions and to help them solve their writing problems. By assigning the tenth edition of *The Bedford Handbook*, you guide students to read deeply, write clearly, and join ongoing research conversations as contributors of ideas.

I am eager to share this handbook with you, knowing that in the new edition you'll find everything you and your students trust and value about *The Bedford Handbook*.

Nancy Sommers

nancy_sommers@harvard.edu

What's new in this edition?

The best college writers succeed because they practice writing, reading, thinking, and researching on a regular basis. *The Bedford Handbook*, Tenth Edition, fosters a culture of practice and is our most practical handbook ever.

Step-by-step instruction will help your students apply writing advice in practical ways and transfer skills to different kinds of writing assignments. More than a dozen new **"How to"** boxes offer the straightforward help that instructors and students want.

HOW TO

Go beyond a Google search

A Google search is a quick way to gain an aerial view of your topic, but not an efficient way to find reliable, authoritative sources. Often a search on Google can return thousands of results, including outdated information and unreliable or biased sources. Good research involves going beyond the instant information available from a quick Google search to gain a deeper understanding of your topic and to establish your authority as a knowledgeable writer.

1. Try *CQ Researcher*. If you are searching for a good topic or seeking to understand the debate around a topic you've chosen, use *CQ Researcher*, available through most college libraries, to jump-start your research. These weekly reports focus on current controversies in government, law, environment, and education; provide pro/con arguments to help you identify positions in the debate; and introduce some key voices in the research conversation.

2. Try online databases available through your school library. Databases such as EBSCO, Academic Search Premier, and JSTOR, designed for academic researchers and vetted by information specialists, lead you to the ideas being reported and debated in the most important and influential publications. You will find articles, studies, and reports from scholarly journals and other widely respected sources written by the key writers and researchers debating your topic.

3. Try Google Scholar (scholar.google.com) for access to academic research. Add words such as debate, disagreements, proponents, or opponents to your search terms: opponents of government regulations of food choices. Another approach is to try using a journalist's questions—Who? When? Where? What? Why?—to refine an online search: Why favor government regulation of food choices?

► How to solve five common problems with thesis statements   22
► How to write helpful peer review comments   44
► How to improve your writing with an editing log   57
► How to draft an analytical thesis statement   109
► How to write a summary of a multimodal text   123
► How to draft a thesis statement for an argument   151
► How to enter a research conversation   532
► How to go beyond a Google search   536
► How to avoid plagiarizing from the Web   550
► How to be a responsible research writer   583
► How to answer the basic question "Who is the author?"   620
► How to cite a source reposted from another source   652
► How to cite course materials   658

More exercises and activities in a wide variety of formats give students more practice opportunities than ever before.

- The **print book** features more exercises in the new edition, including writing and grammar exercises that require rhetorical thinking, research exercises that ask students to practice paraphrasing and summarizing, and writing prompts that encourage students to apply handbook advice to their own writing.

- **LaunchPad Solo for Hacker Handbooks** and *Writer's Help 2.0, Hacker Version*—your two choices for companion media—include 300 exercises (most autoscored), LearningCurve adaptive quizzes, and writing prompts.

New "Writer's choice" boxes on grammar and style topics offer opportunities for students to practice critical thinking at the sentence level. A new **rhetorical approach to grammar coverage** makes this content more teachable by giving instructors flexibility—a way to individualize instruction for students who may need more than a conventional explanation of the rules.

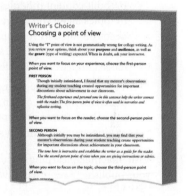

New emphasis on peer review allows students to practice the skills they need to collaborate in college writing environments and beyond.

- Thoroughly revised content in Chapter 2 illustrates best practices for peer review.

- "Writing practice" activities throughout the book ask students to collaborate, provide feedback, and reflect on feedback they've received.

The 2016 MLA guidelines inform all of our MLA coverage, and our revision ensures that you and your students have the most up-to-date advice and models and that your students have ample instruction for conducting responsible research. Two new sample research essays, one in MLA style and one in APA style, model proper formatting and effective writing from sources.

New advice for public speaking/oral presentation prepares students to speak confidently in academic settings and to look ahead to professional and everyday situations that call for oral communication. See page 166.

ForeWords for English makes customizing your handbook easy.

- Prebuilt content modules (12–16 pages each) on a variety of topics allow you to create the handbook that meets the needs of you and your students. Choose from modules on time management, CSE style, business writing, using sentence templates for academic writing, and more.

- You can also define your program and communicate your policies with brief, original, school-specific content such as goals of the writing program, location and hours of the writing center, common syllabus/assignments, and so on.

Visit macmillanlearning.com/forewords/composition or talk to your publisher's representative.

What hasn't changed?

- The handbook **covers a lot of ground**. Even Google can't give students the confidence that comes with a coherent reference that covers all the topics they need in a writing course. *The Bedford Handbook* supports students as they compose for different purposes and audiences and in a variety of genres, as they collaborate, revise and edit, conduct research, document sources, and format their writing.

- It's **easy to use, easy to understand**. The handbook's explanations are brief, accessible, and illustrated by examples. The book's many boxes, charts, checklists, and menus are designed to help users find what they need quickly.

- The handbook provides **authoritative, trustworthy instruction**. Most writing resources on the Web offer *information*, but they don't offer *instruction*. With the tenth edition of *The Bedford Handbook*, students have reference content that has been class-tested by hundreds of thousands of students and instructors.

- The handbook adoption includes the **service and support** you have come to expect from Bedford/St. Martin's. We provide professional resources, professional development workshops, training for digital tools, and quick, personal service when you need it.

Acknowledgments

I am grateful for the expertise, enthusiasm, and classroom experience that so many individuals brought to the tenth edition.

Reviewers

Nora Bacon, University of Nebraska; Garrison Bickerstaff, University of Georgia; Megan Boeshart, Texas State University; Brooke Bovee, Miami Dade College; Steve Brahlek, Palm Beach State College; Edward Coursey, Hillsborough Community College; Pamela Fletcher, St. Catherine University; Edward Glenn, Miami Dade College; Wanda Grimes, Volunteer State Community College; Kay Grossberg, Volunteer State Community College; David Holper, College of the Redwoods; Edmund Jones, Seton Hall University; Matthew Klauza, Palm Beach State College; Matthew Kretchmar, Denison University; Rebecca Mills, California State Polytechnic University; Luis Nazario, Pueblo Community College; Stephanie Noll, Texas State University; Susan North, University of Tennessee at Chattanooga; Annemarie Oldfield, Eastern New Mexico University; Tara O'Neill-Knasick, Hudson Valley Community College; Matthew Sagorski, Miami Dade College; James Suderman, Northwest Florida State College; Tom Treffinger, Greenville Technical College

Editorial advisers

I was thrilled to have the help of the following fellow teachers of writing in shaping a new edition that responds to students' needs, saves teachers time, and reflects current pedagogy.

Cynthia Chanin, Volunteer State Community College
Regina Dilgen, Palm Beach State College
Laura Ellis-Lai, Texas State University
Jan Geyer, Hudson Valley Community College
Shonette Grant, Northern Virginia Community College
Mickey Hall, Volunteer State Community College
Melody Hargraves, St. Johns River State College
Bill Leach, Florida Institute of Technology
Lanie Lundgrin, University of Tennessee at Chattanooga
Alexandra Mason, Miami Dade College
Loren Mitchell, University of Hawaii
Tiffany Mitchell, University of Tennessee at Chattanooga
Jeannine Morgan, St. Johns River State College
Lisa Shaw, Miami Dade College
Ross Wagner, Greenville Technical College
Nancy Wilson, Texas State University

Contributors

I thank the following fellow teachers for smart revisions of important content: Kimberli Huster, ESL specialist at Robert Morris University, updated the advice for multilingual writers, and Sara McCurry, instructor of English at Shasta College, coauthored the new edition of *Teaching with Hacker Handbooks* with Jonathan Cullick, professor of English at Northern Kentucky University. I also thank Robert Koch, director of the Center for Writing Excellence at the University of North Alabama, for drafting content for the new "Writer's choice" rhetorical grammar boxes.

Student contributors

Including sample student writing in each edition of the handbook and its media makes the resources useful for you and your students. I would like to thank these students for letting us adapt their work as models: Ned Bishop, Sophie Harba, Sam Jacobs, Michelle Nguyen, Emilia Sanchez, April Bo Wang, and Ren Yoshida.

Bedford/St. Martin's

A comprehensive handbook is a collaborative writing project, and it is my pleasure to acknowledge and thank the enormously talented Bedford/St. Martin's editorial team, whose focus on students informs each new feature of *The Bedford Handbook.* Edwin Hill, vice president for humanities editorial, and Leasa Burton, senior publisher for composition, offer their commitment to and deep knowledge of the field of composition and the ways in which it is changing. Karen Henry, editorial director for English, has helped shape the book's identity and has guided us with insights about how to continue to meet the needs of the college writer.

Michelle Clark, executive editor, is the editor every author dreams of having—a treasured friend and colleague and an endless source of creativity and clarity. Michelle combines wisdom with patience, imagination with practicality, and hard work with good cheer. Barbara Flanagan, senior media editor, brings unrivaled expertise in documentation—mastering the 2016 MLA update—and organizes our media content. Mara Weible, senior editor, brings to the tenth edition her teacher's sensibility;

I thank her for working with student writer April Wang on a new APA-style research essay. Thanks to Stephanie Thomas, assistant editor, for expertly managing the review and permissions processes and for developing *Teaching with Hacker Handbooks* and other key supplements. And many thanks to Allison Hart, senior media producer, for delivering engaging handbook tools for students in the digital age.

Practical advice from Bedford colleagues Emily Rowin, Joy Fisher Williams, Jimmy Fleming, Nick Carbone, Karita dos Santos, Brendan Baruth, and Harriet Wald—all of whom, like me, spend many hours on the road and in faculty offices—is always treasured. Many thanks to Gregory Erb, senior production editor, who keeps us on schedule and expertly manages the design and composition processes. And thanks to Linda McLatchie, copyeditor, for her thoroughness and attention to detail; to Claire Seng-Niemoeller, text designer, who crafted a clean and more accessible tenth edition of the book; and to John Callahan, designer, who has given the book a strikingly beautiful cover.

Last, but never least, I offer thanks to my own students who, over many years, have shaped my teaching and helped me understand their challenges in becoming college writers. Thanks to my friends and colleagues Suzanne Lane, Maxine Rodburg, Laura Saltz, and Kerry Walk for sustaining conversations about the teaching of writing. And thanks to my family: to Joshua Alper, an attentive reader of life and literature, for his steadfastness across the drafts; to my parents, Walter and Louise Sommers, who encouraged me to write and set me forth on a career of writing and teaching; to my extended family, Ron, Charles Mary, Alexander, Demian, Devin, Liz, Kate, Sam, Terry, Steve, and Yuval, for their good humor and good cheer; and to Rachel and Curran, Alexandra and Brian, witty and wise beyond measure, always generous with their instruction and inspiration in all things that matter. And to Lailah Dragonfly, my granddaughter, thanks for the joy and sweetness you bring to life.

Nancy Sommers

Contents

PREFACE FOR INSTRUCTORS v

Introduction: Why Good Habits Matter 1
Becoming a college writer: Choose topics you care about 2

PART I The Writing Process 3
ONLINE ACTIVITIES 4

1 Exploring, planning, and drafting 5
  a Assessing the writing situation 5
  b Exploring your subject 17
  c Drafting and revising a working thesis 19
  How to solve five common problems with thesis statements 22
  d Drafting a plan 25
  e Drafting an introduction 28
  f Drafting the body 31
  g Drafting a conclusion 33
  h Managing your files 37

2 Revising, editing, and reflecting 38
  a Seeing revision as a social process 38
  b Using peer review; revising with comments 39
  Becoming a college writer: Form a community of readers around you 40
  c Using peer review; giving constructive comments 41
  How to write helpful peer review comments 44
  d Highlights of one student's peer review process 46
  e Approaching global revision in cycles 49
  f Revising and editing sentences 55
  g Proofreading the final manuscript 56
  How to improve your writing with an editing log 57
  h Sample student revision: Literacy narrative 58

i   Preparing a portfolio; reflecting on your writing   62
   Writing guide: How to write a literacy narrative   63
   Writing guide: How to write a reflective letter   70

3   Building effective paragraphs   72
   a   Focusing on a main point   72
   b   Developing the main point   75
   c   Choosing a suitable pattern of organization   76
   d   Making paragraphs coherent   84
   e   Adjusting paragraph length   91

PART II   Academic Reading and Writing   93
   ONLINE ACTIVITIES   94

4   Reading and writing critically   95
   a   Reading actively   95
   Becoming a college writer: Engage with the texts you read   96
   b   Outlining a text to identify main ideas   102
   c   Summarizing to deepen your understanding   104
   d   Analyzing to demonstrate your critical reading   106
   How to draft an analytical thesis statement   109
   Writing guide: How to write an analytical essay   110
   e   Sample student writing: Analysis of an article   112

5   Reading and writing about multimodal texts   115
   a   Reading actively   115
   b   Outlining to identify main ideas   120
   c   Summarizing to deepen your understanding   121
   How to write a summary of a multimodal text   123
   d   Analyzing to demonstrate your critical reading   124
   e   Sample student writing: Analysis of an advertisement   126

6 Reading and writing arguments 130

  a Distinguishing between reasonable and fallacious argumentative tactics 131

    Becoming a college writer: Consider counterarguments 132

  b Distinguishing between legitimate and unfair emotional appeals 139

  c Judging how fairly a writer handles opposing views 143

  d Identifying your purpose and context 146

  e Viewing your audience as a panel of jurors 147

  f Establishing credibility and stating your position 149

  g Backing up your thesis with persuasive lines of argument 150

    How to draft a thesis statement for an argument 151

  h Supporting your claims with specific evidence 152

  i Anticipating objections; countering opposing arguments 155

  j Building common ground 157

  k Sample student writing: Argument 157

    Writing guide: How to write an argument essay 164

  l Remixing a written argument for an oral presentation 166

7 Reading and writing about literature 167

  a Reading actively 167

  b Forming an interpretation 168

  c Drafting a working thesis 172

  d Using evidence from the text; avoiding plot summary 175

  e Observing the conventions of literature papers 178

  f Integrating quotations from the text 179

  g Documenting secondary sources and avoiding plagiarism 183

  h Sample student writing: Literary analysis 187

PART III Clear Sentences 191
ONLINE ACTIVITIES 192

8 Prefer active verbs. 193
  a Active versus passive verbs 194
  b Active versus *be* verbs 194
    Writer's choice: Using the active or the passive voice 195
  c Subject that names the actor 196

9 Balance parallel ideas. 198
  a Parallel ideas in a series 199
  b Parallel ideas presented as pairs 200
  c Repetition of function words 202

10 Add needed words. 204
  a In compound structures 204
  b *that* 205
  c In comparisons 206
  d *a, an,* and *the* 207

11 Untangle mixed constructions. 208
  a Mixed grammar 208
  b Illogical connections 210
  c *is when, is where,* and *reason . . . is because* 211

12 Repair misplaced and dangling modifiers. 212
  a Limiting modifiers 212
  b Misplaced phrases and clauses 213
  c Awkwardly placed modifiers 214
  d Split infinitives 215
  e Dangling modifiers 216

13 Eliminate distracting shifts. 220
  a Point of view (person, number) 220
    Writer's choice: Choosing a point of view 221
  b Verb tense 223
  c Verb mood, voice 225
  d Indirect to direct questions or quotations 226

14 **Emphasize key ideas.** 228

   a Coordination and subordination 228
   b Choppy sentences 230
      Writer's choice: Positioning major and minor ideas 231
   c Ineffective or excessive coordination 236
   d Ineffective subordination 238
   e Excessive subordination 239
   f Other techniques 240

15 **Provide some variety.** 242

   a Sentence openings 242
      Writer's choice: Strengthening with variety 244
   b Sentence structures 245
   c Inverted order 245
   d Question 246

PART IV Word Choice 249
      ONLINE ACTIVITIES 250

16 **Tighten wordy sentences.** 251

   a Redundancies 251
   b Unnecessary repetition 251
   c Empty or inflated phrases 252
   d Simplifying the structure 253
   e Reducing clauses to phrases, phrases to single
      words 254

17 **Choose appropriate language.** 256

   a Jargon 256
      Writer's choice: Using discipline-specific terms 257
   b Pretentious language, euphemisms,
      "doublespeak" 258
   c Obsolete and invented words 260
   d Slang, regional expressions, nonstandard
      English 261
   e Levels of formality 262

f Sexist language   264
g Offensive language   267

18 Find the exact words.   268

a Connotations   269
b Specific, concrete nouns   270
c Misused words   270
d Standard idioms   271
e Clichés   273
f Figures of speech   274

PART V   **Grammatical Sentences**   277
ONLINE ACTIVITIES   278

19 Repair sentence fragments.   279

a Subordinate clauses   281
b Phrases   283
c Other fragmented word groups   284
d Acceptable fragments   285

20 Revise run-on sentences.   287

a Revision with coordinating conjunction   290
   Writer's choice: Clustering ideas in meaningful ways   291
b Revision with semicolon, colon, or dash   292
c Revision by separating sentences   293
d Revision by restructuring   294

21 Make subjects and verbs agree.   297

a Standard subject-verb combinations   297
b Words between subject and verb   297
c Subjects joined with *and*   300
d Subjects joined with *or, nor, either . . . or,* or *neither . . . nor*   301
e Indefinite pronouns   302
f Collective nouns   303
g Subject following verb   304
h Subject, not subject complement   305
i *who, which,* and *that*   306

j Words with plural form, singular meaning 307
k Titles of works, company names, words mentioned as words, gerund phrases 307

22 Make pronouns and antecedents agree. 309

a Singular with singular, plural with plural (indefinite pronouns, generic nouns) 310
b Collective nouns 312
c Antecedents joined with *and* 312
d Antecedents joined with *or, nor, either . . . or*, or *neither . . . nor* 314

23 Make pronoun references clear. 315

a Ambiguous or remote reference 316
b Broad reference of *this, that, which*, and *it* 316
c Implied antecedents 317
d Indefinite use of *they, it*, and *you* 318
e *who* for persons, *which* or *that* for things 319

24 Distinguish between pronouns such as *I* and *me*. 321

a Subjective case for subjects and subject complements 322
b Objective case for objects 322
c Appositives 323
d Pronoun following *than* or *as* 324
e *we* or *us* before a noun 324
f Subjects and objects of infinitives 324
g Pronoun modifying a gerund 325

25 Distinguish between *who* and *whom*. 328

a In subordinate clauses 328
b In questions 330
c As subjects or objects of infinitives 330

26 Choose adjectives and adverbs with care. 332

a Adjectives to modify nouns 332
b Adverbs to modify verbs, adjectives, and other adverbs 334

c *good* and *well*, *bad* and *badly*   335
d Comparatives and superlatives   336
e Double negatives   338

27 Choose appropriate verb forms, tenses, and moods in Standard English.   340

a Irregular verbs   340
b *lie* and *lay*   344
c *-s* (or *-es*) endings   345
d *-ed* endings   348
e Omitted verbs   350
f Verb tense   351
g Subjunctive mood   356

PART VI   Multilingual Writers and ESL Challenges   359

ONLINE ACTIVITIES   360

28 Verbs   361

a Appropriate form and tense   362
b Passive voice   365
c Base form after a modal   368
d Negative verb forms   371
e Verbs in conditional sentences   372
f Verbs followed by gerunds or infinitives   375

29 Articles (*a*, *an*, *the*)   378

a Articles and other noun markers   378
b When to use *the*   380
c When to use *a* or *an*   384
d When not to use *a* or *an*   384
e No articles with general nouns   386
f Articles with proper nouns   387

30 Sentence structure   389

a Linking verb between a subject and its complement   390
b A subject in every sentence   390

   c Repeated nouns or pronouns with the same grammatical function 391

   d Repeated subjects, objects, adverbs in adjective clauses 392

   e Mixed constructions with *although* or *because*   394

   f Placement of adverbs 395

   g Present participles and past participles 396

   h Order of cumulative adjectives 397

31 Prepositions and idiomatic expressions 399

   a Prepositions showing time and place 399

   b Noun (including -*ing* form) after a preposition   400

   c Common adjective + preposition combinations   401

   d Common verb + preposition combinations   402

PART VII   Punctuation 405

      ONLINE ACTIVITIES 406

32 The comma 407

   a Independent clauses joined with *and*, *but*, etc.   407

   b Introductory clauses or phrases 408

   c Items in a series   410

   d Coordinate adjectives   411

   e Nonrestrictive elements   413

   f Transitions, parenthetical expressions, absolute phrases, contrasts 417

   g Direct address, *yes* and *no*, interrogative tags, interjections 419

   h *he said* etc.   419

   i Dates, addresses, titles, numbers   420

33 Unnecessary commas 422

   a Between two words, phrases, or subordinate clauses 422

   b Between a verb and its subject or object   423

   c Before the first or after the last item in a series   423

   d Between cumulative adjectives, an adjective and a noun, or an adverb and an adjective   424

e Before and after restrictive elements 424
f Before essential concluding adverbial elements 425
g After a phrase beginning an inverted sentence 425
h Other misuses 426

34 The semicolon 428

a Independent clauses not joined with a coordinating conjunction 428
b Independent clauses linked with a transitional expression 428
c Series containing internal punctuation 430
d Misuses 430

35 The colon 432

a Before a list, an appositive, a quotation, or a summary 432
b Conventional uses 433
c Misuses 433

36 The apostrophe 434

a Possessive nouns 434
b Possessive indefinite pronouns 436
c Contractions 436
d Not for plural numbers, letters, abbreviations, words as words 436
e Misuses 438

37 Quotation marks 439

a Direct quotations 439
b Quotation within a quotation 441
c Titles of short works 441
d Words as words 442
e With other punctuation marks 442
f Misuses 445

38 End punctuation 447

a The period 447
b The question mark 448
c The exclamation point 448

39 Other punctuation marks 449
  a Dash 449
  b Parentheses 450
  c Brackets 451
  d Ellipsis mark 452
  e Slash 453

PART VIII Mechanics 455
  ONLINE ACTIVITIES 456

40 Abbreviations 457
  a Titles with proper names 457
  b Familiar abbreviations 457
  c Conventional abbreviations 458
  d Units of measurement 458
  e Latin abbreviations 459
  f Plural of abbreviations 459
  g Misuses 460

41 Numbers 461
  a Spelling out 461
  b Using numerals 462

42 Italics 463
  a Titles of works 463
  b Names of ships, spacecraft, and aircraft 464
  c Foreign words 464
  d Words as words, letters as letters, and numbers as numbers 465

43 Spelling 466
  a Spelling rules 466
  b The dictionary 468
  c Words that sound alike 472
  d Commonly misspelled words 473

44 The hyphen 475
  a Compound words 475

b Hyphenated adjectives   476
c Fractions and compound numbers   476
d With certain prefixes and suffixes   477
e To avoid ambiguity or to separate awkward double or triple letters   477
f Word division   477

45 Capitalization   479

a Proper versus common nouns   479
b Titles with proper names   480
c Titles and subtitles of works   481
d First word of a sentence   481
e First word of a quoted sentence   482
f First word after a colon   482

PART IX   Grammar Basics   485
ONLINE ACTIVITIES   486

46 Parts of speech   487

a Nouns   487
b Pronouns   488
c Verbs   491
d Adjectives   493
e Adverbs   494
f Prepositions   496
g Conjunctions   497
h Interjections   498

47 Sentence patterns   499

a Subjects   499
b Verbs, objects, and complements   502
c Pattern variations   506

48 Subordinate word groups   508

a Prepositional phrases   508
b Verbal phrases   510
c Appositive phrases   514

d Absolute phrases 514
e Subordinate clauses 514
Writer's choice: Building credibility with appositives 515

49 Sentence types 519
a Sentence structures 520
b Sentence purposes 522

PART X Researched Writing 523
ONLINE ACTIVITIES 524

50 Thinking like a researcher; gathering sources 525
a Managing the project 525
Becoming a college writer: Join a research conversation 526
b Posing questions worth exploring 528
How to enter a research conversation 532
c Mapping out a search strategy 533
d Searching efficiently; mastering a few shortcuts 534
How to go beyond a Google search 536
e Conducting field research, if appropriate 540
f Writing a research proposal 542

51 Managing information; taking notes responsibly 543
a Maintaining a working bibliography 543
b Keeping track of source materials 544
c Avoiding unintentional plagiarism 544
How to avoid plagiarizing from the Web 550

52 Evaluating sources 552
a Thinking about how sources might contribute to your writing 553
b Selecting sources worth your time and attention 554

c Selecting appropriate versions of online sources 557
d Reading with an open mind and a critical eye 558
e Assessing Web sources with care 561
f Constructing an annotated bibliography 565
Writing guide: How to write an annotated bibliography 567

WRITING MLA PAPERS   569

53 Supporting a thesis 570
a Forming a working thesis 570
b Organizing your ideas 572
c Using sources to inform and support your argument 572
d Drafting an introduction for your thesis 575
e Drafting the paper in an appropriate voice 576

54 Citing sources; avoiding plagiarism 577
a Understanding how the MLA system works 578
b Avoiding plagiarism when quoting, summarizing, and paraphrasing sources 579
How to be a responsible research writer 583
Becoming a college writer: Provide context for sources 584

55 Integrating sources 585
a Summarizing and paraphrasing effectively 585
b Using quotations effectively 587
c Using signal phrases to integrate sources 590
d Synthesizing sources 594

56 MLA documentation style 598
a MLA in-text citations 599
b MLA list of works cited 613
How to answer the basic question "Who is the author?" 620
How to cite a source reposted from another source 652

How to cite course materials 658

   c MLA information notes (optional) 661

57 MLA manuscript format; sample research paper 662

   a MLA manuscript format 662

   b Sample MLA research paper 665

WRITING APA PAPERS 674

58 Supporting a thesis 674

   a Forming a working thesis 675

   b Organizing your ideas 675

   c Using sources to inform and support your argument 676

59 Citing sources; avoiding plagiarism 678

   a Understanding how the APA system works 679

   b Understanding what plagiarism is 680

   c Using quotation marks around borrowed language 680

   d Putting summaries and paraphrases in your own words 681

60 Integrating sources 683

   a Summarizing and paraphrasing effectively 684

   b Using quotations appropriately 685

   c Using signal phrases to integrate sources 687

   d Synthesizing sources 691

61 APA documentation style 693

   a APA in-text citations 695

   b APA list of references 703

62 APA manuscript format; sample research paper 735

   a APA manuscript format 735

   b Sample APA research paper 740

WRITING *CHICAGO* PAPERS 754

63 *Chicago* papers 754
  a Supporting a thesis 755
  b Citing sources; avoiding plagiarism 758
  c Integrating sources 762
  d Documenting sources 768
  e Manuscript format 794
  f Sample *Chicago*-style research paper (excerpt) 797

PART XI Writing in the Disciplines 805
  ONLINE ACTIVITIES 806

64 Learning to write in a discipline 807
  a Finding commonalities across disciplines 807
  b Recognizing the questions that writers in a discipline ask 808
  c Understanding the kinds of evidence that writers in a discipline use 810
  d Becoming familiar with a discipline's language conventions 812
  e Using a discipline's preferred citation style 812

65 Approaching writing assignments in the disciplines 814
  a Writing in psychology 814
  b Writing in business 816
  c Writing in biology 818
  d Writing in nursing 820

APPENDIX: A DOCUMENT DESIGN GALLERY 822
GLOSSARY OF USAGE 834
ANSWERS TO EXERCISES 853
INDEX Index–1

Why good habits matter

College offers many opportunities to learn from the process of writing and revising. As you write, you will use evidence to support your ideas, develop your ability to think carefully, and read and respond to what others have written. In a sociology class, you might write a field report; in a nursing class, a case study; and in a literature class, a critical analysis. By writing in these classes, you contribute your ideas and join writers who share interests, ideas, and ways of communicating with one another.

Developing certain approaches to academic work, often called habits of mind—curiosity, engagement, responsibility, and reflection—will help you write successfully in all of your college courses.

Be curious. What issues intrigue you? What questions need to be explored? Writing is more rewarding when you explore questions you don't have answers to.

Be engaged. Writing is a social activity that brings you into conversations with scholars, instructors, classmates, and others. Writing drafts provides opportunities to request feedback from readers—readers who will help shape your work in progress.

Be responsible. Engaging with the ideas of other writers requires responsibility—to represent their ideas fairly and to acknowledge their contributions to your work.

Be reflective. By examining your decisions, successes, and challenges, you'll be able to figure out what's working and what needs more work and to transfer skills from one writing assignment to the next.

Another good habit, of course, is consulting your *Bedford Handbook* whenever you have a question about writing—whatever the writing assignment.

Becoming a College Writer

curiosity   engagement   responsibility   reflection

Choose topics you care about

"Make connections between yourself and what you are learning. Care about what you are learning, and care about how you are learning." —**Shaye Heyman**, student, University of New Mexico

College writing can seem intimidating, especially when you first try to grasp how expectations for college writing differ from those for high school writing. Something more and something different are being asked of you, but what?

One way to approach each college writing assignment, as Shaye Heyman suggests, is to make the effort to find personal connections with what you are learning. Writing about a topic you care about enables you to write with more authority, confidence, and success. Even when you're not free to choose the topic, you can choose the angle by thinking, "What's at stake here for me (or my family, my community, my school)?"

- Remember a time when something you said or wrote had power or really mattered. What do you think made your words so powerful? Why?

ANDREW RICH/GETTY IMAGES

MORE
Choosing subjects, 1a
Understanding an assignment, page 11
Exploring subjects, 1b

2

The Writing Process

1 Exploring, planning, and drafting 5

2 Revising, editing, and reflecting 38
 Student writing: Literacy narrative 59
 Writing guide: How to write a literacy narrative 63
 Student writing: Reflective letter 66
 Writing guide: How to write a reflective letter 70

3 Building effective paragraphs 72

The Writing Process

ONLINE ACTIVITIES:

 **Writer's Help 2.0**
macmillan learning

writershelp.com/hacker

 **LaunchPad Solo**
macmillan learning

macmillanhighered.com/
launchpadsolo/hacker

Exploring, planning, and drafting	5 Writing practice activities 4 Exercises
Revising, editing, and reflecting	5 Writing practice activities 2 Exercises 3 Sample student papers
Building effective paragraphs	3 Writing practice activities 3 Exercises 3 LearningCurve activities

1 Exploring, planning, and drafting

Writing is a process of figuring out what you think, not a matter of recording already developed thoughts. Since it's not possible to think about everything all at once, most experienced writers handle a piece of writing in stages. You will generally move from planning to drafting to revising, but as your ideas develop, you will find yourself circling back and returning to earlier stages.

Before composing a first draft, spend some time generating ideas. Mull over your subject while listening to music, taking a walk, or driving to work; or jot down inspirations or explore your questions with a willing listener. Consider these questions: What do you find puzzling, striking, or interesting about your subject? What would you like to know more about? Be curious and open to new ideas and different points of view. Explore questions you don't have answers to.

1a Assess the writing situation.

Begin by taking a look at your writing situation. The key elements of a writing situation include the following:

- subject
- purpose
- audience
- genre
- sources of information
- requirements (length, document design, reviewers, deadlines)

It is likely that you will make final decisions about all of these matters later in the writing process—after a first draft, for example—but you can save yourself time by thinking about as many of them as possible in advance. For a quick checklist, see the following chart.

Checklist for assessing the writing situation

Subject

- Has the subject (or a range of possible subjects) been assigned to you, or are you free to choose your own?
- What interests you about your subject? What questions would you like to explore?
- Why is your subject worth writing about? How might readers benefit?
- Do you need to narrow your subject (because of length restrictions, for instance)?

Purpose and audience

- Why are you writing: To inform readers? To persuade them? To call them to action? To offer an interpretation of a text?
- Who are your readers? How well informed are they about the subject? What do you want them to learn?
- How interested and attentive are your readers likely to be? Will they resist any of your ideas? What possible objections will you need to anticipate and counter?
- What is your relationship to your readers: Student to instructor? Citizen to citizen? Expert to novice? Employee to supervisor?

Genre

- What genre (type of writing) does your assignment require: A report? A proposal? An analysis of data? An essay?
- If the genre is not assigned, what genre is appropriate for your subject, purpose, and audience?

CHECKLIST FOR ASSESSING THE WRITING SITUATION *(cont.)*

- What are the expectations and conventions of your assigned genre? For instance, what type of evidence is typically used in the genre?
- Does the genre require a specific design format or method of organization?
- Does the genre require or benefit from visuals, such as photos, drawings, or graphs?

Sources of information

- Where will your information come from: Reading? Research? Direct observation? Interviews? Questionnaires?
- What type of evidence suits your subject, purpose, audience, and genre?
- What documentation style is required: MLA? APA? *Chicago*?

Length and document design

- Do you have any length specifications? If not, what length seems appropriate, given your subject, purpose, audience, and genre?
- Is a particular document format or design required? If so, do you have guidelines to follow or examples to consult?

Deadlines

- What are your deadlines? How much time will you need to allow for the various stages of writing, including proofreading and printing or posting the final draft?

Academic English

What counts as good writing varies from culture to culture and even among groups within cultures. In some situations, you will need to become familiar with the writing styles — such as direct or indirect, personal or impersonal, plain or embellished — that are valued by the culture or discipline for which you are writing.

Subject

Frequently your subject will be given to you. In a psychology class, for example, you might be asked to explain Bruno Bettelheim's Freudian analysis of fairy tales. In a composition course, assignments often ask you to analyze texts and evaluate arguments. In the business world, you may be assigned to draft a marketing plan. When you are free to choose your own subject, let your own curiosity focus your choice. Make connections between yourself and what you are learning. If you are studying television, radio, and the Internet in a communications course, for example, you might ask yourself which of these subjects interests you most. Perhaps you want to learn more about the role streaming video can play in activism and social change. Look through your readings and class notes to see if you can identify questions you'd like to explore further in an essay.

If your interest in a subject stems from your personal experience, you will want to ask what it is about your experience that would interest your audience and why. For example, if you have volunteered at a homeless shelter, you might have spent some time talking to homeless children and learning about their needs. Perhaps you can use your experience to broaden your readers' understanding of the issues, to persuade an organization to fund an after-school program for homeless children, or to propose changes in legislation.

> **MORE HELP**
>
> Effective research writers often start by asking a question.
>
> ► Posing questions for research: 50b

Whether or not you choose your own subject, it's important to be aware of the expectations of each writing situation. The chart on page 11 suggests ways to interpret assignments.

Purpose

Your purpose, or reason for writing, will often be dictated by your writing situation. Perhaps you have been asked to draft a proposal requesting funding for a student organization, to report the results of a psychology experiment, or to write for the school newspaper about the controversy surrounding genetically modified foods. Even though your overall purpose may be fairly obvious in such situations, a closer look at the assignment can help you make some necessary decisions. How detailed should the proposal be? How technical does your psychology professor expect your report to be? Do you want to inform students about the controversy surrounding genetically modified foods or to change their attitudes toward it?

In many writing situations, part of your challenge will be discovering a purpose. Asking yourself why readers should care about what you are saying can help you decide what your purpose might be. Perhaps your subject is magnet schools — schools that draw students from different neighborhoods because of features such as advanced science classes or a concentration on the arts. If you have discussed magnet schools in class, a description of how these schools work probably will not interest you or your readers. But maybe you have discovered that your county's magnet schools are not promoting diversity as had been planned, and you want to call your readers to action.

Although no precise guidelines will lead you to a purpose, you can begin by asking, "Why am I writing?" and "What is my goal?" Identify which one or more of the following aims you hope to accomplish.

PURPOSES FOR WRITING

to inform	to evaluate
to persuade	to recommend
to entertain	to request
to call readers to action	to propose
to change attitudes	to provoke thought
to analyze	to express feelings
to argue	to summarize

Some writers misjudge their own purposes, summarizing when they should be analyzing, or expressing feelings about problems instead of proposing solutions to them. Before beginning any writing task, pause to ask, "Why am I communicating with my readers?" This question will lead you to another important question: "Just who are my readers?"

Audience

Take time to ask questions about your readers and their expectations. Consider questions such as these: Who will be reading your draft? What is your relationship to your readers? What information will your audience need to understand your ideas? The choices you make as you write will tell readers who you think they are (novices or experts, for example) and will show respect for your readers' perspectives.

Academic audiences   In college writing, considerations of audience can be more complex than they seem at first. Your instructors will read your essay, of course, but most instructors play multiple roles while reading. Their first and most obvious roles are as coach and evaluator; but they are also intelligent and objective readers, the kind of people who might reasonably be informed, entertained, or called to action by what you have to say and who want to learn from your insights and ideas.

Some instructors specify an audience, such as readers of a local newspaper, a hypothetical supervisor, or peers in a particular field. Other instructors expect you to imagine an audience appropriate to your purpose, subject, and genre. Still others prefer that you write for a general audience of educated readers—nonspecialists who can be expected to read with a critical eye.

Understanding an assignment

Determining the purpose of an assignment

The wording of an assignment may suggest its purpose. You might be expected to do one or more of the following in a college writing assignment:

- summarize information from textbooks, lectures, or research (See 4c.)
- analyze ideas and concepts (See 4d.)
- take a position on a topic and defend it with evidence (See 6.)
- synthesize (combine ideas from) several sources and create an original argument (See 55d and 60d.)

Understanding how to answer an assignment's question

Many assignments will ask you to answer a *how* or *why* question. You cannot answer such questions using only facts; instead, you will need to take a position. For example, the question "*What* are the survival rates for leukemia patients?" can be answered with facts. The question "*Why* are the survival rates for leukemia patients in one state lower than those in a neighboring state?" must be answered with both facts and interpretation. If a list of questions appears in the assignment, be careful — instructors rarely expect you to answer all the questions in order. Look for topics or themes that will help you ask your own questions.

Recognizing implied questions

When you are asked to *discuss, analyze, agree or disagree with*, or *consider* a topic, your instructor will often expect you to answer a *how* or *why* question.

Discuss the effects of the No Child Left Behind Act on special education programs.	=	*How* has the No Child Left Behind Act affected special education programs?
Consider the recent rise of attention deficit hyper-activity disorder diagnoses.	=	*Why* are diagnoses of attention deficit hyper-activity disorder rising?

Business audiences Writers in the business world often find themselves writing for multiple audiences. A letter to a client, for instance, might be distributed to sales representatives as well. Readers of a report might include people with and without technical expertise, or readers who want details and those who prefer a quick overview.

Public audiences Writers in communities often write to a specific audience—a legislative representative, readers of a local newspaper, fellow members of a social group. With public writing, it is more likely that you are familiar with the views your readers hold and the assumptions they make, so you may be better able to judge how to engage those readers.

For help with considering audience when writing e-mail messages, see the chart on the following page.

Genre

When writing for a college course, pay close attention to the genre, or type of writing, assigned. Each genre is a category of writing meant for a specific purpose and audience, with its own set of agreed-upon expectations and conventions for style, structure, and document design. Sometimes an assignment specifies the genre—an essay in a writing class, a lab report or research proposal in a biology class, a policy memo in a criminal justice class, or an executive summary in a business class. Sometimes the genre is yours to choose, and you need to decide if a particular genre—a poster presentation, an audio essay, a Web page, or a podcast, for example—will help you communicate your purpose and reach readers.

Considering audience when writing e-mail messages

In academic, business, and public contexts, show readers that you value their time. Here are some strategies for writing effective e-mail messages:

- Use a concise, meaningful subject line to help readers sort messages and set priorities.

- State your main point at the beginning so that your reader sees it without scrolling.

- Write concisely; keep paragraphs short.

- Avoid writing in all capital letters or all lowercase letters.

- Proofread for typos and errors that are likely to slow down readers.

You will also want to follow conventions of etiquette and academic integrity. Here are some strategies for writing responsible e-mails:

- E-mail messages can easily be forwarded to others and reproduced. Do not write anything that you would not want attributed to you.

- Do not forward another person's message without asking his or her permission.

- Choose your words carefully. Without hearing your voice or seeing your facial expressions, readers may misunderstand your e-mail message.

- If you write an e-mail message that includes someone else's words — opinions, statistics, song lyrics, and so forth — let your reader know the source for that material and where any borrowed material begins and ends.

It is helpful to think of genre as an opportunity to enter a discipline and join a group of thinkers and writers who share interests, ideas, and ways of communicating with one another. For instance, if you are asked to write a lab report for a biology class or a case study for an education class, you have the opportunity to practice the methods used by scholars in these fields and to communicate with them. For the lab report, your purpose might be to present the results of an experiment; your evidence would be the data you collected while conducting your experiment, and you would use scientific terms expected by your audience. For the case study, your purpose might be to analyze student-teacher interactions in a single classroom; your evidence might be data collected from interviews and observations. (For a discussion of genres in various disciplines, see 65.)

To understand the expectations of different genres—and the opportunities present in different genres—you can begin by asking some of the following questions.

UNDERSTANDING GENRE

If the genre has been assigned, the following questions will help you focus on its expectations.

- Do you have access to samples of writing in the genre that has been assigned?

- Who is the audience? What specialized vocabulary do readers expect in the genre?

- What type of evidence is usually required in the genre?

- What format, organization, and citation style are expected?

If you are free to choose the genre, the following questions will help you focus on its expectations.

- What is your purpose: To argue a position? To instruct? To present a process? To propose a solution? Do you have more than one purpose?

- Who is your audience? What do you know about your readers or viewers?

- What method of presenting information would appeal to your audience: Reasoned paragraphs? Diagrams? Video? Slides?

Sources of information

Where will your evidence—facts, details, and examples—come from? What kind of reading, observation, or research is necessary to meet the expectations of your assignment?

Reading Reading is an important way to deepen your understanding of a topic and expand your perspective. It will be your primary source of information for many college assignments.

Read with an open mind to learn from the insights and research of others. Take notes on your thoughts, impressions, and questions. Your notes can be a way to enter a conversation with the authors of the texts you read. (See 4.) And always keep careful records of any sources you read and consult.

Observation Observation is an excellent means of collecting information about a wide range of subjects, such as gender relationships on a popular television program, the clichéd language of sports announcers, or a current exhibit at the local art museum. For such subjects, do not rely on your memory alone; your information will be fresher and more detailed if you actively collect it, with a notebook, laptop, or voice recorder.

Interviews and surveys Interviews and surveys can supply detailed and interesting information on many subjects. For example, a nursing student interested in the care of terminally ill patients might interview hospice nurses; a criminal justice major might speak with a local judge about alternative sentencing for first offenders.

It is a good idea to record interviews to preserve any vivid quotations that you might want to weave into your essay. Circulating surveys by e-mail or using a survey Web site will facilitate responses. Keep questions simple, and specify a deadline to ensure that you get a reasonable number of replies. (See also 50e.)

Length and format

Writers seldom have complete control over length requirements. Journalists usually write within strict word limits set by their editors, businesspeople routinely aim for conciseness, and most college assignments specify an approximate length.

Your writing situation may also require a certain document format. In the academic world, you may need to learn precise disciplinary and genre conventions for lab reports, critiques, research papers, and so on. For most undergraduate essays, a standard format is acceptable. (See the appendix, pp. 822–33.)

In some writing situations, you will be free to create your own design, complete with headings, lists, and perhaps visuals such as charts and graphs.

EXERCISE 1–1 Narrow three of the following subjects into topics that would be manageable for an essay of two to five pages.

1. The minimum wage
2. Immigration
3. Cyberbullying
4. The cost of a college education
5. Internet privacy

EXERCISE 1–2 Suggest a purpose and an audience for three of the following subjects.

1. Government housing for military veterans
2. What American superhero movies say about Americans

3. Mandatory money management courses for high schoolers
4. Automatic voter registration
5. Students as retail ambassadors (of stores such as Target, American Eagle) on campus

1b Explore your subject.

Experiment with one or more techniques for exploring your subject and discovering your purpose:

- talking and listening
- reading and annotating texts
- asking questions

- brainstorming (listing ideas) and freewriting
- keeping a journal
- blogging

Whatever technique you turn to, the goal is the same: to generate ideas that will lead you to a question, a problem, or a topic that you want to explore further.

Talking and listening

Conversation can help you develop your ideas before you begin to write them down. By talking and listening to others, you can also discover what they find interesting, what they are curious about, and where they disagree with you. If you are writing an argument, you can try it out on listeners with other points of view.

Reading and annotating texts

Reading is an important way to deepen your understanding of a topic, learn from the insights and research of others, and expand your perspective. Annotating a text, written or visual, encourages you to read actively — to highlight key concepts, to note contradictions in an argument, or to raise questions for further research and investigation. (See 4a for an annotated article and 5a for an annotated advertisement.)

Asking questions

Whenever you are writing about ideas, events, or people, whether current or historical, asking questions is one way to get started. You might try the questions journalists routinely ask themselves: *Who? What? When? Where? Why?* and *How?* If you were writing about a negative reaction to a film, for instance, you might want to ask: *Who* objected to the film and *why? What* were the objections, and *when* were they voiced? Such questions will help you investigate your subject to discover important facts.

In academic writing, scholars often generate ideas by posing questions related to a specific discipline. If you are writing in a particular discipline, try to find out which questions its scholars typically explore. Look for clues in assigned readings, assignments, and class discussions to understand how a discipline's questions help you understand its concerns.

Brainstorming and freewriting

Brainstorming and freewriting are good ways to figure out what you know and what questions you have. Write whatever comes to mind without pausing to think about word choice, spelling, or even meaning. The goal is to write quickly and freely to discover what questions are on your mind and what directions you might pursue.

Keeping a journal

A journal is a collection of informal, exploratory, sometimes experimental writing. In a journal, often meant for your eyes only, you can take risks. You might freewrite, pose questions, comment on an interesting idea from one of your classes, or keep a list of questions that occur to you while reading. You might imagine a conversation between yourself and your readers or stage a debate to understand opposing positions.

Blogging

Although a blog is a type of journal, it is a public writing space rather than a private one. You can explore an idea for a paper by blogging about it in different ways or from different angles. Since most blogs have a commenting feature, you can create a conversation by inviting readers to give you feedback—ask questions, make counterarguments, or suggest other sources on a topic.

1c Draft and revise a working thesis statement.

For many types of writing, you will be able to assert your central idea in a sentence or two. Such a statement, which ordinarily appears in the opening paragraph of your finished essay, is called a *thesis*.

Understanding what makes an effective thesis statement

An effective thesis statement is a central idea that conveys your purpose—your reason for writing—and that requires support.

An effective thesis should

- state a position that needs to be explained and supported
- be sharply focused
- use concrete language
- be appropriate for the length requirements of the assignment, not too broad or too narrow
- stand up to the "So what?" question (See p. 21.)

Drafting a working thesis

As you explore your topic, you will begin to see possible ways to focus your material. At this point, try to settle on a *tentative* central idea, or working thesis statement. The more complex your topic, the more your focus will change as you write. Think of your working thesis as preliminary, open for consideration and revision, as you clarify your purpose and consider the expectations

MORE HELP

The thesis statement is central to many types of writing.

▶ Writing arguments: 6
▶ Writing analytical essays: 4, 6f
▶ Writing about multimodal texts: 5
▶ Writing literature papers: 7c
▶ Writing research papers: 53 (MLA), 58 (APA), 63 (*Chicago*)

of your audience. As your ideas develop, you'll need to revisit your working thesis to see whether it represents the position you want to take or whether it can be supported by the sources of evidence you have gathered.

You'll find that the process of answering a question you have posed, resolving a problem you have identified, or taking a position on a debatable topic will focus your thinking and lead you to develop a working thesis. Below, for example, are one student's efforts to pose a question and draft a working thesis for an essay in his ethics course.

QUESTION

Should athletes who enhance their performance through biotechnology be banned from athletic competition?

WORKING THESIS

Athletes who boost their performance through biotechnology should be banned from athletic competition.

The working thesis offers a useful place to start writing — a way to limit the topic and focus a first draft — but it doesn't take into consideration the expectations of readers who will ask "Why?" and "So what?" The student has taken a position — athletes who use performance enhancers should be banned—but he hasn't answered *why* these athletes should be banned. To fully answer his own question, he might push his own thinking with the word *because*.

STRONGER WORKING THESIS

Athletes who boost their performance through biotechnology should be banned from competition *because* biotechnology gives athletes an unfair advantage and disrupts the sense of fair play.

Revising a working thesis

As you move to a clearer and more specific position you want to take, you'll start to see ways to revise your working thesis. You may find that the evidence you have collected supports a different thesis; you may find that your position has changed as you learned more about your topic.

Revision is ongoing; as your ideas evolve, your working thesis will evolve, too. One effective way to revise a working thesis is to put it to the "So what?" test: Can you explain why readers will want to read an essay with this thesis? Can you respond when readers ask "So what?" or "Why does your thesis matter?" Such questions help you consider your audience and purpose—and the expectations of your assignment—as you revise.

For other ideas about revising a thesis, see pages 22–23.

Putting your working thesis to the "So what?" test

Use the following questions to help you revise your working thesis. (The questions continue on page 24.)

- Why would readers want to read an essay with this thesis? How would you respond to a reader who hears your thesis and asks "So what?" or "Why does it matter?"

Solve five common problems with thesis statements

Revising a working thesis is easier if you have a method or an approach. The following problem/solution approach can help you recognize and solve common thesis problems.

1 Common problem: The thesis is a statement of fact.

Solution: Enter a debate by posing a question about your topic that has more than one possible answer. For example: Should the polygraph be used by private employers? Your thesis should be your answer to the question.

Working thesis: *The first polygraph was developed by Dr. John Larson in 1921.*

Revised: *Because the polygraph has not been proved reliable, even under controlled conditions, its use by private employers should be banned.*

2 Common problem: The thesis is a question.

Solution: Take a position on your topic by answering the question you have posed. Your thesis statement should be your answer to the question.

Working thesis: *Would President John F. Kennedy have continued to escalate the war in Vietnam if he had lived?*

Revised: *Although President John F. Kennedy sent the first American troops to Vietnam before he died, an analysis of his foreign policy suggests that he would not have escalated the war had he lived.*

3 **Common problem:** The thesis is too broad.

Solution: Focus on a subtopic of your original topic. Once you have chosen a subtopic, take a position in an ongoing debate and pose a question that has more than one answer. For example: Should people be tested for genetic diseases? Your thesis should be your answer to the question.

Working thesis: *Mapping the human genome has many implications for health and science.*

Revised: *Although scientists can now detect genetic predisposition for specific diseases, policymakers should establish clear guidelines about whom to test and under what circumstances.*

4 **Common problem:** The thesis is too narrow.

Solution: Identify challenging questions that readers might ask about your topic. Then pose a question that has more than one answer. For example: Do the risks of genetic testing outweigh its usefulness? Your thesis should be your answer to the question.

Working thesis: *A person who carries a genetic mutation linked to a particular disease might or might not develop that disease.*

Revised: *Though positive results in a genetic test do not guarantee that the disease will develop, such results can cause psychological trauma; genetic testing should therefore be avoided if possible.*

5 **Common problem:** The thesis is vague.

Solution: Focus your thesis with concrete language and clues about where the essay is headed. Pose a question about the topic that has more than one answer. For example: How does the physical structure of the Vietnam Veterans Memorial shape the experience of the visitors? Your thesis—your answer to the question—should use specific language.

Working thesis: *The Vietnam Veterans Memorial is an interesting structure.*

Revised: *By inviting visitors to see their own reflections in the wall, the Vietnam Veterans Memorial creates a link between the present and the past.*

- Will any readers disagree with this thesis? If so, how might your thesis respond to a counter perspective?

- Is the thesis too obvious? If you cannot come up with interpretations that oppose your own, consider revising your thesis.

- Can you support your thesis with the evidence available?

EXERCISE 1–4   In each of the following pairs, which sentence might work well as a thesis for a short paper? What is the problem with the other one? Is it too factual? Too broad? Too vague? Use the problem/solution approach from pages 22–23 to evaluate each thesis.

1.   a. Many drivers use their cell phones irresponsibly while driving.

   b. Current state laws are inadequate to punish drivers who use their cell phones irresponsibly to text, read e-mail, or per-form other distracting activities.

2.   a. Although Facebook was designed to help college students keep in touch, it actually keeps them apart by discouraging face-to-face interactions and creating an illusion of intimacy.

   b. Facebook was designed to make it easier for people to keep in touch.

3.   a. As we search to define the intelligence of animals, we run the risk of imposing our own understanding of intelligence on animals.

   b. How does the field of animal psychology help humans define intelligence?

4.   a. The high cost of college needs to be reduced because it affects students and their families.

   b. To reduce the high cost of college, more students should be offered opportunities for dual-enrollment courses and a three-year college degree.

5. a. Anorexia nervosa is a dangerous and sometimes deadly eating disorder occurring mainly in young, upper-middle-class teens.

   b. The eating disorder anorexia nervosa is rarely cured by one treatment alone; only by combining drug therapy with psychotherapy and family therapy can the client begin the long journey to wellness.

WRITING PRACTICE

Drafting and revising your working thesis

Exchange drafts with a classmate and put each other's working thesis to the "So what?" test (p. 21). Then use the problem/solution approach to evaluate each other's thesis (pp. 22–23). Discuss how each of you might go about revising your thesis. What do you learn about your working thesis from this discussion? Think about what single piece of advice might help you revise and strengthen your thesis. Then revise your working thesis.

1d Draft a plan.

Many writers draft a plan as part of the early process of drafting a paper. Listing and organizing supporting ideas can help a writer figure out how to flesh out the thesis. Creating outlines, whether informal or formal, can help you make sure your writing is focused and logical and can help you identify any gaps in your support.

When to use an informal outline

You might want to sketch an informal outline to see how you will support your thesis and to figure out a tentative structure for your ideas. Informal outlines can take many forms. Perhaps the most common is simply the thesis followed by a list of major ideas.

Working thesis: Animal testing should be banned because it is bad science and doesn't contribute to biomedical advances.

- Most animals don't serve as good models for the human body.

- Drug therapies can have vastly different effects on different species — 92 percent of all drugs shown to be effective in animal tests fail in human trials.

- Some of the largest biomedical discoveries were made without the use of animal testing.

- The most effective biomedical research methods — tissue engineering and computer modeling — don't use animals.

- Animal studies are not scientifically necessary.

If you began by jotting down a list of ideas, you can turn the list into a rough outline by crossing out some ideas, adding others, and putting the ideas in a logical order.

When to use a formal outline

Early in the writing process, rough outlines have certain advantages: They can be produced quickly, they are obviously tentative, and they can be revised easily. However, a formal outline may be useful later in the writing process, after you have written a rough draft, especially if your topic is complex. A formal outline can help you see whether the parts of your essay work together and whether your essay's structure is logical.

The following formal outline brought order to the research paper that appears in 57b, on regulating healthy eating. The student's thesis is an important part of the outline. Everything else in the outline supports it, directly or indirectly.

FORMAL OUTLINE

Thesis: In the name of public health and safety, state governments have the responsibility to shape public health policies and to regulate healthy eating choices, especially since doing so offers a potentially large social benefit for a relatively small cost.

I.   Debates surrounding food regulation have a long history in the United States.
   A. The 1906 Pure Food and Drug Act guarantees inspection of meat and dairy products.
   B. Such regulations are considered reasonable because consumers are protected from harm with little cost.
   C. Consumers consider reasonable regulations to be an important government function to stop harmful items from entering the marketplace.

II. Even though food meets safety standards, there is a need for further regulation.
   A. The typical American diet — processed sugars, fats, and refined flours — is damaging over time.
   B. Related health risks are diabetes, cancer, and heart problems.
   C. Passing chronic-disease-related legislation is our single most important public health challenge.

III. Food legislation is not a popular solution for most Americans.
   A. A proposed New York City regulation banning the sale of soft drinks greater than twelve ounces failed in 2012, and in California, a proposed soda tax failed in 2011.
   B. Many consumers find such laws to be unreasonable restrictions on freedom of choice.
   C. Opposition to food and beverage regulation is similar to the opposition to early tobacco legislation; the public views the issue as one of personal responsibility.
   D. Counterpoint: Freedom of "choice" is a myth; our choices are heavily influenced by marketing.

IV. The United States has a history of regulations to discourage unhealthy behaviors.
   A. Tobacco-related restrictions faced opposition.
   B. Seat belt laws are a useful analogy.
   C. The public seems to support laws that have a good cost-benefit ratio; the cost of food/beverage regulations is low, and most people agree that the benefits would be high.

V. Americans believe that personal choice is lost when regulations such as taxes and bans are instituted.
   A. Regulations open up the door to excessive control and interfere with cultural and religious traditions.
   B. Counterpoint: Burdens on individual liberty are a reasonable price to pay for large social health benefits.

VI. Public opposition continues to stand in the way of food regulation to promote healthier eating. We must consider whether to allow the costly trend of rising chronic disease to continue in the name of personal choice, or whether we are willing to support the legal changes and public health policies that will reverse that trend.

Planning with headings

When drafting a research paper or a business document, consider using headings to guide your planning and to help your readers follow the organization of your final draft. While drafting, you can insert your working thesis, experiment with possible headings, and type chunks of text beneath each heading. You may need to try grouping your ideas in a few different ways to suit your purpose and audience.

1e Draft an introduction.

Some writers, but not all, begin a paper by drafting the introduction, which introduces the writer's central idea. If you find it difficult to introduce a paper that you have not yet written, try drafting the body first and saving the introduction for later.

Your introduction will usually be a paragraph of 50 to 150 words (in a longer paper, it may be more than one paragraph). Perhaps the most common strategy is to open with a few sentences that engage, or hook, the reader and that establish your purpose for writing and your central idea, or thesis. (See also 1c.) In the following introduction, the thesis is highlighted.

> As the United States industrialized in the nineteenth century, using immigrant labor, social concerns took a backseat to the task of building a prosperous nation. The government did not regulate industries and did not provide an effective safety net for the poor or for those who became sick or injured on the job. Immigrants and the poor did have a few advocates, however. Settlement houses such as Hull-House in Chicago provided information, services, and a place for reform-minded individuals to gather and work to improve the conditions of the urban poor. Alice Hamilton was one of these reformers. Her work at Hull-House spanned twenty-two years and later expanded throughout the nation. Hamilton's efforts helped to improve the lives of immigrants and drew attention and respect to the problems and people that until then had been ignored.
>
> —Laurie McDonough, student

Each sentence leading to your thesis should hook readers by drawing them into the world of the essay and showing them why your essay is worth reading. The chart on page 30 provides strategies for drafting an introduction.

Whether you are writing for a scholarly audience, a professional audience, a public audience, or a general audience, you cannot assume your readers' interest in the topic. The hook should spark readers' curiosity and offer them a reason to continue.

NOTE: Different writing situations call for different introductions. For more examples of effective introductions, see pages 158, 743, and 819.

Strategies for drafting an introduction

Whether you are composing a traditional essay or a multimodal work such as a slide show presentation or a video, the following strategies can provide a hook for your reader:

- Offer a startling statistic or an unusual fact
- Ask a question
- Introduce a quotation or a bit of dialogue
- Provide historical background
- Define a term or concept
- Propose a problem, contradiction, or dilemma
- Use a vivid example or image
- Develop an analogy
- Relate an anecdote

As you draft your introduction, think about your writing situation, especially your genre. For some types of writing, it may be difficult or impossible to express the central idea in a thesis statement; or it may be unwise or unnecessary to put a thesis statement in the essay itself. A literacy narrative, for example, may have a focus too subtle to be distilled in a single sentence. Strictly informative writing, like that found in many business memos or nursing reports, may be difficult to summarize in a thesis. In such

Academic English

If you come from a culture that prefers an indirect approach in writing, you may feel that asserting a thesis early in an essay sounds unrefined and even rude. In the United States, however, readers appreciate a direct approach; when you state your point as directly as possible, you show that you understand your topic and value your readers' time.

instances, do not try to force the central idea into a thesis statement. Instead, think in terms of an overriding purpose and of the genre's conventions and expectations. (See 64d.)

1f Draft the body.

The body of your essay develops support for your thesis, so it's important to have at least a working thesis before you start writing. What does your thesis promise readers? What question are you trying to answer? What problem are you trying to solve? What is your position on the topic? Keep these questions in mind as you draft the body of your essay.

Asking questions as you draft

You may already have written an introduction that includes your working thesis. If not, as long as you have a draft thesis you can begin developing the body and return later to the introduction. If your thesis suggests a plan (see 1e) or if you have sketched a preliminary outline, try to organize your paragraphs accordingly.

Draft the body of your essay by writing at least one paragraph about each supporting point you listed in the planning stage. If you do not have a plan, pause for a few moments and sketch one (see 1d). As you draft the body, keep asking questions; keep anticipating what your readers may need to know.

Often, however, you might not know what you want to say until you have written a draft. It is possible to begin without a plan—assuming you are prepared to treat your first attempt as a "discovery draft" that may be radically rewritten once you discover what you really want to say. Whether or not you have a plan when you begin drafting, you can often figure out a workable order for your ideas by stopping each time you start a new paragraph to think about what your readers will need to know to follow your train of thought.

For more detailed help with drafting and developing paragraphs, see 3.

USING SOURCES RESPONSIBLY: As you draft, keep careful notes and records of any sources you read and consult. If you quote, paraphrase, or summarize a source, include a citation, even in your draft (see 54b, 59, and 63b). You will save time and avoid plagiarism if you follow the rules of citation while drafting.

Adding visuals as you draft

As you draft, you may decide that some of the support for your thesis could come from one or more visuals. Visuals can convey information concisely and powerfully. Charts, graphs, and tables, for example, can simplify complex numerical information. Images — including photographs and diagrams — often express an idea more vividly than words can. Keep in mind that if you download a visual or use published information to create your own visual, you must credit your source. The chart on pages 34–35 describes eight types of visuals and their purposes.

Always consider how a visual conveys your purpose and how your audience might respond to it. Choose visuals to support your writing, not to substitute for it. For an example of an effective use of a visual, see page 160. In writing about the shift from print to online news, student writer Sam Jacobs used a screen shot of a link embedded in a news article to illustrate his argument (see 6k).

Considering format as you draft

Aside from planning visual evidence for your ideas, you will need to think about how to format your paper. Formatting, or designing, your document promotes readability and helps you meet the expectations of your readers and the requirements of the genre. The following questions will help you keep your purpose and audience in mind as you format your document.

- What is the purpose of your document? How can your document format help you achieve this purpose?
- Who are your readers? What are their expectations?
- What format options — layout, margins, line spacing, and font styles — will readers expect?
- How should you place and label any visuals you decide to use?

See the appendix, which starts on page 822, for sample pages from a variety of academic and business documents. Each is annotated to illustrate specific format guidelines.

USING SOURCES RESPONSIBLY: If you create a chart, table, or graph using information from your research, you must cite the source of the information even though the visual is your own. If you download a photograph from the Web or scan an image from a magazine or book, you must credit the person or organization that created it, just as you would cite any other source that you use in a college paper (see 54a, 59a, or 63b, depending on what documentation style your assignment requires).

1g Draft a conclusion.

A conclusion should remind readers of the essay's main idea without repeating it. Often the concluding paragraph can be relatively short. By the end of the essay, readers should already understand your main point; your conclusion drives it home and, perhaps, gives readers something more to consider.

Choosing visuals to suit your purpose

Pie chart

Pie charts compare a part or parts to the whole. Segments of the pie represent percentages of the whole (and always total 100 percent).

Health insurance coverage in the United States (2007)

Bar graph (or line graph)

Bar graphs highlight trends over a period of time or compare numerical data. Line graphs display the same data as bar graphs; the data are graphed as points, and the points are connected with lines.

THE PURSUIT OF PROPERTY
Home ownership rates in the United States

Infographic

An infographic presents data in a visually engaging form. The data are usually numerical, as in bar graphs or line graphs, but they are represented by a graphic element rather than bars or lines.

Just 8% of kids growing up in low-income communities graduate from college by age 24.

Table

Tables display numbers and words in columns and rows. They can be used to organize complicated numerical information into an easily understood format.

Prices of daily doses of AIDS drugs
($US)

Drug	Brazil	Uganda	Côte d'Ivoire	US
3TC (Lamuvidine)	1.66	3.28	2.95	8.70
ddC (Zalcitabine)	0.24	4.17	3.75	8.80
Didanosine	2.04	5.26	3.46	7.25
Efavirenz	5.96	n/a	6.41	13.13
Indinavir	10.32	12.79	9.07	14.93
Nelfinavir	4.14	4.46	4.39	6.47
Nevirapine	5.04	n/a	n/a	8.48
Saquinavir	6.24	7.37	5.52	6.50
Stavudine	0.56	6.19	4.10	9.07
ZDV/3TC	1.44	7.34	n/a	18.78
Zidovudine	1.08	4.34	2.43	10.12

Source: UNAIDS, 2000

CHOOSING VISUALS TO SUIT YOUR PURPOSE (*cont.*)

Photograph

Photographs vividly depict people, scenes, or objects discussed in a text.

Source: Library of Congress, Prints & Photographs Division, Reproduction number LC-DIG-highsm-04024.

Diagram

Diagrams, useful in scientific and technical writing, concisely illustrate processes, structures, or interactions.

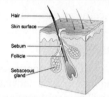

Source: National Institute of Health

Flowchart

Flowcharts show structures (the hierarchy of employees at a company, for example) or steps in a process and their relation to one another. (See also p. 280 for another example.)

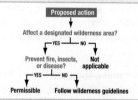

Map

Maps illustrate distances, historical information, or demographics and often use symbols for geographic features and points of interest.

Strategies for drafting a conclusion

In addition to echoing your main idea, a conclusion might do any of
the following:

- Briefly summarize your essay's key points
- Propose a course of action
- Offer a recommendation
- Discuss the topic's wider significance or implications
- Redefine a key term or concept
- Pose a question for future study

To conclude an essay analyzing the shifting roles of women
in the military services, one student discusses her topic's implications for society as a whole.

> As the military continues to train women in jobs formerly
> reserved for men, our understanding of women's roles in
> society will no doubt continue to change. And as news reports
> of women training for and taking part in combat operations
> become commonplace, reports of women becoming CEOs,
> police chiefs, and even president of the United States will cease
> to surprise us. Or perhaps we have already reached this point.
> —Rosa Broderick, student

To make the conclusion memorable and to give a sense of
completion, you might bring readers full circle by returning to
the thesis or including a detail from the introduction. To conclude his argument essay about the shift from print to online
news, student writer Sam Jacobs returns to the phrase "fit to
print" from his introduction and echoes his thesis to show the
wider significance of his argument. (See pp. 158–63.)

> The Internet has enabled consumers to participate in a
> new way in reading, questioning, interpreting, and reporting
> the news. Decisions about appropriate content and coverage
> are no longer exclusively in the hands of news editors.
> Ordinary citizens now have a meaningful voice in the

conversation—a hand in deciding what's "fit to print." Some skeptics worry about the apparent free-for-all and loss of tradition. But the expanding definition of news provides opportunities for consumers to be more engaged with events in their communities, their nations, and the world.

To see more examples of effective conclusions, see pages 129 and 162.

Whatever concluding strategy you choose, keep in mind that an effective conclusion is decisive and unapologetic. Avoid introducing completely new ideas at the end of an essay. And because the conclusion is so closely tied to the rest of the essay in both content and tone, be prepared to revise it or rewrite it as you revise your draft.

1h Manage your files.

Keeping track of all your notes, outlines, rough drafts, and final drafts can be challenging. Writing online in an application such as Google Docs or in a word processing program, however, can make drafting and revising easier. You can undo changes or return to an earlier draft if a revision misfires. If you are using Word or another word processing program, and saving files to your device, the following steps can help you explore drafting and revising possibilities with little risk.

- Create folders and subfolders for each assignment. Save notes, outlines, and drafts together.
- Label revised drafts with different file names and dates ("Ad-analysis-draft-10.7.16.docx" is an earlier version of "Ad-analysis-final-10.19.16.docx").
- Occasionally print hard copies as backup.
- Always record complete bibliographic information about any sources you might use, including visuals.
- Use a comment function to make notes to yourself or to respond to the drafts of peers.

If you are working in Google Drive or another cloud-based storage system, use the revision history tool in the file menu to keep track of different versions of your project as well as reviewers' comments. Also, it's a good idea to use specific names for your files. A name that suggests information about the assignment is useful for you and reviewers. Instead of "English essay," perhaps use "Comp1 persuasive essay Oct 2017."

2 Revising, editing, and reflecting

Revising is rarely a one-step process. Global matters—thesis, purpose, organization, content, and overall strategy—generally receive attention first because global revisions involve bigger changes, including rewrites of paragraphs or whole sections of a paper. Improvements in sentence structure and word choice usually come later. Revising at the sentence level gives you a chance to reconsider whether a particular point could be stronger or clearer or whether a certain word or phrase sends the message you intended.

Editing is a step that is best left for the end of the writing process. It involves identifying errors or patterns of errors, such as using commas and quotation marks correctly, making subjects and verbs agree, or using the right form of a pronoun. See 2b for advice on keeping an editing log.

Writing multiple drafts allows you to write in stages, seek feedback, and strengthen your paper through both revising and editing.

2a See revision as a social process.

To revise is to *re-see*, and the comments you receive from reviewers—instructors, peers, and writing center tutors—will help you re-see your draft from your readers' point of view.

When you ask readers for their comments, revision becomes a social experience, connecting you with the suggestions and insights of readers who help you shape your work in progress. As you write for college courses, form a community of readers around you and seek their feedback.

Feedback gives you perspective on what's working and not working in your draft and keeps the expectations of your readers in mind. Simple questions such as "What would you say is my main idea?" and "Is my draft focused and organized?" will help you see your draft through readers' eyes. The checklist for global revision on page 54 may help you and your reviewers get started.

2b Use peer review: Revise with comments.

Peer review gives you the benefit of real readers and an opportunity to see your draft through their eyes. When peers—classmates and fellow students—read your work, they offer feedback, pointing out where they are intrigued or confused. They offer their insights and suggestions, answer your questions, and help you strengthen your draft. Think of peer review as an opportunity to talk about your writing with a coach, an advocate, who will help you achieve your purpose for writing.

The following guidelines will help you learn from your reviewers' comments and revise successfully.

Be active. Help reviewers understand your purpose for writing and provide background about why you chose your topic, why it matters to you, and what you hope to accomplish in your draft. Let your reviewers know your specific questions and concerns so they can provide focused feedback.

Listen with an open mind. After you've worked hard on a draft, you might be surprised to hear reviewers tell you it still needs more development. Don't take criticism personally. Your readers are responding to your essay, not to you. If comments show that a reviewer doesn't understand what you're trying to do, don't

Becoming a College Writer

curiosity **engagement** responsibility reflection

Form a community of readers around you

"Don't be afraid to seek help with writing. Use all the resources available and ask people to read your drafts. Feedback gives you perspective." —**Donovan Castro**, student, University of Arizona

Have you ever tried writing an entire essay—blank page to final draft—in a single sitting? Was it your best work? Writing and revising multiple drafts allows you to write in stages, seek feedback, and make improvements. Giving yourself time to seek and receive feedback means that a first draft doesn't have to be perfect.

One effective way to approach revision is to form a community of readers around you. As Donovan Castro suggests, use "resources"—instructors, librarians, writing center tutors, classmates—to help you gain perspective on your draft's effectiveness. You might sense that something isn't working, but you don't know why or how to address it. Engage another reader who might help solve a problem. As you write in college, be open to readers' responses and be willing to learn from them.

- You may have had some experience with peer review or feedback groups in the past. Recall one experience that was particularly positive or negative. What do you think made it so?

ANDRESR/SHUTTERSTOCK

MORE
Revising with comments, pages 39–43
Approaching global revision in cycles, 2e

40

be defensive. Instead, consider why your reader is confused, and figure out how to clarify your point. Responding to readers' objections—instead of dismissing them—may strengthen your ideas and make your essay more persuasive. Taking feedback seriously will make you a stronger writer.

Weigh feedback carefully. As you begin revising, you may find yourself sorting through suggestions from many people, including instructors, writing tutors, and peer reviewers. Sometimes these readers will agree, but often their advice will differ. Your reviewers will probably make more suggestions than you can use, so be strategic. It's important to sort through all the comments you receive with your original goals in mind and to focus on global concerns first (see p. 54)—otherwise, you'll be facing the impossible task of trying to incorporate everyone's advice.

Keep a revision and editing log. Make a clear and simple list of the global and sentence-level concerns that keep coming up in most of your reviewers' comments. That list can serve as a starting point each time you revise a paper to help you learn about your strengths and weaknesses as a writer. When you take charge of your own writing in this way, comments will become a valuable resource.

2c Use peer review: Give constructive comments.

Peer review gives you an opportunity to read the work of your classmates and to learn from one another. As you offer advice about how to strengthen a peer's thesis or how to use a visual to convey concise information, you are thinking about the purpose of a thesis and the role of visuals. When you propose a strategy for focusing an introduction or for anticipating a counterargument, you not only help your classmate but also benefit from the process of thinking strategically about revision.

As a peer reviewer, your work is to engage with a writer as a reader. It isn't your job to rewrite, correct, or proofread the work of your peers. It is your job, though, to offer thoughtful, positive, encouraging comments to show peers what they're doing well and how they might build on their strengths as writers.

Strategies for revising with comments

Often the comments you'll receive are written as shorthand commands—"Be specific!"—or as questions—"What is your main point?" Such comments don't immediately show you *how* to revise, but they do identify where revision might improve your draft. Don't hesitate to ask reviewers to explain their comments if you don't understand them. The following sample comments and revision strategies will help you think about how to apply feedback to your own writing—and where to look for help in *The Bedford Handbook*.

The comment: Unfocused introduction

Understanding the comment   When readers point out that your introduction needs to be "focused," the comment often signals that the beginning sentences of your essay are vague, are unconnected to the rest of your essay, and don't establish your purpose for writing.

Strategies for revising

- **Reread your introduction and ask questions.** Are the sentences leading to your thesis specific enough to engage readers and communicate your purpose? Do these sentences lead logically to your thesis? Do they spark your readers' curiosity and offer them a reason to continue reading? (**See 1e.**)

- **Try engaging readers with a "hook"** in your introduction—a question, a quotation, a vivid example, or a startling statistic. (**See the chart on p. 30.**)

The comment: Consider opposing viewpoints

Understanding the comment   When readers suggest that you "consider opposing viewpoints," the comment often signals that you need to recognize and respond to possible objections to your argument.

Strategies for revising

- **Read more** to learn about the debates surrounding the topic. Understand the various sides of your issue so you can anticipate and counter objections to your argument. (**See 50a and 50b.**)

- **Be open-minded.** Although it might seem illogical to introduce opposing arguments, you'll show your knowledge of the topic by recognizing that not everyone draws the same conclusions or holds the same point of view. (**See 6i.**)

- **Introduce and counter objections** with phrases like these: "Some readers might point out that . . ." or "Critics of this view argue that. . . ." (**See p. 156.**)

The comment: *Be specific*

Understanding the comment   When readers say that you need to "be specific," the comment often signals that you could strengthen your writing with
additional details.

Strategies for revising

- **Reread your topic sentence** to understand the focus of the paragraph.
  (**See 3a.**)

- **Ask questions.** Does the paragraph contain claims that need support? Have
  you provided evidence—specific examples, vivid details and illustrations,
  statistics and facts—to help readers understand your ideas and find them
  persuasive? (**See 6h.**)

- **Interpret your evidence**. Remember that details and examples don't speak
  for themselves. You will need to show readers how evidence supports your
  claims. (**See 4d and 55d.**)

The comment: *Cite your sources*

Understanding the comment   When readers point out that you need to
"cite your sources," the comment often signals that you need to acknowledge
and give proper credit to the contributions of others.

Strategies for revising

- **Reread your sentence and ask questions.** Have you properly acknowledged all contributions—words, ideas, facts, or visuals—that you use as
  evidence? Have you given credit to the sources you quote, summarize, or
  paraphrase? Have you made it clear to readers how to locate the source if they
  want to consult it? **See 54 (MLA), 59 (APA), or 63 (*Chicago*)**.

- **Ask your instructor** which documentation style you are required to use—
  MLA, APA, or *Chicago*.

- **Revise** by including an in-text citation for any words, ideas, facts, or visuals
  that you use as evidence—and by including quotation marks around any language borrowed word-for-word from a source. **See 54b (MLA), 59c (APA), or
  63b (*Chicago*).**

Write helpful peer review comments

1 **View yourself as a coach, not a judge.** Think of yourself as asking questions and proposing possibilities, not dictating solutions. Help the writer identify the strengths and limitations of a draft. Try phrasing comments this way: "Have you thought about . . . ?" or "How can you help a reader understand this point?"

2 **Pay attention to global issues first.** Focus on the big picture—purpose, thesis, organization, and content—before sentence structure, word choice, and grammar.

3 **Restate the writer's main idea.** As a reader, you can help the writer see whether he or she is expressing points clearly. Can you follow the writer's train of thought? Restate the writer's thesis and main ideas to check your understanding.

4 **Be specific.** Point to specific places in a draft and show your classmate how, why, and where a draft is effective or confusing. Instead of saying "I like your draft," say exactly what you like: "You use a surprising statistic in your introduction, and it really hooks me as a reader." Or instead of offering a generality such as "Your draft doesn't have much support," give a specific suggestion: "Try putting the data from paragraph three into a graph."

The following excerpt from an online peer review session shows a peer reviewer offering constructive comments.

EXCERPT FROM AN ONLINE PEER REVIEW SESSION

Juan (peer reviewer): *Rachel, your essay makes a great point that credit card companies often hook students on a cycle of spending. But it sounds as if you're blaming students for their spending habits and credit card companies for their deceptive actions. Is this what you want to say?*

Peer reviewer restates writer's main point and asks a question to help her clarify her ideas.

Rachel (writer): *No, I want to keep the focus on the credit card companies. I didn't realize I was blaming students. What could I change?*

Writer takes comment seriously and asks reviewer for specific suggestion.

Juan (reviewer): *In paragraphs three and four, you group all students together as if all students have the same bad spending habits. If students are your audience, you'll be insulting them. What reader is motivated to read something that's alienating? What is your purpose for writing this draft?*

Peer reviewer points to specific places in the draft and asks questions to help writer focus on audience and purpose.

Rachel (writer): *Well . . . It's true that students don't always have good spending habits, but I don't want to blame students. My purpose is to call students to action about the dangers of credit card debt. Any suggestions for narrowing the focus?*

Writer is actively engaged with peer reviewer's comments and doesn't take criticism personally.

Juan (reviewer): *Most students know about the dangers of credit card debt, but they might not know about specific deceptive practices companies use to lure them. Maybe ask yourself what would surprise your audience about these practices.*

Peer reviewer responds as a reader and acts as a coach to suggest possible solutions.

Rachel (writer): *Juan, that's a good idea. I'll try it.*

Writer thanks reviewer for his help and leaves session with a specific revision strategy.

POST COMMENT

WRITING PRACTICE

Using peer review

Exchange drafts with two peers and use the guidelines for receiving and giving comments in 2b and 2c. Help your reviewers understand your purpose for writing. Ask your reviewers if they understand your main idea. What global revision suggestions do they offer to help you strengthen your thesis, organization, and content? Develop three revision goals for your draft based on your reviewers' comments.

2d Highlights of one student's peer review process

Student writer Michelle Nguyen wrote a draft in response to the following assignment:

> How have your experiences with writing, positive or negative, shaped you as a writer? Write a literacy narrative (500–1,000 words) to explore this question. Select one or more key experiences that you think best illustrate how you became the writer you are today. In addition to telling a story, your narrative should make a larger point about learning to write that will be of interest to your readers.

Below is the draft Nguyen submitted to her three peer reviewers. Here are the questions she gave her peer reviewers to focus their feedback.

QUESTIONS FROM NGUYEN TO PEER REVIEWERS

Alex, Brian, and Sameera: Thanks for reading my draft. Here are three questions I have about my draft: Is my focus clear? Is there anything that confuses you? What specifically should I cut or add to strengthen my draft?

ROUGH DRAFT WITH PEER COMMENTS

ROUGH DRAFT

My family used to live in the heart of Hanoi, Vietnam. The neighborhood was small but swamped with crime. Drug addicts scoured the alleys and stole the most mundane things — old clothes, worn slippers, even license plates of motorbikes. Like anyone else in Vietnam in the '90s, we struggled with poverty. There was no entertainment device in our house aside from an 11" black-and-white television. Even then, electricity went off for hours on a weekly basis.

I was particularly close to a Vietnam War veteran. My parents were away a lot, so the old man became like a grandfather to me. He taught me how to ride a bicycle, how to read, how to take care of small pets. He worked sporadically from home, fixing bicycle tires and broken pedals. He was a wrinkly old man who didn't talk much. His vocal cords were damaged during the war, and it caused him pain to speak. In a neighborhood full of screaming babies and angry shop owners and slimy criminals, his home was my quiet haven. I could read and write and think and bond with someone whose worldliness came from his wordlessness.

The tiny house he lived in stood at the far end of our neighborhood. It always smelled of old clothes and forgotten memories. He was a slight man, but his piercing black eyes retained their intensity even after all these years. He must have made one fierce soldier.

"I almost died once," he said, dusting a picture frame. It was one of those rare instances he ever mentioned his life during the war. As he talked, I perched myself on the side of an armchair, rested my head on my tiny hands, and listened intently. I didn't understand

Alex F: You might want to add a title to focus readers.

Sameera K: I really like your introduction. It's so vivid. Think about adding a photo of your neighborhood so readers can relate. What does Hanoi look like?

Brian S: You have great details here to set the scene in Hanoi, but why does it matter that you didn't have an "entertainment device"? Maybe choose the most interesting among all these details.

Brian S: Worldliness came from wordlessness — great phrase! Is this part of your main idea? What is your main idea?

Sameera K: You do a good job of showing us why this Vietnam veteran was important to you, but it seems like this draft is more a story about the man and not about you. What do you want readers to understand about you?

much. I just liked hearing his low, humming voice. The concept of war for me was strictly confined to the classroom, and even then, the details of combat were always murky. The teachers just needed us to know that the communist troops enjoyed a glorious victory.

"I was the only survivor of my unit. 20 guys. All dead within a year. Then they let me go," he said. His voice cracked a little and his eyes misted over as he stared at pictures from his combatant past. "We didn't even live long enough to understand what we were fighting for."

He finished the sentence with a drawn-out sigh, a small set of wrinkles gathering at the end of his eyes. Years later, as I thought about his stories, I started to wonder why he referred to his deceased comrades by the collective pronoun "we." It was as if a little bit of him died on the battlefield with them too.

Three years after my family left the neighborhood, I learned that the old man became stricken with cancer. When I came home the next summer, I visited his house and sat by his sickbed. His shoulder-length mop of salt and pepper hair now dwarfed his rail-thin figure. We barely exchanged a word. He just held my hands tightly until my mother called for me to leave, his skeletal fingers leaving a mark on my pale palms. Perhaps he was trying to transmit to me some of his worldliness and his wisdom. Perhaps he was telling me to go out into the world and live the free life he never had.

Some people say that writers are selfish and vain. The truth is, I learned to write because it gave me peace in the much too noisy world of my Vietnamese childhood. In the quiet of the old man's house, I gazed out the window, listened to my thoughts, and wrote them down. It all started with a story about a wrinkly Vietnam War veteran who didn't talk much.

> **Sameera K:** I'm curious to hear more about you and why this man was so important to you. What did he teach you about writing? What did he see in you?

> **Alex F:** This sentence is confusing. Your draft doesn't seem to be about the selfishness or vanity of writers.

> **Brian S:** What does "it" refer to? I think you're trying to say something important about silence and noise and literacy, but I'm not sure what it is.

After reading her draft and considering the feedback from her classmates, Nguyen realized that she had chosen a good direction but that she hadn't focused her draft to meet the expectations of the assignment. Her classmates offered her valuable suggestions about adding a photograph of her Hanoi neighborhood and clarifying her main idea. With her classmates' specific questions and suggestions in mind and their encouragement to see the undeveloped possibilities in her draft, Nguyen developed some goals for revising.

MICHELLE NGUYEN'S REVISION GOALS

- Add a title.

- Revise introduction to set the scene more dramatically. Use Sameera's idea to include a photo of my neighborhood.

- Make the story my story, not the man's story. Answer Sameera's question: What did the man see in me and I in him? Delete extra material about the old man.

- Answer Brian's question: What is my main idea?

- Follow Brian's suggestion about the connection between wordlessness and worldliness. Make the contrasts sharper between the neighborhood and the man's house.

- Figure out what main idea I'm trying to communicate. See if there is a possible idea in the various contrasts. The surprise was finding writing in silence, not in the noisy exchange of voices in my neighborhood.

See pages 59–61 for Nguyen's revised draft.

2e Approach global revision in cycles.

Revision is more effective when you approach it in cycles, rather than attempting to change everything all at once. Four common cycles of global revision are discussed in this section:

- Engaging the audience
- Sharpening the focus
- Improving the organization
- Strengthening the content

Engaging the audience

Sometimes a rough draft needs an overhaul because it is directed at no particular audience. A good question to ask yourself and your reviewers is the toughest question a reader might ask: "So what?" If your draft can't pass the "So what?" test, you may need to rethink your entire approach.

Once you have made sure that your draft is directed at an audience—readers who have a stake in the topic—you may still need to refine your tone. The tone of a piece of writing expresses the writer's feelings toward the audience and the topic, so it is important to get it right. When you seek responses to your draft, ask your readers about your tone. If they respond that your tone seems self-centered, breezy, bossy, patronizing, or hostile, you'll want to modify it to show respect for your readers.

The following paragraph was drafted by a student who hoped to persuade his audience to buy organic produce.

A PARAGRAPH THAT ALIENATES READERS

If you choose to buy organic produce, you are supporting local farmers as well as demonstrating your opposition to chemical pesticides. As more and more supermarkets carry organic fruits and vegetables, consumers have fewer reasons not to buy organic. Some consumers do not buy organic produce because they are not willing to spend the extra money. But if you care at all about the environment or the small farmer, you should be willing to support organic farms in your area.

When the student asked a classmate to review his draft, his classmate recommended a more diplomatic tone so that readers didn't feel insulted or attacked. The classmate also questioned why he assumed his readers didn't care about the environment.

A PARAGRAPH THAT RESPECTS READERS

By choosing to buy organic produce, you have the opportunity to support local farmers, to oppose the use of chemical pesticides, and to taste some of the freshest produce available. Because more supermarkets carry organic produce than ever, you won't even have to miss out on any of your favorite fruits or vegetables. Although organic produce can be more expensive than conventional produce, the costs are not prohibitive. For example, a pound of organic bananas at my local grocery store is eighty-nine cents, while the conventional bananas are sixty-nine cents a pound. If you can afford this small price difference, you will have the opportunity to make a difference for the environment and for the small farmer.

—Leon Nage, student

Sharpening the focus

A clearly focused draft fixes readers' attention on one central idea and does not stray from that idea. You can sharpen the focus of a draft by clarifying the introduction (especially the thesis) and by deleting any text that is off the point.

Clarifying the introduction   Reread your introduction to see if it clearly states the essay's main idea. To help you revise, ask your reviewers questions such as the following:

- Does the introduction let readers know what to expect?

- Does it make clear the significance of the subject so that readers will want to keep reading?

- Have you included material in the introduction that really belongs in the body? Is your introduction too broad or unfocused?

- Does the thesis accurately state the main idea of the essay?

Deleting text that is off the point Compare the introduction, especially the thesis statement, with the body of the essay. Does the body fulfill the promise of the introduction? If not, you will need to adjust one or the other. Either rebuild the introduction to fit the body or keep the introduction and delete body sentences or paragraphs that stray from its point.

Improving the organization

A draft is well organized when its major divisions are logical and easy to follow. To improve the organization of your draft, you may need to take one or more of the following actions: adding or sharpening topic sentences, moving blocks of text, and inserting headings.

Adding or sharpening topic sentences Topic sentences state the main ideas of the paragraphs in the body of an essay. (See 3a.) You can review the organization of a draft by reading only the topic sentences. Do the topic sentences clearly support the essay's main idea? Can you turn them into a reasonable sentence outline of the paper? (See 1d.) If your draft lacks topic sentences, add them unless you have a good reason for omitting them.

Moving blocks of text Improving the organization of a draft can be as simple as moving a few sentences from one paragraph to another or reordering paragraphs. You may also find that you can clarify the organization of a draft by combining choppy paragraphs or by dividing those that are too long for easy reading. (See 3e.) Often, however, the process is more complex. As you move blocks of text, you may need to supply transitions to make the text fit smoothly in the new positions; you may also need to rework topic sentences to make your new organization clear.

Before moving text, consider sketching a revised outline. Divisions in the outline might become topic sentences in the restructured essay. (See 1d.)

Inserting headings In long documents, such as complex research papers or business reports, headings can help readers follow your organization. Typically, headings are presented as phrases (*The effects of sleep deprivation*), declarative or imperative sentences (*Understand the effects of sleep deprivation*), or questions (*What are the effects of sleep deprivation?*). To draw attention to headings, you can center them, put them in boldface, underline them, use all capital letters, or do some combination of these techniques. (See also 62a for use of headings in APA papers.)

Strengthening the content

In reviewing the content of a draft, first consider whether your argument is sound. You may need to rethink your argument as you revise. Second, consider whether any text (sentences or paragraphs) should be added or deleted, keeping in mind what your readers need to know to understand your ideas. If your purpose is to argue a point, consider how persuasively you have proved your point to an intelligent, thoughtful audience. If your purpose is to inform, be sure that you have presented your ideas clearly and with enough detail to meet readers' needs.

Rethinking your argument A first draft presents you with an opportunity to rethink your argument. You can often deepen your ideas about a subject by asking yourself some hard questions:

- Is your claim more sweeping than the evidence supports?
- Have you left out an important step in the argument?
- Have you dealt fairly with opposing arguments?
- Is your draft free of faulty reasoning? (See 6a.)

Checklist for global revision

Purpose and audience

- Does the draft address a question, a problem, or an issue that readers care about?
- Is the draft appropriate for its audience? Does it address the audience's knowledge of and attitudes toward the subject?
- Is the tone respectful?

Focus

- Is the thesis clear? Is it prominently placed?
- Does the thesis answer a reader's "So what?" question?
- If the draft has no thesis, do you have a good reason for omitting it?

Organization and paragraphing

- Is each paragraph unified around a main point?
- Does each paragraph support and develop the thesis?
- Have you provided organizational cues such as topic sentences and headings?
- Have you presented ideas in a logical order?
- Are any paragraphs too long or too short for easy reading?

Content

- Is the supporting material relevant and persuasive?
- Which ideas need further development? Have you left your readers with any unanswered questions?
- Are the parts proportioned sensibly? Do major ideas receive enough attention?
- Where might you delete redundant or irrelevant material?

Point of view

- Is the dominant point of view—first person (*I* or *we*), second person (*you*), or third person (*he, she, it, one,* or *they*)—appropriate for your purpose and audience? (See 13a.)

Adding text   If any paragraphs or sections of the essay are too skimpy to be clear and convincing (a common problem in rough drafts), add specific facts, details, and examples. You may need to go back to the beginning of the writing process: listing specifics, brainstorming ideas with friends or classmates, perhaps doing more research. As you revise paragraphs, it's helpful to ask questions such as *Why?* and *How?*

Deleting text   Look for sentences and paragraphs that can be cut without serious loss of meaning. Ask your reviewers if they can show you sentences where you have repeated yourself or strayed from your point. Maybe you have given too much emphasis to minor ideas. Cuts may also be necessitated by word limits, such as those imposed by a college assignment or by the realities of a professional environment.

2f Revise and edit sentences.

When you *revise* sentences, you focus on clarity and effectiveness; when you *edit*, you check for correctness. Sentences that are wordy, vague, or rambling may distract readers and make it hard for readers to focus on your purpose or grasp your ideas. Read each sentence slowly to determine if it is as specific and clear as possible. You might find it helpful to read your work aloud and trust your ears to detect awkwardness, wordiness, or a jarring repetition. Your goal as you revise your sentences is to make each word count to keep the attention and interest of your readers.

Here, for example, is a rough-draft paragraph as one student made changes to solve a variety of sentence-level problems.

Although some cities have found creative ways to improve access to public transportation for passengers with physical disabilities, ~~and to fund other programs, there have been problems in~~ our city has struggled with ~~due to the need to address~~ budget constraints and competing ~~needs~~ priorities. ~~This~~ The budget crunch has led citizens to question how funds are distributed~~.~~? For example, last year ~~when~~ city officials voted to use available funds to support ~~had to choose between allocating funds for accessible transportation or allocating funds to~~ after-school programs rather than transportation upgrades~~., they voted for the after-school programs.~~ It is not clear to some citizens why ~~these~~ after-school programs are more important.

The original paragraph was too wordy, a problem that can be addressed through any number of revisions to clarify the meaning of each sentence. The following revision would also be acceptable.

> Some cities have funded improved access to public transportation for passengers with physical disabilities. Because of budget constraints, our city chose to fund after-school programs rather than transportation programs. As a result, citizens have begun to question how funds are distributed and why certain programs are more important than others.

Some of the improvements in the first revision do not involve choice and must be edited to avoid confusion and mis-understanding. For example, the hyphen in *after-school programs* is necessary; a noun must be substituted for the pronoun *these* in the last sentence; and the question mark in the second sentence must be changed to a period.

2g Proofread the final manuscript.

Proofreading is a special kind of reading: a slow and methodi-cal search for misspellings, typographical mistakes, and omit-ted words or word endings. Such errors can be difficult to spot in your own work because you may read what you intended to

Improve your writing with an editing log

An important aspect of becoming a college writer is learning how to identify the grammar, punctuation, and spelling errors that you make frequently. You can use an editing log to keep a list of your common errors, anticipate error patterns, and learn the rules needed to correct the errors.

1 When your instructor or tutor returns a draft, review any errors he or she has identified.

2 Note which errors you commonly make. For example, have you seen "run-on sentence" or "need a transition" in other drafts?

3 Identify the advice in the handbook that will help you correct the errors.

4 Make an entry in your editing log. A suggested format appears below.

SAMPLE EDITING LOG PAGE

Original Sentence

Athletes who use any type of biotechnology give themselves an

unfair advantage they should be banned from competition.

Edited Sentence

Athletes who use any type of biotechnology give themselves an

unfair advantage they should be banned from competition.
　　　　　　　　　, and
　　　　　　　　　　^

Rule or Pattern Applied

To edit a run-on sentence, use a comma and a coordinating

conjunction (*and, but, or*). Handbook, section 20a

write, not what is actually on the page. To fight this natural tendency, try one or more of the following tips.

PROOFREADING TIPS

- Remove distractions and allow yourself ten to fifteen minutes of pure concentration; turn off the TV and your cell phone and find a quiet place, away from people who are talking.

- Proofread out loud, articulating each word as it is actually written.

- Proofread your sentences in reverse order.

- Proofread hard copy pages; mistakes can be difficult to catch on-screen.

- Don't rely too heavily on spell checkers and grammar checkers. Before automatically accepting their changes, consider their accuracy and appropriateness.

- Ask a volunteer (a friend, roommate, or co-worker) to proofread after you. A second reader may catch something you didn't.

2h Sample student revision: Literacy narrative

On pages 47–48, you'll find Michelle Nguyen's first draft, along with the highlights of her peer review process. Comments from her peer reviewers helped Nguyen see her draft through her readers' eyes and to develop a revision plan (see p. 49). One reviewer asked: "What is your main idea?" Another reviewer asked: "What do you want readers to understand about you?" As she revised, Nguyen made both global revisions and sentence-level revisions to clarify her main idea and to delete extra material that might distract readers from her story. Nguyen's final draft, "A Place to Begin," starts on page 59.

Michelle Nguyen

Professor Wilson

English 101

22 September 2015

A Place to Begin

I grew up in the heart of Hanoi, Vietnam — Nhà Dầu — a small but busy neighborhood swamped with crime. Houses, wedged in among cafés and other local businesses (see fig. 1), measured uniformly about 200 square feet, and the walls were so thin that we could hear every heated debate and impassioned disagreement. Drug addicts scoured the vicinity and stole the most mundane things — old clothes, worn slippers, even license plates of motorbikes. It was a neighborhood where dogs howled and kids ran amok and where the earth was always moist and marked with stains. It was the 1990s Vietnam in miniature, with all the turmoil and growing pains of a newly reborn nation.

In a city perpetually inundated with screaming children and slimy criminals, I found my place in the home of a Vietnam War veteran. My parents were away a lot, so the old man became like a grandfather to me. He was a slight man who didn't talk much. His vocal cords had been damaged during the war, and it caused him pain to speak. In his quiet home, I could read and write in the presence of someone whose worldliness grew from his wordlessness.

His tiny house stood at the far end of our neighborhood and always smelled of old clothes and forgotten memories. His wall was plastered with pictures from his combatant past, pictures that told his life story when his own voice couldn't. "I almost died once," he said, dusting a picture frame. It was one of those rare instances he ever mentioned his life during the war.

Nguyen formats her final draft using MLA guidelines.

Nguyen revises her introduction to engage readers with vivid details.

Sentences revised for clarity and specificity.

Nguyen focuses on one key story in response to reviewers' questions.

Nguyen's revisions clarify her main idea.

Marginal annotations indicate MLA-style formatting and effective writing.

Nguyen 2

As her peer reviewers suggested, Nguyen adds a photograph to help readers visualize Hanoi.

Fig. 1. Nhà Dầu neighborhood in Hanoi (personal photograph by author).

I perched myself on the side of the armchair, rested my head on my tiny hands, and listened intently. I didn't understand much. I just liked hearing his low, raspy voice.

Nguyen develops her narrative with dialogue.

"I was the only survivor of my unit. Twenty guys. All dead within a year. Then they let me go."

He finished the sentence with a drawn-out sigh, a small set of wrinkles gathering at the corner of his eye.

I wanted to hear the details of that story yet was too afraid to ask. But the bits and pieces I did hear, I wrote down in a notebook. I wanted to make sure that there were not only photos but also written words to bear witness to the old veteran's existence.

Nguyen revises to keep the focus on her story and not the old man's, as her peer reviewers suggested.

Once, I caught him looking at the jumbled mess of sentences I'd written. I ran to the table and snatched my notebook, my cheeks warmed with a bright tinge of pink. I was embarrassed. But mostly, I was terrified that he'd hate me for stealing his life story and turning it into a collection of words and characters and ambivalent feelings.

"I'm sorry," I muttered, my gaze drilling a hole into the tiled floor.

Quietly, he peeled the notebook from my fingers and placed it back on the table.

In his muted way, with his mouth barely twisted in a smile, he seemed to be granting me permission and encouraging me to keep writing. Maybe he saw a storyteller and a writer in me, a little girl with a pencil and too much free time.

The last time I visited Nhà Dầu was for the veteran's funeral two years ago. It was a cold November afternoon, but the weather didn't dampen the usual tumultuous spirit of the neighborhood. I could hear the jumble of shouting voices and howling dogs, yet it didn't bother me. For a minute I closed my eyes, remembering myself as a little girl with a big pencil, gazing out a window and scribbling words in my first notebook.

Many people think that words emerge from words and from the exchange of voices. Perhaps this is true. But the surprising paradox of writing for me is that I started to write in the presence of silence. It was only in the utter stillness of a Vietnam War veteran's house that I could hear my thoughts for the first time, appreciate language, and find the confidence to put words on a page. With one notebook and a pencil, and with the encouragement of a wordless man to tell his story, I began to write. Sometimes that's all a writer needs, a quiet place to begin.

Nguyen revises her final two paragraphs, circling back to the scene from the introduction, giving the narrative coherence.

Nguyen revises the final paragraph to show readers the significance of her narrative.

Following a peer reviewer's advice, Nguyen chooses words from her final sentence for her title.

WRITING PRACTICE

Learning from a fellow writer

You'll find Michelle Nguyen's rough draft and revision goals on pages 47–49 and her final draft on pages 59–61. With your classmates, discuss Nguyen's revision process. What did she learn from her peers' comments? How did her revision goals focus her revision? What three or four significant changes did she make to strengthen her final draft? Write a brief response: What have you learned about revision from studying the peer comments and Michelle Nguyen's revised draft?

2i Prepare a portfolio; reflect on your writing.

At the end of the semester, your instructor may ask you to submit a portfolio, or collection, of your writing. A writing portfolio often consists of drafts, revisions, and reflections that demonstrate a writer's thinking and learning processes or that showcase the writer's best work. Your instructor may give you the choice of submitting your portfolio on paper or electronically.

As early in the course as possible, be sure you know the answers to the following questions:

- Should the portfolio be a paper collection or an electronic one? Is it your choice?

- Will the portfolio be checked or assessed before the end of the term? If so, when or how often? By whom?

- Are you free to choose any or all of the pieces to include?

- Are you free to include a variety of items (not just rough and final drafts of papers), such as outlines and notes, journal entries, photographs or other visuals, comments from reviewers, sound files, or video clips?

How to write a literacy narrative

A **literacy narrative** allows you to reflect on key reading or writing experiences and to ask: How have my experiences shaped who I am as a reader or writer? A sample literacy narrative begins on page 59.

Key features

- **A well-told narrative** shows readers what happened. Lively details present the sights, sounds, and smells of the world in which the story takes place. Dialogue and action add interest and energy.

- **A main idea or insight** about reading or writing gives a literacy narrative its significance and transforms it from a personal story to one with larger, universal interest.

- **A well-organized narrative**, like all essays, has a beginning, a middle, and an ending and is focused around a thesis or main idea. Narratives can be written in chronological order, in reverse chronological order, or with a series of flashbacks.

- **First-person point of view (I)** gives a narrative immediacy and authenticity. Your voice may be serious or humorous, but it should be appropriate for your main idea.

Thinking ahead: Presenting or publishing

You may have some flexibility in how you present or publish your literacy narrative. If you have the opportunity to submit it as a podcast, a video, or another genre, leave time in your schedule for recording or filming. Also, in seeking feedback, ask reviewers to comment on your plans for using sounds or images.

→

Writing your literacy narrative

Explore

What story will you tell? You can't write about every reading or writing experience or every influential person. Find one interesting experience to focus your narrative. Generate ideas with questions such as the following:

- What challenges have you confronted as a reader or a writer?
- Who were the people who nurtured (or delayed) your reading or writing development?
- What are your best or worst childhood memories of reading or writing?
- What images do you associate with learning to read or write?
- What is significant about the story you want to tell? What larger point do you want readers to take away from your narrative?

Draft

Figure out the best way to tell your story. A narrative isn't a list of "this happened" and then "that happened." It is a focused story with its own logic and order. You don't need to start chronologically. Experiment: What happens if you start in the middle of the story or work in reverse? Try to come up with a tentative organization, and then start to draft.

Revise

Ask reviewers for specific feedback. Here are some questions to guide their comments:

- What main idea do readers take away from your story? Ask them to summarize this idea in one sentence.
- Is the narrative focused around the main idea?
- Are the details vivid? Sufficient? Where might you convey your story more clearly? Would it help to add dialogue? Would visuals deepen the impact of your story?
- Does your introduction bring readers into the world of your story?
- Does your conclusion provide a sense of the story's importance?

- Will your instructor be the primary or only audience for the portfolio? Or will the portfolio be shared with peers or with other instructors?

TIP: Save your notes, drafts, and reviewers' comments for possible use in your portfolio. The more you have assembled, the more you have to choose from to represent your best work. Keep your documents organized in a paper or an electronic file system for easy access. (See 1h.)

Reflection—the process of stepping back periodically to examine your decisions, preferences, strengths, and challenges as a writer—helps you recognize your growth as a writer and is the backbone of portfolio keeping.

When you submit your portfolio for a final evaluation or reading, you may be asked to include a reflective opening statement—a cover letter, an introduction, a preface, a memo, or an essay. Whatever form your reflective piece takes, it could be your most important writing in the course. Reflective writing allows you to do the following:

- show that you can identify the strengths and weaknesses of your writing
- comment on the progress you've made in the course
- understand your own writing process
- demonstrate that you've made good writing decisions
- comment on how you might use skills developed in or experiences from your writing course in other courses in which writing is assigned

Your instructor will expect you to reflect, too, on how *specific* pieces in the portfolio show your development as a writer, as student writer Lucy Bonilla does on pages 66–69.

Check with your instructor about the guidelines for your reflective opening statement.

SAMPLE REFLECTIVE LETTER FOR A PORTFOLIO

Bonilla 1

December 11, 2014
Professor Todd Andersen
Humanities Department
Johnson State College

Dear Professor Andersen,

> Reflective writing can take various forms. Bonilla wrote her reflection as a letter.

This semester has been more challenging than I had anticipated. I have always been a good writer, but I discovered this semester that I had to stretch myself in ways that weren't always comfortable. I learned that if I wanted to reach my readers, I needed to understand

> Reflective writing often calls for first person ("I").

that not everyone sees the world the way I do. I needed to work with my peers and write multiple drafts to understand that a first draft is just a place to start. I have chosen three pieces of writing for my

> Bonilla lists the pieces included in her portfolio by title.

portfolio: "Negi and the Other Girl: Nicknames and Identity," "School Choice Is a Bad Choice," and "Flat-Footed Advertising." Each shows my growth as a writer in different ways, and the final piece was my favorite assignment of the semester.

The peer review sessions that our class held in October helped me with my analytical response paper. My group and I chose to write about "Jíbara," by Esmeralda Santiago, for the Identity unit. My first and second drafts were unfocused. I spent my first draft basically retelling the events of the essay. I think I got stuck doing that because the details of Santiago's essay are so interesting — the biting termites, the burning metal, and the *jíbara* songs on the radio — and because I didn't understand the

> Bonilla comments on a specific area of growth.

differences between summary and analysis. My real progress came when I decided to focus the essay on one image — the mirror hanging in Santiago's small house, a mirror that was hung too high

Bonilla 2

for her to look into. Finding a focus helped me move from listing the events of the essay to interpreting those events. I thought my peers would love my first draft, but they found it confusing. Some of their comments were hard to take, but their feedback (and all the peer feedback I received this semester) helped me see my words through a reader's eyes.

While my Identity paper shows my struggle with focus, my next paper shows my struggle with argument. For my argument essay, I wrote about charter schools. My position is that the existence of charter schools weakens the quality of public schools. In my first draft, my lines of argument were not in the best order. When I revised, I ended the paper with my most powerful argument: Because they refuse to adopt open enrollment policies and are unwilling to admit students with severe learning or behavior problems, charter schools are elitist. While revising, I also introduced a counterargument in my final draft because our class discussion showed me that many of my peers disagree with me. To persuade them, I needed to address their arguments in favor of charter schools. My essay is stronger because I acknowledged that both the proponents and opponents of abandoning charters want improved education for America's children. It took me a while to understand that including counterarguments would actually make my argument more convincing, especially to readers who don't already agree with me. Understanding the importance of counterargument helped me with other writing I did in this course, and it will help me in the writing I do for my major, political science.

Another stretch for me this semester was seeing visuals as texts that are worth more than a five-second response. The final assignment was my favorite because it involved a number of surprises. I wasn't

Even in the reflective document, Bonilla includes elements of good college writing, such as using transitions.

Bonilla reflects on how skills from her writing course will carry over to other courses.

Bonilla 3

so much surprised by the idea that ads make arguments because I understand that they are designed to persuade consumers. What was surprising was being able to see all the elements of a visual and write about how they work together to convey a clear message. For my essay "Flat-Footed Advertising," I chose the EAS Performance Nutrition ad "The New Theory of Evolution for Women." In my summary of the ad, I noted that the woman who follows the EAS program for twelve weeks and "evolves" is compared to modern humans and our evolution from apes as shown in the classic 1966 *March of Progress* illustration (Howell 41). It was these familiar poses of "Nicolle," the woman in the image, that drew me to study this ad.

In my first draft, I made all of the obvious points, looking only literally at the comparison and almost congratulating the company on such a clever use of a classic scientific drawing. Your comments on my draft were a little unsettling because you asked me "So what?" — why would my ideas matter to a reader? You pushed me to consider the ad's assumptions and to question the meaning of the word *evolve*. In my revised essay, I argue that even though Nicolle is portrayed as powerful, satisfied, and "fully evolved," the EAS ad campaign rests on the assumption that performance is best measured by physical milestones. In the end, an ad that is meant to pay homage to woman's strength is in fact demeaning. My essay evolved from draft to draft because I allowed my thinking to change and develop as I revised. I've never revised as much as I did with this final assignment. I actually cared about this essay, and I wanted to show my readers why my argument mattered.

The expectations for college writing are different from those for high school writing. I believe that my portfolio pieces show that I finished this course as a stronger writer. I have learned to take risks in

Bonilla mentions how comments on her draft helped her revise.

In her conclusion, Bonilla summarizes her growth in the course.

my writing and to use the feedback from you and my peers, and now
I know how to acknowledge the points of view of my audience to
be more persuasive. I'm glad to have had the chance to write a
reflection at the end of the course. I hope you enjoy reading this
portfolio and seeing the evolution of my work this semester.

Sincerely,

Lucy Bonilla

Lucy Bonilla

How to write a reflective letter

A **reflective letter** gives you an opportunity to introduce yourself as a writer, to show your progress and key decisions, and to introduce the contents of a portfolio or a significant revision. A sample reflective letter begins on page 66.

Key features

- **First-person perspective (*I*)** gives a reflective statement its individuality and authenticity. You are the writer; you are introducing your work and explaining your choices.

- **A thoughtful tone** shows you examining and learning from your experiences and evaluating your strengths and limitations as a writer. Your honest assessment of your work shows that you are a trustworthy and sincere interpreter of your progress.

- **A focused opening statement** provides readers with specific details to understand the contents and organization of your portfolio.

- **Acknowledgment** of the assistance you received shows that you are responsible to readers and reviewers.

Thinking ahead: Presenting or publishing

You may have some flexibility in how you present or publish a reflective piece for your portfolio. Some instructors require a formal essay; others may ask for a letter. Still others may invite you to submit an audio file. If you are submitting an e-portfolio, chances are that your instructor will require your reflective statement in digital form. If you're publishing for the Web, you may want to insert headings for easier navigation.

Writing your reflective letter

1 Explore

Generate ideas by brainstorming responses to questions such as the following:

- Which piece of writing is your best entry? What does it illustrate about you as a writer, student, or researcher?
- How do the selections in your portfolio illustrate your strengths or challenges?
- What do you learn about your development when you compare your early drafts with your final drafts?
- What do your drafts reveal about your revision process? Examine in detail the revisions you made to one key piece and the changes you want readers to notice.
- How will you use the skills and experiences from your writing course in future courses?

2 Draft

Follow the guidelines given for the form of your reflective statement—an essay, a cover letter, a memo—and focus your reflections to avoid a list-like structure. Experiment with headings and various chronological or thematic groupings. Ask: What have I learned—and how?

3 Revise

Ask reviewers for specific feedback. Here are some questions to guide their comments:

- What major idea do readers take away from your reflective statement? Can they summarize it in one sentence?
- Where in your piece do readers want more reflection and more detailed explanations?
- Is your reflective statement focused and organized?
- Have you used specific passages from drafts, feedback, or other documents from your portfolio to illustrate your reflections?
- Have you explained how you will apply what you learned to future writing assignments?
- What added details might give readers a fuller perspective of your development and your accomplishments in the course?

3 Building effective paragraphs

A paragraph is a group of sentences that focuses on one main point or example. Except for special-purpose paragraphs, such as introductions and conclusions (see 1e and 1g), body paragraphs function to develop and support an essay's main point or thesis. Aim for paragraphs that are well developed, organized, coherent, and neither too long nor too short for easy reading. Note that there is no ideal length for a paragraph, but your instructor may have specific guidelines.

3a Focus on a main point.

A paragraph should be unified around a main point. The point should be clear to readers, and all sentences in the paragraph should relate to it.

Stating the main point in a topic sentence

As readers move into a paragraph, they need to know both where they are in relation to the whole essay and what to expect in the sentences to come. A good topic sentence, a one-sentence summary of the paragraph's main point, acts as a signpost pointing in two directions: backward toward the thesis of the essay and forward toward the body of the paragraph.

Like a thesis statement (see 1c), a topic sentence is more general than the material supporting it. Usually the topic sentence (highlighted in the following example) comes first in the paragraph.

All living creatures manage some form of communication. The dance patterns of bees in their hive help to point the way to distant flower fields or announce successful foraging. Male stickleback fish regularly swim upside-down to indicate outrage in a courtship contest. Male deer and lemurs mark territorial ownership by rubbing their own body secretions on boundary stones or trees. Everyone has seen a frightened dog put his tail between his legs and run in panic. We, too, use gestures, expressions, postures, and movement to give our words point.

— Olivia Vlahos, *Human Beginnings*

In college writing, topic sentences are often necessary for advancing or clarifying lines of an argument and introducing evidence from a source. In the following paragraph on the effects of the 2010 oil spill in the Gulf of Mexico, the writer uses a topic sentence (highlighted) to state that the extent of the threat is unknown before quoting three sources that illustrate her point.

To date, the full ramifications [of the oil spill] remain a question mark. An August report from the National Oceanic and Atmospheric Administration estimated that 75 percent of the oil had "either evaporated or been burned, skimmed, recovered from the wellhead, or dispersed." However, Woods Hole Oceanographic Institution researchers reported that a 1.2-mile-wide, 650-foot-high plume caused by the spill "had and will persist for some time." And University of Georgia scientists concluded that almost 80 percent of the released oil hadn't been recovered and "remains a threat to the ecosystem."

— Michele Berger, "Volunteer Army"

Occasionally the topic sentence may be withheld until the end of the paragraph—but only if the earlier sentences hang together so well that readers perceive their direction, if not their exact point.

Sticking to the point

Sentences that do not support the topic sentence destroy the unity of a paragraph. If the paragraph is otherwise focused, such sentences can simply be deleted or perhaps moved elsewhere. In the following paragraph describing the inadequate facilities in a high school, the information about the chemistry instructor (highlighted) is clearly off the point.

As the result of tax cuts, the educational facilities of Lincoln High School have reached an all-time low. Some of the books date back to 1990 and have long since shed their covers. The few computers in working order must share one printer. The lack of lab equipment makes it necessary for four or five students to work at one table, with most watching rather than performing experiments. Also, the chemistry instructor left to have a baby at the beginning of the semester, and most of the students don't like the substitute. As for the furniture, many of the upright chairs have become recliners, and the desk legs are so unbalanced that they play seesaw on the floor.

EXERCISE 3–1 Underline the topic sentence in the following paragraph and cross out any material that does not clarify or develop the central idea.

Quilt making has served as an important means of social, political, and artistic expression for women. In the nineteenth century, quilting circles provided one of the few opportunities for women to forge social bonds outside of their families. Once a week or more, they came together to sew as well as trade small talk, advice, and news. They used dyed cotton fabrics much like the fabrics quilters use today; surprisingly, quilters' basic materials haven't changed that much over the years. Sometimes the women joined their efforts in support of a politi-cal cause, making quilts that would be raffled to raise money for temperance societies, hospitals for sick and wounded soldiers, and the fight against slavery. Quilt making also afforded women a means of artistic expression at a time when they had few other creative outlets. Within their socially acceptable roles as homemakers, many quilters subtly pushed back at the restrictions placed on them by experimenting with color, design, and technique.

3b Develop the main point.

Though an occasional short paragraph is fine, particularly if it functions as a transition or emphasizes a point, a series of brief paragraphs suggests inadequate development. How much development is enough? That varies, depending on the writer's purpose and audience.

For example, when health columnist Jane Brody wrote a paragraph attempting to convince readers that it is impossible to lose fat quickly, she knew that she would have to present a great deal of evidence because many dieters want to believe the opposite. She did *not* write only the following.

UNDERDEVELOPED PARAGRAPH

When you think about it, it's impossible to lose — as many diets suggest — 10 pounds of *fat* in ten days, even on a total fast. Even a moderately active person cannot lose so much weight so fast. A less active person hasn't a prayer.

This three-sentence paragraph is too skimpy to be convincing. But the paragraph that Brody did write contains enough evidence to convince even skeptical readers.

WELL-DEVELOPED PARAGRAPH

When you think about it, it's impossible to lose — as many . . . diets suggest — 10 pounds of *fat* in ten days, even on a total fast. A pound of body fat represents 3,500 calories. To lose 1 pound of fat, you must expend 3,500 more calories than you consume. Let's say you weigh 170 pounds and, as a moderately active person, you burn 2,500 calories a day. If your diet contains only 1,500 calories, you'd have an energy deficit of 1,000 calories a day. In a week's time that would add up to a 7,000-calorie deficit, or 2 pounds of real fat. In ten days, the accumulated deficit would represent nearly 3 pounds of lost body fat. Even if you ate nothing at all for ten days and maintained your usual level of activity, your caloric deficit would add up to 25,000 calories. . . . At 3,500 calories per pound of fat, that's still only 7 pounds of lost fat.

—Jane Brody, *Jane Brody's Nutrition Book*

3c Choose a suitable pattern of organization.

Although paragraphs (and indeed whole essays) may be patterned in any number of ways, certain patterns of organization occur frequently, either alone or in combination: examples and illustrations, narration, description, process, comparison and contrast, analogy, cause and effect, classification and division, and definition. These patterns (sometimes called *methods of development*) have different uses, depending on the writer's subject and purpose.

Examples and illustrations

Examples, perhaps the most common pattern of development, are appropriate whenever the reader might be tempted to ask, "For example?" Though examples are just selected instances, not a complete catalog, they are enough to suggest the truth of many topic sentences, as in the following paragraph.

Normally my parents abided scrupulously by "The Budget," but several times a year Dad would dip into his battered black strongbox and splurge on some irrational, totally satisfying luxury. Once he bought over a hundred comic books at a flea market, doled out to us thereafter at the tantalizing rate of two a week. He always got a whole flat of pansies, Mom's favorite flower, for us to give her on Mother's Day. One day a boy stopped at our house selling fifty-cent raffle tickets on a sailboat, and Dad bought every ticket the boy had left—three books' worth.

—Connie Hailey, student

Illustrations are extended examples, frequently presented in story form. Because they require several sentences apiece, they are used more sparingly than examples. When well selected, however, they can be a vivid and effective means of developing a point. The writer of the following paragraph uses illustrations to demonstrate that Harriet Tubman, the underground railroad's most famous conductor, was a genius at eluding her pursuers.

Part of [Harriet Tubman's] strategy of conducting was, as in all battle-field operations, the knowledge of how and when to retreat. Numerous allusions have been made to her moves when she suspected that she was in danger. When she feared the party was closely pursued, she would take it for a time on a train southward bound. No one seeing Negroes going in this direction would for an instant suppose them to be fugitives. Once on her return she was at a railroad station. She saw some men reading a poster and she heard one of them reading it aloud. It was a description of her, offering a reward for her capture. She took a southbound train to avert suspicion. At another time when Harriet heard men talking about her, she pretended to read a book which she carried. One man remarked, "This can't be the woman. The one we want can't read or write." Harriet devoutly hoped the book was right side up.

—Earl Conrad, *Harriet Tubman*

Narration

A paragraph of narration tells a story or part of a story. Narrative paragraphs are usually arranged in chronological order, but they may also contain flashbacks, interruptions that take the story back to an earlier time. The following paragraph, from Jane Goodall's *In the Shadow of Man*, recounts one of the author's experiences in the African wild.

> One evening when I was wading in the shallows of the lake to pass a rocky outcrop, I suddenly stopped dead as I saw the sinuous black body of a snake in the water. It was all of six feet long, and from the slight hood and the dark stripes at the back of the neck I knew it to be a Storm's water cobra—a deadly reptile for the bite of which there was, at that time, no serum. As I stared at it an incoming wave gently deposited part of its body on one of my feet. I remained motionless, not even breathing, until the wave rolled back into the lake, drawing the snake with it. Then I leaped out of the water as fast as I could, my heart hammering.
>
> —Jane Goodall, *In the Shadow of Man*

Description

A descriptive paragraph sketches a portrait of a person, place, or thing by using concrete and specific details that appeal to one or more of our senses—sight, sound, smell, taste, and touch. Consider, for example, the following description of the grasshopper invasions that devastated the midwestern landscape in the United States in the late 1860s.

> They came like dive bombers out of the west. They came by the millions with the rustle of their wings roaring overhead. They came in waves, like the rolls of the sea, descending with a terrifying speed, breaking now and again like a mighty surf. They came with the force of a williwaw and they formed a huge, ominous, dark brown cloud that eclipsed the sun. They dipped and touched earth, hitting objects and people like hailstones. But they were not hail. These were *live* demons. They popped, snapped, crackled,

and roared. They were dark brown, an inch or longer in length, plump in the middle and tapered at the ends. They had transparent wings, slender legs, and two black eyes that flashed with a fierce intelligence.

—Eugene Boe, "Pioneers to Eternity"

Process

A process paragraph is structured in chronological order. A writer may choose this pattern either to describe how something is made or done or to explain to readers, step-by-step, how to do something. Here is a paragraph explaining how to perform a "roll cast," a popular fly-fishing technique.

Begin by taking up a suitable stance, with one foot slightly in front of the other and the rod pointing down the line. Then begin a smooth, steady draw, raising your rod hand to just above shoulder height and lifting the rod to the 10:30 or 11:00 position. This steady draw allows a loop of line to form between the rod top and the water. While the line is still moving, raise the rod slightly, then punch it rapidly forward and down. The rod is now flexed and under maximum compression, and the line follows its path, bellying out slightly behind you and coming off the water close to your feet. As you power the rod down through the 3:00 position, the belly of line will roll forward. Follow through smoothly so that the line unfolds and straightens above the water.

—*The Dorling Kindersley Encyclopedia of Fishing*

Comparison and contrast

To compare two subjects is to draw attention to their similarities, although the word *compare* also has a broader meaning that includes a consideration of differences. To contrast is to focus only on differences.

Whether a paragraph stresses similarities or differences, it may be patterned in one of two ways. The two subjects may be presented one at a time, as in the following paragraph of contrast.

> So Grant and Lee were in complete contrast, representing two diametrically opposed elements in American life. Grant was the modern man emerging; beyond him, ready to come on the stage, was the great age of steel and machinery, of crowded cities and a restless, burgeoning vitality. Lee might have ridden down from the old age of chivalry, lance in hand, silken banner fluttering over his head. Each man was the perfect champion of his cause, drawing both his strengths and his weaknesses from the people he led.
>
> —Bruce Catton, "Grant and Lee: A Study in Contrasts"

Or a paragraph may proceed point by point, treating the two subjects together, one aspect at a time. The following paragraph uses the point-by-point method to contrast speeches given by Abraham Lincoln in 1860 and Barack Obama in 2008.

> Two men, two speeches. The men, both lawyers, both from Illinois, were seeking the presidency, despite what seemed their crippling connection with extremists. Each was young by modern standards for a president. Abraham Lincoln had turned fifty-one just five days before delivering his speech. Barack Obama was forty-six when he gave his. Their political experience was mainly provincial, in the Illinois legislature for both of them, and they had received little exposure at the national level—two years in the House of Representatives for Lincoln, four years in the Senate for Obama. Yet each was seeking his party's nomination against a New York senator of longer standing and greater prior reputation—Lincoln against Senator William Seward, Obama against Senator Hillary Clinton.
>
> —Garry Wills, "Two Speeches on Race"

Analogy

Analogies draw comparisons between items that appear to have little in common. Writers turn to analogies for a variety of reasons: to make the unfamiliar seem familiar, to provide a concrete understanding of an abstract topic, to argue a point, or to provoke fresh thoughts or changed feelings about a subject. In the following paragraph, physician Lewis Thomas draws an analogy between the behavior of ants and that of humans.

> Ants are so much like human beings as to be an embarrassment. They farm fungi, raise aphids as livestock, launch armies into wars, use chemical sprays to alarm and confuse enemies, capture slaves. The families of weaver ants engage in child labor, holding their larvae like shuttles to spin out the thread that sews the leaves together for their fungus gardens. They exchange information ceaselessly. They do everything but watch television.
> —Lewis Thomas, "On Societies as Organisms"

Although analogies can be a powerful tool for illuminating a subject, they should be used with caution in arguments. Just because two things may be alike in one respect, we cannot conclude that they are alike in all respects. (See "false analogy," p. 134.)

Cause and effect

When causes and effects are a matter of argument, they are too complex to be reduced to a simple pattern (see p. 134). However, if a writer wishes merely to describe a cause-and-effect relationship that is generally accepted, then the effect may be stated in the topic sentence, with the causes listed in the body of the paragraph.

The fantastic water clarity of the Mount Gambier sinkholes results from several factors. The holes are fed from aquifers holding rainwater that fell decades — even centuries — ago, and that has been filtered through miles of limestone. The high level of calcium that limestone adds causes the silty detritus from dead plants and animals to cling together and settle quickly to the bottom. Abundant bottom vegetation in the shallow sinkholes also helps bind the silt. And the rapid turnover of water prohibits stagnation.

— Hillary Hauser, "Exploring a Sunken Realm in Australia"

Or the paragraph may move from cause to effects, as in this paragraph from a student paper on the effects of the industrial revolution on American farms.

The rise of rail transport in the nineteenth century forever changed American farming — for better and for worse. Farmers who once raised crops and livestock to sustain just their own families could now make a profit by selling their goods in towns and cities miles away. These new markets improved the living standard of struggling farm families and encouraged them to seek out innovations that would increase their profits. On the downside, the competition fostered by the new markets sometimes created hostility among neighboring farm families where there had once been a spirit of cooperation. Those farmers who couldn't compete with their neighbors left farming forever, facing poverty worse than they had ever known.

— Chris Mileski, student

Classification and division

Classification is the grouping of items into categories according to some consistent principle. For example, an elementary school teacher might classify children's books according to their level of difficulty, but a librarian might group them by subject matter. The principle of classification that a writer chooses ultimately depends on the purpose of the classification. The following paragraph classifies species of electric fish.

> Scientists sort electric fishes into three categories. The first comprises the strongly electric species like the marine electric rays or the freshwater African electric catfish and South American electric eel. Known since the dawn of history, these deliver a punch strong enough to stun a human. In recent years, biologists have focused on a second category: weakly electric fish in the South American and African rivers that use tiny voltages for communication and navigation. The third group contains sharks, nonelectric rays, and catfish, which do not emit a field but possess sensors that enable them to detect the minute amounts of electricity that leak out of other organisms.
>
> —Anne and Jack Rudloe, "Electric Warfare: The Fish That Kill with Thunderbolts"

Division takes one item and divides it into parts. As with classification, division should be made according to some consistent principle. The following passage describes the components that make up a baseball.

> Like the game itself, a baseball is composed of many layers. One of the delicious joys of childhood is to take apart a baseball and examine the wonders within. You begin by removing the red cotton thread and peeling off the leather cover—which comes from the hide of a Holstein cow and has been tanned, cut, printed, and punched with holes. Beneath the cover is a thin layer of cotton string, followed by several hundred yards of woolen yarn, which makes up the bulk of the ball. Finally, in the middle is a rubber ball, or "pill," which is a little smaller than a golf ball. Slice into the rubber and you'll find the ball's heart—a cork core. The cork is from Portugal,

the rubber from southeast Asia, the covers are American, and
the balls are assembled in Costa Rica.

—Dan Gutman, *The Way Baseball Works*

Definition

A definition puts a word or concept into a general class and then
provides enough details to distinguish it from others in the same
class. In the following paragraph, the writer defines *crowdsourc-
ing* as a savvy business practice.

> Despite the jargony name, crowdsourcing is a very real
> and important business idea. Definitions and terms vary,
> but the basic idea is to tap into the collective intelligence of
> the public at large to complete business-related tasks that a
> company would normally either perform itself or outsource to
> a third-party provider. Yet free labor is only a narrow part of
> crowdsourcing's appeal. More importantly, it enables managers
> to expand the size of their talent pool while also gaining deeper
> insight into what customers really want.
>
> —Jennifer Alsever, "What Is Crowdsourcing?"

3d Make paragraphs coherent.

When sentences and paragraphs flow from one to another
without discernible bumps, gaps, or shifts, they are said to be
coherent. Coherence can be improved by strengthening the ties
between old information and new. A number of techniques for
strengthening those ties are detailed in this section.

Linking ideas clearly

Readers expect to learn a paragraph's main point in a topic sentence
early in the paragraph. Then, as they move into the body of the
paragraph, they expect to encounter specific details, facts, or examples that support the topic sentence—either directly or indirectly.

If a sentence does not support the topic sentence directly, readers expect it to support another sentence in the paragraph and therefore to support the topic sentence indirectly. The following paragraph begins with a topic sentence. The highlighted sentences are direct supports, and the rest of the sentences are indirect supports.

> Though the open-space classroom works for many children, it is not practical for my son, David. First, David is hyperactive. When he was placed in an open-space classroom, he became distracted and confused. He was tempted to watch the movement going on around him instead of concentrating on his own work. Second, David has a tendency to transpose letters and numbers, a tendency that can be overcome only by individual attention from the instructor. In the open classroom he was moved from teacher to teacher, with each one responsible for a different subject. No single teacher worked with David long enough to diagnose the problem, let alone help him with it. Finally, David is not a highly motivated learner. In the open classroom, he was graded "at his own level," not by criteria for a certain grade. He could receive a B in reading and still be a grade level behind, because he was doing satisfactory work "at his own level."
>
> —Margaret Smith, student

Repeating key words

Repetition of key words is an important technique for gaining coherence. To prevent repetitions from becoming dull, you can use variations of a key word (*hike, hiker, hiking*), pronouns referring to the word (*gamblers . . . they*), and synonyms (*run, spring, race, dash*). In the following paragraph describing plots among indentured servants in the seventeenth century, historian Richard Hofstadter binds sentences together by repeating the key word *plots* and echoing it with a variety of synonyms (which are highlighted).

Plots hatched by several servants to run away together occurred mostly in the plantation colonies, and the few recorded servant uprisings were entirely limited to those colonies. Virginia had been forced from its very earliest years to take stringent steps against mutinous plots, and severe punishments for such behavior were recorded. Most servant plots occurred in the seventeenth century: a contemplated uprising was nipped in the bud in York County in 1661; apparently led by some left-wing offshoots of the Great Rebellion, servants plotted an insurrection in Gloucester County in 1663, and four leaders were condemned and executed; some discontented servants apparently joined Bacon's Rebellion in the 1670's. In the 1680's the planters became newly apprehensive of discontent among the servants "owing to their great necessities and want of clothes," and it was feared they would rise up and plunder the storehouses and ships; in 1682 there were plant-cutting riots in which servants and laborers, as well as some planters, took part.

—Richard Hofstadter, *America at 1750*

Using parallel structures

Parallel structures are frequently used within sentences to underscore the similarity of ideas (see 9). They may also be used to bind together a series of sentences expressing similar information. In the following passage describing folk beliefs, anthropologist Margaret Mead presents similar information in parallel grammatical form.

Actually, almost every day, even in the most sophisticated home, something is likely to happen that evokes the memory of some old folk belief. The salt spills. A knife falls to the floor. Your nose tickles. Then perhaps, with a slightly embarrassed smile, the person who spilled the salt tosses a pinch over his left shoulder. Or someone recites the old rhyme, "Knife falls, gentleman calls." Or as you rub your nose you think, That means a letter. I wonder who's writing?

—Margaret Mead, "New Superstitions for Old"

Maintaining consistency

Coherence suffers whenever a draft shifts confusingly from one point of view to another or from one verb tense to another. (See 13.) In addition, coherence can suffer when new information is introduced with the subject of each sentence. As a rule, a sentence's subject should echo a subject or an object in the previous sentence.

Providing transitions

Transitions help readers move from sentence to sentence; they also alert readers to more global connections of ideas—those between paragraphs or even larger blocks of text.

Sentence-level transitions   Certain words and phrases signal connections between (or within) sentences. Frequently used transitions are included in the chart on page 89.

Skilled writers use transitional expressions with care, making sure, for example, not to use *consequently* when *also* would be more precise. They are also careful to select transitions with an appropriate tone, perhaps preferring *so* to *thus* in an informal piece, *in summary* to *in short* for a scholarly essay.

In the paragraph on the following page, taken from an argument that dinosaurs had the "'right-sized' brains for reptiles of their body size," biologist Stephen Jay Gould uses transitions (highlighted) with skill.

> **Academic English**

Choose transitions carefully and vary them appropriately. Each transition has a different meaning (see the chart on the following page). If you do not use a transition with an appropriate meaning, you might confuse your readers.

▶ Although taking eight o'clock classes may seem

unappealing, coming to school early has its advantages.
For example,
~~Moreover,~~ students who arrive early typically avoid
^

the worst traffic and find the best parking spaces.

I don't wish to deny that the flattened, minuscule head of large bodied Stegosaurus houses little brain from our subjective, top-heavy perspective, but I do wish to assert that we should not expect more of the beast. First of all, large animals have relatively smaller brains than related, small animals. The correlation of brain size with body size among kindred animals (all reptiles, all mammals, for example) is remarkably regular. As we move from small to large animals, from mice to elephants or small lizards to Komodo dragons, brain size increases, but not so fast as body size. In other words, bodies grow faster than brains, and large animals have low ratios of brain weight to body weight. In fact, brains grow only about two-thirds as fast as bodies. Since we have no reason to believe that large animals are consistently stupider than their smaller relatives, we must conclude that large animals require relatively less brain to do as well as smaller animals. If we do not recognize this relationship, we are likely to underestimate the mental power of very large animals, dinosaurs in particular.

—Stephen Jay Gould, "Were Dinosaurs Dumb?"

Common transitions	
TO SHOW ADDITION	and, also, besides, further, furthermore, in addition, moreover, next, too, first, second
TO GIVE EXAMPLES	for example, for instance, to illustrate, in fact, specifically
TO COMPARE	also, in the same manner, similarly, likewise
TO CONTRAST	but, however, on the other hand, in contrast, nevertheless, still, even though, on the contrary, yet, although
TO SUMMARIZE OR CONCLUDE	in short, in summary, in conclusion, to sum up, therefore
TO SHOW TIME	after, as, before, next, during, later, finally, meanwhile, then, when, while, immediately
TO SHOW PLACE OR DIRECTION	above, below, beyond, nearby, opposite, close, to the left
TO INDICATE LOGICAL RELATIONSHIP	if, so, therefore, consequently, thus, as a result, for this reason, because, since

Paragraph-level transitions Paragraph-level transitions usually link the *first* sentence of a new paragraph with the *first* sentence of the previous paragraph. In other words, the topic sentences signal global connections.

Look for opportunities to allude to the subject of a previous paragraph (as summed up in its topic sentence) in the topic sentence of the next one. In his essay "Little Green Lies," Jonathan H. Adler uses this strategy in the following topic sentences, which appear in a passage describing the benefits of plastic packaging.

Consider aseptic packaging, the synthetic packaging for the "juice boxes" so many children bring to school with their lunch. One criticism of aseptic packaging is that it is nearly impossible to recycle, yet on almost every other count, aseptic packaging is environmentally preferable to the packaging alternatives. Not only do aseptic containers not require refrigeration to keep their contents from spoiling, but their manufacture requires less than one-10th the energy of making glass bottles.

What is true for juice boxes is also true for other forms of synthetic packaging. The use of polystyrene, which is commonly (and mistakenly) referred to as "Styrofoam," can reduce food waste dramatically due to its insulating properties. (Thanks to these properties, polystyrene cups are much preferred over paper for that morning cup of coffee.) Polystyrene also requires significantly fewer resources to produce than its paper counterpart.

Transitions between blocks of text   In long essays, you will need to alert readers to connections between blocks of text that are more than one paragraph long. You can do this by inserting transitional sentences or short paragraphs at key points in the essay. Here, for example, is a transitional paragraph from a student research paper. It announces that the first part of the paper (about how apes demonstrate language skills) has come to a close and that the second part (about whether they understand grammar) is about to begin.

Although the great apes have demonstrated significant language skills, one central question remains: Can they be taught to use that uniquely human language tool we call grammar, to learn the difference, for instance, between "ape bite human" and "human bite ape"? In other words, can an ape create a sentence?

Another strategy to help readers move from one block of text to another is to insert headings in your essay. Headings, which usually sit above blocks of text, allow you to announce a new topic boldly, without the need for subtle transitions.

WRITING PRACTICE

Using transitions

Read your current draft and highlight any transitional words you use to show connections between ideas. Then review the list of common transitions on page 89 and consider what words or phrases you might add to help readers follow the progression of your ideas. Revise your draft to use transitions more effectively.

3e If necessary, adjust paragraph length.

Most readers feel comfortable reading paragraphs that range between one hundred and two hundred words. Shorter paragraphs require too much starting and stopping, and longer ones strain readers' attention span. There are exceptions to this guideline, however. Paragraphs longer than two hundred words frequently appear in scholarly writing, where scholars explore complex ideas. Paragraphs shorter than one hundred words occur in newspapers because of narrow columns; in informal essays to quicken the pace; and in business writing and on Web sites, where readers routinely skim for main ideas.

In an essay, the first and last paragraphs will ordinarily be the introduction and the conclusion. These special-purpose paragraphs are likely to be shorter than the paragraphs in the body of the essay. Typically, the body paragraphs will follow the essay's outline: one paragraph per point in short essays, several paragraphs per point in longer ones. Some ideas require more development than others, however, so it is best to be flexible. If an idea stretches to a length unreasonable for a paragraph, you should divide the paragraph, even if you have presented comparable points in the essay in single paragraphs.

Paragraph breaks are not always made for strictly logical reasons. Writers use them for the following reasons as well.

REASONS FOR BEGINNING A NEW PARAGRAPH

- to mark off the introduction and the conclusion
- to signal a shift to a new idea
- to indicate an important shift in time or place
- to emphasize a point (by placing it at the beginning or the end of a paragraph)
- to highlight a contrast
- to signal a change of speakers (in dialogue)
- to provide readers with a needed pause
- to break up text that looks too dense

Beware of using too many short, choppy paragraphs, however. Readers want to see how your ideas connect, and they become irritated when you break their momentum by forcing them to pause every few sentences. Here are some reasons you might have for combining some of the paragraphs in a rough draft.

REASONS FOR COMBINING PARAGRAPHS

- to clarify the essay's organization
- to connect closely related ideas
- to bind together text that looks too choppy

Academic Reading and Writing

4 Reading and writing critically 95

Writing guide: How to write an analytical essay 110

Student writing: Analysis of an article 112

5 Reading and writing about multimodal texts 115

Student writing: Analysis of an advertisement 127

6 Reading and writing arguments 130

Student writing: Argument 158

Writing guide: How to write an argument essay 164

7 Reading and writing about literature 167

Student writing: Literary analysis 188

Academic Reading and Writing

ONLINE ACTIVITIES:

Writer's Help 2.0
macmillan learning

writershelp.com/hacker

LaunchPad Solo
macmillan learning

macmillanhighered.com/
launchpadsolo/hacker

Reading and writing critically	6 Writing practice activities 1 Sample student paper 1 LearningCurve activity
Reading and writing about multimodal texts	4 Writing practice activities 3 Sample student projects
Reading and writing arguments	7 Writing practice activities 1 Exercise 1 Sample student paper 4 LearningCurve activities
Reading and writing about literature	1 Writing practice activity 1 Exercise 2 Sample student papers
Speaking confidently	4 Writing practice activities

4 Reading and writing critically

When you read critically, you read with an open, curious mind to understand both what is said and why. And when you write critically, you respond to a text and its author with thoughtful questions and insights, offering your judgment of *how* the parts of a text contribute to its overall effect. As you write across the disciplines, you will be asked to read, respond to, and analyze a wide range of complex texts—books, articles, essays, reports, and more. To write about these texts, you need to read them actively.

Section 5 offers advice for analyzing multimodal texts.

4a Read actively.

Reading, like writing, is an active process that happens in steps. Most texts, such as the ones assigned in college, don't yield their meaning with one quick reading. Rather, they require you to read and reread to grasp the main points and to comprehend a text's layers of meaning.

When you read actively, you pay attention to details you would miss if you just skimmed a text. First, you read to understand the main ideas. Then you pay attention to your own reactions by making note of what interests, surprises, or puzzles you. Active readers preview a text, annotate it, and then converse with it.

Previewing a text

Previewing—looking quickly through a text before you read—helps you understand the text's basic features and structure. Its title, for example, may reveal an author's purpose; the text's format or design may reveal what kind of text it is—a book, a report,

Becoming a College Writer

Engage with the texts you read

"The best way to become a good writer is to become a good reader. The more you take from a reading, the more you have to give as a writer." —**Carolyn Cremona**, student, Austin Community College

In college, you'll read a range of texts, and you'll be asked to write analytically about the texts you read, to argue with their authors, and to offer your insights about what the texts mean. College reading and writing are intertwined. Becoming a college writer requires you to develop a new habit, as Carolyn Cremona suggests: Become an engaged reader.

You might ask, though, "How can I respond to the work of a writer who has spent decades studying a topic?" This is a natural question. After all, these expectations—offering insights from your reading and taking positions on topics you are learning about—may be new to you. Start by reading slowly and carefully to understand an author's ideas and then reading skeptically enough to question those ideas and converse with the author.

- Think back to a time when you felt strongly about something you read—in or out of school. What made you react so strongly: The topic? The author's message or method (way of communicating)? Your own values or beliefs?

JEKA/SHUTTERSTOCK

MORE
Sample annotated reading, page 97
Asking the "So what?" question, page 100
Guidelines for active reading, page 101

a policy memo, and so on. As you preview, you can browse for illustrations, scan headings, and gain a sense of the text's subsections and intended audience. The more you know about a text before you read it, the easier it will be to dig deeper into it.

Annotating a text

Annotating helps you capture and record your responses to a text. As you annotate, you take notes — you jot down questions and reactions in the margins of the text or on electronic or paper sticky notes. You might circle or underline the author's main points or key ideas. Or you might develop your own system of annotating by placing question marks, asterisks, or stars by the text's thesis or major pieces of evidence. Annotating a text will help you answer the basic question "What is this text about?"

As you annotate and think about a text, you are starting to write about it. Responding with notes helps you frame what *you* want to say about the author's ideas or questions you want to address in response to the text. On a second or third reading, you may notice contradictions — statements the author makes that, put side-by-side, just don't seem to make sense — or surprising insights that may lead to further investigation. Each rereading will raise new questions and lead to a better understanding of the text.

The following example shows how one student, Emilia Sanchez, annotated an article from *CQ Researcher*, a newsletter about social and political issues.

ANNOTATED ARTICLE

Big Box Stores Are Bad for Main Street

BETSY TAYLOR

Opening strategy — the problem is not x, it's y.

There is plenty of reason to be concerned about the proliferation of Wal-Marts and other so-called "big box" stores. The question, however, is not whether or not these types of stores create jobs (although several studies claim they produce a net job loss in local communities) or whether they ultimately save consumers money. The real concern about having a 25-acre slab of concrete with a 100,000 square foot box of stuff land on a town is whether it's good for a community's soul.

> Sentimental—what is a community's soul? I would think job security and a strong economy are better for a community's "soul" than small stores that have to lay people off or close.

> Lumps all big boxes together.

The worst thing about "big boxes" is that they have a tendency to produce Ross Perot's famous "big sucking sound"—sucking the life out of cities and small towns across the country. On the other hand, small businesses are great for a community. They offer more personal service; they won't threaten to pack up and leave town if they don't get tax breaks, free roads and other blandishments; and small-business owners are much more responsive to a customer's needs. (Ever try to complain about bad service or poor quality products to the president of Home Depot?)

> Assumes all small businesses are attentive.

> Logic problem? Why couldn't customer complain to store manager?

Yet, if big boxes are so bad, why are they so successful? One glaring reason is that we've become a nation of hyper-consumers, and the big-box boys know this. Downtown shopping districts comprised of small businesses take some of the efficiency out of overconsumption. There's all that hassle of having to travel from store to store, and having to pull out your credit card so many times. Occasionally, we even find ourselves chatting with the shopkeeper, wandering into a coffee shop to visit with a friend or otherwise wasting precious time that could be spent on acquiring more stuff.

> True?

> Taylor wishes for a time that is long gone or never was.

> Author's "either/or" thinking isn't working. Stores like Home Depot try to encourage a community feel.

But let's face it—bustling, thriving city centers are fun. They breathe life into a community. They allow cities and towns to stand out from each other. They provide an atmosphere for people to interact with each other that just cannot be found at Target, or Wal-Mart or Home Depot.

Community vs. economy. What about prices?

Is it anti-American to be against having a retail giant set up shop in one's community? Some people would say so. On the other hand, if you board up Main Street, what's left of America?

Emotional appeal seems too simplistic.

Conversing with a text

Conversing with a text—responding to a text and its author—helps you move beyond your initial notes to draw conclusions about what you've read. Perhaps you ask additional questions, point out something that doesn't make sense, or explain how the author's points suggest wider implications. As you talk back to a text, you look more closely at how the author works through a topic, and you judge the author's evidence and conclusions. Conversing takes your understanding of a text to the next level. For example, student writer Emilia Sanchez noticed on a first reading that her assigned text closed with an emotional appeal. On a second reading, she questioned whether that emotional appeal was too simplistic.

Many writers use a **double-entry notebook** to converse with a text and its author and to generate ideas and insights. To create one, draw a line down the center of a notebook page or create a two-column table in your word processing program. On the left side, record what the author says; include quotations, sentences, and key terms from the text. On the right side, record your observations and questions. With each rereading of a text, you can return to your notebook to add new insights or questions.

A double-entry notebook allows you to begin to see the difference between what a text says and what it means and to visualize the conversation between you and the author as it develops.

Here is an excerpt from student writer Emilia Sanchez's double-entry notebook.

Ideas from the text	My responses
"The question, however, is not whether or not these types of stores create jobs (although several studies claim they produce a net job loss in local communities) or whether they ultimately save consumers money" (1011).	*Why are big-box stores bad if they create jobs or save people money? Taylor dismisses these possibilities without acknowledging their importance. My family needs to save money and needs jobs more than "chatting with the shopkeeper" (1011).*
"The real concern . . . is whether [big-box stores are] good for a community's soul" (1011). "[S]mall businesses are great for a community" (1011).	*Taylor is missing something here. Are all big-box stores bad? Are all small businesses great? Would getting rid of big-box stores save the "soul" of America? Taylor assumes that small businesses are always better for consumers.*

USING SOURCES RESPONSIBLY: Put quotation marks around words you have copied from the source, and keep an accurate record of page numbers for quotations and ideas.

Asking the "So what?" question

As you read and annotate a text, make sure you understand its thesis, or main idea. Ask yourself: "What is the author's thesis?" Then put the author's thesis to the "So what?" test: "Why does this thesis matter? Why does it need to be argued?" Perhaps you'll conclude that the thesis is too obvious and doesn't matter

Guidelines for active reading

Preview a written text.

- Who is the author? What are the author's credentials?
- What is the author's purpose: To inform? To persuade? To call to action?
- Who is the expected audience?
- When was the text written? Where was it published?
- What kind of text is it: A report? A scholarly article? An ad?

Annotate a written text.

- What surprises, puzzles, or intrigues you about the text?
- What question does the text attempt to answer? Or what problem does it attempt to solve?
- What is the author's thesis, or main idea?
- What type of evidence does the author provide to support the thesis? How persuasive is this evidence?

Converse with a written text.

- What are the strengths and limitations of the text?
- Has the author drawn conclusions that you want to question? Do you have a different interpretation of the evidence?
- Does the text raise questions that it does not answer?
- Does the author consider opposing points of view? Does the author seem to treat sources fairly?

Ask the "So what?" question.

- Why does the author's thesis need to be argued, explained, or explored? What's at stake?
- What has the author overlooked or failed to consider in presenting this thesis? What's missing?
- Could a reasonable person draw different conclusions?
- To put an author's thesis to the "So what?" test, use phrases like the following: *The author overlooks this important point: . . .* and *The author's argument is convincing because. . . .*

at all—or that it matters so much that you feel the author stopped short and overlooked key details. Or perhaps you'll think that a reasonable person might draw different conclusions about the issue. You'll be in a stronger position to analyze a text after putting its thesis to the "So what?" test.

WRITING PRACTICE

Reading as a writer

Use the guidelines for active reading on page 101 to guide your reading of an assigned text. Annotate to identify the author's thesis and supporting evidence. Pay particular attention to key words, ideas, and passages. Start a conversation by questioning any assumptions and by putting the author's thesis to the "So what?" test. Write responses to as many of the questions in the guidelines as you can. How do the guidelines for active reading help you become a questioning reader?

4b Outline a text to identify main ideas.

You are probably familiar with using an outline as a planning tool to help you organize your ideas. An outline is a useful tool for reading, too. Outlining a text—identifying its main idea and major parts—can be an important step in your reading process.

As you outline, look closely for a text's thesis statement (main idea) and topic sentences because they serve as important signposts for readers. A thesis statement often appears in the introduction, usually in the first or second paragraph. Topic sentences often can be found at the beginning of body paragraphs, where they announce a shift to a new idea. (See 1e and 3a.)

Put the author's thesis and key points in your own words. Here, for example, are the points Emilia Sanchez identified as she prepared to write her summary and analysis of the text printed on pages 97–99. Notice that Sanchez does not simply trace the author's ideas paragraph by paragraph; instead, she sums up the article's central points.

OUTLINE OF "BIG BOX STORES ARE BAD FOR MAIN STREET"

Thesis: Whether or not they take jobs away from a community or offer low prices to consumers, we should be worried about "big-box" stores like Wal-Mart, Target, and Home Depot because they harm communities by taking the life out of downtown shopping districts.

I.   Small businesses are better for cities and towns than big-box stores are.

   A. Small businesses offer personal service; big-box stores do not.

   B. Small businesses don't make demands on community resources as big-box stores do.

   C. Small businesses respond to customer concerns; big-box stores do not.

II. Big-box stores are successful because they cater to consumption at the expense of benefits to the community.

   A. Buying everything in one place is convenient.

   B. Shopping at small businesses may be inefficient, but it provides opportunities for socializing.

   C. Downtown shopping districts give each city or town a special identity.

Conclusion: Although some people say that it's anti-American to oppose big-box stores, actually these stores threaten the communities that make up America by encouraging buying at the expense of the traditional interactions of Main Street.

Reading online

For many college assignments, you will be asked to read online sources. It is tempting to skim and browse online texts rather than read them carefully. When you skim a text, you are less likely to remember what you have read and less inclined to reread to grasp layers of meaning.

The following strategies will help you read critically online.

Read slowly. Instead of sweeping your eyes across the page, consciously slow down the pace of your reading to focus on each sentence.

Avoid multitasking. Close other applications, especially messaging and social media. If you follow a link for background or the definition of a term, return to the text immediately.

Annotate electronically. Use software tools—such as sticky notes, highlighting, and commenting features—to record your thoughts as you read online texts.

Print the text. If you prefer to read and annotate printed texts, make a copy for close reading and note taking. Be sure to record information about the online source so that you can find it again, if needed, and cite it properly.

4c Summarize to deepen your understanding.

Your goal in summarizing a text is to state the work's main ideas and key points simply, objectively, and accurately in your own words. Writing a summary does not require you to judge the author's ideas; it requires you to *understand* the author's ideas. In summarizing, you condense information, put an author's ideas in your own words, and test your understanding of what a text says. If you have sketched a brief outline of the text (see 4b), refer to it as you draft your summary.

> **MORE HELP**
>
> Knowing how to summarize a source is a key research skill.
>
> ▶ Using summaries in researched writing: 51c

Following is Emilia Sanchez's summary of the article that is printed on pages 97–99.

In her essay "Big Box Stores Are Bad for Main Street," Betsy Taylor argues that chain stores harm communities by taking the life out of downtown shopping districts. Explaining that a community's "soul" is more important than low prices or consumer convenience, she argues that small businesses are better than stores like Home Depot and Target because they emphasize personal interactions and don't place demands on a community's resources. Taylor asserts that big-box stores are successful because "we've become a nation of hyper-consumers" (1011), although the convenience of shopping in these stores comes at the expense of benefits to the community. She concludes by suggesting that it's not "anti-American" to oppose big-box stores because the damage they inflict on downtown shopping districts extends to America itself.

—Emilia Sanchez, student

Guidelines for writing a summary

- In the first sentence, mention the title of the text, the name of the author, and the author's thesis.

- Maintain a neutral tone; be objective.

- As you present the author's ideas, use the third-person point of view and the present tense: *Taylor argues.* . . . (If you are writing in APA style, see 60c.)

- Keep your focus on the text. Don't state the author's ideas as if they were your own.

- Put all or most of your summary in your own words; if you borrow a phrase or a sentence from the text, put it in quotation marks and give the page number in parentheses.

- Limit yourself to presenting the text's key points.

- Be concise; make every word count.

4d Analyze to demonstrate your critical reading.

Whereas a summary most often answers the question of *what* a text says, an analysis looks at *how* a text conveys its main idea. As you read and reread a text—previewing, annotating, and conversing—you are forming a judgment of it. When you analyze

MORE HELP

Writing about a text often requires you to quote directly from the text.

▶ Guidelines for using quotation marks: 51c

that text, you say to readers: "Here's my reading of this text. This is what the text means and why it matters." Assignments calling for an analysis of a text vary widely, but they usually ask you to look at how the text's parts contribute to its central argument or purpose, often with the aim of judging its evidence or overall effect.

Balancing summary with analysis

If you have written a summary of a text, you may find it useful to refer to the main points of the summary as you write your analysis. Your readers may or may not be familiar with the text you are analyzing, so you need to summarize the text briefly to help readers understand the basis of your analysis. The following strategies will help you balance summary with analysis.

- Remember that readers are interested in your ideas about the text.

- Pose questions that lead to an interpretation or a judgment of the text rather than to a summary. The questions on page 101 can help steer you away from summary and toward analysis.

- Focus your analysis on the text's thesis and main ideas or some prominent feature of the reading.

- Pay attention to your topic sentences to make sure they signal analysis.

- Ask reviewers to give you feedback: Do you summarize too much and need to analyze more?

Here is an example of how student writer Emilia Sanchez balances summary with analysis in her essay about Betsy Taylor's article (see pp. 97–99). Before stating her thesis, Sanchez summarizes the article's purpose and central idea.

Summary

[In her essay "Big Box Stores Are Bad for Main Street," Betsy Taylor focuses not on the economic effects of large chain stores but on the effects these stores have on the "soul" of America. She argues that stores like Home Depot, Target, and Wal-Mart are bad for America because they draw people out of downtown shopping districts and cause them to focus on consumption. In contrast, she believes that small businesses are good for America because they provide personal attention, encourage community interaction, and make each city and town unique.]

Analysis

[But Taylor's argument is unconvincing because it is based on sentimentality—on idealized images of a quaint Main Street—rather than on the roles that businesses play in consumers' lives and communities.]

Drafting an analytical thesis statement

An effective thesis statement for analytical writing responds to a question about a text or tries to resolve a problem in the text. Remember that your thesis shouldn't state what the reading is *about*. In other words, your thesis isn't the same as the text's thesis or main idea. Your thesis presents your judgment of the text's argument.

If Emilia Sanchez had started her analysis of "Big Box Stores Are Bad for Main Street" (pp. 97–99) with the following thesis statement, she merely would have repeated the main idea of the article.

> **MORE HELP**
>
> When you analyze a text, you weave words and ideas from the source into your own writing.
>
> ▶ Quoting or paraphrasing: 55b (MLA), 60b (APA), 63c (*Chicago*)
>
> ▶ Using signal phrases: 55c (MLA), 60c (APA), 63c (*Chicago*)

INEFFECTIVE THESIS STATEMENT: Big-box stores such as Wal-Mart and Home Depot promote consumerism by offering endless goods at low prices, but they do nothing to promote community.

Instead, Sanchez wrote the following thesis statement, which offers her judgment of Taylor's argument.

EFFECTIVE THESIS STATEMENT: By ignoring the complex economic relationship between large chain stores and their communities, Taylor incorrectly assumes that simply getting rid of big-box stores would have a positive effect on America's communities.

Using analysis in other disciplines

Emilia Sanchez analyzes an author's argument by breaking it down in order to understand it. She looks first at the author's language choices, then she addresses the author's assumptions, and then she scrutinizes a specific claim.

You may be asked to do this kind of rhetorical analysis in a composition class, and you may already be familiar with literary analysis, which is often assigned in high school. If you are preparing for a career in the social sciences, however, you may have to analyze data and draw conclusions. As an engineering student, you will analyze the design of products and processes. A health studies major might be assigned to analyze a proposed healthcare policy. Analysis—a careful, methodical study of parts in order to make judgments about the whole—is an important academic skill.

Draft an analytical thesis statement

Analysis begins with asking questions about a text. As you draft your thesis, your questions will help you form a judgment about the text. Let these steps guide you as you develop an analytical thesis statement.

1 Review your notes to remind yourself of the author's main idea, supporting evidence, and, if possible, his or her purpose (reason for writing) and audience (intended reader).

2 Ask *what, why,* or *how* questions such as the following: What has the author overlooked or failed to consider? Why might a reasonable person draw a conclusion different from the author's? How does the text complicate or clarify something you've been thinking about or reading about?

3 Write your thesis as an answer to the questions you have posed or the resolution of a problem you have identified in the text. Remember that your thesis isn't the same as the text's thesis. Your thesis presents your judgment of the text.

4 Test your thesis. Is your position clear? Is your position debatable? The answer to both questions should be yes.

5 Revise your thesis. Why does your position matter? Put your working thesis to the "So what?" test (see p. 100). Consider adding a *because* clause to your thesis (see p. 21).

How to write an analytical essay

An **analysis** of a text allows you to examine the parts of a text to understand *what* it means and *how* it makes its meaning. Your goal is to offer your judgment of the text and to persuade readers to see it through your analytical perspective. A sample analytical essay begins on page 112.

Key features

- **A careful and critical reading** of a text reveals what the text says, how it works, and what it means. In an analytical essay, you pay attention to the details of the text, especially its thesis and evidence.

- **A thesis that offers a clear judgment** of a text anchors your analysis. Your thesis might be the answer to a question you have posed about a text or the resolution of a problem you have identified in the text.

- **Support for the thesis** comes from evidence in the text. You summarize, paraphrase, and quote passages that support the claims you make about the text.

- **A balance of summary and analysis** helps readers who may not be familiar with the text you are analyzing. Summary answers the question of *what* a text says; an analysis looks at *how* a text makes its point.

Thinking ahead: Presenting and publishing

You may have the opportunity to present or publish your analysis in the form of a multimodal text such as a slide show presentation. Consider how adding images or sound might strengthen your analysis or help you to better reach your audience. (See 5.)

Writing your analytical essay

1
Explore

Generate ideas for your analysis by brainstorming responses to questions such as the following:

- What is the text about?
- What do you find most interesting, surprising, or puzzling about this text?
- What is the author's thesis or central idea? Put the author's thesis to the "So what?" test. (See p. 100.)
- What do your annotations of the text reveal about your response to it?

2
Draft

- Draft a working thesis to focus your analysis. Remember that your thesis is not the same as the author's thesis. Your thesis presents *your* judgment of the text.
- Draft a plan to organize your paragraphs. Your introductory paragraph will briefly summarize the text and offer your thesis. Your body paragraphs will support your thesis with evidence from the text. Your conclusion will pull together the major points and show the significance of your analysis.
- Identify specific words, phrases, and sentences as evidence to support your thesis.

3
Revise

Ask your reviewers to give you specific comments. You can use the following questions to guide their feedback.

- Is the introduction effective and engaging?
- Is summary balanced with analysis?
- Does the thesis offer a clear judgment of the text?
- What objections might other writers pose to your analysis?
- Is the analysis well organized? Are there clear topic sentences and transitions?
- Have you provided sufficient evidence? Have you analyzed the evidence?
- Have you cited words, phrases, or sentences that are summarized or quoted?

WRITING PRACTICE

Seeking peer review

Use the Writing Guide for analyzing a text (pp. 110–11) to help you draft your analysis. Share your draft with a peer, and ask for specific comments. For example, does your draft accomplish its purpose? Does your analysis present your *judgment* of the text (not just a summary)? Use the questions in the Writing Guide to direct your peer review. Write three to five revision goals.

4e Sample student writing: Analysis of an article

Following is Emilia Sanchez's complete essay. Sanchez used MLA (Modern Language Association) style to format her paper and cite the source. A guide to writing an analytical essay appears on pages 110–11.

Sanchez 1

Emilia Sanchez

Professor Goodwin

English 10

23 October 2015

Rethinking Big-Box Stores

Opening briefly summarizes the article's purpose and thesis.

In her essay "Big Box Stores Are Bad for Main Street," Betsy Taylor focuses not on the economic effects of large chain stores but on the effects these stores have on the "soul" of America. She argues that stores like Home Depot, Target, and Wal-Mart are bad for America because they draw people out of downtown shopping districts and cause them to focus on consumption. In contrast, she believes that small businesses are good for America because they provide personal attention, encourage community interaction, and make each city

Marginal annotations indicate MLA-style formatting and effective writing.

Sanchez 2

and town unique. But Taylor's argument is unconvincing because it is based on sentimentality—on idealized images of a quaint Main Street—rather than on the roles that businesses play in consumers' lives and communities. By ignoring the complex economic relationship between large chain stores and their communities, Taylor incorrectly assumes that simply getting rid of big-box stores would have a positive effect on America's communities.

Sanchez begins to analyze Taylor's argument.

Thesis expresses Sanchez's judgment of Taylor's article.

Taylor's use of colorful language reveals that she has a sentimental view of American society and does not understand economic realities. In her first paragraph, Taylor refers to a big-box store as a "25-acre slab of concrete with a 100,000 square foot box of stuff" that "land[s] on a town," evoking images of a powerful monster crushing the American way of life (1011). But she oversimplifies a complex issue. Taylor does not consider that many downtown business districts failed long before chain stores moved in, when factories and mills closed and workers lost their jobs. In cities with struggling economies, big-box stores can actually provide much-needed jobs. Similarly, while Taylor blames big-box stores for harming local economies by asking for tax breaks, free roads, and other perks, she doesn't acknowledge that these stores also enter into economic partnerships with the surrounding communities by offering financial benefits to schools and hospitals.

Signal phrase introduces quotations from the source; Sanchez uses an MLA in-text citation.

Sanchez identifies and challenges Taylor's assumptions.

Taylor's assumption that shopping in small businesses is always better for the customer also seems driven by nostalgia for an old-fashioned Main Street rather than by the facts. While she may be right that many small businesses offer personal service and are responsive to customer complaints, she does not consider that many customers appreciate the service at big-box stores. Just as customer service is better at some small businesses than at others, it is impossible to generalize about service at all big-box stores. For example, customers

Clear topic sentence announces a shift to a new topic.

Sanchez refutes Taylor's claim.

Sanchez 3

depend on the lenient return policies and the wide variety of products
at stores like Target and Home Depot.

Taylor blames big-box stores for encouraging American "hyper-
consumerism," but she oversimplifies by equating big-box stores
with bad values and small businesses with good values. Like her
other points, this claim ignores the economic and social realities of
American society today. Big-box stores do not force Americans to buy
more. By offering lower prices in a convenient setting, however, they
allow consumers to save time and purchase goods they might not
be able to afford from small businesses. The existence of more small
businesses would not change what most Americans can afford, nor
would it reduce their desire to buy affordable merchandise.

Taylor may be right that some big-box stores have a negative
impact on communities and that small businesses offer certain
advantages. But she ignores the economic conditions that support
big-box stores as well as the fact that Main Street was in decline before
the big-box store arrived. Getting rid of big-box stores will not bring back
a simpler America populated by thriving, unique Main Streets; in reality,
Main Street will not survive if consumers cannot afford to shop there.

*Sanchez treats
the author fairly.*

*Conclusion returns
to the thesis and
shows the wider
significance of
Sanchez's analysis.*

Sanchez 4

*Work cited page
is in MLA style.*

Work Cited

Taylor, Betsy. "Big Box Stores Are Bad for Main Street." *CQ Researcher,*
vol. 9, no. 44, 1999, p. 1011.

5 Reading and writing about multimodal texts

In many of your college classes, you'll have the opportunity to read and write about multimodal texts, such as advertisements, maps, videos, and Web sites. Multimodal texts combine one or more of the following modes to convey meaning: words, static images, moving images, and sound. You might, for instance, be asked to analyze an advertisement for a composition course, a map for a geology course, or a YouTube video for a sociology course.

Writing about multimodal texts differs from writing about written texts—a video is a different kind of text from a report, of course—but there are also similarities. All texts can be approached in a critical way. You can engage with them by studying how they work to communicate their message and by discovering within them something that is surprising, interesting, and worthy of analysis.

The strategies and advice offered in section 4 for critically reading and writing about texts also apply to multimodal texts. In this section, you'll find additional advice specific to analyzing multimodal texts.

5a Read actively.

Any multimodal text can be read—that is, examined to understand *what* it says and *how* it communicates its purpose and reaches its audience. Like written texts, multimodal texts don't speak for themselves; they don't reveal their meaning with a quick glance or a casual scan. Rather, you need to read and reread, questioning and conversing with them with an open, critical mind.

When you read a multimodal text, you are reading more than words; you might also be reading a text's design and composition—and perhaps even its pace and volume. Your work involves understanding the modes—words, images, and sound—separately and then analyzing how the modes work together—the interaction among words, images, and sound. As you read a multimodal text, pay attention to the details that make up the entire composition.

When you read multimodal text, you'll find it helpful to preview, annotate, and converse with the text.

> **MORE HELP**
>
> Integrating visuals (images and some multimodal texts) can strengthen your writing.
> ▸ Adding visuals to your draft: page 32
> ▸ Choosing visuals to suit your purpose: pages 34–35

Previewing a multimodal text

Previewing starts when you look at the basic details of a multimodal text and pay attention to first impressions. You ask questions about the text's subject matter and design, its context and composer or creator, and its purpose and intended audience. The more you can gather from a first look, the easier it will be to dig deeper into the meaning of a text.

The following questions will help you to preview a multimodal text.

- What kind of text is it: An advertisement? A video? A slide show?

- What is your first reaction to the text? Does it elicit an emotional response?

- What strikes you right away about the various modes—words, images (moving or static), or sound? Does one mode seem to stand out more than the others?

- What do the subject matter and design suggest about the intended audience?

What will it take before we respect the planet?

Multimodal texts, such as this World Wildlife Fund (WWF) ad, combine modes. Here, words and an image work together to communicate an idea.

Annotating a multimodal text

Annotating a text — jotting down observations and questions — helps you read actively to answer the question "What is this text about?" In annotating, you generate ideas by paying close attention to each mode. You notice what surprises and intrigues you about the text, and you observe what is present and absent. For example, you might question the choice of music in an audio essay and wonder what this choice implies about the intended audience. Or in viewing a public service video, you might notice the presence of black-and-white photographs and the absence of words and question how these design choices serve the video's message.

The following guidelines will help you annotate a multimodal text.

- **Identify the different modes used and examine them separately.** Thinking about each mode on its own is a helpful first step to evaluating the text as a whole. What modes are present—written words, static images, moving images, or sound?

- **Identify the role of each mode within the text.** For example, do written words convey information? Does audio evoke an emotional response?

- **Identify the features of each mode.** How do various features help convey the text's meaning and serve its purpose? For example, if written words are the mode being used, are they boldface or italic, large or small, black or in color? What differences do these features make?

- **Keep track of details.** For example, if you are making notes about an audio or a video file, include a time stamp with each observation so that you can easily find that moment again to check your notes or to include a clip in your analysis: *04:21 The music stops abruptly, and a single word, "Care," appears on-screen.*

The example on page 119 shows how one student, Ren Yoshida, annotated an advertisement.

Conversing with a multimodal text

Conversing with a text—or responding to a text and its author—helps you move beyond your early notes to form judgments about the text you're examining. You might choose to examine the choice of mode—why the message is conveyed in moving images rather than printed words, for example—or the features of the mode—why the background music becomes much louder at one point. You might point out something that is puzzling, contradictory, or provocative about the relationship between two modes.

empowering
FARMERS

When you choose Equal Exchange fairly traded coffee, tea or chocolate, you join a network that empowers farmers in Latin America, Africa, and Asia to:

- Stay on their land
- Care for the environment
- Farm organically
- Support their family
- Plan for the future

www.equalexchange.coop

Photo: Jesus Choqueheranca de Quevero,
Coffee farmer & CEPICAFE Cooperative member, Peru

ANNOTATED ADVERTISEMENT

What is being exchanged?

Why is "fairly traded" so difficult to read?

"Empowering" — why in an elegant font? Who is empowering farmers?
"Farmers" in all capital letters. Shows strength?

Straightforward design and not much text.

Outstretched hands. Is she giving a gift? Inviting a partnership?

Hands: heart-shaped, foregrounded.

Raw coffee is earthy, natural.

Positive verbs: consumers choose, join, empower; farmers stay, care, farm, support, plan.

What does it mean to join a network?

How do consumers know their money helps farmers stay on their land?

In his annotations on the Equal Exchange ad, Ren Yoshida asks why two words, *empowering* and *farmers*, are in different fonts (see p. 119) and why the farmer's hands are outstretched. As Yoshida moves beyond his annotations to form judgments about the text, he focuses his attention on the contradictions between the ad's emotional and logical appeals. He notices that the ad appeals to consumers' emotions, yet such appeals raise logical questions about what is being exchanged and who is becoming empowered.

Many writers use a double-entry notebook to converse with a text and generate ideas for writing (see pp. 99–100 for guidelines on creating a double-entry notebook and sample entries). As you record details and features of a multimodal text on the left side of the notebook page and your own responses on the right side, you can visualize the conversation as it develops.

WRITING PRACTICE

Reading a multimodal text

Use the advice on previewing, annotating, and conversing with a multimodal text (pp. 116–20) to guide your active reading. Pay attention to details and to what surprises or interests you about the text. If you could talk with the composer of the text, what questions would you ask? Exchange notes and questions with a classmate. Then reflect on how the process of reading and questioning a multimodal text helps you understand the text and form a judgment about it.

5b Outline to identify main ideas.

When you outline a text, you identify its main idea or purpose and its major parts. One way to outline a multimodal text is to try to define its main idea or purpose and sketch a list of its key elements. Because ads, Web sites, and videos may not explicitly state a purpose, you may have to puzzle it out from the details in the work.

Here is the informal outline Ren Yoshida developed as he prepared to write an analysis of the advertisement printed on page 119. Notice that Yoshida makes an attempt to state the ad's purpose and sum up its message.

INFORMAL OUTLINE OF EQUAL EXCHANGE ADVERTISEMENT

Purpose: To persuade consumers that they can improve the lives of organic farmers and their families by purchasing Equal Exchange coffee.

Key features:

- The farmer's heart-shaped hands are outstretched, offering the viewer partnership and the product of her hard work.
- The raw coffee is surprisingly fruitlike and fresh—natural and healthy looking.
- A variety of fonts are used for emphasis, such as the elegant font for "empowering."
- Consumer support leads to a higher quality of life for the farmers and for all people, since these farmers care for the environment and plan for the future.
- The simplicity of the design reflects the simplicity of the exchange. The consumer only has to buy a cup of coffee to make a difference.

Conclusion: Equal Exchange is selling more than a product—coffee. It is selling the message that together farmers and consumers hold the future of land, environment, farms, and families in their hands.

5c Summarize to deepen your understanding.

Writing a summary does not require you to judge a text's ideas; it requires you to understand them. Your goal in summarizing a multimodal text is to state the work's central idea and key points simply, objectively, and accurately, in your own words, and usually in paragraph form. As you summarize the central idea, use the third-person point of view and the present tense. If you have sketched a brief outline of the text (see 5b), refer to it as you draft your summary.

To summarize a multimodal text, begin with essential information such as who composed the text and why, who the intended audience is, and when and where the work appeared. Briefly explain the text's main idea or message and identify its key features.

MORE HELP

Knowing how to summarize is a key research skill.

▸ Summarizing written texts: 4c

▸ Summarizing researched sources: 51c

Divide the summary into a few major and perhaps minor ideas. Since a summary must be fairly short, you must be selective about what is most important.

Here is the summary Ren Yoshida developed as he prepared to write an analysis of the advertisement on page 119. Notice that he composes the summary in his own words, uses the third-person point of view ("The Equal Exchange advertisement is . . ."), and uses present tense ("The ad suggests . . .").

> The Equal Exchange advertisement is selling the message that together farmers and consumers hold the future of the planet in their hands. At the center of the ad is a farmer whose outstretched hands, full of raw coffee, offer the fruit of her labor and a partnership with consumers. The ad suggests that in a global world producers and consumers are bound together. A cup of coffee is more than just a morning ritual; a cup of coffee is part of an equal exchange that empowers farmers to stay on their land and empowers consumers to do the right thing.
>
> — Ren Yoshida, student

Write a summary of a multimodal text

1 In the first two sentences, mention the title of the text and the name of the composer (or the sponsoring organization or company), and provide some brief information about the context—where the text appeared and when, why, and for whom the text was composed.

2 State the text's central idea or message.

3 Maintain a neutral tone; be objective.

4 As you present the text's ideas, use the third-person point of view and the present tense: *The focus of the Uber advertisement is. . . . Devaney uses the infographic to argue. . . .* (If you are writing in APA style, see 60c.) Limit yourself to presenting the text's major points.

5 Keep your focus on the text. Don't state the text's or composer's ideas as if they were your own.

6 Put your summary in your own words; if you borrow a phrase or a sentence from the text, put it in quotation marks and cite the text (see 51c).

5d Analyze to demonstrate your critical reading.

Whereas a summary most often answers the question of *what* a text says, an analysis looks at *how* a text conveys its main idea or message. As you read and reread a multimodal text—previewing, annotating, and conversing—you are forming a judgment of it. Your analysis says to readers: "Here's my reading of this text. This is what the text means and why it matters." When you are assigned to analyze a text such as a pamphlet, a podcast, or a PowerPoint slide, you will usually be expected to look at how the different parts of the multimodal work (use of words, sounds, images) contribute to its central purpose, often with the aim of judging how effective the text is in achieving its purpose.

Guidelines for analyzing a multimodal text

- What is your first impression of the text? What details in the text create this response?

- When and why was the text created? Where did the text appear?

- What clues suggest the text's intended audience? What assumptions are being made about the audience?

- What is the thesis, central idea, or message of the text? Do you find it persuasive?

- Does this text tell a story? How would you sum up the story?

- What modes are used, and why? How do the modes work together?

- How do the arrangement of sounds or design details—images, illustrations, colors, fonts, perspective—help convey the text's meaning or serve its purpose?

Balancing summary with analysis

If you have written a summary of a text, you may find it useful to refer to the main points of the summary as you write your analysis. Your readers may or may not be familiar with the multimodal text you are analyzing and will need at least some summary to ground your analysis. For example, student writer Ren Yoshida summarized the Equal Exchange advertisement on page 119 by describing part of the text first, allowing readers to get their bearings, and then moving to an analytical statement about that particular part of the text.

Summary

Analysis

[A farmer, her hardworking hands full of coffee beans, reaches out from an Equal Exchange advertisement. The hands, in the shape of a heart, offer to consumers the fruit of the farmer's labor. The ad's message is straightforward: in choosing Equal Exchange, consumers become global citizens, partnering with farmers to help save the planet.] [Suddenly, a cup of coffee is more than just a morning ritual; a cup of coffee is a moral choice that empowers both consumers and farmers.]

The following strategies will help you balance summary with analysis.

- Remember that readers are interested in your ideas about a text.

- Pose questions that lead to an interpretation or a judgment of a text rather than to a summary. The questions on page 124 can help steer you away from summary and toward analysis.

- Focus your analysis on a few significant details (fonts, use of color, sounds, images) rather than presenting a list of every detail.

- As you draft, pay attention to your topic sentences to make sure they signal analysis.

- Ask reviewers to give you feedback: Do you summarize too much and need to analyze more?

Drafting an analytical thesis statement

An effective thesis statement for analytical writing about a multimodal text responds to a question about the text or tries to resolve a problem in the text. Remember that your thesis isn't the same as the text's main idea. Your thesis presents your judgment of the text's argument. If your draft thesis restates the text's message, return to the questions you asked earlier in the process as you revise.

> **INEFFECTIVE THESIS STATEMENT**
>
> Consumers who purchase coffee from farmers in the Equal Exchange network are helping farmers stay on their land.

The thesis is ineffective because it summarizes the ad; it doesn't present an analysis. Ren Yoshida focused the thesis by questioning a single detail in the work.

> **QUESTIONS**
>
> The ad promises an equal exchange, but is the exchange equal between consumers and farmers? Do the words *equal exchange* and *empowering farmers* appeal to consumers' emotions?

> **EFFECTIVE THESIS STATEMENT**
>
> Although the ad works successfully on an emotional level, it is less successful on a logical level because of its promise for an equal exchange between consumers and farmers.

5e Sample student writing: Analysis of an advertisement

On the following pages is Ren Yoshida's analysis of the Equal Exchange advertisement that appears on page 119.

Ren Yoshida

Professor Marcotte

English 101

4 November 2015

Sometimes a Cup of Coffee Is Just a Cup of Coffee

A farmer, her hardworking hands full of coffee
beans, reaches out from an Equal Exchange advertisement
("Empowering"). The hands, in the shape of a heart, offer to
consumers the fruit of the farmer's labor. The ad's message is
straightforward: in choosing Equal Exchange, consumers become
global citizens, partnering with farmers to help save the planet.
Suddenly, a cup of coffee is more than just a morning ritual; a cup
of coffee is a moral choice that empowers both consumers and
farmers. This simple exchange appeals to a consumer's desire to
be a good person—to protect the environment and do the right
thing. Yet the ad is more complicated than it first seems, and
its design raises some logical questions about such an exchange.
Although the ad works successfully on an emotional level, it is
less successful on a logical level because of its promise for an
equal exchange between consumers and farmers.

The focus of the ad is a farmer, Jesus Choqueheranca de
Quevero, and, more specifically, her outstretched, cupped hands. Her
hands are full of red, raw coffee, her life's work. The ad successfully
appeals to consumers' emotions, assuming they will find the farmer's
welcoming face and hands, caked with dirt, more appealing than
startling statistics about the state of the environment or the number
of farmers who lose their land each year. It seems almost rude not to
accept the farmer's generous offering since we know her name and,
as the ad implies, have the choice to "empower" her. In fact, how

The source is
cited in the text.
No page number
is available for the
online source.

Yoshida
summarizes the
content of the ad.

Thesis expresses
Yoshida's analysis
of the ad.

Details show how
the ad appeals
to consumers'
emotions.

Yoshida interprets
details such as the
farmer's hands.

Marginal annotations indicate MLA-style formatting and effective writing.

Yoshida 2

can a consumer resist helping the farmer "[c]are for the environment" and "[p]lan for the future," when it is a simple matter of choosing the right coffee? The ad sends the message that our future is a global future in which producers and consumers are bound together.

First impressions play a major role in the success of an advertisement. Consumers are pulled toward a product, or pushed away, by an ad's initial visual and emotional appeal. Here, the intended audience is busy people, so the ad tries to catch viewers' attention and make a strong impression immediately. Yet with a second or third viewing, consumers might start to ask some logical questions about Equal Exchange before buying their morning coffee. Although the farmer extends her heart-shaped hands to consumers, they are not actually buying a cup of coffee or the raw coffee directly from her. In reality, consumers are buying from Equal Exchange, even if the ad substitutes the more positive word *choose* for *buy*. Furthermore, consumers aren't actually empowering the farmer; they are joining "a network that empowers farmers." The idea of a network makes a simple transaction more complicated. How do consumers know their money helps farmers "[s]tay on their land" and "[p]lan for the future" as the ad promises? They don't.

The ad's design elements raise questions about the use of the key terms *equal exchange* and *empowering farmers*. The Equal Exchange logo suggests symmetry and equality, with two red arrows facing each other, but the words of the logo appear almost like an eye exam poster, with each line decreasing in font size and clarity. The words *fairly traded* are tiny. Below the logo, the words *empowering farmers* are presented in contradictory fonts. *Empowering* is written in a flowing, cursive font, almost the opposite of what might be considered empowering, whereas

Yoshida begins to challenge the logic of the ad.

Words from the ad serve as evidence.

Clear topic sentence announces a shift.

Summary of the ad's key features serves Yoshida's analysis.

Yoshida 3

farmers is written in a plain, sturdy font. The ad's varying fonts
communicate differently and make it hard to know exactly what is
being exchanged and who is becoming empowered.

What is being exchanged? The logic of the ad suggests that
consumers will improve the future by choosing Equal Exchange. The
first exchange is economic: consumers give one thing—dollars—and
receive something in return—a cup of coffee—and the farmer stays
on her land. The second exchange is more complicated because it
involves a moral exchange. The ad suggests that if consumers don't
choose "fairly traded" products, farmers will be forced off their land and
the environment destroyed. This exchange, when put into motion by
consumers choosing to purchase products not "fairly traded," has negative
consequences for both consumers and farmers. The message of the ad is
that the actual exchange taking place is not economic but moral; after
all, nothing is being bought, only chosen. Yet the logic of this exchange
quickly falls apart. Consumers aren't empowered to become global
citizens simply by choosing Equal Exchange, and farmers aren't
empowered to plan for the future by consumers' choices. And even if all
this empowerment magically happened, there is nothing equal about such
an exchange.

Advertisements are themselves about empowerment—
encouraging viewers to believe they can become someone or do
something by identifying, emotionally or logically, with a product.
In the Equal Exchange ad, consumers are emotionally persuaded to
identify with a farmer whose face is not easily forgotten and whose
heart-shaped hands hold a collective future. On a logical level,
though, the ad raises questions because empowerment, although a
good concept to choose, is not easily or equally exchanged. Sometimes
a cup of coffee is just a cup of coffee.

Yoshida shows why
his thesis matters.

Conclusion includes
a detail from the
introduction.

Conclusion returns
to Yoshida's thesis.

Yoshida 4

Work Cited

"Empowering Farmers." Equal Exchange, equalexchange.coop/.
Advertisement. Accessed 14 Oct. 2015.

6 Reading and writing arguments

Many of your college assignments will ask you to read and write arguments about debatable issues. The questions being debated might be matters of public policy (*Should corporations be allowed to advertise on public school property?* or *What is the least dangerous way to dispose of hazardous waste?*), or they might be scholarly issues (*What role do genes play in determining behavior?* or *What were the causes of the Vietnam War?*). On such questions, reasonable people may disagree.

As you read arguments across the disciplines and enter into academic or public policy debates, pay attention to the questions being asked, the evidence being presented, and the various positions being argued. It's helpful to approach all arguments with an open, curious mind. You'll find the critical reading strategies introduced in section 4—previewing, annotating, and conversing with texts—to be useful as you ask questions about an argument's logic, evidence, and use of appeals. Many arguments can stand up to critical scrutiny. Sometimes, however, a line of argument that at first seems reasonable turns out to be illogical, unfair, or both.

As you write for various college courses, you'll be asked to take positions in academic debates, propose solutions to problems, and persuade readers to accept your arguments. Just as you evaluate arguments with openness, you'll want to construct arguments with the same openness—acknowledging disagreements and opposing views and presenting your arguments fully and fairly to your readers.

See sections 6a–6c for advice about reading arguments. Sections 6d–6k address writing arguments.

6a Distinguish between reasonable and fallacious argumentative tactics.

When you evaluate an argument, look closely at the reasoning and evidence behind it. Some unreasonable argumentative tactics are known as *logical fallacies*. Most of the fallacies—such as hasty generalizations and false analogies—are misguided or dishonest uses of legitimate strategies. The examples in this section suggest when such strategies are reasonable and when they are not.

Generalizing (inductive reasoning)

Writers and thinkers generalize all the time. We look at a sample of data and conclude that data we have not observed will most likely conform to what we have seen. From a spoonful of soup, we conclude just how salty the whole bowl will be. After numerous unpleasant experiences with an airline, we decide to book future flights with a competitor.

Becoming a College Writer

Consider counterarguments

"Understand the argument you want to make, but also figure out why readers might disagree with your position. At the heart of a good argument is disagreement."

—**Geily Gonzalez**, student, Miami Dade College

Many college writing assignments invite you to take a position in a debate. It isn't enough simply to offer your opinion and assume readers won't have their own. You want to approach arguments, those you read and write, with an open mind—one that sees "disagreement" as useful.

Reasonable people disagree on topics worth debating. Becoming a college writer requires that you take time to reflect on the disagreements in debates that you enter—to think through your own point of view *and* other points of view.

You might worry that if you include counterarguments in your writing, you will contradict yourself. In fact, you will show your understanding of the complexity of the debate and the importance of fairness.

MICHAELJUNG/SHUTTERSTOCK

● We are surrounded by disagreements—those that we can follow in the media and those that we follow or engage in personally. Reflect on this question: Why is fairness important in arguing a position?

● **MORE**
Handling opposing views, 6c
Countering opposing arguments, 6i
Sample argument essay, 6k

When we draw a conclusion from an array of facts, we are engaged in inductive reasoning. Such reasoning deals in probability, not certainty. For a conclusion to be highly probable, it must be based on evidence that is sufficient, representative, and relevant. (See the chart on p. 135.)

Academic English

Many hasty generalizations contain words such as *all, ever, always,* and *never,* when qualifiers such as *most, many, usually,* and *seldom* would be more accurate.

The fallacy known as *hasty generalization* is a conclusion based on insufficient or unrepresentative evidence.

HASTY GENERALIZATION

In a single year, scores on standardized tests in California's public schools rose by ten points. Therefore, more children than ever are succeeding in America's public school systems.

Data from one state, even a large one, do not justify a conclusion about the whole United States.

A *stereotype* is a hasty generalization about a group. Here are a few examples.

STEREOTYPES

Women are bad bosses.
Politicians are corrupt.
Children are always curious.

Stereotyping is common because of our human tendency to perceive selectively. We tend to see what we want to see; we notice evidence confirming our already-formed opinions and fail to notice evidence to the contrary. For example, if you have concluded that politicians are corrupt, your stereotype will be confirmed by news reports of legislators being indicted—even though every day the media describe conscientious officials serving the public honestly and well.

Drawing analogies

An analogy points out a similarity between two things that are otherwise different. Analogies can be an effective means of arguing a point. It is not always easy to draw the line between a reasonable and an unreasonable analogy. At times, however, an analogy is clearly off base, in which case it is called a *false analogy*.

FALSE ANALOGY

If we can send a spacecraft to Mars, we should be able to find a cure for the common cold.

How are these ideas related? The writer has falsely assumed that because two things are alike in one respect, they must be alike in others. Exploring the solar system and finding a cure for the common cold are both scientific challenges, but the problems confronting medical researchers are quite different from those solved by space scientists.

Tracing causes and effects

Demonstrating a connection between causes and effects is rarely simple. For example, to explain why a chemistry course has a high failure rate, you would begin by listing possible causes: inadequate preparation of students, poor teaching, lack of qualified tutors, and so on. Next you would investigate each possible

Testing inductive reasoning

Though inductive reasoning leads to probable and not absolute truth, you can assess a conclusion's likely probability by asking three questions. This chart shows how to apply those questions to a sample conclusion based on a survey.

CONCLUSION   The majority of students on our campus would volunteer at least five hours a week in a community organization if the school provided a placement service for volunteers.

EVIDENCE   In a recent survey, 723 of 1,215 students questioned said they would volunteer at least five hours a week in a community organization if the school provided a placement service for volunteers.

1. Is the evidence sufficient?

That depends. On a small campus (3,000 students), the pool of students surveyed would be sufficient for market research, but on a large campus (30,000), 1,215 students are only 4 percent of the population. If those 4 percent were known to be truly representative of the other 96 percent, however, even such a small sample would be sufficient (see question 2).

2. Is the evidence representative?

Only if those responding to the survey reflect the characteristics of the entire student population: age, gender, race, field of study, number of extracurricular commitments, and so on. If most of those surveyed are majors in a field like social work, the researchers should question the survey's conclusion.

3. Is the evidence relevant?

Yes. The survey results are directly linked to the conclusion. A survey about the number of hours students work for pay would not be relevant because it would not be about *choosing to volunteer.*

cause. Only after investigating the possible causes would you be able to weigh the relative impact of each cause and suggest appropriate remedies.

Because cause-and-effect reasoning is so complex, it is not surprising that writers frequently oversimplify it. In particular, writers sometimes assume that because one event follows another, the first is the cause of the second. This common fallacy is known as *post hoc*, from the Latin *post hoc, ergo propter hoc*, meaning "after this, therefore because of this."

> **POST HOC FALLACY**
>
> Since Governor Cho took office, unemployment among minorities in the state has decreased by 7 percent. Governor Cho should be applauded for reducing unemployment among minorities.

Is the governor solely responsible for the decrease? Are there other reasons? The writer must show that Governor Cho's policies are responsible for the decrease in unemployment; it is not enough to show that the decrease followed the governor's taking office.

Weighing options

Especially when reasoning about problems and solutions, writers must weigh options. To be fair, a writer should mention the full range of options, showing why one is superior to the others or might work well in combination with others.

It is unfair to suggest that there are only two alternatives when in fact there are more. Writers who set up a false choice between their preferred option and one that is clearly unsatisfactory are guilty of the *either . . . or* fallacy.

> **EITHER . . . OR FALLACY**
>
> Our current war against drugs has not worked. Either we should legalize drugs or we should turn the drug war over to our armed forces and let them fight it.

Are these the only solutions—legalizing drugs and calling out the army? Other options, such as funding for drug abuse prevention programs, are possible.

Making assumptions

An assumption is a claim that is taken to be true—without the need of proof. Most arguments are based to some extent on assumptions since writers rarely have the time and space to prove all the conceivable claims on which their argument is based. For example, someone arguing about the best means of limiting population growth in developing countries might assume that the goal of limiting population growth is worthwhile. For most audiences, there would be no need to articulate this assumption or to defend it.

There is a danger, however, in failing to spell out and prove a claim that is clearly controversial. Consider the following short argument, in which a key claim is missing.

ARGUMENT WITH MISSING CLAIM

Violent crime is increasing. Therefore, we should vigorously enforce the death penalty.

The writer seems to be assuming both that the death penalty deters violent criminals and that it is a fair punishment—and that most readers will agree. These are not reasonable assumptions; the writer will need to state and support both claims.

When a missing claim is an assertion that few would agree with, we say that a writer is guilty of a *non sequitur* (Latin for "does not follow").

NON SEQUITUR

Christopher gets plenty of sleep; therefore, he will be a successful student in the university's pre-med program.

Does it take more than sleep to be a successful student? The missing claim—that people with good sleep habits always make successful students—would be hard to prove.

Deducing conclusions (deductive reasoning)

When we deduce a conclusion, we put things together, like any good detective. We establish that a general principle is true, that a specific case is an example of that principle, and that therefore a particular conclusion about that case is a certainty.

Deductive reasoning can often be structured in a three-step argument called a *syllogism*. The three steps are the major premise, the minor premise, and the conclusion.

1. Anything that increases radiation in the environment is dangerous to public health. (Major premise)

2. Nuclear reactors increase radiation in the environment. (Minor premise)

3. Therefore, nuclear reactors are dangerous to public health. (Conclusion)

The major premise is a generalization. The minor premise is a specific case. The conclusion follows from applying the generalization to the specific case.

Deductive arguments break down if one of the premises is not true or if the conclusion does not follow logically from the premises. In the following short argument, the major premise is very likely untrue.

UNTRUE PREMISE

The police do not give speeding tickets to people driving less than five miles per hour over the limit. Dominic is driving fifty-nine miles per hour in a fifty-five-mile-per-hour zone. Therefore, the police will not give Dominic a speeding ticket.

The conclusion is true only if the premises are true. If the police sometimes give tickets for driving less than five miles per hour over the limit, Dominic cannot safely conclude that he will avoid a ticket.

In the following argument, both premises might be true, but the conclusion does not follow logically from them.

CONCLUSION DOES NOT FOLLOW

All members of our club ran in this year's Boston Marathon. Jay ran in this year's Boston Marathon. Therefore, Jay is a member of our club.

The fact that Jay ran the race is no guarantee that he is a member of the club. Presumably, many runners are nonmembers.

Assuming that both premises are true, the following argument holds up.

CONCLUSION FOLLOWS

All members of our club ran in this year's Boston Marathon. Jay is a member of our club. Therefore, Jay ran in this year's Boston Marathon.

6b Distinguish between legitimate and unfair emotional appeals.

There is nothing wrong with appealing to readers' emotions. After all, many issues worth arguing about have an emotional as well as a logical dimension. Even the Greek logician Aristotle lists *pathos* (emotion) as a legitimate argumentative tactic. For example, in an essay criticizing big-box stores (see pp. 97–99), writer Betsy Taylor has a good reason for tugging at readers' emotions: Her subject is the decline of city and town life. In her conclusion, Taylor appeals to readers' emotions by invoking their national pride.

LEGITIMATE EMOTIONAL APPEAL

Is it anti-American to be against having a retail giant set up shop in one's community? Some people would say so. On the other hand, if you board up Main Street, what's left of America?

Emotional appeals, however, are frequently misused. Many of the arguments we see in popular media, for instance, strive to win our sympathy rather than our intelligent agreement. A television commercial suggesting that you will be thin, attractive, and happy if you drink a certain diet beverage is making a pitch to emotions. So is a political speech that recommends electing a candidate because he is a devoted husband and father of five who also serves as a volunteer firefighter on weekends.

The following passage illustrates several types of unfair emotional appeals.

UNFAIR EMOTIONAL APPEALS

This progressive proposal to build a ski resort in the state park has been carefully researched by Western Trust, the largest bank in the state; furthermore, it is favored by a majority of the local merchants. The only opposition comes from tree huggers who care more about trees than they do about people. One of their leaders was actually arrested for disturbing the peace several years ago.

Words with strong positive or negative connotations, such as *progressive* and *tree hugger,* are examples of *biased language.* Attacking the people who hold a belief (environmentalists) rather than refuting their argument is called *ad hominem,* a Latin term meaning "to the man." Associating a prestigious name (Western Trust) with the writer's side is called *transfer.* Claiming that an idea should be accepted because a large number of people (the majority of merchants) are in favor of it is called the

Advertising makes use of ethical, logical, and emotional appeals to persuade consumers to buy a product or embrace a brand. This Patagonia ad makes an ethical appeal with its copy that invites customers to rethink their purchasing practices.

bandwagon appeal. Bringing in irrelevant issues (the arrest) is a *red herring*, named after a trick used in fox hunts to mislead the dogs by dragging a smelly fish across the trail.

Evaluating ethical, logical, and emotional appeals as a reader

Ancient Greek rhetoricians distinguished among three kinds of appeals used to influence readers — ethical, logical, emotional. As you evaluate arguments, identify these appeals and question their effectiveness. Are they appropriate for the audience and the argument? Are they balanced and legitimate or lopsided and misleading?

EVALUATING ETHICAL, LOGICAL, AND EMOTIONAL APPEALS AS A READER (*cont.*)

Ethical appeals (*ethos*)

Ethical arguments call upon a writer's character, knowledge, and authority. Ask questions such as the following when you evaluate the ethical appeal of an argument.

- Is the writer informed and trustworthy? How does the writer establish authority and credibility?

- Is the writer fair-minded and unbiased? How does the writer establish reasonableness and good judgment?

- Does the writer use sources knowledgeably and responsibly?

- How does the writer describe the views of others and deal with opposing views?

Logical appeals (*logos*)

Reasonable arguments appeal to readers' sense of logic, rely on evidence, and use inductive and deductive reasoning. Ask questions such as the following to evaluate the logical appeal of an argument.

- Is the evidence sufficient, representative, and relevant?

- Is the reasoning sound?

- Does the argument contain any logical fallacies or unwarranted assumptions?

- Are there any missing or mistaken premises?

Emotional appeals (*pathos*)

Emotional arguments appeal to readers' beliefs and values. Ask questions such as the following to evaluate the emotional appeal of an argument.

- What values or beliefs does the writer address, either directly or indirectly?

- Are the emotional appeals legitimate and fair?

- Does the writer oversimplify or dramatize an issue?

- Do the emotional arguments highlight or shift attention away from the evidence?

EXERCISE 6-1 In the following paragraph, identify the type of appeal used in the preceding sentence: *ethos* (ethical appeal), *logos* (logical appeal), or *pathos* (emotional appeal).

Elderspeak, the use of pet names such as "dear" and "sweetie" directed toward older adults, is generally intended as an endearment. However, the use of such language suggests a view of seniors as childlike or cognitively impaired. It should be no surprise, then, that older adults find these pet names condescending and demeaning (*ethos / logos / pathos*). Unfortunately, the effects of elderspeak go far beyond insulting older adults. Health care professionals have found that residents in nursing facilities, even those with dementia, respond to patronizing language by becoming uncooperative, aggressive, or depressed. In a 2009 study published in the *American Journal of Alzheimer's Disease and Other Dementias*, Ruth Herman and Kristine L. Williams reported that older adults responded to elderspeak by resisting care, yelling, or crying ("Elderspeak's Influence") (*ethos / logos / pathos*). Surprisingly, despite widely published research on the negative effects of elderspeak, the worst offenders are health care workers, the very people we trust to treat our elderly family members with respect and dignity — and the very people who are old enough to know better (*ethos / logos / pathos*).

6c Judge how fairly a writer handles opposing views.

The way in which a writer deals with opposing views is telling. Some writers address the arguments of the opposition fairly, conceding points when necessary and countering others, all in a civil spirit. Other writers will do almost anything to win an argument: either ignoring opposing views altogether or misrepresenting such views and attacking their proponents.

Writers build credibility — *ethos* — by addressing opposing arguments fairly. As you read arguments, assess the credibility of your sources by looking at how they deal with views not in agreement with their own.

Describing the views of others

Some writers and speakers deliberately misrepresent the views of others. One way they do this is by setting up a "straw man," a character so weak that he is easily knocked down. The *straw man* fallacy consists of an oversimplification or outright distortion of opposing views. For example, in a California debate over attempts to control the mountain lion population, pro-lion groups characterized their opponents as trophy hunters bent on shooting harmless animals. In truth, hunters were only one faction of those who saw a need to control the lion population.

During the District of Columbia's struggle for voting representation, some politicians set up a straw man, as shown in the following example.

STRAW MAN FALLACY

Washington, DC, residents are lobbying for statehood. Giving a city such as the District of Columbia the status of a state would be unfair.

The straw man wanted statehood. In fact, most DC citizens lobbied for voting representation in any form, not necessarily through statehood.

Quoting opposing views

Writers often quote the words of writers who hold opposing views. In general, this is a good idea, for it assures some level of fairness and accuracy. At times, though, both the fairness and the accuracy are an illusion.

A source may be misrepresented when it is quoted out of context. All quotations are to some extent taken out of context, but a fair writer will explain the context to readers. To select a provocative sentence from a source and to ignore the more moderate sentences surrounding it is both unfair and misleading. Sometimes a writer deliberately distorts a source through the device of ellipsis dots. Ellipsis dots [. . .] tell readers that words have been omitted

---

> ### Checklist for reading and evaluating arguments
>
> - What is the writer's thesis, or central claim?
> - Are there any gaps in reasoning? Does the argument contain any logical fallacies (see 6a)?
> - What assumptions does the argument rest on? Are any of the assumptions unstated?
> - What appeals—ethical, logical, or emotional—does the writer make? Are these appeals effective?
> - What kind of evidence does the writer use to support his or her claims? Can you find alternative interpretations of the evidence?
> - How does the writer handle opposing views?
> - If you are not persuaded by the writer's argument, what counterarguments could you make to the writer?

---

from the original source. When those words are crucial to an author's meaning, omitting them is obviously unfair. (See also 39d.)

ORIGINAL SOURCE

Johnson's *History of the American West* is riddled with inaccuracies and astonishing in its blatantly racist description of the Indian wars.

—B. R., reviewer

MISLEADING QUOTATION

According to B. R., Johnson's *History of the American West* is "astonishing in its . . . description of the Indian wars."

EXERCISE 6–2   Explain what is illogical in the following brief arguments. It may be helpful to identify the logical fallacy or fallacies by name. Answers appear in the back of the book.

a.   My roommate, who is an engineering major, is taking a course called Structures of Tall Buildings. All engineers have to know how to design tall buildings.

b.   If you're old enough to vote, you're old enough to drink. Therefore, the drinking age should be lowered to eighteen.

c. If you're not part of the solution, you're part of the problem.

d. American students could be outperforming students in schools around the globe if it weren't for the outmoded, behind-the-times thinking of many statewide education departments.

e. Charging a fee for curbside trash pickup will encourage everyone to recycle more because no one in my town likes to spend extra money.

WRITING PRACTICE

Evaluating an argument

Using the checklist for reading and evaluating arguments on page 145, evaluate the argument in student writer Sam Jacobs's essay on pages 158–63. Do you find Jacobs's argument persuasive? Is it logical and fair? Does Jacobs present himself as a trustworthy and credible writer? What led you to your conclusion? If you had an opportunity to talk with him, what counterarguments would you present?

6d When writing arguments, identify your purpose and context.

Evaluating the arguments of other writers prepares you to construct your own. When you ask questions about the logic and evidence of the arguments you read, you become more aware of such needs in your own writing. And when you pose objections to arguments, you more readily anticipate and counter objections to your own arguments.

In constructing an argument, you take a stand on a debatable issue. Your purpose is to explain your understanding of the truth about a subject or to propose the best solution to a problem, reasonably and logically, without being combative. Your aim is to persuade your readers to reconsider their positions by offering new reasons to question existing viewpoints.

It's best to start by informing yourself about the debate or conversation around a subject, sometimes called its *context*. If you are planning to write about the subject of offshore drilling, you might want to read sources that shed light on the social context (the concerns of consumers, the ideas of lawmakers, the proposals of environmentalists) and sources that may inform you about

MORE HELP

Supporting your claims with evidence from sources can make your argument more effective.

▶ Conducting research: 50

the intellectual context (scientific or theoretical responses by geologists, oceanographers, or economists) in which the debate is played out. Because your readers may be aware of the social and intellectual contexts in which your issue is grounded, you will be at a disadvantage if you are not informed. Conduct some research before preparing your argument. Consulting even a few sources can help to deepen your understanding of the conversation around the issue.

6e View your audience as a panel of jurors.

Do not assume that your audience already agrees with you. Instead, envision skeptical readers who, like a panel of jurors, will make up their minds after listening to all sides of the argument. If you are arguing a public policy issue, you may want to aim your paper at readers who represent a variety of positions. In the case of a debate over

MORE HELP

You may need to consider a specific audience for your argument.

▶ Analyzing your audience: 1a

▶ Writing in a particular discipline, such as business or psychology: 65

offshore drilling, for example, imagine a jury that represents those who have a stake in the matter: consumers, policymakers, and environmentalists.

At times, you can deliberately narrow your audience. If you are working within a word limit, for example, you might not have the space in which to address the concerns of all interested parties. Or you might be primarily interested in reaching just a segment of a larger audience, such as consumers. Once you target a specific audience, it's helpful to think about what kinds of arguments and evidence will appeal to that audience.

Using ethical, logical, and emotional appeals as a writer

To construct a convincing argument, you must establish your credibility (*ethos*) and appeal to your readers' sense of logic and reason (*logos*) as well as to their values and beliefs (*pathos*). When using these appeals, make sure they are appropriate for your audience and your argument.

Ethical appeals (*ethos*)

To accept your argument, a reader must perceive you as trustworthy, fair, and reasonable. When you acknowledge alternative positions, you build common ground with readers and gain their trust by showing that you are knowledgeable about the arguments relevant to your subject. And when you use sources responsibly (summarizing, paraphrasing, or quoting the views of others respectfully), you inspire readers' confidence in your judgment.

Logical appeals (*logos*)

To persuade readers, you need to appeal to their sense of logic and sound reasoning. When you provide sufficient evidence, you offer readers logical support for your argument. And when you clarify the assumptions that underlie your arguments and avoid logical fallacies, you appeal to readers' desire for reason.

Emotional appeals (*pathos*)

To establish common ground with readers, you need to appeal to their beliefs and values as well as to their minds. When you offer readers vivid examples, surprising statistics, or compelling visuals, you engage readers and deepen their interest in your argument. And when you balance emotional appeals with logical appeals, you highlight the human dimension of an issue to show readers why they should care about your argument.

> **Academic English**
>
> Some cultures value writers who argue with force; other cultures value writers who argue subtly or indirectly. Academic audiences in the United States will expect your writing to be assertive and confident—neither aggressive nor passive. You can create an assertive tone by acknowledging different positions and supporting your ideas with specific evidence.
>
> **TOO AGGRESSIVE**   Of course only registered organ donors should be eligible for organ transplants. It's selfish and shortsighted to think otherwise.
>
> **TOO PASSIVE**   I might be wrong, but I think that maybe people should have to register as organ donors if they want to be considered for a transplant.
>
> **ASSERTIVE TONE**   If only registered organ donors are eligible for transplants, more people will register as donors.
>
> If you are uncertain about the tone of your work, ask for help at your school's writing center.

6f In your introduction, establish credibility and state your position.

When you are constructing an argument, make sure your introduction includes a thesis statement that establishes your position on the issue you have chosen to debate. In the sentences leading up to the thesis, establish your credibility (*ethos*) with readers by showing that you are knowledgeable and

> **MORE HELP**
>
> When you write an argument, you state your position in a thesis.
>
> ▸ Writing effective thesis statements: 1c, 1e

fair-minded. If possible, build common ground (*pathos*) with readers who may not at first agree with your views, and show them why they should consider your thesis.

In the following introduction, student writer Kevin Smith presents himself as someone worth listening to. Because Smith introduces both sides of the debate, readers are likely to approach his essay with an open mind.

Smith shows that he is familiar with the legal issues surrounding school prayer.

Although the Supreme Court has ruled against prayer in public schools on First Amendment grounds, many people still feel that prayer should be allowed. Such people value prayer as a practice central to their faith and believe that prayer is a way for schools to reinforce moral principles. They also compellingly point out a paradox in the First Amendment itself: at what point does the separation of church and state restrict the freedom of those who wish to practice their religion? What proponents of school prayer fail to realize, however, is that the Supreme Court's decision, although it was made on legal grounds, makes sense on religious grounds as well. Prayer is too important to be trusted to our public schools.

Smith is fair-minded, presenting the views of both sides.

Thesis builds common ground.

—Kevin Smith, student

TIP: A good way to test a thesis while drafting and revising is to imagine a counterargument to your argument (see 6i). If you can't think of an opposing point of view, rethink your thesis and ask a classmate or writing center tutor to respond to your argument.

6g Back up your thesis with persuasive lines of argument.

Arguments of any complexity contain lines of argument that, when taken together, might reasonably persuade readers that the thesis has merit. On page 152, for example, are the main lines of argument that student writer Sam Jacobs used in his paper about the shift from print to online news (see pp. 158–63).

Draft a thesis statement for an argument

1 Identify the various positions in the debate you're writing about. At the heart of a good argument are debate and disagreement. An argumentative thesis takes a clear position on a debatable issue and is supported by evidence. Identify the points in the debate on which there is disagreement. Consider your own questions and thoughts about the topic.

2 Review any notes you have taken to clarify your own thoughts about the debate.

3 Pose a question that has not been dealt with sufficiently yet. Write this question either in your draft or in your notes to guide your thinking. An open-ended question will make a stronger thesis. If your question can be answered with yes or no, add *why* or *how* to it.

4 Write your thesis as an answer to your question. Include the topic, your position, and any language that might preview the organization of your argument or might show why you are making the argument.

5 Test your thesis. Is your position clear? Is your position debatable? The answer to both questions should be yes.

6 Revise your thesis. Why does your position matter? Put your working thesis to the "So what?" test (see p. 100). Consider adding a *because* clause to your thesis (see p. 21).

CENTRAL CLAIM

Thesis: The shift from print to online news provides unprecedented opportunities for readers to become more engaged with the news, to hold journalists accountable, and to participate as producers, not simply as consumers.

SUPPORTING CLAIMS

- Print news has traditionally had a one-sided relationship with its readers, delivering information for passive consumption.
- Online news invites readers to participate in a collaborative process—to question and even contribute to the content.
- Links within news stories provide transparency, allowing readers to move easily from the main story to original sources, related articles, or background materials.
- Technology has made it possible for readers to become news producers—posting text, audio, images, and video of news events.
- Citizen journalists can provide valuable information, sometimes more quickly than traditional journalists can.

If you sum up your main lines of argument, as Jacobs did, you will have a rough outline of your essay. In your paper, you will provide evidence for each of these claims.

6h Support your claims with specific evidence.

You will need to support your central claim and any subordinate claims with evidence: facts, statistics, examples and illustrations, visuals (charts, slides, photos), expert opinion, and so on. Debatable topics require that you consult some sources. As you read through or view the sources, you will learn more about the arguments and counterarguments at the center of your debate.

USING SOURCES RESPONSIBLY: Remember that you must document any sources you use as evidence. Documentation gives credit to authors and shows readers how to locate a source in case they want to assess its credibility or explore the issue further.

Using facts and statistics

A fact is something that is known with certainty because it has been objectively verified: The capital of Wyoming is Cheyenne. Carbon has an atomic weight of 12. John F. Kennedy was assassinated on November 22, 1963. Statistics are collections of numerical facts: Alcohol use is a factor in nearly 40 percent of traffic fatalities. More than four in ten businesses in the United States are owned by women.

> **MORE HELP**
>
> Sources, when used responsibly, can provide evidence to support an argument.
>
> ▶ Paraphrasing, summarizing, and quoting sources: 51c
>
> ▶ Punctuating direct quotations: 37a
>
> ▶ Citing sources: 54b (MLA), 59b (APA), 63b (*Chicago*)

Most arguments are supported at least to some extent by facts and statistics. For example, in the following passage the writer uses statistics to show that college students' credit card debt is declining.

> A recent study revealed that undergraduates are relying less on credit cards and are carrying lower debt than they did five years ago. The study credits the change to wider availability of grant and scholarship money. The average credit card debt per college undergraduate dropped more than 70% from $3,173 in 2008 to $925 in 2013 (Papadimitriou).

Writers often use statistics in selective ways to bolster their own positions. If you suspect that a writer's handling of statistics is not fair, track down the original sources for those statistics or read authors with opposing views, who may give you a fuller understanding of the numbers.

Using examples and illustrations

Examples and illustrations (extended examples, often in story form) rarely prove a point by themselves, but when used in combination with other forms of evidence, they flesh out an argument with details and specific instances and bring it to life. Because examples are often concrete and sometimes vivid, they can reach readers in ways that statistics and abstract ideas cannot.

In a paper arguing that online news provides opportunities for readers that print does not, Sam Jacobs describes how regular citizens using only cell phones and laptops helped save lives during Hurricane Katrina by sending important updates to the rest of the world.

> Citizen reporting made a difference in the wake of Hurricane Katrina in 2005. Armed with cell phones and laptops, regular citizens relayed critical news updates in a rapidly developing crisis, often before traditional journalists were even on the scene.

Using visuals

Visuals — charts, graphs, diagrams, photographs — can support your argument by providing vivid and detailed evidence and by capturing your readers' attention. Bar or line graphs, for instance, describe and organize complex statistical data; photographs can immediately convey abstract ideas; a map can illustrate geography. (See pp. 34–35.)

As you consider using visual evidence, ask yourself the following questions:

- Is the visual accurate, credible, and relevant?

- How will the visual appeal to readers: Logically? Ethically? Emotionally?

- How will the visual evidence function? Will it provide background information? Present complex numerical information? Lend authority? Refute counterarguments?

Citing expert opinion

Although they are no substitute for careful reasoning of your own, the views of an expert can contribute to the force of your argument. For example, to help make the case that print journalism has a one-sided relationship with its readers, student writer Sam Jacobs integrates an expert's key description.

> With the rise of the Internet, however, this model has been criticized by journalists such as Dan Gillmor, founder of the Center for Citizen Media, who argues that traditional print journalism treats "news as a lecture," whereas online news is "more of a conversation" (xxiv).

When you rely on expert opinion, make sure that your source is an expert in the field you are writing about. In some cases, you may need to provide credentials showing why your source is worth listening to, such as listing the person's position or title alongside his or her name. When including expert testimony in your paper, you can summarize or paraphrase the expert's opinion or you can quote the expert's exact words. You will of course need to document the source, as Jacobs did.

6i Anticipate objections; counter opposing arguments.

Readers who already agree with you need no convincing, but skeptical readers may resist your arguments. To be willing to give up a position that seems reasonable, readers need to see that another position is even more reasonable. In addition to presenting your own case, therefore, you should consider the opposing arguments and attempt to counter them.

It might seem at first that drawing attention to an opposing point of view or contradictory evidence would weaken your argument. But by anticipating and countering objections to your argument, you show yourself as a reasonable and well-informed writer who has a thorough understanding of the significance of the issue.

Anticipating and countering objections

To anticipate a possible objection to your argument, consider the following questions.

- Could a reasonable person draw a different conclusion from your facts or examples?
- Might a reader question any of your assumptions or offer an alternative explanation?
- Is there any evidence that might weaken your position?

The following questions may help you respond to a potential objection.

- Can you concede the point to the opposition but challenge the point's importance or usefulness?
- Can you explain why readers should consider a new perspective or question a piece of evidence?
- Should you explain how your position responds to contradictory evidence?
- Can you suggest a different interpretation of the evidence?

When you write, use phrasing to signal to readers that you're about to present an objection. Often the signal phrase can go in the lead sentence of a paragraph.

Critics of this view argue that . . .

Some readers might point out that . . .

Researchers challenge these claims by . . .

There is no best place in an essay to deal with opposing views. Often it is useful to summarize the opposing position early in your essay. After stating your thesis but before developing your own arguments, you might have a paragraph that takes up the most important counterargument. Or you can anticipate objections paragraph by paragraph as you develop your case. Wherever you decide to address opposing arguments, you will enhance your credibility if you explain the arguments of others accurately and fairly.

6j Build common ground.

As you counter opposing arguments, try to seek out one or two assumptions you might share with readers who do not initially agree with your views. If you can show that you share their concerns, your readers will be more likely to accept that your argument is valid. For example, to persuade people opposed to controlling the deer population with a regulated hunting season, a state wildlife commission would have to show that it too cares about preserving deer and does not want them to die needlessly. Having established these values in common, the commission might be able to persuade critics that reducing the total number of deer prevents starvation caused by overpopulation.

People believe that intelligence and decency support their side of an argument. To be persuaded, they must see these qualities in your argument. Otherwise, they will persist in their opposition.

6k Sample student writing: Argument

In the paper that begins on the next page, student writer Sam Jacobs argues that the shift from print to online news benefits readers by providing them with new opportunities to produce news and to think more critically as consumers of news. Notice how he appeals to his readers by presenting opposing views fairly before providing his own arguments.

In writing the paper, Jacobs consulted both print and online sources. When he quotes, summarizes, or paraphrases information from a source, he cites the source with an MLA (Modern Language Association) in-text citation. Citations in the paper refer readers to the list of works cited at the end of the paper. (For more details about citing sources, see 54.)

For a guide to writing an argument essay, see pages 164–65.

Jacobs 1

Sam Jacobs

Professor Alperini

English 101

5 November 2013

From Lecture to Conversation:

Redefining What's "Fit to Print"

In his opening sentences, Jacobs provides background for his thesis.

"All the news that's fit to print," the motto of the *New York Times* since 1896, plays with the word *fit*, asserting that a news story must be newsworthy and must not exceed the limits of the printed page. The increase in online news consumption, however, challenges both meanings of the word *fit*, allowing producers and consumers alike to rethink who decides which topics are worth covering and how extensive that coverage should be. Any cultural shift usually means that something is lost, but in this case there are clear gains. The shift from print to online news provides unprecedented opportunities for readers to become more engaged with the news, to hold journalists accountable, and to participate as producers, not simply as consumers.

Thesis states the main point.

Jacobs does not need a citation for common knowledge.

Guided by journalism's code of ethics—accuracy, objectivity, and fairness—print news reporters have gathered and delivered stories according to what editors decide is fit for their readers. Except for op-ed pages and letters to the editor, print news has traditionally had a one-sided relationship with its readers. The print news media's reputation for objective reporting has been held up as "a stop sign" for readers, sending a clear message that no further inquiry is necessary (Weinberger). With the rise of the Internet, however, this model has been criticized by journalists such as Dan Gillmor, founder of the Center for Citizen Media, who argues that traditional print journalism treats "news as a lecture," whereas online news is "more of a conversation"

Source is cited in MLA style.

Marginal annotations indicate MLA-style formatting and effective writing.

Jacobs 2

(xxiv). Print news arrives on the doorstep every morning as a fully formed lecture, a product created without participation from its readership. By contrast, online news invites readers to participate in a collaborative process—to question and even help produce the content.

One of the most important advantages online news offers over print news is the presence of built-in hyperlinks, which carry readers from one electronic document to another. If readers are curious about the definition of a term, the roots of a story, or other perspectives on a topic, links provide a path. Links help readers become more critical consumers of information by engaging them in a totally new way. For instance, the link embedded in the story "Credit-Shy: Younger Generation Is More Likely to Stick to a Cash-Only Policy" (Sapin) allows readers to find out more about the financial trends of young adults and provides statistics that confirm the article's accuracy (see fig. 1). Other links in the article widen the conversation. These kinds of links give readers the opportunity to conduct their own evaluation of the evidence and verify the journalist's claims.

Links provide a kind of transparency impossible in print because they allow readers to see through online news to the "sources, disagreements, and the personal assumptions and values" that may have influenced a news story (Weinberger). The International Center for Media and the Public Agenda underscores the importance of news organizations letting "customers in on the often tightly held little secrets of journalism." To do so, they suggest, will lead to "accountability and accountability leads to credibility" ("Openness"). These tools alone don't guarantee that news producers will be responsible and trustworthy, but they encourage an open and transparent environment that benefits news consumers.

> Transition moves from Jacobs's main argument to specific examples.

> Jacobs clarifies key terms (*transparency* and *accountability*).

Jacobs 3

Jacobs develops the thesis.

Not only has technology allowed readers to become more critical news consumers, but it also has helped some to become news producers. The Web gives ordinary people the power to report on the

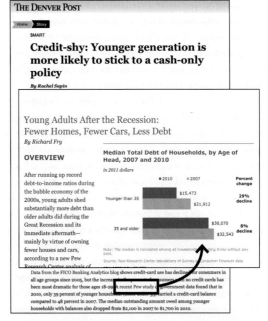

Fig. 1. Links embedded in online news articles allow readers to move from the main story to original sources, related articles, or background materials. The link in this online article (Sapin) points to a statistical report by the Pew Research Center, the original source of the author's data on young adults' spending practices.

day's events. Anyone with an Internet connection can publish on blogs and Web sites, engage in online discussion forums, and contribute video and audio recordings. Citizen journalists with laptops, cell phones, and digital camcorders have become news producers alongside large news organizations.

Not everyone embraces the spread of unregulated news reporting online. Critics point out that citizen journalists are not necessarily trained to be fair or ethical, for example, nor are they subject to editorial oversight. Acknowledging that citizen reporting is more immediate and experimental, critics also question its accuracy and accountability: "While it has its place . . . it really isn't journalism at all, and it opens up information flow to the strong probability of fraud and abuse. . . . Information without journalistic standards is called gossip," writes David Hazinski in the *Atlanta Journal-Constitution* (23A). In his book *Losing the News*, media specialist Alex S. Jones argues that what passes for news today is in fact "pseudo news" and is "far less reliable" than traditional print news (27). Even a supporter like Gillmor is willing to agree that citizen journalists are "nonexperts," but he argues that they are "using technology to make a profound contribution, and a real difference" (140).

Citizen reporting made a difference in the wake of Hurricane Katrina in 2005. Armed with cell phones and laptops, regular citizens relayed critical news updates in a rapidly developing crisis, often before traditional journalists were even on the scene. In 2006, the enormous contributions of citizen journalists were recognized when the New Orleans *Times-Picayune* received the Pulitzer Prize in public service for its online coverage—largely citizen-generated—of Hurricane Katrina. In recognizing the paper's "meritorious public

Opposing views are presented fairly.

Jacobs counters opposing arguments.

A vivid example helps Jacobs make his point.

Jacobs 5

service," the Pulitzer Prize board credited the newspaper's blog for "heroic, multi-faceted coverage of [the storm] and its

Jacobs uses specific evidence for support.

aftermath" ("2006"). Writing for the *Online Journalism Review*, Mark Glaser emphasizes the role that blog updates played in saving storm victims' lives. Further, he calls the *Times-Picayune*'s partnership with citizen journalists a "watershed for online journalism."

Conclusion echoes the thesis without repeating it.

The Internet has enabled consumers to participate in a new way in reading, questioning, interpreting, and reporting the news. Decisions about appropriate content and coverage are no longer exclusively in the hands of news editors. Ordinary citizens now have a meaningful voice in the conversation—a hand in deciding what's "fit to print." Some skeptics worry about the apparent free-for-all and loss of tradition. But the expanding definition of news provides opportunities for consumers to be more engaged with events in their communities, their nations, and the world.

Works Cited

Gillmor, Dan. *We the Media: Grassroots Journalism by the People,
     for the People*. O'Reilly Media, 2006.

Glaser, Mark. "NOLA.com Blogs and Forums Help Save Lives after
     Katrina." *OJR: The Online Journalism Review*, Knight Digital
     Media Center, 13 Sept. 2005, www.ojr.org/050913glaser/.

Hazinski, David. "Unfettered 'Citizen Journalism' Too Risky." *Atlanta
     Journal-Constitution*, 13 Dec. 2007, p. 23A. *General OneFile*,
     go.galegroup.com/ps/.

Jones, Alex S. *Losing the News: The Future of the News That Feeds
     Democracy*. Oxford UP, 2009.

"Openness and Accountability: A Study of Transparency in Global Media
     Outlets." *ICMPA: International Center for Media and the Public
     Agenda*, 2006, www.icmpa.umd.edu/pages/studies/transparency/
     main.html.

Sapin, Rachel. "Credit-Shy: Younger Generation Is More
     Likely to Stick to a Cash-Only Policy." *The Denver Post*,
     26 Aug. 2013, www.denverpost.com/ci_23929523/
     credit-shy-younger-generation-stick-cash-only-policy.

"The 2006 Pulitzer Prize Winners: Public Service." *The Pulitzer Prizes*,
     Columbia U, www.pulitzer.org/prize-winners-by-year/2006.
     Accessed 21 Oct. 2013.

Weinberger, David. "Transparency Is the New Objectivity." *Joho the
     Blog*, 19 July 2009, www.hyperorg.com/blogger/2009/07/19/
     transparency-is-the-new-objectivity/.

Works cited page uses MLA style.

List is alphabetized by authors' last names (or by title when a work has no author).

Access date is used for a Web source that has no update date.

How to write an argument essay

Composing an **argument** gives you the opportunity to propose a reasonable solution to a debatable issue. You say to your readers: "Here is my position, here is the evidence that supports the position, and here is my response to other positions on the issue." A sample argument essay begins on page 158.

Key features

- **A thesis, stated as a clear position on a debatable issue,** frames an argument essay. The issue is debatable because reasonable people disagree about it.

- **An examination of the issue's context** indicates why the issue is important, why readers should care about it, or how your position fits into the debates surrounding the topic.

- **Sufficient, representative, and relevant evidence** supports the argument's claims. Evidence needs to be specific and persuasive; quoted, summarized, or paraphrased fairly and accurately; and cited correctly.

- **Opposing positions are summarized and countered.** By anticipating and countering objections to your position, you establish common ground with readers and show yourself as a reasonable and well-informed writer.

Thinking ahead: Presenting or publishing

You may have some flexibility in how you present or publish your argument. If you submit your argument as an audio or video essay, make sure you understand the genre's conventions and think through how your voice or a combination of sounds and images can help you establish your *ethos*. If you are taking a position on a local issue, consider publishing your argument in the form of a newspaper op-ed or letter to the editor. The benefit? A real-world audience.

Writing your argument

Explore

Generate ideas by brainstorming responses to questions such as the following.

- What is the debate around your issue? What sources will help you learn more about your issue?
- What position will you take? Why does your position need to be argued?
- What evidence supports your position? What evidence makes you question your position?
- What types of appeals—*ethos, logos, pathos*—might you use to persuade readers? How will you build common ground with your readers?

Draft

Try to figure out the best way to structure your argument. A typical outline might include the following steps: Capture readers' attention; state your position; give background information; outline your major claims with specific evidence; recognize and respond to opposing points of view; and end by reinforcing your point and why it matters.

As you draft, think about the best order for your claims. You could organize by strength, building to your strongest argument (instead of starting with your strongest), or by concerns your audience might have.

Revise

Ask your reviewers for specific feedback. Here are some questions to guide their comments.

- Is the thesis clear? Is the issue debatable?
- Is the evidence persuasive? Is more needed?
- Is your argument organized logically?
- Are there any flaws in your reasoning or assumptions that weaken the argument?
- Have you presented yourself as a knowledgeable, trustworthy writer?
- Does the conclusion pull together your entire argument? How might the conclusion be more effective?

6l Remix a written argument essay for an oral presentation.

You may be assigned to adapt an argument essay for delivery to a listening audience. Speaking and writing draw on many of the same skills. Effective speakers, like effective writers, identify their purpose, audience, and context. They project themselves as informed and reasonable, establish common ground with listeners, and use specific, memorable language and persuasive techniques to capture their audience's attention.

Student writer Sam Jacobs revised his argument essay as he prepared a speaking script. Compare the first paragraph of Jacobs's essay (p. 158) with the opening lines for his oral presentation.

Good afternoon, everyone. I'm Sam Jacobs.

Today I want to explore this question: How do consumers benefit from reading news online? But first let me have a quick show of hands: How many of you read news online? If you answered yes, you are part of the 71% of young Americans, ages 18 to 29, who read their news online, according to the Pew Center. We've grown up in a digital generation, consuming news on every possible mobile device, especially our cell phones. Most of us don't miss the newspaper arriving on the doorstep every morning. And because we expect to read news online, we take it for granted. But if we take it for granted, we might miss the benefits of participating as producers of news, not simply as consumers. The three benefits I want to explore are . . .

Jacobs starts with his key question and engages the audience immediately.

Jacobs uses a source responsibly and integrates it well.

Friendly opening establishes a relationship with the audience.

Establishes common ground with the audience.

Jacobs repeats words and phrases for emphasis and uses signposts to make it easier for his listeners to follow his ideas.

7 Reading and writing about literature

All good writing about literature attempts to answer a question, spoken or unspoken, about the text.

- How does street language function in Gwendolyn Brooks's "We Real Cool"?

- Why does Margaret Atwood make so many biblical allusions in *The Handmaid's Tale*?

- How does Suzanne Collins critique modern society in *The Hunger Games*?

- Why does Hamlet hesitate for so long before killing his uncle, King Claudius?

The goal of a literature analysis should be to answer such questions with a meaningful and persuasive interpretation.

7a Be an active reader.

Responding to literature starts with becoming an engaged and active reader. Read the work through once, closely and carefully. Think of it as speaking to you: What is it telling you? Asking you? Trying to make you feel? Then go back and read it a second time. Rereading is a central part of the process of developing an analysis. If the work provides an introduction and footnotes, read them as well. They may provide key information. Use the dictionary to look up words unfamiliar to you or words with connotations that may influence the work's meaning.

As you read and reread, interact with the work by posing questions and looking for possible answers. The chart on pages 171–72 suggests some questions about literature that may help you become a more engaged, active reader.

Annotating the work

Annotating the work—in other words, interacting with the text by taking notes—is a way to focus your reading, capture your responses, and prepare for a class discussion. The first time you read the work through, you may want to indicate passages you find especially significant or puzzling—with a pencil or highlighter or by taking notes electronically. On a more careful rereading, pay particular attention to those passages, and jot down your ideas and reactions in a notebook or (if you own the text) on the pages. As you annotate, you can try out ideas and develop your questions and perspectives about the work. (See 4a for an annotated article.)

Discussing the work

Understanding literature can be a social experience, and class discussions often lead to interesting insights about a literary work, perhaps by calling attention to details that you took little notice of on a first reading. Discussions don't always occur face-to-face. In many classes, they happen online in discussion forums, chat rooms, blogs, or wikis. On the following page is a set of blog posts about a character in Joyce Carol Oates's short story "Where Are You Going, Where Have You Been?"

7b Form an interpretation.

After rereading, taking notes, and perhaps discussing the work, you are ready to form an interpretation—your understanding of the meaning of details in the work. At this stage, try to focus on one aspect of the work. Look through your notes and annotations for recurring questions and insights.

Conversation about a subject

Dr. Connolly's Blog | ENG 101, Section 4

①

Who is Arnold Friend?

Posted by **Professor Barbara Connolly**, Thu Mar 5, 2015 4:36 PM

At one point during the story, Arnold Friend demands, "Don't you know who I am?" Who do you think he is? Does the reader or Connie ever really know?

View comments | Add a comment

---

3 comments on
"Who is Arnold Friend?" Original post

②

Posted by **Zoe Marshall**, Thu Mar 5, 2015 7:23 PM
I think we're not supposed to know who Arnold Friend is. When he first arrives at Connie's house, she asks him, "Who the hell do you think you are?" but Arnold ignores her question by changing the subject. He never tells her who he really is, only that he's her friend and her lover.

Posted by **Jon Fietze**, Thu Mar 5, 2015 8:04 PM
I found a lot of parallels between Arnold and the wolf in "Little Red Riding Hood." For example, Connie notices Arnold's hair, his teeth, and his grin. It reminded me of that part in "Little Red Riding Hood" when Little Red says, "Oh, Grandmother, what big teeth you have!"

Posted by **Yuko Yoshikawa**, Thu Mar 5, 2015 11:11 PM
I was thinking the same thing. Plus, Arnold seems like he's dressing up to hide who he is. Connie thinks that his hair is like a wig and later that his face is a mask. It reminded me of when the wolf puts on the grandmother's clothing to trick Little Red Riding Hood, just like Arnold is trying to trick Connie.

1 Instructor's prompt.

2 A series of student responses to the prompt.

Focusing on a central issue

In writing an analysis of literature, you will focus on a central issue. Your job isn't to say everything about the work that can possibly be said. It is to develop a sustained, in-depth interpretation that illuminates the work in some specific way. For example, you may think that *Huckleberry Finn* is an interesting book because it not only contains humor and brilliant descriptions of scenery but also tells a serious story of one boy's development. But to develop this general response into an interpretation, you will have to find a focus. For example, you might address the ways in which the runaway slave Jim uses humor to preserve his dignity. Or you might examine the ironic contradictions between what Huck says and what his heart tells him.

Asking questions that lead to an interpretation

Good interpretations generally arise from good questions. What is it about the work that puzzles or intrigues you? What do you want to know more about? By asking yourself such questions, you will push yourself beyond your first impressions to deeper insights.

In writing an analysis, you might answer questions about literary techniques, such as the author's handling of plot, setting, or character. Or you could respond to questions about social context as well—what a work reveals about the time and culture in which it was written. Both kinds of questions are included in the chart on pages 171–72.

Often you will find yourself writing about both technique and social context. For example, Margaret Peel, a student who wrote an essay on Langston Hughes's poem "Ballad of the Landlord," addressed the following question, which touches on both language and race:

How does the poem's language—through its four voices—dramatize the experience of a black man in a society dominated by whites?

Questions to ask about literature

Questions about technique

Plot: What central conflicts drive the plot? Are they internal (within a character) or external (between characters or between a character and a force)? How are conflicts resolved?

Setting: Does the setting (time and place) create an atmosphere, give an insight into a character, suggest symbolic meanings, or hint at the theme of the work?

Character: What seems to motivate the central characters? Do any characters change significantly? If so, what have they learned from their experiences? Do contrasts between characters highlight important themes?

Point of view: Does the point of view—the perspective from which the story is narrated or the poem is spoken—influence our understanding of events? Does the narration reveal the character traits of the speaker, or does the speaker merely observe others? Is the narrator innocent, naive, or deceitful?

Theme: Does the work have an overall theme (a central insight about people or a truth about life, for example)? If so, how do details in the work illuminate this theme?

Language: Does language—formal or informal, standard or dialect, ordinary or poetic, cool or passionate—reveal the character of speakers? How do metaphors, similes, and sensory images contribute to the work? How do recurring images enrich the work and hint at its meaning?

Questions about social context

Historical context: What does the work reveal about—or how was it shaped by—the time and place in which it was written? Does the work appear to promote or undermine a philosophy that was popular in its time, such as feminism in the mid-twentieth century?

Class: How does social class shape or influence characters' choices and actions? How does class affect the way characters view or are viewed by others? What economic struggles or power relationships does the work reflect or depict? →

QUESTIONS TO ASK ABOUT LITERATURE (*cont.*)

Race and culture: Are any characters portrayed as being caught between cultures: between a traditional and an emerging culture, for example? Are any characters engaged in a conflict with society because of their race or ethnic background? Does the work celebrate a specific culture and its traditions?

Gender: Are any characters' choices restricted because of gender? What are the power relationships between the sexes? Do any characters resist the gender roles that society has assigned to them? Do other characters choose to conform to those roles?

Archetypes (or universal types): Does a character, an image, or a plot fit a pattern—a type—that has been repeated in stories throughout history and across cultures? (For example, nearly every culture has stories about heroes, quests, redemption, and revenge.) How is an archetypal character, image, or plot line similar to or different from others within the same universal type?

In the introduction of your paper, you will usually announce your interpretation in a one- or two-sentence thesis. The thesis answers the central question that you posed. Here, for example, is Margaret Peel's two-sentence thesis:

> Langston Hughes's "Ballad of the Landlord" is narrated through four voices, each with its own perspective on the poem's action. These opposing voices—of a tenant, a landlord, the police, and the press—dramatize a black man's experience in a society dominated by whites.

7c Draft a working thesis.

A thesis, which often appears in the introduction, announces an essay's main point (see also 1e and 53a). When planning your paper, it is helpful to have a working thesis in mind. This working thesis will reflect the current state of your thinking about the work and will likely change as you plan and draft. In a literature analysis, your thesis will answer the central question that you have asked about the work. Putting your working thesis and notes into an informal outline can help you organize your ideas.

Drafting a thesis

When drafting your thesis, aim for a strong, assertive summary of your interpretation. Here, for example, is a successful thesis taken from a student essay, together with the central question the student had posed.

QUESTION

What is the significance of the explorer Robert Walton in Mary Shelley's novel *Frankenstein*?

THESIS

Through the character of Walton, Shelley suggests that the most profound and useful sort of knowledge is not a knowledge of nature's secrets but a knowledge of the limits of knowledge itself.

As in other college writing, the thesis of a literature paper should not be too factual, too broad, or too vague (see 1c). For an essay on Mark Twain's *Huckleberry Finn*, the first three examples would all make weak thesis statements.

TOO FACTUAL

As a runaway slave, Jim is in danger from the law.

TOO BROAD

In *Huckleberry Finn*, Mark Twain criticizes mid-nineteenth-century American society.

TOO VAGUE

Huckleberry Finn is Twain's most exciting work.

The following thesis statement is sharply focused and presents a central idea that requires discussion and support. It connects a general point (that Twain objects to empty piety) to those specific aspects of the novel the paper will address (Huck's status as narrator, Huck's comments on religion).

EFFECTIVE THESIS

Because Huckleberry Finn is a naive narrator, his comments on conventional religion function ironically at every turn, allowing Twain to poke fun at empty piety.

Sketching an outline

Your thesis may strongly suggest a method of organization, in which case you will have little difficulty jotting down your essay's key points. Consider, for example, the following informal outline, based on a thesis that leads naturally to a three-part organization.

Thesis: In Zora Neale Hurston's novel *Their Eyes Were Watching God*, Janie grows into independence through a series of marriages: first to Logan Killicks, who treats her as a source of farm labor; next to Jody Starks, who sees her as a symbol of his own power; and then to Tea Cake, with whom she shares a passionate and satisfying love that leads her to self-discovery.

- Marriage to Logan Killicks: arranged by grandmother, Janie as labor, runs away
- Marriage to Jody Starks: Eatonville, Jody as mayor, violence, Jody's death
- Marriage to Tea Cake: younger man, love, shooting, return to Eatonville

Whether to use an informal or a formal outline (see 1d) is to some extent a matter of personal preference. For most purposes, you will probably find that an informal outline is sufficient, perhaps even preferable.

Drafting an introduction that announces your interpretation

The introduction to a literature analysis is usually one paragraph long. In most cases, you will want to begin the paragraph with a few sentences that provide context for your thesis and to end it with a thesis that sums up your interpretation. You may also want to note the question or issue that motivated your interpretation. In this way, you will help your readers understand not only what your idea or thesis *is* but also why it *matters*.

The following is an introductory paragraph announcing a student's interpretation of one aspect of the novel *Frankenstein*; the thesis is highlighted.

> In Mary Shelley's novel *Frankenstein*, Walton's ambition as an explorer, to find a passage to the North Pole, mirrors Frankenstein's ambition as a scientist, to discover and master the secret of life. But where Frankenstein is ultimately destroyed by his quest for knowledge, Walton turns back from his quest when he learns of Frankenstein's fate. Walton's story might seem unimportant, but paired with Frankenstein's, it keeps us from missing one of the novel's most important themes. Through the character of Walton, Shelley suggests that the most profound and useful sort of knowledge is not a knowledge of nature's secrets but a knowledge of the limits of knowledge itself.

7d Support your interpretation with evidence from the text; avoid plot summary.

Your thesis and preliminary outline will point you toward details in the text relevant to your interpretation. As you begin drafting the body of your paper, make good use of those details.

Supporting your interpretation

As a rule, each paragraph in the body of your paper should focus on some aspect of your overall interpretation and should include a topic sentence that states the main idea of the paragraph. The rest of the paragraph should present details and quotations from the work that back up your interpretation. In the following paragraph, which develops part of the organization sketched on page 174, the topic sentence comes first. It sums up the significance of Janie's marriage to Logan Killicks in Zora Neale Hurston's novel *Their Eyes Were Watching God*.

Topic sentence

Janie finds her marriage to Logan Killicks unsatisfying because she did not choose him and cannot love him. The marriage is arranged by Janie's grandmother and caretaker, Nanny, so that Janie will have a secure home after Nanny dies. When Janie objects to the marriage, Nanny tells her, "'Tain't Logan Killicks Ah wants you to have, baby, it's protection" (15). Janie marries Logan even though she does not love him. She "wait[s] for love to begin" (22), but love never comes. At first, Logan dotes on Janie, but as time passes he demands more and more work from her. Although she works hard in the kitchen, he wants her to perform traditionally masculine tasks such as chopping wood, plowing fields, and shoveling manure. When Janie suggests that they each have their roles—"Youse in yo' place and Ah'm in mine"—Logan asserts his authority over her and doesn't seem to relate to her as family: "You ain't got no particular place. It's wherever Ah need yuh" (31). As husband and wife, Janie and Logan are estranged from each other. Janie tells him, "You ain't done me no favor by marryin' me" (31). Janie's leaving the marriage is the first step in her growing independence.

Notice that the writer has quoted dialogue from the novel to lend both flavor and substance to her interpretation (quotations are cited with page numbers). Notice too that the writer is *interpreting* the work: She is not merely summarizing the plot.

Avoiding simple plot summary

In a literature paper, it is tempting to rely heavily on plot summary and avoid interpretation. You can resist this temptation by paying special attention to your topic sentences.

> **DRAFT: A TOPIC SENTENCE THAT LEADS TO PLOT SUMMARY**
>
> As they drift down the river on a raft, Huck and Jim have many philosophical discussions.

> **REVISED: A TOPIC SENTENCE THAT ANNOUNCES AN INTERPRETATION**
>
> The theme of growing moral awareness is reinforced by the many philosophical discussions between Huck and Jim as they drift down the river on a raft.

Remember that readers are interested in your ideas about a work—the questions you are asking and the details you find significant. To avoid simple plot summary, keep the following strategies in mind as you write.

- When you write for an academic audience, you can assume that most readers have read the work. You need to include some summary as background, but the emphasis should be on your ideas and your interpretation of the work.

- Pose questions that lead to an interpretation or a judgment of the work rather than to a summary. The questions in the chart on pages 171–72 can help steer you away from summary and toward interpretation.

- Read your essay out loud. If you hear yourself listing events from the work, stop and revise.

- Rather than organizing your paper according to the work's sequence of events, organize it in a way that brings out the relationship among your ideas.

7e Observe the conventions of literature papers.

The academic discipline of English literature has certain conventions, or standard practices, that scholars in the field use when writing about literature. These conventions help scholars contribute their ideas clearly and efficiently. If you follow these conventions, you will enhance your credibility and enable your readers to focus more easily on your ideas.

Referring to authors, titles, and characters

The first time you refer to an author of a literary work or a secondary source, such as a critical essay, use the author's full name: *Virginia Woolf is known for her experimental novels.* In subsequent references, you may use the last name only: *Woolf's early work was largely overlooked.* As a rule, do not use personal titles such as *Mr.* or *Ms.* or *Dr.* when referring to authors.

When you mention the title of a short story, an essay, or a short or medium-length poem, put the title in quotation marks: "The Progress of Love" by Alice Munro (see 37c). Italicize the titles of novels, nonfiction books, plays, and long poems: *The Fourth Hand* by John Irving (see 42a).

Using the present tense to describe fictional events

Perhaps because fictional events have not actually occurred in the past, the literary convention is to describe them in the present tense. Until you become used to this convention, you may find yourself shifting between present and past tense. As you revise your draft, make sure that you have used the present tense consistently.

NOTE: See also page 180 on avoiding shifts in tenses when you integrate quotations into your own text.

7f Integrate quotations from the text.

Integrating quotations from a literary text can lend vivid support to your argument, but keep most quotations fairly short. Excessive use of long quotations may interrupt the flow of your interpretation. (The examples in this section use MLA style for citing sources. See 56a for details.)

Introducing literary quotations

When introducing quotations from a literary work, make sure that you don't confuse the author with the narrator of a story, the speaker of a poem, or a character in a story or play. Instead of naming the author, you can refer to the narrator or speaker—or to the work itself.

INAPPROPRIATE

Poet Andrew Marvell describes his fear of death like this: "But at my back I always hear / Time's wingèd chariot hurrying near" (21-22).

APPROPRIATE

Addressing his beloved, the speaker of the poem argues that death gives them no time to waste: "But at my back I always hear / Time's wingèd chariot hurrying near" (21-22).

APPROPRIATE

The poem "To His Coy Mistress" says as much about fleeting time and death as it does about sexual passion. Its most powerful lines are "But at my back I always hear / Time's wingèd chariot hurrying near" (21-22).

In the last example, you could mention the author as well: *Andrew Marvell's poem "To His Coy Mistress" says as much. . . .*

Although the author is mentioned, readers will not confuse him with the speaker of the poem.

Providing context for quotations

When you quote the words of a narrator, speaker, or character in a literary work, you should name who is speaking and provide a context for the quoted words. In the following example, the quoted language is from Shirley Jackson's short story "The Lottery."

> When a neighbor suggests that the lottery should be abandoned, Old
> Man Warner responds, "There's *always* been a lottery" (284).

Avoiding shifts in tense when quoting

Because it is conventional to write about literature in the present tense (see p. 178) and because literary works often use other tenses, you will need to exercise some care when weaving quotations into your own writing. One student's draft of an essay on Nadine Gordimer's short story "Friday's Footprint" included the following awkward sentence, in which the present-tense main verb *sees* is followed by the past-tense verb *blushed* in the quotation.

TENSE SHIFT

> When Rita <u>sees</u> Johnny's relaxed attitude, "she <u>blushed</u>, like a wave of
> illness" (159).

When revising, the writer considered two ways to avoid the shift from present to past tense: to paraphrase the reference to Rita's blushing and reduce the length of the quotation or to change the verb in the quotation to the present tense, using brackets to indicate the change. (For advice on using brackets to indicate changes in a quotation, see 39c.)

REVISION 1

When Rita sees Johnny's relaxed attitude, she is overcome with embarrassment, "like a wave of illness" (159).

REVISION 2

When Rita sees Johnny's relaxed attitude, "she blushe[s], like a wave of illness" (159).

Citing quotations

MLA guidelines for citing quotations differ somewhat for short stories or novels, poems, and plays.

Short stories or novels   To cite a passage from a short story or a novel, use a page number in parentheses after the quoted words.

> The narrator of Madeleine Thien's "Simple Recipes" remembers a conversation in which her mother described guilt as something one could "shrink" and "compress." After a time, according to the mother, "you can blow it off your body like a speck of dirt" (12).

When a quotation is five lines or longer, set it off from the text by indenting one-half inch from the left margin; when you set a quotation off from the text, do not use quotation marks. Put the parenthetical citation after the final mark of punctuation.

> Sister's tale begins with "I," and she makes every event revolve around herself, even her sister's marriage:
>
>> I was getting along fine with Mama, Papa-Daddy, and Uncle Rondo until my sister Stella-Rondo just separated from her husband and came back home again. Mr. Whitaker! Of course I went with Mr. Whitaker first, when he first appeared here

in China Grove, taking "Pose Yourself" photos, and Stella-Rondo broke us up. (46)

Poems   To cite lines from a poem, use line numbers in parentheses at the end of the quotation. For the first reference, use the word "lines": (lines 1-2). Thereafter use just the numbers: (12-13).

The opening lines of Frost's "Fire and Ice" strike a conversational tone: "Some say the world will end in fire, / Some say in ice" (1-2).

Enclose quotations of three or fewer lines of poetry in quotation marks within your text, and indicate line breaks with a slash, as in the example just given. (See also 39e and item 25 on pp. 609–10.)

When you quote four or more lines of poetry, set the quotation off from the text by indenting one-half inch and omit the quotation marks. Put the line numbers in parentheses after the final mark of punctuation.

Plays   To cite lines from a play, include the act number, scene number, and line numbers (as many of these as are available) in parentheses at the end of the quotation. Separate the numbers with periods, and use arabic numerals (1, 2, 3) unless your instructor prefers roman numerals.

Two attendants silently watch as the sleepwalking Lady Macbeth subconsciously struggles with her guilt: "Here's the smell of the blood still. All the perfumes of Arabia will not sweeten this little hand" (5.1.50-51).

If no act, scene, or line numbers are available, use a page number.

When a quotation from a play takes up four or fewer typed lines in your paper and is spoken by only one character, put quotation marks around it and run it into the text of your essay, as in the previous example. If the quotation consists of two or three lines from a verse play, use a slash for line breaks, as for poetry (see p. 182). When a dramatic quotation by a single character is five typed lines or longer (or more than three lines in a verse play), treat it like a passage from a short story or a novel (see p. 181): Indent the quotation one-half inch from the left margin and omit quotation marks. Include the citation in parentheses after the final mark of punctuation.

When quoting dialogue between two or more characters in a play, set the quotation off from the text. Type each character's name in all capital letters at a one-half inch indent from the left margin. Indent subsequent lines under the character's name an additional one-quarter inch.

> In the opening act of *Translations*, Friel pointedly contrasts the monolingual Captain Lancey with the multilingual Irish:
>> HUGH. . . . [Lancey] then explained that he does not speak Irish. Latin? I asked. None. Greek? Not a syllable. He speaks—on his own admission—only English; and to his credit he seemed suitably verecund—James?
>> JIMMY. *Verecundus*—humble.
>> HUGH. Indeed—he voiced some surprise that we did not speak his language. (act 1)

7g Document secondary sources appropriately and avoid plagiarism.

Many times, an analysis of literature relies wholly on the primary source—the literary work under discussion. In addition to relying on primary sources, some analyses draw on secondary sources: essays of literary criticism, a biography or autobiography of the author, or histories of the era in which the work was written. When you use secondary sources, you must document them with MLA in-text citations and a list of works cited as explained in 56. (For an example of a paper that uses secondary sources, see pp. 188–90.)

Keep in mind that even when you use secondary sources, your main goal should be to develop your own understanding and interpretation of the literary work.

Whenever you use secondary sources, you must document them to avoid plagiarism. Plagiarism is unacknowledged borrowing of a source's words or ideas. (See 54b.)

Documenting secondary sources

Most literature papers use the documentation system recommended by the Modern Language Association (MLA). This system of documentation is discussed in detail in 56.

MLA recommends in-text citations that refer readers to a list of works cited. An in-text citation names the author of the source, often in a signal phrase, and gives the page number in parentheses. At the end of the paper, a list of works cited provides publication information about the sources used in the paper.

MLA IN-TEXT CITATION

Finding Butler's science fiction novel *Xenogenesis* more hopeful than *Frankenstein*, Theodora Goss and John Paul Riquelme note that "[h]uman and creature never bridge their differences in Shelley's narrative, but in Butler's they do . . ." (437).

SAMPLE ENTRY IN THE LIST OF WORKS CITED

Goss, Theodora, and John Paul Riquelme. "From Superhuman to Posthuman: The Gothic Technological Imaginary in Mary Shelley's *Frankenstein* and Octavia Butler's *Xenogenesis*." *Modern Fiction Studies*, vol. 53, no. 3, Fall 2007, pp. 434-59.

As you document secondary sources with in-text citations and a list of works cited, you will need to consult 56a and 56b.

Avoiding plagiarism; being responsible

The rules about plagiarism are the same for literary papers as for other academic and research writing (see 51c and 54 for important details). To be fair and ethical, you must acknowledge your responsibility to the writers of any sources you use. If another critic's work suggested an interpretation to you or if someone else's research clarified an obscure point, it is your responsibility to cite the source. In addition to citing the source, you must place any borrowed language in quotation marks and credit the author. In the following example, the plagiarized words are highlighted.

ORIGINAL SOURCE

Here again Glaspell's story reflects a larger truth about the lives of rural women. Their isolation induced madness in many. The rate of insanity in rural areas, especially for women, was a much-discussed subject in the second half of the nineteenth century.

—Elaine Hedges, "Small Things Reconsidered: 'A Jury of Her Peers,'" p. 59

PLAGIARISM

Glaspell may or may not want us to believe that Minnie Wright's murder of her husband is an insane act, but Minnie's loneliness and isolation certainly could have driven her mad. As Elaine Hedges notes, the rate of insanity in rural areas, especially for women, was a much-discussed subject in the second half of the nineteenth century (59).

BORROWED LANGUAGE IN QUOTATION MARKS

Glaspell may or may not want us to believe that Minnie Wright's murder of her husband is an insane act, but Minnie's loneliness and isolation certainly could have driven her mad. As Elaine Hedges notes, "The rate of insanity in rural areas, especially for women, was a much-discussed subject in the second half of the nineteenth century" (59).

Sometimes writers plagiarize unintentionally because they have difficulty paraphrasing a source's ideas. In the first paraphrase of the following source, the writer has copied the highlighted words (without quotation marks) and followed the sentence structure of the source too closely, merely plugging in synonyms (*prowess* for *skill*, *respect* for *esteem*, and so on).

ORIGINAL SOURCE

Mothers [in the late nineteenth century] were advised to teach their daughters to make small, exact stitches, not only for durability but as a way of instilling habits of patience, neatness, and diligence. But such stitches also became a badge of one's needlework skill, a source of self-esteem and of status, through the recognition and admiration of other women.

— Elaine Hedges, "Small Things Reconsidered:
'A Jury of Her Peers,'" p. 62

PLAGIARISM: UNACCEPTABLE BORROWING

One of the final clues in the story, the irregular stitching in Minnie's quilt patches, connects immediately with Mrs. Hale and Mrs. Peters. In the late nineteenth century, explains Elaine Hedges, small, exact stitches were valued not only for their durability. They became a badge of one's prowess with the needle, a source of self-respect and of prestige, through the recognition and approval of other women (62).

ACCEPTABLE PARAPHRASE

One of the final clues in the story, the irregular stitching in Minnie's quilt patches, connects immediately with Mrs. Hale and Mrs. Peters. In the late nineteenth century, explains Elaine Hedges, precise needlework was valued for more than its strength. It was a source of pride to women, a way of gaining status in the community of other women (62).

Although the acceptable version uses a few words found in the source, it does not borrow entire phrases without quotation marks or closely mimic the structure of the original. To write an acceptable paraphrase, resist the temptation to look at the source while you write; instead, write from memory. When you write from memory, you will be more likely to use your own words. Ask yourself, "What is the author's meaning?" and then in your own words state your understanding of the author's basic point.

7h Sample student writing: Literary analysis

Following are pages from a sample essay that analyzes a literary work. Dan Larson uses evidence from the primary source, a short story, as well as from secondary sources, essays written by literary critics.

Larson 1

Dan Larson

Professor Duncan

English 102

19 April 2013

The Transformation of Mrs. Peters:

An Analysis of "A Jury of Her Peers"

In Susan Glaspell's 1917 short story "A Jury of Her Peers,"
two women accompany their husbands and a county attorney to an
isolated house where a farmer named John Wright has been choked
to death in his bed with a rope. The chief suspect is Wright's wife,
Minnie, who is in jail awaiting trial. The sheriff's wife, Mrs. Peters, has
come along to gather some personal items for Minnie, and Mrs. Hale
has joined her. Early in the story, Mrs. Hale sympathizes with Minnie
and objects to the way the male investigators are "snoopin' round and
criticizin'" her kitchen (249). In contrast, Mrs. Peters shows respect
for the law, saying that the men are doing "no more than their duty"
(249). By the end of the story, however, Mrs. Peters has joined
Mrs. Hale in a conspiracy of silence, lied to the men, and committed
a crime—hiding key evidence. What causes this dramatic change?

One critic, Leonard Mustazza, argues that Mrs. Hale recruits
Mrs. Peters "as a fellow 'juror' in the case, moving the sheriff's wife
away from her sympathy for her husband's position and towards
identification with the accused wom[a]n" (494). While this is true,
Mrs. Peters also reaches insights on her own. Her observations in the
kitchen lead her to understand Minnie's grim and lonely plight as the
wife of an abusive farmer, and her identification with both Minnie and
Mrs. Hale is strengthened as the men conducting the investigation
trivialize the lives of women.

The opening lines
name the story and
establish context.

Present tense is
used to describe
details from the
story.

Quotations from
the story are cited
with page numbers
in parentheses.

The opening
paragraph ends
with Larson's
research question.

The thesis asserts
Larson's main point.

Marginal annotations indicate MLA-style formatting and effective writing.

Larson 2

The first evidence that Mrs. Peters reaches understanding on her own surfaces in the following passage:

> The sheriff's wife had looked from the stove to the sink—
> to the pail of water which had been carried in from
> outside. . . . That look of seeing into things, of seeing
> through a thing to something else, was in the eyes of
> the sheriff's wife now. (251-52)

Something about the stove, the sink, and the pail of water connects with her own experience, giving Mrs. Peters a glimpse into the life of Minnie Wright. The details resonate with meaning.

Social historian Elaine Hedges argues that such details, which evoke the drudgery of a farm woman's work, would not have been lost on Glaspell's readers in 1917. Hedges tells us what the pail and the stove, along with another detail from the story—a dirty towel on a roller—would have meant to women of the time. Laundry was a dreaded all-day affair. Water had to be pumped, hauled, and boiled; then the wash was rubbed, rinsed, wrung through a wringer, carried outside, and hung on a line to dry. "What the women see, beyond the pail and the stove," writes Hedges, "are the hours of work it took Minnie to produce that one clean towel" (56).

On her own, Mrs. Peters discovers clues about the motive for the murder. Her curiosity leads her to pick up a sewing basket filled with quilt pieces and then to notice something strange: a sudden row of badly sewn stitches. "What do you suppose she was so—nervous about?" asks Mrs. Peters (252). A short time later, Mrs. Peters spots another clue, an empty birdcage. Again she observes details on her own, in this case a broken door and hinge, suggesting that the cage has been roughly handled.

A long quotation is set off by indenting; no quotation marks are needed; ellipsis dots indicate a sentence omitted from the source.

Larson summarizes ideas from a secondary source and then quotes from that source; he names the author in a signal phrase and gives a page number in parentheses.

Topic sentences present Larson's interpretation.

Larson 7

Works Cited

The works cited page lists the primary source (Glaspell's story) and secondary sources.

Ben-Zvi, Linda. "'Murder, She Wrote': The Genesis of Susan Glaspell's
    Trifles." *Susan Glaspell: Essays on Her Theater and Fiction*,
    edited by Ben-Zvi, U of Michigan P, 1995, pp. 19-48. Originally
    published in *Theatre Journal*, vol. 44, no. 2, May 1992, pp.
    141-62.

Glaspell, Susan. "A Jury of Her Peers." *Literature and Its Writers: A
    Compact Introduction to Fiction, Poetry, and Drama,* edited by
    Ann Charters and Samuel Charters, 6th ed., Bedford/St. Martin's,
    2013, pp. 243-58.

Hedges, Elaine. "Small Things Reconsidered: 'A Jury of Her Peers.'"
    Susan Glaspell: Essays on Her Theater and Fiction, edited by
    Linda Ben-Zvi, U of Michigan P, 1995, pp. 49-69. Originally
    published in *Women's Studies*, vol. 12, no. 1, 1986, pp. 80-110.

Mustazza, Leonard. "Generic Translation and Thematic Shift in Susan
    Glaspell's *Trifles* and 'A Jury of Her Peers.'" *Studies in Short
    Fiction*, vol. 26, no. 4, 1989, pp. 489-96.

PART III

Clear Sentences

8 Prefer active verbs. 193

9 Balance parallel ideas. 198

10 Add needed words. 204

11 Untangle mixed constructions. 208

12 Repair misplaced and dangling modifiers. 212

13 Eliminate distracting shifts. 220

14 Emphasize key ideas. 228

15 Provide some variety. 242

Clear Sentences

ONLINE ACTIVITIES:

 **Writer's Help 2.0**
macmillan learning

writershelp.com/hacker

 **LaunchPad Solo**
macmillan learning

macmillanhighered.com/
launchpadsolo/hacker

Active verbs	5 Exercises 1 LearningCurve activity
Parallelism	5 Exercises 1 LearningCurve activity
Needed words	4 Exercises
Mixed constructions	4 Exercises
Misplaced and dangling modifiers	8 Exercises 1 LearningCurve activity
Shifts	7 Exercises 1 LearningCurve activity
Sentence emphasis	8 Exercises 1 LearningCurve activity
Sentence variety	2 Exercises

8 Prefer active verbs.

As a rule, choose an active verb and pair it with a subject that names the person or thing doing the action. Active verbs express meaning more emphatically and vigorously than their weaker counterparts—verbs in the passive voice and forms of the verb *be*.

PASSIVE	The pumps *were destroyed* by a surge of power.
***BE* VERB**	A surge of power *was* responsible for the destruction of the pumps.
ACTIVE	A surge of power *destroyed* the pumps.

Verbs in the passive voice lack strength because their subjects receive the action instead of doing it. Forms of the verb *be* (*be, am, is, are, was, were, being, been*) lack vigor because they convey no action.

Although passive verbs and the forms of *be* have legitimate uses, choose an active verb whenever possible.

Even among active verbs, some are more vigorous and colorful than others. Carefully selected verbs can energize a piece of writing.

▶ The goalie crouched low, ~~reached~~ swept out his stick, and ~~sent~~ hooked the rebound away from the mouth of the net.

Academic English

Although you may be tempted to avoid the passive voice completely, keep in mind that some writing situations call for it, especially scientific writing. For appropriate uses of the passive voice, see page 195; for advice about forming the passive voice, see 28b and 47c.

8a Choose the active voice or the passive voice depending on your writing situation.

In the active voice, the subject does the action; in the passive voice, the subject receives the action (see also 47c). Although both voices are grammatically correct, the active voice is usually more effective because it is clearer and more direct.

ACTIVE	Hernando *caught* the fly ball.
PASSIVE	The fly ball *was caught* by Hernando.

Passive sentences often identify the actor in a *by* phrase, as in the preceding example. Sometimes, however, that phrase is omitted, and who or what is responsible for the action becomes unclear: *The fly ball was caught.*

Most of the time, you will want to emphasize the actor, so you should use the active voice. To replace a passive verb with an active one, make the actor the subject of the sentence.

> The settlers stripped the land of timber before realizing
> ▶ ~~The land was stripped of timber before the settlers realized~~
> ^
> the consequences of their actions.

The revision emphasizes the actors (*settlers*) by naming them in the subject.

In much scientific writing, the passive voice properly emphasizes an experiment or a process, not the researcher. Check with your instructor for the preference in your discipline.

8b Replace *be* verbs that result in dull or wordy sentences.

Not every *be* verb needs replacing. The forms of *be* (*be, am, is, are, was, were, being, been*) work well when you want to link a subject to a noun that clearly renames it or to an adjective that

Writer's Choice
Using the active or the passive voice

You will usually choose whether to write in the active voice or the passive voice. While your instructors often expect you to use the active voice, some situations and fields of study will require you to write in the passive voice. This choice will be influenced primarily by your **purpose** but also by your **audience's expectations** and the **genre** in which you are writing (see 1a).

To emphasize the actor and not the receiver of the action, choose the active voice.

ACTIVE   <u>State officials forced</u> nearly 28,000 Hawaiians to leave their homes after the earthquake.

This sentence focuses on the government's displacing the people. Emphasizing the state's action may be better for the writer whose purpose is to make an argument about that action.

To focus attention on the receiver of the action, choose the passive voice.

PASSIVE   Nearly <u>28,000 Hawaiians were forced</u> to leave their homes after the earthquake.

This sentence focuses on the people displaced by the earthquake. Emphasizing the number of homeless Hawaiians may be better for the writer whose purpose is to discuss how the earthquake affected residents.

What idea are you emphasizing in your sentence? Considering your purpose and audience, what would be more effective—focusing on the actor or the person or thing being acted on? It's your choice.

describes it: *Orchard House was the home of Louisa May Alcott. The harvest will be bountiful after the summer rains.*

Be verbs also are essential as helping verbs before present participles (*is flying, are disappearing*) to express ongoing action: *Derrick was fighting the fire when his wife went into labor.* (See 27f.)

If using a *be* verb makes a sentence needlessly dull and wordy, however, consider replacing it. Often a phrase following the verb contains a noun or an adjective (such as *violation, resistant*) that suggests a more vigorous, active verb (*violate, resist*).

▶ Burying nuclear waste in Antarctica would ~~be in violation of~~ *violate* an international treaty.

Violate is less wordy and more vigorous than *be in violation of.*

▶ When Rosa Parks ~~was resistant to~~ *resisted* giving up her seat on the bus, she became a civil rights hero.

Resisted is stronger than *was resistant to.*

8c As a rule, choose a subject that names the person or thing doing the action.

In weak, unemphatic prose, both the actor and the action may be buried in sentence elements other than the subject and the verb. In the following weak sentence, for example, both the actor and the action appear in prepositional phrases, word groups that readers often don't notice.

WEAK	The institution of the New Deal had the effect of reversing some of the economic inequalities of the Great Depression.
EMPHATIC	The New Deal reversed some of the economic inequalities of the Great Depression.

Consider the subjects and verbs of the two versions—*institution had* versus *New Deal reversed*. The latter expresses the writer's point more emphatically.

▶ ~~The use of~~ **p**ure oxygen can ~~cause~~ heal~~ing in~~ wounds that
  ^

are otherwise untreatable.

In the original sentence, the subject and verb—*use can cause*—express the point blandly. *Oxygen can heal* makes the point more emphatically and directly.

EXERCISE 8–1 Revise any weak, unemphatic sentences by replacing passive verbs or *be* verbs with active alternatives. You may need to name in the subject the person or thing doing the action. If a sentence is emphatic, do not change it. Possible revisions appear in the back of the book.

The ranger doused the campfire before giving us
The campfire was doused by the ranger before we were given
  ^
a ticket for unauthorized use of a campsite.

a. The Prussians were victorious over the Saxons in 1745.

b. The entire operation is managed by Ahmed, the producer.

c. The sea kayaks were expertly paddled by the tour guides.

d. At the crack of rocket and mortar blasts, I jumped from the top bunk and landed on my buddy below, who was crawling on the floor looking for his boots.

e. There were shouting protesters on the courthouse steps.

EXERCISE 8–2 For each writing situation below, decide whether it is more appropriate to use the active voice or the passive voice.

a. You are writing a research paper explaining the effects of a deadly bacterial outbreak in a remote Chilean village. (active / passive)

b.   You are writing a letter to the editor, praising an emergency medical technician whose quick action saved an injured motorist. (active / passive)

c.   You are writing a summary of the procedure you used in an experiment for your biology class. (active / passive)

d.   To accompany your résumé, you must write a cover letter explaining your recent accomplishments as a manager. (active / passive)

e.   You must fill out an incident report, explaining in detail how your actions led to a collision between the forklift you were operating and a wall of fully-stocked shelves. (active / passive)

9   Balance parallel ideas.

If two or more ideas are parallel, they are easier to grasp when expressed in parallel grammatical form. Single words should be balanced with single words, phrases with phrases, clauses with clauses.

A kiss can be a comma, a question mark, or an exclamation point.   —Mistinguett

This novel is not to be tossed lightly aside, but to be hurled with great force.   —Dorothy Parker

In matters of principle, stand like a rock; in matters of taste, swim with the current.   —Thomas Jefferson

Writers often use parallelism to create emphasis. (See p. 241.)

9a Balance parallel ideas in a series.

Readers expect items in a series to appear in parallel grammatical form. When one or more of the items violate readers' expectations, a sentence will be needlessly awkward.

▶ Children who study music also learn confidence,
                 creativity.
  discipline, and ~~they are creative.~~
           ∧

The revision presents all the items in the series as nouns: *confidence,*
discipline, and *creativity.*

▶ Impressionist painters believed in focusing on ordinary

  subjects, capturing the effects of light on those subjects,
      using
  and ~~to use~~ short brushstrokes.
     ∧

The revision uses *-ing* forms for all the items in the series: *focusing,*
capturing, and *using.*

▶ Racing to get to work on time, Sam drove down the middle
                               ignored
  of the road, ran one red light, and two stop signs.
                                ∧

The revision adds a verb to make the three items parallel: *drove,*
ran, and *ignored.*

In headings and lists, aim for as much parallelism as the
content allows.

Headings

Headings on the same level of organization should be written in
parallel form—as single words, phrases, or clauses.

PHRASES AS HEADINGS

Safeguarding Earth's atmosphere

Charting the path to sustainable energy

Conserving global forests

INDEPENDENT CLAUSES AS HEADINGS

Ask the patient to describe current symptoms.

Take a detailed medical history.

Record the patient's vital signs.

Lists

Lists are usually introduced with an independent clause followed by a colon. Lists are most readable when they are presented in parallel grammatical form. Like headings, lists might consist of words, phrases, or clauses. The following list consists of parallel noun phrases.

> Renewable energy technologies include the following: hydroelectric power, solar power, wind energy, and geothermal energy.

9b Balance parallel ideas presented as pairs.

When pairing ideas, underscore their connection by expressing them in similar grammatical form. Paired ideas are usually connected in one of these ways:

- with a coordinating conjunction such as *and, but,* or *or*

- with a pair of correlative conjunctions such as *either . . . or* or *not only . . . but also*

- with a word introducing a comparison, usually *than* or *as*

Parallel ideas linked with coordinating conjunctions

Coordinating conjunctions (*and, but, or, nor, for, so,* and *yet*) link ideas of equal importance. When those ideas are closely parallel in content, they should be expressed in parallel grammatical form.

▶ Emily Dickinson's poetry features the use of dashes and
the capitalization of
~~capitalizing~~ common words.
^

The revision balances the nouns *use* and *capitalization.*

▶ Many states are reducing property taxes for home owners
extending
and ~~extend~~ tax credits to renters.
^

The revision balances the verb *reducing* with the verb *extending.*

Parallel ideas linked with correlative conjunctions

Correlative conjunctions come in pairs: *either . . . or, neither . . . nor, not only . . . but also, both . . . and, whether . . . or.* Make sure that the grammatical structure following the second half of the pair is the same as that following the first half.

▶ Thomas Edison was not only a prolific inventor but also ~~was~~

a successful entrepreneur.

The words *a prolific inventor* follow *not only,* so *a successful entrepreneur* should follow *but also.* Repeating *was* creates an unbalanced effect.

to
▶ The clerk told me either to change my flight or take the train.
^

To change my flight, which follows *either,* should be balanced with *to take the train,* which follows *or.*

Comparisons linked with than *or* as

In comparisons linked with *than* or *as*, the elements being compared should be expressed in parallel grammatical structure.

▶ It is easier to speak in abstractions than ~~grounding~~ one's

    to ground

    thoughts in reality.

To speak is balanced with *to ground*.

▶ In Pueblo culture, according to Silko, ~~to write~~ down the

    writing

    stories of a tribe is not the same as "keeping track of all the

    stories" (290).

When you are quoting from a source, parallel grammatical structure—such as *writing . . . keeping*—helps create continuity between your sentence and the words from the source. (See 56a on citing sources in MLA style.)

Comparisons should also be logical and complete. (See 10c.)

9c Repeat function words to clarify parallels.

Function words such as prepositions (*by, to*) and subordinating conjunctions (*that, because*) signal the grammatical nature of the word groups to follow. Although you can sometimes omit them, be sure to include them whenever they signal parallel structures that readers might otherwise miss.

▶ Our study revealed that left-handed students were more likely

                                    that

    to have trouble with classroom desks and rearranging

    desks for exam periods was useful.

A second subordinating conjunction helps readers sort out the two parallel ideas: *that* left-handed students have trouble with classroom desks and *that* rearranging desks was useful.

EXERCISE 9–1 Edit the following sentences to correct faulty parallelism. Possible revisions appear in the back of the book.

> Rowena began her workday by pouring a cup of coffee and
> *checking*
> ~~checked~~ her e-mail.
> ^

a. Police dogs are used for finding lost children, tracking criminals, and the detection of bombs and illegal drugs.

b. Hannah told her rock-climbing partner that she bought a new harness and of her desire to climb Otter Cliffs.

c. It is more difficult to sustain an exercise program than starting one.

d. During basic training, I was not only told what to do but also what to think.

e. Jan wanted to drive to the wine country or at least Sausalito.

EXERCISE 9–2 Revise the following paragraph to balance parallel ideas.

Community service can provide tremendous benefits not only for the organization receiving the help but the volunteer providing the help, too. This dual benefit idea is behind a recent move to make community service hours a graduation requirement in high schools across the country. For many nonprofit organizations, seeking volunteers is often smarter financially than to hire additional employees. For many young people, community service positions can help develop empathy, being committed, and leadership. Opponents of the trend argue that volunteerism should not be mandatory, but research shows that community service requirements are keeping students engaged in school and lower dropout rates dramatically. Parents, school administrators, and people who are leaders in the community all seem to favor the new initiatives.

10 Add needed words.

Sometimes writers leave out words intentionally, and the meaning of the sentence is not affected. But leaving out words can occasionally cause confusion for readers or make the sentence ungrammatical. Readers need to see at a glance how the parts of a sentence are connected.

Multilingual

Languages sometimes differ in the need for certain words. In particular, be alert for missing articles, verbs, subjects, or expletives. See 29, 30a, and 30b.

10a Add words needed to complete compound structures.

In compound structures, words are often left out for economy: *Tom is a man who means what he says and [who] says what he means.* Such omissions are acceptable as long as the omitted words are common to both parts of the compound structure.

If a sentence defies grammar or idiom because an omitted word is not common to both parts of the compound structure, the simplest solution is to put the word back in.

▶ Advertisers target customers whom they identify through
    who
    demographic research or have purchased their product in
                                    ^
    the past.

The word *who* must be included because *whom . . . have purchased* is
not grammatically correct.

▶ Mayor Davis never has and never will accept~~accepted~~ a bribe.

> *Has . . . accept* is not grammatically correct.

▶ Many South Pacific islanders still believe and live by~~in~~

ancient laws.

> *Believe . . . by* is not idiomatic in English. (For a list of common idioms, see 18d.)

NOTE: Even when the omitted word is common to both parts of the compound structure, occasionally it must be inserted to avoid ambiguity.

> *My* favorite *professor* and *mentor* influenced my choice of a career. [Professor and mentor are the same person.]

> *My* favorite *professor* and *my mentor* influenced my choice of a career. [Professor and mentor are two different people; *my* must be repeated.]

10b Add the word *that* if there is any danger of misreading without it.

If there is no danger of misreading, the word *that* may be omitted when it introduces a subordinate clause. *The value of a principle is the number of things* [*that*] *it will explain.* When a sentence might be misread without *that*, however, it is necessary to include the word.

▶ In his famous obedience experiments, psychologist Stanley
Milgram discovered ~~that~~ ordinary people were willing to inflict

physical pain on strangers.

> Milgram didn't discover ordinary people; he discovered that ordinary people were willing to inflict pain on strangers. The word *that* tells readers to expect a clause, not just *ordinary people*, as the direct object of *discovered*.

10c Add words needed to make comparisons logical and complete.

Comparisons should be made between items that are alike. To compare unlike items is illogical and distracting.

▶ The forests of North America are much more extensive
than Europe.
^ those of

Forests must be compared with forests, not with all of Europe.

▶ Some say that Ella Fitzgerald's renditions of Cole Porter's
songs are better than any other ~~singer.~~
^ singer's.

Ella Fitzgerald's renditions cannot logically be compared with a singer. The revision uses the possessive form *singer's*, with the word *renditions* being implied.

Sometimes the word *other* must be inserted to make a comparison logical.

▶ Jupiter is larger than any planet in our solar system.
^ other

Jupiter is a planet, and it cannot be larger than itself.

Sometimes the word *as* must be inserted to make a comparison grammatically complete.

▶ The city of Lowell is as old, if not older than, the neighboring
^ as
city of Lawrence.

The construction *as old* is not complete without a second *as*: *as old as . . . the neighboring city of Lawrence.*

Comparisons should be complete enough to ensure clarity. The reader should understand what is being compared.

INCOMPLETE   Brand X is less salty.

COMPLETE   Brand X is less salty than Brand Y.

Finally, comparisons should leave no ambiguity for readers. If a sentence lends itself to more than one interpretation, revise the sentence to state clearly which interpretation you intend. In the following ambiguous sentence, two interpretations are possible.

AMBIGUOUS   Ken helped me more than my roommate.

CLEAR   Ken helped me more than *he helped* my roommate.

CLEAR   Ken helped me more than my roommate *did.*

10d Add the articles *a, an,* and *the* where necessary for grammatical completeness.

It is not always necessary to repeat articles with paired items: *We bought a computer and printer.* However, if one of the items requires *a* and the other requires *an,* both articles must be included.

▸ We bought a computer and ^{an} antivirus program.

Articles are sometimes omitted in recipes and other instructions that are meant to be followed while they are being read. In nearly all other forms of writing, whether formal or informal, such omissions are inappropriate.

Multilingual

Choosing and using articles can be challenging for multilingual writers. See 29.

EXERCISE 10–1 Add any words needed for grammatical or logical completeness in the following sentences. Possible revisions appear in the back of the book.

>   *that*
> **The officer feared the prisoner would escape.**
>   ^

a. A grapefruit or orange is a good source of vitamin C.

b. The women entering the military academy can expect haircuts as short as the male cadets.

c. Looking out the family room window, Sarah saw her favorite tree, which she had climbed as a child, was gone.

d. The graphic designers are interested and knowledgeable about producing posters for the balloon race.

e. The Great Barrier Reef is larger than any coral reef in the world.

11 Untangle mixed constructions.

A mixed construction contains sentence parts that do not sensibly fit together. The mismatch may be a matter of grammar or of logic.

11a Untangle the grammatical structure.

Once you begin a sentence, your choices are limited by the range of grammatical patterns in English. (See 47 and 48.) You cannot begin with one grammatical plan and switch without warning to another. Often you must rethink the purpose of the sentence and revise.

MIXED   For most drivers who have a blood alcohol content of .05 percent double their risk of causing an accident.

The writer begins the sentence with a long prepositional phrase and makes it the subject of the verb *double*. But a prepositional phrase can serve only as a modifier; it cannot be the subject of a sentence.

REVISED   For most drivers who have a blood alcohol content of .05 percent, the risk of causing an accident is doubled.

REVISED   Most drivers who have a blood alcohol content of .05 percent double their risk of causing an accident.

In the first revision, the writer begins with the prepositional phrase and finishes the sentence with a proper subject and verb (*risk . . . is doubled*). In the second revision, the writer stays with the original verb (*double*) and begins the sentence another way, making *drivers* the subject of *double*.

▶ ~~When the country elects~~ a president is the most important
Electing
^
responsibility in a democracy.

The adverb clause *When the country elects a president* cannot serve as the subject of the verb *is*. The revision replaces the adverb clause with a gerund phrase, a word group that can function as a subject. (See 48a and 48b.)

▶ Although the United States is a wealthy nation, ~~but~~ more

than 20 percent of our children live in poverty.

The coordinating conjunction *but* cannot link a subordinate clause (*Although the United States . . .*) with an independent clause (*more than 20 percent of our children live in poverty*).

Occasionally a mixed construction is so tangled that it defies grammatical analysis. When this happens, back away from the sentence, rethink what you want to say, and then rewrite the sentence.

MIXED　　In the whole-word method, children learn to recognize entire words rather than by the phonics method in which they learn to sound out letters and groups of letters.

REVISED　　The whole-word method teaches children to recognize entire words; the phonics method teaches them to sound out letters and groups of letters.

Multilingual

English does not allow double subjects, nor does it allow an object or an adverb to be repeated in an adjective clause. Unlike some other languages, English does not allow a noun and a pronoun to be repeated in a sentence if they have the same grammatical function. See 30c and 30d.

▶ My father ~~he~~ moved to Peru before he met my mother.

11b Straighten out the logical connections.

The subject and the predicate (the verb and its modifiers) should make sense together; when they don't, the error is known as *faulty predication*.

▶ The court decided that ~~Tiffany's welfare~~ ^{Tiffany} would not be safe living with her drug-addicted parents.

Tiffany, not her welfare, would not be safe.

▶ Under the revised plan, the elderly/ ^{double personal exemption for the} ~~who now receive a double personal exemption,~~ will be abolished.

The exemption, not the elderly, will be abolished.

An appositive is a noun that renames a nearby noun. When an appositive and the noun it renames are not logically equivalent, the error is known as *faulty apposition.* (See 48c.)

► ~~The tax accountant,~~ Tax accounting, a very lucrative profession, requires intelligence, patience, and attention to mathematical detail.

The tax accountant is a person, not a profession.

11c Avoid *is when, is where,* and *reason . . . is because* constructions.

In formal English, many readers object to *is when, is where,* and *reason . . . is because* constructions on either grammatical or logical grounds. Grammatically, the verb *is* (as well as *are, was,* and *were*) should be followed by a noun that renames the subject or by an adjective that describes the subject, not by an adverb clause beginning with *when, where,* or *because.* (See 47b and 48e.) Logically, the words *when, where,* and *because* suggest relations of time, place, and cause—relations that do not always make sense with *is, are, was,* or *were.*

► Anorexia nervosa is ~~where people~~ a disorder suffered by people who think they are too fat and diet to the point of starvation.

Where refers to places. Anorexia nervosa is a disorder, not a place.

► The ~~reason the~~ experiment failed ~~is~~ because conditions in the lab were not sterile.

The writer might have changed *because* to *that* (*The reason the experiment failed is that conditions in the lab were not sterile*), but the preceding revision is more concise.

> **EXERCISE 11–1** Edit the following sentences to untangle mixed constructions. Possible revisions appear in the back of the book.

> Taking
> ~~By taking~~ the oath of allegiance made Ling a US citizen.
>   ^

a. Using surgical gloves is a precaution now worn by dentists to prevent contact with patients' blood and saliva.

b. A physician, the career my brother is pursuing, requires at least ten years of challenging work.

c. The reason the pharaohs had bad teeth was because tiny particles of sand found their way into Egyptian bread.

d. Recurring bouts of flu among team members set a record for number of games forfeited.

e. In this box contains the key to your future.

12 Repair misplaced and dangling modifiers.

Modifiers, whether they are single words, phrases, or clauses, should point clearly to the words they modify. As a rule, related words should be kept together.

12a Put limiting modifiers in front of the words they modify.

Limiting modifiers such as *only, even, almost, nearly,* and *just* should appear in front of a verb only if they modify the verb: *At first, I couldn't even touch my toes, much less grasp them.* If they limit the meaning of some other word in the sentence, they should be placed in front of that word.

► The literature reveals that students ~~only~~ learn new vocabulary
  only
  ^
words when they are encouraged to read.
  ^

Only limits the meaning of the *when* clause.

                                 just
► If you ~~just~~ interview chemistry majors, your picture of the
       ^

student response to the new policies will be incomplete.

The adverb *just* limits the meaning of *chemistry majors*, not *interview*.

When the limiting modifier *not* is misplaced, the sentence
usually suggests a meaning the writer did not intend.

                           not
► In the US in 1860, all black southerners were ~~not~~ slaves.
                                              ^

The original sentence says that no black southerners were slaves.
The revision makes the writer's real meaning clear: Some (but not
all) black southerners were slaves.

12b Place phrases and clauses so that readers can see at a glance what they modify.

Although phrases and clauses can appear at some distance
from the words they modify, make sure your meaning is clear.
When phrases or clauses are oddly placed, absurd misreadings
can result.

MISPLACED   The soccer player returned to the clinic where he
             had undergone emergency surgery in 2010 in a
             limousine sent by Adidas.

REVISED   Traveling in a limousine sent by Adidas, the soccer
             player returned to the clinic where he had under-
             gone emergency surgery in 2010.

The revision corrects the false impression that the soccer player underwent emergency surgery in a limousine.

> *On the walls*
> ~~There~~ are many pictures of comedians who have performed
> ^
> at Gavin's **.** ~~on the walls.~~
> ^

The comedians weren't performing on the walls; the pictures were on the walls.

Occasionally the placement of a modifier leads to an ambiguity—a squinting modifier. In such a case, two revisions will be possible, depending on the writer's intended meaning.

AMBIGUOUS	The exchange students we met for coffee occasionally questioned us about our latest slang.
CLEAR	The exchange students we occasionally met for coffee questioned us about our latest slang.
CLEAR	The exchange students we met for coffee questioned us occasionally about our latest slang.

In the original version, it was not clear whether the meeting or the questioning happened occasionally. Both revisions eliminate the ambiguity.

12c Move awkwardly placed modifiers.

As a rule, a sentence should flow from subject to verb to object, without lengthy detours along the way. When a long adverbial word group separates a subject from its verb, a verb from its object, or a helping verb from its main verb, the result is often awkward.

> ~~Hong Kong,~~ After more than 150 years of British rule, was ^A   ^Hong Kong

> transferred back to Chinese control in 1997.

There is no reason to separate the subject, *Hong Kong*, from the verb, *was transferred*, with a long phrase.

Multilingual

English does not allow an adverb to appear between a verb and its object. See 30f.

> Yolanda lifted ~~easily~~ the fifty-pound weight. ^easily

12d Avoid split infinitives when they are awkward.

An infinitive consists of *to* plus the base form of a verb: *to think, to breathe, to dance.* When a modifier appears between *to* and the verb, an infinitive is said to be "split": *to carefully balance, to completely understand.*

When a long word or a phrase appears between the parts of the infinitive, the result is usually awkward.

> ~~The~~ patient should try to ~~if possible~~ avoid going up and If possible, the ^

> down stairs.

Attempts to avoid split infinitives can result in equally awkward sentences. When alternative phrasing sounds unnatural, most experts allow—and even encourage—splitting the infinitive.

AWKWARD	We decided actually to enforce the law.
BETTER	We decided to actually enforce the law.

At times, neither the split infinitive nor its alternative sounds particularly awkward. In such situations, it is usually better not to split the infinitive, especially in formal writing.

> Nursing students learn to ~~accurately~~ record a patient's
>   accurately.
> vital signs/
>   ^

EXERCISE 12–1   Edit the following sentences to correct misplaced or awkwardly placed modifiers. Possible revisions appear in the back of the book.

              in a telephone survey
Answering questions can be annoying. ~~in a telephone~~
                               ^   ^
~~survey.~~

a.   More research is needed to effectively evaluate the risks posed by volcanoes in the Pacific Northwest.

b.   Many students graduate with debt from college totaling more than fifty thousand dollars.

c.   It is a myth that humans only use 10 percent of their brains.

d.   A coolhunter is a person who can find in the unnoticed corners of modern society the next wave of fashion.

e.   All geese do not fly beyond Narragansett for the winter.

12e Repair dangling modifiers.

A dangling modifier fails to refer logically to any word in the sentence. Dangling modifiers are easy to repair, but they can be hard to recognize, especially in your own writing.

Recognizing dangling modifiers

Dangling modifiers are usually word groups (such as verbal phrases) that suggest but do not name an actor. When a sentence opens with such a modifier, readers expect the subject of the next clause to name the actor. If it doesn't, the modifier dangles.

▶ **Understanding the need to create checks and balances on** the framers of
power, the Constitution divided the government into three
∧
branches.

The framers of the Constitution (not the document itself) understood the need for checks and balances.

                            women were often denied
▶ **After completing seminary training, ~~women's~~ access to the**
∧
priesthood. ~~has often been denied.~~
∧

Women (not their access to the priesthood) complete the training.

The following sentences illustrate four common kinds of dangling modifiers.

DANGLING   *Deciding to join the navy,* the recruiter enthusiastically pumped Joe's hand. [Participial phrase]

DANGLING   *Upon entering the doctor's office,* a skeleton caught my attention. [Preposition followed by a gerund phrase]

DANGLING   *To satisfy her mother,* the piano had to be practiced every day. [Infinitive phrase]

DANGLING   *Though not eligible for the clinical trial,* the doctor prescribed the drug for Ethan on compassionate grounds. [Elliptical clause with an understood subject and verb]

These dangling modifiers falsely suggest that the recruiter decided to join the navy, that the skeleton entered the doctor's office, that the piano intended to satisfy the mother, and that the doctor was not eligible for the clinical trial.

Although most readers will understand the writer's intended meaning in such sentences, the inadvertent humor can be distracting.

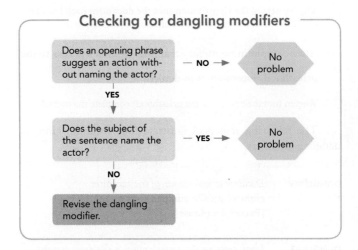

Checking for dangling modifiers

Does an opening phrase suggest an action without naming the actor? — **NO** → No problem

↓ **YES**

Does the subject of the sentence name the actor? — **YES** → No problem

↓ **NO**

Revise the dangling modifier.

Repairing dangling modifiers

To repair a dangling modifier, you can revise the sentence in one of two ways:

- Name the actor in the subject of the sentence.
- Name the actor in the modifier.

Depending on your sentence, one of these revision strategies may be more appropriate than the other.

ACTOR NAMED IN SUBJECT

I noticed
▶ Upon entering the doctor's office, a skeleton. ~~caught my~~
    ^   ^
~~attention.~~

Jing-mei had to practice
▶ To satisfy her mother, the piano ~~had to be practiced~~
                                      ^
every day.

ACTOR NAMED IN MODIFIER

When Joe decided
▶ ~~Deciding~~ to join the navy, the recruiter enthusiastically
    ^   his
pumped ~~Joe's~~ hand.
        ^

Ethan was
▶ Though not eligible for the clinical trial, the doctor
    ^   him
prescribed the drug for ~~Ethan~~ on compassionate grounds.
                          ^

NOTE: You cannot repair a dangling modifier just by moving
it. Consider, for example, the sentence about the skeleton.
If you put the modifier at the end of the sentence (*A skeleton caught my attention upon entering the doctor's office*), you
are still suggesting — absurdly, of course — that the skeleton
entered the office. The only way to avoid the problem is to
put the word *I* in the sentence, either as the subject or in the
modifier.

I noticed
▶ Upon entering the doctor's office, a skeleton. ~~caught my~~
    ^   ^
~~attention.~~

As I entered
▶ ~~Upon entering~~ the doctor's office, a skeleton caught my
    ^
attention.

EXERCISE 12–6   Edit the following sentences to correct dangling modifiers. Most sentences can be revised in more than one way. Possible revisions appear in the back of the book.

> *a student must complete*
> **To acquire a degree in almost any field, two science courses.**
> **must be completed.**

a.   To complete an online purchase with a credit card, the expiration date and the security code must be entered.

b.   Though only sixteen, UCLA accepted Martha's application.

c.   Settled in the cockpit, the pounding of the engine was muffled only slightly by my helmet.

d.   After studying polymer chemistry, computer games seemed less complex to Phuong.

e.   When a young man, my mother enrolled me in tap dance classes.

13 Eliminate distracting shifts.

This section can help you avoid unnecessary shifts that might distract or confuse your readers: shifts in point of view, in verb tense, in mood or voice, or from indirect to direct questions or quotations.

13a Make the point of view consistent in person and number.

The point of view of a piece of writing is the perspective from which it is written: first person (*I* or *we*), second person (*you*), or third person (*he, she, it, one, they,* or any noun).

Writer's Choice
Choosing a point of view

Using the "I" point of view is not grammatically wrong for college writing. As you review your options, think about your **purpose** and **audience**, as well as the **genre** (type of writing) expected. When in doubt, ask your instructor.

When you want to focus on your experience, choose the first-person point of view.

FIRST PERSON

Though initially intimidated, I found that my mentor's observations during my student teaching created opportunities for important discussions about achievement in our classroom.

The firsthand experience and personal tone in this sentence help the writer connect with the reader. The first-person point of view is often used in narrative and reflective writing.

When you want to focus on the reader, choose the second-person point of view.

SECOND PERSON

Although initially you may be intimidated, you may find that your mentor's observations during your student teaching create opportunities for important discussions about achievement in your classroom.

The tone here is instructive and establishes the writer as a guide for the reader. Use the second-person point of view when you are giving instructions or advice.

When you want to focus on the topic, choose the third-person point of view.

THIRD PERSON

Although initially they may be intimidated, many student teachers find that their mentor's observations during their student teaching create opportunities for important discussions about achievement in the classroom.

This sentence focuses on the topic, not on the writer or the reader. Use the third-person point of view when you are arguing a point or presenting information.

Once you make a choice, *stick with it.* Shifting points of view within a piece of writing confuses your reader.

The *I* (or *we*) point of view, which emphasizes the writer, is a good choice for informal letters and writing based primarily on personal experience. The *you* point of view, which emphasizes the reader, works well for giving advice or explaining how to do something. The third-person point of view, which emphasizes the subject, is appropriate in formal academic and professional writing.

Writers who have trouble settling on an appropriate point of view sometimes shift confusingly from one to another. The solution is to choose a suitable perspective and stay with it.

▶ **Our class practiced rescuing a victim trapped in a wrecked**
                                We
car. We learned to dismantle the car with the essential
                            our   our
tools. ~~You~~ were graded on ~~your~~ speed and ~~your~~ skill in
              ^   ^   ^
freeing the victim.

The writer should have stayed with the *we* point of view. *You* is inappropriate because the writer is not addressing readers directly. *You* should not be used in a vague sense meaning "anyone." (See 23d.)

                 You need
▶ ~~One needs~~ a password and a credit card number to access
      ^
the database. You will be billed at an hourly rate.

You is an appropriate choice because the writer is giving advice directly to readers.

EXERCISE 13–1 Edit the following paragraph to eliminate distracting shifts in point of view (person and number). Create two versions. First, imagine that this is an introductory paragraph designed to engage the reader with a personal story; write it in the first person (using *I* and *we*). Can you think of other contexts in which the first-person point of view would be the best choice? Then write the paragraph in the third person (using *people* and *they*). In what contexts would this version be the best choice?

> When online dating first became available, many people thought that it would simplify romance. We believed that you could type in a list of criteria—sense of humor, college education, green eyes, good job—and a database would select the perfect mate. Thousands of people signed up for services and filled out their profiles, confident that true love was only a few mouse clicks away. As it turns out, however, virtual dating is no easier than traditional dating. I still have to contact the people I find, exchange e-mails and phone calls, and meet him in the real world. Although a database might produce a list of possibilities and screen out obviously undesirable people, you can't predict chemistry. More often than not, people who seem perfect online just don't click in person. Electronic services do help a single person expand their pool of potential dates, but it's no substitute for the hard work of romance.

13b Maintain consistent verb tenses.

Consistent verb tenses clearly establish the time of the actions being described. When a passage begins in one tense and then shifts without warning and for no reason to another, readers are distracted and confused.

> ► There was no way I could fight the current and win. Just as I
> was losing hope, a stranger ~~jumps~~ off a passing boat and ^jumped^
> ~~swims~~ toward me. ^swam^

The writer thought that the present tense (*jumps, swims*) would convey immediacy and drama. But having begun in the past tense (*could fight, was losing*), the writer should follow through in the past tense.

Writers often encounter difficulty with verb tenses when writing about literature. Because fictional events occur outside the time frames of real life, the past tense and the present tense may seem equally appropriate. The literary convention, however, is to describe fictional events consistently in the present tense. (See 7e.)

▶ **The scarlet letter is a punishment sternly placed on Hester's**

$\overset{\text{is}}{\underset{\wedge}{\text{breast by the community, and yet it}\ \cancel{\text{was}}\ \text{a fanciful and}}}$

imaginative product of Hester's own needlework.

EXERCISE 13–3 Edit the following paragraphs to eliminate distracting shifts in tense.

The English colonists who settled in Massachusetts received assistance at first from the local Indian tribes, but by 1675 there had been friction between the two groups for many years. In that year, Metacomet, whom the colonists called Philip, leads the Wampanoag tribe in the first of a series of attacks on the colonial settlements. The war, known as King Philip's War, rages on for more than a year and leaves three thousand Indians and six hundred colonists dead. Metacomet's attempt to retain his power failed. He too is killed, and the colonists sell his wife and children into slavery.

The Indians did not leave records of their encounters with the English, but the settlers recorded some of their experiences. One of the few accounts to survive was written by a captured colonist, Mary Rowlandson. She is a minister's wife who is kidnapped by Indians and held captive in 1676. Her history, *A Narrative of the Captivity and Restoration of Mrs. Mary Rowlandson*, tells the story of her experiences with the Wampanoags. Although it did not paint a completely balanced picture of the Indians, Rowlandson's story, which is considered a classic early American text, showed its author to be a keen observer of life in an Indian camp.

13c Make verbs consistent in mood and voice.

Unnecessary shifts in the mood of a verb can be distracting and confusing to readers. There are three moods in English: the *indicative*, used for facts, opinions, and questions; the *imperative*, used for orders or advice; and the *subjunctive*, used in certain contexts to express wishes or conditions contrary to fact (see 27g).

The following passage shifts confusingly from the indicative to the imperative mood.

▶ The counselor advised us to spread out our core requirements
    She also suggested that we
over two or three semesters. ~~Also,~~ pay attention to pre-
                          ^
requisites for elective courses.

The writer began by reporting the counselor's advice in the indicative mood (*counselor advised*) and switched to the imperative mood (*pay attention*); the revision puts both sentences in the indicative.

A verb may be in either the active voice (with the subject doing the action) or the passive voice (with the subject receiving the action). (See 8a.) If a writer shifts without warning from one to the other, readers may be left wondering why.

▶ Each student completes a self-assessment/, ~~The self-assessment~~
                              gives it
                                          exchanges ^
~~is then given~~ to the teacher, and a copy ~~is exchanged~~ with
            ^   ^
a classmate.

Because the passage began in the active voice (*student completes*) and then switched to the passive (*self-assessment is given, copy is exchanged*), readers are left wondering who gives the self-assessment to the teacher and the classmate. The active voice, which is clearer and more direct, leaves no ambiguity.

13d Avoid sudden shifts from indirect to direct questions or quotations.

An indirect question reports a question without asking it: *We asked whether we could visit Miriam.* A direct question asks directly: *Can we visit Miriam?* Sudden shifts from indirect to direct questions are awkward. In addition, sentences containing such shifts are impossible to punctuate because indirect questions must end with a period and direct questions must end with a question mark. (See 38b.)

▶ I wonder whether Karla knew of the theft and, if so, ~~did~~
   whether she reported
   ~~she report~~ it to the police~~?~~.

The revision poses both questions indirectly. The writer could also ask both questions directly: *Did Karla know of the theft, and, if so, did she report it to the police?*

An indirect quotation reports someone's words without quoting word-for-word: *Annabelle said that she is a Virgo.* A direct quotation presents the exact words of a speaker or writer, set off with quotation marks: *Annabelle said, "I am a Virgo."* Unannounced shifts from indirect to direct quotations are distracting and confusing, especially when the writer fails to insert the necessary quotation marks, as in the following example.

▶ The patient said she had been experiencing heart palpitations
   asked me to
  and ~~please~~ run as many tests as possible to find the
  problem.

The revision reports the patient's words indirectly. The writer also could quote the words directly: *The patient said, "I have been experiencing heart palpitations. Please run as many tests as possible to find the problem."*

EXERCISE 13–5 Edit the following sentences to make the verbs consistent in mood and voice and to eliminate distracting shifts from indirect to direct questions or quotations. Possible revisions appear in the back of the book.

As a public relations intern, I wrote press releases, managed

the Web site, and ~~all phone calls were fielded by me.~~
fielded all phone calls.

a. An incredibly talented musician, Ray Charles mastered R&B, soul, and gospel styles. Even country music was performed well by him.

b. Environmentalists point out that shrimp farming in Southeast Asia is polluting water and making farmlands useless. They warn that action must be taken by governments before it is too late.

c. The samples were observed for five days before we detected any growth.

d. In his famous soliloquy, Hamlet contemplates whether death would be preferable to his difficult life and, if so, is he capable of committing suicide?

e. The lawyer told the judge that Miranda Hale was innocent and allow her to prove the allegations false.

EXERCISE 13–6 Edit the following sentences to eliminate distracting shifts. Possible revisions appear in the back of the book.

For many first-year engineering students, adjusting to a

rigorous course load can be so challenging that ~~you~~
they

sometimes feel overwhelmed.

a. A courtroom lawyer needs to have more than a touch of theater in their blood.

b. The interviewer asked whether we had brought our proof of citizenship and did we bring our passports?

c. The experienced reconnaissance scout knows how to make fast decisions and use sophisticated equipment to keep their team from being detected.

d. After the animators finish their scenes, the production designer arranges the clips according to the storyboard. Synchronization notes must also be made for the sound editor and the composer.

e. Madame Defarge is a sinister figure in Dickens's *A Tale of Two Cities*. On a symbolic level, she represents fate; like the Greek Fates, she knitted the fabric of individual destiny.

14 Emphasize key ideas.

Within each sentence, emphasize your point by expressing it in the subject and verb of an independent clause, the words that receive the most attention from readers (see 14a–14e).

Within longer stretches of prose, you can draw attention to ideas deserving special emphasis by using a variety of techniques, often involving an unusual twist or some element of surprise (see 14f).

14a Coordinate equal ideas; subordinate minor ideas.

When combining two or more ideas in one sentence, you have two choices: coordination or subordination. Choose coordination to indicate that the ideas are equal or nearly equal in importance.

Choose subordination to indicate that one idea is less important than another.

Coordination

Coordination draws attention equally to two or more ideas. To coordinate single words or phrases, join them with a coordinating conjunction or with a pair of correlative conjunctions: *bananas and strawberries; not only a lackluster plot but also inferior acting* (see 46g).

To coordinate independent clauses—word groups that express a complete thought and that can stand alone as a sentence—join them with a comma and a coordinating conjunction or with a semicolon:

, and	, for
, but	, so
, or	, yet
, nor	;

The semicolon is often accompanied by a conjunctive adverb such as *moreover, furthermore, therefore,* or *however* or by a transitional phrase such as *for example, in other words,* or *as a matter of fact.* (For a longer list, see p. 233.)

Assume, for example, that your intention is to draw equal attention to the following two ideas.

> Social networking Web sites offer ways for people to connect in the virtual world. They do not replace face-to-face forms of social interaction.

To coordinate these ideas, you can join them with a comma and the coordinating conjunction *but* or with a semicolon and the conjunctive adverb *however.*

Social networking Web sites offer ways for people to connect in the virtual world, but they do not replace face-to-face forms of social interaction.

Social networking Web sites offer ways for people to connect in the virtual world; however, they do not replace face-to-face forms of social interaction.

It is important to choose a coordinating conjunction or conjunctive adverb appropriate to your meaning. In the preceding example, the two ideas contrast with each other, calling for *but* or *however*. (For specific coordination strategies, see the chart on p. 233.)

Subordination

To give unequal emphasis to two or more ideas, express the major idea in an independent clause and place any minor ideas in subordinate clauses or phrases. (For specific subordination strategies, see the chart on p. 234.)

Let your intended meaning determine which idea you emphasize. Thinking about your purpose and your audience often helps you decide which ideas deserve emphasis.

14b Combine choppy sentences.

Short sentences demand attention, so you should use them primarily for emphasis. Too many short sentences, one after the other, make for a choppy style.

If an idea is not important enough to deserve its own sentence, try combining it with a sentence close by. Put any minor ideas in subordinate structures such as phrases or subordinate clauses. (See 48.)

Writer's Choice
Positioning major and minor ideas

There are many ways to organize the ideas in a sentence. If your **purpose** is to convey one particular idea to your readers, put that major idea in the main part of the sentence, and place minor ideas in a subordinate word group to de-emphasize them. Consider these two ideas about social networking sites.

Social networking Web sites offer ways for people to connect in the virtual world.

Social networking sites do not replace face-to-face forms of social interaction.

To stress the ways that people can *connect* in the virtual world, the writer should subordinate — or de-emphasize — the idea about the limitations.

> ———————— MINOR IDEA ————————
> Although they do not replace face-to-face forms of social interaction,
> ———————— MAJOR IDEA ————————
> social networking Web sites offer ways for people to connect in the
> virtual world.
>
> *The writer might be arguing that joining sites such as LinkedIn is the best way to broaden the range of job opportunities for college graduates.*

To focus on the *limitations* of the virtual world, the writer should subordinate the idea about the ways people connect on these Web sites.

> ———————— MINOR IDEA ————————
> Although social networking Web sites offer ways for people to connect
> ———————— MAJOR IDEA ————————
> in the virtual world, they do not replace face-to-face forms of social
> interaction.
>
> *The writer might be arguing that personal contact is still the best way to build professional relationships.*

When you have both major and minor ideas in a sentence, put your main idea in the independent clause and tuck minor ideas into subordinate word groups.

▶ The Parks Department keeps the use of insecticides to a
                   because the
minimum/ ~~The~~ city is concerned about the environment.
          ^

The writer wanted to emphasize that the Parks Department mini-
mizes its use of chemicals, so she put the reason in a subordinate
clause beginning with *because*.

▶ The Chesapeake and Ohio Canal, ~~is~~ a 184-mile waterway
                             ^

constructed in the 1800s/, ~~It~~ was a major source of
                   ^

transportation for goods during the Civil War.

A minor idea is now expressed in an appositive phrase (*a 184-mile
waterway constructed in the 1800s*).

Although subordination is ordinarily the most effective
technique for combining short, choppy sentences, coordination
is appropriate when the ideas are equal in importance.

▶ On January 1, lawmakers raised the minimum wage/
                                and
~~Lawmakers~~ opened doors for thousands of poor families.
  ^

Combining two short sentences by joining their predicates
(*raised . . . opened*) is an effective coordination technique.

Multilingual

Unlike some other languages, English does not repeat objects or
adverbs in adjective clauses. The relative pronoun (*that*, *which*,
whom) or relative adverb (*where*) in the adjective clause represents the
object or adverb. See 30d.

▶ The apartment that we rented ~~it~~ needed repairs.

The pronoun *it* cannot repeat the relative pronoun *that*.

Using coordination to combine sentences of equal importance

1. Consider using a comma and a coordinating conjunction. (See 32a.)

, and	, but	, or	, nor
, for	, so	, yet	

   ▶ In Orthodox Jewish funeral ceremonies, the shroud is
   a simple linen vestment/, ~~The~~ coffin is plain wood.
     and the

2. Consider using a semicolon with a conjunctive adverb or a transitional phrase. (See 34b.)

also	however	next
as a result	in addition	now
besides	in fact	of course
consequently	in other words	otherwise
finally	in the first place	still
for example	meanwhile	then
for instance	moreover	therefore
furthermore	nevertheless	thus

   ▶ Alicia scored well on the SAT/; ~~She also~~ had excellent
     in addition, she

   grades and a record of community service.

3. Consider using a semicolon alone. (See 34a.)

   ▶ In youth we learn/; ~~In~~ age we understand.
     in

Using subordination to combine sentences of unequal importance

1. Consider putting the less important idea in a subordinate clause beginning with one of the following words. (See 48e.)

after	before	that	which
although	even though	unless	while
as	if	until	who
as if	since	when	whom
because	so that	where	whose

▶ ~~When~~ Elizabeth Cady Stanton proposed a convention to discuss the status of women in America/, Lucretia Mott agreed.

▶ My sister owes much of her recovery to a yoga program/ ~~She~~ *that she* began ~~the program~~ three years ago.

2. Consider putting the less important idea in an appositive phrase. (See 48c.)

▶ Karate, ~~is~~ a discipline based on the philosophy of nonviolence/, ~~It~~ teaches the art of self-defense.

3. Consider putting the less important idea in a participial phrase. (See 48b.)

▶ ~~American essayist Cheryl Peck was~~ Encouraged by friends to write about her life/, ~~She~~ *American essayist Cheryl Peck* began combining humor and irony in her essays about being overweight.

EXERCISE 14–1 Use the coordination or subordination technique in brackets to combine each pair of independent clauses. Possible revisions appear in the back of the book.

Ted Williams was one of the best hitters in the history of

baseball, but he

~~baseball. He~~ **never won a World Series ring.** [*Use a comma*
^

and a coordinating conjunction.]

a. Williams played for the Boston Red Sox from 1939 to 1960. He managed the Washington Senators and Texas Rangers for several years after retiring as a player. [*Use a comma and a coordinating conjunction.*]

b. In 1941, Williams finished the season with a batting average of .406. No player has hit over .400 for a season since then. [*Use a semicolon.*]

c. Williams acknowledged that Joe DiMaggio was a better all-around player. Williams felt that he was a better hitter than DiMaggio. [*Use the subordinating conjunction* although.]

d. Williams was a stubborn man. He always refused to tip his cap to the crowd after a home run because he claimed that fans were fickle. [*Use a semicolon and the transitional phrase* for example.]

e. Williams's relationship with the media was unfriendly at best. He sarcastically called baseball writers the "knights of the keyboard" in his memoir. [*Use a semicolon.*]

EXERCISE 14-2   Combine the following sentences by subordinating minor ideas or by coordinating ideas of equal importance. You must decide which ideas are minor because the sentences are given out of context. Possible revisions appear in the back of the book.

Agnes, ~~was a girl I worked with/.~~ ~~She~~ was a hyperactive child.

a. The X-Men comic books and Japanese woodcuts of kabuki dancers were part of Marlena's research project on popular culture. They covered the tabletop and the chairs.

b. Our waitress was costumed in a kimono. She had painted her face white. She had arranged her hair in a beehive.

c. Students can apply for a spot in the leadership program. The program teaches thinking and communication skills.

d. Shore houses were flooded. Beaches were washed away. Brant's Lighthouse was swallowed by the sea.

e. Laura Thackray was an engineer at Volvo. She addressed women's safety needs. She designed a pregnant crash-test dummy.

14c Avoid ineffective or excessive coordination.

Coordinate structures are appropriate only when you intend to draw readers' attention equally to two or more ideas: *Professor Liu praises loudly, and she criticizes softly.* If one idea is more important than another—or if a coordinating conjunction does not clearly signal the relationship between the ideas—you should subordinate the less important idea.

INEFFECTIVE COORDINATION	Closets were taxed as rooms, and most colonists stored their clothes in chests or clothespresses.
IMPROVED WITH SUBORDINATION	Because closets were taxed as rooms, most colonists stored their clothes in chests or clothespresses.

The revision subordinates the less important idea (*closets were taxed as rooms*). Notice that the subordinating conjunction *Because* signals the relation between the ideas more clearly than the coordinating conjunction *and*.

Because it is so easy to string ideas together with *and*, writers often rely too heavily on coordination in their rough drafts. The cure for excessive coordination is simple: Look for opportunities to tuck minor ideas into subordinate clauses or phrases.

> *When shareholders*
> ► ~~Shareholders~~ exchanged investment tips at the company's
>   ^
>
> annual meeting, ~~and~~ they learned that different approaches
>
> can yield similar results.

The minor idea has become a subordinate clause beginning with *When*.

> *After four hours,*
> ► ~~Four hours went by, and~~ a rescue truck finally arrived, but
>   ^
>
> by that time we had been evacuated in a helicopter.

Three independent clauses were excessive. The least important idea has become a prepositional phrase.

EXERCISE 14–8 The following sentences show coordinated ideas (ideas joined with a coordinating conjunction or a semicolon). Restructure the sentences by subordinating minor ideas. You must decide which ideas are minor because the sentences are given out of context. Possible revisions appear in the back of the book.

> *where they*
> The rowers returned to shore , ~~and~~ had a party on the beach
>   ^
> *to celebrate*
> ~~and celebrated~~ the start of the season.
> ^

a. These particles are known as "stealth liposomes," and they can hide in the body for a long time without detection.

b.   Irena is a competitive gymnast and majors in biochemistry; her goal is to apply her athletic experience and her science degree to a career in sports medicine.

c.   Students, textile workers, and labor unions have loudly protested sweatshop abuses, so apparel makers have been forced to examine their labor practices.

d.   IRC (Internet relay chat) was developed in a European university; it was created as a way for a group of graduate students to talk about projects from their dorm rooms.

e.   The cafeteria's new menu has an international flavor, and it includes everything from enchiladas and pizza to pad thai and sauerbraten.

14d Do not subordinate major ideas.

If a sentence buries its major idea in a subordinate construction, readers may not give the idea enough attention. Make sure to express your major idea in an independent clause and to subordinate any minor ideas.

▶ Harry S. Truman, who was the unexpected winner of the *defeated Thomas E. Dewey,*

1948 presidential election/. ~~defeated Thomas E. Dewey.~~

The writer wanted to focus on Truman's unexpected victory, but the original sentence buried this information in an adjective clause. The revision puts the more important idea in an independent clause and tucks the less important idea into an adjective clause (*who defeated Thomas E. Dewey*).

▶ *As*
I was driving home from my new job, heading down

Ranchitos Road, ~~when~~ my car suddenly overheated.

The writer wanted to emphasize that the car overheated, not the fact of driving home. The revision expresses the major idea in an independent clause and places the less important idea in an adverb clause (*As I was driving home from my new job*).

14e Do not subordinate excessively.

In attempting to avoid short, choppy sentences, writers sometimes go to the opposite extreme, putting more subordinate ideas into a sentence than its structure can bear. If a sentence collapses of its own weight, occasionally it can be restructured. More often, however, such sentences must be divided.

▶ In *Animal Liberation*, Peter Singer argues that animals possess nervous systems and can feel pain. ~~and that~~ H̲e believes that "the ethical principle on which human equality rests requires us to extend equal consideration to animals" (1).

Excessive subordination makes it difficult for the reader to focus on the quoted passage. By splitting the original sentence into two separate sentences, the writer draws attention to Peter Singer's main claim, that humans should give "equal consideration to animals." (See 56a on citing sources in MLA style.)

EXERCISE 14–10   In each of the following sentences, the idea that the writer wished to emphasize is buried in a subordinate construction. Restructure each sentence so that the independent clause expresses the major idea, as indicated in brackets, and lesser ideas are subordinated. Possible revisions appear in the back of the book.

Although
Catherine has weathered many hardships, ~~although~~ she has rarely become discouraged. [*Emphasize that Catherine has rarely become discouraged.*]

a. Gina worked as an aide for the relief agency, distributing food and medical supplies. [*Emphasize distributing food and medical supplies.*]

b. Janbir spent every Saturday learning tabla drumming, noticing with each hour of practice that his memory for complex patterns was growing stronger. [*Emphasize Janbir's memory.*]

c. The rotor hit, gouging a hole about an eighth of an inch deep in my helmet. [*Emphasize that the rotor gouged a hole in the helmet.*]

d. My grandfather, who raised his daughters the old-fashioned way, was born eighty years ago in Puerto Rico. [*Emphasize how the grandfather raised his daughters.*]

e. The Narcan reversed the depressive effect of the drug, saving the patient's life. [*Emphasize that the patient's life was saved.*]

14f Experiment with techniques for gaining emphasis.

By experimenting with certain techniques, usually involving some element of surprise, you can draw attention to ideas that deserve special emphasis. Use such techniques sparingly, however, or they will lose their punch. The writer who tries to emphasize everything ends up emphasizing nothing.

Using sentence endings for emphasis

You can highlight an idea simply by withholding it until the end of a sentence. The technique works something like a punch line. In the following example, the sentence's meaning is not revealed until its very last word.

> "The only completely consistent people are the dead."
> — Aldous Huxley

Two types of sentences that withhold information until the end are the inversion and the periodic sentence. The *inversion* reverses the normal subject-verb order, placing the subject at the end, where it receives unusual emphasis. (See also 15c.)

> "In golden pots are hidden the most deadly poisons."
> — Thomas Draxe

The *periodic* sentence opens with a pile-up of modifiers and withholds the subject and verb until the end.

PERIODIC

> "Twenty-five years ago, at the age of thirteen, while hiking in the mountains near my hometown of Vancouver, Washington, I came face-to-face with a legend."   — Tom Weitzel, student

Using parallel structure for emphasis

Parallel grammatical structure draws special attention to paired ideas or to items in a series. (See 9.) When parallel ideas are paired, the emphasis falls on words that underscore comparisons or contrasts, especially when they occur at the end of a phrase or clause.

> "We must *stop talking* about the *American dream* and *start listening* to the *dreams of Americans*."   — Reubin Askew

In a parallel series, the emphasis falls at the end, so it is generally best to end with the most dramatic or climactic item in the series.

> "My uncle often talks about growing up in Sudan — playing soccer, eating goat stew, and dodging bullets."
> — Alec Hamza, student

Using punctuation for emphasis

Obviously the exclamation point can add emphasis, but you should not overuse it. As a rule, the exclamation point is more appropriate in dialogue than in ordinary prose.

A dash or a colon may be used to draw attention to word groups worthy of special attention. (See 35a, 35b, and 39a.)

> "The middle of the road is where the white line is — and that's the worst place to drive."
> — Robert Frost

> "I turned to see what the anemometer read: The needle had pegged out at 106 knots."
> — Jonathan Shilk, student

Occasionally, a pair of dashes may be used to highlight a word or an idea.

> "They carried the land itself—Vietnam, the place, the soil—a powdery orange-red dust that covered their boots and fatigues and faces."
> —Tim O'Brien

15 Provide some variety.

When a rough draft is filled with too many sentences that begin the same way or have the same structure, try injecting some variety—as long as you can do so without sacrificing clarity or ease of reading.

15a Vary your sentence openings.

Most sentences in English begin with the subject, move to the verb, and continue to the object, with modifiers tucked in along the way or put at the end. For the most part, such sentences are fine. Put too many of them in a row, however, and they become monotonous.

Adverbial modifiers are easily movable when they modify verbs; they can often be inserted ahead of the subject. Such modifiers might be single words, phrases, or clauses.

> *Eventually a*
> ▶ ~~A~~ few drops of sap ~~eventually~~ began to trickle into the
>   ^
>   aluminum bucket.

Like most adverbs, *eventually* does not need to appear close to the verb it modifies (*began*).

> *Just as the sun was coming up, a*
> ▶ ~~A~~ pair of black ducks flew over the pond. ~~just as the sun was~~
>   ^   ^
>   ~~coming up.~~

The adverb clause, which modifies the verb *flew*, is as clear at the beginning of the sentence as it is at the end.

Adjectives and participial phrases can frequently be moved to the beginning of a sentence without loss of clarity.

> *Dejected and withdrawn,*
> ▶ Edward/ ~~dejected and withdrawn,~~ nearly gave up his search
>   ^
>   for a job.

TIP: When beginning a sentence with an adjective or a participial phrase, make sure that the subject of the sentence names the person or thing described in the introductory phrase. If it doesn't, the phrase will dangle. (See 12e.)

Writer's Choice
Strengthening with variety

If you look at a whole paragraph in your draft, you may have difficulty seeing the individual sentences. If a particular passage sounds repetitive, try listing the sentences one after the other so that you can review them.

> I have always loved trains.
>
> As a young boy, I watched the trains from a hillside overlooking the rail yard.
>
> I remember the individual cars rolling down the hill.
>
> I remember how they would couple with other cars.
>
> Sometimes I would hear a loud boom, which always surprised me.

When seen in this format, the sentences look monotonous and sound dull — *I did this, I remember that.* . . . To engage the **audience** and to bring readers into the experience, narrative writing needs variety and detail.

To reduce the repetition, try varying the sentence structure.

REVISED SENTENCES	I have always loved trains, even as a young boy.
	From a hillside overlooking the rail yard, I would watch individual cars roll down the track to couple with other cars.
	The *BOOM!* — the sound of two cars joining — always surprised me.
REVISED PARAGRAPH	I have always loved trains, even as a young boy. From a hillside overlooking the rail yard, I would watch individual cars roll down the track to couple with other cars. The *BOOM!* — the sound of two cars joining — always surprised me.
	In the revision, the sentences don't all begin in the same way, and the writer has provided details of sight and sound so that readers can experience the memory.

When you revise for variety, keep your audience in mind. Choose details specific enough to engage the reader, and add some variety to your sentence structure.

15b Use a variety of sentence structures.

A writer should not rely too heavily on simple sentences and compound sentences, for the effect tends to be both monotonous and choppy. (See 14b and 14c.) Too many complex or compound-complex sentences, however, can be equally monotonous. If your style tends to one or the other extreme, try to achieve a better mix of sentence types.

The major sentence types are illustrated in the following sentences, all taken from Flannery O'Connor's "The King of the Birds," an essay describing the author's pet peafowl.

SIMPLE	Frequently the cock combines the lifting of his tail with the raising of his voice.
COMPOUND	Any chicken's dusting hole is out of place in a flower bed, but the peafowl's hole, being the size of a small crater, is more so.
COMPLEX	The peacock does most of his serious strutting in the spring and summer when he has a full tail to do it with.
COMPOUND-COMPLEX	The cock's plumage requires two years to attain its pattern, and for the rest of his life, this chicken will act as though he designed it himself.

For a fuller discussion of sentence types, see 49a.

15c Try inverting sentences occasionally.

A sentence is inverted if it does not follow the normal subject-verb-object pattern (see 47c). Many inversions sound artificial and should be avoided except in the most formal contexts. But if an inversion sounds natural, it can provide a welcome touch of variety.

▶ *Set at the top two corners of the stage were huge*
~~Huge~~ lavender hearts outlined in bright white lights. ~~were~~
     ^   ^
~~set at the top two corners of the stage.~~

In the revision, the subject, *hearts*, appears after the verb, *were set.*
Notice that the two parts of the verb are also inverted—and separated from each other (*Set ... were*)—without any awkwardness or
loss of meaning.

Inverted sentences are used for emphasis as well as for
variety (see 14f).

15d Consider adding an occasional question.

An occasional question can provide a change of pace, especially at
the beginning of a paragraph, where it engages the reader's interest.

> Virginia Woolf, in her book *A Room of One's Own*, wrote
> that in order for a woman to write fiction she must have two
> things, certainly: a room of her own (with key and lock) and
> enough money to support herself.
> *What then are we to make of Phillis Wheatley, a slave,
> who owned not even herself?* This sickly, frail black girl who
> required a servant of her own at times—her health was so
> precarious—and who, had she been white, would have been
> easily considered the intellectual superior of all the women and
> most of the men in the society of her day. [Italics added.]
> — Alice Walker

EXERCISE 15-1   Improve sentence variety in each of the following sentences by using the technique suggested in brackets.
Possible revisions appear in the back of the book.

To protect endangered marine turtles, *fishing*
~~Fishing~~ crews place turtle excluder devices in fishing nets.
     ^   ^
~~to protect endangered marine turtles.~~ [*Begin the sentence*

with the adverbial infinitive phrase.]

a. The exhibits for insects and spiders are across the hall from the fossils exhibit. [*Invert the sentence.*]

b. Sayuri becomes a successful geisha after growing up desperately poor in Japan. [*Move the adverb phrase to the beginning of the sentence.*]

c. Researchers have been studying Mount St. Helens for years. They believe that a series of earthquakes in the area may have caused the 1980 eruption. [*Combine the sentences into a complex sentence. See also 49a.*]

d. Ice cream typically contains 10 percent milk fat. Premium ice cream may contain up to 16 percent milk fat and has considerably less air in the product. [*Combine the two sentences as a compound sentence.*]

e. The economy may recover more quickly than expected if home values climb. [*Move the adverb clause to the beginning of the sentence.*]

EXERCISE 15-2 Edit the following paragraph to increase sentence variety.

Making architectural models is a skill that requires patience and precision. It is an art that illuminates a design. Architects come up with a grand and intricate vision. Draftspersons convert that vision into blueprints. The model maker follows the blueprints. The model maker builds a miniature version of the structure. Modelers can work in traditional materials like wood and clay and paint. Modelers can work in newer materials like Styrofoam and liquid polymers. Some modelers still use cardboard, paper, and glue. Other modelers prefer glue guns, deformable plastic, and thin aluminum and brass wire. The modeler may seem to be making a small mess in the early stages of model building. In the end the modeler has completed a small-scale structure. Architect Rem Koolhaas has insisted that plans reveal the logic of a design. He has argued that models expose the architect's vision. The model maker's art makes this vision real.

PART IV

Word Choice

16 Tighten wordy sentences. 251

17 Choose appropriate language. 256

18 Find the exact words. 268

Word Choice

ONLINE ACTIVITIES:

writershelp.com/hacker

macmillanhighered.com/
launchpadsolo/hacker

Wordy sentences	5 Exercises
Appropriate language	5 Exercises 1 LearningCurve activity
Exact words	6 Exercises 1 LearningCurve activity

16   Tighten wordy sentences.

Long sentences are not necessarily wordy, nor are short sentences always concise. A sentence is wordy if it can be tightened without loss of meaning.

16a Eliminate redundancies.

Writers often repeat themselves unnecessarily, thinking that expressions such as *cooperate together*, *yellow in color*, or *basic essentials* add emphasis to their writing. In reality, such redundancies do just the opposite. There is no need to say the same thing twice.

>   works
> ▶ Daniel ~~is now employed~~ at a private rehabilitation center
>
>   ^
> ~~working~~ as a registered physical therapist.

Though modifiers ordinarily add meaning to the words they modify, occasionally they are redundant.

> ▶ Sylvia ~~very quickly~~ scribbled her name, address, and phone
>
> number on a greasy napkin.

The word *scribbled* already suggests that Sylvia wrote *very quickly*.

16b Avoid unnecessary repetition of words.

Though words may be repeated deliberately, for effect, repetitions will seem awkward if they are clearly unnecessary. When a more concise version is possible, choose it.

► Our fifth patient, in room six, is a mentally ill. ~~patient.~~

grow
► The best teachers help each student ~~become a better~~
~~student~~ both academically and emotionally.

16c Cut empty or inflated phrases.

An empty phrase can be cut with little or no loss of meaning. Common examples are introductory word groups that weaken the writer's authority by apologizing or hedging: *in my opinion, I think that, it seems that, one must admit that,* and so on.

O
► ~~In my opinion,~~ our current immigration policy is misguided.

Readers understand without being told that they are hearing the writer's opinion.

Inflated phrases can be reduced to a word or two without loss of meaning.

INFLATED	CONCISE
along the lines of	like
as a matter of fact	in fact
at the present time	now, currently
at this point in time	now, currently
because of the fact that	because
by means of	by
due to the fact that	because
for the purpose of	for
have the ability to	be able to, can
in order to	to
in spite of the fact that	although, though
in the event that	if
in the final analysis	finally
in the neighborhood of	about

16d Simplify the structure.

If the structure of a sentence is needlessly indirect, try simplifying it. Look for opportunities to strengthen the verb.

▶ The financial analyst claimed that because of volatile

market conditions she could not ~~make an~~ estimate ~~of~~ the

company's future profits.

The verb *estimate* is more vigorous and concise than *make an estimate of*.

The colorless verbs *is*, *are*, *was*, and *were* frequently generate excess words.

studied
▶ Investigators ~~were involved in studying~~ the effect of classical
⌃
music on unborn babies.

The revision is more direct and concise. The action (*studying*), originally appearing in a subordinate structure, has become a strong verb, *studied*.

The expletive constructions *there is* and *there are* (or *there was* and *there were*) can also lead to wordy sentences. The same is true of expletive constructions beginning with *it*. (See 47c.)

A
▶ ~~There is~~ ⱥnother module ~~that~~ tells the story of Charles
⌃
Darwin and introduces the theory of evolution.

Finally, verbs in the passive voice may be needlessly indirect. When the active voice expresses your meaning as effectively, use it. (See 8a.)

16e Reduce clauses to phrases, phrases to single words.

Word groups functioning as modifiers can often be made more compact. Look for any opportunities to reduce clauses to phrases or phrases to single words.

▶ We took a side trip to Monticello, ~~which was~~ the home of

Thomas Jefferson.

  this
▶ In ~~the~~ essay, ~~that follows,~~ I argue against Immanuel
  ^   ^
         problematic
Kant's claim that we should not lie under any
  ^

circumstances/. ~~which is a problematic claim.~~
  ^

EXERCISE 16–1 Edit the following sentences to reduce wordiness. Possible revisions appear in the back of the book.

  even though
The Wilsons moved into the house ~~in spite of the fact that~~
  ^

the back door was only ten yards from the train tracks.

a. Martin Luther King Jr. was a man who set a high standard for future leaders to meet.

b. Alice has been deeply in love with cooking since she was little and could first peek over the edge of a big kitchen tabletop.

c. In my opinion, Bloom's race for the governorship is a futile exercise.

d. It is pretty important in being a successful graphic designer to have technical knowledge and at the same time an eye for color and balance.

e. Your task will be to set up digital mail communications capabilities for all employees in the company.

EXERCISE 16–2 Edit the following business memo to reduce wordiness.

To: District managers
From: Margaret Davenport, Vice President
Subject: Customer database

It has recently been brought to my attention that a percentage of our sales representatives have been failing to log reports of their client calls in our customer database each and every day. I have also learned that some representatives are not checking the database on a routine basis.

Our clients sometimes receive a multiple number of sales calls from us when a sales representative is not cognizant of the fact that the client has been contacted at a previous time. Repeated telephone calls from our representatives annoy our customers. These repeated telephone calls also portray our company as one that is lacking in organization.

Effective as of immediately, direct your representatives to do the following:

- Record each and every customer contact in the customer database at the end of each day, without fail.

- Check the database at the very beginning of each day to ensure that telephone communications will not be initiated with clients who have already been called.

Let me extend my appreciation to you for cooperating in this important matter.

17 Choose appropriate language.

Language is appropriate when it suits your subject, engages your audience, and blends naturally with your own voice.

To some extent, your choice of language will be governed by the conventions of the genre in which you are writing. When in doubt about the conventions of a particular genre—lab reports, essays, business memos, and so on—consult your instructor or look at models written by experts in the field.

17a Avoid jargon, except in specialized writing situations.

Jargon is specialized language used among members of a trade, profession, or group. Use jargon only when readers will be familiar with it and when plain English will not do as well.

| JARGON | We outsourced the work to an outfit in Ohio because we didn't have the bandwidth to tackle it in-house. |
| REVISED | We hired a company in Ohio because we had too few employees to do the work. |

Broadly defined, jargon includes puffed-up language designed more to impress readers than to inform them. The following are examples from business, government, higher education, and the military, with plain English alternatives in parentheses.

ameliorate (improve)   indicator (sign)
commence (begin)   optimal (best, most favorable)
components (parts)   parameters (boundaries, limits)
endeavor (try)   peruse (read, look over)
exit (leave)   prior to (before)
facilitate (help)   utilize (use)
impact (v.) (affect)   viable (workable)

Writer's Choice
Using discipline-specific terms

In general, try to minimize jargon and instead use plain language in your writing. Some disciplines, however, have specific terminology that is not only standard but also expected. When you use a discipline's terms effectively, you show yourself to be a member of that community and increase your authority with your **audience**.

For example, the following terms have specialized meanings in chemistry and economics and are understood by readers in those disciplines.

absolute	deadweight loss	hybridization
consumer surplus	degenerate	utility

UNNECESSARY USE OF A SPECIALIZED TERM

Although America's love affair with the automobile has not diminished, more Americans have embraced automotive *hybridization* as their concern for the environment has grown.

In this example, hybridization *is not discipline-specific. The writer has used the word to sound impressive.*

NECESSARY USE OF A SPECIALIZED TERM

As shown, sp^2 *hybridization* leaves one nonhybridized *p* orbital.

Here, hybridization *has a specific meaning for chemists.*

When writing for a specific disciplinary audience, familiarize yourself with the language and terminology of the discipline (through course readings and other materials). Use discipline-specific terms only when you know that you and your readers understand their meaning. Doing so will help you make effective word choices.

Sentences filled with jargon are hard to read, and they are often wordy as well.

▶ The CEO should ~~dialogue~~ talk with investors about ~~partnering~~ working with clients to ~~purchase~~ buy land in ~~economically deprived zones~~ poor neighborhoods.

17b Avoid pretentious language, most euphemisms, and "doublespeak."

Hoping to sound profound or poetic, some writers embroider their thoughts with large words and flowery phrases. Such pretentious language is so ornate and wordy that it obscures the writer's meaning.

▶ Taylor's ~~employment of multihued means of expression draws~~ use of colorful language reveals that she has a ~~back the curtains and lets slip the~~ nostalgic ~~vantage point~~ view of ~~from which she observes~~ American society ~~as well as her~~ and does not ~~lack of comprehension of~~ understand economic realities.

The writer of the original sentence had turned to a thesaurus (a dictionary of synonyms and antonyms) in an attempt to sound authoritative. When such a writer gains enough confidence to speak in his or her own voice, pretentious language disappears.

Euphemisms—nice-sounding words or phrases substituted for words thought to sound harsh or ugly—are sometimes appropriate. Many cultures, for example, accept euphemisms when speaking or writing about excretion (*I have to go to the bathroom*) or sexual intercourse (*They did not sleep together*). We may also use euphemisms out of concern for someone's feelings. Telling parents, for example, that their daughter is "unmotivated" is more sensitive than saying she's lazy. Tact or politeness, then, can justify an occasional euphemism.

Most euphemisms, however, are needlessly evasive or even deceitful. Like pretentious language, they obscure the intended meaning.

EUPHEMISM	PLAIN ENGLISH
adult entertainment	pornography
preowned automobile	used car
economically deprived	poor
negative savings	debts
strategic withdrawal	retreat, defeat
revenue enhancers	taxes
chemical dependency	drug addiction
downsize	lay off, fire
correctional facility	prison

The term *doublespeak* applies to any deliberately evasive or deceptive language, including euphemisms. Doublespeak is especially common in politics and business. A military retreat is described as *tactical redeployment*; *enhanced interrogation* is a euphemism for "torture"; and *downsizing* really means "firing employees."

EXERCISE 17–1 Edit the following sentences to eliminate jargon, pretentious or flowery language, euphemisms, and doublespeak. You may need to make substantial changes in some sentences. Possible revisions appear in the back of the book.

> After two weeks in the legal department, Sue has ~~worked~~ mastered
> ~~into~~ the routine, ~~of the office,~~ office and her ~~functional and self-management skills have~~ performance has exceeded all expectations.

a. In my youth, my family was under the constraints of difficult financial circumstances.

b. In order that I may increase my expertise in the area of delivery of services to clients, I feel that participation in this conference will be beneficial.

c. The prophetic meteorologist cautioned the general populace regarding the possible deleterious effects of the impending tempest.

d. Governmentally sanctioned investigations into the continued value of after-school programs indicate a perceived need in the public realm at large.

e. Passengers should endeavor to finalize the customs declaration form prior to exiting the aircraft.

EXERCISE 17–2   Edit the following e-mail message to eliminate jargon.

Dear Ms. Jackson:

We members of the Nakamura Reyes team value our external partnering arrangements with Creative Software, and I look forward to seeing you next week at the trade show in Fresno. Per Mr. Reyes, please let me know when you'll have some downtime there so that he and I can conduct a strategizing session with you concerning our production schedule. It's crucial that we all be on the same page re our 2015–2016 product release dates.

Before we have some face time, however, I have some findings to share. Our customer-centric approach to the new products will necessitate that user testing periods trend upward. The enclosed data should help you effectuate any adjustments to your timeline; let me know ASAP if you require any additional information to facilitate the above.

Before we convene in Fresno, Mr. Reyes and I will agendize any further talking points. Thanks for your help.

Sincerely,

Sylvia Nakamura

17c Avoid obsolete and invented words.

Although dictionaries list obsolete words such as *recomfort* and *reechy*, these words are not appropriate for current use. Invented words or expressions (called *neologisms*) are too recently created to be part of Standard English. Many fade out of use without becoming standard. *YOLO* and *MOOC* are neologisms that may not last. *Prequel* and *e-mail* are no longer neologisms; they have become Standard English. Avoid using invented words in formal writing unless they are given in the dictionary as standard or unless no other word expresses your meaning.

17d In most contexts, avoid slang, regional expressions, and nonstandard English.

Slang is an informal and sometimes private vocabulary that expresses the solidarity of a group such as teenagers, rap musicians, or sports fans; it is subject to more rapid change than Standard English. For example, the slang teenagers use to express approval changes every few years; *cool, groovy, neat, awesome, phat,* and *sick* have replaced one another within the last three decades. Sometimes slang becomes so widespread that it is accepted as standard vocabulary. *Jazz,* for example, started out as slang but is now a standard term for a style of music.

Although slang has a certain vitality, it is a code that not everyone understands, and it is very informal. Therefore, it is inappropriate in most written work.

▶ When the server crashed unexpectedly, three hours of ^ we lost

  unsaved data. ~~went down the tubes.~~
  ^

▶ The government's "filth" guidelines for food will ~~gross you~~ ^ disgust you.

  ~~out.~~

Regional expressions are common to a group in a geographic area. *Let's talk with the bark off* (for *Let's speak frankly*) is an expression in the southern United States, for example. Regional expressions have the same limitations as slang and are therefore inappropriate in most writing.

▶ John was four blocks from the house before he remembered

to ~~cut~~ the headlights. ~~on.~~
    ^turn on   ^

▶ Seamus wasn't ~~for~~ sure, but he thought the whales might

be migrating during his visit to Oregon.

Standard English is the language used in all academic, business, and professional fields. Nonstandard English is spoken by people with a common regional or social heritage. Although nonstandard English may be appropriate when spoken within a close group, it is out of place in most formal and informal writing.

▶ The governor said he ~~don't~~ know if he will approve the
                          ^doesn't
budget without the clean air provision.

If you speak a nonstandard dialect, try to identify the ways in which your dialect differs from Standard English. Look especially for the following features of nonstandard English, which commonly cause problems in writing.

Misusing verb forms such as *began* and *begun* (See 27a.)

Leaving -*s* endings off verbs (See 27c.)

Leaving -*ed* endings off verbs (See 27d.)

Leaving out necessary verbs (See 27e.)

Using double negatives (See 26e.)

17e Choose an appropriate level of formality.

In deciding on a level of formality, consider both your subject and your audience. Does the subject demand a dignified treatment, or is a relaxed tone more suitable? Will readers be put off if you assume too close a relationship with them, or might you alienate them by seeming too distant?

For most college and professional writing, some degree of formality is appropriate. In a job application letter, for example, it is a mistake to sound too breezy and informal.

> **TOO INFORMAL**   I'd like to get that sales job you've got on the Web site.
>
> **MORE FORMAL**   I would like to apply for the position of sales manager advertised on LinkedIn.

Informal writing is appropriate for private letters, personal e-mail and text messages, and business correspondence between close associates. Like spoken conversation, informal writing allows contractions (*don't*, *I'll*) and colloquial words (*kids*, *kinda*). Vocabulary and sentence structure are rarely complex.

In choosing a level of formality, above all be consistent. When a writer's voice shifts from one level of formality to another, readers receive mixed messages.

> ▶ Once a pitcher for the Blue Jays, Jorge shared with me
> the secrets of his trade. His lesson ~~commenced~~ [began] with his
> famous curveball, ~~implemented~~ [thrown] by tucking the little finger
> behind the ball. Next he ~~elucidated~~ [revealed] the mysteries of the
> sucker pitch, a slow ball coming behind a fast windup.

Words such as *commenced* and *elucidated* are inappropriate for the subject matter, and they clash with informal terms such as *sucker pitch* and *fast windup*.

Revise the following passage twice. First, use a level of formality appropriate for a newspaper editorial directed toward a general audience. Then use a level of formality appropriate for a blog post directed at young adults.

> In pop culture, college grads who return home to live with the folks are seen as good-for-nothing losers who mooch off their families. And many older adults seem to feel that the trend of moving back home after school, which was rare in their day, is becoming too commonplace today. But society must realize that a cultural shift is taking place. Most young adults want to live on their own ASAP, but they graduate with heaps of debt and need some time to become financially stable. College tuition and the cost of housing have increased way more than salary increases in the past half century. Also, the job market is tighter and more jobs require advanced degrees than in the past. So before people go off on college graduates who move back into their parents' house for a spell, they must indeed consider all the facts.

17f Avoid sexist language.

Sexist language is language that stereotypes or demeans women or men. Using nonsexist language is a matter of courtesy—of respect for and sensitivity to the feelings of others.

Recognizing sexist language

Some sexist language is easy to recognize because it reflects genuine contempt for women: referring to a woman as a "chick," for example, or calling a lawyer a "lady lawyer."

Other forms of sexist language are less blatant. The following practices, while they may not result from conscious sexism, reflect stereotypical thinking: referring to members of one profession as exclusively male or exclusively female (teachers as women or engineers as men, for instance) or using different conventions when naming or identifying women and men.

STEREOTYPICAL LANGUAGE

After a nursing student graduates, *she* must face a difficult state board examination. [Not all nursing students are women.]

Running for city council are Boris Stotsky, an attorney, and *Mrs.* Cynthia Jones, a professor of English and *mother of three*. [The title *Mrs.* and the phrase *mother of three* are irrelevant.]

All executives' *wives* are invited to the welcome dinner. [Not all executives are men.]

Still other forms of sexist language result from outdated traditions. The pronouns *he*, *him*, and *his*, for instance, were traditionally used to refer generically to persons of either sex. Nowadays, to avoid sexist usage, some writers substitute the female pronouns (*she*, *her*, *hers*) alternately with the male pronouns.

GENERIC PRONOUNS

A journalist is motivated by *his* deadline.

A good interior designer treats *her* clients' ideas respectfully.

But both forms are sexist—for excluding one sex entirely and for making assumptions about the members of particular professions.

Similarly, the nouns *man* and *men* were once used to refer generically to persons of either sex. Current usage demands gender-neutral terms for references to both men and women.

INAPPROPRIATE	APPROPRIATE
chairman	chairperson, moderator, chair, head
clergyman	member of the clergy, minister, rabbi, imam
congressman	representative, legislator
fireman	firefighter
mailman	mail carrier, postal worker, letter carrier
to man	to operate, to staff
mankind	people, humans

INAPPROPRIATE	APPROPRIATE
manpower	personnel, staff
policeman	police officer
salesman	salesperson, sales associate, salesclerk
weatherman	forecaster, meteorologist

Revising sexist language

When revising sexist language, you may be tempted to substitute *he or she* and *his or her*. These terms are inclusive but wordy; fine in small doses, they can become awkward when repeated throughout an essay. A better revision strategy is to write in the plural; yet another strategy is to recast the sentence so that the problem does not arise.

SEXIST

A journalist is motivated by *his* deadline.

A good interior designer treats *her* clients' ideas respectfully.

ACCEPTABLE BUT WORDY

A journalist is motivated by *his or her* deadline.

A good interior designer treats *his or her* clients' ideas respectfully.

BETTER: USING THE PLURAL

Journalists are motivated by *their* deadlines.

Good interior designers treat *their* clients' ideas respectfully.

BETTER: RECASTING THE SENTENCE

A journalist is motivated by *a* deadline.

A good interior designer treats clients' ideas respectfully.

For more examples of these revision strategies, see 22.

EXERCISE 17–6 Edit the following sentences to eliminate sexist language or sexist assumptions. Possible revisions appear in the back of the book.

Scholarship athletes   their
~~A scholarship athlete~~ must be as concerned about ~~his~~
          ^   they are   their   ^
academic performance as ~~he is~~ about ~~his~~ athletic
                          ^   ^
performance.

a.   Mrs. Geralyn Farmer, who is the mayor's wife, is the chief sur-
     geon at University Hospital. Dr. Paul Green is her assistant.

b.   Every applicant wants to know how much he will earn.

c.   An elementary school teacher should understand the concept of
     nurturing if she intends to be effective.

d.   An obstetrician needs to be available to his patients at all hours.

e.   If man does not stop polluting his environment, mankind will perish.

EXERCISE 17–7   Eliminate sexist language or sexist assumptions
in the following job posting for an elementary school teacher.

We are looking for qualified women for the position of
elementary school teacher. The ideal candidate should have a
bachelor's degree, a state teaching certificate, and one year of
student teaching. She should be knowledgeable in all elementary subject areas, including science and math. While we want
our new teacher to have a commanding presence in the classroom, we are also looking for motherly characteristics such as
patience and trustworthiness. She must be able to both motivate an entire classroom and work with each student one-on-
one to assess his individual needs. She must also be comfortable
communicating with the parents of her students. For salary and
benefits information, including maternity leave policy, please
contact the Martin County School Board. Any qualified applicant
should submit her résumé by March 15.

17g Revise language that may offend groups of people.

Your writing should be respectful and free of stereotypical,
biased, or other offensive language. Be especially careful when
describing or labeling people. Labels can become dated, and it

is important to recognize when their use is no longer acceptable. When naming groups of people, choose labels that the groups currently use to describe themselves. For example, *Negro* is not an acceptable label for African Americans; instead of *Eskimo*, use *Inuit*; for other native peoples, name the specific group when possible.

▶ North Dakota takes its name from the ~~Indian~~ ^Lakota^ word

meaning "friend" or "ally."

▶ Many ^Asian^ ~~Oriental~~ immigrants have recently settled in our

town.

Negative stereotypes (such as "drives like a teenager" or "sour as a spinster") are of course offensive. But you should avoid stereotyping a person or a group even if you believe your generalization to be positive.

▶ It was no surprise that Greer, ~~a Chinese American,~~ ^*an excellent math and science student,*^ was

selected for the honors chemistry program in her

sophomore year.

18 Find the exact words.

Two reference works (or their online equivalents) will help you find words to express your meaning exactly: a good dictionary, such as *The American Heritage Dictionary* or *Merriam-Webster* online, and a collection of synonyms and antonyms, such as *Roget's International Thesaurus.*

TIP: Do not turn to a thesaurus in search of flowery or impressive words. Look instead for words that exactly express your meaning.

18a Select words with appropriate connotations.

In addition to their strict dictionary meanings (or *denotations*), words have *connotations*, emotional colorings that affect how readers respond to them. The word *steel* denotes "commercial iron that contains carbon," but it also calls up a cluster of images associated with steel. These associations give the word its connotations — cold, hard, smooth, unbending.

If the connotation of a word does not seem appropriate for your purpose, your audience, or your subject matter, you should change the word. When a more appropriate synonym does not come quickly to mind, consult a dictionary or a thesaurus.

▶ When American soldiers returned home after World War II,
  left
many women ~~abandoned~~ their jobs in favor of marriage.
            ^

The word *abandoned* is too negative for the context.

                                              sweat
▶ As I covered the boats with marsh grass, the ~~perspiration~~
                                              ^
I had worked up evaporated in the wind, and the cold

morning air seemed even colder.

The term *perspiration* is too dainty for the context, which suggests vigorous exercise.

EXERCISE 18-1 Use a dictionary and a thesaurus to find at least four synonyms for each of the following words. Be prepared to explain any slight differences in meaning.

1. decay (verb)
2. difficult (adjective)
3. hurry (verb)
4. pleasure (noun)
5. secret (adjective)
6. talent (noun)

18b Prefer specific, concrete nouns.

Unlike general nouns, which refer to broad classes of things, specific nouns point to particular items. *Film*, for example, names a general class, *fantasy film* names a narrower class, and *The Golden Compass* is more specific still. Other examples: *team, football team, Denver Broncos; music, symphony, Beethoven's Ninth*.

Unlike abstract nouns, which refer to qualities and ideas (*justice, beauty, realism, dignity*), concrete nouns point to immediate, often sensory experience and to physical objects (*steeple, asphalt, lilac, stone, garlic*).

Specific, concrete nouns express meaning more vividly than general or abstract ones. Although general and abstract language is sometimes necessary to convey your meaning, use specific, concrete words whenever possible.

▶ The senator spoke about the challenges of the future:
  pollution, dwindling resources, and terrorism.
  ~~the environment and world peace.~~
  ^

Nouns such as *thing, area, aspect, factor*, and *individual* are especially dull and imprecise.

                                                    motherhood, and memory.
▶ Toni Morrison's *Beloved* is about slavery, ~~among other things.~~
                                                    ^

18c Do not misuse words.

If a word is not in your active vocabulary, you may find yourself misusing it, sometimes with embarrassing consequences. When in doubt, check the dictionary.

climbing
▶ The fans were ~~migrating~~ up the bleachers in search of seats.
    ^

        permeated
▶ The Internet has so ~~diffused~~ our culture that it touches all

segments of society.
    ^

Also be alert for misused word forms—using a noun such as *absence* or *significance*, for example, when your meaning requires the adjective *absent* or *significant*.

    persistent
▶ Most dieters are not ~~persistence~~ enough to make a
    ^

permanent change in their eating habits.

EXERCISE 18–2 Edit the following sentences to correct misused words. Possible revisions appear in the back of the book.

These days the training required for a ballet dancer is
all-absorbing.
~~all-absorbent.~~
    ^

a. We regret this delay; thank you for your patients.

b. Ada's plan is to require education and experience to prepare herself for a position as property manager.

c. Serena Williams, the penultimate competitor, has earned millions of dollars just in endorsements.

d. Many people take for granite that public libraries have up-to-date computer systems.

e. The affect of Gao Xingjian's novels on other Chinese exiles is hard to gauge.

18d Use standard idioms.

Idioms are speech forms that follow no easily specified rules. The English say "Bernice went *to hospital*," an idiom strange to American ears, which are accustomed to hearing *the* in front of *hospital*. Native speakers of a language seldom have problems with idioms, but prepositions (such as *with, to, at,* and *of*) sometimes cause trouble, especially when they follow certain verbs and adjectives. When in doubt, consult a dictionary.

UNIDIOMATIC	IDIOMATIC
abide with (a decision)	abide by (a decision)
according with	according to
agree to (an idea)	agree with (an idea)
angry at (a person)	angry with (a person)
capable to	capable of
comply to	comply with
desirous to	desirous of
different than (a person or thing)	different from (a person or thing)
intend on doing	intend to do
off of	off
plan on doing	plan to do
preferable than	preferable to
prior than	prior to
superior than	superior to
sure and	sure to
think on	think of, about
try and	try to
type of a	type of

Multilingual

Because idioms follow no particular rules, you must learn them individually. You may find it helpful to keep a list of idioms that you frequently encounter in conversation and in reading.

EXERCISE 18-5 Edit the following sentences to eliminate errors in the use of idiomatic expressions. If a sentence is correct, write "correct" after it. Possible revisions appear in the back of the book.

> by
> We agreed to abide ~~with~~ the decision of the judge.

a. Queen Anne was so angry at Sarah Churchill that she refused to see her again.

b. Jean-Pierre's ambitious travel plans made it impossible for him to comply with the residency requirement for in-state tuition.

c. The parade moved off of the street and onto the beach.

d. The frightened refugees intend on making the dangerous trek across the mountains.

e. What type of a wedding are you planning?

18e Do not rely heavily on clichés.

The pioneer who first announced that he had "slept like a log" no doubt amused his companions with a fresh, unlikely comparison. Today, however, that comparison is a cliché, a saying that can no longer add emphasis or surprise.

To see just how dully predictable clichés are, put your hand over the right-hand column in the following list and then finish the phrases on the left.

cool as a	cucumber
beat around	the bush
blind as a	bat
busy as a	bee, beaver
crystal	clear
dead as a	doornail
out of the frying pan and	into the fire
light as a	feather
like a bull	in a china shop

playing with	fire
starting out at the bottom	of the ladder
water under the	bridge
white as a	sheet, ghost
avoid clichés like the	plague

The solution for clichés is simple: Delete them or rewrite them.

▶ **When I received a full scholarship from my second-**
   ~~**choice school, I**~~ *felt pressured to settle for second best.*
   choice school, I ~~found myself between a rock and a~~
   ~~hard place.~~

Sometimes you can write around a cliché by adding an element of surprise. One student revised a cliché about butterflies in her stomach like this:

> If all of the action in my stomach is caused by butterflies, there must be a horde of them, with horseshoes on.

The image of butterflies wearing horseshoes is fresh and unlikely, not predictable like the original cliché.

18f Use figures of speech with care.

A figure of speech is an expression that uses words imaginatively (rather than literally) to make abstract ideas concrete. Most often, figures of speech compare two seemingly unlike things to reveal surprising similarities.

In a *simile*, the writer makes the comparison explicitly, usually by introducing it with *like* or *as*: *By the time cotton had to be picked, Grandfather's neck was as red as the clay he plowed.* In a *metaphor*, the *like* or *as* is omitted, and the comparison is implied. For example, in the Old Testament Song of Solomon, a young woman compares the man she loves to a fruit tree: *With great delight I sat in his shadow, and his fruit was sweet to my taste.*

Although figures of speech are useful devices, writers sometimes use them without thinking through the images they evoke. The result is sometimes a *mixed metaphor*, the combination of two or more images that don't make sense together.

▶ Crossing Utah's salt flats in his new convertible, my father flew ~~at jet speed.~~
~~under a full head of steam.~~
^

Flew suggests an airplane, whereas *under a full head of steam* suggests a steamboat or a train. To clarify the image, the writer should stick with one comparison or the other.

▶ Our manager decided to put all controversial issues

~~in a holding pattern~~ on a back burner until after the annual

meeting.

Here the writer is mixing airplanes and stoves. Simply deleting one of the images corrects the problem.

EXERCISE 18–8   Edit the following sentences to replace worn-out expressions and to clarify mixed figures of speech. Possible revisions appear in the back of the book.

the color drained from his face.
When he heard about the accident, ~~he turned white as a~~
^
~~sheet.~~

a.   John stormed into the room like a bull in a china shop.

b. Some people insist that they'll always be there for you, even when they haven't been before.

c. The Cubs easily beat the Mets, who were in the soup early in the game today at Wrigley Field.

d. We ironed out the sticky spots in our relationship.

e. My mother accused me of beating around the bush when in fact I was just talking off the top of my head.

Grammatical Sentences

19 Repair sentence fragments. 279

20 Revise run-on sentences. 287

21 Make subjects and verbs agree. 297

22 Make pronouns and antecedents agree. 309

23 Make pronoun references clear. 315

24 Distinguish between pronouns such as *I* and *me*. 321

25 Distinguish between *who* and *whom*. 328

26 Choose adjectives and adverbs with care. 332

27 Choose appropriate verb forms, tenses, and moods in Standard English. 340

PART V

Grammatical Sentences

ONLINE ACTIVITIES:

 **Writer's Help 2.0**
macmillan learning

writershelp.com/hacker

 **LaunchPad Solo**
macmillan learning

macmillanhighered.com/
launchpadsolo/hacker

Sentence fragments 6 Exercises
1 LearningCurve activity

Run-on sentences 6 Exercises
1 LearningCurve activity

Subject-verb agreement 5 Exercises
1 LearningCurve activity

Pronoun-antecedent 5 Exercises
agreement 1 LearningCurve activity

Pronoun reference 4 Exercises
1 LearningCurve activity

Pronoun case 7 Exercises

Adjectives and adverbs 3 Exercises
1 LearningCurve activity

Standard English verb forms 9 Exercises
1 LearningCurve activity

19 Repair sentence fragments.

A sentence fragment is a word group that pretends to be a sentence. Sentence fragments are easy to recognize when they appear out of context, like these:

> When the cat leaped onto the table.

> Running for the bus.

When fragments appear next to related sentences, however, they are harder to spot.

> We had just sat down to dinner. When the cat leaped onto the table.

> I tripped and twisted my ankle. Running for the bus.

Recognizing sentence fragments

To be a sentence, a word group must consist of at least one full independent clause. An independent clause includes a subject and a verb, and it either stands alone or could stand alone.

To test whether a word group is a complete sentence or a fragment, use the flowchart on page 280. By using the flowchart, you can see exactly why *When the cat leaped onto the table* is a fragment: It has a subject (*cat*) and a verb (*leaped*), but it begins with a subordinating word (*When*). *Running for the bus* is a fragment because it lacks a subject and a verb (*Running* is a verbal, not a verb). (See also 48b and 48e.)

Test for fragments

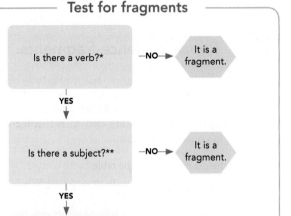

Is there a verb?* —NO→ It is a fragment.

YES

Is there a subject?** —NO→ It is a fragment.

YES

Is the word group merely a subordinate clause (because it begins with a word such as *because* or *when*)?*** —YES→ It is a fragment.

NO

It is a sentence.

*Do not mistake verbals for verbs. A verbal is a verb form (such as *walking, to act*) that does not function as a verb of a clause. (See 48b.)

**The subject of a sentence may be *you*, understood but not present in the sentence. (See 47a.)

***A sentence may open with a subordinate clause, but the sentence must also include an independent clause. (See 19a and 49a.)

If you find any fragments, try one of these methods of revision (see 19a–19c):

1. Attach the fragment to a nearby sentence.
2. Rewrite the fragment as a complete sentence.

Multilingual

Unlike some other languages, English requires a subject and a verb in every sentence (except in commands, where the subject *you* is understood but not present: *Sit down*). See 30a and 30b.

It is
▶ ~~Is~~ often hot and humid during the summer.
  ^

       are
▶ Students usually very busy at the end of the semester.
    ^

Repairing sentence fragments

You can repair most fragments in one of two ways:

- Pull the fragment into a nearby sentence.

- Rewrite the fragment as a complete sentence.

                  when
▶ We had just sat down to dinner/ ~~When~~ the cat leaped onto
                                ^

the table.

  Running for the bus,
▶ I tripped and sprained my ankle. ~~Running for the bus.~~
  ^

19a Attach fragmented subordinate clauses or turn them into sentences.

A subordinate clause is patterned like a sentence, with both a subject and a verb, but it begins with a word that marks it as subordinate. The following words commonly introduce subordinate clauses.

after	before	so that	until	while
although	even though	than	when	who
as	how	that	where	whom
as if	if	though	whether	whose
because	since	unless	which	why

Subordinate clauses function within sentences as adjectives, as adverbs, or as nouns. They cannot stand alone. (See 48e.)

Most fragmented clauses beg to be pulled into a sentence nearby.

▶ Americans have come to fear the West Nile virus/~~Because~~ it is transmitted by the common mosquito.

     because [inserted above]

Because introduces a subordinate clause, so it cannot stand alone. (For punctuation of subordinate clauses appearing at the end of a sentence, see 33f.)

▶ Although psychiatrist Peter Kramer expresses concerns about Prozac/, ~~Many~~ other doctors believe that the benefits of antidepressants outweigh the risks.

     many [inserted above]

Although introduces a subordinate clause, so it cannot stand alone. (For punctuation of subordinate clauses at the beginning of a sentence, see 32b.)

If a fragmented clause cannot be attached to a nearby sentence or if you feel that attaching it would be awkward, try turning the clause into a sentence. The simplest way to do this is to delete the opening word or words that mark it as subordinate.

▶ Population increases and uncontrolled development are taking a deadly toll on the environment. ~~So that across~~ the globe, fragile ecosystems are collapsing.

     Across [inserted above]

19b Attach fragmented phrases or turn them into sentences.

Like subordinate clauses, phrases function within sentences as adjectives, as adverbs, or as nouns. They cannot stand alone. Fragmented phrases are often prepositional or verbal phrases; sometimes they are appositives, words or word groups that rename nouns or pronouns. (See 48a, 48b, and 48c.)

Often a fragmented phrase may simply be pulled into a nearby sentence.

▶ The archaeologists worked slowly. ~~Examining~~ *examining* and

labeling every pottery shard they uncovered.

The word group beginning with *Examining* is a verbal phrase.

▶ The patient displayed symptoms of ALS. ~~A~~ *a* neuro-

degenerative disease.

A neurodegenerative disease is an appositive renaming the noun *ALS*. (For punctuation of appositives, see 32e.)

If a fragmented phrase cannot be pulled into a nearby sentence effectively, turn the phrase into a sentence. You may need to add a subject, a verb, or both.

▶ In the training session, Jamie explained how to access our

new database. ~~Also~~ *She also taught us* how to submit expense reports and

request vendor payments.

The revision turns the fragmented phrase into a sentence by adding a subject and a verb.

19c Attach other fragmented word groups or turn them into sentences.

Other word groups that are commonly fragmented include parts of compound predicates, lists, and examples introduced by *for example, in addition,* or similar expressions.

Parts of compound predicates

A predicate consists of a verb and its objects, complements, and modifiers (see 47b). A compound predicate includes two or more predicates joined with a coordinating conjunction such as *and, but,* or *or.* Because the parts of a compound predicate have the same subject, they should appear in the same sentence.

▶ The woodpecker finch of the Galápagos Islands carefully
     selects a twig of a certain size and shape/. ~~And~~ ^and^ then uses this
     tool to pry out grubs from trees.

> The subject is *finch,* and the compound predicate is *selects . . . and . . . uses.* (For punctuation of compound predicates, see 33a.)

Lists

To correct a fragmented list, often you can attach it to a nearby sentence with a colon or a dash. (See 35a and 39a.)

▶ It has been said that there are only three indigenous
     American art forms/: ~~Musical~~ ^musical^ comedy, jazz, and soap opera.

Sometimes terms such as *especially, namely, like,* and *such as* introduce fragmented lists. Such fragments can usually be attached to the preceding sentence.

▶ In the twentieth century, the South produced some great

American writers, ~~Such~~ ^such^ as Flannery O'Connor, William

Faulkner, Alice Walker, Tennessee Williams, and Thomas

Wolfe.

Examples introduced by for example, in addition, or similar expressions

Other expressions that introduce examples or explanations can lead to unintentional fragments. Although you may begin a sentence with some of the following words or phrases, make sure that what follows has a subject and a verb.

also	for example	mainly
and	for instance	or
but	in addition	that is

Often the easiest solution is to turn the fragment into a sentence.

▶ In his memoir, Primo Levi describes the horrors of living

in a concentration camp. For example, ^he worked^ ~~working~~ without

food and ^suffered^ ~~suffering~~ emotional abuse.

The writer corrected this fragment by adding a subject — *he* — and substituting verbs for the verbals *working* and *suffering*.

19d Exception: A fragment may be used for effect.

Writers occasionally use sentence fragments for special purposes.

FOR EMPHASIS   Following the dramatic Americanization of their children, even my parents grew more publicly confident. *Especially my mother.*

— Richard Rodriguez

TO ANSWER A QUESTION	Are these new drug tests 100 percent reliable? *Not in the opinion of most experts.*
TRANSITIONS	*And now the opposing arguments.*
EXCLAMATIONS	*Not again!*
IN ADVERTISING	*Fewer carbs. Improved taste.*

Although fragments are sometimes appropriate, writers and readers do not always agree on when they are appropriate. That's why you will find it safer to write in complete sentences.

EXERCISE 19–1 Repair any fragment by attaching it to a nearby sentence or by rewriting it as a complete sentence. If a word group is correct, write "correct" after it. Possible revisions appear in the back of the book.

> One Greek island that should not be missed is Mykonos/. A
>
> vacation spot for Europeans and a playground for the rich.

a. Listening to the CD her sister had sent, Mia was overcome with a mix of emotions. Happiness, homesickness, and nostalgia.

b. Cortés and his soldiers were astonished when they looked down from the mountains and saw Tenochtitlán. The magnificent capital of the Aztecs.

c. Although my spoken Spanish is not very good. I can read the language with ease.

d. There are several reasons for not eating meat. One reason being that dangerous chemicals are used throughout the various stages of meat production.

e. To learn how to sculpt beauty from everyday life. This is my intention in studying art and archaeology.

EXERCISE 19–2 Repair each fragment in the following passage by attaching it to a sentence nearby or by rewriting it as a complete sentence.

Digital technology has revolutionized information delivery. Forever blurring the lines between information and entertainment. Yesterday's readers of books and newspapers are today's readers of e-books and blogs. Countless readers have moved on from print information entirely. Choosing instead to point, click, and scroll their way through a text online or on an e-reader. Once a nation of people spoon-fed television commercials and the six o'clock evening news. We are now seemingly addicted to YouTube and social media. Remember the family trip when Dad or Mom wrestled with a road map? On the way to St. Louis or Seattle? No wrestling is required with a GPS device. Unless it's Mom and Dad wrestling over who gets to program the address. Accessing information now seems to be America's favorite pastime. John Horrigan, associate director for research at the Pew Internet and American Life Project, reports that nearly half of American adults are "elite" users of technology. Who are "highly engaged" with digital content. As a country, we embrace information and communication technologies. Which now include iPods, smartphones, and tablets. Among children and adolescents, social media and other technology use are well established. For activities like socializing, gaming, and information gathering.

20 Revise run-on sentences.

Run-on sentences are independent clauses that have not been joined correctly. An independent clause is a word group that can stand alone as a sentence. (See 49a.) When two independent clauses appear in one sentence, they must be joined in one of these ways:

- with a comma and a coordinating conjunction (*and*, *but*, *or*, *nor*, *for*, *so*, *yet*)

- with a semicolon (or occasionally with a colon or a dash)

Recognizing run-on sentences

There are two types of run-on sentences. When a writer puts no mark of punctuation and no coordinating conjunction between independent clauses, the result is called a *fused sentence*.

┌─────── INDEPENDENT CLAUSE ───────┐ ┌───────
FUSED Air pollution poses risks to all humans it can be

── INDEPENDENT CLAUSE ──┐
deadly for asthma sufferers.

A far more common type of run-on sentence is the *comma splice*—two or more independent clauses joined with a comma but without a coordinating conjunction. In some comma splices, the comma appears alone.

COMMA Air pollution poses risks to all humans, it can be
SPLICE deadly for asthma sufferers.

In other comma splices, the comma is accompanied by a joining word that is *not* a coordinating conjunction. There are only seven coordinating conjunctions in English: *and, but, or, nor, for, so,* and *yet.*

COMMA Air pollution poses risks to all humans, however, it can
SPLICE be deadly for asthma sufferers.

However is a transitional expression, not a coordinating conjunction, and cannot be used with only a comma to join two independent clauses (see 20b).

Revising run-on sentences

To revise a run-on sentence, you have four choices (see pp. 289–90).

1. Use a comma and a coordinating conjunction (*and, but, or, nor, for, so, yet*).

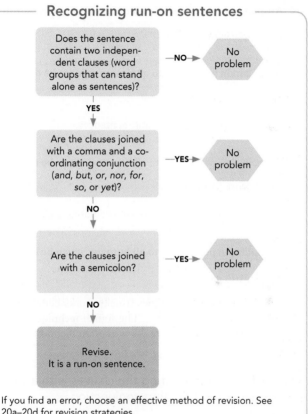

Recognizing run-on sentences

Does the sentence contain two independent clauses (word groups that can stand alone as sentences)? —**NO**→ No problem

YES ↓

Are the clauses joined with a comma and a co-ordinating conjunction (*and, but, or, nor, for, so,* or *yet*)? —**YES**→ No problem

NO ↓

Are the clauses joined with a semicolon? —**YES**→ No problem

NO ↓

Revise.
It is a run-on sentence.

If you find an error, choose an effective method of revision. See 20a–20d for revision strategies.

> but
> ▶ Air pollution poses risks to all humans, it can be deadly for
> ^
>
> people with asthma.

2. Use a semicolon (or, if appropriate, a colon or a dash). A semicolon may be used alone; it can also be accompanied by a transitional expression.

▶ Air pollution poses risks to all humans/; it can be deadly

for people with asthma.

however,
▶ Air pollution poses risks to all humans/; it can be deadly for

people with asthma.

3. Make the clauses into separate sentences.

It
▶ Air pollution poses risks to all humans/. it can be deadly for

people with asthma.

4. Restructure the sentence; try subordinating a clause.

Although air
▶ ~~Air~~ pollution poses risks to all humans, it can be deadly for

people with asthma.

One of these revision techniques usually works better than the others for a particular sentence. The fourth technique, the one requiring the most extensive revision, is often the most effective.

20a Consider separating the clauses with a comma and a coordinating conjunction.

There are seven coordinating conjunctions in English: *and, but, or, nor, for, so,* and *yet.* When a coordinating conjunction joins independent clauses, it is usually preceded by a comma. (See 32a.)

but
▶ Some lesson plans include exercises, completing them

should not be the focus of all class periods.

Writer's Choice
Clustering ideas in meaningful ways

When you draft, you may rush to write down your ideas before you forget them. Writers at all levels of experience do this. When you're generating ideas, you may not worry too much about grammar and punctuation, so you may end up with some run-on sentences. In later drafts you will need to revise so that your **audience** understands your meaning.

RUN-ON SENTENCE   Students can succeed in college by attending classes and keeping up with homework, visiting instructors during office hours can also be important, participating in campus events and clubs can help students succeed, too.

Several ideas compete for attention in this draft sentence:

- Students can succeed in college.
- Attending classes is important.
- Doing homework is important.
- Visiting instructors during office hours is important.
- Participating in campus events can help students succeed.
- Participating in campus clubs can help students succeed.

As a writer, ask yourself: How can I cluster the ideas in a way that best communicates my meaning?

POSSIBLE REVISION   Students can succeed in college by attending classes and keeping up with homework, by visiting instructors during office hours, and by participating in campus events and clubs.

POSSIBLE REVISION   In addition to attending class and keeping up with homework, students can succeed in college by visiting instructors during office hours. Participating in campus events and clubs is another way to foster success.

In each revision, the ideas are clustered, making the passage easier to read. The first revision places equal emphasis on all the different actions students can take to succeed in college. The second revision focuses on the importance of communicating with instructors.

Identifying, separating, and grouping ideas—all with your **purpose** and **audience** in mind—can help you revise run-on sentences.

▶ Many government officials privately admit that the poly-

graph is unreliable, ~~however,~~ *yet* they continue to use it as a

security measure.

However is a transitional expression, not a coordinating conjunction, so it cannot be used with only a comma to join independent
clauses. (See also 20b.)

20b Consider separating the clauses with a semicolon, a colon, or a dash.

When the independent clauses are closely related and their relation is clear without a coordinating conjunction, a semicolon is
an acceptable method of revision. (See 34a.)

▶ Tragedy depicts the individual confronted with the fact

of death/; comedy depicts the adaptability of human nature.

A semicolon is required between independent clauses that
have been linked with a transitional expression (such as *however, therefore, moreover, in fact,* or *for example*). For a longer list,
see 34b.

▶ The timber wolf looks like a German shepherd/; however,

the wolf has longer legs, larger feet, and a wider head.

▶ In his film adaptation of the short story "Killings," director

Todd Field changed key details of the plot/; in fact, he

added whole scenes that do not appear in the story.

A colon or a dash may be more appropriate if the first independent clause introduces the second or if the second clause

summarizes or explains the first. (See 35a and 39a.) In formal writing, the colon is usually preferred to the dash.

▶ Nuclear waste is hazardous; ~~this~~ ^This^ is an indisputable fact.

▶ The female black widow spider is often a widow of her own making, she has been known to eat her partner after mating.

A colon is an appropriate method of revision if the first independent clause introduces a quoted sentence.

▶ Nobel Peace Prize winner Al Gore had this to say about climate change: "The truth is that our circumstances are not only new; they are completely different than they have ever been in all of human history."

20c Consider making the clauses into separate sentences.

▶ Why should we spend money on space exploration? We ~~we~~ have enough underfunded programs here on Earth.

A question and a statement should be separate sentences.

▶ Some studies have suggested that sexual relationships set bonobos apart from common chimpanzees. According ~~according~~ to Stanford (1998), these differences have been exaggerated.

Using a comma alone to join two independent clauses creates a comma splice. (See also 61a on citing sources in APA style.)

NOTE: When two quoted independent clauses are divided by explanatory words, make each clause its own sentence.

▶ "It's always smart to learn from your mistakes," quipped my

supervisor/. "It's even smarter to learn from the mistakes of
　　　　　　 ^ "It's

others."

20d Consider restructuring the sentence, perhaps by subordinating one of the clauses.

If one of the independent clauses is less important than the other, turn the less important clause into a subordinate clause or phrase. (For more about subordination, see 14, especially the chart on p. 234.)

▶ One of the most famous advertising slogans is Wheaties

　　　　　　　　　　　　　　　　　　 which
cereal's "Breakfast of Champions," it associated the cereal
　　　　　　　　　　　　　　　　 ^

with famous athletes.

　 Although many
▶ Many scholars dismiss the abominable snowman of the
　^

Himalayas as a myth, some scientists claim it may be a

kind of ape.

▶ Mary McLeod Bethune, was the seventeenth child of former
　　　　　　　　　　　 ^

slaves, she founded the National Council of Negro Women

in 1935.

Minor ideas in these sentences are now expressed in subordinate clauses or phrases.

EXERCISE 20–1   Revise the following run-on sentences using the method of revision suggested in brackets. Possible revisions appear in the back of the book.

> *Because*
> **Orville had been obsessed with his weight as a teenager, he**
>   ^
> **rarely ate anything sweet.** [*Restructure the sentence.*]

a. The city had one public swimming pool, it stayed packed with children all summer long. [*Restructure the sentence.*]

b. The building is being renovated, therefore at times we have no heat, water, or electricity. [*Use a comma and a coordinating conjunction.*]

c. The view was not what the travel agent had described, where were the rolling hills and the shimmering rivers? [*Make two sentences.*]

d. Walker's coming-of-age novel is set against a gloomy scientific backdrop, the Earth's rotation has begun to slow down. [*Use a semicolon.*]

e. City officials had good reason to fear a major earthquake, most of the business district was built on landfill. [*Use a colon.*]

EXERCISE 20–2   Revise any run-on sentences using a technique that you find effective. If a sentence is correct, write "correct" after it. Possible revisions appear in the back of the book.

> **Crossing so many time zones on an eight-hour flight, I knew**
>   *but*
> **I would be tired when I arrived, ~~however,~~ I was too excited**
>   ^
> **to sleep on the plane.**

a. Wind power for the home is a supplementary source of energy, it can be combined with electricity, gas, or solar energy.

b. Aidan viewed Sofia Coppola's *Lost in Translation* three times and then wrote a paper describing the film as the work of a mysterious modern painter.

c. In the Middle Ages, the streets of London were dangerous places, it was safer to travel by boat along the Thames.

d. "He's not drunk," I said, "he's in a state of diabetic shock."

e. Are you able to endure extreme angle turns, high speeds, frequent jumps, and occasional crashes, then supermoto racing may be a sport for you.

EXERCISE 20–3 In the following rough draft, revise any run-on sentences.

Some parents and educators argue that requiring uniforms in public schools would improve student behavior and performance. They think that uniforms give students a more professional attitude toward school, moreover, they believe that uniforms help create a sense of community among students from diverse backgrounds. But parents and educators should consider the drawbacks to requiring uniforms in public schools.

Uniforms do create a sense of community, they do this, however, by stamping out individuality. Youth is a time to express originality, it is a time to develop a sense of self. One important way young people express their identities is through the clothes they wear. The self-patrolled dress code of high school students may be stricter than any school-imposed code, nevertheless, trying to control dress habits from above will only lead to resentment or to mindless conformity.

If children are going to act like adults, they need to be treated like adults, they need to be allowed to make their own choices. Telling young people what to wear to school merely prolongs their childhood. Requiring uniforms undermines the educational purpose of public schools, which is not just to teach facts and figures but to help young people grow into adults who are responsible for making their own choices.

21 Make subjects and verbs agree.

In the present tense, verbs agree with their subjects in number (singular or plural) and in person (first, second, third): *I sing, you sing, she sings, we sing, they sing.* Even if your ear recognizes the standard subject-verb combinations in 21a, you will no doubt encounter tricky situations such as those described in 21b–21k.

21a Learn to recognize standard subject-verb combinations.

This section describes the basic guidelines for making present-tense verbs agree with their subjects. The present-tense ending *-s* (or *-es*) is used on a verb if its subject is third-person singular (*he, she, it,* and singular nouns); otherwise the verb takes no ending. Consider, for example, the present-tense forms of the verbs *love* and *try,* given at the beginning of the chart on page 298.

The verb *be* varies from this pattern; it has special forms in *both* the present and the past tense (see the end of the chart).

If you aren't sure of the standard forms, use the charts on pages 298 and 299 as you proofread your work. See also 27c on *-s* endings of regular and irregular verbs.

21b Make the verb agree with its subject, not with a word that comes between.

Word groups often come between the subject and the verb. Such word groups, usually modifying the subject, may contain a noun that at first appears to be the subject. By mentally stripping away such modifiers, you can isolate the noun that is in fact the subject.

Subject-verb agreement at a glance

Present-tense forms of *love* and *try* (typical verbs)

	SINGULAR		PLURAL	
FIRST PERSON	I	love	we	love
SECOND PERSON	you	love	you	love
THIRD PERSON	he/she/it*	loves	they**	love

	SINGULAR		PLURAL	
FIRST PERSON	I	try	we	try
SECOND PERSON	you	try	you	try
THIRD PERSON	he/she/it*	tries	they**	try

Present-tense forms of *have*

	SINGULAR		PLURAL	
FIRST PERSON	I	have	we	have
SECOND PERSON	you	have	you	have
THIRD PERSON	he/she/it*	has	they**	have

Present-tense forms of *do* (including negative forms)

	SINGULAR		PLURAL	
FIRST PERSON	I	do/don't	we	do/don't
SECOND PERSON	you	do/don't	you	do/don't
THIRD PERSON	he/she/it*	does/doesn't	they**	do/don't

Present-tense and past-tense forms of *be*

	SINGULAR		PLURAL	
FIRST PERSON	I	am/was	we	are/were
SECOND PERSON	you	are/were	you	are/were
THIRD PERSON	he/she/it*	is/was	they**	are/were

*And singular nouns (*child*, *Roger*)

**And plural nouns (*children*, *the Mannings*)

When to use the -s (or -es) form of a present-tense verb

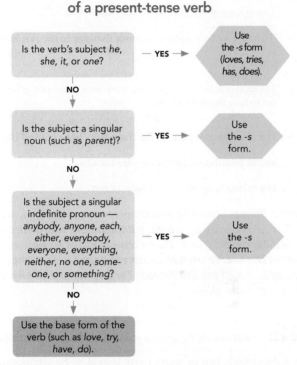

Is the verb's subject *he, she, it,* or *one*? — **YES** → Use the *-s* form (*loves, tries, has, does*).

NO ↓

Is the subject a singular noun (such as *parent*)? — **YES** → Use the *-s* form.

NO ↓

Is the subject a singular indefinite pronoun — *anybody, anyone, each, either, everybody, everyone, everything, neither, no one, someone,* or *something*? — **YES** → Use the *-s* form.

NO ↓

Use the base form of the verb (such as *love, try, have, do*).

EXCEPTION: Choosing the correct present-tense form of *be* (*am, is,* or *are*) is not quite so simple. See the chart on the previous page for both present- and past-tense forms of *be*.

MULTILINGUAL TIP: Do not use the *-s* form of a verb if it follows a modal verb such as *can, must,* or *should* or another helping verb. (See 28c.)

The *samples* on the tray in the lab *need* testing.

▶ High levels of air pollution causes damage to the respiratory

tract.

The subject is *levels*, not *pollution*. Strip away the phrase *of air pollu-tion* to hear the correct verb: *levels cause*.

has

▶ The slaughter of pandas for their pelts ~~have~~ caused the

panda population to decline drastically.

The subject is *slaughter*, not *pandas* or *pelts*.

NOTE: Phrases beginning with the prepositions *as well as*, *in addi-tion to*, *accompanied by*, *together with*, and *along with* do not make a singular subject plural. *The governor as well as his press secretary was on the plane.* To emphasize that two people were on the plane, the writer could use *and* instead: *The governor and his press secre-tary were on the plane.*

21c Treat most subjects joined with *and* as plural.

A subject with two or more parts is said to be compound. If the parts are connected with *and*, the subject is nearly always plural.

Leon and Jan often *jog* together.

▶ The Supreme Court's willingness to hear the case and

have

its affirmation of the original decision ~~has~~ set a new

precedent.

EXCEPTIONS: When the parts of the subject form a single unit or when they refer to the same person or thing, treat the subject as singular.

> Fish and chips was a last-minute addition to the menu.

> Sue's friend and adviser was surprised by her decision.

When a compound subject is preceded by *each* or *every*, treat it as singular.

> Each tree, shrub, and vine needs to be sprayed.

> Every car, truck, and van is required to pass inspection.

This exception does not apply when a compound subject is followed by *each*: *Alan and Marcia each have different ideas.*

21d With subjects joined with *or* or *nor* (or with *either . . . or* or *neither . . . nor*), make the verb agree with the part of the subject nearer to the verb.

> A driver's *license* or credit *card is* required.

> A driver's *license* or two credit *cards are* required.

▶ If an infant or a child ~~have~~ *has* a high fever, call a doctor.

▶ Neither the chief financial officer nor the marketing

> managers ~~was~~ *were* able to convince the client to reconsider.

> The verb must be matched with the part of the subject closer to it: *child has* in the first sentence, *managers were* in the second.

NOTE: If one part of the subject is singular and the other is plural, put the plural one last to avoid awkwardness.

21e Treat most indefinite pronouns as singular.

Indefinite pronouns are pronouns that do not refer to specific persons or things. The following commonly used indefinite pronouns are singular.

anybody	each	everyone	nobody	somebody
anyone	either	everything	no one	someone
anything	everybody	neither	nothing	something

Many of these words appear to have plural meanings, and they are often treated as such in casual speech. In formal written English, however, they are nearly always treated as singular.

Everyone on the team *supports* the coach.

▶ Each of the essays ~~have~~ has been graded.

▶ Nobody who participated in the clinical trials ~~were~~ was given a placebo.

The subjects of these sentences are *Each* and *Nobody*. These indefinite pronouns are third-person singular, so the verbs must be *has* and *was*.

A few indefinite pronouns (*all, any, none, some*) may be singular or plural depending on the noun or pronoun they refer to.

SINGULAR   *Some* of our *luggage was* lost.

None of his *advice makes* sense.

PLURAL   *Some* of the *rocks are* slippery.

None of the *eggs were* broken.

NOTE: When the meaning of *none* is emphatically "not one," *none* may be treated as singular: *None* [meaning "Not one"] *of the eggs was broken.* Using *not one* is sometimes clearer: *Not one of the eggs was broken.*

21f Treat collective nouns as singular unless the meaning is clearly plural.

Collective nouns such as *jury, committee, audience, crowd, troop, family,* and *couple* name a class or a group. In American English, collective nouns are nearly always treated as singular: They emphasize the group as a unit. Occasionally, when there is some reason to draw attention to the individual members of the group, a collective noun may be treated as plural. (See also 22b.)

SINGULAR   The *class respects* the teacher.

PLURAL   The *class are* debating among themselves.

To underscore the notion of individuality in the second sentence, many writers would add a clearly plural noun.

PLURAL   The class *members are* debating among themselves.

▶ The board of trustees ~~meet~~ *meets* in Denver twice a year.

  The board as a whole meets; there is no reason to draw attention to its individual members.

▶ A young couple ~~was~~ *were* arguing about politics while holding hands.

  The meaning is clearly plural. Only separate individuals can argue and hold hands.

NOTE: The phrase *the number* is treated as singular, *a number* as plural.

SINGULAR   *The number* of school-age children *is* declining.

PLURAL   *A number* of children *are* attending the wedding.

NOTE: In general, when fractions or units of measurement are used with a singular noun, treat them as singular; when they are used with a plural noun, treat them as plural.

SINGULAR   *Three-fourths* of the salad *has* been eaten.

SINGULAR   Twenty *inches* of wallboard *was* covered with mud.

PLURAL   *One-fourth* of the drivers *were* texting.

PLURAL   Two *pounds* of blueberries *were* used to make the pie.

21g Make the verb agree with its subject even when the subject follows the verb.

Verbs ordinarily follow subjects. When this normal order is reversed, it is easy to become confused. Sentences beginning with *there is* or *there are* (or *there was* or *there were*) are inverted; the subject follows the verb.

There *are* surprisingly few *honeybees* left in southern China.

▶ There ~~was~~ a social worker and a journalist at the meeting.
   were

The subject, *worker and journalist,* is plural, so the verb must be *were.*

Occasionally you may decide to invert a sentence for variety or effect. When you do so, check to make sure that your subject and verb agree.

▶ Of particular concern ~~is~~ *are* penicillin and tetracycline, antibiotics used to make animals more resistant to disease.

The subject, *penicillin and tetracycline*, is plural, so the verb must be *are*.

21h Make the verb agree with its subject, not with a subject complement.

One basic sentence pattern in English consists of a subject, a linking verb, and a subject complement: *Jack is a lawyer.* Because the subject complement (*lawyer*) names or describes the subject (*Jack*), it is sometimes mistaken for the subject. (See 47b on subject complements.)

These *exercises are* a way to test your ability to perform under pressure.

▶ A tent and a sleeping bag ~~is~~ *are* the required equipment.

Tent and bag is the subject, not *equipment*.

▶ A major force in today's economy ~~are~~ *is* children—as consumers, decision makers, and trend spotters.

Force is the subject, not *children*. If the corrected version seems too awkward, make *children* the subject: *Children are a major force in today's economy—as consumers, decision makers, and trend spotters.*

21i *Who, which,* and *that* take verbs that agree with their antecedents.

Like most pronouns, the relative pronouns *who, which,* and *that* have antecedents, nouns or pronouns to which they refer. Relative pronouns used as subjects of subordinate clauses take verbs that agree with their antecedents.

ANT PN   V

Take a *course that prepares* you for classroom management.

One of the

Constructions such as *one of the students who* [or *one of the things that*] cause problems for writers. Do not assume that the antecedent must be *one.* Instead, consider the logic of the sentence.

▶ Our ability to use language is one of the things that sets us

apart from animals.

The antecedent of *that* is *things,* not *one.* Several things set us apart from animals.

Only one of the

When the word *only* comes before *one,* you are safe in assuming that *one* is the antecedent of the relative pronoun.

▶ Veronica was the only one of the first-year Spanish

               was

students who ~~were~~ fluent enough to apply for the exchange

program.

The antecedent of *who* is *one,* not *students.* Only one student was fluent enough.

21j Words such as *athletics*, *economics*, *mathematics*, *physics*, *politics*, *statistics*, *measles*, and *news* are usually singular, despite their plural form.

▶ Politics ~~are~~ `is` among my mother's favorite pastimes.

EXCEPTIONS: Occasionally some of these words, especially *mathematics*, *economics*, *politics*, and *statistics*, have plural meanings: *Office politics often sway decisions about hiring and promotion. The economics of the building plan are prohibitive.*

21k Titles of works, company names, words mentioned as words, and gerund phrases are singular.

▶ *Lost Cities* ~~describe~~ `describes` the discoveries of fifty ancient civilizations.

▶ Delmonico Brothers ~~specialize~~ `specializes` in organic produce and additive-free meats.

▶ *Controlled substances* ~~are~~ `is` a euphemism for illegal drugs.

A gerund phrase consists of an *-ing* verb form followed by any objects, complements, or modifiers (see 48b). Treat gerund phrases as singular.

▶ Encountering long hold times ~~make~~ `makes` customers impatient with telephone tech support.

EXERCISE 21–1 Edit the following sentences to eliminate problems with subject-verb agreement. If a sentence is correct, write "correct" after it. Answers appear in the back of the book.

> were
> Jack's first days in the military ~~was~~ grueling.
>   ^

a. One of the main reasons for elephant poaching are the profits received from selling the ivory tusks.

b. Not until my interview with Dr. Hwang were other possibilities opened to me.

c. A number of students in the seminar was aware of the importance of joining the discussion.

d. Batik cloth from Bali, blue and white ceramics from Delft, and a bocce ball from Turin has made Angelie's room the talk of the dorm.

e. The board of directors, ignoring the wishes of the neighborhood, has voted to allow further development.

EXERCISE 21–2 For each sentence in the following passage, underline the subject (or compound subject) and then select the verb that agrees with it. (If you have trouble identifying the subject, consult 47a.)

Loggerhead sea turtles (migrate / migrates) thousands of miles before returning to their nesting location every two to three years. The nesting season for loggerhead turtles (span / spans) the hottest months of the summer. Although the habitat of Atlantic loggerheads (range / ranges) from Newfoundland to Argentina, nesting for these turtles (take / takes) place primarily along the southeastern coast of the United States. Female turtles that have reached sexual maturity (crawl / crawls) ashore at night to lay their eggs. The cavity that serves as a nest for the eggs (is / are) dug out with the female's strong flippers. Deposited into each nest (is / are) anywhere from fifty to two hundred spherical eggs, also known as a *clutch*. After a two-month incubation period, all eggs in the clutch (begin / begins) to hatch, and within a few days the young turtles attempt to make their way into the ocean. A major cause of the loggerhead's decreasing numbers (is / are) natural predators such as raccoons,

birds, and crabs. Beach erosion and coastal development also
(threaten / threatens) the turtles' survival. For example, a crowd
of curious humans or lights from beachfront residences (is / are)
enough to make the female abandon her nesting plans and
return to the ocean. Since only one in one thousand loggerheads
survives to adulthood, special care should be taken to protect
this threatened species.

22 Make pronouns and antecedents agree.

A pronoun is a word that substitutes for a noun. (See 46b.)
Many pronouns have antecedents, nouns or pronouns to which
they refer. A pronoun and its antecedent agree when they are
both singular or both plural.

SINGULAR   *Dr. Ava Berto* finished *her* rounds.

PLURAL   The hospital *interns* finished *their* rounds.

Multilingual

The pronouns *he, his, she, her, it,* and *its* must agree in gender (masculine, feminine, or neuter) with their antecedents, not with the words
they modify.

   Steve visited *his* [not *her*] sister in Seattle.

22a Do not use plural pronouns to refer to singular antecedents.

Writers are frequently tempted to use plural pronouns to refer to two kinds of singular antecedents: indefinite pronouns and generic nouns.

Indefinite pronouns

Indefinite pronouns refer to nonspecific persons or things. Even though some of the following indefinite pronouns may seem to have plural meanings, treat them as singular in formal English.

anybody	each	everyone	nobody	somebody
anyone	either	everything	no one	someone
anything	everybody	neither	nothing	something

Everyone performs at *his or her* [not *their*] own fitness level.

When a plural pronoun refers mistakenly to a singular indefinite pronoun, you can usually choose one of three options for revision:

1. Replace the plural pronoun with *he or she* (or *his or her*).

2. Make the antecedent plural.

3. Rewrite the sentence so that no problem of agreement exists.

▶ When someone travels outside the United States for the
        he or she needs
first time, ~~they need~~ to apply for a passport.
        ^

        people travel
▶ When ~~someone travels~~ outside the United States for the
        ^
first time, they need to apply for a passport.

> Anyone who
> ~~When someone~~ travels outside the United States for the
>   needs
> first time,/~~they need~~ to apply for a passport.

Because the *he or she* construction is wordy, often the second
or third revision strategy is more effective. Using *he* (or *his*) to
refer to persons of either sex, while less wordy, is considered
sexist, as is using *she* (or *her*) for all persons. Some writers
alternate male and female pronouns throughout a text, but the
result is often awkward. See 17f and the chart on page 313 for
strategies that avoid sexist usage.

NOTE: If you change a pronoun from singular to plural (or vice
versa), check to be sure that the verb agrees with the new pronoun (see 21e).

Generic nouns

A generic noun represents a typical member of a group, such as
a typical student, or any member of a group, such as any lawyer.
Although generic nouns may seem to have plural meanings, they
are singular.

Every *runner* must train rigorously if *he or she wants* [not *they
want*] to excel.

When a plural pronoun refers mistakenly to a generic noun,
you will usually have the same three revision options as mentioned on page 310 for indefinite pronouns.

>   he or she wants
> A medical student must study hard if ~~they want~~ to succeed.

> Medical students
> ~~A medical student~~ must study hard if they want to succeed.

> A medical student must study hard ~~if they want~~ to succeed.

22b Treat collective nouns as singular unless the meaning is clearly plural.

Collective nouns such as *jury*, *committee*, *audience*, *crowd*, *class*, *troop*, *family*, *team*, and *couple* name a group. Ordinarily the group functions as a unit, so the noun should be treated as singular; if the members of the group function as individuals, however, the noun should be treated as plural. (See also 21f.)

AS A UNIT   The *committee* granted *its* permission to build.

AS INDIVIDUALS   The *committee* put *their* signatures on the document.

When treating a collective noun as plural, many writers prefer to add a clearly plural antecedent such as *members* to the sentence: *The members of the committee put their signatures on the document.*

▶ Defense attorney Clarence Darrow surprisingly urged the

jury to find his client, John Scopes, guilty so that he could

appeal the case to a higher court. The jury complied,
its
returning ~~their~~ verdict in only nine minutes.
      ^

There is no reason to draw attention to the individual members of the jury, so *jury* should be treated as singular.

22c Treat most compound antecedents joined with *and* as plural.

In 1987, *Reagan and Gorbachev* held a summit where *they* signed the Intermediate-Range Nuclear Forces Treaty.

Choosing a revision strategy that avoids sexist language

Because many readers object to sexist language, avoid using *he*, *him*, and *his* (or *she*, *her*, and *hers*) to refer to both men and women. Also try to avoid the wordy expressions *he or she* and *his or her*. More graceful alternatives are usually possible.

Use an occasional *he or she* (or *his or her*).

> In our office, everyone works at ~~their~~ own pace.
> *his or her*

Make the antecedent plural.

> ~~An employee~~ on extended disability leave may continue their life insurance.
> *Employees*

Recast the sentence.

> The amount of vacation time a federal worker may accrue depends on ~~their~~ length of service.

> ~~If a~~ child ~~is~~ born to parents who are both tall, ~~they have~~ a high chance of being tall.
> *A* ... *has*

> A year later someone finally admitted ~~that they were~~ involved in the kidnapping.
> *to being*

> In his autobiography, Benjamin Franklin suggests that anyone can achieve success ~~as long as they live~~ a virtuous life and ~~work~~ hard.
> *by living* ... *working*

22d With compound antecedents joined with *or* or *nor* (or with *either . . . or* or *neither . . . nor*), make the pronoun agree with the nearer antecedent.

Either *Bruce* or *Tom* should receive first prize for *his* poem.

Neither the *mouse* nor the *rats* could find *their* way through the maze.

NOTE: If one of the antecedents is singular and the other plural, as in the second example, put the plural one last to avoid awkwardness.

EXCEPTION: If one antecedent is male and the other female, do not follow the traditional rule. The sentence *Either Bruce or Elizabeth should receive first prize for her short story* makes no sense. The best solution is to recast the sentence: *The prize for best short story should go to either Bruce or Elizabeth.*

EXERCISE 22-1 Edit the following sentences to eliminate problems with pronoun-antecedent agreement. Most of the sentences can be revised in more than one way, so experiment before choosing a solution. If a sentence is correct, write "correct" after it. Possible revisions appear in the back of the book.

Recruiters
~~The recruiter~~ may tell the truth, but there is much that they
  ^

choose not to tell.

a. Every presidential candidate must appeal to a wide variety of ethnic and social groups if they want to win the election.

b. David lent his motorcycle to someone who allowed their friend to use it.

c. The trainer motioned for everyone to move their arms in wide, slow circles.

d. The parade committee was unanimous in its decision to allow all groups and organizations to join the festivities.

e. The applicant should be bilingual if they want to qualify for this position.

EXERCISE 22–2 Edit the following paragraph to eliminate problems with pronoun-antecedent agreement or sexist language.

A common practice in businesses is to put each employee in their own cubicle. A typical cubicle resembles an office, but their walls don't reach the ceiling. Many office managers feel that a cubicle floor plan has its advantages. Cubicles make a large area feel spacious. In addition, they can be moved around so that each new employee can be accommodated in his own work area. Of course, the cubicle model also has problems. Typically, an employee is not as happy with a cubicle as they would be with a traditional office. Also, productivity can suffer. Neither a manager nor a frontline worker can ordinarily do their best work in a cubicle because of noise and lack of privacy. Each worker can hear his neighbors tapping on keyboards, making phone calls, and muttering under their breath.

23 Make pronoun references clear.

Pronouns substitute for nouns; they are a kind of shorthand. In a sentence like *After Andrew intercepted the ball, he kicked it as hard as he could,* the pronouns *he* and *it* substitute for the nouns *Andrew* and *ball.* The word a pronoun refers to is called its *antecedent.*

23a Avoid ambiguous or remote pronoun reference.

Ambiguous pronoun reference occurs when a pronoun could refer to two possible antecedents.

The pitcher broke when Gloria set it
▶ ~~When Gloria set the pitcher~~ on the glass-topped table~~, it broke.~~

          "You have
▶ Tom told James~~, that he had~~ won the lottery.*"*

What broke—the pitcher or the table? Who won the lottery—Tom or James? The revisions eliminate the ambiguity.

Remote pronoun reference occurs when a pronoun is too far away from its antecedent for easy reading.

▶ After the court ordered my ex-husband to pay child support,

he refused. Eight months later, the judge ordered him to make

payments directly to the court, which would in turn pay me.
                                          my ex-husband
After six months, payments stopped. Again he was

summoned to appear in court.

The pronoun *he* was too distant from its antecedent, *ex-husband*, which appeared several sentences earlier.

23b Generally, avoid broad reference of *this*, *that*, *which*, and *it*.

For clarity, the pronouns *this*, *that*, *which*, and *it* should ordinarily refer to specific antecedents rather than to whole ideas or sentences. When a pronoun's reference is needlessly broad, either replace the pronoun with a noun or supply an antecedent to which the pronoun clearly refers.

▶ By advertising on television, pharmaceutical companies

gain exposure for their prescription drugs. Patients
      the ads
respond to ~~this~~ by requesting drugs they might not need.
             ∧

The writer substituted the noun *ads* for the pronoun *this*, which referred broadly to the idea expressed in the preceding sentence.

▶ Romeo and Juliet were both too young to have acquired
                a fact
much wisdom, ~~and~~ that accounts for their rash actions.
             ∧

The writer added an antecedent (*fact*) that the pronoun *that* clearly refers to.

23c Do not use a pronoun to refer to an implied antecedent.

A pronoun should refer to a specific antecedent, not to a word that is implied but not present in the sentence.

                                          the braids
▶ After braiding Ann's hair, Sue decorated ~~them~~ with
                                          ∧
ribbons.

The pronoun *them* referred to Ann's braids (implied by the term *braiding*), but the word *braids* did not appear in the sentence.

Modifiers, such as possessives, cannot serve as antecedents. A modifier may strongly imply the noun that a pronoun might logically refer to, but it is not itself that noun.

> In ~~Jamaica Kincaid's~~ "Girl," ~~she~~ describes the advice a
> ^ Jamaica Kincaid
> mother gives her daughter, including the mysterious
> warning not to be "the kind of woman who the baker won't
> let near the bread" (454).

Using the possessive form of an author's name to introduce a
source leads to a problem later in this sentence: The pronoun *she*
cannot refer logically to a possessive modifier (*Jamaica Kincaid's*).
The revision substitutes the noun *Jamaica Kincaid* for the pronoun
she, thereby eliminating the problem. (For more on writing with
sources in MLA style, see 55.)

23d Avoid the indefinite use of *they*, *it*, and *you*.

Do not use the pronoun *they* to refer indefinitely to persons who
have not been specifically mentioned. *They* should always refer to
a specific antecedent.

> In June, ~~they~~ voted to charge a fee for students to
> ^ the school board
> participate in sports and music programs.

The word *it* should not be used indefinitely in constructions
such as *It is said on television . . .* or *In the article, it says that. . . .*

> ~~In the~~ encyclopedia ~~it~~ states that male moths can smell
> ^ The
> female moths from several miles away.

The pronoun *you* is appropriate only when the writer is
addressing the reader directly: *Once you have kneaded the dough,
let it rise in a warm place.* Except in informal contexts, however,
you should not be used to mean "anyone in general." Use a noun
instead.

> Ms. Pickersgill's *Guide to Etiquette* stipulates that ~~you~~
> a guest
> should not arrive at a party too early or leave too late.

23e To refer to persons, use *who*, *whom*, or *whose*, not *which* or *that*.

In most contexts, use *who*, *whom*, or *whose* to refer to persons, and use *which* or *that* to refer to animals or things. *Which* is reserved only for animals or things, so it is impolite to use it to refer to persons.

> All thirty-two women in the study, half of ~~which~~ were
> whom
> unemployed for more than six months, reported higher
> self-esteem after job training.

Although *that* is sometimes used to refer to persons, many readers will find such references dehumanizing. It is more polite to use a form of *who*—a word reserved for people.

> During the two-day festival El Día de los Muertos (Day of
> the Dead), Mexican families celebrate loved ones ~~that~~ have
> who
> died.

NOTE: Occasionally *whose* may be used to refer to animals and things to avoid the awkward *of which* construction.

> whose
> A local school, ~~the~~ name ~~of which~~ will be in tomorrow's
> paper, has received the Governor's Gold Medal for
> outstanding community service.

EXERCISE 23–1   Edit the following sentences to correct errors in pronoun reference. In some cases, you will need to decide on an antecedent that the pronoun might logically refer to. Possible revisions appear in the back of the book.

Although Apple makes the most widely recognized tablet

device, other companies have gained a share of the market.

The competition
~~This~~ has kept prices from skyrocketing.

a.   They say that engineering students should have hands-on experience with dismantling and reassembling machines.

b.   She had decorated her living room with posters from chamber music festivals. This led her date to believe that she was interested in classical music. Actually she preferred rock.

c.   In my high school, you didn't need to get all A's to be considered a success; you just needed to work to your ability.

d.   Marianne told Jenny that she was worried about her mother's illness.

e.   Though Lewis cried for several minutes after scraping his knee, eventually it subsided.

EXERCISE 23–2   Edit the following passage to correct errors in pronoun reference. In some cases, you will need to decide on an antecedent that the pronoun might logically refer to.

Since its launch in the 1980s, the Internet has grown to be one of the largest communications forums in the world. The Internet was created by a team of academics who were building on a platform that government scientists had started developing in the 1950s. They initially viewed it as a noncommercial enterprise that would serve only the needs of the academic and technical communities. But with the introduction of user-friendly browser technology in the 1990s, it expanded tremendously. By the late 1990s, many businesses were connecting to the Internet with high-speed broadband and fiber-optic connections, which is also true of home users today. Accessing information, shopping, gaming, and communicating are easier than ever before. This, however, can lead to some possible drawbacks. You forfeit privacy when you search, shop, game, and communicate. They say that avoiding disclosure of personal information and routinely adjusting your privacy settings on social media sites are the best ways to protect yourself on the Internet.

24 Distinguish between pronouns such as *I* and *me*.

The personal pronouns in the following chart change what is known as *case form* according to their grammatical function in a sentence. Pronouns functioning as subjects or subject complements appear in the *subjective* case; those functioning as objects appear in the *objective* case; and those showing ownership appear in the *possessive* case.

	SUBJECTIVE CASE	OBJECTIVE CASE	POSSESSIVE CASE
SINGULAR	I	me	my
	you	you	your
	he/she/it	him/her/it	his/her/its
PLURAL	we	us	our
	you	you	your
	they	them	their

Pronouns in the subjective and objective cases are frequently confused. Most of the rules in this section specify when to use one or the other of these cases (*I* or *me*, *he* or *him*, and so on). Section 24g explains a special use of pronouns and nouns in the possessive case.

24a Use the subjective case (*I, you, he, she, it, we, they*) for subjects and subject complements.

When personal pronouns are used as subjects, ordinarily your ear will tell you the correct pronoun. Problems sometimes arise, however, with compound word groups containing a pronoun, so it is not always safe to trust your ear.

▶ Joel ran away because his stepfather and ~~him~~ had argued.
     _{he}

His stepfather and he is the subject of the verb *had argued.*
If we strip away the words *his stepfather and,* the correct pronoun becomes clear: *he had argued* (not *him had argued*).

When a pronoun is used as a subject complement (a word following a linking verb), your ear may mislead you, since the incorrect form is frequently heard in casual speech. (See "subject complement," 47b.)

▶ During the Lindbergh trial, Bruno Hauptmann repeatedly
   denied that the kidnapper was ~~him.~~
                                    _{he.}

If kidnapper was he seems too stilted, rewrite the sentence: *During the Lindbergh trial, Bruno Hauptmann repeatedly denied that he was the kidnapper.*

24b Use the objective case (*me, you, him, her, it, us, them*) for all objects.

When a personal pronoun is used as a direct object, an indirect object, or the object of a preposition, ordinarily your ear will lead you to the correct pronoun. When an object is compound, however, you may occasionally become confused.

▶ Janice was indignant when she realized that the salesclerk
   was insulting her mother and ~~she.~~
                                 _{her.}

Her mother and her is the direct object of the verb *was insulting.*
Strip away the words *her mother and* to hear the correct pronoun:
was insulting her (not *was insulting she*).

► The most traumatic experience for her father and ~~I~~ *me* occurred

long after her operation.

Her father and me is the object of the preposition *for.* Strip away the
words *her father and* to test for the correct pronoun: *for me* (not *for I*).

When in doubt about the correct pronoun, some writers try
to avoid making the choice by using a reflexive pronoun such as
myself. Using a reflexive pronoun in such situations is nonstandard.

► Nidra gave my cousin and ~~myself~~ *me* some good tips on

traveling in New Delhi.

My cousin and me is the indirect object of the verb *gave.* For correct
uses of *myself*, see the glossary of usage at the back of the book.

24c Put an appositive and the word to which it refers in the same case.

Appositives are noun phrases that rename nouns or pronouns.
A pronoun used as an appositive has the same function (usually
subject or object) as the word(s) it renames.

► The managers, Dr. Bell and ~~me,~~ *I,* could not agree on a plan.

The appositive *Dr. Bell and I* renames the subject, *managers.*
Test: *I could not agree* (not *me could not agree*).

► The reporter found only two witnesses, the bicyclist and ~~I.~~ *me.*

The appositive *the bicyclist and me* renames the direct object,
witnesses. Test: *found me* (not *found I*).

24d Following *than* or *as*, choose the pronoun that expresses your meaning.

When a comparison begins with *than* or *as*, your choice of a pronoun will depend on your intended meaning. To test for the correct pronoun, mentally complete the sentence: *My roommate likes football more than I [do].*

▶ In our report on nationalized health care in the United

   States, we argued that Canadians are better off than ~~us.~~ we.
                                                              ^

    We is the subject of the verb *are*, which is understood: *Canadians are better off than we [are].* If the correct English seems too formal, you can always add the verb.

▶ We respected no other candidate as much as ~~she.~~ her.
                                                         ^

    This sentence means that we respected no other candidate as much as *we respected her. Her* is the direct object of the understood verb *respected.*

24e For *we* or *us* before a noun, choose the pronoun that would be appropriate if the noun were omitted.

▶ ~~Us~~ We tenants would rather fight than move.
  ^

▶ Management is shortchanging ~~we~~ us tenants.
                                    ^

    No one would say *Us would rather fight than move* or *Management is shortchanging we.*

24f Use the objective case for subjects and objects of infinitives.

An infinitive is the word *to* followed by the base form of a verb. (See 48b.) Subjects of infinitives are an exception to the rule that subjects must be in the subjective case. Whenever an infinitive has a subject, it must be in the objective case. Objects of infinitives also are in the objective case.

> Sue asked John and ~~I~~ *me* to drive the mayor and ~~she~~ *her* to the
>
> airport.

John and me is the subject of the infinitive *to drive; mayor and her* is the direct object of the infinitive.

24g Use the possessive case to modify a gerund.

A pronoun that modifies a gerund or a gerund phrase should be in the possessive case (*my, our, your, his, her, its, their*). A gerund is a verb form ending in *-ing* that functions as a noun. Gerunds frequently appear in phrases; when they do, the whole gerund phrase functions as a noun. (See 48b.)

> The chances of ~~you~~ *your* being hit by lightning are about two
>
> million to one.

Your modifies the gerund phrase *being hit by lightning.*

Nouns as well as pronouns may modify gerunds. To form the possessive case of a noun, use an apostrophe and an *-s* (*victim's*) or just an apostrophe (*victims'*). (See 36a.)

> The old order in France paid a high price for the ~~aristocracy~~ *aristocracy's*
>
> exploiting the lower classes.

The possessive noun *aristocracy's* modifies the gerund phrase *exploiting the lower classes.*

Gerund phrases should not be confused with participial phrases, which function as adjectives, not as nouns: *We saw him driving a yellow convertible.* Here *driving a yellow convertible* is a participial phrase modifying the pronoun *him*. (See 48b.)

The choice between the objective case and the possessive case depends on the meaning you intend; sometimes the distinction is subtle.

> We watched *them* dancing.
>
> We watched *their* dancing.

In the first sentence, the emphasis is on the people; we watched *them*, and they happened to be dancing. In the second sentence, the emphasis is on the dancing; we watched the *dancing*—a noun form modified by the possessive *their*.

NOTE: Do not use the possessive if it creates an awkward effect. Try to reword the sentence instead.

AWKWARD	The president agreed to the applications' being reviewed by a faculty committee.
REVISED	The president agreed that the applications could be reviewed by a faculty committee.
REVISED	The president agreed that a faculty committee could review the applications.

EXERCISE 24–1   Edit the following sentences to eliminate errors in pronoun case. If a sentence is correct, write "correct" after it. Answers appear in the back of the book.

> Grandfather cuts down trees for neighbors much younger
>   he.
> than ~~him.~~
>   ^

a. Rick applied for the job even though he heard that other candidates were more experienced than he.

b. The volleyball team could not believe that the coach was she.

c. She appreciated him telling the truth in such a difficult situation.

d. The director has asked you and I to draft a proposal for a new recycling plan.

e. Five close friends and myself rented an SUV, packed it with food, and drove two hundred miles to Mardi Gras.

EXERCISE 24–2   In the following paragraph, choose the correct pronoun in each set of parentheses.

We may blame television for the number of products based on characters in children's TV shows — from Big Bird to SpongeBob — but in fact merchandising that capitalizes on a character's popularity started long before television. Raggedy Ann began as a child's rag doll, and a few years later books about (she / her) and her brother, Raggedy Andy, were published. A cartoonist named Johnny Gruelle painted a cloth face on a family doll and applied for a patent in 1915. Later Gruelle began writing and illustrating stories about Raggedy Ann, and in 1918 (he / him) and a publisher teamed up to publish the books and sell the dolls. He was not the only one to try to sell products linked to children's stories. Beatrix Potter published the first of many Peter Rabbit picture books in 1902, and no one was better than (she / her) at making a living from spin-offs. After Peter Rabbit and Benjamin Bunny became popular, Potter began putting pictures of (they / them) and their little animal friends on merchandise. Potter had fans all over the world, and she understood (them / their) wanting to see Peter Rabbit not only in books but also on teapots and plates and lamps and other furnishings for the nursery. Potter and Gruelle, like countless others before and since, knew that entertaining children could be a profitable business.

25 Distinguish between *who* and *whom.*

The choice between *who* and *whom* (or *whoever* and *whomever*) occurs primarily in subordinate clauses and in questions. *Who* and *whoever*, subjective-case pronouns, are used for subjects and subject complements. *Whom* and *whomever*, objective-case pronouns, are used for objects. (See 25a and 25b.)

An exception to this general rule occurs when the pronoun functions as the subject of an infinitive (see 25c). See also 24f.

Consult the chart on page 331 for a summary of the trouble spots with *who* and *whom.*

25a Use *who* and *whom* correctly in subordinate clauses.

When *who* and *whom* (or *whoever* and *whomever*) introduce subordinate clauses, their case is determined by their function *within the clause they introduce.*

In the following two examples, the pronouns *who* and *whoever* function as the subjects of the clauses they introduce.

▶ First prize goes to the runner ~~whom~~ ^{who} earns the most points.

> The subordinate clause is *who earns the most points.* The verb of the clause is *earns*, and its subject is *who.*

▶ Maya Angelou's *I Know Why the Caged Bird Sings* should be read by ~~whomever~~ ^{whoever} is interested in the effects of racial prejudice on children.

The writer selected the pronoun *whomever*, thinking that it was the object of the preposition *by*. However, the object of the preposition is the entire subordinate clause *whoever is interested in the effects of racial prejudice on children*. The verb of the clause is *is*, and the subject of the verb is *whoever*.

When functioning as an object in a subordinate clause, *whom* (or *whomever*) also appears out of order, before the subject and verb. To choose the correct pronoun, you can mentally restructure the clause.

► You will work with our senior traders, ~~who~~ whom you will meet later.

The subordinate clause is *whom you will meet later*. The subject of the clause is *you*, and the verb is *will meet*. *Whom* is the direct object of the verb. The correct choice becomes clear if you mentally restructure the clause: *you will meet whom*.

When functioning as the object of a preposition in a subordinate clause, *whom* is often separated from its preposition.

► The tutor ~~who~~ whom I was assigned to was very supportive.

Whom is the object of the preposition *to*. In this sentence, the writer might choose to drop *whom*: *The tutor I was assigned to was very supportive*.

NOTE: Inserted expressions such as *they know*, *I think*, and *she says* should be ignored in determining whether to use *who* or *whom*.

► The speech pathologist reported a particularly difficult session with a stroke patient ~~whom~~ who she knew was suffering from aphasia.

Who is the subject of *was suffering*, not the object of *knew*.

25b Use *who* and *whom* correctly in questions.

When *who* and *whom* (or *whoever* and *whomever*) are used to open questions, their case is determined by their function within the question.

Who
▶ ~~Whom~~ was responsible for creating that computer virus?
^

Who is the subject of the verb *was*.

When *whom* functions as the object of a verb or the object of a preposition in a question, it appears out of normal order. To choose the correct pronoun, mentally restructure the question.

Whom
▶ ~~Who~~ did the Democratic Party nominate in 1952?
^

Whom is the direct object of the verb *did nominate*. This becomes clear if you restructure the question: *The Democratic Party did nominate whom in 1952?*

25c Use *whom* for subjects or objects of infinitives.

An infinitive is the word *to* followed by the base form of a verb. (See 48b.) Subjects of infinitives are an exception to the rule that subjects must be in the subjective case. The subject of an infinitive must be in the objective case. Objects of infinitives also are in the objective case.

whom
▶ When it comes to money, I know ~~who~~ to believe.
^

The infinitive phrase *whom to believe* is the direct object of the verb *know*, and *whom* is the subject of the infinitive *to believe*.

NOTE: In spoken English, *who* is often used when the correct *whom* sounds too stuffy. Although some readers will accept constructions like *Who* [not *Whom*] *did Senator Boxer replace?* in informal written English, it is safer to use *whom* in formal English.

Checking for problems with *who* and *whom*

In subordinate clauses (25a)

Isolate the subordinate clause. Then read its subject, verb, and any objects, restructuring the clause if necessary. Some writers find it helpful to substitute *he* for *who* and *him* for *whom*.

> Samuels hoped to become the business partner of (whoever/whomever) found the treasure.
>
> TEST: . . . *whoever* found the treasure. [. . . *he* found the treasure.]
>
> Ada always seemed to be bestowing a favor on (whoever/whomever) she worked for.
>
> TEST: . . . she worked for *whomever*. [. . . she worked for *him*.]

In questions (25b)

Read the subject, verb, and any objects, rearranging the sentence structure if necessary.

> (Who/Whom) conferred with Roosevelt and Stalin at Yalta in 1945?
>
> TEST: *Who* conferred . . . ?
>
> (Who/Whom) did the committee nominate?
>
> TEST: The committee did nominate *whom*?

EXERCISE 25–1   Edit the following sentences to eliminate errors in the use of *who* and *whom* (or *whoever* and *whomever*). If a sentence is correct, write "correct" after it. Answers appear in the back of the book.

> whom
> **What is the address of the artist ~~who~~ Antonio hired?**
>   ^

a. Arriving late for rehearsal, we had no idea who was supposed to dance with whom.

b. The environmental policy conference featured scholars who I had never heard of.

c. Whom did you support in last month's election for student government president?

d. Daniel always gives a holiday donation to whomever needs it.

e. So many singers came to the audition that Natalia had trouble deciding who to select for the choir.

26 Choose adjectives and adverbs with care.

Adjectives modify nouns or pronouns. They usually come before the word they modify; occasionally they function as complements following the word they modify. Adverbs modify verbs, adjectives, or other adverbs. (See 46d and 46e.)

Many adverbs are formed by adding *-ly* to adjectives (*normal, normally; smooth, smoothly*). But don't assume that all words ending in *-ly* are adverbs or that all adverbs end in *-ly*. Some adjectives end in *-ly* (*lovely, friendly*), and some adverbs don't (*always, here, there*). When in doubt, consult a dictionary.

> **Multilingual**
>
> Placement of adjectives and adverbs can be a tricky matter for multilingual writers. See 30f and 30h.

26a Use adjectives to modify nouns.

Adjectives ordinarily precede the nouns they modify. But they can also function as subject complements or object complements, following the nouns they modify.

> **Multilingual**
>
> In English, adjectives are not pluralized to agree with the words they modify: *The red* [not *reds*] *roses were a surprise.*

Subject complements

A subject complement follows a linking verb and completes the meaning of the subject. (See 47b.) When an adjective functions as a subject complement, it describes the subject.

Justice is *blind.*

Problems can arise with verbs such as *smell, taste, look,* and *feel,* which sometimes, but not always, function as linking verbs. If the word following one of these verbs describes the subject, use an adjective; if the word following the verb modifies the verb, use an adverb.

ADJECTIVE   The detective looked *cautious.*

ADVERB   The detective looked *cautiously* for fingerprints.

The adjective *cautious* describes the detective; the adverb *cautiously* modifies the verb *looked.*

Linking verbs suggest states of being, not actions. Notice, for example, the different meanings of *looked* in the preceding examples. To look cautious suggests the state of being cautious; to look cautiously is to perform an action in a cautious way.

▶ The lilacs in our backyard smell especially ~~sweetly~~ this
    sweet
    ^

year.

The verb *smell* suggests a state of being, not an action. Therefore, it should be followed by an adjective, not an adverb.

▶ The drawings looked ~~well~~ after the architect made changes.
    good
    ^

The verb *looked* is a linking verb suggesting a state of being, not an action. The adjective *good* is appropriate following the linking verb to describe *drawings.* (See also 26c.)

Object complements

An object complement follows a direct object and completes its meaning. (See 47b.) When an adjective functions as an object complement, it describes the direct object.

> Sorrow makes *us wise*.

Object complements occur with verbs such as *call, consider, create, find, keep,* and *make.* When a modifier follows the direct object of one of these verbs, use an adjective to describe the direct object; use an adverb to modify the verb.

ADJECTIVE	The referee called the plays *perfect*.
ADVERB	The referee called the plays *perfectly*.

The first sentence means that the referee considered the plays to be perfect; the second means that the referee did an excellent job of calling the plays.

26b Use adverbs to modify verbs, adjectives, and other adverbs.

When adverbs modify verbs (or verbals), they nearly always answer the question When? Where? How? Why? Under what conditions? How often? or To what degree? When adverbs modify adjectives or other adverbs, they usually qualify or intensify the meaning of the word they modify. (See 46e.)

Adjectives are often used incorrectly in place of adverbs in casual or nonstandard speech.

> ► The travel arrangement worked out ~~perfect~~ perfectly for everyone.

> ► The manager must see that the office runs ~~smooth~~ smoothly and ~~efficient~~ efficiently.

The adverb *perfectly* modifies the verb *worked out;* the adverbs *smoothly* and *efficiently* modify the verb *runs.*

▶ The chance of recovering lost property looks ~~real~~ *really* slim.

> Only adverbs can modify adjectives or other adverbs. *Really* intensifies the meaning of the adjective *slim*.

26c Distinguish between *good* and *well*, *bad* and *badly*.

Good is an adjective (*good performance*). *Well* is an adverb when it modifies a verb (*speak well*). The use of the adjective *good* in place of the adverb *well* to modify a verb is nonstandard and especially common in casual speech.

▶ We were glad that Sanya had done ~~good~~ *well* on the CPA exam.

> The adverb *well* modifies the verb *had done*.

Confusion can arise because *well* is an adjective when it modifies a noun or pronoun and means "healthy" or "satisfactory" (*The babies were well and warm*).

▶ Adrienne did not feel ~~good~~ *well*, but she performed anyway.

> As an adjective following the linking verb *did feel*, *well* describes Adrienne's health.

Bad is always an adjective and should be used to describe a noun; *badly* is always an adverb and should be used to modify a verb. The adverb *badly* is often used inappropriately to describe a noun, especially following a linking verb.

▶ The sisters felt ~~badly~~ *bad* when they realized they had left their brother out of the planning.

> The adjective *bad* is used after the linking verb *felt* to describe the noun *sisters*.

26d Use comparatives and superlatives with care.

Most adjectives and adverbs have three forms: the positive, the comparative, and the superlative.

POSITIVE	COMPARATIVE	SUPERLATIVE
soft	softer	softest
fast	faster	fastest
friendly	friendlier	friendliest
carefully	more carefully	most carefully
bad	worse	worst
good	better	best

Comparative versus superlative

Use the comparative to compare two things, the superlative to compare three or more.

▶ Which of these two low-carb drinks is ~~best?~~ better?

▶ Though Shaw and Jackson are impressive, Zhao is the ~~more~~ most qualified of the three candidates running for state senator.

Forming comparatives and superlatives

To form comparatives and superlatives of most one- and two-syllable adjectives, use the endings -er and -est: smooth, smoother, smoothest; easy, easier, easiest. With longer adjectives, use more and most (or less and least for downward comparisons): exciting, more exciting, most exciting; helpful, less helpful, least helpful.

Some one-syllable adverbs take the endings *-er* and *-est* (*fast, faster, fastest*), but longer adverbs and all of those ending in *-ly* form the comparative and superlative with *more* and *most* (or *less* and *least*).

The comparative and superlative forms of some adjectives and adverbs are irregular: *good, better, best; well, better, best; bad, worse, worst; badly, worse, worst.*

► The Kirov is the ~~talentedest~~ ballet company we have seen.
      most talented

► According to our projections, sales at local businesses will
      be ~~worser~~ than those at the chain stores this winter.
      worse

Double comparatives or superlatives

Do not use double comparatives or superlatives. When you have added *-er* or *-est* to an adjective or adverb, do not also use *more* or *most* (or *less* or *least*).

► Of all her family, Julia is the ~~most~~ happiest about the move.

► All the polls indicated that Gore was more ~~likelier~~ to win
      than Bush.
      likely

Absolute concepts

Avoid expressions such as *more straight, less perfect, very round,* and *most unique.* Either something is unique or it isn't. It is illogical to suggest that absolute concepts come in degrees.

► That is the most ~~unique~~ wedding gown I have ever seen.
      unusual

► The painting is ~~priceless~~ because it is signed.
      valuable

26e Avoid double negatives.

Standard English allows two negatives only if a positive meaning is intended: *The orchestra was not unhappy with its performance* (meaning that the orchestra was happy). Using a double negative to emphasize a negative meaning is nonstandard.

Negative modifiers such as *never*, *no*, and *not* should not be paired with other negative modifiers or with negative words such as *neither*, *none*, *no one*, *nobody*, and *nothing*.

▶ The city is not doing ~~nothing~~ ^{anything} to see that the trash is

 collected during the strike.

   The double negative *not . . . nothing* is nonstandard.

The modifiers *hardly*, *barely*, and *scarcely* are considered negatives in Standard English, so they should not be used with negatives such as *not*, *no one*, or *never*.

▶ Maxine is so weak that she ~~can't~~ ^{can} hardly climb stairs.

EXERCISE 26–1   Edit the following sentences to eliminate errors in the use of adjectives and adverbs. If a sentence is correct, write "correct" after it. Answers appear in the back of the book.

> We weren't surprised by how ~~good~~ ^{well} the sidecar racing team
>
> flowed through the tricky course.

a. Do you expect to perform good on the nursing board exam next week?

b. With the budget deadline approaching, our office hasn't hardly had time to handle routine correspondence.

c. When I worked in a flower shop, I learned that some flowers smell surprisingly bad.

d. The customer complained that he hadn't been treated nice by the agent on the phone.

e. Of all the smart people in my family, Uncle Roberto is the most cleverest.

EXERCISE 26–2 Edit the following passage to eliminate errors in the use of adjectives and adverbs.

Doctors recommend that to give skin the most fullest protection from ultraviolet rays, people should use plenty of sunscreen, limit sun exposure, and wear protective clothing. The commonest sunscreens today are known as "broad spectrum" because they block out both UVA and UVB rays. These lotions don't feel any differently on the skin from the old UVA-only types, but they work best at preventing premature aging and skin cancer.

Many sunscreens claim to be waterproof, but they won't hardly provide adequate coverage after extended periods of swimming or perspiring. To protect good, even waterproof sunscreens should be reapplied liberal and often. All areas of exposed skin, including ears, backs of hands, and tops of feet, need to be coated good to avoid burning or damage. Some people's skin reacts bad to PABA, or para-aminobenzoic acid, so PABA-free (hypoallergenic) sunscreens are widely available. In addition to recommending sunscreen, doctors almost unanimously agree that people should stay out of the sun when rays are the most strongest—between 10:00 a.m. and 3:00 p.m.— and should limit time in the sun. They also suggest that people wear long-sleeved shirts, broad-brimmed hats, and long pants whenever possible.

27 Choose appropriate verb forms, tenses, and moods in Standard English.

In speech, some people use verb forms and tenses that match a home dialect or variety of English. In writing, use Standard English verb forms unless you are quoting nonstandard speech or using alternative forms for literary effect. (See 17d.)

Except for the verb *be*, all verbs in English have five forms. The following list shows the five forms and provides a sample sentence in which each might appear.

BASE FORM	Usually I (*walk*, *ride*).
PAST TENSE	Yesterday I (*walked*, *rode*).
PAST PARTICIPLE	I have (*walked*, *ridden*) many times before.
PRESENT PARTICIPLE	I am (*walking*, *riding*) right now.
-S FORM	He/she/it (*walks*, *rides*) regularly.

The verb *be* has eight forms instead of the usual five: *be, am, is, are, was, were, being, been.*

27a Choose Standard English forms of irregular verbs.

For all regular verbs, the past-tense and past-participle forms are the same (ending in *-ed* or *-d*), so there is no danger of confusion. This is not true, however, for irregular verbs, such as the following.

BASE FORM	PAST TENSE	PAST PARTICIPLE
go	went	gone
break	broke	broken
fly	flew	flown

The past-tense form always occurs alone, without a helping verb. It expresses action that occurred entirely in the past: *I rode to work yesterday. I walked to work last Tuesday.* The past participle is used with a helping verb. It forms the perfect tenses with *has*, *have*, or *had*; it forms the passive voice with *be, am, is, are, was, were, being,* or *been.* (See 46c for a complete list of helping verbs and 27f for a survey of tenses.)

PAST TENSE   Last July, we *went* to Seoul.

HELPING VERB + PAST PARTICIPLE   We *have gone* to Seoul twice.

The list of common irregular verbs beginning on the next page will help you distinguish between the past tense and the past participle. Choose the past-participle form if the verb in your sentence requires a helping verb; choose the past-tense form if the verb does not require a helping verb. (See verb tenses in 27f.)

>   saw
> ▶ Yesterday we ~~seen~~ a documentary about Isabel Allende.
>   ^
>
> The past-tense *saw* is required because there is no helping verb.

>   stolen
> ▶ The pickup truck was apparently ~~stole~~ while the driver
>   ^
> ate lunch.

>   fallen
> ▶ By Friday, the stock market had ~~fell~~ two hundred points.
>   ^
>
> Because of the helping verbs *was* and *had*, the past-participle forms are required: *was stolen, had fallen.*

When in doubt about the Standard English forms of irregular verbs, consult the list on pages 342–44 or look up the base form of the verb in the dictionary, which also lists any irregular forms. (If no additional forms are listed in the dictionary, the verb is regular, not irregular.)

Common irregular verbs

BASE FORM	PAST TENSE	PAST PARTICIPLE
arise	arose	arisen
awake	awoke, awaked	awaked, awoke, awoken
be	was, were	been
beat	beat	beaten, beat
become	became	become
begin	began	begun
bend	bent	bent
bite	bit	bitten, bit
blow	blew	blown
break	broke	broken
bring	brought	brought
build	built	built
burst	burst	burst
buy	bought	bought
catch	caught	caught
choose	chose	chosen
cling	clung	clung
come	came	come
cost	cost	cost
deal	dealt	dealt
dig	dug	dug
dive	dived, dove	dived
do	did	done
draw	drew	drawn
dream	dreamed, dreamt	dreamed, dreamt
drink	drank	drunk
drive	drove	driven
eat	ate	eaten
fall	fell	fallen
fight	fought	fought
find	found	found
fly	flew	flown
forget	forgot	forgotten, forgot
freeze	froze	frozen
get	got	gotten, got

BASE FORM	PAST TENSE	PAST PARTICIPLE
give	gave	given
go	went	gone
grow	grew	grown
hang (execute)	hanged	hanged
hang (suspend)	hung	hung
have	had	had
hear	heard	heard
hide	hid	hidden
hurt	hurt	hurt
keep	kept	kept
know	knew	known
lay (put)	laid	laid
lead	led	led
lend	lent	lent
let (allow)	let	let
lie (recline)	lay	lain
lose	lost	lost
make	made	made
prove	proved	proved, proven
read	read	read
ride	rode	ridden
ring	rang	rung
rise (get up)	rose	risen
run	ran	run
say	said	said
see	saw	seen
send	sent	sent
set (place)	set	set
shake	shook	shaken
shoot	shot	shot
shrink	shrank	shrunk
sing	sang	sung
sink	sank	sunk
sit (be seated)	sat	sat
slay	slew	slain
sleep	slept	slept
speak	spoke	spoken

BASE FORM	PAST TENSE	PAST PARTICIPLE
spin	spun	spun
spring	sprang	sprung
stand	stood	stood
steal	stole	stolen
sting	stung	stung
strike	struck	struck, stricken
swear	swore	sworn
swim	swam	swum
swing	swung	swung
take	took	taken
teach	taught	taught
throw	threw	thrown
wake	woke, waked	waked, woken
wear	wore	worn
win	won	won
wring	wrung	wrung
write	wrote	written

27b Distinguish among the forms of *lie* and *lay*.

Writers and speakers frequently confuse the various forms of *lie* (meaning "to recline or rest on a surface") and *lay* (meaning "to put or place something"). *Lie* is an intransitive verb; it does not take a direct object: *The tax forms lie on the table.* The verb *lay* is transitive; it takes a direct object: *Please lay the tax forms on the table.* (See 47b.)

In addition to confusing the meaning of *lie* and *lay*, writers and speakers are often unfamiliar with the Standard English forms of these verbs.

BASE FORM	PAST TENSE	PAST PARTICIPLE	PRESENT PARTICIPLE
lie ("recline")	lay	lain	lying
lay ("put")	laid	laid	laying

▶ Sue was so exhausted that she ~~laid~~ lay down for a nap.

The past-tense form of *lie* ("to recline") is *lay*.

> lain
> The patient had ~~laid~~ in an uncomfortable position all night.
> ^

The past-participle form of *lie* ("to recline") is *lain*. If the correct English seems too stilted, recast the sentence: *The patient had been lying in an uncomfortable position all night.*

> laid
> The prosecutor ~~lay~~ the pistol on a table close to the jurors.
> ^

The past-tense form of *lay* ("to place") is *laid*.

> lying
> Letters dating from 1915 were ~~laying~~ in a corner of the chest.
> ^

The present participle of *lie* ("to rest on a surface") is *lying*.

EXERCISE 27–1 Edit the following sentences to eliminate problems with irregular verbs. If a sentence is correct, write "correct" after it. Answers appear in the back of the book.

saw
The ranger ~~seen~~ the forest fire ten miles away.
^

a. When I get the urge to exercise, I lay down until it passes.

b. Grandmother had drove our new hybrid to the sunrise church service, so we were left with the van.

c. A pile of dirty rags was laying at the bottom of the stairs.

d. How did the game know that the player had went from the room with the blue ogre to the hall where the gold was heaped?

e. Abraham Lincoln took good care of his legal clients; the contracts he drew for the Illinois Central Railroad could never be broke.

27c Use -*s* (or -*es*) endings on present-tense verbs that have third-person singular subjects.

All singular nouns (*child, tree*) and the pronouns *he, she,* and *it* are third-person singular; indefinite pronouns such as *everyone* and *neither* are also third-person singular. When the subject of a sentence is third-person singular, its verb takes an *-s* or *-es* ending in the present tense. (See also 21.)

	SINGULAR		PLURAL	
FIRST PERSON	I	know	we	know
SECOND PERSON	you	know	you	know
THIRD PERSON	he/she/it	knows	they	know
	child	knows	parents	know
	everyone	knows		

▶ My neighbor ~~drive~~ ^drives^ to Marco Island every weekend.

▶ McBride ~~argue~~ ^argues^ that hip-hop "represents a deeper dream: a better life" (560).

▶ Sulfur dioxide ~~turn~~ ^turns^ leaves yellow and ~~dissolve~~ ^dissolves^ marble.

The subjects *neighbor, McBride,* and *sulfur dioxide* are third-person singular, so the verbs must end in *-s.*

TIP: Do not add the *-s* ending to the verb if the subject is not third-person singular. The writers of the following sentences added *-s* endings where they don't belong.

▶ I prepares system specifications for every installation.

The writer mistakenly concluded that the *-s* ending belongs on present-tense verbs used with *all* singular subjects, not just *third-person* singular subjects. The pronoun *I* is first-person singular, so its verb does not require the *-s.*

▶ The wood floors requires continual sweeping.

The writer mistakenly thought that the verb needed an *-s* ending because of the plural subject. But the *-s* ending is used only on present-tense verbs with third-person *singular* subjects.

Has *versus* have

In the present tense, use *has* with third-person singular subjects; all other subjects require *have*.

	SINGULAR		PLURAL	
FIRST PERSON	I	have	we	have
SECOND PERSON	you	have	you	have
THIRD PERSON	he/she/it	has	they	have

▶ This respected musician almost always ~~have~~ has a message to convey in his work.

> The subject, *musician*, is third-person singular, so the verb should be *has*.

▶ My law classes ~~has~~ have helped me understand contracts.

> The subject, *classes*, is third-person plural, so Standard English requires the verb *have*. *Has* is used only with third-person singular subjects.

Does *versus* do *and* doesn't *versus* don't

In the present tense, use *does* and *doesn't* with third-person singular subjects; all other subjects require *do* and *don't*.

	SINGULAR		PLURAL	
FIRST PERSON	I	do/don't	we	do/don't
SECOND PERSON	you	do/don't	you	do/don't
THIRD PERSON	he/she/it	does/doesn't	they	do/don't

▶ Grandfather really ~~don't~~ doesn't have a place to call home.

> *Grandfather* is third-person singular, so the verb should be *doesn't*.

Am, is, and are; was and were

The verb *be* has three forms in the present tense (*am, is, are*) and two in the past tense (*was, were*).

	SINGULAR		PLURAL	
FIRST PERSON	I	am/was	we	are/were
SECOND PERSON	you	are/were	you	are/were
THIRD PERSON	he/she/it	is/was	they	are/were

> were
▶ Did you think you ~~was~~ going to drown?
>   ^

The subject *you* is second-person singular, so the verb should be *were*.

27d Do not omit *-ed* endings on verbs.

Speakers who do not fully pronounce *-ed* endings sometimes omit them unintentionally in writing. Failure to pronounce *-ed* endings is common in many dialects and in informal speech even in Standard English. In the following frequently used words and phrases, for example, the *-ed* ending is not always fully pronounced.

advised	developed	prejudiced	supposed to
asked	fixed	pronounced	used to
concerned	frightened	stereotyped	

When a verb is regular, both the past tense and the past participle are formed by adding *-ed* (or *-d*) to the base form of the verb.

Past tense

Use the ending *-ed* or *-d* to express the past tense of regular verbs. The past tense is used when the action occurred entirely in the past.

▶ In 1998, journalist Barbara Ehrenreich ~~decide~~ to try to live
    decided

on minimum wage.

▶ Last summer, my counselor ~~advise~~ me to ask my graphic
    advised

arts instructor for help.

Past participles

Past participles are used in three ways: (1) following *have, has,* or *had* to form one of the perfect tenses; (2) following *be, am, is, are, was, were, being,* or *been* to form the passive voice; and (3) as adjectives modifying nouns or pronouns. The perfect tenses are listed on page 352, and the passive voice is discussed in 8a. For a discussion of participles as adjectives, see 48b.

▶ Robin has ~~ask~~ the Office of Student Affairs for more
    asked

housing staff for next year.

> *Has asked* is the present perfect tense (*have* or *has* followed by a past participle).

▶ Though it is not a new phenomenon, domestic violence is
    publicized
now ~~publicize~~ more than ever.

> *Is publicized* is a verb in the passive voice (a form of *be* followed by a past participle).

▶ All kickboxing classes end in a cool-down period to stretch
    tightened
~~tighten~~ muscles.

> The past participle *tightened* functions as an adjective modifying the noun *muscles*.

27e Do not omit needed verbs.

Although Standard English allows some linking verbs and help-ing verbs to be contracted in informal contexts, it does not allow them to be omitted.

Linking verbs, used to link subjects to subject complements, are frequently a form of *be*: *be, am, is, are, was, were, being, been*. (See 47b.) Some of these forms may be contracted (*I'm, she's, we're, you're, they're*), but they should not be omitted altogether.

▶ When we quiet in the evening, we can hear the crickets.
^are^

▶ Sherman Alexie a Native American author whose stories
^is^

   have been made into a film.

Helping verbs, used with main verbs, include forms of *be, do*, and *have* and the modal verbs *can, will, shall, could, would, should, may, might*, and *must*. (See 46c.) Some helping verbs may be contracted (*he's leaving, we'll celebrate, they've been told*), but they should not be omitted altogether.

▶ We been in Chicago since last Thursday.
^have^

▶ Do you know someone who be good for the job?
^would^

Multilingual

Some languages do not require a linking verb between a subject and its complement. English, however, requires a verb in every sentence. See 30a.

▶ Every night, I read a short book to my daughter. When I
^am^

   too busy, my husband reads to her.

EXERCISE 27–5   Edit the following sentences to eliminate problems with *-s* and *-ed* verb forms and with omitted verbs. If a sentence is correct, write "correct" after it. Answers appear in the back of the book.

> *covers*
> The Pell Grant sometimes ~~cover~~ the student's full tuition.
> ^

a. The glass sculptures of the Swan Boats was prominent in the brightly lit lobby.

b. Visitors to the glass museum were not suppose to touch the exhibits.

c. Our church has all the latest technology, even a close-circuit television.

d. Christos didn't know about Marlo's promotion because he never listens. He always talking.

e. Most psychologists agree that no one performs well under stress.

27f Choose the appropriate verb tense.

Tenses indicate the time of an action in relation to the time of the speaking or writing about that action.

The most common problem with tenses—shifting confusingly from one tense to another—is discussed in section 13. Other problems with tenses are detailed in this section, after the following survey of tenses.

Survey of tenses

Tenses are classified as present, past, and future, with simple, perfect, and progressive forms for each.

Simple tenses   The simple tenses indicate relatively simple time relations. The *simple present* tense is used primarily for actions occurring at the same time they are being discussed or for actions occurring regularly. The *simple past* tense is used for actions completed in the past. The *simple future* tense is used for actions that will occur in the future. In the following table, the simple tenses are given for the regular verb *walk*, the irregular verb *ride*, and the highly irregular verb *be*.

SIMPLE PRESENT

SINGULAR		PLURAL	
I	walk, ride, am	we	walk, ride, are
you	walk, ride, are	you	walk, ride, are
he/she/it	walks, rides, is	they	walk, ride, are

SIMPLE PAST

SINGULAR		PLURAL	
I	walked, rode, was	we	walked, rode, were
you	walked, rode, were	you	walked, rode, were
he/she/it	walked, rode, was	they	walked, rode, were

SIMPLE FUTURE

I, you, he/she/it, we, they   will walk, ride, be

Perfect tenses More complex time relations are indicated by the perfect tenses. A verb in one of the perfect tenses (a form of *have* plus the past participle) expresses an action that was or will be completed at the time of another action.

PRESENT PERFECT

I, you, we, they	have walked, ridden, been
he/she/it	has walked, ridden, been

PAST PERFECT

I, you, he/she/it, we, they   had walked, ridden, been

FUTURE PERFECT

I, you, he/she/it, we, they   will have walked, ridden, been

Progressive forms The simple and perfect tenses have progressive forms that describe actions in progress. A progressive verb consists of a form of *be* followed by a present participle. The progressive forms are not normally used with certain verbs, such as *believe, know, hear,* and *seem.*

PRESENT PROGRESSIVE

I	am walking, riding, being
he/she/it	is walking, riding, being
you, we, they	are walking, riding, being

PAST PROGRESSIVE

I, he/she/it	was walking, riding, being
you, we, they	were walking, riding, being

FUTURE PROGRESSIVE

I, you, he/she/it, we, they	will be walking, riding, being

PRESENT PERFECT PROGRESSIVE

I, you, we, they	have been walking, riding, being
he/she/it	has been walking, riding, being

PAST PERFECT PROGRESSIVE

I, you, he/she/it, we, they	had been walking, riding, being

FUTURE PERFECT PROGRESSIVE

I, you, he/she/it, we, they	will have been walking, riding, being

Multilingual

See 28a for more specific examples of verb tenses that can be challenging for multilingual writers.

Special uses of the present tense

Use the present tense when expressing general truths, when writing about literature, and when quoting, summarizing, or paraphrasing an author's views.

General truths or scientific principles should appear in the present tense unless such principles have been disproved.

▶ Galileo taught that the earth ~~revolved~~ around the sun.
  revolves

Because Galileo's teaching has not been discredited, the verb should be in the present tense. The following sentence, however, is acceptable: *Ptolemy taught that the sun revolved around the earth.*

When writing about a work of literature, you may be tempted to use the past tense. The convention in the humanities, however, is to describe fictional events in the present tense.

▶ In Masuji Ibuse's *Black Rain*, a child ~~reached~~ for a
  reaches

  pomegranate in his mother's garden, and a moment later

  he ~~was~~ dead, killed by the blast of the atomic bomb.
  is

When you are quoting, summarizing, or paraphrasing the author of a nonliterary work, use present-tense verbs such as *writes, reports, asserts*, and so on to introduce the source. This convention is usually followed even when the author is dead (unless a date or the context specifies the time of writing).

▶ Dr. Jerome Groopman ~~argued~~ that doctors are
  argues

  "susceptible to the subtle and not so subtle efforts of the

  pharmaceutical industry to sculpt our thinking" (9).

In MLA style, signal phrases are written in the present tense, not the past tense. (See also 55c.)

APA NOTE: When you are documenting a paper with the APA (American Psychological Association) style of in-text citations, use past tense verbs such as *reported* or *demonstrated* or present perfect verbs such as *has reported* or *has demonstrated* to introduce the source. (See 60c.)

The past perfect tense

The past perfect tense consists of a past participle preceded by *had* (*had worked, had gone*). This tense is used for an action already completed by the time of another past action or for an action already completed at some specific past time.

> Everyone *had spoken* by the time I arrived.

> I pleaded my case, but Paula *had made up* her mind.

Writers sometimes use the simple past tense when they should use the past perfect.

▶ By the time dinner was served, the guest of honor left.
^had

The past perfect tense is needed because the action of leaving was already completed at a specific past time (when dinner was served).

Some writers tend to overuse the past perfect tense. Do not use the past perfect if two past actions occurred at the same time.

▶ When Ernest Hemingway lived in Cuba, he ~~had written~~
^wrote

For Whom the Bell Tolls.

Sequence of tenses with infinitives and participles

An infinitive is the base form of a verb preceded by *to*. (See 48b.) Use the present infinitive to show action at the same time as or later than the action of the verb in the sentence.

▶ Barb had hoped to ~~have paid~~ the bill by May 1.
                    ^
               pay

The action expressed in the infinitive (*to pay*) occurred later than the action of the sentence's verb (*had hoped*).

Use the perfect form of an infinitive (*to have* followed by the past participle) for an action occurring earlier than that of the verb in the sentence.

▶ Dan would like to ~~join~~ the navy, but he could not swim.
                    ^
             have joined

The liking occurs in the present; the joining would have occurred in the past.

Like the tense of an infinitive, the tense of a participle is governed by the tense of the sentence's verb. Use the present participle (ending in *-ing*) for an action occurring at the same time as that of the sentence's verb.

> *Hiking* the Appalachian Trail, we spotted many wildflowers.

Use the past participle (such as *given* or *helped*) or the present perfect participle (*having* plus the past participle) for an action occurring before that of the verb.

> *Discovered* off the coast of Florida, the Spanish galleon yielded many treasures.

> *Having worked* her way through college, Lee graduated debt-free.

27g Use the subjunctive mood in the few contexts that require it.

There are three moods in English: the *indicative*, used for facts, opinions, and questions; the *imperative*, used for orders or advice; and the *subjunctive*, used in certain contexts to express wishes, requests, or conditions contrary to fact. For many writers, the subjunctive causes the most problems.

Forms of the subjunctive

In the subjunctive mood, present-tense verbs do not change form to indicate the number and person of the subject (see 21). Instead, the subjunctive uses the base form of the verb (*be, drive, employ*) with all subjects. Also, in the subjunctive mood, there is only one past-tense form of *be: were* (never *was*).

> It is important that you *be* [not *are*] prepared for the interview.

> We asked that she *drive* [not *drives*] more slowly.

> If I *were* [not *was*] you, I'd try a new strategy.

Uses of the subjunctive

The subjunctive mood appears only in a few contexts: in contrary-to-fact clauses beginning with *if* or expressing a wish; in *that* clauses following verbs such as *ask, insist, recommend, request*, and *suggest*; and in certain set expressions.

In contrary-to-fact clauses beginning with *if* When a subordinate clause beginning with *if* expresses a condition contrary to fact, use the subjunctive *were* in place of *was*.

> ▶ If I ~~was~~ a member of Congress, I would vote for that bill.
>   *were*

> ▶ The astronomers would be able to see the moons of Jupiter tonight if the weather ~~was~~ clearer.
>   *were*

> The writer is not a member of Congress, and the weather is not clear.

Do not use the subjunctive mood in *if* clauses expressing conditions that exist or may exist.

> If Dana *wins* the contest, she will leave for Barcelona in June.

In contrary-to-fact clauses expressing a wish In formal English, use the subjunctive *were* in clauses expressing a wish or desire.

INFORMAL	I wish that Dr. Vaughn *was* my professor.
FORMAL	I wish that Dr. Vaughn *were* my professor.

In *that* clauses following verbs such as *ask*, *insist*, *request*, and *suggest* Because requests have not yet become reality, they are expressed in the subjunctive mood.

> be
> ▶ Professor Moore insists that her students ~~are~~ on time.
>   ^

> file
> ▶ We recommend that Lambert ~~files~~ form 1050 soon.
>   ^

In certain set expressions The subjunctive mood, once more widely used, remains in certain set expressions: *Be that as it may, as it were, far be it from me,* and so on.

EXERCISE 27–9 Edit the following sentences to eliminate errors in verb tense or mood. If a sentence is correct, write "correct" after it. Answers appear in the back of the book.

> had been
> After the path ~~was~~ plowed, we were able to walk in the park.
>   ^

a. The palace of Knossos in Crete is believed to have been destroyed by fire around 1375 BCE.

b. Watson and Crick discovered the mechanism that controlled inheritance in all life: the workings of the DNA molecule.

c. When city planners proposed rezoning the waterfront, did they know that the mayor promised to curb development in that neighborhood?

d. Tonight's concert begins at 9:30. If it was earlier, I'd consider going.

e. The math position was filled by the instructor who had been running the tutoring center.

PART VI

Multilingual Writers and ESL Challenges

28 Verbs 361

29 Articles (*a, an, the*) 378

30 Sentence structure 389

31 Prepositions and idiomatic expressions 399

Multilingual Writers and ESL Challenges

ONLINE ACTIVITIES:

 Writer's Help 2.0
macmillan learning

writershelp.com/hacker

 LaunchPad Solo
macmillan learning

macmillanhighered.com/
launchpadsolo/hacker

Verbs for multilingual
writers

8 Exercises
1 LearningCurve activity

Articles for multilingual
writers

4 Exercises
1 LearningCurve activity

Sentence structure for
multilingual writers

8 Exercises
1 LearningCurve activity

Prepositions and idiomatic
expressions for multilingual
writers

2 Exercises
1 LearningCurve activity

This part of *The Bedford Handbook* is primarily for multilingual writers. You may find this section helpful if you learned English as a second language (ESL) or if you speak a language other than English with your friends and family.

Besides concentrating on specific points of grammar and usage, you can strengthen your English-language skills by reading, writing, listening to, and speaking English in a variety of settings.

- **Reading:** To familiarize yourself with the ways in which other writers use the language, you can read textbooks, with a focus on vocabulary and sentence patterns, or read fiction or nonfiction books, newspapers, magazines, and Web sites to absorb popular uses of language.

- **Writing:** You will write in your college courses, but you also can practice your skills by writing e-mail messages or blog posts for various audiences or by keeping a personal journal.

- **Listening:** Paying attention to and following directions in class can help you focus on academic conversation. Listening to speakers on campus, to friends, or to TV or radio programs can help you understand colloquial usage.

- **Speaking:** Conversing with English-speaking friends privately or in class discussions can help you develop an "ear" for pronunciation and appropriate usage in various situations.

28 Verbs

Both native and nonnative speakers of English encounter challenges with verbs. Section 28 focuses on specific challenges that multilingual writers sometimes face. You can find more help with verbs in other sections in the book:

making subjects and verbs agree (21)

using irregular verb forms (27a, 27b)

leaving off verb endings (27c, 27d)

choosing the correct verb tense (27f)

avoiding inappropriate uses of the passive voice (8a)

28a Use the appropriate verb form and tense.

This section offers a brief review of English verb forms and tenses. For additional help, see 27 and 46c.

Basic verb forms

Every main verb in English has five forms, which are used to create all of the verb tenses in Standard English. The following chart shows these forms for the regular verb *help* and the irregular verbs *give* and *be*. See 27a for a list of other common irregular verbs.

Basic verb forms			
	REGULAR VERB *HELP*	IRREGULAR VERB *GIVE*	IRREGULAR VERB *BE**
BASE FORM	help	give	be
PAST TENSE	helped	gave	was, were
PAST PARTICIPLE	helped	given	been
PRESENT PARTICIPLE	helping	giving	being
-S FORM	helps	gives	is

*Be also has the forms *am* and *are*, which are used in the present tense.

Verb tenses commonly used in the active voice

For descriptions and examples of all verb tenses, see 27f. For verb tenses commonly used in the passive voice, see the chart beginning on page 366.

Simple tenses
For general facts, states of being, habitual actions

Simple present	**Base form or -s form**
• general facts	College students often *study* late at night.
• states of being	Water *becomes* steam at 100 degrees centigrade.
• habitual, repetitive actions	We *donate* to a different charity each year.
• scheduled future events	The train *arrives* tomorrow at 6:30 p.m.

Note: For uses of the present tense in writing about literature, see page 354.

Simple past	**Base form + -ed or -d or irregular form**
• completed actions at a specific time in the past	The storm *destroyed* their property. She *drove* to Montana three years ago.
• facts or states of being in the past	When I was young, I usually *walked* to school with my sister.

Simple future	***will* + base form**
• future actions, promises, or predictions	I *will exercise* tomorrow. The snowfall *will begin* around midnight.

Simple progressive forms
For continuing actions

Present progressive	***am, is, are* + present participle**
• actions in progress at the present time, not continuing indefinitely	The students *are taking* an exam in Room 105. The valet *is parking* the car.
• future actions (with *leave, go, come, move,* etc.)	I *am leaving* tomorrow morning.

VERB TENSES COMMONLY USED IN THE ACTIVE VOICE (cont.)

Past progressive   **was, were + present participle**

- actions in progress at a specific time in the past

They *were swimming* when the storm struck.

- *was going to, were going to* for past plans that did not happen

We *were going* to drive to Florida for spring break, but the car broke down.

Note: Some verbs are not normally used in the progressive: *appear, believe, belong, contain, have, hear, know, like, need, see, seem, taste, understand,* and *want.*

     want
▶ I ~~am wanting~~ to see August Wilson's *Radio Golf.*

Perfect tenses
For actions that happened before another present or past time

Present perfect   **has, have + past participle**

- repetitive or constant actions that began in the past and continue to the present

I *have loved* cats since I was a child. Alicia *has worked* in Kenya for ten years.

- actions that happened at an unknown or unspecific time in the past

Stephen *has visited* Bogotá three times.

Past perfect   **had + past participle**

- actions that began or occurred before another time in the past

She *had* just *crossed* the street when the runaway car crashed into the building.

Note: For more on the past perfect, see 27f. For uses of the past perfect in conditional sentences, see 28e.

VERB TENSES COMMONLY USED IN THE ACTIVE VOICE (*cont.*)

Perfect progressive forms
For continuous past actions before another present or past time

Present perfect progressive	**has, have + been + present participle**
• continuous actions that began in the past and continue to the present	Yolanda *has been trying* to get a job in Boston for five years.

Past perfect progressive	***had + been + present participle***
• actions that began and continued in the past until another past action	By the time I moved to Georgia, I *had been supporting* myself for five years.

Verb tenses

Section 27f describes all the verb tenses in English, showing the forms of a regular verb, an irregular verb, and the verb *be* in each tense. The chart beginning on page 363 provides more details about the tenses commonly used in the active voice in writing; the chart beginning on page 366 gives details about tenses commonly used in the passive voice.

28b To write a verb in the passive voice, use a form of *be* with the past participle.

When a sentence is written in the passive voice, the subject receives the action instead of doing it. (See 47c.)

> The solution *was measured* by the lab assistant.

> Melissa *was taken* to the theater.

To form the passive voice, use a form of *be*—*am, is, are, was, were, being, be,* or *been*—followed by the past participle of the

Verb tenses commonly used in the passive voice

For details about verb tenses in the active voice, see pages 363–65.

Simple tenses (passive voice)

Simple present   *am, is, are* + past participle
- general facts   Breakfast *is served* daily.
- habitual, repetitive actions   The receipts *are counted* every night.

Simple past   *was, were* + past participle
- completed past actions   He *was punished* for being late.

Simple future   *will be* + past participle
- future actions, promises,   The decision *will be made* by the
  or predictions   committee next week.

Simple progressive forms (passive voice)

Present progressive   *am, is, are* + *being* + past participle
- actions in progress at the   The new stadium *is being built* with
  present time   private money.
- future actions (with *leave,*   Jo *is being moved* to a new class next
  go, come, move, etc.)   month.

Past progressive   *was, were* + *being* + past participle
- actions in progress at a   We thought we *were being followed.*
  specific time in the past

Perfect tenses (passive voice)

Present perfect   *has, have* + *been* + past participle
- actions that began in   The flight *has been delayed* because
  the past and continue   of storms in the Midwest.
  to the present
- actions that happened at   Wars *have been fought* throughout
  an unknown or unspecific   history.
  time in the past

VERB TENSES COMMONLY USED IN THE PASSIVE VOICE (*cont.*)

Past perfect	*had* + *been* + past participle
• actions that began or occurred before another time in the past	He *had been given* all the hints he needed to complete the puzzle.

Note: Future progressive, future perfect, and perfect progressive forms are not used in the passive voice.

main verb: *was chosen, are remembered.* (Sometimes a form of *be* follows another helping verb: *will be considered, could have been broken.*)

> ~~written~~
> ▶ *Dreaming in Cuban* was ~~writing~~ by Cristina García.
>   ∧

In the passive voice, the past participle *written*, not the present participle *writing*, must follow *was* (the past tense of *be*).

> tested.
> ▶ The child is being ~~test.~~
>   ∧

The past participle *tested*, not the base form *test*, must be used with *is being* to form the passive voice.

For details on forming the passive in various tenses, consult the chart on pages 366–67. (The active voice is generally stronger and more direct than the passive voice. The passive voice does have appropriate uses; see 8a and 47c.)

NOTE: Only transitive verbs, those that take direct objects, may be used in the passive voice. Intransitive verbs such as *occur, happen, sleep, die, become,* and *fall* are not used in the passive. (See 47b.)

> ▶ The accident ~~was~~ happened suddenly.

EXERCISE 28–1 Revise the following sentences to correct errors in verb forms and tenses in the active and the passive voice. You may need to look at 27a for the correct form of some irregular verbs and at 27f for help with tenses. Answers appear in the back of the book.

> begins
> **The meeting ~~begin~~ tonight at 7:30.**
>   ^

a. In the past, tobacco companies deny any connection between smoking and health problems.

b. The volunteer's compassion has touch many lives.

c. I am wanting to register for a summer tutoring session.

d. By the end of the year, the state will have test 139 birds for avian flu.

e. The golfers were prepare for all weather conditions.

28c Use the base form of the verb after a modal.

The modal verbs are *can, could, may, might, must, shall, should, will,* and *would.* (*Ought to* is also considered a modal verb.) The modals are used with the base form of a verb to show ability, certainty, necessity, permission, obligation, or possibility.

Modals and the verbs that follow them do not change form to indicate tense. For a summary of modals and their meanings, see the chart on pages 369–70. (See also 27e.)

>   launch
> ▶ **The art museum will ~~launches~~ its fundraising campaign**
>   ^
> **next month.**

The modal *will* must be followed by the base form *launch,* not the present tense *launches.*

Modals and their meanings

can

- general ability (present)

  Ants *can survive* anywhere, even in space. Jorge *can run* a marathon faster than his brother.

- informal requests or permission

  Can you *tell* me where the light is? Sandy *can borrow* my calculator.

could

- general ability (past)

  Lea *could read* when she was only three years old.

- polite, informal requests or permission

  Could you *give* me that pen?

may

- formal requests or permission

  May I *see* the report? Students *may park* only in the yellow zone.

- possibility

  I *may try* to finish my homework tonight, or I *may wake up* early and *finish* it tomorrow.

might

- possibility

  Funding for the language lab *might double* by 2020.

Note: *Might* usually expresses a stronger possibility than *may*.

must

- necessity (present or future)

  To be effective, welfare-to-work programs *must provide* access to job training.

- strong probability

  Amy *must be* nervous. [She is probably nervous.]

- near certainty (present or past)

  I *must have left* my wallet at home. [I almost certainly left my wallet at home.] →

MODALS AND THEIR MEANINGS (*cont.*)

should	
• suggestions or advice	Diabetics *should drink* plenty of water every day.
• obligations or duties	The government *should protect* citizens' rights.
• expectations	The books *should arrive* soon. [We expect the books to arrive soon.]

will	
• certainty	If you don't leave now, you *will be* late for your rehearsal.
• requests	*Will* you *help* me study for my psychology exam?
• promises and offers	Jonah *will arrange* the carpool.

would	
• polite requests	*Would* you *help* me carry these books? I *would like* some coffee. [*Would like* is more polite than *want*.]
• habitual or repeated actions (in the past)	Whenever Elena needed help with sewing, she *would call* her aunt.

► The translator could ~~spoke~~ _{^speak} many languages, so the

ambassador hired her for the Asian tour.

The modal *could* must be followed by the base form *speak*, not the past tense *spoke*.

TIP: Do not use *to* before a main verb that follows a modal.

► Gina can ~~to~~ drive us home if we miss the last train.

For the use of modals in conditional sentences, see 28e.

EXERCISE 28–4 Edit the following sentences to correct errors in the use of verb forms with modals. You may find it helpful to consult the chart on pages 369–70. If a sentence is correct, write "correct" after it. Answers appear in the back of the book.

We should ~~to~~ order pizza for dinner.

a. A major league pitcher can to throw a baseball more than ninety-five miles per hour.

b. The writing center tutor will helps you revise your essay.

c. A reptile must adjusted its body temperature to its environment.

d. In some states, individuals may renew a driver's license online.

e. My uncle, a cartoonist, could sketched a face in less than a minute.

28d To make negative verb forms, add *not* in the appropriate place.

If the verb is the simple present or past tense of *be* (*am, is, are, was, were*), add *not* after the verb.

> George is *not* a member of the club.

For simple present-tense verbs other than *be*, use *do* or *does* plus *not* before the base form of the verb. (For the correct forms of *do* and *does*, see the chart on p. 347.)

▶ Mariko not want more dessert.
        ^ does

▶ Mariko does not wants more dessert.

For simple past-tense verbs other than *be*, use *did* plus *not* before the base form of the verb.

▶ They did not ~~planted~~ corn this year.
         ^ plant

In a verb phrase consisting of one or more helping verbs and a present or past participle (*is watching*, *were living*, *has played*, *could have been driven*), use the word *not* after the first helping verb.

▶ Inna should have ~~not~~ gone dancing last night.
             ^*not*

▶ Sarvesh is ~~no~~ singing this weekend.
          ^*not*

NOTE: English allows only one negative in an independent clause to express a negative idea; using more than one is an error known as a *double negative* (see 26e for more on double negatives to express a positive idea).

▶ We could not find ~~no~~ books about the history of our school.
             ^*any*

28e In a conditional sentence, choose verb tenses according to the type of condition expressed in the sentence.

Conditional sentences contain two clauses: a subordinate clause (usually starting with *if*, *when*, or *unless*) and an independent clause. The subordinate clause (sometimes called the *if* or *unless* clause) states the condition or cause; the independent clause states the result or effect. In each example in this section, the subordinate clause (*if* clause) is marked SUB, and the independent clause is marked IND. (See 48e, on subordinate clauses.)

Factual

Factual conditional sentences express relationships based on facts. If the relationship is a scientific truth, use the present tense in both clauses.

        ┌──── SUB ────┐ ┌─ IND ─┐
If water *cools* to 32 degrees Fahrenheit, it *freezes*.

If the sentence describes a condition that is (or was) habitually true, use the same tense in both clauses.

> ┌─────── SUB ───────┐ ┌─────── IND ───────┐
> When Sue *jogs* along the canal, her dog *runs* ahead of her.

> ┌─────── SUB ───────┐ ┌─── IND ───┐
> Whenever the coach *asked* for help, I *volunteered*.

Predictive

Predictive conditional sentences are used to predict the future or to express future plans or possibilities. To form a predictive sentence, use a present-tense verb in the subordinate clause; in the independent clause, use the modal *will, can, may, should,* or *might* plus the base form of the verb.

> ┌─────── SUB ───────┐ ┌─────── IND ───────┐
> If you *practice* regularly, your tennis game *should improve*.

> ┌─────── IND ───────┐ ┌─── SUB ───┐
> We *will lose* our remaining wetlands unless we *act* now.

TIP: In all types of conditional sentences (factual, predictive, and speculative), *if* or *unless* clauses do not use the modal verb *will*.

>   passes
> ▶ If Liv ~~will pass~~ her history test, she will graduate this year.
>   ^

Speculative

Speculative conditional sentences express unlikely, contrary-to-fact, or impossible conditions. English uses the past or past perfect tense in the *if* clause, even for conditions in the present or the future.

Unlikely possibilities If the condition is possible but unlikely in the present or the future, use the past tense in the subordinate clause; in the independent clause, use *would, could,* or *might* plus the base form of the verb.

```
        ┌──── SUB ────┐ ┌──── IND ────┐
```
If I *won* the lottery, I *would travel* to Egypt.

The writer does not expect to win the lottery. Because this is a possible but unlikely present or future situation, the past tense is used in the subordinate clause.

Conditions contrary to fact In conditions that are currently unreal or contrary to fact, use the past-tense verb *were* (not *was*) in the *if* clause for all subjects. (See also 27g, on the subjunctive mood.)

>   were
> ► If I ~~was~~ president, I would make children's issues a priority.
>   ^

The writer is not president, so *were* is correct in the *if* clause.

Events that did not happen In a conditional sentence that speculates about an event that did not happen or was impossible in the past, use the past perfect tense in the *if* clause; in the independent clause, use *would have*, *could have*, or *might have* with the past participle. (See also past perfect tense, p. 364.)

```
        ┌──── SUB ────┐ ┌────────── IND ──────────┐
```
If I *had saved* more money, I *would have visited* Laos last year.

The writer did not save more money and did not travel to Laos. This sentence shows a possibility that did not happen.

EXERCISE 28–7   Edit the following sentences to correct problems with verbs. In some cases, more than one revision is possible. Possible revisions appear in the back of the book.

>   had
> If I ~~have~~ time, I would study both French and Russian next
>   ^
> semester.

a. The electrician might have discovered the broken circuit if she went through the modules one at a time.

b. If Verena wins a scholarship, she would go to graduate school.

c. Whenever a rainbow appears after a storm, everybody came out to see it.

d. Sarah did not understood the terms of her internship.

e. If I live in Budapest with my cousin Szusza, she would teach me Hungarian cooking.

28f Become familiar with verbs that may be followed by gerunds or infinitives.

A gerund is a verb form that ends in *-ing* and is used as a noun: *sleeping, dreaming.* An infinitive is the word *to* plus the base form of the verb: *to sleep, to dream.* The word *to* is an infinitive marker, not a preposition, in this use. (See 48b.)

A few verbs may be followed by either a gerund or an infinitive; others may be followed by a gerund but not by an infinitive; still others may be followed by an infinitive but not by a gerund.

Verb + gerund or infinitive (no change in meaning)

The following commonly used verbs may be followed by a gerund or an infinitive, with little or no difference in meaning:

begin	hate	love
continue	like	start

I love *skiing.* I love *to ski.*

Verb + gerund or infinitive (change in meaning)

With a few verbs, the choice of a gerund or an infinitive changes the meaning dramatically:

forget	remember	stop	try

She stopped *speaking* to Lucia. [She no longer spoke to Lucia.]

She stopped *to speak* to Lucia. [She paused so that she could speak to Lucia.]

Verb + gerund

These verbs may be followed by a gerund but not by an infinitive:

admit	discuss	imagine	put off	risk
appreciate	enjoy	miss	quit	suggest
avoid	escape	postpone	recall	tolerate
deny	finish	practice	resist	

Bill enjoys *playing* [not *to play*] the piano.

Jamie quit *smoking*.

Verb + infinitive

These verbs may be followed by an infinitive but not by a gerund:

agree	decide	manage	plan	wait
ask	expect	mean	pretend	want
beg	help	need	promise	wish
claim	hope	offer	refuse	would like

Jill has offered *to water* [not *watering*] the plants while we are away.

Joe finally managed *to find* a parking space.

A few of these verbs may be followed either by an infinitive directly or by a noun or pronoun plus an infinitive:

ask	help	promise	would like
expect	need	want	

We asked *to speak* to the congregation.

We asked *Rabbi Abrams to speak* to our congregation.

Verb + noun or pronoun + infinitive

With certain verbs in the active voice, a noun or pronoun must come between the verb and the infinitive that follows it. The noun or pronoun usually names a person who is affected by the action of the verb.

advise	convince	order	tell
allow	encourage	persuade	urge
cause	have ("own")	remind	warn
command	instruct	require	

The class encouraged Luis to tell the story of his escape.

The counselor *advised Haley to take* four courses instead of five.

Verb + noun or pronoun + unmarked infinitive

An unmarked infinitive is an infinitive without *to*. A few verbs (often called *causative verbs*) may be followed by a noun or pronoun and an unmarked infinitive.

have ("cause")	let ("allow")
help	make ("force")

▶ Rose had the attendant ~~to~~ wash the windshield.

▶ Fredo made me ~~to~~ carry his book for him.

Help can be followed by a noun or pronoun and either an unmarked or a marked infinitive.

Emma *helped Brian wash* the dishes.

Emma *helped Brian to wash* the dishes.

NOTE: The infinitive is used in some typical constructions with *too* and *enough*.

TOO + ADJECTIVE + INFINITIVE
The gift is *too large to wrap*.

ENOUGH + NOUN + INFINITIVE

Our emergency pack has *enough bottled water to last* a week.

ADJECTIVE + *ENOUGH* + INFINITIVE

Some of the hikers felt *strong enough to climb* another thousand feet.

EXERCISE 28–10   Form sentences by adding gerund or infinitive constructions to the following sentence openings. In some cases, more than one kind of construction is possible. Possible answers appear in the back of the book.

Please remind your sister to call me.
          ^

a.   I enjoy

b.   The tutor told Samantha

c.   The team hopes

d.   Ricardo and his brothers miss

e.   Jon remembered

29   Articles (*a, an, the*)

Articles (*a, an, the*) are part of a category of words known as *noun markers* or *determiners*.

29a Be familiar with articles and other noun markers.

Standard English uses noun markers to help identify the nouns that follow. In addition to articles (*a, an,* and *the*), noun markers include the following:

- possessive nouns, such as *Elena's* (See 36a.)

- possessive pronoun/adjectives: *my, your, his, her, its, our, their* (See 46b.)

- demonstrative pronoun/adjectives: *this, that, these, those* (See 46b.)

- quantifiers: *all, any, each, either, every, few, many, more, most, much, neither, several, some,* and so on (See 29d.)

- numbers: *one, twenty-three,* and so on

Using articles and other noun markers

Articles and other noun markers always appear before nouns; sometimes other modifiers, such as adjectives and adverbs, come between a noun marker and a noun.

> ART N
> Felix is reading a book about mythology.

> ART ADJ N
> We took an exciting trip to Alaska last summer.

> NOUN
> MARKER ADV ADJ N
> That very delicious meal was expensive.

In most cases, do not use an article with another noun marker.

▶ ~~The~~ Natalie's older brother lives in Wisconsin.

Expressions like *a few, the most,* and *all the* are exceptions: *a few potatoes, all the rain.* See also 29d.

Types of articles and types of nouns

To choose an appropriate article for a noun, you must first determine whether the noun is *common* or *proper, count* or *noncount, singular* or *plural*, and *specific* or *general.* The chart on pages 381–82 describes the types of nouns.

Articles are classified as *indefinite* and *definite.* The indefinite articles, *a* and *an*, are used with general nouns. The definite article, *the*, is used with specific nouns. (The last section of the chart on p. 382 explains general and specific nouns.)

A and *an* both mean "one" or "one among many." Use *a* before a consonant sound: *a banana, a vacation, a happy child, a united family.* Use *an* before a vowel sound: *an eggplant, an uncle, an honorable person.* (See also *a, an* in the glossary of usage.)

The shows that a noun is specific; use *the* with one or more than one specific thing: *the newspaper, the soldiers.*

29b Use *the* with most specific common nouns.

The definite article, *the*, is used with most nouns—both count and noncount—that the reader can identify specifically. Usually the identity will be clear to the reader for one of the following reasons. (See the chart on pp. 381–82.)

1. The noun has been previously mentioned.

                                             the
   ▶ A truck cut in front of our van. When truck skidded a few
                                                    ^

   seconds later, we almost crashed into it.

   The article *A* is used before *truck* when the noun is first mentioned. When the noun is mentioned again, it needs the article *the* because readers can now identify which truck skidded—the one that cut in front of the van.

2. A phrase or clause following the noun restricts its identity.

                                      the
   ▶ Bryce warned me that GPS in his car was not working.
                                          ^

   The phrase *in his car* identifies the specific GPS.

Types of nouns

Common or proper

Common nouns	**Examples**	
• name general persons, places, things, or ideas	religion	beauty
	knowledge	student
• begin with lowercase	rain	country

Proper nouns	**Examples**	
• name specific persons, places, things, or ideas	Hinduism	President Adams
	Philip	Washington Monument
• begin with capital letter	New Jersey	Supreme Court
	Vietnam	Renaissance

Count or noncount (common nouns only)

Count nouns	**Examples**
• name persons, places, things, or ideas that can be counted	girl, girls
	city, cities
	goose, geese
• have plural forms	philosophy, philosophies

Noncount nouns	**Examples**	
• name things or abstract ideas that cannot be counted	water	patience
	silver	knowledge
	furniture	air
• cannot be made plural		

Note: See the chart on page 386 for lists of commonly used noncount nouns.

TYPES OF NOUNS (cont.)

Singular or plural (both common and proper)

Singular nouns (count and noncount)

- represent one person, place, thing, or idea

Examples

backpack	rain
country	beauty
woman	Nile River
achievement	Block Island

Plural nouns (count only)

- represent more than one person, place, thing, or idea
- must be count nouns

Examples

backpacks	Ural Mountains
countries	Falkland Islands
women	achievements

Specific (definite) or general (indefinite) (count and noncount)

Specific nouns

- name persons, places, things, or ideas that can be identified within a group of the same type

Examples

The students in Professor Martin's *class* should study.

The airplane carrying *the senator* was late.

The furniture in *the truck* was damaged.

General nouns

- name categories of persons, places, things, or ideas (often plural)

Examples

Students should study.

Books bridge *gaps* between *cultures*.

The airplane has made commuting between *cities* easy.

NOTE: Descriptive adjectives do not necessarily make a noun specific. A specific noun is one that readers can identify within a group of nouns of the same type.

▶ If I win the lottery, I will buy ~~the~~ *a* brand-new bright red sports car.

> The reader cannot identify which specific brand-new bright red sports car the writer will buy. Even though *car* has many adjectives in front of it, it is a general noun in this sentence.

3. A superlative adjective such as *best* or *most intelligent* makes the noun's identity specific. (See also 26d.)

▶ Our petite daughter dated *the* tallest boy in her class.

> The superlative *tallest* makes the noun *boy* specific. Although there might be several tall boys, only one boy can be the tallest.

4. The noun describes a unique person, place, or thing.

▶ During an eclipse, one should not look directly at *the* sun.

> There is only one sun in our solar system, so its identity is clear.

5. The context or situation makes the noun's identity clear.

▶ Please don't slam *the* door when you leave.

> Both the speaker and the listener know which door is meant.

6. The noun is singular and refers to a scientific class or category of items (most often animals, musical instruments, and inventions).

▶ ~~Tin~~ *The tin* whistle is common in traditional Irish music.

> The writer is referring to the tin whistle as a class of musical instruments.

29c Use *a* (or *an*) with common singular count nouns that refer to "one" or "any."

If a count noun refers to one unspecific item (not a whole category), use the indefinite article, *a* or *an*. *A* and *an* usually mean "one among many" but can also mean "any one." (See the chart on p. 385.)

▶ My English professor asked me to bring ^*a* dictionary to class.

> The noun *dictionary* refers to "one unspecific dictionary" or "any dictionary."

▶ We want to rent ^*an* apartment close to the lake.

> The noun *apartment* refers to "any apartment close to the lake," not a specific apartment.

29d Use a quantifier such as *some* or *more*, not *a* or *an*, with a noncount noun to express an approximate amount.

Do not use *a* or *an* with noncount nouns. Also do not use numbers or words such as *several* or *many*; they must be used with plural nouns, and noncount nouns do not have plural forms. (See the chart on p. 386 for lists of commonly used noncount nouns.)

▶ Dr. Snyder gave us ~~an~~ information about the Peace Corps.

▶ Do you have ~~many~~ money with you?

You can use quantifiers such as *enough*, *less*, and *some* to suggest approximate amounts or nonspecific quantities of noncount nouns: *a little salt, any homework, enough wood, less information, much pollution.*

Choosing articles for common nouns

Use *the*

• if the reader has enough information to identify the noun specifically	**COUNT:** Please turn on *the lights*. We're going to *the zoo* tomorrow.
	NONCOUNT: *The food* throughout Italy is excellent.

Use *a* or *an*

• if the noun refers to one item *and* if the item is singular but not specific	**COUNT:** Bring *a pencil* to class. Charles wrote *an essay* about his first job.

Note: Do not use *a* or *an* with plural or noncount nouns.

Use a quantifier (*enough, many, some*, etc.)

• if the noun represents an unspecified amount of something	**COUNT (PLURAL):** Amir showed us *some photos* of India. *Many turtles* return to the same nesting site each year.
• if the amount is more than one but not all items in a category	**NONCOUNT:** We didn't get *enough rain* this summer.

Note: Sometimes no article conveys an unspecified amount: *Amir showed us photos of India.*

Use no article

• if the noun represents all items in a category	**COUNT (PLURAL):** *Students* can attend the show for free.
• if the noun represents a category in general	**NONCOUNT:** *Coal* is a natural resource.

Note: *The* is occasionally used when a singular count noun refers to all items in a class or a specific category: *The bald eagle is no longer endangered in the United States.*

Commonly used noncount nouns
Food and drink
beef, bread, butter, candy, cereal, cheese, cream, meat, milk, pasta, rice, salt, sugar, water, wine
Nonfood substances
air, cement, coal, dirt, gasoline, gold, paper, petroleum, plastic, rain, silver, snow, soap, steel, wood, wool
Abstract nouns
advice, anger, beauty, confidence, courage, employment, fun, happiness, health, honesty, information, intelligence, knowledge, love, poverty, satisfaction, wealth
Other
biology (and other areas of study), clothing, equipment, furniture, homework, jewelry, luggage, machinery, mail, money, news, poetry, pollution, research, scenery, traffic, transportation, violence, weather, work
Note: A few noncount nouns (such as *love*) can also be used as count nouns: *He had two loves: music and archery.*

29e Do not use articles with nouns that refer to all of something or something in general.

When a noncount noun refers to all of its type or to a concept in general, it is not marked with an article.

> Kindness
> ▶ ~~The kindness~~ is a virtue.
>   ^
>
> The noun represents kindness in general; it does not represent a specific type of kindness, such as *the kindness he showed me after my mother's death.*

▶ In some places, ~~the~~ rice is preferred to all other grains.

The noun *rice* represents rice in general. To refer to a specific type or serving of rice, the definite article is appropriate: *The rice my husband served last night is the best I've ever tasted.*

In most cases, when you use a count noun to represent a general category, make the noun plural. Do not use unmarked singular count nouns to represent whole categories.

Fountains are
▶ ~~Fountain is~~ an expensive element of landscape design.
  ^
Fountains is a count noun that represents fountains in general.

EXCEPTION: In some cases, *the* can be used with singular count nouns to represent a class or specific category: *The Chinese alligator is smaller than the American alligator.* See also number 6 in 29b.

29f Do not use articles with most singular proper nouns. Use *the* with most plural proper nouns.

Since singular proper nouns are already specific, they typically do not need an article: *Prime Minister Cameron, Jamaica, Lake Huron, Mount Etna.*

There are, however, many exceptions. In most cases, if the proper noun consists of a common noun with modifiers (adjectives or an *of* phrase), use *the* with the proper noun.

                the
▶ We visited Great Wall of China last year.
             ^
                                          the
▶ Rob wants to be a translator for Central Intelligence Agency.
                                          ^

The is used with most plural proper nouns: *the McGregors, the Bahamas, the Finger Lakes, the United States.*

Geographic names create problems because there are so many exceptions to the rules. When in doubt, consult the chart on page 388, check a dictionary, or ask a native speaker.

Using *the* with geographic nouns

When to omit *the*

streets, squares, parks	Ivy Street, Union Square, Denali National Park
cities, states, counties	Miami, New Mexico, Bee County
most countries, continents	Italy, China, South America, Africa
bays, single lakes	Tampa Bay, Lake Geneva
single mountains, islands	Mount Everest, Crete

When to use *the*

country names with *of* phrase	the United States (of America), the People's Republic of China
large regions, deserts	the East Coast, the Sahara
peninsulas	the Baja Peninsula, the Sinai Peninsula
oceans, seas, gulfs	the Pacific Ocean, the Dead Sea, the Persian Gulf
canals and rivers	the Panama Canal, the Amazon
mountain ranges	the Rocky Mountains, the Alps
groups of islands	the Solomon Islands

EXERCISE 29–1   Edit the following sentences for proper use of articles and nouns. If a sentence is correct, write "correct" after it. Answers appear in the back of the book.

~~The~~ Josefina's dance routine was flawless.

a.   Doing volunteer work often brings a satisfaction.

b.   As I looked out the window of the plane, I could see the Cape Cod.

c.   Melina likes to drink her coffees with lots of cream.

d.   Recovering from abdominal surgery requires patience.

e.   I completed the my homework assignment quickly.

EXERCISE 29–2   Articles have been omitted from the following description of winter weather. Insert the articles *a*, *an*, and *the* where English requires them and be prepared to explain the reasons for your choices.

> Many people confuse terms *hail*, *sleet*, and *freezing rain*. Hail normally occurs in thunderstorm and is caused by strong updrafts that lift growing chunks of ice into clouds. When chunks of ice, called hailstones, become too heavy to be carried by updrafts, they fall to ground. Hailstones can cause damage to crops, windshields, and people. Sleet occurs during winter storms and is caused by snowflakes falling from layer of cold air into warm layer, where they become raindrops, and then into another cold layer. As they fall through last layer of cold air, raindrops freeze and become small ice pellets, forming sleet. When it hits car windshield or windows of house, sleet can make annoying racket. Driving and walking can be hazardous when sleet accumulates on roads and sidewalks. Freezing rain is basically rain that falls onto ground and then freezes after it hits ground. It causes icy glaze on trees and any surface that is below freezing.

30 Sentence structure

Although their structure can vary widely, sentences in English generally flow from subject to verb to object or complement: *Bears eat fish.* This section focuses on the major challenges that multilingual students face when writing sentences in English. For more details on the parts of speech and the elements of sentences, consult sections 46–49.

30a Use a linking verb between a subject and its complement.

Some languages, such as Russian and Turkish, do not use linking verbs (*is, are, was, were*) between subjects and complements (nouns or adjectives that rename or describe the subject). Every English sentence, however, must include a verb. For more on linking verbs, see 27e.

> ▶ Jim ^is^ intelligent.

> ▶ Many streets in San Francisco ^are^ very steep.

30b Include a subject in every sentence.

Some languages, such as Spanish and Japanese, do not require a subject in every sentence. Every English sentence, however, needs a subject. Commands are an exception: The subject *you* is understood but not present in the sentence ([*You*] *Give me the book*).

> ▶ Your aunt is very energetic. ~~Seems~~ ^She seems^ young for her age.

The word *it* is used as the subject of a sentence describing the weather or temperature, stating the time, indicating distance, or suggesting an environmental fact.

> ▶ ~~Is~~ ^It is^ raining in the valley and snowing in the mountains.

> ▶ ~~Is~~ ^It is^ 9:15 a.m.

In most English sentences, the subject appears before the verb. Some sentences, however, are inverted: The subject comes after the verb. In these sentences, a placeholder called an *expletive* (*there* or *it*) often comes before the verb.

EXP   V ┌──── S ────┐   ┌──── S ────┐ V
There are many people here today. (Many people are here today.)

There is
▶ ~~Is~~ an apple pie in the refrigerator.
  ^

              there are
▶ As you know, many religious sects in India.
                  ^

Notice that the verb agrees with the subject that follows it: *apple pie is, sects are.* (See 21g.)

Sometimes an inverted sentence has an infinitive (*to work*) or a noun clause (*that she is intelligent*) as the subject. In such sentences, the placeholder *it* is needed before the verb. (Also see 48b and 48e.)

EXP V   ┌── S ──┐   ┌── S ──┐   V
It is important to study daily. (To study daily is important.)

                    it
▶ Because the road is flooded, is necessary to change our route.
                                ^

TIP: The words *here* and *there* are not used as subjects. When they mean "in this place" (*here*) or "in that place" (*there*), they are adverbs, which are never subjects.

              It   *there.*
▶ I just returned from Japan. ~~There~~ is very beautiful~~/~~
                              ^   ^

  This school   *that school*
▶ ~~Here~~ offers a master's degree in physical therapy; ~~there~~ has
  ^   ^

  only a bachelor's program.

30c Do not use both a noun and a pronoun to perform the same grammatical function in a sentence.

English does not allow a subject to be repeated in its own clause.

▶ The doctor ~~she~~ advised me to cut down on salt.

The pronoun *she* cannot repeat the subject, *doctor.*

Do not add a pronoun even when a word group comes between the subject and the verb.

▶ **The watch that I lost on vacation ~~it~~ was in my backpack.**

The pronoun *it* cannot repeat the subject, *watch*.

Some languages allow "topic fronting," placing a word or phrase (a "topic") at the beginning of a sentence and following it with an independent clause that explains something about the topic. This form is not allowed in English because the sentence seems to start with one subject but then introduces a new subject in an independent clause.

$\overbrace{}^{\text{TOPIC}}$ $\overbrace{}^{\text{IND CLAUSE}}$

INCORRECT   The seeds I planted them last fall.

The sentence can be corrected by bringing the topic (*seeds*) into the independent clause.

                                   the seeds
▶ ~~The seeds~~ I planted ~~them~~ last fall.
                   ∧

30d Do not repeat a subject, an object, or an adverb in an adjective clause.

Adjective clauses begin with relative pronouns (*who*, *whom*, *whose*, *which*, *that*) or relative adverbs (*when*, *where*). Relative pronouns usually serve as subjects or objects in the clauses they introduce; another word in the clause cannot serve the same function. Relative adverbs should not be repeated by other adverbs later in the clause.

$\overbrace{}^{\text{ADJ CLAUSE}}$

The cat ran under the car that was parked on the street.

▶ **The cat ran under the car that ~~it~~ was parked on the street.**

The relative pronoun *that* is the subject of the adjective clause, so the pronoun *it* cannot be added as a subject.

▶ Myrna enjoyed the investment seminars that she attended

~~them~~ last week.

The relative pronoun *that* is the object of the verb *attended*. The pronoun *them* cannot also serve as an object.

Sometimes the relative pronoun is understood but not present in the sentence. In such cases, do not add another word with the same function as the omitted pronoun.

▶ Myrna enjoyed the investment seminars she attended ~~them~~

last week.

The relative pronoun *that* is understood after *seminars* even though it is not present in the sentence.

If the clause begins with a relative adverb, do not use another adverb with the same meaning later in the clause.

▶ The office where I work ~~there~~ is one hour from the city.

The adverb *there* cannot repeat the relative adverb *where*.

EXERCISE 30–1 In the following sentences, add needed subjects or expletives and delete any repeated subjects, objects, or adverbs. Answers appear in the back of the book.

The new geology professor is the one whom we saw ~~him~~ on TV.

a. Are some cartons of ice cream in the freezer.
b. I don't use the subway because am afraid.
c. The prime minister she is the most popular leader in my country.
d. We tried to get in touch with the same manager whom we spoke to him earlier.
e. Recently have been a number of earthquakes in Turkey.

30e Avoid mixed constructions beginning with *although* or *because*.

A word group that begins with *although* cannot be linked to a word group that begins with *but* or *however*. The result is an error called a *mixed construction* (see also 11a). Similarly, a word group that begins with *because* cannot be linked to a word group that begins with *so* or *therefore*.

If you want to keep *although* or *because*, drop the other linking word.

▶ Although Nikki Giovanni is best known for her poetry for adults, ~~but~~ she has written several books for children.

▶ Because German and Dutch are related languages, ~~therefore~~ tourists from Berlin can usually read a few signs in Amsterdam.

If you want to keep the other linking word, omit *although* or *because*.

▶ ~~Although~~ Nikki Giovanni is best known for her poetry for adults, but she has written several books for children.

▶ ~~Because~~ German and Dutch are related languages,; therefore, tourists from Berlin can usually read a few signs in Amsterdam.

For advice about using commas and semicolons with linking words, see 32a and 34b.

30f Do not place an adverb between a verb and its direct object.

Adverbs modifying verbs can appear in various positions: at the beginning or end of a sentence, before or after a verb, or between a helping verb and its main verb.

> *Slowly*, we drove along the rain-slick road.

> Mia handled the teapot *very carefully*.

> Martin *always* wins our tennis matches.

> Christina is *rarely* late for our lunch dates.

> My daughter has *often* spoken of you.

> The election results were being *closely* followed by analysts.

However, an adverb cannot appear between a verb and its direct object.

carefully
► Mother wrapped ~~carefully~~ the gift.
                ^

The adverb *carefully* cannot appear between the verb, *wrapped*, and its direct object, *the gift*.

EXERCISE 30–4   Edit the following sentences for proper sentence structure. If a sentence is correct, write "correct" after it. Possible revisions appear in the back of the book.

slowly.
She peeled ~~slowly~~ the banana./
                              ^

a.   Although freshwater freezes at 32 degrees Fahrenheit, however ocean water freezes at 28 degrees Fahrenheit.

b.   Because we switched cable packages, so our channel lineup has changed.

c.   The competitor mounted confidently his skateboard.

d. My sister performs well the *legong*, a Balinese dance.
e. Because product development is behind schedule, we will have to launch the product next spring.

30g Distinguish between present participles and past participles used as adjectives.

Both present and past participles may be used as adjectives. The present participle always ends in *-ing*. Past participles usually end in *-ed, -d, -en, -n,* or *-t.* (See 27a.)

PRESENT PARTICIPLES   confusing, speaking, boring
PAST PARTICIPLES   confused, spoken, bored

Like all other adjectives, participles can come before nouns; they also can follow linking verbs, in which case they describe the subject of the sentence. (See 47b.)

Use a present participle to describe a person or thing *causing or stimulating an experience.*

The *boring lecture* put us to sleep. [The lecture caused boredom.]

Use a past participle to describe a person or thing *undergoing an experience.*

The *audience* was *bored and restless.* [The audience experienced boredom.]

Participles that describe emotions or mental states often cause the most confusion.

annoying/annoyed	exhausting/exhausted
boring/bored	fascinating/fascinated
confusing/confused	frightening/frightened
depressing/depressed	satisfying/satisfied
exciting/excited	surprising/surprised

EXERCISE 30–7 Edit the following sentences for proper use of present and past participles. If a sentence is correct, write "correct" after it. Answers appear in the back of the book.

> *excited*
> **Danielle and Monica were very ~~exciting~~ to be going to a**
>   ^
> **Broadway show for the first time.**

a. Listening to everyone's complaints all day was irritated.

b. The long flight to Singapore was exhausted.

c. His skill at chess is amazing.

d. After a great deal of research, the scientist made a fascinated discovery.

e. Surviving that tornado was one of the most frightened experiences I've ever had.

30h Place cumulative adjectives in an appropriate order.

Adjectives usually come before the nouns they modify and may also come after linking verbs. (See 46d and 47b.)

>   ADJ   N   V ADJ
> Janine wore a new necklace. Janine's necklace was new.

Cumulative adjectives, which cannot be joined by the word *and* or separated by commas, must come in a particular order. If you use cumulative adjectives before a noun, see the chart on page 398. The chart is only a guide; don't be surprised if you encounter exceptions. (See also 33d.)

>   *stained red plastic*
> ▶ **My dorm room has only a desk and a ~~plastic red stained~~**
>   ^
> **chair.**

Order of cumulative adjectives

FIRST **ARTICLE OR OTHER NOUN MARKER** a, an, the, her, Joe's, two, many, some

EVALUATIVE WORD attractive, dedicated, delicious, ugly, disgusting

SIZE large, enormous, small, little

LENGTH OR SHAPE long, short, round, square

AGE new, old, young, antique

COLOR yellow, blue, crimson

NATIONALITY French, Peruvian, Vietnamese

RELIGION Catholic, Protestant, Jewish, Muslim

MATERIAL silver, walnut, wool, marble

LAST **NOUN/ADJECTIVE** tree (as in *tree* house), kitchen (as in *kitchen* table)

THE NOUN MODIFIED house, coat, bicycle, bread, woman, coin

My large blue wool coat is in the attic.

EXERCISE 30–10   Using the chart on this page as necessary, arrange the following modifiers and nouns in their proper order. Answers appear in the back of the book.

two new French racing bicycles
new, French, two, bicycles, racing

a. sculptor, young, an, Vietnamese, intelligent

b. dedicated, a, priest, Catholic

c. old, her, sweater, blue, wool

d. delicious, Joe's, Scandinavian, bread

e. many, boxes, jewelry, antique, beautiful

31 Prepositions and idiomatic expressions

31a Become familiar with prepositions that show time and place.

The most frequently used prepositions in English are *at*, *by*, *for*, *from*, *in*, *of*, *on*, *to*, and *with*. Prepositions can be difficult to master because the differences among them are subtle and idiomatic. The chart on page 401 is limited to three troublesome prepositions that show time and place: *at*, *on*, and *in*.

Not every possible use is listed in the chart, so don't be surprised when you encounter exceptions and idiomatic uses that you must learn one at a time. For example, in English a person rides *in* a car but *on* a bus, plane, train, or subway.

► My first class starts ~~on~~ *at* 8:00 a.m.

► The farmers go to market ~~in~~ *on* Wednesday.

EXERCISE 31–1 In the following sentences, replace prepositions that are not used correctly. You may need to refer to the chart on page 401. If a sentence is correct, write "correct" after it. Answers appear in the back of the book.

> The play begins ~~on~~ *at* 7:20 p.m.

a. Whenever we eat at the Centerville Café, we sit at a small table on the corner of the room.

b. In the 1990s, entrepreneurs created new online businesses in record numbers.

c. In Thursday, Nancy will attend her first home repair class at the community center.

d. Alex began looking for her lost mitten in another location.

e. We decided to go to a restaurant because there was no fresh food on the refrigerator.

31b Use nouns (including *-ing* forms) after prepositions.

In a prepositional phrase, use a noun (not a verb) after the preposition. Sometimes the noun will be a gerund, the *-ing* verb form that functions as a noun (see 48b).

▶ Our student government is good at ~~save~~ money.
                                       saving

Distinguish between the preposition *to* and the infinitive marker *to*. If *to* is a preposition, it should be followed by a noun or a gerund.

▶ We are dedicated to ~~help~~ the poor.
                        helping

If *to* is an infinitive marker, it should be followed by the base form of the verb.

▶ We want to ~~helping~~ the poor.
               help

To test whether *to* is a preposition or an infinitive marker, insert a word that you know is a noun after the word *to*. If the noun makes sense in that position, *to* is a preposition. If the noun does not make sense after *to*, then *to* is an infinitive marker.

Zoe is addicted *to* _____.
They are planning *to* _____.

In the first sentence, a noun (such as *magazines*) makes sense after *to*, so *to* is a preposition and should be followed by a noun or a gerund: Zoe is addicted *to magazines*. Zoe is addicted *to running*.

_At_, _on_, and _in_ to show time and place	
Showing time	
AT	*at* a specific time: *at* 7:20, *at* dawn, *at* dinner
ON	*on* a specific day or date: *on* Tuesday, *on* June 4
IN	*in* a part of a 24-hour period: *in* the afternoon, *in* the daytime [but *at* night]
	in a year or month: *in* 2008, *in* July
	in a period of time: finished *in* three hours
Showing place	
AT	*at* a meeting place or location: *at* home, *at* the club
	at the edge of something: sitting *at* the desk
	at the corner of something: turning *at* the intersection
	at a target: throwing the snowball *at* Lucy
ON	*on* a surface: placed *on* the table, hanging *on* the wall
	on a street: the house *on* Spring Street
	on an electronic medium: *on* television, *on* the Internet
IN	*in* an enclosed space: *in* the garage, *in* an envelope
	in a geographic location: *in* San Diego, *in* Texas
	in a print medium: *in* a book, *in* a magazine

In the second sentence, a noun (such as *magazines*) does not make sense after *to*, so *to* is an infinitive marker and must be followed by the base form of the verb: They are planning *to build* a new school.

31c Become familiar with common adjective + preposition combinations.

Some adjectives appear only with certain prepositions. These expressions are idiomatic and may be different from the combinations used in your native language.

Adjective + preposition combinations

accustomed to	connected to	guilty of	preferable to
addicted to	covered with	interested in	proud of
afraid of	dedicated to	involved in	responsible for
angry with	devoted to	involved with	
ashamed of	different from	known as	satisfied with
aware of	engaged in	known for	scared of
committed to	engaged to	made of (*or* made from)	similar to
concerned about	excited about		tired of
	familiar with	married to	worried about
concerned with	full of	opposed to	

▶ Paula is married ~~with~~ ^to^ Jon.

Check an ESL dictionary for combinations that are not listed in the chart above.

31d Become familiar with common verb + preposition combinations.

Many verbs and prepositions appear together in idiomatic phrases. Pay special attention to the combinations that are different from the combinations used in your native language.

▶ Your success depends ~~of~~ ^on^ your effort.

Check an ESL dictionary for combinations that are not listed in the chart on page 403.

Verb + preposition combinations

agree with	compare with	forget about	speak to (*or* speak with)
apply to	concentrate on	happen to	stare at
approve of	consist of	hope for	succeed at
arrive at	count on	insist on	succeed in
arrive in	decide on	listen to	take advantage of
ask for	depend on	participate in	take care of
believe in	differ from	rely on	think about
belong to	disagree with	reply to	think of
care about	dream about	respond to	wait for
care for	dream of	result in	wait on
compare to	feel like	search for	

Punctuation

32 The comma 407

33 Unnecessary commas 422

34 The semicolon 428

35 The colon 432

36 The apostrophe 434

37 Quotation marks 439

38 End punctuation 447

39 Other punctuation marks 449

Punctuation

ONLINE ACTIVITIES:

writershelp.com/hacker

macmillanhighered.com/
launchpadsolo/hacker

The comma   8 Exercises
                                    1 LearningCurve activity

Unnecessary commas   3 Exercises

The semicolon and the colon   6 Exercises
                                    1 LearningCurve activity

The apostrophe   4 Exercises
                                    1 LearningCurve activity

Quotation marks   3 Exercises
                                    1 LearningCurve activity

Other punctuation marks   3 Exercises

32 The comma

The comma was invented to help readers. Without it, sentence parts can collide into one another unexpectedly, causing misreadings.

CONFUSING	If you cook Elmer will do the dishes.
CONFUSING	While we were eating a rattlesnake approached our campsite.

Add commas in the logical places (after *cook* and *eating*), and suddenly all is clear. No longer is Elmer being cooked, the rattlesnake being eaten.

Various rules have evolved to prevent such misreadings and to speed readers along through complex grammatical structures. Those rules are detailed in this section. (Section 33 explains when not to use commas.)

32a Use a comma before a coordinating conjunction joining independent clauses.

When a coordinating conjunction connects two or more independent clauses—word groups that could stand alone as separate sentences—a comma must be placed before the conjunction. There are seven coordinating conjunctions in English: *and, but, or, nor, for, so,* and *yet.*

A comma tells readers that one independent clause has come to a close and that another is about to begin.

▶ The department sponsored a seminar on college survival

skills, and it also hosted a barbecue for new students.
 ^

EXCEPTION: If the two independent clauses are short and there is no danger of misreading, the comma may be omitted.

> The plane took off and we were on our way.

TIP: As a rule, do *not* use a comma with a coordinating conjunction that joins only two words, phrases, or subordinate clauses. (See 33a. See also 32c for commas with coordinating conjunctions joining three or more elements.)

▶ **A good money manager controls expenses/ and invests**

surplus dollars to meet future needs.

The word group following *and* is not an independent clause; it is the second half of a compound predicate (*controls . . . and invests*).

32b Use a comma after an introductory clause or phrase.

The most common introductory word groups are clauses and phrases functioning as adverbs. Such word groups usually tell when, where, how, why, or under what conditions the main action of the sentence occurred. (See 48a, 48b, and 48e.)

A comma tells readers that the introductory clause or phrase has come to a close and that the main part of the sentence is about to begin.

▶ **When Irwin was ready to iron, his cat tripped on the cord.**

Without the comma, readers may think that Irwin is ironing his cat. The comma signals that *his cat* is the subject of a new clause, not part of the introductory one.

EXCEPTION: The comma may be omitted after a short adverb clause or phrase if there is no danger of misreading. *In no time we were at 2,800 feet.*

Sentences also frequently begin with participial phrases that function as adjectives, describing the noun or pronoun immediately following them. The comma tells readers that they are about to learn the identity of the person or thing described; therefore, the comma is usually required even when the phrase is short. (See 48b.)

▶ **Buried under layers of younger rocks, the earth's oldest rocks contain no fossils.**

NOTE: Other introductory word groups include transitional expressions and absolute phrases (see 32f).

EXERCISE 32–1 Add or delete commas where necessary in the following sentences. If a sentence is correct, write "correct" after it. Answers appear in the back of the book.

Because we had been saving molding for a few weeks, we had enough wood to frame all thirty paintings.

a. Alisa brought the injured bird home, and fashioned a splint out of Popsicle sticks for its wing.

b. Considered a classic of early animation *The Adventures of Prince Achmed* used hand-cut silhouettes against colored backgrounds.

c. If you complete the evaluation form and return it within two weeks you will receive a free breakfast during your next stay.

d. After retiring from the New York City Ballet in 1965, legendary dancer Maria Tallchief went on to found the Chicago City Ballet.

e. Roger had always wanted a handmade violin but he couldn't afford one.

EXERCISE 32–2 Add or delete commas where necessary in the following sentences. If a sentence is correct, write "correct" after it. Answers appear in the back of the book.

> The car had been sitting idle for a month, so the battery was
>
> completely dead.

a. J. R. R. Tolkien finished writing his draft of *The Lord of the Rings* trilogy in 1949 but the first book wasn't published until 1954.

b. In the first two minutes of its ascent the space shuttle had broken the sound barrier and reached a height of over twenty-five miles.

c. German shepherds can be gentle guide dogs or they can be fierce attack dogs.

d. Some former professional cyclists admit that the use of performance-enhancing drugs is widespread in cycling but they argue that no rider can be competitive without doping.

e. As an intern, I learned most aspects of the broadcasting industry but I never learned about fundraising.

32c Use a comma between all items in a series.

When three or more items are presented in a series, those items should be separated from one another with commas. Items in a series may be single words, phrases, or clauses.

> ▶ Langston Hughes's poetry is concerned with race, justice,
>
> and the diversity of the African American experience.

Although some writers view the last comma in a series as optional, most experts advise using the comma because its omission can result in ambiguity or misreading.

> ▶ My uncle willed me all of his property, houses, and boats.

Did the uncle will his property *and* houses *and* boats—or simply his property, consisting of houses and boats? If the former meaning is intended, a comma is necessary to prevent ambiguity.

32d Use a comma between coordinate adjectives not joined with *and*. Do not use a comma between cumulative adjectives.

When two or more adjectives each modify a noun separately, they are coordinate.

> Roberto is a *warm, gentle, affectionate* father.

If the adjectives can be joined with *and*, the adjectives are coordinate, so you should use commas: *warm* and *gentle* and *affectionate* (*warm, gentle, affectionate*).

Adjectives that do not modify the noun separately are cumulative.

> *Three large gray* shapes moved slowly toward us.

Beginning with the adjective closest to the noun *shapes*, these modifiers lean on one another, piggyback style, with each modifying a larger word group. *Gray* modifies *shapes*, *large* modifies *gray shapes*, and *three* modifies *large gray shapes*. Cumulative adjectives cannot be joined with *and* (not *three* and *large* and *gray shapes*).

COORDINATE ADJECTIVES

▶ Should patients with severe‸ irreversible brain damage be put on life support systems?

Adjectives are coordinate if they can be connected with *and*: *severe and irreversible*.

CUMULATIVE ADJECTIVES

▶ Ira ordered a rich/ chocolate/ layer cake.

Ira didn't order a cake that was rich and chocolate and layer. He ordered a *layer cake* that was *chocolate*, a *chocolate layer cake* that was *rich*.

EXERCISE 32–5 Add or delete commas where necessary in the following sentences. If a sentence is correct, write "correct" after it. Answers appear in the back of the book.

> We gathered our essentials, took off for the great outdoors, and ignored the fact that it was Friday the 13th.

a. The cold impersonal atmosphere of the university was unbearable.
b. An ambulance threaded its way through police cars, fire trucks and irate citizens.
c. The *1812 Overture* is a stirring, magnificent piece of music.
d. After two broken arms, three cracked ribs and one concussion, Ken quit the varsity football team.
e. My cat's pupils had constricted to small black shining slits.

EXERCISE 32–6 Add or delete commas where necessary in the following sentences. If a sentence is correct, write "correct" after it. Answers appear in the back of the book.

> Good social workers excel in patience, diplomacy, and positive thinking.

a. NASA's rovers on Mars are equipped with special cameras that can take close-up high-resolution pictures of the terrain.
b. A baseball player achieves the triple crown by having the highest batting average, the most home runs, and the most runs batted in during the regular season.
c. If it does not get enough sunlight, a healthy green lawn can turn into a shriveled brown mess within a matter of days.
d. Love, vengeance, greed and betrayal are common themes in Western literature.
e. Many experts believe that shark attacks on surfers are a result of the sharks' mistaking surfboards for small, injured seals.

32e Use commas to set off nonrestrictive (nonessential) elements. Do not use commas to set off restrictive (essential) elements.

Certain word groups that modify nouns or pronouns can be restrictive or nonrestrictive—that is, essential or not essential to the meaning of a sentence. These word groups are usually adjective clauses, adjective phrases, or appositives.

Restrictive elements

A restrictive element defines or limits the meaning of the word it modifies; it is therefore essential to the meaning of the sentence and is not set off with commas. If you remove a restrictive modifier from a sentence, the meaning changes significantly, becoming more general than you intended.

> **RESTRICTIVE (NO COMMAS)**
> The campers need clothes *that are durable*.
>
> Scientists *who study the earth's structure* are called geologists.

The first sentence does not mean that the campers need clothes in general. The intended meaning is more limited: The campers need durable clothes. The second sentence does not mean that scientists in general are called geologists; only those scientists who specifically study the earth's structure are called geologists. The italicized word groups are essential and are therefore not set off with commas.

Nonrestrictive elements

A nonrestrictive modifier describes a noun or pronoun whose meaning has already been clearly defined or limited. Because the modifier contains nonessential or parenthetical information, it is set off with commas. If you remove a nonrestrictive element from a sentence, the meaning does not change dramatically. Some meaning may be lost, but the defining characteristics of the person or thing described remain the same.

NONRESTRICTIVE (WITH COMMAS)

The campers need sturdy shoes, *which are expensive.*

The scientists, *who represented eight different universities,* met to review applications for the prestigious Advancements in Science Award.

In the first sentence, the campers need sturdy shoes, and the shoes happen to be expensive. In the second sentence, the scientists met to review applications for the award; that they represented eight different universities is informative but not critical to the meaning of the sentence. The nonessential information in both sentences is set off with commas.

NOTE: Often it is difficult to tell whether a word group is restrictive or nonrestrictive without seeing it in context and considering the writer's meaning. Both of the following sentences are grammatically correct, but their meaning is slightly different.

The dessert made with fresh raspberries was delicious.

The dessert, made with fresh raspberries, was delicious.

In the first example, the phrase *made with fresh raspberries* tells readers which of two or more desserts the writer is referring to. In the example with commas, the phrase merely adds information about one dessert.

Adjective clauses

Adjective clauses are patterned like sentences, containing subjects and verbs, but they function within sentences as modifiers of nouns or pronouns. They always follow the word they modify, usually immediately. Adjective clauses begin with a relative pronoun (*who, whom, whose, which, that*) or with a relative adverb (*where, when*). (See also 48e.)

Nonrestrictive adjective clauses are set off with commas; restrictive adjective clauses are not.

NONRESTRICTIVE CLAUSE (WITH COMMAS)

▶ Ed's house, which is located on thirteen acres, was completely furnished with bats in the rafters and mice in the kitchen.

The adjective clause *which is located on thirteen acres* does not restrict the meaning of *Ed's house*; the information is nonessential and is therefore set off with commas.

RESTRICTIVE CLAUSE (NO COMMAS)

▶ The giant panda that was born at the San Diego Zoo in 2003 was sent to China in 2007.

Because the adjective clause *that was born at the San Diego Zoo in 2003* identifies one particular panda out of many, the information is essential and is therefore not set off with commas.

NOTE: Use *that* only with restrictive (essential) clauses. Many writers prefer to use *which* only with nonrestrictive (nonessential) clauses, but usage varies.

Adjective phrases

Prepositional or verbal phrases functioning as adjectives may be restrictive or nonrestrictive. Nonrestrictive phrases are set off with commas; restrictive phrases are not.

NONRESTRICTIVE PHRASE (WITH COMMAS)

▶ The helicopter, with its million-candlepower spotlight illuminating the area, circled above.

The *with* phrase is nonessential because its purpose is not to specify which of two or more helicopters is being discussed. The phrase is not required for readers to understand the meaning of the sentence.

RESTRICTIVE PHRASE (NO COMMAS)

▶ One corner of the attic was filled with newspapers⁄ dating

from the early 1900s.

Dating from the early 1900s restricts the meaning of *newspapers*, so
the comma should be omitted.

Appositives

An appositive is a noun or noun phrase that renames a nearby
noun. Nonrestrictive appositives are set off with commas; restrictive appositives are not.

NONRESTRICTIVE APPOSITIVE (WITH COMMAS)

▶ Darwin's most important book, *On the Origin of Species,*
was the result of many years of research.

Most important restricts the meaning to one book, so the appositive
On the Origin of Species is nonrestrictive and should be set off with
commas.

RESTRICTIVE APPOSITIVE (NO COMMAS)

▶ The song⁄ "Viva la Vida⁄" was blasted out of huge

amplifiers at the concert.

Once they've read *song*, readers still don't know precisely which
song the writer means. The appositive following *song* restricts its
meaning, so the appositive should not be set off with commas.

> **EXERCISE 32–9**   Add or delete commas where necessary in the
following sentences. If a sentence is correct, write "correct" after it.
Answers appear in the back of the book.

My sister, who plays center on the Sparks, now lives at
The Sands, a beach house near Los Angeles.

a. Choreographer Alvin Ailey's best-known work *Revelations* is more than just a crowd-pleaser.

b. Twyla Tharp's contemporary ballet *Push Comes to Shove* was made famous by the Russian dancer Baryshnikov. [*Tharp has written more than one contemporary ballet.*]

c. The glass sculptor sifting through hot red sand explained her technique to the other glassmakers. [*There is more than one glass sculptor.*]

d. A member of an organization, that provides job training for teens, was also appointed to the education commission.

e. Brian Eno who began his career as a rock musician turned to meditative compositions in the late 1970s.

32f Use commas to set off transitional and parenthetical expressions, absolute phrases, and word groups expressing contrast.

Transitional expressions

Transitional expressions serve as bridges between sentences or parts of sentences. They include conjunctive adverbs such as *however, therefore,* and *moreover* and transitional phrases such as *for example, as a matter of fact,* and *in other words.* (For complete lists of these expressions, see 34b.)

When a transitional expression appears between independent clauses in a compound sentence, it is preceded by a semicolon and is usually followed by a comma. (See 34b.)

▶ Minh did not understand our language; moreover, he was unfamiliar with our customs.

When a transitional expression appears at the beginning of a sentence or in the middle of an independent clause, it is usually set off with commas.

▶ **Natural foods are not always salt-free; celery, for example, contains more sodium than most people think.**

EXCEPTION: If a transitional expression blends smoothly with the rest of the sentence, calling for little or no pause in reading, it does not need to be set off with a comma. Expressions such as *also, at least, certainly, consequently, indeed, of course, moreover, no doubt, perhaps, then,* and *therefore* do not always call for a pause.

Alice's bicycle is broken; *therefore* you will need to borrow Sue's.

Parenthetical expressions

Expressions that are distinctly parenthetical, providing only supplemental information, should be set off with commas. They interrupt the flow of a sentence or appear at the end as afterthoughts.

▶ **Evolution, as far as we know, doesn't work this way.**

Absolute phrases

An absolute phrase, which modifies the whole sentence, usually consists of a noun followed by a participle or participial phrase. (See 48d.) Absolute phrases may appear at the beginning or at the end of a sentence and should be set off with commas.

┌─────── ABSOLUTE PHRASE ───────┐
  N PARTICIPLE
The sun appearing for the first time in a week, we were at last able to begin the archaeological dig.

▶ **Elvis Presley made music industry history in the 1950s, his records having sold more than ten million copies.**

NOTE: Do not insert a comma between the noun and the participle in an absolute construction.

▶ The next contestant/ being five years old, the host adjusted the height of the microphone.

Word groups expressing contrast

Sharp contrasts beginning with words such as *not*, *never*, and *unlike* are set off with commas.

▶ Unlike Robert, Celia loved dance contests.

32g Use commas to set off nouns of direct address, the words *yes* and *no*, interrogative tags, and mild interjections.

▶ Forgive me, Angela, for forgetting your birthday.

▶ The film was faithful to the book, wasn't it?

32h Use commas with expressions such as *he said* to set off direct quotations.

▶ In his "Letter from Birmingham Jail," Martin Luther King Jr. wrote, "We know through painful experience that freedom is never voluntarily given by the oppressor; it must be demanded by the oppressed" (225).

See 37 on the use of quotation marks and pages 609–10 on citing literary sources in MLA style.

32i Use commas with dates, addresses, titles, and numbers.

Dates

In dates, set off the year with a pair of commas.

▶ On December 12, 1890, orders were sent out for the arrest
of Sitting Bull.

EXCEPTIONS: Commas are not needed if the date is inverted or if only the month and year are given: 15 April 2009; January 2018.

Addresses

The elements of an address or a place name are separated with commas. A zip code, however, is not preceded by a comma.

▶ Please send the package to Greg Tarvin at 708 Spring
Street, Washington, IL 61571.

Titles

If a title follows a name, set off the title with a pair of commas.

▶ Ann Hall, MD, has been appointed to the board of trustees.

Numbers

In numbers more than four digits long, use commas to separate the numbers into groups of three, starting from the right. In numbers four digits long, a comma is optional.

    3,500 [*or* 3500]   100,000   5,000,000

EXCEPTIONS: Do not use commas in street numbers, zip codes, telephone numbers, or years with four or fewer digits.

EXERCISE 32–11 This exercise covers the major uses of the comma described in 32a–32e. Add or delete commas where necessary. If a sentence is correct, write "correct" after it. Answers appear in the back of the book.

> **Even though our brains actually can't focus on two tasks at a time, many people believe they can multitask.**

a. Cricket which originated in England is also popular in Australia, South Africa and India.

b. At the sound of the starting pistol the horses surged forward toward the first obstacle, a sharp incline three feet high.

c. After seeing an exhibition of Western art Gerhard Richter escaped from East Berlin, and smuggled out many of his notebooks.

d. Corrie's new wet suit has an intricate, blue pattern.

e. We replaced the rickety, old, spiral staircase with a sturdy, new ladder.

EXERCISE 32–12 This exercise covers the major uses of the comma described in 32a–32f. Edit the following paragraph to correct any comma errors.

> Hope for Paws, a nonprofit rescue organization in Los Angeles tells many sad stories of animal abuse and neglect. Most of the stories, however have happy endings. One such story involves Woody, a dog left behind, after his master died. For a long lonely year, Woody took refuge under a neighbor's shed, waiting in vain, for his master's return. He survived on occasional scraps from his neighbors who eventually contacted Hope for Paws. When rescuers reached Woody, they found a malnourished, and frightened dog who had one blind eye and dirty, matted, fur. Gently, Woody was pulled from beneath the shed, and taken to the home of a volunteer, who fosters orphaned pets. There, Woody was fed, shaved, bathed and loved. Woody's story had the happiest of endings, when a family adopted him. Now Woody has a new forever home and he is once again a happy, well-loved dog.

EXERCISE 32–13 This exercise covers all uses of the comma. Add or delete commas where necessary in the following sentences. If a sentence is correct, write "correct" after it. Answers appear in the back of the book.

> "Yes, dear, you can have dessert," my mother said.
>   ∧

a. On January 15, 2012 our office moved to 29 Commonwealth Avenue, Mechanicsville VA 23111.

b. The coach having bawled us out thoroughly, we left the locker room with his harsh words ringing in our ears.

c. Ms. Carlson you are a valued customer whose satisfaction is very important to us.

d. Mr. Mundy was born on July 22, 1939 in Arkansas, where his family had lived for four generations.

e. Her board poised at the edge of the half-pipe, Nina waited her turn to drop in.

33 Unnecessary commas

Many common misuses of the comma result from a misunderstanding of the major comma rules presented in 32.

33a Do not use a comma with a coordinating conjunction that joins only two words, phrases, or subordinate clauses.

Though a comma should be used before a coordinating conjunction joining independent clauses (see 32a) or with a series of three or more elements (see 32c), these rules should not be extended to other compound word groups.

▶ Ron discovered a leak⁄ and came back to fix it.

The coordinating conjunction *and* links two verbs in a compound predicate: *discovered* and *came*.

▶ We knew that she had won⁄ but that the election was close.

The coordinating conjunction *but* links two subordinate clauses, each beginning with *that*.

33b Do not use a comma to separate a verb from its subject or object.

A sentence should flow from subject to verb to object without unnecessary pauses. Commas may appear between these major sentence elements only when a specific rule calls for them.

▶ Zoos large enough to give the animals freedom to roam⁄

are becoming more popular.

The comma should not separate the subject, *Zoos*, from the verb, *are becoming*.

33c Do not use a comma before the first or after the last item in a series.

Though commas are required between items in a series (32c), do not place them either before or after the whole series.

▶ Other causes of asthmatic attacks are⁄ stress, change in

temperature, and cold air.

▶ Ironically, even novels that focus on horror, evil, and

alienation⁄ often have themes of spiritual renewal and

redemption as well.

33d Do not use a comma between cumulative adjectives, between an adjective and a noun, or between an adverb and an adjective.

Commas are required between coordinate adjectives (those that can be joined with *and*), but they do not belong between cumulative adjectives (those that cannot be joined with *and*). (For a full discussion, see 32d.)

▶ In the corner of the closet, we found an old⁄ maroon hatbox.

A comma should never be used between an adjective and the noun that follows it.

▶ It was a senseless, dangerous⁄ mission.

Nor should a comma be used between an adverb and an adjective that follows it.

▶ Deer are often responsible for severely⁄ damaged crops.

33e Do not use commas to set off restrictive elements.

Restrictive elements are modifiers or appositives that restrict the meaning of the nouns they follow. Because they are essential to the meaning of the sentence, they are not set off with commas. (For a full discussion of restrictive and nonrestrictive elements, see 32e.)

▶ Drivers⁄ who think they own the road⁄ make cycling a

dangerous sport.

The modifier *who think they own the road* restricts the meaning of *Drivers* and is essential to the meaning of the sentence. Putting commas around the *who* clause falsely suggests that all drivers think they own the road.

▶ Margaret Mead's book/ *Coming of Age in Samoa/* stirred

up considerable controversy when it was published in 1928.

Since Mead wrote more than one book, the appositive contains information essential to the meaning of the sentence.

33f Do not use a comma to set off a concluding adverb clause that is essential for meaning.

When adverb clauses introduce a sentence, they are nearly always followed by a comma (see 32b). When they conclude a sentence, however, they are not set off by commas if their content is essential to the meaning of the earlier part of the sentence. Adverb clauses beginning with *after, as soon as, because, before, if, since, unless, until,* and *when* are usually essential.

▶ Don't visit Paris at the height of the tourist season/ unless

you have booked hotel reservations.

Without the *unless* clause, the meaning of the sentence might at first seem broader than the writer intended.

When a concluding adverb clause is nonessential, it should be preceded by a comma. Clauses beginning with *although, even though, though,* and *whereas* are usually nonessential.

▶ The lecture seemed to last only a short time, although the
^
clock said it had gone on for more than an hour.

33g Do not use a comma after a phrase that begins an inverted sentence.

Though a comma belongs after most introductory phrases (see 32b), it does not belong after phrases that begin an inverted sentence. In an inverted sentence, the subject follows the verb, and a phrase that ordinarily would follow the verb is moved to the beginning (see 47c).

▶ At the bottom of the hill/ sat the stubborn mule.

33h Avoid other common misuses of the comma.

Do not use a comma in the following situations.

AFTER A COORDINATING CONJUNCTION (*AND, BUT, OR, NOR, FOR, SO, YET*)

▶ Occasionally TV talk shows are performed live, but/ more often they are taped.

AFTER *SUCH AS* OR *LIKE*

▶ Shade-loving plants such as/ begonias, impatiens, and coleus can add color to a shady garden.

AFTER *ALTHOUGH*

▶ Although/ the air was balmy, the water was cold.

BEFORE A PARENTHESIS

▶ Though Sylvia's ACT score was low/ (only 24), her application essay was superior.

TO SET OFF AN INDIRECT (REPORTED) QUOTATION

▶ Samuel Goldwyn once said/ that a verbal contract isn't worth the paper it's written on.

WITH A QUESTION MARK OR AN EXCLAMATION POINT

▶ "Why don't you try it?⁄ " she coaxed. "You can't do any

worse than the rest of us."

EXERCISE 33-1 Delete any unnecessary commas in the following sentences. If a sentence is correct, write "correct" after it. Answers appear in the back of the book.

In his Silk Road Project, Yo-Yo Ma incorporates work by

musicians such as⁄ Kayhan Kalhor and Richard Danielpour.

a. After the morning rains cease, the swimmers emerge from their cottages.

b. Tricia's first artwork was a bright, blue, clay dolphin.

c. Some modern musicians, (trumpeter Jon Hassell is an example) blend several cultural traditions into a unique sound.

d. Myra liked hot, spicy foods such as, chili, kung pao chicken, and buffalo wings.

e. On the display screen, was a soothing pattern of light and shadow.

EXERCISE 33-2 Delete unnecessary commas in the following passage.

Each spring since 1970, New Orleans has hosted the Jazz and Heritage Festival, an event that celebrates the music, food, and culture, of the region. Although, it is often referred to as "Jazz Fest," the festival typically includes a wide variety of musical styles such as, gospel, Cajun, blues, zydeco, and, rock and roll. Famous musicians who have appeared regularly at Jazz Fest, include Dr. John, B. B. King, and Aretha Franklin. Large stages are set up throughout the fairgrounds in a way, that allows up to ten bands to play simultaneously without any sound overlap. Food tents are located throughout the festival, and offer popular, local dishes like crawfish Monica, jambalaya, and fried, green tomatoes. Following Hurricane Katrina in 2005, Jazz Fest revived quickly, and attendance has steadily increased each year. Fans, who cannot attend the festival, still enjoy the music by downloading MP3 files, and watching performances online.

34 The semicolon

The semicolon is used to connect major sentence elements of equal grammatical rank.

34a Use a semicolon between closely related independent clauses not joined with a coordinating conjunction.

When two independent clauses appear in one sentence, they are usually linked with a comma and a coordinating conjunction (*and, but, or, nor, for, so, yet*). If the clauses are closely related and the relation is clear without a conjunction, they may be linked with a semicolon instead.

> In film, a low-angle shot makes the subject look powerful; a high-angle shot does just the opposite.

A semicolon must be used whenever a coordinating conjunction has been omitted between independent clauses. To use merely a comma creates a type of run-on sentence known as a *comma splice*. (See 20.)

> ▶ In 1800, a traveler needed six weeks to get from New York
>
> to Chicago ̸; in 1860, the trip by train took only two days.
>   ^

34b Use a semicolon between independent clauses linked with a transitional expression.

Transitional expressions include conjunctive adverbs and transitional phrases.

CONJUNCTIVE ADVERBS

accordingly	furthermore	moreover	still
also	hence	nevertheless	subsequently
anyway	however	next	then
besides	incidentally	nonetheless	therefore
certainly	indeed	now	thus
consequently	instead	otherwise	
conversely	likewise	similarly	
finally	meanwhile	specifically	

TRANSITIONAL PHRASES

after all	even so	in fact
as a matter of fact	for example	in other words
as a result	for instance	in the first place
at any rate	in addition	on the contrary
at the same time	in conclusion	on the other hand

When a transitional expression appears between independent clauses, it is preceded by a semicolon and usually followed by a comma.

▶ Many corals grow very gradually/; in fact, the creation of

a coral reef can take centuries.

When a transitional expression appears in the middle or at the end of the second independent clause, the semicolon goes *between the clauses*.

▶ Biologists have observed laughter in primates other than

humans/; chimpanzees, however, sound more like they are

panting than laughing.

Transitional expressions should not be confused with the coordinating conjunctions *and, but, or, nor, for, so,* and *yet,* which are preceded by a comma when they link independent clauses. (See 32a.)

34c Use a semicolon between items in a series containing internal punctuation.

▶ Classic science fiction sagas are *Star Trek*, with Mr.

Spock/; *Battlestar Galactica*, with its Cylons/; and *Star*
       ^   ^

Wars, with Han Solo, Luke Skywalker, and Darth Vader.

Without the semicolons, the reader would have to sort out the major groupings, distinguishing between important and less important pauses according to the logic of the sentence. By inserting semicolons at the major breaks, the writer does this work for the reader.

34d Avoid common misuses of the semicolon.

Do not use a semicolon in the following situations.

BETWEEN A SUBORDINATE CLAUSE AND THE REST OF THE SENTENCE

▶ Although children's literature was added to the National

Book Awards in 1969/, it has had its own award, the
                    ^

Newbery Medal, since 1922.

BETWEEN AN APPOSITIVE AND THE WORD IT REFERS TO

▶ The scientists were fascinated by the species *Argyroneta*

aquatica/, a spider that lives underwater.
          ^

TO INTRODUCE A LIST

▶ Some of my favorite celebrities have their own blogs/:
                                                      ^
Ashton Kutcher, Beyoncé, and Zach Braff.

BETWEEN INDEPENDENT CLAUSES JOINED BY *AND*, *BUT*, *OR*, *NOR*, *FOR*, *SO*, OR *YET*

▶ Five of the applicants had worked with spreadsheets⁄, but
   ∧
only one was familiar with database management.

EXCEPTION: If one or both of the independent clauses contains a comma, you may use a semicolon with a coordinating conjunction between the clauses.

EXERCISE 34–1 Add commas or semicolons where needed in the following well-known quotations. If a sentence is correct, write "correct" after it. Answers appear in the back of the book.

"If an animal does something, we call it instinct; if we do the
                              ∧   ∧
same thing, we call it intelligence."   —Will Cuppy
          ∧

a. "Do not ask me to be kind just ask me to act as though I were."
                                             —Jules Renard

b. "When men talk about defense they always claim to be protecting women and children but they never ask the women
   and children what they think."   —Pat Schroeder

c. "When I get a little money I buy books if any is left I buy food
   and clothes."   —Desiderius Erasmus

d. "America is a country that doesn't know where it is going but
   is determined to set a speed record getting there."
                                           —Laurence J. Peter

e. "Wit has truth in it wisecracking is simply calisthenics with
   words."   —Dorothy Parker

EXERCISE 34–2 Edit the following sentences to correct errors in the use of the comma and the semicolon. If a sentence is correct, write "correct" after it. Answers appear in the back of the book.

Love is blind; envy has its eyes wide open.
            ∧

a. Strong black coffee will not sober you up, the truth is that time
   is the only way to get alcohol out of your system.

b. Margaret was not surprised to see hail and vivid lightning, conditions had been right for violent weather all day.

c. There is often a fine line between right and wrong; good and bad; truth and deception.

d. My mother always says that you can't learn common sense; either you're born with it or you're not.

e. Severe, unremitting pain is a ravaging force; especially when the patient tries to hide it from others.

35 The colon

The colon is used primarily to call attention to the words that follow it. In addition, the colon has some conventional uses.

35a Use a colon after an independent clause to direct attention to a list, an appositive, a quotation, or a summary or an explanation.

A LIST

The daily exercise routine should include at least the following: twenty knee bends, fifty sit-ups, and five minutes of running in place.

AN APPOSITIVE

My roommate seems to live on two things: snacks and social media.

A QUOTATION

Consider the words of Benjamin Franklin: "There never was a good war or a bad peace."

A SUMMARY OR AN EXPLANATION

Faith is like love: It cannot be forced.

The novel is clearly autobiographical: The author even gives his own name to the main character.

NOTE: For other ways of introducing quotations, see "Introducing quoted material" on pages 443–45. When an independent clause follows a colon, begin with a capital letter. Some disciplines use a lowercase letter instead. See 45f for variations.

35b Use a colon according to convention.

SALUTATION IN A LETTER Dear Editor:

HOURS AND MINUTES 5:30 p.m.

PROPORTIONS The ratio of women to men was 2:1.

TITLE AND SUBTITLE *The Glory of Hera: Greek Mythology and the Greek Family*

BIBLIOGRAPHIC ENTRIES Boston: Bedford/St. Martin's, 2015

CHAPTER AND VERSE IN SACRED TEXT Luke 2:14, Qur'an 67:3

35c Avoid common misuses of the colon.

A colon must be preceded by a full independent clause. Therefore, avoid using it in the following situations.

BETWEEN A VERB AND ITS OBJECT OR COMPLEMENT

▶ Some important vitamins found in vegetables are⫻ vitamin A, thiamine, niacin, and vitamin C.

BETWEEN A PREPOSITION AND ITS OBJECT

▶ The heart's two pumps each consist of⫻ an upper chamber, or atrium, and a lower chamber, or ventricle.

AFTER *SUCH AS*, *INCLUDING*, OR *FOR EXAMPLE*

▶ The NCAA regulates college athletic sports, including͵

basketball, baseball, softball, and football.

EXERCISE 35–1   Edit the following sentences to correct errors in the use of the comma, the semicolon, or the colon. If a sentence is correct, write "correct" after it. Answers appear in the back of the book.

Lifting the cover gently, Luca found the source of the odd

sound͵: a marble in the gears.
     ^

a. We always looked forward to Thanksgiving in Vermont: It was our only chance to see our Grady cousins.

b. If we have come to fight, we are far too few, if we have come to die, we are far too many.

c. The travel package includes: a round-trip ticket to Athens, a cruise through the Cyclades, and all hotel accommodations.

d. The news article portrays the land use proposal as reckless; although 62 percent of the town's residents support it.

e. Psychologists Kindlon and Thompson (2000) offer parents a simple starting point for raising male children, "Teach boys that there are many ways to be a man" (p. 256).

36 The apostrophe

36a Use an apostrophe to indicate that a noun is possessive.

Possessive nouns usually indicate ownership, as in *Tim's hat* or *the lawyer's desk*. Frequently, however, ownership is only loosely implied: *the tree's roots, a day's work.* If you are not sure whether a noun is possessive, try turning it into an *of* phrase: *the roots of the tree, the work of a day.* (Pronouns also have possessive forms. See 36b and 36e.)

When to add -'s

1. If the noun does not end in *-s*, add *-'s*.

   Luck often propels a rock musician's career.

   The Children's Defense Fund is a nonprofit organization that supports programs for poor and minority children.

2. If the noun is singular and ends in *-s* or an *s* sound, add *-'s* to indicate possession.

   Lois's sister spent last year in India.

   Her article presents an overview of Marx's teachings.

NOTE: To avoid potentially awkward pronunciation, some writers use only the apostrophe with a singular noun ending in *-s*: *Sophocles'*.

When to add only an apostrophe

If the noun is plural and ends in *-s*, add only an apostrophe.

   Both diplomats' briefcases were searched by guards.

Joint possession

To show joint possession, use *-'s* or (*-s'*) with the last noun only; to show individual possession, make all nouns possessive.

   Have you seen Joyce and Greg's new camper?

   John's and Marie's expectations of marriage couldn't have been more different.

Joyce and Greg jointly own one camper. John and Marie individually have different expectations.

Compound nouns

If a noun is compound, use *-'s* (or *-s'*) with the last element.

> My father-in-law's memoir about his childhood in Sri Lanka was published in October.

36b Use an apostrophe and -s to indicate that an indefinite pronoun is possessive.

Indefinite pronouns refer to no specific person or thing: *everyone, someone, no one, something.* (See 46b.)

> Someone's raincoat has been left behind.

36c Use an apostrophe to mark omissions in contractions and numbers.

In a contraction, the apostrophe takes the place of one or more missing letters. *It's* stands for *it is, can't* for *cannot.*

> It's a shame that Frank can't go on the tour.

The apostrophe is also used to mark the omission of the first two digits of a year (*the class of '12*) or years (*the '60s generation*).

36d Do not use an apostrophe in certain situations.

An apostrophe typically is not used to pluralize numbers, letters, abbreviations, and words mentioned as words. Note the few exceptions and be consistent throughout your paper.

Plural of numbers

Do not use an apostrophe in the plural of any numbers.

> Oksana skated nearly perfect figure 8s.

> The 1920s are known as the Jazz Age.

Plural of letters

Italicize the letter and use roman (regular) font style for the -*s* ending. (Do not italicize academic grades.)

> Two large *P*s were painted on the door.

> He received two Ds for the first time in his life.

EXCEPTIONS: To avoid misreading, use an apostrophe to form the plural of lowercase letters and the capital letters *A* and *I*.

> Beginning readers often confuse *b*'s and *d*'s.

> Students with straight A's earn high honors.

MLA NOTE: MLA recommends using an apostrophe for the plural of single capital and lowercase letters: *H's, p's.*

Plural of abbreviations

Do not use an apostrophe to pluralize an abbreviation.

> Harriet has thirty DVDs on her desk.

> Marco earned two PhDs before his thirtieth birthday.

Plural of words mentioned as words

Generally, omit the apostrophe to form the plural of words mentioned as words. If the word is italicized, the -*s* ending appears in roman (regular) type.

> We've heard enough *maybe*s.

Words mentioned as words may also appear in quotation marks. When you choose this option, use the apostrophe.

> We've heard enough "maybe's."

36e Avoid common misuses of the apostrophe.

Do not use an apostrophe with nouns that are not possessive or with the possessive pronouns *its*, *whose*, *his*, *hers*, *ours*, *yours*, and *theirs*.

►   Some ~~outpatient's~~ outpatients have special parking permits.

►   Each area has ~~it's~~ its own conference room.

It's means "it is." The possessive pronoun *its* contains no apostrophe despite the fact that it is possessive.

►   We attended a reading by Junot Díaz, ~~who's~~ whose work focuses on the Dominican immigration experience.

Who's means "who is." The possessive pronoun is *whose*.

EXERCISE 36–1   Edit the following sentences to correct errors in the use of the apostrophe. If a sentence is correct, write "correct" after it. Answers appear in the back of the book.

Our favorite barbecue restaurant is Poor ~~Richards~~ Richard's Ribs.

a.   This diet will improve almost anyone's health.

b.   The innovative shoe fastener was inspired by the designers young son.

c.   Each days menu features a different European country's dish.

d.   Sue worked overtime to increase her families earnings.

e.   Ms. Jacobs is unwilling to listen to students complaints about computer failures.

EXERCISE 36–2   Edit the following passage to correct errors in the use of the apostrophe.

Its never too soon to start holiday shopping. In fact, some people choose to start shopping as early as January, when last seasons leftover's are priced at their lowest. Many stores try to lure customers in with promise's of savings up to 90 percent.

Their main objective, of course, is to make way for next years inventory. The big problem with postholiday shopping, though, is that there isn't much left to choose from. Store's shelves have been picked over by last-minute shoppers desperately searching for gifts. The other problem is that its hard to know what to buy so far in advance. Next year's hot items are anyones guess. But proper timing, mixed with lot's of luck and determination, can lead to good purchases at great price's.

37 Quotation marks

Writers use quotation marks primarily to enclose direct quotations of another person's spoken or written words. You will also find these other uses and exceptions:

- for quotations within quotations (single quotation marks: 37b)
- for titles of short works (37c)
- for words used as words (37d)
- with other marks of punctuation (37e)
- with brackets and ellipsis marks (39c and 39d)
- no quotation marks for indirect quotations, paraphrases, and summaries (p. 440)
- no quotation marks for long quotations (p. 440)

37a Use quotation marks to enclose direct quotations.

Direct quotations of a person's words, whether spoken or written, must be in quotation marks.

> "Twitter," according to social media researcher Jameson Brown, "is the best social network for brand to customer engagement."

In dialogue, begin a new paragraph to mark a change in speaker.

> "Mom, his name is Willie, not William. A thousand times I've told you, it's *Willie*."
>
> "Willie is a derivative of William, Lester. Surely his birth certificate doesn't have Willie on it, and I like calling people by their proper names."
>
> "Yes, it does, ma'am. My mother named me Willie K. Mason."
>
> —Gloria Naylor

If a single speaker utters more than one paragraph, introduce each paragraph with a quotation mark, but do not use a closing quotation mark until the end of the speech.

Exception: indirect quotations

Do not use quotation marks around indirect quotations. An indirect quotation reports someone's ideas without using that person's exact words. In academic writing, indirect quotation is called *paraphrase* or *summary*. (See 51c.)

> Social media researcher Jameson Brown finds Twitter the best social media tool for companies that want to reach their consumers.

Exception: long quotations

Long quotations of prose or poetry are generally set off from the text by indenting. Quotation marks are not used because the indented format tells readers that the quotation is taken word-for-word from the source.

> After making an exhaustive study of the historical record, James Horan evaluates Billy the Kid like this:
>
> > The portrait that emerges of [the Kid] from the thousands of pages of affidavits, reports, trial transcripts, his letters, and his testimony is neither the mythical Robin Hood nor the stereotyped

adenoidal moron and pathological killer. Rather Billy appears
as a disturbed, lonely young man, honest, loyal to his friends,
dedicated to his beliefs, and betrayed by our institutions and the
corrupt, ambitious, and compromising politicians in his
time. (158)

The number in parentheses is a citation handled according to
MLA style (see 56a). (For details about citing long quotations
from poetry, see "Citing quotations" in 7f.)

MLA, APA, and *Chicago* have specific guidelines for what
constitutes a long quotation and how it should be indented (see
pp. 589, 687, and 764, respectively).

37b Use single quotation marks to enclose a quotation within a quotation.

Megan Marshall notes that Elizabeth Peabody's school focused
on "not merely 'teaching' but 'educating children morally and
spiritually as well as intellectually from the first'" (107).

37c Use quotation marks around the titles of short works.

Short works include newspaper and magazine articles, poems,
short stories, songs, episodes of television and radio programs,
and chapters or subdivisions of books.

James Baldwin's story "Sonny's Blues" tells the story of two
brothers who come to understand each other's suffering.

NOTE: Titles of long works such as books, plays, television and
radio programs, films, magazines, and so on are put in italics.
(See 42a.)

37d Quotation marks may be used to set off words used as words.

Although words used as words are ordinarily italicized (see 42d), quotation marks are also acceptable. Be consistent throughout your paper.

> The terms "migrant" and "refugee" are frequently confused.

> The terms *migrant* and *refugee* are frequently confused.

37e Use punctuation with quotation marks according to convention.

This section describes the conventions American publishers use in placing various marks of punctuation inside or outside quotation marks. It also explains how to punctuate when introducing quoted material. (For the use of quotation marks in MLA, APA, and *Chicago* styles, see 56a, 61a, and 63d, respectively. The examples in this section show MLA style.)

Periods and commas

Place periods and commas inside quotation marks.

> "I'm here as part of my service-learning project," I told the classroom teacher. "I'm hoping to become a reading specialist."

This rule applies to single quotation marks as well as double quotation marks. (See 37b.) It also applies to all uses of quotation marks: for quoted material, for titles of works, and for words used as words.

EXCEPTION: In MLA- and APA-style parenthetical in-text citations, the period follows the citation in parentheses (see p. 443).

James M. McPherson comments, approvingly, that the Whigs "were not averse to extending the blessings of American liberty, even to Mexicans and Indians" (48).

Colons and semicolons

Put colons and semicolons outside quotation marks.

Harold wrote, "I regret that I am unable to attend the fundraiser for ALS research"; his letter, however, came with a substantial contribution.

Question marks and exclamation points

Put question marks and exclamation points inside quotation marks unless they apply to the whole sentence.

Dr. Abram's first question on the first day of class was "What three goals do you have for the course?"

Have you heard the old proverb "Do not climb the hill until you reach it"?

In the first sentence, the question mark applies only to the quoted question. In the second sentence, the question mark applies to the whole sentence.

NOTE: In MLA and APA styles for a quotation that ends with a question mark or an exclamation point, the parenthetical citation and a period should follow the entire quotation.

Rosie Thomas asks, "Is nothing in life ever straight and clear, the way children see it?" (77).

Introducing quoted material

After a word group introducing a quotation, choose a colon, a comma, or no punctuation at all, whichever is appropriate in context.

Formal introduction If a quotation is formally introduced, a colon is appropriate. A formal introduction is a full independent clause, not just an expression such as *he writes* or *she remarked*.

> Thomas Friedman provides a challenging yet optimistic view of the future: "We need to get back to work on our country and on our planet. The hour is late, the stakes couldn't be higher, the project couldn't be harder, the payoff couldn't be greater" (25).

Expression such as *he writes* If a quotation is introduced with an expression such as *he writes* or *she remarked*—or if it is followed by such an expression—a comma is needed.

> "With regard to air travel," Stephen Ambrose notes, "Jefferson was a full century ahead of the curve" (53).

> "Unless another war is prevented it is likely to bring destruction on a scale never before held possible and even now hardly conceived," Albert Einstein wrote in the aftermath of the atomic bomb (29).

Blended quotation When a quotation is blended into the writer's own sentence, either a comma or no punctuation is appropriate, depending on the way in which the quotation fits into the sentence structure.

> The future champion could, as he put it, "float like a butterfly and sting like a bee."

> Virginia Woolf wrote in 1928 that "a woman must have money and a room of her own if she is to write fiction" (4).

Beginning of sentence If a quotation appears at the beginning of a sentence, use a comma after it unless the quotation ends with a question mark or an exclamation point.

> "I've always thought of myself as a reporter," American poet Gwendolyn Brooks has stated (162).

> "What is it?" she asked, bracing herself.

Interrupted quotation If a quoted sentence is interrupted by explanatory words, use commas to set off the explanatory words. If two successive quoted sentences from the same source are interrupted by explanatory words, use a comma before the explanatory words and a period after them.

> "Everyone agrees journalists must tell the truth," Bill Kovach and Tom Rosenstiel write. "Yet people are befuddled about what 'the truth' means" (37).

37f Avoid common misuses of quotation marks.

Do not use quotation marks to draw attention to familiar slang, to disown trite expressions, or to justify an attempt at humor.

▶ The economist estimated that single-family home prices

would decline another 5 percent by the end of the year,

emphasizing that this was only a ⸓ballpark figure.⸓

Do not use quotation marks around the title of your own essay.

EXERCISE 37–1 Add or delete quotation marks as needed and make any other necessary changes in punctuation in the following sentences. If a sentence is correct, write "correct" after it. Answers appear in the back of the book.

> Gandhi once said, ⌃"An eye for an eye only ends up making
> the whole world blind.⌃"

a. As for the advertisement "Sailors have more fun", if you consider chipping paint and swabbing decks fun, then you will have plenty of it.

b. Even after forty minutes of discussion, our class could not agree on an interpretation of Robert Frost's poem "The Road Not Taken."

c. After winning the lottery, Juanita said that "she would give half the money to charity."

d. After the movie, Vicki said, "The reviewer called this flick "trash of the first order." I guess you can't believe everything you read."

e. "Cleaning your house while your kids are still growing," said Phyllis Diller, "is like shoveling the walk before it stops snowing."

EXERCISE 37–2 Add or delete quotation marks as needed and make any other necessary changes in punctuation in the following passage. Citations should conform to MLA style (see 56a).

In his article The Moment of Truth, former vice president Al Gore argues that global warming is a genuine threat to life on Earth and that we must act now to avoid catastrophe. Gore calls our situation a "true *planetary emergency*" and cites scientific evidence of the greenhouse effect and its consequences (170-71). "What is at stake, Gore insists, is the survival of our civilization and the habitability of the Earth (197)." With such a grim predicament at hand, Gore questions why so many political and economic leaders are reluctant to act. "Is it simply more convenient to ignore the warnings," he asks (171)?

The crisis, of course, will not go away if we just pretend it isn't there. Gore points out that in Chinese two symbols form the character for the word crisis. The first of those symbols means "danger", and the second means "opportunity." The danger we face, he claims, is accompanied by "unprecedented opportunity." (172) Gore contends that throughout history we have won battles against seemingly unbeatable evils such as slavery and fascism and that we did so by facing the truth and choosing the moral high ground. Gore's final appeal is to our humanity:

"Ultimately, [the fight to end global warming] is not about any scientific discussion or political dialogue; it is about who we are as human beings. It is about our capacity to transcend our limitations, to rise to this new occasion. To see with our hearts, as well as our heads, the response that is now called for." (244)

Gore feels that the fate of our world rests in our own hands, and his hope is that we will make the choice to save the planet.

Source of quotations: Al Gore, "The Moment of Truth," *Vanity Fair*, May 2006, pp. 170+.

38 End punctuation

38a The period

Use a period to end all sentences except direct questions or genuine exclamations. Also use periods in abbreviations according to convention.

To end sentences

Most sentences should end with a period. A sentence that reports a question instead of asking it directly (an indirect question) should end with a period, not a question mark.

▶ The professor asked whether talk therapy was more

beneficial than antidepressants~~?~~.
                                      ^

If a sentence is not a genuine exclamation, it should end with a period, not an exclamation point. (See also 38c.)

▶ After years of working her way through school, Geeta

finally graduated with high honors~~!~~.
                                     ^

In abbreviations

A period is conventionally used in abbreviations of titles and Latin words or phrases, including the time designations for morning and afternoon.

Mr.	i.e.	a.m. (or AM)
Ms.	e.g.	p.m. (or PM)
Dr.	etc.	

NOTE: If a sentence ends with a period marking an abbreviation, do not add a second period.

Do not use a period with US Postal Service abbreviations for states: MD, TX, CA.

Current usage is to omit the period in abbreviations of organization names, academic degrees, and designations for eras.

NATO	UNESCO	UCLA	BS	BC
IRS	AFL-CIO	NIH	PhD	BCE

38b The question mark

A direct question should be followed by a question mark.

What is the horsepower of a 777 engine?

TIP: Do not use a question mark after an indirect question, one that is reported rather than asked directly. Use a period instead.

▶ He asked me who was teaching the math course this year~~?~~.
                                                          ^

38c The exclamation point

Use an exclamation point after a word group or sentence to express exceptional feeling or to provide special emphasis. The exclamation point is rarely appropriate in academic writing.

When Gloria entered the room, I switched on the lights, and we all yelled, "Surprise!"

TIP: Do not overuse the exclamation point.

▶ In the fisherman's memory, the fish lives on, increasing in

length and weight with each passing year, until at last it is

big enough to shade a fishing boat~~!~~.
                                   ^
This sentence is emphatic enough without an exclamation point.

EXERCISE 38–1   Add appropriate end punctuation in the following paragraph.

Although I am generally rational, I am superstitious I never walk under ladders or put shoes on the table If I spill the salt, I go into frenzied calisthenics picking up the grains and tossing them over my left shoulder As a result of these curious activities, I've always wondered whether knowing the roots of superstitions would quell my irrational responses Superstition has it, for example, that one should never place a hat on the bed This superstition arises from a time when head lice were common and placing a guest's hat on the bed stood a good chance of spreading lice through the host's bed Doesn't this make good sense And doesn't it stand to reason that, if I know that my guests don't have lice, I shouldn't care where their hats go Of course it does It is fair to ask, then, whether I have changed my ways and place hats on beds Are you kidding I wouldn't put a hat on a bed if my life depended on it

39 Other punctuation marks

39a The dash

When typing, use two hyphens to form a dash (--). Do not put spaces before or after the dash. If your word processing program has what is known as an "em-dash" (—), you may use it instead, with no space before or after it.

Use a dash to set off parenthetical material that deserves emphasis.

> Everything that went wrong—from the peeping Tom at her window last night to my head-on collision today—we blamed on our move.

Use a dash to set off appositives that contain commas. An appositive is a noun or noun phrase that renames a nearby noun. Ordinarily most appositives are set off with commas (32e), but when the appositive itself contains commas, a pair of dashes helps readers see the relative importance of all the pauses.

> In my hometown, people's basic needs—food, clothing, and shelter—are less costly than in a big city like Los Angeles.

A dash can also be used to introduce a list, a restatement, an amplification, or a dramatic shift in tone or thought.

> Along the wall are the bulk liquids—sesame seed oil, honey, safflower oil, and that half-liquid "peanuts only" peanut butter.
>
> In his last semester, Peter tried to pay more attention to his priorities—applying to graduate school and getting financial aid.
>
> Everywhere we looked there were little kids—a bag of Skittles in one hand and their mommy or daddy's sleeve in the other.
>
> Kiere took a few steps back, came running full speed, kicked a mighty kick—and missed the ball.

In the first two examples, the writer could also use a colon. (See 35a.) The colon is more formal than the dash and not quite as dramatic.

TIP: Unless there is a specific reason for using the dash, avoid it. Unnecessary dashes create a choppy effect.

39b Parentheses

Use parentheses to enclose supplemental material, minor digressions, and afterthoughts.

> Nurses record patients' vital signs (temperature, pulse, and blood pressure) several times a day.

Use parentheses to enclose letters or numbers labeling items in a series.

> Regulations stipulated that only the following equipment could be used on the survival mission: (1) a knife, (2) thirty feet of parachute line, (3) a book of matches, (4) two ponchos, (5) an E tool, and (6) a signal flare.

TIP: Rough drafts are likely to contain unnecessary parentheses. As writers head into a sentence, they often think of additional details, using parentheses to work them in as best they can. Such sentences usually can be revised to add the details without parentheses.

> ▶ Researchers have said that seventeen million ~~(estimates run~~ ^*from*^ ~~as high as~~ ^*to*^ twenty-three million~~)~~ Americans have diabetes. ^

39c Brackets

Use brackets to enclose any words or phrases that you have inserted into an otherwise word-for-word quotation.

> *Audubon* reports that "if there are not enough young to balance deaths, the end of the species [California condor] is inevitable" (4).

The sentence quoted from the *Audubon* article did not contain the words *California condor* (since the context of the full article made clear what species was meant), so the writer needed to add the name in brackets.

The Latin word "sic" in brackets indicates that an error in a quoted sentence appears in the original source.

> According to the review, Nelly Furtado's performance was brilliant, "exceding [sic] the expectations of even her most loyal fans."

Do not overuse "sic," however, since calling attention to others' mistakes can appear snobbish. The preceding quotation, for example, might have been paraphrased instead: *According to the review, even Nelly Furtado's most loyal fans were surprised by the brilliance of her performance.*

NOTE: For advice on using "sic" in MLA, APA, and *Chicago* styles, see 55b, 60b, and 63c, respectively.

39d The ellipsis mark

The ellipsis mark consists of three spaced periods. Use an ellipsis mark to indicate that you have deleted words from an otherwise word-for-word quotation.

> Shute acknowledges that treatment for autism can be expensive: "Sensory integration therapy . . . can cost up to $200 an hour" (82).

If you delete a full sentence or more in the middle of a quoted passage, use a period before the three ellipsis dots.

> "If we don't properly train, teach, or treat our growing prison population," says Luis Rodríguez, "somebody else will. . . . This may well be the safety issue of the new century" (16).

TIP: Ordinarily, do not use the ellipsis mark at the beginning or at the end of a quotation. Readers will understand that the quoted material is taken from a longer passage. (If you have cut some words from the end of the final quoted sentence, however, MLA requires an ellipsis mark.)

In quoted poetry, use a full line of ellipsis dots to indicate that you have dropped a line or more from the poem, as in this example from "To His Coy Mistress" by Andrew Marvell:

> Had we but world enough, and time,
> This coyness, lady, were no crime.
> . . . .
> But at my back I always hear
> Time's wingèd chariot hurrying near; (1-2, 21-22)

39e The slash

Use the slash to separate two or three lines of poetry that have been run into your text. Add a space both before and after the slash.

> In the opening lines of "Jordan," George Herbert pokes gentle fun at popular poems of his time: "Who says that fictions only and false hair / Become a verse? Is there in truth no beauty?" (1-2).

Four or more lines of poetry should be handled as an indented quotation. (See p. 182.)

The slash may occasionally be used to separate paired terms such as *pass/fail* and *producer/director*. Do not use a space before or after the slash. Be sparing in this use of the slash. In particular, avoid the use of *and/or*, *he/she*, and *his/her*. Instead of using *he/she* and *his/her* to solve sexist language problems, you can usually find more graceful alternatives. (See 17f and 22a.)

EXERCISE 39–1 Edit the following sentences to correct errors in punctuation, focusing especially on appropriate use of the dash, parentheses, brackets, the ellipsis mark, and the slash. If a sentence is correct, write "correct" after it. Answers appear in the back of the book.

> Social insects/——bees, for example/——are able to
> communicate complicated messages to one another.

a. A client left his/her cell phone in our conference room after the meeting.

b. The films we made of Kilauea—on our trip to Hawaii Volcanoes National Park—illustrate a typical spatter cone eruption.

c. Although he was confident in his course selections, Greg chose the pass/fail option for Chemistry 101.

d. Of three engineering fields, chemical, mechanical, and materials, Keegan chose materials engineering for its application to toy manufacturing.

e. The writer Chitra Divakaruni explained her work with other Indian American immigrants: "Many women who came to Maitri [a women's support group in San Francisco] needed to know simple things like opening a bank account or getting citizenship. . . . Many women in Maitri spoke English, but their English was functional rather than emotional. They needed someone who understands their problems and speaks their language."

PART VIII

Mechanics

40 Abbreviations 457
41 Numbers 461
42 Italics 463
43 Spelling 466
44 The hyphen 475
45 Capitalization 479

455

Mechanics

ONLINE ACTIVITIES: **Writer's Help 2.0**
macmillan learning

writershelp.com/hacker

 LaunchPad Solo
macmillan learning

macmillanhighered.com/
launchpadsolo/hacker

Abbreviations and numbers — 4 Exercises

Italics — 2 Exercises
1 LearningCurve activity

Spelling and hyphenation — 3 Exercises

Capitalization — 2 Exercises
1 LearningCurve activity

40 Abbreviations

In the text of a paper, use abbreviations only when they are clearly appropriate and universally understood (such as *Dr.*, *a.m.*, *PhD*, and so on). This section provides details about common abbreviations and about how to handle abbreviations that might not be familiar to your readers.

40a Use standard abbreviations for titles immediately before and after proper names.

TITLES BEFORE PROPER NAMES	TITLES AFTER PROPER NAMES
Mr. Rafael Zabala	William Albert Sr.
Ms. Nancy Linehan	Thomas Hines Jr.
Dr. Margaret Simmons	Robert Simkowski, MD
Rev. John Stone	Mia Chin, LLD

Do not abbreviate a title if it is not used with a proper name. *My history professor* (not *prof.*) *is an expert on race relations in South Africa.*

Avoid redundant titles such as *Dr. Amy Day, MD*. Choose one title or the other: *Dr. Amy Day* or *Amy Day, MD*.

40b Use abbreviations only when you are sure your readers will understand them.

Familiar abbreviations for the names of organizations, companies, countries, academic degrees, and common terms, written without periods, are generally acceptable (see page 458).

| CIA | FBI | MD | NAACP |
| NBA | CEO | PhD | DVD |

Talk show host Conan O'Brien is a Harvard graduate with a BA in history.

When using an unfamiliar abbreviation (such as *NASW* for National Association of Social Workers) or a potentially ambiguous abbreviation (such as *AMA*, which can refer to either the American Medical Association or the American Management Association), write the full name followed by the abbreviation in parentheses at the first mention of the name. Then use just the abbreviation throughout the rest of the paper.

NOTE: An abbreviation that can be pronounced as a word is called an *acronym*: *NATO, MADD, SWAT.*

40c Use BC, AD, a.m., p.m., No., and $ only with specific dates, times, numbers, and amounts.

The abbreviation *BC* ("before Christ") follows a date, and *AD* ("*anno Domini*") precedes a date. Acceptable alternatives are *BCE* ("before the common era") and *CE* ("common era"), both of which follow a date.

40 BC (or 40 BCE)	4:00 a.m. (or AM)	No. 12 (or no. 12)
AD 44 (or 44 CE)	6:00 p.m. (or PM)	$150

Avoid using *a.m., p.m., No.,* or *$* when not accompanied by a specific numeral: *in the morning* (not *in the a.m.*).

40d Units of measurement

The following are typical abbreviations for units of measurement. Most social sciences and related fields use metric units (*km, mg*), but in other fields and in everyday use, US standard units (*mi, lb*) are typical. Generally, use abbreviations for units when they appear with numerals; spell out the units when they are used alone or when they are used with spelled-out numbers (see also 41a).

METRIC UNITS	US STANDARD UNITS
m, cm, mm	yd, ft, in.
km, kph	mi, mph
kg, g, mg	lb, oz

Results were measured in pounds.

Runners in the 5-km race had to contend with pouring rain.

Use no periods after abbreviations for units of measurement, except the abbreviation for "inch" (*in.*), to distinguish it from the preposition *in*.

40e Be sparing in your use of Latin abbreviations.

Latin abbreviations are acceptable in notes and bibliographies.

cf. (Latin *confer*, "compare")

e.g. (Latin *exempli gratia*, "for example")

et al. (Latin *et alia*, "and others")

etc. (Latin *et cetera*, "and so forth")

i.e. (Latin *id est*, "that is")

N.B. (Latin *nota bene*, "note well")

In the text of a paper in most academic fields, use the appropriate English phrases.

40f Plural of abbreviations

To form the plural of most abbreviations, add *-s*, without an apostrophe: *PhDs*, *DVDs*. Do not add *-s* to indicate the plural of units of measurement: *mm* (not *mms*), *lb* (not *lbs*), *in.* (not *ins.*).

40g Avoid inappropriate abbreviations.

In academic writing, abbreviations for the following are not commonly accepted.

> **PERSONAL NAMES** Charles (not Chas.)
>
> **DAYS OF THE WEEK** Monday (not Mon.)
>
> **HOLIDAYS** Christmas (not Xmas)
>
> **MONTHS** January, February, March (not Jan., Feb., Mar.)
>
> **COURSES OF STUDY** political science (not poli. sci.)
>
> **DIVISIONS OF WRITTEN WORKS** chapter, page (not ch., p.)
>
> **STATES AND COUNTRIES** Massachusetts (not MA or Mass.)
>
> **PARTS OF A BUSINESS NAME** Adams Lighting Company (not Adams Lighting Co.); Kim and Brothers (not Kim and Bros.)

NOTE: Use abbreviations for units of measurement when they are preceded by numerals (*13 cm*). Do not abbreviate them when they are used alone. See 40d.

EXCEPTION: Abbreviate states and provinces in complete addresses, and always abbreviate *DC* when used with *Washington.*

EXERCISE 40–1   Edit the following sentences to correct errors in abbreviations. If a sentence is correct, write "correct" after it. Answers appear in the back of the book.

> <u>Christmas</u>   <u>Tuesday.</u>
> This year ~~Xmas~~ will fall on a ~~Tues.~~
>   ^   ^

a.   Since its inception, the BBC has maintained a consistently high standard of radio and television broadcasting.

b.   Some combat soldiers are trained by govt. diplomats to be sensitive to issues of culture, history, and religion.

c.   Mahatma Gandhi has inspired many modern leaders, including Martin Luther King Jr.

d.   A gluten-free diet is not always the best strategy for shedding lbs.

e.   The work of Dr. Khan, a psych. professor and researcher, has helped practitioners better understand post-traumatic stress.

41   Numbers

41a Follow the conventions in your discipline for spelling out or using numerals to express numbers.

In the humanities, which generally follow Modern Language Association (MLA) style, use numerals only for specific numbers larger than one hundred: *353; 1,020.* Spell out numbers one hundred and below and large round numbers: *eleven, thirty-five, fifteen million.* Treat related numbers in a passage consistently: *The survey found that 9 of the 157 students had not taken a course on alcohol use.*

The social sciences and other disciplines that follow American Psychological Association (APA) style use numerals for all but the numbers one through nine. Spell out numbers from one to nine even when they are used with related numerals in a passage: *The survey found that nine of the 157 respondents had not taken a course on alcohol use.* (An exception is the abstract of a paper, where numerals are used for all numbers. See 62a.)

If a sentence begins with a number, spell out the number or rewrite the sentence.

> One hundred fifty
> ▶ ~~150~~ children in our program need expensive dental
>   ^
> treatment.

Rewriting the sentence may be less awkward if the number is long: *In our program, 150 children need expensive dental treatment.*

41b Use numerals according to convention in dates, addresses, and so on.

> **DATES** July 4, 1776; 56 BC; AD 30
>
> **ADDRESSES** 77 Latches Lane, 519 West 42nd Street
>
> **PERCENTAGES** 55 percent (or 55%)
>
> **FRACTIONS, DECIMALS** ⅞, 0.047
>
> **SCORES** 7 to 3, 21–18
>
> **STATISTICS** average age 37, average weight 180
>
> **SURVEYS** 4 out of 5
>
> **EXACT AMOUNTS OF MONEY** $105.37, $106,000
>
> **DIVISIONS OF BOOKS** volume 3, chapter 4, page 189
>
> **DIVISIONS OF PLAYS** act 3, scene 3 (or act III, scene iii)
>
> **TIME OF DAY** 4:00 p.m., 1:30 a.m.

NOTE: When not using *a.m.* or *p.m.*, write out the time in words (*two o'clock in the afternoon, twelve noon, seven in the morning*).

EXERCISE 41–1 Edit the following sentences to correct errors in the use of numbers. If a sentence is correct, write "correct" after it. Answers appear in the back of the book.

> $3.06
> By the end of the evening, Ashanti had only ~~three dollars~~
> ^
> ~~and six cents~~ left.

a. The carpenters located 3 maple timbers, 21 sheets of cherry, and 10 oblongs of polished ebony for the theater set.

b. The program's cost is well over one billion dollars.

c. The score was tied at 5–5 when the momentum shifted and carried the Standards to a decisive 12–5 win.

d. 8 students in the class had been labeled "learning disabled."

e. The Vietnam Veterans Memorial in Washington, DC, had fifty-eight thousand one hundred thirty-two names inscribed on it when it was dedicated in 1982.

42 Italics

This section describes conventional uses for italics. (If your instructor prefers underlining, simply substitute underlining for italics in the examples in this section.)

Some computer and online applications do not allow for italics. To indicate words that should be italicized, you can use underscore marks or asterisks before and after the words.

> I am planning to write my senior thesis on _The Hunger Games_.

NOTE: Excessive use of italics to emphasize words or ideas, especially in academic writing, is distracting and should be avoided.

42a Italicize the titles of works according to convention.

Titles of the following types of works should be italicized.

TITLES OF BOOKS *The Color Purple, The Round House*

MAGAZINES *Time, Scientific American, Slate*

NEWSPAPERS the *Baltimore Sun,* the *Orlando Sentinel*

PAMPHLETS *Common Sense, Facts about Marijuana*

LONG POEMS *The Waste Land, Paradise Lost*

PLAYS *In the Heights, Wicked*

FILMS *Casablanca, Argo*

TELEVISION PROGRAMS *The Voice, Frontline*

RADIO PROGRAMS *All Things Considered*

MUSICAL COMPOSITIONS *Porgy and Bess*

CHOREOGRAPHIC WORKS *Brief Fling*

WORKS OF VISUAL ART *American Gothic*

VIDEO GAMES *Everquest, Call of Duty*

DATABASES [MLA] *JSTOR*

WEB SITES [MLA] *Salon, Google*

COMPUTER SOFTWARE OR APPS [MLA] *Photoshop, Instagram*

The titles of other works—including short stories, essays, episodes of radio and television programs, songs, and short poems — are enclosed in quotation marks. (See 37c.)

NOTE: Do not use italics when referring to the Bible, titles of books in the Bible (Genesis, not *Genesis*), or titles of legal documents (the Constitution, not the *Constitution*).

42b Italicize the names of specific ships, spacecraft, and aircraft.

Queen Mary 2, Endeavour, Wright Flyer

The success of the Soviets' *Sputnik* energized the US space program.

42c Italicize foreign words used in an English sentence.

Shakespeare's Falstaff is a comic character known for both his excessive drinking and his general *joie de vivre*.

EXCEPTION: Do not italicize foreign words that have become a standard part of the English language—"laissez-faire," "fait accompli," "modus operandi," and "per diem," for example.

42d Italicize words mentioned as words, letters mentioned as letters, and numbers mentioned as numbers.

Tomás assured us that the chemicals could probably be safely mixed, but his *probably* stuck in our minds.

Some toddlers have trouble pronouncing the letters *f* and *s*.

A big *3* was painted on the stage door.

NOTE: Quotation marks may be used instead of italics to set off words mentioned as words. (See 37d.)

EXERCISE 42–1 Edit the following sentences to correct errors in the use of italics. If a sentence is correct, write "correct" after it. Answers appear in the back of the book.

We had a lively discussion about Gini Alhadeff's memoir

The Sun at Midday. *Correct*

a. Howard Hughes commissioned the Spruce Goose, a beautifully built but thoroughly impractical wooden aircraft.

b. The old man *screamed* his anger, *shouting* to all of us, "I will not leave my money to you worthless layabouts!"

c. I learned the Latin term ad infinitum from an old nursery rhyme about fleas: "Great fleas have little fleas upon their back to bite 'em, / Little fleas have lesser fleas and so on ad infinitum."

d. Cinema audiences once gasped at hearing the word *damn* in *Gone with the Wind.*

e. Neve Campbell's lifelong interest in ballet inspired her involvement in the film "The Company," which portrays a season with the Joffrey Ballet.

43 Spelling

You learned to spell from repeated experience with words in both reading and writing. As you proofread, you can probably tell if a word doesn't look quite right. In such cases, the solution is simple: Look up the word in the dictionary. (See 43b.)

43a Become familiar with the major spelling rules.

i before e except after c

In general, use *i* before *e* except after *c* and except when sounded like *ay*, as in *neighbor* and *weigh*.

I BEFORE E	relieve, believe, sieve, niece, fierce, frieze
E BEFORE I	receive, deceive, sleigh, freight, eight
EXCEPTIONS	seize, either, weird, height, foreign, leisure

Suffixes

Final silent -e Generally, drop a final silent *-e* when adding a suffix that begins with a vowel. Keep the final *-e* if the suffix begins with a consonant.

combine, combination	achieve, achievement
desire, desiring	care, careful
prude, prudish	entire, entirety
remove, removable	gentle, gentleness

Words such as *changeable*, *judgment*, *argument*, and *truly* are exceptions.

Final -y When adding *-s* or *-d* to words ending in *-y*, ordinarily change *-y* to *-ie* when the *-y* is preceded by a consonant but not when it is preceded by a vowel.

comedy, comedies   monkey, monkeys
dry, dried   play, played

With proper names ending in *-y*, however, do not change the *-y* to *-ie* even if it is preceded by a consonant: *the Doughertys.*

Final consonants If a final consonant is preceded by a single vowel *and* the consonant ends a one-syllable word or a stressed syllable, double the consonant when adding a suffix beginning with a vowel.

bet, betting   occur, occurrence
commit, committed

Plurals

-s or -es Add *-s* to form the plural of most nouns; add *-es* to singular nouns ending in *-s*, *-sh*, *-ch*, and *-x*.

table, tables   church, churches
paper, papers   dish, dishes

Ordinarily add *-s* to nouns ending in *-o* when the *-o* is preceded by a vowel. Add *-es* when it is preceded by a consonant.

radio, radios   hero, heroes
video, videos   tomato, tomatoes

Other plurals To form the plural of a hyphenated compound word, add *-s* to the chief word even if it does not appear at the end.

mother-in-law, mothers-in-law

English words derived from other languages such as Latin, Greek, or French sometimes form the plural as they would in their original language.

medium, media   chateau, chateaux
criterion, criteria

Multilingual

Spelling varies slightly among English-speaking countries. Variations can be confusing for some multilingual students in the United States. Following is a list of some common words with different American and British spellings. Consult a dictionary for others.

AMERICAN	BRITISH
canceled, traveled	cancelled, travelled
color, humor	colour, humour
judgment	judgement
check	cheque
realize, apologize	realise, apologise
defense	defence
anemia, anesthetic	anaemia, anaesthetic
theater, center	theatre, centre
fetus	foetus
mold, smolder	mould, smoulder
civilization	civilisation
connection, inflection	connexion, inflexion
licorice	liquorice

43b Become familiar with your dictionary.

A good dictionary, whether print or online—such as *The Random House College Dictionary* or *Merriam-Webster* online—is an indispensable writer's aid.

A sample print dictionary entry, taken from *The American Heritage Dictionary of the English Language*, appears on this page. A sample online dictionary entry, taken from *Merriam-Webster* online, appears on page 470.

Print dictionary entry

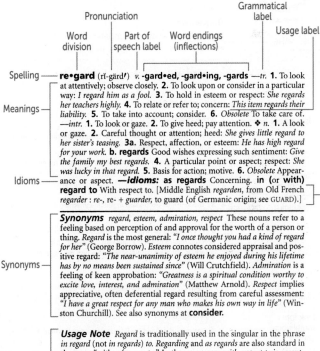

Grammatical label

Pronunciation

Word division · Part of speech label · Word endings (inflections) · Usage label

Spelling — **re•gard** (rĭ-gärd′) *v.* **-gard•ed, -gard•ing, -gards** —*tr.* **1.** To look at attentively; observe closely. **2.** To look upon or consider in a particular way: *I regard him as a fool.* **3.** To hold in esteem or respect: *She regards her teachers highly.* **4.** To relate or refer to; concern: *This item regards their liability.* **5.** To take into account; consider. **6.** *Obsolete* To take care of. —*intr.* **1.** To look or gaze. **2.** To give heed; pay attention. ❖ *n.* **1.** A look or gaze. **2.** Careful thought or attention; heed: *She gives little regard to her sister's teasing.* **3a.** Respect, affection, or esteem: *He has high regard for your work.* **b. regards** Good wishes expressing such sentiment: *Give the family my best regards.* **4.** A particular point or aspect; respect: *She was lucky in that regard.* **5.** Basis for action; motive. **6.** *Obsolete* Appearance or aspect. —**idioms: as regards** Concerning. **in** (or **with**) **regard to** With respect to. [Middle English *regarden*, from Old French *regarder* : *re-*, re- + *guarder*, to guard (of Germanic origin); see GUARD.]

Synonyms *regard, esteem, admiration, respect* These nouns refer to a feeling based on perception of and approval for the worth of a person or thing. *Regard* is the most general: *"I once thought you had a kind of regard for her"* (George Borrow). *Esteem* connotes considered appraisal and positive regard: *"The near-unanimity of esteem he enjoyed during his lifetime has by no means been sustained since"* (Will Crutchfield). *Admiration* is a feeling of keen approbation: *"Greatness is a spiritual condition worthy to excite love, interest, and admiration"* (Matthew Arnold). *Respect* implies appreciative, often deferential regard resulting from careful assessment: *"I have a great respect for any man who makes his own way in life"* (Winston Churchill). See also synonyms at **consider.**

Usage Note *Regard* is traditionally used in the singular in the phrase *in regard* (not *in regards*) *to. Regarding* and *as regards* are also standard in the sense "with reference to." In the same sense *with respect to* is acceptable, but *respecting* is not. • *Respects* is sometimes considered preferable to *regards* in the sense of "particulars": *In some respects* (not *regards*) *the books are alike.*

Meanings · Idioms · Synonyms · Usage note

Word origin (etymology)

Online dictionary entry

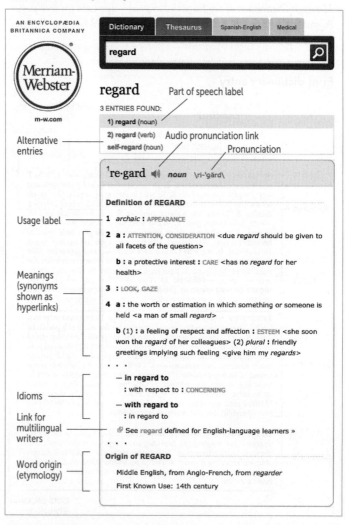

AN ENCYCLOPÆDIA BRITANNICA COMPANY

Merriam-Webster

m-w.com

Dictionary | Thesaurus | Spanish-English | Medical

regard 🔍

regard — Part of speech label

3 ENTRIES FOUND:

1) regard (noun)
2) regard (verb) — Audio pronunciation link
self-regard (noun)

Alternative entries

Pronunciation

¹**re·gard** 🔊 *noun* \ri-ˈgärd\

Definition of REGARD

Usage label —

1 *archaic* : APPEARANCE

2 a : ATTENTION, CONSIDERATION <due *regard* should be given to all facets of the question>

b : a protective interest : CARE <has no *regard* for her health>

Meanings (synonyms shown as hyperlinks)

3 : LOOK, GAZE

4 a : the worth or estimation in which something or someone is held <a man of small *regard*>

b (1) : a feeling of respect and affection : ESTEEM <she soon won the *regard* of her colleagues> (2) *plural* : friendly greetings implying such feeling <give him my *regards*>

. . .

Idioms —

— **in regard to**
: with respect to : CONCERNING

— **with regard to**
: in regard to

Link for multilingual writers —

📖 See *regard* defined for English-language learners »

. . .

Word origin (etymology)

Origin of REGARD

Middle English, from Anglo-French, from *regarder*

First Known Use: 14th century

Spelling, word division, pronunciation

The main entry (*re·gard* in the sample entries) shows the correct spelling of the word. When there are two correct spellings of a word (as in *collectible, collectable*), both are given, with the preferred spelling usually appearing first.

The dot between *re* and *gard* separates the two syllables and indicates where the word should be divided if it can't fit at the end of a typed line (see 44f). When a word is compound, the main entry shows how to write it: as one word (*crossroad*), as a hyphenated word (*cross-stitch*), or as two words (*cross section*).

The word's pronunciation is given just after the main entry. The accents indicate which syllables are stressed; the other marks are explained in the dictionary's pronunciation key. Many online entries include an audio link to a voice pronouncing the word.

Word endings and grammatical labels

When a word takes endings to indicate grammatical functions (called *inflections*), the endings are listed in boldface, as with *-garded*, *-garding*, and *-gards* in the sample print entry (p. 469).

Labels for the parts of speech and for other grammatical terms are sometimes abbreviated, as they are in the print entry. The most commonly used abbreviations are these:

n.	noun	adj.	adjective
pl.	plural	adv.	adverb
sing.	singular	pron.	pronoun
v.	verb	prep.	preposition
tr.	transitive verb	conj.	conjunction
intr.	intransitive verb	interj.	interjection

Meanings, word origin, synonyms, and antonyms

Sometimes a word can be used as more than one part of speech (*regard*, for instance, can be used as either a verb or a noun). In such a case, all the meanings for one part of speech are given before all the meanings for another, as in the sample entries.

In both the print and online versions, the origin of the word, called its *etymology*, appears after all of the word's meanings.

Synonyms, words similar in meaning to the main entry, are frequently listed. In the sample print entry, the dictionary draws distinctions in meaning among the various synonyms. In the online entry, synonyms appear as hyperlinks. Antonyms, which do not appear in the sample entries, are words having a meaning opposite from that of the main entry.

Usage

Usage labels indicate when, where, or under what conditions a particular meaning for a word is appropriately used. Common labels are *informal* (or *colloquial*), *slang*, *archaic*, *poetic*, *nonstandard*, *dialect*, *obsolete*, and *British*. In the sample print entry, two meanings of *regard* are labeled *obsolete* because they are no longer in use. The sample online entry (p. 470) has one meaning labeled *archaic*.

Dictionaries sometimes include usage notes as well. Advice in the notes is based on the opinions of many experts and on actual usage in current publications.

43c Discriminate between words that sound alike but have different meanings.

Words that sound alike or nearly alike but have different meanings and spellings are called *homophones*. The following sets of words are commonly confused. A careful writer will double-check their every use. (See also the glossary of usage at the back of the book.)

> affect (verb: to exert an influence)
> effect (verb: to accomplish; noun: result)
>
> its (possessive pronoun: of or belonging to it)
> it's (contraction of *it is* or *it has*)

loose (adjective: free, not securely attached)
lose (verb: to fail to keep, to be deprived of)

principal (adjective: most important; noun: head of a school)
principle (noun: a fundamental guideline or truth)

their (possessive pronoun: belonging to them)
they're (contraction of *they are*)
there (adverb: that place or position)

who's (contraction of *who is* or *who has*)
whose (possessive form of *who*)

your (possessive pronoun: belonging to you)
you're (contraction of *you are*)

43d Be alert to commonly misspelled words.

absence	athlete	conscientious	existence
accidentally	attendance	conscious	extraordinary
accommodate	basically	criticism	familiar
achievement	beautiful	criticize	fascinate
acknowledge	beginning	decision	February
acquaintance	believe	definitely	foreign
acquire	benefited	descendant	forty
address	bureau	desperate	fourth
all right	business	different	friend
amateur	calendar	disastrous	government
analyze	cemetery	eighth	grammar
answer	changeable	eligible	harass
apparently	column	embarrass	height
appearance	commitment	emphasize	humorous
arctic	committed	environment	incidentally
argument	committee	especially	incredible
arithmetic	competitive	exaggerated	independence
arrangement	conceivable	exercise	indispensable
ascend	conscience	exhaust	inevitable

intelligence	pamphlet	pronunciation	sincerely
irrelevant	parallel	publicly	sophomore
irresistible	particularly	quiet	strictly
knowledge	pastime	quite	subtly
library	permanent	quizzes	succeed
license	permissible	receive	surprise
lightning	perseverance	recognize	thorough
loneliness	phenomenon	referred	tomorrow
maintenance	physically	restaurant	tragedy
maneuver	practically	rhythm	transferred
marriage	precede	roommate	truly
mathematics	preference	sandwich	unnecessarily
mischievous	preferred	schedule	usually
necessary	prejudice	seize	vacuum
noticeable	presence	separate	villain
occasion	prevalent	sergeant	weird
occurred	privilege	siege	whether
occurrence	proceed	similar	writing

EXERCISE 43–1 The following memo has been run through a spell checker. Proofread it carefully, editing the spelling and typographical errors that remain.

November 2, 2015

To: Patricia Wise
From: Constance Mayhew
Subject: Express Tours annual report

Thank you for agreeing to draft the annual report for Express Tours. Before you begin you're work, let me outline the initial steps.

First, its essential for you to include brief profiles of top management. Early next week, I'll provide profiles for all manages accept Samuel Heath, who's biographical information is being revised. You should edit these profiles carefully and than format them according to the enclosed instructions. We may ask you to include other employee's profiles at some point.

Second, you should arrange to get complete financial information for fiscal year 2015 from our comptroller, Richard Chang. (Helen Boyes, to, can provide the necessary figures.) When you get this information, precede according tot he plans we discuss in yesterday's meeting. By the way, you will notice from the figures that the sale of our Charterhouse division did not significantly effect net profits.

Third, you should e-mail first draft of the report by December 14. Of coarse, you should proofread you writing.

I am quiet pleased that you can take on this project. If I can answers questions, don't hesitate to call.

44 The hyphen

In addition to the guidelines in this section, a dictionary will help you make decisions about hyphenation.

44a Consult the dictionary to determine how to treat a compound word.

The dictionary indicates whether to treat a compound word as hyphenated (*water-repellent*), as one word (*waterproof*), or as two words (*water table*). If the compound word is not in the dictionary, treat it as two words.

▶ The prosecutor chose not to cross-examine any witnesses.

▶ All students are expected to record their data in a small
note‿book.

▶ Alice walked through the looking⁄glass into a backward
world.

44b Hyphenate two or more words used together as an adjective before a noun.

▶ Today's teachers depend on both traditional textbook
material and Web‿delivered content.

▶ Richa Gupta is not yet a well‿known candidate.

Generally, do not use a hyphen when such compounds follow
the noun.

▶ After our television campaign, Richa Gupta will be
well⁄known.

Do not use a hyphen to connect -*ly* adverbs to the words
they modify.

▶ A slowly⁄moving truck tied up traffic.

44c Hyphenate fractions and certain numbers when they are spelled out.

For numbers written as words, use a hyphen in all fractions (*two-
thirds*) and in all forms of compound numbers from twenty-one
to ninety-nine (*thirty-five*, *sixty-seventh*).

44d Use a hyphen with the prefixes *all-*,
ex- (meaning "former"), and *self-* and with the
suffix *-elect*.

▶ The private foundation is funneling more money into

self-help projects.

▶ The Student Senate bylaws require the president-elect to

attend all senate meetings before the transfer of office.

44e Use a hyphen in certain words to avoid
ambiguity.

Without the hyphen, there would be no way to distinguish between
words such as *re-creation* and *recreation*.

Bicycling in the city has always been my favorite form of
recreation.

The film was praised for its astonishing re-creation of
nineteenth-century London.

Hyphens are sometimes used to separate awkward double or
triple letters in compound words (*anti-intellectual*, *cross-stitch*).

44f Check for correct word breaks when words
must be divided at the end of a line.

Some word processing programs and other computer applications automatically generate word breaks at the ends of lines.
In academic writing, it's best to set your computer application
not to hyphenate automatically. This setting will ensure that

only words already containing a hyphen (such as *long-distance*, *pre-Roman*) will be hyphenated at the ends of lines.

E-mail addresses and URLs need special attention when they occur at the end of a line of text or in bibliographic citations. You must make a decision about hyphenation in each case.

Do not insert a hyphen to divide electronic addresses. Instead, break an e-mail address after the @ symbol or before a period. It is common practice to break a URL before most marks of punctuation. (For variations in MLA, APA, and *Chicago* styles, see 57a, 62a, and 63e, respectively.)

> Thousands of primary documents are available at docsteach .org/documents, a site organized by historical eras.

EXERCISE 44–1 Edit the following sentences to correct errors in hyphenation. If a sentence is correct, write "correct" after it. Answers appear in the back of the book.

Émile Zola's first readers were scandalized by his slice‿of‿life

novels.

a. Gold is the seventy-ninth element in the periodic table.
b. The swiftly-moving tugboat pulled alongside the barge and directed it away from the oil spill in the harbor.
c. The Moche were a pre-Columbian people who established a sophisticated culture in ancient Peru.
d. Your dog is well-known in our neighborhood.
e. Road-blocks were set up along all the major highways leading out of the city.

45 Capitalization

In addition to the rules in this section, a good dictionary can tell you when to use capital letters.

45a Capitalize proper nouns and words derived from them; do not capitalize common nouns.

Proper nouns are the names of specific persons, places, and things. All other nouns are common nouns. The following types of words are usually capitalized: names of deities, religions, religious followers, sacred books; words of family relationship used as names; particular places; nationalities and their languages, races, tribes; educational institutions, departments, particular courses; government departments, organizations, political parties; historical movements, periods, events, documents; and trade names.

PROPER NOUNS	COMMON NOUNS
God (used as a name)	a god
Book of Common Prayer	a sacred book
Uncle Pedro	my uncle
Father (used as a name)	my father
Lake Superior	a picturesque lake
the Capital Center	a center for advanced studies
the South	a southern state
Wrigley Field	a baseball stadium
University of Wisconsin	a state university
Geology 101	geology
the Democratic Party	a political party
the Enlightenment	the eighteenth century
Advil	a painkiller

Months, holidays, and days of the week are treated as proper nouns; the seasons and numbers of the days of the month are not.

> Our academic year begins on a Tuesday in early September, right after Labor Day.

> Graduation is in late spring, on the second of June.

EXCEPTION: Capitalize Fourth of July (or July Fourth) when referring to the holiday.

Names of school subjects are capitalized only if they are names of languages. Names of particular courses are capitalized.

> This semester Lee is taking math, physics, French, and English.

> Professor Obembe offers Modern American Fiction to graduate students.

The terms *Web* and *Internet* are typically capitalized, but related common nouns are not: *home page, operating system.* Usage varies widely, however, so check with your instructor about whether you should follow the guidelines for MLA, APA, or *Chicago* style (See 57a, 62a, or 63e, respectively).

CAUTION: Do not capitalize common nouns to make them seem important.

45b Capitalize titles of persons when used as part of a proper name but usually not when used alone.

> Professor Margaret Barnes; Dr. Sinyee Sein; John Scott Williams Jr.

> District Attorney Marshall was reprimanded for badgering the witness.

> The district attorney was elected for a two-year term.

> Usage varies when the title of an important public figure is used alone: *The president* [or *President*] *vetoed the bill.*

45c Capitalize titles according to convention.

In both titles and subtitles of works mentioned in the text of a paper, major words such as nouns, pronouns, verbs, adjectives, and adverbs should be capitalized. Minor words such as articles, prepositions, and coordinating conjunctions are not capitalized unless they are the first or last word of a title or subtitle. (In APA style, also capitalize all words of four or more letters. See 62a.)

Capitalize the second part of a hyphenated term in a title if it is a major word but not if it is a minor word. Capitalize chapter titles and the titles of other major divisions of a work following the same guidelines used for titles of complete works.

> *Seizing the Enigma: The Race to Break the German U-Boat Codes*
> *A River Runs through It*
> "I Want to Hold Your Hand"
> *The Canadian Green Page*

To see why some of the titles in the list are italicized and some are put in quotation marks, see 42a and 37c.

Titles of works are handled differently in the APA reference list. See "Preparing the list of references" in 62a.

45d Capitalize the first word of a sentence.

The first word of a sentence should be capitalized. When a sentence appears within parentheses, capitalize its first word unless the parentheses appear within another sentence.

> Early detection of breast cancer significantly increases survival rates. (See table 2.)

> Early detection of breast cancer significantly increases survival rates (see table 2).

45e Capitalize the first word of a quoted sentence but not a quoted word or phrase.

> Loveless writes, "If failing schools are ever to be turned around, much more must be learned about how schools age as institutions" (25).

> Russell Baker has written that in this country, sports are "the opiate of the masses" (46).

If a quoted sentence is interrupted by explanatory words, do not capitalize the first word after the interruption. (See also 37e.)

> "If you want to go out," he said, "tell me now."

When quoting poetry, copy the poet's capitalization exactly. Many poets capitalize the first word of every line of poetry; a few contemporary poets dismiss capitalization altogether.

> it was the week   that
> i felt the city's narrow breezes rush about
> me   —Don L. Lee

45f Capitalize the first word after a colon if it begins an independent clause.

If a group of words following a colon could stand on its own as a complete sentence, capitalize the first word.

> Clinical trials called into question the safety profile of the drug: A high percentage of participants reported hypertension and kidney problems.

Preferences vary among academic disciplines. See 57a, 62a, and 63e.

Always use lowercase for a list or an appositive that follows a colon (see 35a).

Students were divided into two groups: residents and commuters.

EXERCISE 45–1 Edit the following sentences to correct errors in capitalization. If a sentence is correct, write "correct" after it. Answers appear in the back of the book.

>   *G*   *C*
> **On our trip to the West, we visited the grand canyon and the**
> *G*   *S* *D*
> **great salt desert.**

a. Assistant dean Shirin Ahmadi recommended offering more world language courses.

b. We went to the Mark Taper Forum to see a production of *Angels in America*.

c. Kalindi has an ambitious semester, studying differential calculus, classical hebrew, brochure design, and greek literature.

d. Lydia's Aunt and Uncle make modular houses as beautiful as modernist works of art.

e. We amused ourselves on the long flight by discussing how Spring in Kyoto stacks up against Summer in London.

Grammar Basics

46 Parts of speech 487

47 Sentence patterns 499

48 Subordinate word groups 508

49 Sentence types 519

Grammar Basics

ONLINE ACTIVITIES:

Writer's Help 2.0
macmillan learning

writershelp.com/hacker

LaunchPad Solo
macmillan learning

macmillanhighered.com/
launchpadsolo/hacker

Nouns and pronouns	6 Exercises 1 LearningCurve activity
Verbs	3 Exercises 1 LearningCurve activity
Adjectives and adverbs	5 Exercises 1 LearningCurve activity
Prepositions and conjunctions	4 Exercises 1 LearningCurve activity
All parts of speech	2 Exercises
Sentence patterns	9 Exercises
Subordinate word groups: Phrases	7 Exercises
Subordinate word groups: Clauses	5 Exercises
Sentence types	2 Exercises

46 Parts of speech

Traditional grammar recognizes eight parts of speech: noun, pronoun, verb, adjective, adverb, preposition, conjunction, and interjection. Many words can function as more than one part of speech. For example, depending on its use in a sentence, the word *paint* can be a noun (*The paint is wet*) or a verb (*Please paint the ceiling next*).

46a Nouns

A noun is the name of a person, place, thing, or concept.

       N   N   N
The *lion* in the *cage* growled at the *zookeeper*.

Nouns sometimes function as adjectives modifying other nouns. Because of their dual roles, nouns used in this manner may be called *noun/adjectives*.

    N/ADJ   N/ADJ
The *leather* notebook was tucked in the *student's* backpack.

Nouns are classified in a variety of ways. *Proper* nouns are capitalized, but *common* nouns are not (see 45a). For clarity, writers choose between *concrete* and *abstract* nouns (see 18b). The distinction between *count* nouns and *noncount* nouns can be especially helpful to multilingual writers (see 29a). Most nouns have singular and plural forms; *collective* nouns may be either singular or plural, depending on how they are used (see 21f and 22b). *Possessive* nouns require an apostrophe (see 36a).

EXERCISE 46–1   Underline the nouns (and noun/adjectives) in the following sentences. Answers appear in the back of the book.

The best <u>part</u> of <u>dinner</u> was the <u>chef's</u> newest <u>dessert</u>.

a. The stage was set for a confrontation of biblical proportions.

b. The courage of the mountain climber was an inspiration to the rescuers.

c. The need to arrive before the guest of honor motivated us to navigate the thick fog.

d. The defense attorney made a final appeal to the jury.

e. A national museum dedicated to women artists opened in 1987.

46b Pronouns

A pronoun is a word used in place of a noun. Usually the pronoun substitutes for a specific noun, known as its *antecedent*.

> ANT   PN
> When the *battery* wears down, we recharge *it*.

Although most pronouns function as substitutes for nouns, some can function as adjectives modifying nouns. Such pronouns may be called *pronoun/adjectives*.

> PN/ADJ
> *That* bird was at the same window yesterday morning.

Pronouns are classified in the following ways.

Personal pronouns   Personal pronouns refer to specific persons or things. They always function as substitutes for nouns.

> *Singular:* I, me, you, she, her, he, him, it
>
> *Plural:* we, us, you, they, them

Possessive pronouns Possessive pronouns indicate ownership.

Singular: my, mine, your, yours, her, hers, his, its

Plural: our, ours, your, yours, their, theirs

Some of these possessive pronouns function as adjectives modifying nouns: *my, your, his, her, its, our, their.*

Intensive and reflexive pronouns Intensive pronouns emphasize a noun or another pronoun (The senator *herself* met us at the door). Reflexive pronouns name a receiver of an action identical with the doer of the action (Paula cut *herself*).

Singular: myself, yourself, himself, herself, itself

Plural: ourselves, yourselves, themselves

Relative pronouns Relative pronouns introduce subordinate clauses functioning as adjectives (The writer *who won the award* refused to accept it). The relative pronoun, in this case *who*, also points back to a noun or pronoun that the clause modifies (*writer*). (See 48e.)

who, whom, whose, which, that

The pronouns *whichever, whoever, whomever, what,* and *whatever* are sometimes considered relative pronouns, but they introduce noun clauses and do not point back to a noun or pronoun. (See "Noun clauses" in 48e.)

Interrogative pronouns Interrogative pronouns introduce questions (*Who* is expected to win the election?).

who, whom, whose, which, what

Demonstrative pronouns Demonstrative pronouns identify or point to nouns. Frequently they function as adjectives (*This* chair is my favorite), but they may also function as substitutes for nouns (*This* is my favorite chair).

> this, that, these, those

Indefinite pronouns   Indefinite pronouns refer to nonspecific persons or things. Most are always singular (*everyone, each*); some are always plural (*both, many*); a few may be singular or plural (see 21e). Most indefinite pronouns function as substitutes for nouns (*Something* is burning), but some can also function as adjectives (*All* campers must check in at the lodge).

all	anything	everyone	nobody	several
another	both	everything	none	some
any	each	few	no one	somebody
anybody	either	many	nothing	someone
anyone	everybody	neither	one	something

Reciprocal pronouns   Reciprocal pronouns refer to individual parts of a plural antecedent (By turns, the penguins fed *one another*).

> each other, one another

NOTE: See also pronoun-antecedent agreement (22), pronoun reference (23), distinguishing between pronouns such as *I* and *me* (24), and distinguishing between *who* and *whom* (25).

EXERCISE 46–5   Underline the pronouns (and pronoun/adjectives) in the following sentences. Answers appear in the back of the book.

> <u>We</u> enjoyed the video <u>that</u> the fifth graders produced as
>
> <u>their</u> final project.

a.   The governor's loyalty was his most appealing trait.

b.   In the fall, the geese that fly south for the winter pass through our town in huge numbers.

c. As Carl Sandburg once said, even he himself did not understand some of his poetry.

d. I appealed my parking ticket, but you did not get one.

e. Angela did not mind gossip as long as no one gossiped about her.

46c Verbs

The verb of a sentence usually expresses action (*jump, think*) or being (*is, become*). It is composed of a main verb possibly preceded by one or more helping verbs.

> MV
> The horses *exercise* every day.

> HV   MV
> The task force report *was* not *completed* on schedule.

> HV HV   MV
> No one *has been defended* with more passion than our pastor.

Notice that words, usually adverbs, can intervene between the helping verb and the main verb (was *not* completed). (See 46e.)

Helping verbs

There are twenty-three helping verbs in English: forms of *have, do,* and *be,* which may also function as main verbs; and nine modals, which function only as helping verbs. *Have, do,* and *be* change form to indicate tense; the nine modals do not.

FORMS OF *HAVE, DO,* AND *BE*

have, has, had

do, does, did

be, am, is, are, was, were, being, been

MODALS

can, could, may, might, must, shall, should, will, would

The verb phrase *ought to* is often classified as a modal as well.

Main verbs

The main verb of a sentence is always the kind of word that would change form if put into these test sentences:

BASE FORM	Usually I (*walk, ride*).
PAST TENSE	Yesterday I (*walked, rode*).
PAST PARTICIPLE	I have (*walked, ridden*) many times before.
PRESENT PARTICIPLE	I am (*walking, riding*) right now.
***-S* FORM**	Usually he/she/it (*walks, rides*).

If a word doesn't change form when slipped into the test sentences, you can be certain that it is not a main verb. For example, the noun *revolution*, though it may seem to suggest action, can never function as a main verb. Try to make it behave like one (*Today I revolution . . . Yesterday I revolutioned . . .*) and you'll see why.

When both the past-tense and the past-participle forms of a verb end in *-ed*, the verb is regular (*walked, walked*). Otherwise, the verb is irregular (*rode, ridden*). (See 27a.)

The verb *be* is highly irregular, having eight forms instead of the usual five: the base form *be*; the present-tense forms *am, is,* and *are*; the past-tense forms *was* and *were*; the present participle *being*; and the past participle *been*. Helping verbs combine with main verbs to create tenses. (See 28a.)

NOTE: Some verbs are followed by words that look like prepositions but are so closely associated with the verb that they are a part of its meaning. These words are known as *particles*. Common verb-particle combinations include *bring up, call off, drop off, give in, look up, run into,* and *take off.*

TIP: For more information about using verbs, see these sections of the handbook: active verbs (8), subject-verb agreement (21), Standard English verb forms (27), verb tense and mood (27f and 27g), and multilingual/ESL challenges with verbs (28).

EXERCISE 46–9 Underline the verbs in the following sentences, including helping verbs and particles. If a verb is part of a contraction (such as *is* in *isn't* or *would* in *I'd*), underline only the letters that represent the verb. Answers appear in the back of the book.

The ground under the pine trees <u>wasn't</u> wet from the rain.

a. My grandmother always told me a soothing story before bed.
b. There were fifty apples on the tree before the frost killed them.
c. Morton brought down the box of letters from the attic.
d. Stay on the main road and you'll arrive at the base camp.
e. The fish struggled vigorously but was trapped in the net.

46d Adjectives

An adjective is a word used to modify, or describe, a noun or pronoun. An adjective usually answers one of these questions: Which one? What kind of? How many?

ADJ
the *frisky* horse [Which horse?]

ADJ   ADJ
cracked old plates [What kind of plates?]

ADJ
nine months [How many months?]

ADJ
qualified applicants [What kind of applicants?]

Adjectives usually precede the words they modify. They may also follow linking verbs, in which case they describe the subject. (See 47b.)

ADJ
The decision was *unpopular*.

The definite article *the* and the indefinite articles *a* and *an* are also classified as adjectives.

ART   ART   ART
A defendant should be judged on *the* evidence provided to *the* jury, not on hearsay.

Some possessive, demonstrative, and indefinite pronouns can function as adjectives: *their, its, this, all* (see 46b). And nouns can function as adjectives when they modify other nouns: *apple pie* (the noun *apple* modifies the noun *pie*; see 46a).

TIP: You can find more details about using adjectives in 26. If you are a multilingual writer, you may find help with articles and specific uses of adjectives in 29, 30g, and 30h.

46e Adverbs

An adverb is a word used to modify, or qualify, a verb (or verbal), an adjective, or another adverb. It usually answers one of these questions: When? Where? How? Why? Under what conditions? To what degree?

Pull *firmly* on the emergency handle. [Pull how?]

Read the text *first* and *then* complete the exercises. [Read when? Complete when?]

Place the flowers *here*. [Place where?]

Adverbs modifying adjectives or other adverbs usually intensify or limit the intensity of the word they modify.

ADV
Be *extremely* kind, and you will have many friends.

ADV
We proceeded *very* cautiously in the dark house.

The words *not* and *never* are classified as adverbs. A word such as *cannot* contains the helping verb *can* and the adverb *not*. The word *can't* contains the helping verb *can* and a contracted form of *not* (see 36c).

TIP: You can find more details about using adverbs in 26b–26d. Multilingual writers can find more about the placement of adverbs in 30f.

EXERCISE 46–13   Underline the adjectives and circle the adverbs in the following sentences. If a word is a noun or pronoun functioning as an adjective, underline it and mark it as a noun/adjective or pronoun/adjective. Also treat the articles *a*, *an*, and *the* as adjectives. Answers appear in the back of the book.

Finding an available room during the convention was (not) easy.

a.   Generalizations lead to weak, unfocused essays.
b.   The Spanish language is wonderfully flexible.
c.   The wildflowers smelled especially fragrant after the steady rain.
d.   I'd rather be slightly hot than bitterly cold.
e.   The cat slept soundly in its wicker basket.

46f Prepositions

A preposition is a word placed before a noun or a pronoun to form a phrase that modifies another word in the sentence. The prepositional phrase functions as an adjective or an adverb.

> P   P   P
> The winding road *to* the summit travels *past* craters *from* an extinct volcano.

To the summit functions as an adjective modifying the noun *road*; *past craters* functions as an adverb modifying the verb *travels*; *from an extinct volcano* functions as an adjective modifying the noun *craters*. (For more on prepositional phrases, see 48a.)

English has a limited number of prepositions. The most common are included in the following list.

about	beside	from	outside	toward
above	besides	in	over	under
across	between	inside	past	underneath
after	beyond	into	plus	unlike
against	but	like	regarding	until
along	by	near	respecting	unto
among	concerning	next	round	up
around	considering	of	since	upon
as	despite	off	than	with
at	down	on	through	within
before	during	onto	throughout	without
behind	except	opposite	till	
below	for	out	to	

Some prepositions are more than one word long. *Along with, as well as, in addition to, next to,* and *rather than* are examples.

TIP: Prepositions are used in idioms such as *capable of* and *dig up* (see 18d). For specific issues for multilingual writers, see 31.

46g Conjunctions

Conjunctions join words, phrases, or clauses, and they indicate the relation between the elements joined.

Coordinating conjunctions A coordinating conjunction is used to connect grammatically equal elements. (See 9b and 14a.) The coordinating conjunctions are *and, but, or, nor, for, so,* and *yet.*

> The sociologist interviewed children *but* not their parents.
>
> Write clearly, *and* your readers will appreciate your efforts.

In the first sentence, *but* connects two noun phrases; in the second, *and* connects two independent clauses.

Correlative conjunctions Correlative conjunctions come in pairs; they connect grammatically equal elements.

> either . . . or
>
> neither . . . nor
>
> not only . . . but also
>
> whether . . . or
>
> both . . . and

> *Either* the painting was brilliant *or* it was a forgery.

Subordinating conjunctions A subordinating conjunction introduces a subordinate clause and indicates the relation of the clause to the rest of the sentence. (See 48e.) The most common subordinating conjunctions are *after, although, as, as if, because, before, if, in order that, once, since, so that, than, that, though,* *unless, until, when, where, whether,* and *while.* (For a complete list, see p. 517.)

> *When* the fundraiser ends, we expect to have raised more than half a million dollars.

Conjunctive adverbs   Conjunctive adverbs connect independent clauses and indicate the relation between the clauses. They can be used with a semicolon to join two independent clauses in one sentence, or they can be used alone with an independent clause. The most common conjunctive adverbs are *finally, furthermore, however, moreover, nevertheless, similarly, then, therefore,* and *thus.* (For a complete list, see p. 429.)

> The photographer failed to take a light reading; *therefore,* all the pictures were underexposed.

> During the day, the kitten sleeps peacefully. *However,* when night falls, the kitten is wide awake and ready to play.

Conjunctive adverbs can appear at the beginning or in the middle of a clause.

> When night falls, *however,* the kitten is wide awake and ready to play.

TIP: The ability to distinguish between conjunctive adverbs and coordinating conjunctions will help you avoid run-on sentences and make punctuation decisions (see 20, 32a, and 32f). The ability to recognize subordinating conjunctions will help you avoid sentence fragments (see 19).

46h Interjections

An interjection is a word used to express surprise or emotion (*Oh! Hey! Wow!*).

47 Sentence patterns

The vast majority of English sentences conform to one of these five patterns:

> subject/verb/subject complement
>
> subject/verb/direct object
>
> subject/verb/indirect object/direct object
>
> subject/verb/direct object/object complement
>
> subject/verb

Adverbial modifiers (single words, phrases, or clauses) may be added to any of these patterns, and they may appear nearly anywhere—at the beginning, in the middle, or at the end.

Predicate is the grammatical term given to the verb plus its objects, complements, and adverbial modifiers.

47a Subjects

The subject of a sentence names whom or what the sentence is about. The simple subject is always a noun or pronoun; the complete subject consists of the simple subject and any words or word groups modifying the simple subject.

The complete subject

To find the complete subject, ask Who? or What?, insert the verb, and finish the question. The answer is the complete subject.

┌────── COMPLETE SUBJECT ──────┐
The devastating effects of famine can last for many years.

Who or what can last for many years? *The devastating effects of famine.*

┌─────────────── COMPLETE SUBJECT ───────────────┐

Adventure novels that contain multiple subplots are often made into successful movies.

Who or what are often made into movies? *Adventure novels that contain multiple subplots.*

COMPLETE
┌──── SUBJECT ────┐

In our program, student teachers work full-time for ten months.

Who or what works full-time for ten months? *Student teachers.* Notice that *In our program, student teachers* is not a sensible answer to the question. (It is not safe to assume that the subject must always appear first in a sentence.)

The simple subject

To find the simple subject, strip away all modifiers in the complete subject. This includes single-word modifiers such as *the* and *devastating*, phrases such as *of famine*, and subordinate clauses such as *that contain multiple subplots.*

┌SS┐
The devastating effects of famine can last for many years.

┌SS┐
Adventure novels that contain multiple subplots are often made into successful movies.

A sentence may have a compound subject containing two or more simple subjects joined with a coordinating conjunction such as *and, but,* or *or.*

┌──── SS ────┐   ┌SS┐
Great commitment and a little luck make a successful actor.

Understood subjects

In imperative sentences, which give advice or issue commands, the subject is understood but not actually present in the sentence. The subject of an imperative sentence is understood to be *you*.

> [*You*] Put your hands on the steering wheel.

Subject after the verb

Although the subject ordinarily comes before the verb (*The planes took off*), occasionally it does not. When a sentence begins with *There is* or *There are* (or *There was* or *There were*), the subject follows the verb. In such inverted constructions, the word *There* is an expletive, an empty word serving merely to get the sentence started.

> ⌐ SS ⌐
> There are *eight planes waiting to take off.*

Occasionally a writer will invert a sentence for effect.

> ⌐ SS ⌐
> Joyful is *the child whose school closes for snow.*

Joyful is an adjective, so it cannot be the subject. Turn this sentence around and its structure becomes obvious.

> The *child* whose school closes for snow is joyful.

In questions, the subject frequently appears between the helping verb and the main verb.

> HV ┌─── SS ───┐ MV
> Do *Kenyan marathoners* train year-round?

TIP: The ability to recognize the subject of a sentence will help you edit for fragments (19), subject-verb agreement (21), pronouns such as *I* and *me* (24), missing subjects (30b), and repeated subjects (30c).

EXERCISE 47–1 In the following sentences, underline the complete subject and write *SS* above the simple subject(s). If the subject is an understood *you*, insert *you* in parentheses. Answers appear in the back of the book.

       ┌─SS─┐   ┌─SS─┐
Parents and their children often look alike.

a. The hills and mountains seemed endless, and the snow atop them glistened.
b. In foil fencing, points are scored by hitting an electronic target.
c. Do not stand in the aisles or sit on the stairs.
d. There were hundreds of fireflies in the open field.
e. The evidence against the defendant was staggering.

47b Verbs, objects, and complements

Section 46c explains how to find the verb of a sentence. A sentence's verb is classified as linking, transitive, or intransitive, depending on the kinds of objects or complements the verb can (or cannot) take.

Linking verbs and subject complements

Linking verbs connect the subject to a subject complement, a word or word group that completes the meaning of the subject by renaming or describing it.

If the subject complement renames the subject, it is a noun or noun equivalent (sometimes called a *predicate noun*).

┌──────────────── S ────────────────┐ ┌─ V ─┐
A phone call requesting personal information may be

┌─SC─┐
a scam.

If the subject complement describes the subject, it is an adjective or adjective equivalent (sometimes called a *predicate adjective*).

$$\overset{\text{S}}{\overbrace{\text{Last month's temperatures}}} \overset{\text{V}}{\text{were}} \overset{\text{SC}}{\text{mild.}}$$

Whenever they appear as main verbs (rather than helping verbs), the forms of *be*—*be, am, is, are, was, were, being, been*—usually function as linking verbs. In the preceding examples, for instance, the main verbs are *be* and *were*.

Verbs such as *appear, become, feel, grow, look, make, seem, smell, sound,* and *taste* are linking when they are followed by a word or word group that renames or describes the subject.

$$\overset{\text{S}}{\overbrace{\text{As it thickens,}}} \overset{\text{S}}{\overbrace{\text{the sauce}}} \overset{\text{V}}{\overbrace{\text{will look}}} \overset{\text{SC}}{\text{unappealing.}}$$

Transitive verbs and direct objects

A transitive verb takes a direct object, a word or word group that names a receiver of the action.

$$\overset{\text{S}}{\overbrace{\text{The hungry cat}}} \overset{\text{V}}{\text{clawed}} \overset{\text{DO}}{\overbrace{\text{the bag of dry food.}}}$$

The simple direct object is always a noun or pronoun, in this case *bag.* To find it, simply strip away all modifiers.

Transitive verbs usually appear in the active voice, with the subject doing the action and a direct object receiving the action. Active-voice sentences can be transformed into passive, with the subject receiving the action. (See 47c.)

Transitive verbs, indirect objects, and direct objects

The direct object of a transitive verb is sometimes preceded by an indirect object, a noun or pronoun telling to whom or for whom the action of the sentence is done.

$$\overset{\text{S}}{\text{You}} \overset{\text{V}}{\text{give}} \overset{\text{IO}}{\text{her}} \overset{\text{DO}}{\overbrace{\text{some yarn,}}} \text{and} \overset{\text{S}}{\text{she}} \overset{\text{V}}{\overbrace{\text{will knit}}} \overset{\text{IO}}{\text{you}} \overset{\text{DO}}{\overbrace{\text{a scarf.}}}$$

The simple indirect object is always a noun or pronoun. To test for an indirect object, insert the word *to* or *for* before the word or word group in question. If the sentence makes sense, the word or word group is an indirect object.

You give [to] *her* some yarn, and she will knit [for] *you* a scarf.

An indirect object may be turned into a prepositional phrase using *to* or *for*: *You give some yarn to her, and she will knit a scarf for you.*

Only certain transitive verbs take indirect objects. Some examples are *ask, bring, find, get, give, hand, lend, make, offer, pay, promise, read, send, show, teach, tell, throw,* and *write.*

Transitive verbs, direct objects, and object complements

The direct object of a transitive verb is sometimes followed by an object complement, a word or word group that renames or describes the object.

> S   V DO ┌──── OC ────┐
> People often consider chivalry a thing of the past.

> ┌── S ──┐ V DO ┌──── OC ────┐
> The kiln makes clay firm and strong.

When the object complement renames the direct object, it is a noun or pronoun (such as *thing*). When it describes the direct object, it is an adjective (such as *firm* and *strong*).

Intransitive verbs

Intransitive verbs take no objects or complements.

> ┌──── S ────┐ V
> The audience laughed.

> ┌──── S ────┐ V
> The driver accelerated in the straightaway.

Nothing receives the actions of laughing and accelerating in these sentences, so the verbs are intransitive. Notice that such verbs may or may not be followed by adverbial modifiers. In the second sentence, *in the straightaway* is an adverbial prepositional phrase modifying *accelerated*.

NOTE: The dictionary will tell you whether a verb is transitive or intransitive. Some verbs can be both transitive and intransitive.

TRANSITIVE	Sandra *flew* her small plane over the canyon.
INTRANSITIVE	A flock of migrating geese *flew* overhead.

In the first example, *flew* has a direct object that receives the action: *her small plane*. In the second example, the verb is followed by an adverb (*overhead*), not by a direct object.

EXERCISE 47–5 Label the subject complements and direct objects in the following sentences, using the labels *SC* and *DO*. If a subject complement or a direct object consists of more than one word, bracket and label all of it. Answers appear in the back of the book.

> ┌——DO——┐
> **The sharp right turn confused most drivers.**

a. Textbooks are innovative.
b. Samurai warriors never fear death.
c. Successful coaches always praise their players' efforts.
d. St. Petersburg was the capital of the Russian Empire for two centuries.
e. The medicine tasted bitter.

EXERCISE 47–6 Each of the following sentences has either an indirect object followed by a direct object or a direct object followed by an object complement. Label the objects and complements, using the labels *IO*, *DO*, and *OC*. If an object or a complement consists of more than one word, bracket and label all of it. Answers appear in the back of the book.

$$\overbrace{\hspace{3cm}}^{DO}\ \overbrace{\hspace{1.5cm}}^{OC}$$
Most people consider their own experience normal.

a. Stress can make adults and children weary.
b. The dining hall offered students healthy meal choices.
c. Consider the work finished.
d. We showed the agent our tickets, and she gave us boarding passes.
e. Zita has made community service her priority this year.

47c Pattern variations

Although most sentences follow one of the five patterns listed on page 499, variations of these patterns commonly occur in questions, commands, sentences with delayed subjects, and passive transformations.

Questions and commands

Questions are sometimes patterned in normal word order, with the subject preceding the verb.

$$\overset{S}{}\ \overbrace{\hspace{1.5cm}}^{V}$$
Who will have the most hits this season?

Often, the pattern of a question is inverted, with the subject appearing between the helping verb and the main verb or after the verb.

HV S MV
Will he have the most hits this season?

$$\overset{V}{}\ \overbrace{\hspace{2cm}}^{S}$$
Why is the number of hits an important statistic?

In commands, the subject of the sentence is an understood *you.*

S   V
[You] Pay attention to the road.

Sentences with delayed subjects

Writers sometimes choose to delay the subject of a sentence to achieve a special effect such as suspense or humor.

> V ┌──── S ────┐
> Behind the phony tinsel of Hollywood lies the real tinsel.

The subject of the sentence is also delayed in sentences opening with the expletive *There* or *It*. When used as expletives, the words *There* and *It* have no strict grammatical function; they serve merely to get the sentence started.

> V ┌──────── S ────────┐
> There are thirty thousand spectators in the stadium.

> V ┌──── S ────┐
> It is best to avoid trans fats.

The subject in the second example is an infinitive phrase. (See 48b.)

Passive transformations

Transitive verbs, those that can take direct objects, usually appear in the active voice. In the active voice, the subject does the action, and a direct object receives the action.

> ┌──── S ────┐ V ┌──── DO ────┐
> **ACTIVE** The fireworks display dazzled the viewers on the
>
> Esplanade.

Sentences in the active voice may be transformed into the passive voice, with the subject receiving the action instead.

> ┌──────── S ────────┐ HV MV
> **PASSIVE** The viewers on the Esplanade were dazzled by the
> fireworks display.

What was once the direct object (*the viewers on the Esplanade*) has become the subject in the passive-voice transformation, and the original subject appears in a prepositional phrase beginning with *by*. The *by* phrase is frequently omitted in passive-voice constructions.

PASSIVE   The viewers on the Esplanade were dazzled.

Verbs in the passive voice can be identified by their form alone. The main verb is always a past participle, such as *dazzled* (see 46c), preceded by a form of *be* (*be, am, is, are, was, were, being, been*): *were dazzled*. Sometimes adverbs intervene (*were usually dazzled*).

TIP: Avoid using the passive voice when the active voice would be more appropriate (see 8a).

48 Subordinate word groups

Subordinate word groups include phrases and clauses. Phrases are subordinate because they lack a subject and a verb; they are classified as prepositional, verbal, appositive, and absolute (see 48a–48d). Subordinate clauses have a subject and a verb, but they begin with a word (such as *although, that,* or *when*) that marks them as subordinate (see 48e).

48a Prepositional phrases

A prepositional phrase begins with a preposition such as *at, by, for, from, in, of, on, to,* or *with* (see 46f) and usually ends with a noun or noun equivalent: *on the table, for him, by sleeping late.* The noun or noun equivalent is known as the *object of the preposition*.

Prepositional phrases function as adjectives or as adverbs. As an adjective, a prepositional phrase nearly always appears immediately following the noun or pronoun it modifies.

The hut had *walls of mud.*

Adjective phrases usually answer one or both of the questions Which one? and What kind of? If we ask Which walls? or What kind of walls? we get a sensible answer: *walls of mud.*

Adverbial prepositional phrases usually modify the verb, but they can also modify adjectives or other adverbs. When a prepositional phrase modifies the verb, it can appear nearly anywhere in a sentence.

James *walked* his dog *on a leash.*

Sabrina *will in time adjust* to life in Ecuador.

During a mudslide, the terrain *can change* drastically.

If a prepositional phrase is movable, you can be certain that it is adverbial.

> *In the cave,* the explorers found well-preserved prehistoric drawings.

> The explorers found well-preserved prehistoric drawings *in the cave.*

Adverbial word groups usually answer one of these questions: When? Where? How? Why? Under what conditions? To what degree?

> James walked his dog *how? On a leash.*

> Sabrina will adjust to life in Ecuador *when? In time.*

The terrain can change drastically *under what conditions*? *During a mudslide.*

In questions and subordinate clauses, a preposition may appear after its object.

What are you afraid *of*?

We avoided the bike trail *that* John had warned us *about*.

EXERCISE 48–1 Underline the prepositional phrases in the following sentences. Tell whether each one is an adjective phrase or an adverb phrase and what it modifies in the sentence. Answers appear in the back of the book.

Flecks <u>of mica</u> glittered <u>in the new granite floor</u>. (Adjective phrase modifying "Flecks"; adverb phrase modifying "glittered")

a. In northern Italy, we met many people who speak German as their first language.

b. William completed the three-mile hike through the thick forest with ease.

c. To my boss's dismay, I was late for work again.

d. The traveling exhibit of Mayan artifacts gave viewers new insight into pre-Columbian culture.

e. In 2002, the euro became the official currency in twelve European countries.

48b Verbal phrases

A verbal is a verb form that does not function as the verb of a clause. Verbals include infinitives (the word *to* plus the base form of the verb), present participles (the *-ing* form of the verb), and past participles (the verb form usually ending in *-d, -ed, -n, -en,* or *-t*). (See 27a and 46c.)

	PRESENT	PAST
INFINITIVE	**PARTICIPLE**	**PARTICIPLE**
to dream	dreaming	dreamed
to choose	choosing	chosen
to build	building	built
to grow	growing	grown

Instead of functioning as the verb of a clause, a verbal functions as an adjective, a noun, or an adverb.

ADJECTIVE	*Broken* promises cannot be fixed.
NOUN	Constant *complaining* becomes wearisome.
ADVERB	Can you wait *to celebrate*?

Verbals with objects, complements, or modifiers form verbal phrases.

In my family, *singing loudly* is more appreciated than *singing well*.

Governments exist *to protect the rights of minorities.*

Like verbals, verbal phrases function as adjectives, nouns, or adverbs. Verbal phrases are ordinarily classified as participial, gerund, and infinitive.

Participial phrases

Participial phrases always function as adjectives. Their verbals are either present participles (such as *dreaming, asking*) or past participles (such as *stolen, reached*).

Participial phrases frequently appear immediately following the noun or pronoun they modify.

Congress shall make no *law abridging the freedom of speech*

or of the press.

Participial phrases are often movable. They can precede the word they modify.

Being a weight-bearing joint, the *knee* is among the most frequently injured.

They may also appear at some distance from the word they modify.

Last night we saw a *play* that affected us deeply, *written with profound insight into the lives of immigrants.*

Gerund phrases

Gerund phrases are built around present participles (verb forms that end in *-ing*), and they always function as nouns: usually as subjects, subject complements, direct objects, or objects of a preposition.

    ⎡——— S ———⎤
Rationalizing a fear can eliminate it.

      ⎡——— SC ———⎤
The key to good sauce is browning the mushrooms.

      ⎡——— DO ———⎤
Lizards usually enjoy sunning themselves.

The American Heart Association has documented the benefits
    ⎡——— OBJ OF PREP ———⎤
of diet and exercise in reducing the risk of heart attack.

Infinitive phrases

Infinitive phrases, usually constructed around *to* plus the base form of the verb (*to call, to drink*), can function as nouns, as adjectives, or as adverbs. When functioning as a noun, an infinitive phrase may appear in almost any noun slot in a sentence, usually as a subject, subject complement, or direct object.

┌────── S ──────┐
To live without health insurance is risky.

┌────────────── DO ──────────────┐
The orchestra wanted to make its premier season memorable.

Infinitive phrases functioning as adjectives usually appear immediately following the noun or pronoun they modify.

The Nineteenth Amendment gave women the *right to vote.*

The infinitive phrase modifies the noun *right.* Which right? *The right to vote.*

Adverbial infinitive phrases usually qualify the meaning of the verb, telling when, where, how, why, under what conditions, or to what degree an action occurred.

Volunteers *rolled up* their pants *to wade through the flood waters.*

NOTE: In some constructions, the infinitive is unmarked; that is, the *to* does not appear. (See 28f.)

Graphs and charts can help researchers [*to*] *present complex data.*

EXERCISE 48–6 Underline the verbal phrases in the following sentences. Tell whether each phrase is participial, gerund, or infinitive and how each is used in the sentence. Answers appear in the back of the book.

Do you want to watch that documentary? (Infinitive phrase used as direct object of "Do want")

a. Updating your software will fix the computer glitch.
b. The challenge in decreasing the town budget is identifying non-essential services.

c.   Cathleen tried to help her mother by raking the lawn.

d.   Understanding little, I had no hope of passing my biology final.

e.   Working with animals gave Steve a sense of satisfaction.

48c Appositive phrases

Appositive phrases describe nouns or pronouns. Instead of modifying nouns or pronouns, however, appositive phrases rename them. In form they are nouns or noun equivalents.

> Bloggers, *conversationalists at heart*, are the online equivalent of radio talk show hosts.

Appositives are said to be "in apposition to" the nouns or pronouns they rename. *Conversationalists at heart* is in apposition to the noun *Bloggers*.

48d Absolute phrases

An absolute phrase modifies a whole clause or sentence, not just one word. It consists of a noun or noun equivalent usually followed by a participial phrase.

> *Her words reverberating in the hushed arena*, the senator urged the crowd to support her former opponent.

48e Subordinate clauses

Subordinate clauses are patterned like sentences, having subjects and verbs and sometimes objects or complements. But they function within sentences as adjectives, adverbs, or nouns. They cannot stand alone as complete sentences.

A subordinate clause usually begins with a subordinating conjunction or a relative pronoun. The chart on page 517 classifies these words according to the kinds of clauses (adjective, adverb, or noun) they introduce.

Writer's Choice
Building credibility with appositives

Appositives rename a noun or pronoun. Writers often use them to help an **audience** better understand a person or thing or to give that person or thing fuller context. Consider the following pair of sentences.

> Helene Aumais surprised everyone by winning the Crescent City 10k road race.

> Helene Aumais, a woman who had never run more than a mile before last month, surprised everyone by winning the Crescent City 10k road race.

In the second example, the writer uses an appositive to give more information about Helene Aumais, the subject of the sentence, and to suggest to readers why the win was so surprising.

As a college research writer, you will often use appositives to build your own credibility as you cite sources within your own text. To come across as a knowledgeable researcher who draws on relevant and reliable sources of information, you can give the credentials for your source in an appositive phrase.

CITATION WITH NO CREDENTIALS	According to John Dunlosky, regular use of practice tests "can substantially boost student learning" (14).
CITATION WITH CREDENTIALS	According to John Dunlosky, a researcher and professor of psychology at Kent State University, regular use of practice tests "can substantially boost student learning" (14).
	The first sentence, while not incorrect, may prompt your readers to question who John Dunlosky is and, further, why anyone should care. The second sentence adds language that suggests Dunlosky's authority on the subject and that positions you as a credible researcher.

As a research writer, you use sources to help you fulfill your purpose — to inform or to persuade — and to help you meet the needs of your audience. Choosing to use appositives to introduce sources builds your credibility as a researcher.

Adjective clauses

Adjective clauses modify nouns or pronouns, usually answering the question Which one? or What kind of? Most adjective clauses begin with a relative pronoun (*who, whom, whose, which,* or *that*). In addition to introducing the clause, the relative pronoun points back to the noun that the clause modifies.

The coach chose *players who would benefit from intense drills.*

A *book that goes unread* is a writer's worst nightmare.

Relative pronouns are sometimes "understood."

The things [*that*] *we cherish most* are the things [*that*] *we might lose.*

Occasionally an adjective clause is introduced by a relative adverb, usually *when, where,* or *why.*

The aging actor returned to the *stage where he had made his debut as Hamlet half a century earlier.*

The parts of an adjective clause are often arranged as in sentences (subject/verb/object or complement).

S   V   DO

Sometimes it is our closest friends who disappoint us.

Frequently, however, the object or complement appears first, out of the normal order of subject/verb/object.

DO S   V

They can be the very friends whom we disappoint.

TIP: For punctuation of adjective clauses, see 32e and 33e. For advice about avoiding repeated words in adjective clauses, see 30d.

Words that introduce subordinate clauses

Words introducing adjective clauses

Relative pronouns: that, which, who, whom, whose

Relative adverbs: when, where, why

Words introducing adverb clauses

Subordinating conjunctions: after, although, as, as if, because, before, even though, if, in order that, since, so that, than, that, though, unless, until, when, where, whether, while

Words introducing noun clauses

Relative pronouns: which, who, whom, whose

Other pronouns: what, whatever, whichever, whoever, whomever

Other subordinating words: how, if, that, when, whenever, where, wherever, whether, why

---

Adverb clauses

Adverb clauses modify verbs, adjectives, or other adverbs, usually answering one of these questions: When? Where? Why? How? Under what conditions? To what degree? They always begin with a subordinating conjunction (such as *after*, *although*, *because*, *that*, *though*, *unless*, or *when*). (For a complete list, see the chart on this page.)

When the sun went down, the hikers *prepared* their camp.

Kate *would have made* the team *if she hadn't broken her ankle.*

Adverb clauses are usually movable when they modify a verb. In the preceding examples, for instance, the adverb clauses can be moved without affecting the meaning of the sentences.

The hikers prepared their camp *when the sun went down.*

If she hadn't broken her ankle, Kate would have made the team.

When an adverb clause modifies an adjective or an adverb, it is not movable; it must appear next to the word it modifies. In the following examples, the *when* clause modifies the adjective *Uncertain,* and the *than* clause modifies the adverb *better.*

Uncertain *when the baby would be born,* Ray and Leah stayed close to home.

Jackie can dance better *than I can walk.*

Adverb clauses are sometimes elliptical, with some of their words being understood but not appearing in the sentence.

When [it is] renovated, the dorm will hold six hundred students.

Noun clauses

A noun clause functions just like a single-word noun, usually as a subject, a subject complement, a direct object, or an object of a preposition. It usually begins with one of the following words: *how, if, that, what, whatever, when, where, whether, which, who, whoever, whom, whomever, whose, why.* (For a complete list, see the chart on p. 517.)

┌────── S ──────┐
Whoever leaves the house last must double-lock the door.

┌────────────── DO ──────────────┐
Copernicus argued that the sun is the center of the universe.

The subordinating word introducing the clause may or may not play a significant role in the clause. In the preceding examples, *Whoever* is the subject of its clause, but *that* does not perform a function in its clause.

As with adjective clauses, the parts of a noun clause may appear in normal order (subject/verb/object or complement) or out of their normal order.

S   V   ┌──DO──┐
Loyalty is what keeps a friendship strong.

        DO   S   V
New Mexico is where we live.

EXERCISE 48–10 Underline the subordinate clauses in the following sentences. Tell whether each clause is an adjective clause, an adverb clause, or a noun clause and how it is used in the sentence. Answers appear in the back of the book.

Show the committee the latest draft <u>before you print the</u>

<u>final report</u>. (*Adverb clause modifying "Show"*)

a. The city's electoral commission adjusted the voting process so that every vote would count.

b. A marketing campaign that targets baby boomers may not appeal to young professionals.

c. After the Tambora volcano erupted in the southern Pacific in 1815, no one realized that it would contribute to the "year without a summer" in Europe and North America.

d. The concept of peak oil implies that at a certain point there will be no more oil to extract from the earth.

e. Details are easily overlooked when you are rushing.

49 Sentence types

Sentences are classified in two ways: according to their structure (simple, compound, complex, and compound-complex) and according to their purpose (declarative, imperative, interrogative, and exclamatory).

49a Sentence structures

Depending on the number and the types of clauses they contain, sentences are classified as simple, compound, complex, or compound-complex.

Clauses come in two varieties: independent and subordinate. An independent clause contains a subject and a predicate, and it either stands alone or could stand alone as a sentence. A subordinate clause also contains a subject and a predicate, but it functions within a sentence as an adjective, an adverb, or a noun; it cannot stand alone. (See 48e.)

Simple sentences

A simple sentence is one independent clause with no subordinate clauses.

———————— INDEPENDENT CLAUSE ————————
Without a passport, Eva could not visit her grandparents in

Hungary.

A simple sentence may contain compound elements—a compound subject, verb, or object, for example—but it does not contain more than one full sentence pattern. The following sentence is simple because its two verbs (*comes in* and *goes out*) share a subject (*Spring*).

———————— INDEPENDENT CLAUSE ————————
Spring comes in like a lion and goes out like a lamb.

Compound sentences

A compound sentence is composed of two or more independent clauses with no subordinate clauses. The independent clauses are usually joined with a comma and a coordinating conjunction (*and*, *but*, *or*, *nor*, *for*, *so*, *yet*) or with a semicolon. (See 14a.)

> INDEPENDENT CLAUSE · INDEPENDENT CLAUSE
> The car broke down, but a rescue van arrived within minutes.

> INDEPENDENT CLAUSE · INDEPENDENT CLAUSE
> A shark was spotted near shore; people left immediately.

Complex sentences

A complex sentence is composed of one independent clause with one or more subordinate clauses. (See 48e.)

ADJECTIVE
> SUBORDINATE CLAUSE
> The pitcher who won the game is a rookie.

ADVERB
> SUBORDINATE CLAUSE
> If you leave late, take a cab home.

NOUN
> SUBORDINATE CLAUSE
> What matters most to us is a quick commute.

Compound-complex sentences

A compound-complex sentence contains at least two independent clauses and at least one subordinate clause. The following sentence contains two independent clauses, each of which contains a subordinate clause.

> INDEPENDENT CLAUSE · INDEPENDENT CLAUSE
> SUB CL
> Tell the doctor how you feel, and she will decide whether

> SUB CL
> you can go home.

49b Sentence purposes

Writers use declarative sentences to make statements, imperative sentences to issue requests or commands, interrogative sentences to ask questions, and exclamatory sentences to make exclamations.

DECLARATIVE	The echo sounded in our ears.
IMPERATIVE	Love your neighbor.
INTERROGATIVE	Did the better team win tonight?
EXCLAMATORY	We're here to save you!

EXERCISE 49–1 Identify the following sentences as simple, compound, complex, or compound-complex. Identify the subordinate clauses and classify them according to their function: adjective, adverb, or noun. (See 48e.) Answers appear in the back of the book.

The deli in Courthouse Square was crowded with lawyers

at lunchtime. (Simple)

a. Fires that are ignited in dry areas spread especially quickly.

b. The early Incas were advanced; they used a calendar and developed a decimal system.

c. Elaine's jacket was too thin to block the wintry air.

d. Before we leave for the station, we always check the Amtrak Web site.

e. Decide when you want to leave, and I will be there to pick you up.

PART X

Researched Writing

50 Thinking like a researcher; gathering sources 525

51 Managing information; taking notes responsibly 543

52 Evaluating sources 552

WRITING MLA PAPERS

53 Supporting a thesis 570

54 Citing sources; avoiding plagiarism 577

55 Integrating sources 585

56 Documenting sources 598

57 Manuscript format; sample research paper 662

WRITING APA PAPERS

58 Supporting a thesis 674

59 Citing sources; avoiding plagiarism 678

60 Integrating sources 683

61 Documenting sources 693

62 Manuscript format; sample research paper 735

WRITING *CHICAGO* PAPERS

63 *Chicago* papers 754

Researched Writing

ONLINE ACTIVITIES:

writershelp.com/hacker

macmillanhighered.com/
launchpadsolo/hacker

Thinking like a researcher | 4 Writing practice activities
| 1 Exercise

Managing information | 1 Writing practice activity

Evaluating sources | 1 Writing practice activity

Writing MLA papers | 1 Writing practice activity
| 22 Exercises
| 1 LearningCurve activity
| 1 Sample student essay

Writing APA papers | 29 Exercises
| 1 LearningCurve activity
| 1 Sample student essay

Writing *Chicago* papers | 24 Exercises
| 1 Sample student essay

50 Thinking like a researcher; gathering sources

A college research assignment asks you to pose questions worth exploring, read widely in search of possible answers, interpret what you read, draw reasoned conclusions, and support those conclusions with evidence. In short, it asks you to enter a research conversation by being *in* conversation with other writers and thinkers who have explored and studied your topic. As you listen to and learn from the voices already in the conversation, you'll find entry points where you can add your own insights and ideas.

Becoming a confident researcher means figuring out how to respond to and engage with ideas and how to present your ideas alongside other people's thoughts. It also requires embracing the idea that writing with sources is a process that takes time. As your ideas evolve, you may find that the process leads you in unexpected directions—perhaps new questions in the conversation require you to create a new search strategy, find additional sources, and challenge your initial assumptions. Keep an open mind throughout the process, be curious, and enjoy the work of finding answers to questions that matter to you.

50a Manage the project.

When you get started on a research project, you need to understand the assignment, choose a direction, and ask questions about your topic. The following tips will help you manage the beginning phase of research.

Managing time

When you receive your assignment, set a realistic schedule of deadlines. Think about how much time you might need for each

Becoming a College Writer

Join a research conversation

"Pursue your research with passion and energy. Find out what has been written about your topic, but also what's missing from the conversation." —**Stephen Thacker,** student, University of Alabama

You probably have conducted research in the past—perhaps to seek information or report what others have said about a topic. For college research, you'll be asked to go beyond reporting the views of others; you'll develop your own authority by stating your positions and *contributing* your ideas to ongoing conversations. Becoming a college writer requires you to engage with, learn from, and question the ideas of experts in order to shape your own ideas.

One approach is to start with your own curiosity: What problems interest you? What topics do you want to learn more about? Read and view a wide range of sources, and try to understand not only what has been written about an issue but also, as Thacker suggests, "what's missing from the conversation." Asking such questions can help you find entry points in a debate.

- Think about issues you care about—either because you have strong opinions about them or because they affect you, your family, or your community. Write briefly about one issue: What new angle might you bring? What's "missing from the conversation"?

MAKSIM SHMELJOV/SHUTTERSTOCK

MORE
Assessing the writing situation, 1a
Posing questions worth exploring, 50b

526

Thinking like a researcher

To develop your authority as a researcher, you need to think like a researcher — asking questions, becoming informed through reading and evaluating sources, and citing sources to acknowledge other researchers.

Be curious. What topics and debates do you care about? What problems do you want to help solve? What makes you concerned? Explore your topic from multiple perspectives, and let your curiosity drive your project.

Be engaged. Learn how to use your library's research tools. Once you find promising sources, let one source lead you to another; follow clues (in the list of works cited, if one exists) to learn who else has written about your topic. Listen to the key voices in the research conversation — and then respond.

Be responsible. Use sources to develop and support your ideas rather than patching them together to let them speak for you. From the start of your research project, keep careful track of sources you read or view (see 51), place quotation marks around words copied from sources, and maintain accurate records for all bibliographic information.

Be reflective. Keep a research log, and use your log to explore various points you are developing and to pose counterarguments to your research argument. Research is never a straightforward path, so use your log to reflect on the evolution of your project as well as your evolution as a researcher.

---

step of your project. One student created a calendar to map out her tasks for a research paper (see p. 529), keeping in mind that some tasks might overlap or need to be repeated.

Getting the big picture

As you consider a possible research topic, set aside some time to learn what people are saying about it by reading sources on the Web or in databases. Ask yourself questions such as these:

- What aspects of the topic are generating the most debate?
- Why and how are people disagreeing?
- Which approaches seem the most intriguing?

Once you have an aerial view of the topic and are familiar with some of the existing research, you can zoom in closer to examine subtopics and debates that look interesting.

Keeping a research log

Research is a process. As your topic evolves, you may find yourself asking new questions that require you to create a new search strategy, find additional sources, and revise your initial assumptions. A research log — a notebook or a set of digital files — helps you maintain orderly records of the sources you read and your ideas about those sources. Keeping an accurate source trail and working bibliography and separating your own insights and ideas from those of your sources will help you become both a more efficient and more responsible researcher.

50b Pose questions worth exploring.

Every research project starts with questions. Working within the guidelines of your assignment, come up with a few preliminary questions that seem worth researching — questions that you are interested in exploring, that you feel would engage your audience, and about which there is substantial debate. You'll find the research process more rewarding and meaningful if you choose questions that you care about.

Here, for example, are a few students' preliminary research questions.

- Why are boys diagnosed with attention deficit disorder more often than girls are?

- Do nutritional food labels inform consumers or confuse them?

- Under what circumstances should juvenile offenders be tried and treated as adults?

Sample calendar for a research assignment

2	3	4	5	6	7	8
	Receive and analyze the assignment.	Pose questions you might explore. →→	→→→ Talk with a reference librarian; plan a → search strategy.	Start research log.	Settle on a topic; narrow the focus.	Revise research questions. Locate → sources.
9	**10**	**11**	**12**	**13**	**14**	**15**
Read, take notes, and → compile a working bibliography. →			→→	Draft a working thesis and an outline.	Draft the paper. →	
16	**17**	**18**	**19**	**20**	**21**	**22**
→ Draft the paper. →		→→	Visit the writing center for feedback.	Do additional → research if needed.		→→
23	**24**	**25**	**26**	**27**	**28**	**29**
Ask peers for feedback. Revise the paper; → if necessary, revise the thesis. →			→→	Prepare a list of → works cited.		Proofread the final draft. →
30	**31**					
Proofread the final draft. →	Submit the final draft.					

As you think about possible questions, choose those that are focused (not too broad), challenging (not just factual), and grounded (not too speculative) as possible entry points in a conversation.

Choosing a focused question

If your initial question is too broad, given the length of the paper you plan to write, look for ways to restrict your focus (see also "Subject" on p. 8). Here, for example, is how two students refined their initial questions.

TOO BROAD	FOCUSED
What are the benefits of stricter auto emissions standards?	How will stricter auto emissions standards create new auto industry jobs and make US carmakers more competitive in the world market?
What causes depression?	How has the widespread use of antidepressant drugs affected teenage suicide rates?

Choosing a challenging question

Your research paper will be more interesting to both you and your audience if you base it on an intellectually challenging line of inquiry. Avoid factual questions that fail to provoke thought or engage readers in a debate; such questions lead to reports or lists of facts, not to researched arguments.

TOO FACTUAL	CHALLENGING
Is autism on the rise?	Why is autism so difficult to treat?
Where is wind energy being used?	What makes wind farms economically viable?

You will need to address a factual question in the course of answering a more challenging one. For example, if you were writing about promising treatments for autism, you would no doubt answer the question "What is autism?" at some point in your paper and even analyze competing definitions of autism to help support your arguments about the challenges of treating the condition. It would be unproductive, however, to use the factual question as the focus for the entire paper.

Choosing a grounded question

Make sure that your research question is grounded, not too speculative. Although speculative questions—such as those that address morality or beliefs—are worth asking in a research paper, they are unsuitable central questions. For most college courses, the central argument of a research paper should be grounded in facts and should not be based entirely on beliefs.

TOO SPECULATIVE	GROUNDED
Is it wrong to share pornographic personal photos by cell phone?	What role should the US government play in regulating mobile content?
Do medical scientists have the right to experiment on animals?	How have technical breakthroughs made medical experiments on animals increasingly unnecessary?

Testing a research question

- Does the question allow you to enter into a research conversation that you care about?
- Is the question flexible enough to allow for many possible answers?
- Is the question focused, challenging, and grounded?
- Put the question to the "So what?" test. Can you show readers why the question needs to be asked and why the answer matters? (See p. 21.)

Enter a research conversation

A college research project asks you to be in conversation with writers and researchers who have studied your topic — responding to their ideas and positions and contributing your own insights to move the conversation forward. As you pose preliminary research questions, you may wonder where and how to step into a research conversation.

1 **Identify the experts and ideas in the conversation.** Ask: Who are the major writers and most influential people researching your topic? What are their credentials? What positions have they taken? How and why do the experts disagree?

2 **Identify any gaps in the conversation.** What is missing from the conversation? Where are the gaps in the existing research? What questions haven't been asked yet? What positions need to be challenged?

3 **Try using an orienting statement** to help you find a point of entry.

- *On one side of the debate is position X, on the other side is Y, but there is a middle position, Z.*

- *The conventional view about the problem needs to be challenged because . . .*

- *Key details in this debate that have been overlooked are . . .*

- *Researchers have drawn conclusion X from the evidence, but one could also draw conclusion Y.*

50c Map out a search strategy.

A search strategy is a systematic plan for locating sources. To create a search strategy appropriate for your research question, it may help to consult a librarian and take a look at your library's Web site, which will give you an overview of available resources.

No single search strategy works for every topic. For some topics, it may be useful to search for information in newspapers, magazines, and Web sites. For others, the best sources might be found in scholarly journals and books. Still other topics might be enhanced by field research—interviews, surveys, or direct observation.

With the help of a librarian, each of the students whose research essays can be found in this handbook constructed a search strategy appropriate for his or her research question.

Sophie Harba (See her full research paper in 57b.) Sophie Harba's topic, the role of government in legislating food choices, is the subject of lively debates in scholarly articles and in publications aimed at the general public. To find information on her topic, Harba decided to

- search the Web to locate current news, government publications, and information from organizations that focus on the issues surrounding government regulation of food

- check a library database for current peer-reviewed research articles

- use the library catalog to search for a recently published book that was cited in a blog post on her topic and on several well-respected Web sites

April Wang (See her full paper in 62b.) April Wang's topic, the role of technology in the shift from teacher-delivered to student-centered learning, is the subject of educational studies as well as articles and books aimed at both educators and the general public. To find information on her topic, Wang decided to

- search Google Scholar and *CQ Researcher* to learn what aspects of her topic are generating the most debate

- listen to a TED talk to deepen her understanding about educational technology

- search specialized databases related to education and technology for recent scholarly articles and reports

- track down a scholarly article that several of her sources cited as an influential study

Ned Bishop (See pages from his paper in 63f.) Ned Bishop's topic, Nathan Bedford Forrest's role in the Fort Pillow massacre during the Civil War, has been investigated and debated by historians. Given the nature of his historical topic, Bishop consulted a reference librarian and decided to

- locate books through the library's online catalog

- locate scholarly articles by searching a database specializing in history sources

- locate newspaper articles from 1864 by searching a historical newspaper database

- use the Web to track down additional primary documents mentioned in his sources

See 52a for more on assessing how different sources might contribute to your paper.

50d Search efficiently; master a few shortcuts to finding good sources.

Most students use a combination of library databases and the Web in their research. You can save yourself a lot of time by becoming an efficient searcher.

Using the library

The Web site hosted by your college library is full of useful information. In addition to dozens of databases and links to other references, many libraries offer online subject guides as well as one-on-one help from reference librarians through e-mail or chat. You can save yourself a lot of time if you get advice from your instructor, a librarian, or your library's Web site about the best place to start your search for sources.

Visiting your library can also be helpful. You can talk personally with reference librarians, who can show you what resources are available, help you refine your keywords for catalog or database searches, or suggest ways to narrow your search.

Savvy searchers cut down on the clutter of a broad search by adding additional search terms, limiting a search to recent publications, or clicking on a database option to look at only one type of source, such as peer-reviewed articles, if that's what is needed. When looking for books, you can broaden a catalog search by asking "What kind of book might contain the information I need?"

Using the Web

When using a search engine, it's a good idea to use terms that are as specific as possible and to enclose search phrases in quotation marks. You can refine your search by date or domain; for example, *autism site:.gov* will search for information about autism on government Web sites. Use clues in what you find (such as organizations or government agencies that seem particularly informative) to refine your search.

As you examine sites, look for "about" links to learn about the site's author or sponsoring agency. Examine URLs for clues. Those that contain .k12 may be intended for young audiences; URLs ending in .gov lead to official information from US government entities. URLs may also offer clues about the country of origin: .au for Australia, .uk for United Kingdom, .in for India, and so on. If you aren't sure where a page originated,

Go beyond a Google search

A Google search is a quick way to gain an aerial view of your topic, but not an efficient way to find reliable, authoritative sources. Often a search on Google can return thousands of results, including outdated information and unreliable or biased sources. Good research involves going beyond the instant information available from a quick Google search to gain a deeper understanding of your topic and to establish your authority as a knowledgeable writer.

1 Try *CQ Researcher*. If you are searching for a good topic or seeking to understand the debate around a topic you've chosen, use *CQ Researcher*, available through most college libraries, to jump-start your research. These weekly reports focus on current controversies in government, law, environment, and education; provide pro/con arguments to help you identify positions in the debate; and introduce some key voices in the research conversation.

2 Try online databases available through your school library. Databases such as EBSCO, Academic Search Premier, and JSTOR, designed for academic researchers and vetted by information specialists, lead you to the ideas being reported and debated in the most important and influential publications. You will find articles, studies, and reports from scholarly journals and other widely respected sources written by the key writers and researchers debating your topic.

3 Try Google Scholar (scholar.google.com) for access to academic research. Add words such as *debate, disagreements, proponents,* or *opponents* to your search terms: *opponents of government regulations of food choices.* Another approach is to try using a journalist's questions—Who? When? Where? What? Why?—to refine an online search: *Why favor government regulation of food choices?*

Check URLs for clues about sponsorship

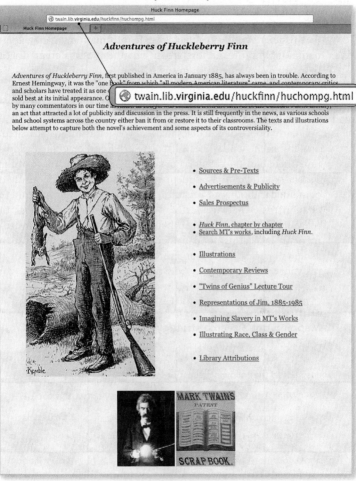

This source, from an internal page of a Web site, provides no indication of an author or a sponsor. Shortening the URL to http://twain.lib.virginia.edu/ leads to a main page that lists a university literature professor as the author and the University of Virginia Library as the sponsor.

erase everything in the URL after the first slash in your address bar; the result should be the root page of the site, which may offer useful information about the site's purpose and audience (see p. 537). Avoid sites that provide information but no explanation of who the authors are or why the site was created. For more on evaluating Web sites, see 52e.

Using bibliographies and citations as shortcuts

Scholarly books and articles list the works the author has cited, usually at the end. These lists are useful shortcuts to additional reliable sources on your topic. For example, most of the scholarly articles that student writer Sophie Harba consulted contained citations to related research studies. Through these citations, she quickly located other sources and a network of relevant research related to her topic, the role of the government in legislating food choices. Even popular sources such as news articles, videos, and interviews may refer to additional relevant sources that may be worth tracking down.

WRITING PRACTICE

Mapping out a search strategy

Draft notes about your preliminary research questions and your search terms. After you've done some searching and reading, write answers to the following questions:

- What is the current debate or controversy about this topic?

- In which online or print publications is the debate taking place?

- Who are the most influential people in this debate?

Show your notes to a reference librarian and ask for feedback about whether the sources you have found are the most influential and authoritative. Based on the comments you receive, revise your search strategy and clarify your search terms.

Tips for smart searching

For currency. News outlets such as the *New York Times* and the BBC, think tanks, government agencies, and advocacy groups may provide appropriate sources for your research. You can often limit a search to the most recent year, month, week, or day.

For authority. Keep an eye out for experts being cited in sources you examine. Following the trail of citation may lead you to sources by those experts—or the organizations they represent—that may be even more helpful. You can limit a Google search by type of Web site and type of source. Add *site:.gov* to focus on government sources or *filetype:pdf* to zero in on reports and research papers as PDF files.

For scholarship. Use a library database to look for reports of original research written by the people who conducted it. Scholarly articles provide information about where the authors work (such as universities or research centers), use a formal writing style, and include footnotes or a bibliography. Don't rule out an article just because it's long. Read the abstract or the introductory paragraphs and the conclusion to see if the source is worth further investigation.

For context. Books are important sources in many fields such as history, philosophy, and sociology, and they often do a better job than scholarly articles of putting ideas in context. You may find a single chapter or even a few pages that are just what you need to gain a deeper perspective. Consider publication dates with your topic in mind.

For firsthand authenticity. In some academic disciplines, primary sources may be required. In historical research, for example, a primary source is one that originated in the historical period under discussion or is a firsthand account from a witness. In the sciences, a primary source (sometimes called a *primary article*) is a published report of research written by the scientist who conducted it. For more information, see page 559.

50e Conduct field research, if appropriate.

Your own field research can enhance or be the focus of a writing project. For a composition class, for example, you might interview a local politician about a current issue, such as the initiation of a city bike-share program. For a sociology class, you might conduct a survey regarding campus trends in community service.

RESEARCH TIP: Colleges and universities often require researchers to submit projects to an institutional review board (IRB) if the research involves human subjects outside a classroom setting. Before administering a survey or conducting other fieldwork, check with your instructor to see if IRB approval is required.

Interviewing

Interviews can often shed new light on a topic. Look for an expert who has firsthand knowledge of the subject, or seek out someone whose personal experience provides a valuable perspective on your topic.

When asking for an interview, be clear about who you are, what the purpose of the interview is, and how you would prefer to conduct it: via e-mail, over the phone, or in person. Plan for the interview by writing down a series of questions. Try to avoid closed questions with yes or no answers. Instead, ask open questions that lead to facts, anecdotes, and opinions that will add a meaningful dimension to your paper.

INEFFECTIVE (CLOSED) INTERVIEW QUESTIONS

How many years have you spent studying childhood obesity?

Is your work interesting?

EFFECTIVE (OPEN) INTERVIEW QUESTIONS

What are some current interpretations of the causes of childhood obesity?

What treatments have you found to be most effective? Why do you think they work?

USING SOURCES RESPONSIBLY: When quoting your source (the interviewee) in your paper, be accurate and fair. To ensure accuracy, you might ask permission to record the interview or conduct it by e-mail.

Surveying opinion

For some topics, you need expert opinion and scholarly research. For others, you may find it useful to survey opinions through written questionnaires, phone or e-mail polls, or questions posted on a social media site. Many people resist long questionnaires, so for a good response rate, limit your questions with your purpose in mind.

Surveys with yes/no questions or multiple-choice options can be completed quickly, and the results are easy to tally. You may also want to ask a few open-ended questions to elicit more individual responses, some of which may be worth quoting in your paper.

SAMPLE YES/NO QUESTION

Do you favor government regulation of snack food ingredients?

SAMPLE OPEN-ENDED QUESTION

What experiences have you had with government regulation of snack food ingredients?

Other field methods

Your firsthand visits to and observations of significant places, people, or events can enhance a research project in a variety of disciplines. If you aren't able to schedule an in-person visit to an organization, a company, or a historic site, you may find useful information on an official Web site or a phone number or e-mail address to use to contact a representative, who may grant you an interview, send materials, or make useful suggestions.

50f Write a research proposal.

One effective way to manage your project and focus your thinking is to write a research proposal. A proposal gives you an opportunity to look back—to remind you why you chose your topic—and to look forward—to predict any difficulties or obstacles that might arise during your project. In a research proposal, you identify the research question you plan to explore, the sources you plan to use, and the feasibility of the project, given the time and resources available. As you take stock of your project, you also have the opportunity to receive feedback about your proposed research question and search strategy.

The following questions will help you organize your proposal.

- **Research question.** What question will you be exploring? Why does this question need to be asked? What do you hope to learn from the project?

- **Research conversation.** What have you learned so far about the debate or specific research conversation you will enter? What entry point have you found to offer your own insights and ideas?

- **Search strategy.** Explain your search strategy: What kinds of sources will you use to explore your question? What sources will be most useful, and why? How will you locate a variety of sources (primary/secondary, textual/visual, field/library)?

- **Research challenges.** What challenges, if any, do you anticipate (locating sufficient sources, managing the project, finding a position to take)? What resources are available to help you meet these challenges?

51 Managing information; taking notes responsibly

An effective researcher is a good record keeper. Whether you decide to keep records in your research log or in a file on your computer, you will need methods for managing information: maintaining a working bibliography (see 51a), keeping track of source materials (see 51b), and taking notes without plagiarizing your sources (see 51c). (For more on avoiding plagiarism, see 54 for MLA style, 59 for APA style, and 63b for *Chicago* style.)

51a Maintain a working bibliography.

Keep a record of any sources you read or view. This record, called a *working bibliography*, will help you compile the list of sources that will appear at the end of your paper. The format of this list depends on the documentation style you are using (for MLA style, see 56b; for APA style, see 61b; for *Chicago* style, see 63d). Using the proper style in your working bibliography will ensure that you have all the information you need to correctly cite any sources you use. (See 52f for advice on using your working bibliography as the basis for an annotated bibliography.)

Most researchers save bibliographic information from the library's catalog and databases and from the Web. The information you need is given in the chart on pages 545–46. If you download a visual, gather the same information as for a print source.

For Web sources, some bibliographic information may not be available, but spend time looking for it before assuming that it doesn't exist. When information isn't available on the home page, you may have to drill into the site, following links to interior pages. (See also pp. 535 and 562 for more details about finding bibliographic information in online sources.)

51b Keep track of source materials.

The best way to keep track of source materials is to save a copy of each potential source as you conduct your research. Many database services will allow you to e-mail, save, or print citations or full texts of articles, and you can easily download, copy, or take screen shots of information from the Web.

Working with photocopies, printouts, and electronic files—as opposed to relying on memory or hastily written notes—has several benefits. You can highlight key passages, perhaps even color-coding them to reflect topics in your outline. You can get a head start on note taking. Finally, you reduce the chances of unintentional plagiarism since you will be able to compare your use of a source in your paper with the actual source, not just with your notes.

USING SOURCES RESPONSIBLY: Be especially careful when using copy-and-paste functions in electronic files. Some researchers plagiarize their sources because they lose track of which words came from sources and which are their own. To prevent unintentional plagiarism, put quotation marks around any source text that you copy during your research.

51c As you take notes, avoid unintentional plagiarism.

When you take notes and jot down ideas, be careful not to borrow exact language from your sources. Even if you half-copy the author's sentences—either by mixing the author's phrases with your own without using quotation marks or by plugging your synonyms into the author's sentence structure—you are committing plagiarism, a serious academic offense. (For examples of this kind of plagiarism, sometimes referred to as *patchwriting*, see 54b, 59b, and 63b.)

To take notes responsibly, make sure you understand the ideas in the source. What are the major arguments? What is the evidence? Then, resist the temptation to look at the source

Information to collect for a working bibliography

For an entire book

- All authors; any editors or translators
- Title and subtitle
- Edition (if not the first)
- Publication information: city, publisher, and date
- Medium: print, Web, and so on
- Date you accessed the source (for an online source)

For an article

- All authors of the article
- Title and subtitle of the article
- Title of the journal, magazine, or newspaper
- Date; volume, issue, and page numbers
- Medium: print, Web, DVD, and so on
- Date you accessed the source (for an online source)

For an article retrieved from a database (in addition to the information above)

- Name of the database
- Accession number or other number assigned by the database
- Digital object identifier (DOI), if there is one
- URL of the database home page or of the journal's home page, if there is no DOI
- Date you accessed the source

INFORMATION TO COLLECT FOR A WORKING BIBLIOGRAPHY (cont.)

For a Web source (including visual, audio, and multimedia sources)

- All authors, editors, or composers of the source
- Editor or compiler of the Web source, if there is one
- Title and subtitle of the source
- Title of the longer work, if the source is contained in a longer work
- Title of the Web site
- Print publication information for the source, if available
- Online page or paragraph numbers (only if the source provides them)
- Date of online publication (or latest update)
- Sponsor or publisher of the site
- Date you accessed the source
- URL or permalink of the page on which the source appears

NOTE: For the exact bibliographic format to use in your working bibliography and in the final paper, see 56b (MLA), 61b (APA), or 63d (*Chicago*).

as you take notes — except when you are quoting. Keep the source close by so that you can check for accuracy, but don't try to put ideas in your own words with the source's sentences in front of you. When you need to quote a source, make sure you copy the words exactly and put quotation marks around them.

For strategies for avoiding plagiarism when using sources from the Web, see page 550.

There are three kinds of note taking: summarizing, paraphrasing, and quoting. Be sure to keep track of exact page references for all three types of notes; you will need the page numbers later if you use the information in your paper.

Summarizing without plagiarizing

A summary condenses information, perhaps reducing a chapter to a short paragraph or a paragraph to a single sentence. A summary should be written in your own words; if you use phrases from the source, put them in quotation marks.

Academic English

Even in the early stages of note taking, it is important to keep in mind that in the United States written texts are considered an author's property. (This "property" isn't a physical object, so it is often referred to as *intellectual property*.) The author (or the publisher) owns the language as well as any original ideas contained in the writing, whether the source is published in print, online, or in electronic form. When you use another author's property in your own writing, you are required to follow certain conventions for citing the material, or you risk committing *plagiarism*.

Here is a passage about marine pollution from a National Oceanic and Atmospheric Administration (NOAA) Web site. Following the passage are the student's annotations—notes and questions that help him figure out the meaning—and then his summary of the passage. (The bibliographic information is recorded in MLA style.)

ORIGINAL SOURCE

A question that is often posed to the NOAA Marine Debris Program (MDP) is "How much debris is actually out there?" The MDP has recognized the need for this answer as well as the growing interest and value of citizen science. To that end, the MDP is developing and testing two types of monitoring and assessment protocols: 1) rigorous scientific survey and 2) volunteer at-sea visual survey. These types of monitoring programs are necessary in order to compare marine debris,

composition, abundance, distribution, movement, and impact
data on national and global scales.

> —NOAA Marine Debris Program. "Efforts and Activities
> Related to the 'Garbage Patches.'" *Marine Debris*,
> 2012, pm22100.net/docs/pdf/enercoop/pollutions/
> noaa-plastiques.pdf.

ORIGINAL SOURCE WITH STUDENT ANNOTATIONS

⌐ by whom?   *ocean ⌐*   *⌐ trash*

A question that is often posed to the NOAA Marine Debris

Program (MDP) is "How much debris is actually out there?"

The MDP has recognized the need for this answer as well as the

growing interest and value of citizen science. To that end, the MDP

ways of gathering information ⌐

is developing and testing two types of monitoring and assessment

protocols: 1) rigorous scientific survey and 2) volunteer at-sea

visual survey. These types of monitoring programs are necessary

kinds of materials ⌐   *⌐ how much?*

in order to compare marine debris, composition, abundance,

⌐ why it matters

distribution, movement, and impact data on national and global

scales.

SUMMARY

Source: NOAA Marine Debris Program. "Efforts and Activities Related
to the 'Garbage Patches.'" *Marine Debris,* 2012, pm22100.net/
docs/pdf/enercoop/pollutions/noaa-plastiques.pdf.

Having to field citizens' questions about the size of debris fields in
Earth's oceans, the Marine Debris Program, an arm of the US National
Oceanic and Atmospheric Administration, is currently implementing
methods to monitor and draw conclusions about our oceans' patches
of pollution (NOAA Marine Debris Program).

Paraphrasing without plagiarizing

Like a summary, a paraphrase is written in your own words; but whereas a summary reports significant information in fewer words than the source, a paraphrase retells the information in roughly the same number of words. If you retain occasional choice phrases from the source, use quotation marks so that later you will know which phrases are not your own. If you paraphrase a source, you must still cite the source.

As you read the following paraphrase of the original source (see p. 547), notice that the language is significantly different from that in the original.

PARAPHRASE

Source: NOAA Marine Debris Program. "Efforts and Activities Related to the 'Garbage Patches.'" *Marine Debris*, 2012, pm22100.net/docs/pdf/enercoop/pollutions/noaa-plastiques.pdf.

Citizens concerned and curious about the amount, makeup, and locations of debris patches in our oceans have been pressing NOAA's Marine Debris Program for answers. In response, the organization is preparing to implement plans and standards for expert study and nonexpert observation, both of which will yield results that will be helpful in determining the significance of the pollution problem (NOAA Marine Debris Program).

Academic English

When you are summarizing and paraphrasing ideas from a source, keep these guidelines in mind:

- **Avoid replacing a source's words with synonyms.** Word-by-word substitutions can be awkward because meaning in English often comes from phrases and whole sentences.

- **Determine the meaning of the source.** A topic sentence can often be the clue to understanding the passage.

- **Present your understanding of the author's meaning.** Focus on the overall idea in the source rather than the individual words.

Avoid plagiarizing from the Web

1 **Understand what plagiarism is.** When you use another author's intellectual property—language, visuals, or ideas—in your own writing without giving proper credit, you commit a kind of academic theft called *plagiarism*.

2 **Treat Web sources the same way you treat print sources.** Language, data, or images that you find on the Web must be cited, even if the material is in the public domain (older works no longer protected by copyright law) or is publicly accessible on free sites. When you use material from Web sites sponsored by federal, state, or municipal governments (.gov sites) or by nonprofit organizations (.org sites), you must acknowledge that material, too, as intellectual property owned by those agencies.

3 **Keep track of words borrowed from sources.** When you copy and paste passages from Web sources to an electronic file, put quotation marks around any words that you have inserted into your own work. Develop a system for distinguishing between your words and those of your sources and to indicate whether you have summarized, paraphrased, or quoted an author's words.

4 **Avoid Web sites that sell essays.** Some sites that appear to offer legitimate writing support actually *sell* college essays. Submitting a paper that you have purchased, or even using material from such a paper, is cheating and is considered plagiarism.

For details on avoiding plagiarism while working with sources, see 54b (MLA), 59b (APA), and 63b (*Chicago*).

Using quotation marks to avoid plagiarizing

A quotation consists of the exact words from a source. In your notes, put all quoted material in quotation marks; do not assume that you will remember later which words, phrases, and passages you have quoted and which are your own. When you quote, be sure to copy the words of your source exactly, including punctuation and capitalization.

QUOTATION

Source: NOAA Marine Debris Program. "Efforts and Activities Related to the 'Garbage Patches.'" *Marine Debris*, 2012, pm22100.net/docs/pdf/enercoop/pollutions/noaa-plastiques.pdf.

The NOAA Marine Debris Program has noted that, as our oceans become increasingly polluted, surveillance is "necessary in order to compare marine debris, composition, abundance, distribution, movement, and impact data on national and global scales."

EXERCISE 51–1 Summarize the following passage from a research source. Use MLA-style in-text citation.

Just last year, a systematic review and meta-analysis of studies looking at long-term consumption of coffee and the risk of cardiovascular disease was published. The researchers found 36 studies involving more than 1,270,000 participants. The combined data showed that those who consumed a moderate amount of coffee, about three to five cups a day, were at the lowest risk for problems. Those who consumed five or more cups a day had no higher risk than those who consumed none.

Source: Carroll, Aaron E. "More Consensus on Coffee's Effect on Health Than You Might Think." *The New York Times*, 11 May 2015, nyti.ms/1lw1yZ8.

EXERCISE 51–2 Paraphrase the following passage from a research source. Use MLA-style in-text citation.

The historical legacy of physical and cultural genocide is thus firmly imprinted in the memory of World War II, and for the 400

Navajo Code Talkers, who worked from within the U.S. Marine Corps to clandestinely communicate across the Pacific theater, the irony was even more striking: their native language, which had been subject to systematic attempts of extermination and which they were forbidden to use, was now turning into a crucial device to win the war.

Source: Däwes, Birgit. "Transnational Debts: The Cultural Memory of Navajo Code Talkers in World War II." *American Studies Journal*, no. 59, 2015, www.asjournal.org/59-2015/cultural-memory-of-navajo-code-talkers-in-world-war-ii/.

52 Evaluating sources

You can often locate hundreds of potential sources for your topic—far more than you will have time to read. Your challenge will be to determine what kinds of sources you need and to zero in on a reasonable number of trustworthy sources. This kind of decision making is referred to as *evaluating sources*. When you evaluate a source, you make a judgment about how useful the source is to your project.

Evaluating sources isn't something you do in one sitting. Being an effective researcher doesn't mean following a formula (*find some sources > evaluate those sources > write the paper*). Rather, it means looking at the process as more dynamic. After you do some planning, searching, and reading, for example, you may reflect on the information you have and conclude that you need to rethink your research question—and so you may return to assessing the kinds of sources you need. Or you may be midway through drafting your paper when you begin to question a particular source's credibility, at which point you return to searching and reading.

Viewing evaluation as a process

When you use sources in writing, make a habit of evaluating, or judging the value of, those sources at each stage of your project. The following questions may help.

Evaluate as you PLAN

What kinds of sources do I need?

What do I need these sources to help me do: Define? Persuade? Inform?

Evaluate as you SEARCH

How can I find reliable sources that help me answer my research question?

Which sources will help me build my credibility as a researcher?

Evaluate as you READ

What positions do these sources take in the debate on my topic? What are their biases?

How do these sources inform my own understanding of the topic and the position I will take?

Evaluate as you WRITE

How do the sources I've chosen help me make my point?

How do my own ideas fit into the conversation on my research topic?

52a Think about how sources might contribute to your writing.

How you plan to use sources in your paper will affect how you evaluate them. Not every source must directly support your thesis; sources can have a range of functions in a paper. They can do any of the following:

- provide background information or context for your topic
- explain terms or concepts that your readers might not understand
- provide evidence for your argument

- lend authority to your argument
- identify a gap or contradiction in the conversation
- offer counterarguments and alternative interpretations to your argument

As you plan, you will need to think through the kinds of sources that will help you fulfill your purpose. For some examples of how student writers use sources for a variety of purposes, see 53c and 58c.

52b Select sources worth your time and attention.

As you search for sources in databases, the library catalog, and search engines, you're likely to get many more results than you can read or use. This section explains how to scan through the results for the most promising sources, and how to evaluate them as you preview them, to see whether they meet your needs.

Scanning search results

As you scan through a list of search results, watch for clues indicating whether a source might be useful for your purposes or not worth pursuing. You will need to use somewhat different strategies when scanning search results from a database, a library catalog, and a Web search engine.

Databases Most databases list at least the following information, which can help you decide if a source is relevant, current, and scholarly (see the chart on p. 557).

Title and brief description (How relevant?)

Date (How current?)

Name of periodical or other publication (How scholarly?)

Length (How extensive in coverage?)

Many databases allow you to sort your list of results by relevance or date; sorting may help you scan the information more efficiently.

Library catalogs   The library's catalog usually lists basic information about books, periodicals, DVDs, and other material—enough to give you a first impression (see also p. 535). As in database search results, the title and date of publication of books and other sources listed in the catalog will often be your first clues about whether the source is worth consulting. If a title looks interesting, you can click on it for information about the subject matter and length. For books or other long sources, such as reports, a table of contents may also be available.

Web search engines   Reliable and unreliable sources live side-by-side online. As you scan through search results, look for the following clues about the probable relevance, currency, and reliability of a Web site.

> The title, keywords, headings, and lead-in text
> (How relevant?)
>
> A date (How current?)
>
> An indication of the site's sponsor or purpose
> (How reliable?)
>
> The URL, especially the domain name extension: for example, .com, .edu, .gov, or .org (How relevant? How reliable?)

Previewing sources

Once you have decided that a source looks promising, preview it quickly to see whether it lives up to its promise. Evaluating as you search, rejecting irrelevant or unreliable sources before actually reading them, can save you time.

PREVIEWING AN ARTICLE

- Consider the publication in which the article is printed. Is it a scholarly journal (see the chart on p. 557)? A popular magazine? A newspaper with a national reputation?

- For a magazine or journal article, look for an abstract or a statement of purpose at the beginning; also look for a summary at the end.

- For a newspaper article, focus on the headline and the opening paragraphs for relevance.

- Scan any headings and look at any visuals — charts, graphs, diagrams, or illustrations — that might indicate the article's focus and scope.

PREVIEWING A WEB SITE

- Check to see if the sponsor is a reputable organization, a government agency, or a university. Is the group likely to look at only one side of a debatable issue?

- If you have landed on an internal page of a site and no author or sponsor is evident, try navigating to the home page, either through a link or by truncating (shortening) the URL (see p. 537).

- Try to determine the purpose of the Web site. Is the site trying to sell a product? Promote an idea? Inform the public? Is the purpose consistent with your research?

- If the Web site includes statistical data (tables, graphs, charts), can you tell how and by whom the statistics were compiled? Is research cited?

- Find out when the site was created or last updated. Is it current enough for your purposes?

PREVIEWING A BOOK

- Glance through the table of contents, keeping your research question in mind. Even if the entire book is not relevant, parts of it may be useful.

Determining if a source is scholarly

For many college assignments, you will be asked to use scholarly sources. These are written by experts for a knowledgeable audience and usually go into more depth than books and articles written for a general audience. (Scholarly sources are sometimes called *refereed* or *peer-reviewed* because the work is evaluated by experts in the field before publication.) To determine if a source is scholarly, you should look for the following:

- Formal language and presentation
- Authors who are academics or scientists
- Footnotes or a bibliography documenting the works cited by the author in the source
- Original research and interpretation (rather than a summary of other people's work)
- Quotations from and analysis of primary sources (in humanities disciplines such as literature, history, and philosophy)
- A description of research methods or a review of related research (in the sciences and social sciences)

NOTE: In some databases, searches can be limited to refereed or peer-reviewed journals.

- Scan the preface in search of a statement of the author's purposes.
- Use the index to look up a few words related to your topic.
- If a chapter looks useful, read its opening and closing paragraphs and skim any headings.

52c Select appropriate versions of online sources.

An online source may appear as an abstract, an excerpt, or a full-text work. It is important to distinguish among these versions of sources and to use a complete version of a source, preferably one with page numbers, for your research.

Abstracts and excerpts are shortened versions of complete works. An abstract—a summary of a work's contents—might appear in a database record for a source and can give you clues about the usefulness of the source for your paper. An excerpt is the first few sentences or paragraphs of a newspaper or magazine article and sometimes appears in a list of results from an online search.

Abstracts and excerpts often provide enough information for you to determine whether the complete article would be useful for your paper. Both are brief (usually fewer than five hundred words) and generally do not contain enough information to function alone as sources in a research paper. Reading the complete article is the best way to understand the author's argument before referring to it in your own writing. If an article is available in multiple file formats, work with the file that includes page numbers; these are useful for accurate note taking and citation.

52d Read with an open mind and a critical eye.

As you begin reading the sources you have chosen, keep an open mind. Do not let your personal beliefs prevent you from listening to new ideas and opposing viewpoints. Be curious about the wide range of positions in the research conversation you are entering. Your research question should guide you as you engage your sources.

When you read critically, you are examining an author's assumptions, assessing evidence, and weighing conclusions. Reading critically means

- reading carefully (*What does the source say?*)
- reading skeptically (*Are any of the author's points or conclusions problematic?*)

- reading evaluatively (*How does this source help me make my argument?*)

To see one student's careful reading of a source text, see 5a.

USING SOURCES RESPONSIBLY: Take time to read the entire source to understand its author's arguments, assumptions, and conclusions. Try to avoid taking quotations from the first few pages of a source before you understand whether the words and ideas are representative of the work as a whole.

Distinguishing between primary and secondary sources

As you begin assessing evidence in a source, determine whether you are reading a primary or a secondary source. Primary sources include original documents such as letters, diaries, films, legislative bills, laboratory studies, field research reports, and eyewitness accounts. Secondary sources are commentaries on primary sources — another writer's opinions about or interpretation of a primary source.

Although a primary source is not necessarily more reliable than a secondary source, it has the advantage of being a firsthand account. You can better evaluate what a secondary source says if you have first read any primary sources it discusses.

Being alert for signs of bias

Bias is a way of thinking, a tendency to be partial, that prevents people and publications from viewing a topic objectively. Both in print and online, some sources are more objective than others. If you are exploring the rights of organizations like WikiLeaks to distribute sensitive government documents over the Internet, for example, you may not find objective, unbiased information in a US State Department report. If you are researching timber harvesting practices, you are likely to encounter bias in publications sponsored by environmental groups. As you read sources,

> ## Evaluating all sources
>
> ### Checking for signs of bias
>
> - Does the author or publisher endorse political or religious views that could affect objectivity?
> - Is the author or publisher associated with a special-interest group, such as PETA or the National Rifle Association, that might present only one side of an issue?
> - Are alternative views presented and addressed? How fairly does the author treat opposing views? (See 6c.)
> - Does the author's language show signs of bias? (See 6b.)
>
> ### Assessing an argument
>
> - What is the author's central claim or thesis?
> - How does the author support this claim—with relevant and sufficient evidence or with just a few anecdotes or emotional examples?
> - Are statistics consistent with those you encounter in other sources? Have they been used fairly? Does the author explain where the statistics come from?
> - Are any of the author's assumptions questionable?
> - Does the author consider opposing arguments and refute them persuasively? (See 6c.)
> - Does the author use flawed logic? (See 6a.)

however, you need not reject those that are biased. Publications that are known to be reputable can be editorially biased. As a researcher, you will need to consider any suspected bias as you assess the source. If you are uncertain about a source's special interests, seek the help of a reference librarian.

Like publishers, some authors are more objective than others. If you have reason to believe that a writer is particularly biased, you will want to assess his or her arguments with special care. For a list of questions worth asking, see the chart on page 560.

Assessing the author's argument

In nearly all subjects worth writing about, there is some element of argument, so expect to encounter authors who disagree. In fact, areas of disagreement give you entry points in a research conversation. The questions in the chart on page 560 can help you weigh the strengths and weaknesses of each author's arguments.

> **MORE HELP**
>
> Good college writers read critically.
> ▸ Judging whether a source is reasonable: 6a
> ▸ Judging whether a source is fair: 6c

52e Assess Web sources with care.

Sources found on the Web can provide valuable information, but verifying their credibility may take time. Before using a Web source in your paper, make sure you know who created the material and for what purpose. Sites with reliable information can stand up to careful scrutiny. For a checklist on evaluating Web sources by considering authorship, sponsorship, purpose and audience, and currency, see the chart on page 562.

WRITING PRACTICE

Evaluating sources you find on the Web

Using the guidelines on page 562, evaluate two Web sources that you've selected for your research project. Evaluate the authorship, sponsorship, purpose, audience, and currency for each site. Based on your evaluation, are these sources credible? Reliable? Right for your project? Use your research log to reflect on the usefulness of these Web sources for your project.

Evaluating sources you find on the Web

Authorship

- Does the Web site or document have an author? You may need to dig to find the author's name. If you have landed directly on an internal page of a site, for example, you may need to navigate to the home page or find an "about this site" link.

- If there is an author, can you tell whether he or she is knowledgeable and credible? When the author's credentials aren't listed on the site itself, look for links to the author's home page, which may provide evidence of his or her expertise.

Sponsorship

- Who, if anyone, sponsors the site? The sponsor of a site is often named and described on the home page.

- What does the URL tell you? The domain name extension often indicates the type of group hosting the site: commercial (.com), educational (.edu), nonprofit (.org), governmental (.gov), military (.mil), or network (.net). URLs may also indicate a country of origin: .uk (United Kingdom) or .jp (Japan), for instance.

Purpose and audience

- Why was the site created: To argue a position? To sell a product? To inform readers?

- Who is the site's intended audience?

Currency

- How current is the site? Check for the date of publication or the latest update, often located at the bottom of the home page or at the beginning or end of an internal page.

- How current are the site's links? If many of the links no longer work, the site may be too dated for your purposes.

Evaluating a Web site: Checking reliability

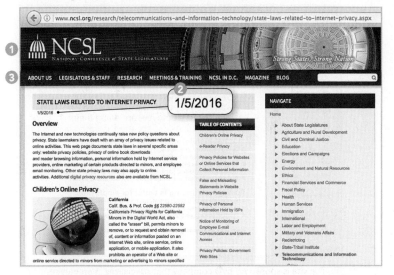

1 This page on Internet monitoring and workplace privacy appears on a Web site sponsored by the National Conference of State Legislatures. The NCSL is a bipartisan group that functions as a clearinghouse of ideas and research of interest to state lawmakers. It is also a lobby for state issues before the US government. The domain ending .org marks this sponsor as a nonprofit organization.

2 A clear date of publication shows currency.

3 An "About Us" page suggests that this is a credible organization whose credentials can be verified.

Evaluating a Web site: Checking purpose

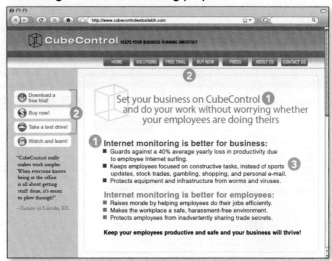

1 The site is sponsored by a company that specializes in employee-monitoring software.

2 Repeated links for trial downloads and purchase suggest the site's intended audience: consumers seeking to purchase software (probably not researchers seeking detailed information about employees' use of the Internet in the workplace).

3 The site appears to provide information and even shows statistics from studies, but ultimately the purpose of the site is to sell a product.

Assessing multimodal sources with your research question in mind

You may find that, for your topic, the best sources are videos such as public service ads or interviews delivered as podcasts or blog posts that include opinion, data, or graphics. Though these are generally not considered scholarly sources, such sources may be perfectly appropriate given your topic, your purpose, and your audience. When student writer Sophie Harba entered a debate about the rise of chronic diseases from harmful diets, she used a graph from the US Department of Agriculture to demonstrate the dangers of the typical American diet. (See her essay on pages 666–73.) The graph added needed evidence to help her answer her research question: Should the government enact laws to regulate eating choices? The guidelines in the chart on page 562 will be helpful as you evaluate multimodal sources.

52f Construct an annotated bibliography.

Section 51a describes how to write a working bibliography, a document that helps you keep track of publication information for all the sources you may be considering for your project.

You may be assigned to write an *annotated bibliography*, a more formal document in which you summarize and evaluate the sources you have read—at least the most promising ones. Writing brief sentences summarizing key points of a source will help you identify how the source relates to your argument and to your other sources and will help you judge whether the source is relevant and appropriate for your project. Evaluating your sources' ideas will help you separate them from your own and from each other, and it will also help you move toward a draft in which you synthesize sources and present your own research thesis. (See 55d and 60d for more on synthesis.) An annotated bibliography asks you to think about how each source helps you take your place in the debate you have entered.

For more help with writing an annotated bibliography, see the Writing Guide on pages 567–68.

SAMPLE ANNOTATED BIBLIOGRAPHY ENTRY (MLA STYLE)

Resnik, David. "Trans Fat Bans and Human Freedom."
American Journal of Bioethics, vol. 10, no. 3, Mar.
2010, pp. 27-32.

Summarize the source using present tense.

Evaluate the source for bias and relevance.

Annotations should be three to seven sentences long.

Evaluate the source for its contribution to the research project.

In this scholarly article, bioethicist David Resnik argues that bans on unhealthy foods threaten our personal freedom. He claims that researchers don't have enough evidence to know whether banning trans fats will save lives or money; all we know is that such bans restrict dietary choices. Resnik explains why most Americans oppose food restrictions, noting our multiethnic and regional food traditions as well as our resistance to government limitations on personal freedoms. He acknowledges that few people would miss eating trans fats, but he fears that bans on such substances could lead to widespread restrictions on red meat, sugary sodas, and other foods known to have harmful effects. Resnik offers a well-reasoned argument, but he goes too far by insisting that all proposed food restrictions will do more harm than good. This article contributes important perspectives on American resistance to government intervention in food choice and counters arguments in other sources that support the idea of food legislation to advance public health.

How to write an annotated bibliography

An **annotated bibliography** gives you an opportunity to summarize, evaluate, and record publication information for your sources before drafting your research paper. You summarize each source to understand its main ideas; you evaluate each source for accuracy, quality, and relevance. Finally, you reflect, asking yourself how the source will contribute to your research project. A sample annotated bibliography entry appears on page 566.

Key features

- **A list of sources arranged in alphabetical order by author** includes complete bibliographic information for each source.
- **A brief entry for each source** is typically one hundred to two hundred words.
- **A summary** of each source states the work's main ideas and key points briefly and accurately. The summary is written in the third person and the present tense. Summarizing helps you test your understanding of a source and convey its meaning responsibly.
- **An evaluation** of the source's role and usefulness in your project includes an assessment of the source's strengths and limitations, the author's qualifications and expertise, and the function of the source in your project. Evaluating a source helps you analyze how the source fits into your project and separate the source's ideas from your own.

Thinking ahead: Presenting or publishing

You may be asked to submit your annotated bibliography electronically. If this is the case, and if any of your sources are from the Web, you may want to format some of the text as hyperlinks to make it easier for your readers to access the sources if they need to do so.

Writing your annotated bibliography

1 Explore

For each source, begin by brainstorming responses to questions such as the following.

- What is the purpose of the source? Who is its intended audience?
- What is the author's thesis? What evidence supports the thesis?
- Do you agree or disagree with the author's conclusions?
- What qualifications and expertise does the author bring? Does the author have any biases or make any questionable assumptions?
- Why do you think this source is useful for your project?
- How does this source relate to the other sources in your bibliography?

2 Draft

- Arrange the sources in alphabetical order by author (or by title for works with no author).
- Provide consistent bibliographic information for each source. For the exact bibliographic format, see 56b (MLA), 61b (APA), or 63d (*Chicago*).
- Start your summary by identifying the thesis and purpose of the source as well as the credentials of the source's author.
- Keep your research question in mind. How does this source contribute to your project? How does it help you take your place in the conversation?

3 Revise

Ask reviewers for specific feedback. Here are some questions to guide their comments.

- Is each source summarized clearly? Have you identified the author's main idea?
- For each source, have you made a clear judgment about how and why the source is useful for your project?
- Have you used quotation marks around exact words from a source?

Writing MLA papers

BRIEF DIRECTORY

53 Supporting a thesis, 570
54 Citing sources; avoiding plagiarism, 577
55 Integrating sources, 585
56 Documenting sources, 598
        Directory to MLA in-text citation models, 599
        Directory to MLA works cited models, 611
57 Manuscript format; sample research paper, 662

Most English instructors and some humanities instructors will ask you to document your sources with the Modern Language Association (MLA) system of citations described in section 56.

When writing an MLA paper that is based on sources, you face three main challenges: (1) supporting a thesis, (2) citing your sources accurately and avoiding plagiarism, and (3) integrating source material effectively.

Examples in sections 53–55 are drawn from a student's research about the role of government in legislating food choices. Sophie Harba's research paper, in which she argues that state governments have the responsibility to advance health policies and to regulate healthy eating choices, appears on pages 666–73.

NOTE: For advice on finding and evaluating sources and on managing information in all your college courses, see 50–52.

53 Supporting a thesis

Most research assignments ask you to form a thesis, or main idea, and to support that thesis with well-organized evidence. (See also 1c.)

53a Form a working thesis.

Once you have read a variety of sources, considered your issue from different perspectives, and chosen an entry point in the research conversation (see 50b), you are ready to form a working thesis to focus your project: a one-sentence (or occasionally a two-sentence) statement of your central idea. (See also 1c and 53d.) The working thesis expresses more than your opinion; it expresses your informed, reasoned answer to your research question—a question about which people might disagree. As you learn more about your subject, your ideas may change, and your working thesis will evolve, too. You can revise your thesis as you draft.

In a research paper, your thesis will answer the central research question that you pose (see 50b). Here, for example, are student writer Sophie Harba's research question and working thesis.

RESEARCH QUESTION

Should the government enact laws to regulate healthy eating choices?

WORKING THESIS

Government has the responsibility to regulate healthy eating choices because of the rise of chronic diseases.

After you have written a rough draft and perhaps done more reading, you may decide to revise your thesis, as Harba did, to give it a sharper and more specific focus.

REVISED THESIS

In the name of public health and safety, state governments have the responsibility to advance health policies and to regulate healthy eating choices, especially since doing so offers a potentially large social benefit for a relatively small cost.

The thesis usually appears at the end of the introductory paragraph. To read Sophie Harba's thesis in her introduction, see page 666.

Testing your thesis

Keeping the following guidelines in mind will help you develop an effective thesis statement.

- A thesis should take a position that needs to be argued and supported. It should not be a fact or description.

- A thesis should match the scope of the research project. If your thesis is too broad, explore a subtopic of your original topic. If your thesis is too narrow, ask a research question that has more than one answer.

- A thesis should be focused. Avoid vague words such as *interesting* or *good*. Use concrete language and make sure your thesis lets readers know your position.

- A thesis should stand up to the "So what?" question. Ask yourself why readers should care about your thesis. If your thesis matters to you, your readers are more likely to find your ideas engaging.

WRITING PRACTICE

Testing your working thesis

Exchange your research question and working thesis with a classmate. Use the guidelines on this page and focus your feedback on questions such as these: Does your thesis answer your research question and take a position that needs to be argued? Is your working thesis a debatable claim—in other words, might some readers disagree with you? Using your classmate's feedback, revise your working thesis.

53b Organize your ideas.

The body of your paper will consist of evidence in support of your thesis. It will be useful to sketch an informal plan that helps you begin to organize your ideas. Sophie Harba, for example, used this simple plan to outline the structure of her argument:

- Debates about the government's role in regulating food have a long history in the United States.

- Some experts argue that we should focus on the dangers of unhealthy eating habits and on preventing chronic diseases linked to diet.

- But food regulations are not a popular solution because many Americans object to government restrictions on personal choice.

- Food regulations designed to prevent chronic disease don't ask Americans to give up their freedom; they ask Americans to see health as a matter of public good.

After you have written a rough draft, a formal outline can help you organize your argument (see 1d).

53c Use sources to inform and support your argument.

The source materials you have gathered will help you support and develop your argument. Sources can play several different roles to support your thesis and develop your points.

Providing background information or context

You can use facts and statistics to support generalizations or to establish the importance of your topic, as student writer Sophie

Harba does to demonstrate the social benefits of laws designed to prevent chronic disease.

> To give just one example, Marion Nestle, New York University professor of nutrition and public health, notes that "a 1% reduction in intake of saturated fat across the population would prevent more than 30,000 cases of coronary heart disease annually and save more than a billion dollars in health care costs" (7).

Explaining terms or concepts

If readers are unfamiliar with a term or a concept, you will want to define or explain it; or if your argument depends on a term with multiple meanings, you will want to explain your use of the term. Quoting or paraphrasing a source can help you define terms and concepts in accessible language. Harba defines the term *refined grains* as part of her claim that the typical American diet is getting less healthy over time.

> A diet that is low in nutritional value and high in sugars, fats, and refined grains—grains that have been processed to increase shelf life but that sacrifice fiber, iron, and B vitamins—can be damaging over time (United States, Dept. of Agriculture and Dept. of Health and Human Services 36).

Supporting your claims

As you develop your argument, back up your assertions with facts, examples, and other evidence from your research. (See also 6h.) Harba, for example, uses factual evidence to make the point that the typical American diet is damaging.

> Michael Pollan, who has written extensively about Americans' unhealthy eating habits, cites the Centers for Disease Control in arguing that "fully three quarters of US health care spending goes to treat chronic diseases, most of which are preventable and linked to diet: heart disease, stroke, type 2 diabetes, and at least a third of all cancers."

Lending authority

Expert opinion can add weight and credibility to your argument. (See also 6h.) But don't rely on experts to make your points for you. State your ideas in your own words and, when appropriate, cite the judgment of an authority in the field to support your position.

> Debates surrounding the government's role in regulating food have a long history in the United States. According to Lorine Goodwin, a food historian, nineteenth-century reformers who sought to purify the food supply were called "fanatics" and "radicals" by critics who argued that consumers should be free to buy and eat what they want (77).

Anticipating and countering objections

Do not ignore sources that seem contrary to your position. Instead, use them to give voice to opposing points of view and to state potential objections to your argument before you counter them (see 6i). By anticipating her readers' argument that many Americans oppose laws to limit what they eat, Sophie Harba creates an opportunity to counter that objection and build common ground with her readers.

> Why is the public largely resistant to laws that would limit unhealthy choices or penalize those choices with so-called fat taxes? Many consumers and civil rights advocates find such laws to be an unreasonable restriction on individual freedom of choice. As health policy experts Mello et al. point out, opposition to food and beverage regulation is similar to the opposition to early tobacco legislation: the public views the issue as one of personal responsibility rather than one requiring government intervention (2602). In other words, if a person eats unhealthy food and becomes ill as a result, that is his or her choice. But those who favor legislation claim that freedom of choice is a myth because of the strong influence of food and beverage industry marketing on consumers' dietary habits.

53d Draft an introduction for your thesis.

In a research paper, readers are accustomed to seeing the thesis statement—the paper's main point—at the end of the first or second paragraph. The advantage of putting it in the first paragraph is that readers can easily recognize your position. The advantage of delaying the thesis until the second paragraph is that you can provide a fuller context for your main idea. Check with your instructor about any expectations he or she might have for the location of your thesis.

As you draft your introduction, you may revise your working thesis, either because you have refined your thinking or because new wording fits more smoothly into the context you have created for it.

In addition to stating your thesis, an introduction should hook readers by capturing their attention (see 1e). For example, in your first sentence or two you might introduce readers to the research conversation by connecting your topic to a recent news item or by pointing to emerging trends in an academic discipline. Other strategies are to pose a puzzling problem or to cite a surprising statistic. Student writer Sophie Harba begins her paper by engaging readers with her research question. She then highlights the research conversation around the question before offering her perspective in her thesis.

SAMPLE INTRODUCTION FOR A RESEARCH PAPER

Should the government enact laws to regulate healthy eating choices? Many Americans would answer an emphatic "No," arguing that what and how much we eat should be left to individual choice rather than unreasonable laws. Others might argue that it would be unreasonable for the government not to enact legislation, given the rise of

Writer hooks readers with a question.

Writer presents the research conversation around her question.

chronic diseases that result from harmful diets. In this
debate, both the definition of reasonable regulations and
the role of government to legislate food choices are at stake.
In the name of public health and safety, state governments
have the responsibility to shape health policies and to
regulate healthy eating choices, especially since doing so
offers a potentially large social benefit for a relatively small
cost.

Writer presents
her thesis.

53e Draft the paper in an appropriate voice.

A chatty, breezy voice is usually not appropriate in a research
paper, but neither is a vague, timid one.

TOO CHATTY

What's up with these people who think food isn't important
and don't want the government in their kitchen? People
who are against food regulation seem so irrational and
unreasonable.

MORE FORMAL

Why is the public largely resistant to laws that would limit
unhealthy choices or penalize those choices with so-called fat
taxes? Many consumers and civil rights advocates find such
laws to be an unreasonable restriction on individual freedom
of choice.

TOO VAGUE

It has been concluded that a majority of Americans don't want
the government to restrict their food access.

MORE SPECIFIC

According to a nationwide poll, 75 percent of Americans are
opposed to laws that restrict or put limitations on access to
unhealthy foods (Neergaard and Agiesta).

TOO TIMID

I may not be an expert on food policy, but it seems to me that eating unhealthy foods contributes to chronic disease and lots of other problems.

MORE AUTHORITATIVE

Mounting scientific evidence points to unhealthy foods as a significant contributing factor to chronic disease, which we know is straining our health care system, decreasing our quality of life, and leading to unnecessary premature deaths.

54 Citing sources; avoiding plagiarism

In a research paper, you will draw on the work of other writers, and you must document their contributions by citing your sources. Sources are cited for two reasons:

1. to tell readers where your information comes from — so that they can assess its reliability and, if interested, find and read the original source

2. to give credit to the writers from whom you have borrowed words and ideas

Borrowing another writer's language, sentence structures, or ideas without proper acknowledgment is a form of dishonesty known as *plagiarism*.

You must include a citation when you quote from a source, when you summarize or paraphrase, and when you borrow facts that are not common knowledge (see 54b).

54a Understand how the MLA system works.

Most English professors and some humanities professors require the MLA (Modern Language Association) system of in-text citations. Here, briefly, is how the MLA citation system usually works. (See 56 for more details and model citations. See 57b for a sample research paper with in-text citations and a works cited list in MLA style.)

1. The source is introduced by a signal phrase that names its author.
2. The material being cited is followed by a page number in parentheses (unless the source is unpaginated, as many Web sources are).
3. At the end of the paper, a list of works cited (arranged alphabetically by authors' last names) gives complete publication information for the source.

IN-TEXT CITATION

Bioethicist David Resnik emphasizes that such policies "open the door to excessive government control over food, which could restrict dietary choices, interfere with cultural, ethnic, and religious traditions, and exacerbate socioeconomic inequalities" (31).

ENTRY IN THE LIST OF WORKS CITED

Resnik, David. "Trans Fat Bans and Human Freedom." *American Journal of Bioethics*, vol. 10, no. 3, Mar. 2010, pp. 27-32.

NOTE: This basic MLA format varies for different types of sources. For a detailed discussion as well as other models, see section 56.

54b Avoid plagiarism when quoting, summarizing, and paraphrasing sources.

In a research paper, you draw on the work of other writers, and you must document their contributions by citing your sources. When you acknowledge your sources, you avoid plagiarism, a serious academic offense. (See also 51c.)

In general, these three acts are considered plagiarism:

1. failing to cite quotations and borrowed ideas
2. failing to enclose borrowed language in quotation marks
3. failing to put summaries and paraphrases in your own words

Definitions of plagiarism may vary; it's a good idea to find out how your school defines academic dishonesty.

Citing quotations and borrowed ideas

You must cite all direct quotations. You must also cite any ideas borrowed from a source: summaries and paraphrases; statistics and other specific facts; and visuals such as cartoons, graphs, and diagrams.

The only exception is common knowledge—information that your readers could easily find in any number of general sources. For example, a quick search could tell you that Joel Coen directed *Fargo* in 1996 and that Emily Dickinson published only a handful of her many poems during her lifetime.

As a rule, when you have seen information repeatedly in your reading, you don't need to cite it. However, when information has appeared in only one or two sources, when it is highly specific (as with statistics), or when it is controversial, you should cite the source. If a topic is new to you and you are not sure what is considered common knowledge or what is controversial, ask your instructor or a reference librarian. When in doubt, cite the source. (See 56 for details.)

Enclosing borrowed language in quotation marks

To indicate that you are using a source's exact phrases or sentences, you must enclose them in quotation marks unless they have been set off from the text by indenting (see 55b). To omit the quotation marks is to claim—falsely—that the language is your own, as in the example below. Such an omission is plagiarism even if you have cited the source.

ORIGINAL SOURCE

Although these policies may have a positive impact on human health, they open the door to excessive government control over food, which could restrict dietary choices, interfere with cultural, ethnic, and religious traditions, and exacerbate socioeconomic inequalities.

—David Resnik, "Trans Fat Bans and Human Freedom," p. 31

PLAGIARISM

Bioethicist David Resnik points out that policies to ban trans fats may protect human health, but they open the door to excessive government control over food, which could restrict dietary choices and interfere with cultural, ethnic, and religious traditions (31).

BORROWED LANGUAGE IN QUOTATION MARKS

Bioethicist David Resnik points out that policies to ban trans fats may protect human health, but they "open the door to excessive government control over food, which could restrict dietary choices, interfere with cultural, ethnic, and religious traditions, and exacerbate socioeconomic inequalities" (31).

Putting summaries and paraphrases in your own words

Summaries and paraphrases are written in your own words. A summary condenses information from a source; a paraphrase uses roughly the same number of words as the original source to convey the information. When you summarize or paraphrase, it is not enough to name the source; you must restate the source's meaning using your own language. (See also 51c and 55a.) Half-copying the author's sentences by using the author's phrases in your own sentences without quotation marks or by plugging synonyms into the author's sentence structure (sometimes called patchwriting) is a form of plagiarism.

The first paraphrase of the following source is plagiarized. Even though the source is cited, too much of the language in the student's paraphrase is borrowed from the original. The highlighted strings of words have been copied exactly (without quotation marks). In addition, the writer has closely echoed the sentence structure of the source, merely substituting some synonyms (*interfere with lifestyle choices* for *paternalistic intervention into lifestyle choices*, for example).

ORIGINAL SOURCE

[A]ntiobesity laws encounter strong opposition from some quarters on the grounds that they constitute paternalistic intervention into lifestyle choices and enfeeble the notion of personal responsibility. Such arguments echo those made in the early days of tobacco regulation.

> —Michelle M. Mello et al., "Obesity—the New Frontier of Public Health Law," p. 2602

PLAGIARISM: UNACCEPTABLE BORROWING

Health policy experts Mello et al. argue that antiobesity laws encounter strong opposition from some quarters because they interfere with lifestyle choices and decrease the feeling of personal responsibility. These arguments mirror those made in the early days of tobacco regulation (2602).

To avoid plagiarizing an author's language, resist the temptation to look at the source while you are summarizing or paraphrasing. After you have read the passage you want to paraphrase, set the source aside. Ask yourself, "What is the author's meaning?" In your own words, state your understanding of the author's ideas.

Return to the source and check that you haven't used the author's language or sentence structure or misrepresented the author's ideas. Following these steps will help you avoid plagiarizing the source. When you fully understand another writer's meaning, you can more easily and accurately represent those ideas in your own words.

ACCEPTABLE PARAPHRASE

As health policy experts Mello et al. point out, opposition to food and beverage regulation is similar to the opposition to early tobacco legislation: the public views the issue as one of personal responsibility rather than one requiring government intervention (2602).

EXERCISE 54–1 Summarize the following passage from a research source. Then paraphrase the same source. Use MLA-style in-text citation.

Until recently, school-readiness skills weren't high on anyone's agenda, nor was the idea that the youngest learners might be disqualified from moving on to a subsequent stage. But now that kindergarten serves as a gatekeeper, not a welcome mat, to elementary school, concerns about school preparedness kick in earlier and earlier. A child who's supposed to read by the end of kindergarten had better be getting ready in preschool.

Source: Christakis, Erika. "How the New Preschool Is Crushing Kids." *The Atlantic*, Jan./Feb. 2016, p. 18.

Be a responsible research writer

Using good citation habits is the best way to avoid plagiarizing sources and to demonstrate your responsibility as a researcher.

1 Cite your sources as you write drafts. Don't wait until your final draft is complete to add citations. Include a citation when you quote from a source, when you summarize or paraphrase, and when you borrow facts that are not common knowledge.

2 Place quotation marks around direct quotations, both in your notes and in your drafts.

3 Check each quotation, summary, and paraphrase against the source to make certain you aren't misrepresenting the source. Also be sure that your language and sentence structure differ from those in the original passage.

4 Provide a full citation in your works cited. It is not sufficient to cite a source only in the body of your paper; you must also provide complete publication information for each source in a list of works cited.

Becoming a College Writer

Provide context for sources

> "When you write with sources, don't make quotations
> stand on their own. You have to support a quotation on
> either side (leading into it and then analyzing it) and give it a
> place to stand."   —**Danielle Novotny,** student, Brandeis University

It's an exciting moment when you think you've found the
perfect quotation to support a
point you're making in a researched essay. It's tempting to let
this quotation make your
point for you. However, when you write papers for college
courses, papers in which you are expected to make a
contribution to the conversation about a subject, remember that
you are in charge of the conversation. You shape the argument
with your words and ideas, making, as Danielle Novotny suggests,
"a place" for each source.

Becoming a college writer requires you not only to use evidence,
integrating sources into your argument and acknowledging their
contributions to your thinking, but also to put that evidence into a
context that will help readers understand your ideas — your stand on
the issue.

● Writing a research paper is a common requirement in college
  courses. What do you find challenging about using sources?
  What does it mean to you to be a researcher who is "in charge
  of the conversation" when you write a research essay?

584   ● **MORE**
Putting source materials in context, 55c

55 Integrating sources

Your research writing draws on and borrows from the work of others to help you develop and support your ideas. As you conduct research, you gather language and ideas from your sources that you might want to use in your paper. Section 54 shows you how to acknowledge sources to avoid plagiarism. This section will help you integrate those sources into your paper so that readers understand how your use of quotation, summary, and paraphrase contributes to your argument.

As you integrate sources, you need to find a balance between the words of your sources and your own voice. Readers should always know who is speaking in your paper—you or your source. You can use several strategies to integrate sources into your paper while maintaining your own voice.

- Use sources as concisely as possible so that your own thinking and voice aren't lost (55a and 55b).

- Use signal phrases and avoid dropping quotations into your paper without indicating the boundary between your words and the source's words (55c).

- Discuss and analyze your sources to show readers how each source supports your argument and how the sources relate to one another (55d).

55a Summarize and paraphrase effectively.

In your academic writing, keep the emphasis on your ideas and your language; use your own words to summarize and to paraphrase sources and to explain your points. Whether you choose to summarize or paraphrase a source depends on your purpose.

Summarizing

When you summarize a source, you express another writer's ideas in your own words, condensing the author's key points and using fewer words than the author.

WHEN TO USE A SUMMARY

- When a passage is lengthy and you want to condense a chapter to a short paragraph or a paragraph to a single sentence

- When you want to state the source's main ideas simply and briefly in your own words

- When you want to compare arguments or ideas from various sources

- When you want to provide readers with an understanding of the source's argument before you respond to it or launch your own

Paraphrasing

When you paraphrase, you express an author's ideas in your own words, using approximately the same number of words and details as in the source.

WHEN TO USE A PARAPHRASE

- When the ideas and information are important but the author's exact words are not needed for accuracy or emphasis

- When you want to restate the source's ideas in your own words

- When you need to simplify and explain a technical or complicated source

- When you need to reorder a source's ideas

Even though you use your own words to summarize and paraphrase, the original idea remains the intellectual property of the author, so you must include a citation. (See 54b.)

55b Use quotations effectively.

When you quote a source, you borrow some of the author's exact words and enclose them in quotation marks. Quotation marks show your readers that both the idea and the words belong to the author.

WHEN TO USE QUOTATIONS

- When language is especially vivid or expressive
- When exact wording is needed for technical accuracy
- When it is important to let the debaters of an issue explain their positions in their own words
- When the words of an authority lend weight to an argument
- When the language of a source is the topic of your discussion (as in an analysis or interpretation)

Limiting your use of quotations

Although it is tempting to insert many quotations in your paper and to use your own words only for connecting passages, do not quote excessively.

It is not always necessary to quote full sentences from a source. To reduce your reliance on the words of others, you can often integrate language from a source into your own sentence structure.

> Resnik acknowledges that his argument relies on the "slippery slope" fallacy, but he insists that "social and political pressures" regarding food regulations make his concerns valid (31).

Using the ellipsis mark and brackets

Two useful marks of punctuation, the ellipsis mark and brackets, allow you to keep quoted material to a minimum and to integrate it smoothly into your text.

The ellipsis mark To condense a quoted passage, you can use the ellipsis mark (three periods, with spaces between) to indicate that you have left words out. What remains must be grammatically complete.

> In Mississippi, legislators passed "a ban on bans—a law that
> forbids . . . local restrictions on food or drink" (Conly A23).

The writer has omitted from the source the words *municipalities to place* before *local restrictions* to condense the quoted material.

On the rare occasions when you want to leave out one or more full sentences, use a period before the three ellipsis dots.

> Legal scholars Gostin and Gostin argue that "individuals have limited
> willpower to defer immediate gratification for longer-term health benefits.
> . . . A person understands that high-fat foods or a sedentary lifestyle will
> cause adverse health effects, or that excessive spending or gambling will
> cause financial hardship, but it is not always easy to refrain" (217).

Ordinarily, do not use an ellipsis mark at the beginning or at the end of a quotation. Your readers will understand that the quoted material is taken from a longer passage, so such marks are not necessary. The only exception occurs when you have dropped words at the end of the final quoted sentence. In such cases, put three ellipsis dots before the closing quotation mark and parenthetical reference.

USING SOURCES RESPONSIBLY: Make sure omissions and ellipsis marks do not distort the meaning of your source.

Brackets   Brackets allow you to insert your own words into quoted material. You can insert words in brackets to clarify a confusing reference or to keep a sentence grammatical in your context. You also use brackets to indicate that you are changing a letter from capital to lowercase (or vice versa) to fit into your sentence.

> Neergaard and Agiesta argue that "a new poll finds people are split
> on how much the government should do to help [find solutions to the
> national health crisis]—and most draw the line at attempts to force
> healthier eating."

In this example, the writer inserted words in brackets to clarify the meaning of *help*.

To indicate an error such as a misspelling in a quotation, insert [sic], including the brackets, right after the error.

> "While Americans of every race, gender and ethnicity are affected by this disease, diabetes disproportionately effects [sic] minority populations."

Do not overuse [sic] to call attention to errors in a source. Sometimes paraphrasing is a better option. (See 39c.)

Setting off long quotations

When you quote more than four typed lines of prose or more than three lines of poetry, set off the quotation by indenting it one-half inch from the left margin.

Long quotations should be introduced by an informative sentence, often followed by a colon. Quotation marks are unnecessary because the indented format tells readers that the passage is taken word-for-word from the source.

> In response to critics who claim that laws aimed at stopping us from eating whatever we want are an assault on our freedom of choice, Conly offers a persuasive counterargument:
>
> > [L]aws aren't designed for each one of us individually. Some of us can drive safely at 90 miles per hour, but we're bound by the same laws as the people who can't, because individual speeding laws aren't practical. Giving up a little liberty is something we agree to when we agree to live in a democratic society that is governed by laws. (A23)

Notice that at the end of an indented quotation the parenthetical citation goes outside the final mark of punctuation. (When a quotation is run into your text, the opposite is true. See the sample citations at the top of p. 588.)

55c Use signal phrases to integrate sources.

Whenever you include a paraphrase, summary, or direct quotation of another writer's work in your paper, prepare your readers for it with introductory words called a *signal phrase*. A signal phrase usually names the author of the source and often provides some context for the source material.

Using signal phrases in MLA papers

To avoid monotony, try to vary both the language and the placement of your signal phrases.

Model signal phrases

Michael Pollan, who has written extensively about Americans' unhealthy eating habits, argues that ". . ."

As health policy experts Mello et al. point out, ". . ."

Marion Nestle, New York University professor of nutrition and public health, notes, ". . ."

Conly offers a persuasive counterargument: ". . ."

Verbs in signal phrases

acknowledges	comments	endorses	reasons
adds	compares	grants	refutes
admits	confirms	illustrates	rejects
agrees	contends	implies	reports
argues	declares	insists	responds
asserts	denies	notes	suggests
believes	disputes	observes	thinks
claims	emphasizes	points out	writes

When you write a signal phrase, choose a verb that is appropriate for the way you are using the source. Are you providing background, explaining a concept, supporting a claim, lending authority, or refuting a belief (see 53c)?

NOTE: MLA style calls for verbs in the present or present perfect tense (*argues*, *has argued*) to introduce source material unless you include a date that specifies the time of the original author's writing.

Marking boundaries

Readers need to move from your words to the words of a source without feeling a jolt. Avoid dropping quotations into the text without warning. Instead, provide clear signal phrases, including at least the author's name, to indicate the boundary between your words and the source's words. (The signal phrase is highlighted in the second example.)

DROPPED QUOTATION

Laws designed to prevent chronic disease by promoting healthier food and beverage consumption also have potential economic benefits. "[A] 1% reduction in the intake of saturated fat across the population would prevent more than 30,000 cases of coronary heart disease annually and would save more than a billion dollars in health care costs" (Nestle 7).

QUOTATION WITH SIGNAL PHRASE

Laws designed to prevent chronic disease by promoting healthier food and beverage consumption also have potential economic benefits. Marion Nestle, New York University professor of nutrition and public health, notes that "a 1% reduction in the intake of saturated fat across the population would prevent more than 30,000 cases of coronary heart disease annually and would save more than a billion dollars in health care costs" (7).

Establishing authority

The first time you mention a source, include in the signal phrase the author's title, credentials, or experience to help your readers recognize the source's authority and your own credibility as a responsible researcher who has located reliable sources. (Signal phrases are highlighted in the next two examples.)

SOURCE WITH NO CREDENTIALS

Michael Pollan notes that "[t]he Centers for Disease Control estimates that fully three quarters of US health care spending goes to treat chronic diseases, most of which are preventable and linked to diet: heart disease, stroke, type 2 diabetes, and at least a third of all cancers."

SOURCE WITH CREDENTIALS

Journalist Michael Pollan, who has written extensively about Americans' unhealthy eating habits, notes that "[t]he Centers for Disease Control estimates that fully three quarters of US health care spending goes to treat chronic diseases, most of which are preventable and linked to diet: heart disease, stroke, type 2 diabetes, and at least a third of all cancers."

Introducing summaries and paraphrases

Introduce most summaries and paraphrases with a signal phrase that names the author and places the material in the context of your argument. Readers will then understand that everything between the signal phrase and the parenthetical citation summarizes or paraphrases the cited source.

Without the signal phrase (highlighted) in the following example, readers might think that only the quotation at the end is being cited, when in fact the whole paragraph is based on the source.

To improve public health, advocates such as Bowdoin College philosophy professor Sarah Conly contend that it is the government's duty to prevent people from making harmful choices whenever feasible and whenever public benefits outweigh the costs. In response to critics who claim that laws aimed at stopping us from eating whatever we want are an assault on our freedom of choice, Conly asserts that "laws aren't designed for each one of us individually" (A23).

When the context makes clear where the cited material begins, you may omit the signal phrase and include the author's last name in parentheses.

Using signal phrases with statistics and other facts

When you cite a statistic or another specific fact, a signal phrase is often not necessary. Readers usually will understand that the citation refers to the statistic or fact (not the whole paragraph).

> Seventy-five percent of Americans are opposed to laws that restrict or put limitations on access to unhealthy foods (Neergaard and Agiesta).

Putting source material in context

Readers should not have to guess why source material appears in your paper. A signal phrase can help you make the connection between your own ideas and those of another writer by clarifying how the source will contribute to your paper (see 52a).

If you use another writer's words, you must explain how they relate to your argument. Quotations don't speak for themselves; you must support them by creating a context for readers. Sandwich each quotation between sentences of your own: Introduce the quotation with a signal phrase, and follow it with interpretive comments that link the quotation to your paper's argument (see also 55d).

QUOTATION WITH EFFECTIVE CONTEXT (QUOTATION SANDWICH)

In response to critics who claim that laws aimed at stopping us from eating whatever we want are an assault on our freedom of choice, Conly offers a persuasive counterargument:

> [L]aws aren't designed for each one of us individually. Some of us can drive safely at 90 miles per hour, but we're bound by the same laws as the people who can't, because individual speeding laws aren't practical. Giving up a little liberty is something we agree to when we agree to live in a democratic society that is governed by laws. (A23)

As Conly suggests, we need to change our either/or thinking (either we have complete freedom of choice *or* we have government regulations and lose our freedom) and instead need to see health as a matter of public good, not individual liberty.

55d Synthesize sources.

When you synthesize multiple sources in a research paper, you create a conversation about your research topic. Your argument includes your active analysis and integration of ideas, not just a series of quotations and paraphrases. Your synthesis will show how your sources relate to one another; one source may support, extend, or counter the ideas of another. Not every source has to "speak" to another in a research paper, but readers should be able to see how each one functions in your argument (see 52a).

Considering how sources relate to your argument

Before you integrate sources and show readers how they relate to one another, consider how each one might contribute to your own argument. As student writer Sophie Harba became more informed about her research topic, she asked herself these questions: *What have I learned from my sources? Which sources might support my ideas or illustrate the points I want to make? What counterarguments do I need to address to strengthen my position?* She annotated a passage from one of her sources—a nonprofit group's assertion that our choices about food are skewed by marketing messages.

STUDENT NOTES ON THE ORIGINAL SOURCE

useful factual information ⟶

The food and beverage industry spends approximately $2 billion per year marketing to children.   —"Facts on Junk Food"

⌐ could use this to counter the point about
personal choice in Mello et al.

Placing sources in conversation

You can show readers how the ideas of one source relate to those of another by connecting and analyzing the ideas in your own voice. After all, you've done the research and thought through the issues, so you should control the conversation. When you effectively synthesize sources, the emphasis is still on your own writing; the thread of your argument should be easy to identify and to understand, with or without your sources.

SAMPLE SYNTHESIS

Student writer

Why is the public largely resistant to laws that would limit unhealthy choices or penalize those choices with so-called fat taxes? Many consumers and civil rights advocates find such laws to be an unreasonable restriction on individual freedom of choice. As health policy experts Mello et al. point out, opposition to food and beverage regulation is similar to the opposition to early tobacco legislation: the public views the issue as one of personal responsibility rather than one requiring government intervention (2602). In other words, if a person eats unhealthy food and becomes ill as a result, that is his or her choice. But those who favor legislation claim that freedom of choice is a myth because of the strong influence of food and beverage industry marketing on consumers' dietary habits. According to one nonprofit health advocacy group, food and beverage companies spend roughly two billion dollars per year marketing directly to children. As a result, kids see about four thousand ads per year encouraging them to consume unhealthy food and drinks ("Facts"). As was the case with antismoking laws passed in recent decades, taxes and legal restrictions on junk food sales could help to counter the strong marketing messages that promote unhealthy products.

Student writer — Source 1 — Student writer — Source 2 — Student writer

Student writer Sophie Harba sets up her synthesis with a question.

A signal phrase indicates how the source contributes to Harba's argument and shows that the idea that follows is not her own.

Harba interprets a paraphrased source.

Harba uses a source to support her counterargument.

The United States has a history of state and local public health laws that have successfully promoted a particular behavior by punishing an undesirable behavior. The decline in tobacco use as a result of antismoking taxes and laws is perhaps the most obvious example. Another example is legislation requiring the use of seat belts, which have significantly reduced fatalities in car crashes.

Harba uses a statistic to extend the argument and follows the source with a closing thought of her own.

One government agency reports that seat belt use saved an average of more than fourteen thousand lives per year in the United States between 2000 and 2010 (United States, Dept. of Transportation, Natl. Highway Traffic Safety Administration 231). Perhaps seat belt laws have public support because the cost of wearing a seat belt is small, especially when compared with the benefit of saving fourteen thousand lives per year.

Source 3

Student writer

In this synthesis, Harba uses her own analysis to shape the conversation among her sources. She does not simply string quotations together or allow them to overwhelm her writing. She guides her readers through a conversation about a variety of laws that could promote and have promoted public health. She finds points of intersection among her sources, acknowledges the contributions of others in the research conversation, and shows readers, in her own voice, how the various sources support her argument.

When synthesizing sources, ask yourself the following questions:

- How do your sources address your research question?

- How do your sources respond to each other's ideas?

- Have you varied the function of sources — to provide background, to explain concepts, to lend authority, and to anticipate counterarguments?

- Do you connect and analyze sources in your own voice?

- Is your own argument easy to identify and to understand, with or without your sources?

Reviewing an MLA paper: Use of sources

Use of quotations

- Have you used quotation marks around borrowed language (unless it has been set off from the text)? (See 54b.)

- Have you checked that quoted language is word-for-word accurate? If not, do ellipsis marks or brackets indicate the omissions or changes? (See pp. 587–89.)

- Does a clear signal phrase (usually naming the author) prepare readers for each quotation and for the purpose the quotation serves? (See 55c.)

- Does a parenthetical citation follow each quotation? (See 56a.)

- Have you sandwiched each quotation between sentences of your own to put the source in context? (See 55c.)

Use of summaries and paraphrases

- Are summaries and paraphrases free of plagiarized wording? (See 54b.)

- Are summaries and paraphrases documented with parenthetical citations? (See 54b and 56a.)

- Do readers know where the cited material begins? In other words, does a signal phrase mark the boundary between your words and the summary or paraphrase? Or does the context alone make clear exactly what you are citing? (See 55c.)

- Does a signal phrase prepare readers for the purpose the summary or paraphrase has in your argument?

Use of statistics and other facts

- Are statistics and facts (other than common knowledge) documented with parenthetical citations? (See 54b and 56a.)

- If there is no signal phrase, will readers understand exactly which facts are being cited? (See 55c.)

56 MLA documentation style

In English and other humanities classes, you may be asked to use the MLA (Modern Language Association) system for documenting sources, which is set forth in the *MLA Handbook*, 8th edition (MLA, 2016).

MLA recommends in-text citations that refer readers to a list of works cited. A typical in-text citation names the author of the source, often in a signal phrase, and gives a page number in parentheses. At the end of the paper, the list of works cited provides publication information about the source; the list is alphabetized by authors' last names (or by titles for works without authors). There is a direct connection between the in-text citation and the alphabetical listing. In the following example, that connection is highlighted in orange.

MORE HELP

A works cited list includes all the sources cited in the text of a paper.

▶ MLA works cited list: 56b
▶ Preparing the list of works cited: 57a
▶ Sample lists of works cited: pages 190, 672

IN-TEXT CITATION

Bioethicist David Resnik emphasizes that such policies, despite their potential to make our society healthier, "open the door to excessive government control over food, which could restrict dietary choices, interfere with cultural, ethnic, and religious traditions, and exacerbate socioeconomic inequalities" (31).

ENTRY IN THE LIST OF WORKS CITED

Resnik, David. "Trans Fat Bans and Human Freedom." *American Journal of Bioethics*, vol. 10, no. 3, Mar. 2010, pp. 27-32.

For a list of works cited that includes this entry, see page 672.

Directory to MLA in-text citation models

General guidelines for signal phrases and page numbers

1. Author named in a signal phrase, 600

2. Author named in parentheses, 601

3. Author unknown, 601

4. Page number unknown, 601

5. One-page source, 602

Variations on the general guidelines

6. Two authors, 602

7. Three or more authors, 602

8. Organization as author, 603

9. Authors with the same last name, 603

10. Two or more works by the same author, 603

11. Two or more works in one citation, 604

12. Repeated citations from the same source, 604

13. Encyclopedia or dictionary entry, 605

14. Multivolume work, 605

15. Entire work, 605

16. Selection in an anthology or a collection, 606

17. Government document, 606

18. Historical document, 606

19. Legal source, 607

20. Visual such as a table, a chart, or another graphic, 607

21. Personal communication and social media, 608

22. Web source, 608

23. Indirect source (source quoted in another source), 608

Literary works and sacred texts

24. Literary work without parts or line numbers, 609

25. Verse play or poem, 609

26. Novel with numbered divisions, 610

27. Sacred text, 610

56a MLA in-text citations

MLA in-text citations are made with a combination of signal phrases and parenthetical references. A signal phrase introduces information taken from a source (a quotation, summary, paraphrase, or fact); usually the signal phrase includes the author's name. The parenthetical reference comes after the cited material, often at the end of the sentence. It includes at least a page number (except for unpaginated sources, such as those found on the Web). In the models in 56a, the elements of the in-text citation are highlighted in orange.

IN-TEXT CITATION

Resnik acknowledges that his argument relies on "slippery slope" thinking, but he insists that "social and political pressures" regarding food regulation make his concerns valid (31).

Readers can look up the author's last name in the alphabetized list of works cited, where they will learn the work's title and other publication information. If readers decide to consult the source, the page number will take them straight to the cited passage.

General guidelines for signal phrases and page numbers

Items 1–5 explain how the MLA system usually works for all sources—in print, on the Web, in other media, and with or without authors and page numbers. Items 6–27 give variations on the basic guidelines.

1. Author named in a signal phrase   Ordinarily, introduce the material being cited with a signal phrase that includes the author's name. In addition to preparing readers for the source, the signal phrase allows you to keep the parenthetical citation brief.

According to Lorine Goodwin, a food historian, nineteenth-century reformers who sought to purify the food supply were called "fanatics" and "radicals" by critics who argued that consumers should be free to buy and eat what they want (77).

The signal phrase—*According to Lorine Goodwin*—names the author; the parenthetical citation gives the page number of the book in which the quoted words may be found.

Notice that the period follows the parenthetical citation. When a quotation ends with a question mark or an exclamation point, leave the end punctuation inside the quotation mark and add a period after the parenthetical citation.

Burgess asks a critical question: "How can we think differently about food labeling?" (51).

2. Author named in parentheses If you do not give the author's name in a signal phrase, put the last name in parentheses along with the page number (if the source has one). Use no punctuation between the name and the page number: (Moran 351).

According to a nationwide poll, 75% of Americans are opposed to laws that restrict or put limitations on access to unhealthy foods (Neergaard and Agiesta).

3. Author unknown If a source has no author, the works cited entry will begin with the title. In your in-text citation, either use the complete title in a signal phrase or use a short form of the title in parentheses. Titles of books and other long works are italicized; titles of articles and other short works are put in quotation marks (see also p. 663).

As a result, kids see nearly four thousand ads per year encouraging them to eat unhealthy food and drinks ("Facts").

NOTE: If the author is a corporation or a government agency, see items 8 and 17 on pages 603 and 606, respectively.

4. Page number unknown Do not include the page number if a work lacks page numbers, as is the case with many Web sources. Do not use page numbers from a printout from a Web site. (When the pages of a Web source are stable, as in PDF files, supply a page number in your in-text citation.)

Michael Pollan points out that "cheap food" actually has "significant costs—to the environment, to public health, to the public purse, even to the culture."

If a source has numbered paragraphs or sections, use "par." (or "pars.") or "sec." (or "secs.") in the parentheses: (Smith, par. 4). Notice that a comma follows the author's name.

5. One-page source   If the source is one page long, MLA allows (but does not require) you to omit the page number. It's a good idea to include the page number because without it readers may not know where your citation ends or, worse, may not realize that you have provided a citation at all.

NO PAGE NUMBER IN CITATION

Sarah Conly uses John Stuart Mill's "harm principle" to argue that citizens need their government to intervene to prevent them from taking harmful actions—such as driving too fast or buying unhealthy foods—out of ignorance of the harm they can do. But government intervention may overstep in the case of food choices.

PAGE NUMBER IN CITATION

Sarah Conly uses John Stuart Mill's "harm principle" to argue that citizens need their government to intervene to prevent them from taking harmful actions—such as driving too fast or buying unhealthy foods—out of ignorance of the harm they can do (A23). But government intervention may overstep in the case of food choices.

Variations on the general guidelines

This section describes the MLA guidelines for handling a variety of situations not covered in items 1–5.

6. Two authors   Name the authors in a signal phrase, as in the following example, or include their last names in the parenthetical reference: (Gostin and Gostin 214).

As legal scholars Gostin and Gostin explain, "[I]nterventions that do not pose a truly significant burden on individual liberty" are justified if they "go a long way towards safeguarding the health and well-being of the populace" (214).

7. Three or more authors   Give the first author's name followed by "et al." (Latin for "and others") in the signal phrase and in the parenthetical citation.

The study was extended for two years, and only after results were reviewed by an independent panel did the researchers publish their findings (Blaine et al. 35).

8. Organization as author   When the author is a corporation or an organization, name that author either in the signal phrase or in the parentheses. (For a government agency as author, see item 17 on p. 606.)

The American Diabetes Association estimates that the cost of diagnosed diabetes in the United States in 2012 was $245 billion.

In the list of works cited, the American Diabetes Association is treated as the author and alphabetized under *A.* When you give the organization name in the text, spell out the name; when you use it in parentheses, abbreviate common words in the name: "Assn.," "Dept.," "Natl.," "Soc.," and so on.

The cost of diagnosed diabetes in the United States in 2012 was estimated at $245 billion (Amer. Diabetes Assn.).

9. Authors with the same last name   If your list of works cited includes works by two or more authors with the same last name, include the author's first name in the signal phrase or first initial in the parentheses.

One approach to the problem is to introduce nutrition literacy at the K-5 level in public schools (E. Chen 15).

10. Two or more works by the same author   Mention the title of the work in the signal phrase or include a short version of the title in the parentheses.

The American Diabetes Association tracks trends in diabetes across age groups. In 2012, more than 200,000 children and adolescents had diabetes ("Fast"). Because of an expected dramatic increase in diabetes in young people over the next forty years, the association encourages medical professionals to develop "strategies for implementing childhood obesity prevention programs and primary prevention programs for youth at risk of developing type 2 diabetes" ("Number").

Titles of articles and other short works are placed in quotation marks; titles of books and other long works are italicized. (See also p. 663.)

In the rare case when both the author's name and a short title must be given in parentheses, separate them with a comma.

Researchers have estimated that "the number of youth with type 2 [diabetes] could quadruple and the number with type 1 could triple" by 2050, "with an increasing proportion of youth with diabetes from minority populations" (Amer. Diabetes Assn., "Number").

11. Two or more works in one citation   To cite more than one source in the parentheses, list the authors (or titles) in alphabetical order and separate them with semicolons.

The prevalence of early-onset Type 2 diabetes has been well documented (Finn 68; Sharma 2037; Whitaker 118).

It may be less distracting to use an information note for multiple citations (see 56c).

12. Repeated citations from the same source   When you are writing about a single work, you do not need to include the author's name each time you quote from or paraphrase the work. After you mention the author's name at the beginning of your paper, you may include just the page number in your parenthetical citations.

In Susan Glaspell's short story "A Jury of Her Peers," two women accompany their husbands and a county attorney to an isolated house where a farmer named John Wright has been choked to death in his bed with a rope. The chief suspect is Wright's wife, Minnie, who is in jail awaiting trial. The sheriff's wife, Mrs. Peters, has come along to gather some personal items for Minnie, and Mrs. Hale has joined her. Early in the story, Mrs. Hale sympathizes with Minnie and objects to the way the male investigators are "snoopin' round and criticizin'" her kitchen (249). In contrast, Mrs. Peters shows respect for the law, saying that the men are doing "no more than their duty" (249).

In a paper with multiple sources, if you are citing a source more than once in a paragraph, you may omit the author's name after the first mention in the paragraph as long as it is clear that you are still referring to the same source.

13. Encyclopedia or dictionary entry   When an encyclopedia or a dictionary entry does not have an author, it will be alphabetized in the list of works cited under the word or entry that you consulted (see item 28, p. 633). Either in your text or in your parenthetical citation, mention the word or entry. No page number is required because readers can look up the word or entry.

The word *crocodile* has a complex etymology ("Crocodile").

14. Multivolume work   If your paper cites more than one volume of a multivolume work, indicate in the parentheses the volume you are referring to, followed by a colon and the page number.

In his studies of gifted children, Terman describes a pattern of accelerated language acquisition (2: 279).

If you cite only one volume of a multivolume work, you will include the volume number in the list of works cited and will not need to include it in the parentheses. (See the second example in item 38 on p. 639.)

15. Entire work   Use the author's name in a signal phrase or a parenthetical citation. There is no need to use a page number.

Pollan explores the issues surrounding food production and consumption from a political angle.

16. Selection in an anthology or a collection Put the name of the author of the selection (not the editor of the anthology) in the signal phrase or the parentheses.

> In "Love Is a Fallacy," the narrator's logical teachings disintegrate when Polly declares that she should date Petey because "[h]e's got a raccoon coat" (Shulman 391).

In the list of works cited, the work is alphabetized under *Shulman*, the author of the story, not under the name of the editor of the anthology. (See item 35 on p. 638.)

> Shulman, Max. "Love Is a Fallacy." *Current Issues and Enduring Questions*, edited by Sylvan Barnet and Hugo Bedau, 9th ed., Bedford/St. Martin's, 2011, pp. 383-91.

17. Government document When a government agency is the author, you will alphabetize it in the list of works cited under the name of the government, such as United States or Great Britain (see item 70 on p. 657). For this reason, you must name the government as well as the agency in your in-text citation. (See item 8 on p. 603 about abbreviations in parenthetical citations.)

> One government agency reports that seat belt use saved an average of more than fourteen thousand lives per year in the United States between 2000 and 2010 (United States, Dept. of Transportation, Natl. Highway Traffic Safety Administration 231).

18. Historical document For a historical document, such as the United States Constitution or the Canadian Charter of Rights and Freedoms, provide the document title, neither italicized nor in quotation marks, along with relevant article and section numbers. In parenthetical citations, use common abbreviations such as "art." and "sec." and abbreviations of well-known titles: (US Const., art. 1, sec. 2).

> While the United States Constitution provides for the formation of
> new states (art. 4, sec. 3), it does not explicitly allow or prohibit the
> secession of states.

Cite other historical documents as you would any other work, by
the first element in the works cited entry (see item 72 on p. 659).

19. Legal source   For a legislative act (law) or court case, name
the act or case either in a signal phrase or in parentheses. Italicize
the names of cases but not the names of acts. (See also items 73
and 74 on pp. 659–60.)

> The Jones Act of 1917 granted US citizenship to Puerto Ricans.

> In 1857, Chief Justice Roger B. Taney declared in *Dred Scott v. Sandford*
> that blacks, whether enslaved or free, could not be citizens of the
> United States.

20. Visual such as a table, a chart, or another graphic   To cite a
visual that has a figure number in the source, use the abbreviation
"fig." and the number in place of a page number in your parenthetical citation: (Manning, fig. 4). If you refer to the figure in your
text, spell out the word "figure."

To cite a visual that does not have a figure number in a print
source, use the visual's title or a description in your text and cite
the author and page number as for any other source.

For a visual not in a print source, identify the visual in your
text and then in parentheses use the first element in the works
cited entry: the artist's or photographer's name or the title of the
work. (See items 64–69 on pp. 654–57.)

> Photographs such as *Woman Aircraft Worker* (Bransby) and *Women
> Welders* (Parks) demonstrate the US government's attempt to document
> the contributions of women during World War II.

21. Personal communication and social media Cite personal letters, personal interviews, e-mail messages, and social media posts by the name listed in the works cited entry, as you would for any other source. Identify the type of source in your text if you feel it is necessary for clarity. (See items 27d, 29c, and 75–79 in section 56b.)

22. Web source Your in-text citation for a source from the Web should follow the same guidelines as for other sources. If the source lacks page numbers but has numbered paragraphs, sections, or divisions, use those numbers with the appropriate abbreviation in your parenthetical citation: "par.," "sec.," "ch.," and so on. Do not add such numbers if the source does not use them; simply give the author or title in your in-text citation.

> Julian Hawthorne points out profound differences between his father and Ralph Waldo Emerson but concludes that, in their lives and their writing, "together they met the needs of nearly all that is worthy in human nature" (ch. 4).

23. Indirect source (source quoted in another source) When a writer's or a speaker's quoted words appear in a source written by someone else, begin the parenthetical citation with the abbreviation "qtd. in." (See also item 12 on p. 622.) In the following example, Gostin and Gostin are the authors of the source given in the works cited list; the source contains a quotation by Beauchamp.

> Public health researcher Dan Beauchamp has said that "public health practices are 'communal in nature, and concerned with the well-being of the community as a whole and not just the well-being of any particular person'" (qtd. in Gostin and Gostin 217).

Literary works and sacred texts

Literary works and sacred texts are usually available in a variety of editions. Your list of works cited will specify which edition you are using, and your in-text citation will usually consist of a page number from the edition you consulted (see item 24). When possible, give enough information — such as book parts, play divisions, or line numbers — so that readers can locate the cited passage in any edition of the work (see items 25–27).

24. Literary work without parts or line numbers Many literary works, such as most short stories and many novels and plays, do not have parts or line numbers. In such cases, simply cite the page number.

> At the end of Kate Chopin's "The Story of an Hour," Mrs. Mallard drops dead upon learning that her husband is alive. In the final irony of the story, doctors report that she has died of a "joy that kills" (25).

25. Verse play or poem For verse plays, give act, scene, and line numbers that can be located in any edition of the work. Use arabic numerals and separate the numbers with periods.

> In Shakespeare's *King Lear*, Gloucester, blinded for suspected treason, learns a profound lesson from his tragic experience: "A man may see how this world goes / with no eyes" (4.2.148-49).

For a poem, cite the part, stanza, and line numbers, if it has them, separated by periods.

> The Green Knight claims to approach King Arthur's court "because the praise of you, prince, is puffed so high, / And your manor and your men are considered so magnificent" (1.12.258-59).

For poems that are not divided into numbered parts or stanzas, use line numbers. For a first reference, use the word "lines": (lines 5-8). Thereafter use just the numbers: (12-13).

26. Novel with numbered divisions When a novel has numbered divisions, put the page number first, followed by a semicolon, and then the book, part, or chapter in which the passage may be found. Use abbreviations such as "bk.," "pt.," and "ch."

> One of Kingsolver's narrators, teenager Rachel, pushes her vocabulary beyond its limits. For example, Rachel complains that being forced to live in the Congo with her missionary family is "a sheer tapestry of justice" because her chances of finding a boyfriend are "dull and void" (117; bk. 2, ch. 10).

27. Sacred text When citing a sacred text such as the Bible or the Qur'an, name the edition you are using in your works cited entry (see item 39 on p. 639). In your parenthetical citation, give the book, chapter, and verse (or their equivalent), separated with periods. Common abbreviations for books of the Bible are acceptable.

> Consider the words of Solomon: "If your enemy is hungry, give him bread to eat; and if he is thirsty, give him water to drink" (*Oxford Annotated Bible*, Prov. 25.21).

The title of a sacred work is italicized when it refers to a specific edition of the work, as in the preceding example. If you refer to the book in a general sense in your text, neither italicize it nor put it in quotation marks (see also the note on p. 464 in section 42a).

> The Bible and the Qur'an provide allegories that help readers understand how to lead a moral life.

Directory to MLA works cited models

General guidelines for listing authors

1. Single author, 614
2. Two authors, 614
3. Three or more authors, 614
4. Organization or company as author, 617
5. No author listed, 617
   a. Article or other short work, 617
   b. Television program, 618
   c. Book, entire Web site, or other long work, 618
6. Two or more works by the same author, 618
7. Two or more works by the same group of authors, 618
8. Editor or translator, 619
9. Author with editor or translator, 619
10. Graphic narrative or other illustrated work, 619
    a. Author first, 619
    b. Illustrator first, 621
    c. Author and illustrator the same person, 621
11. Author using a pseudonym (pen name) or screen name, 621
12. Author quoted by another author (indirect source), 622

Articles and other short works

13. Basic format for an article or other short work, 623
    a. Print, 623
    b. Web, 623
    c. Database, 623
14. Article in a journal, 623
    a. Print, 623

b. Online journal, 625
c. Database, 625
15. Article in a magazine, 625
    a. Print (monthly), 625
    b. Print (weekly), 627
    c. Web, 627
    d. Database, 627
16. Article in a newspaper, 627
    a. Print, 628
    b. Web, 628
    c. Database, 628
17. Abstract or executive summary, 628
    a. Abstract of an article, 629
    b. Abstract of a paper, 629
    c. Abstract of a dissertation, 629
    d. Executive summary, 629
18. Article with a title in its title, 629
19. Editorial, 630
20. Unsigned article, 630
21. Letter to the editor, 630
22. Comment on an online article, 630
23. Paper or presentation at a conference, 631
24. Book review, 631
    a. Print, 631
    b. Web, 631
    c. Database, 632
25. Film review or other review, 632
    a. Print, 632
    b. Web, 632
26. Performance review, 632
27. Interview, 633
    a. Print, 633
    b. Web, 633

Directory to MLA works cited models (*cont.*)

c. Television or radio, 633

d. Personal, 633

28. Article in a dictionary or an encyclopedia (including a wiki), 633

    a. Print, 634

    b. Web, 634

29. Letter, 634

    a. Print, 634

    b. Web, 634

    c. Personal, 635

Books and other long works

30. Basic format for a book, 635

    a. Print book or e-book, 635

    b. Web, 635

    c. Database, 637

31. Parts of a book, 637

    a. Foreword, introduction, preface, or afterword, 637

    b. Chapter in a book, 637

32. Book with a title in its title, 637

33. Book in a language other than English, 638

34. Entire anthology or collection, 638

35. One selection from an anthology or a collection, 638

36. Two or more selections from an anthology or a collection, 638

37. Edition other than the first, 639

38. Multivolume work, 639

39. Sacred text, 639

40. Book in a series, 642

41. Republished book, 642

42. Pamphlet, brochure, or newsletter, 642

43. Dissertation, 642

    a. Published, 642

b. Unpublished, 642

44. Proceedings of a conference, 643

45. Manuscript, 643

Web sites and parts of Web sites

46. An entire Web site, 643

    a. Web site with author or editor, 643

    b. Web site with organization as author, 644

    c. Web site with no author, 644

    d. Web site with no title, 644

47. Short work from a Web site, 644

    a. Short work with author, 644

    b. Short work with no author, 645

48. Long work from a Web site, 645

49. Entire blog, 645

50. Blog post or comment, 645

51. Academic course or department home page, 647

Audio, visual, and multimedia sources

52. Podcast, 648

53. Film, 648

54. Supplementary material accompanying a film, 649

55. Video or audio from the Web, 649

56. Video game, 649

57. Computer software or app, 650

58. Television or radio episode or program, 650

    a. Broadcast, 650

    b. Web, 651

59. Transcript, 651

60. Performance, 651

61. Lecture or public address, 653

Directory to MLA works cited models (*cont.*)

a. Live, 653
b. Web, 654
62. Musical score, 654
63. Sound recording, 654
64. Work of art, 654
   a. Original, 655
   b. Web, 655
   c. Reproduction (print), 655
65. Photograph, 655
   a. Original, 655
   b. Web, 656
   c. Reproduction (print), 656
66. Cartoon, 656
67. Advertisement, 656
68. Visual such as a table, a chart, or another graphic, 656

69. Map, 657

Government and legal documents

70. Government document, 657
71. Testimony before a legislative body, 659
72. Historical document, 659
73. Legislative act (law), 659
74. Court case, 660

Personal communication and social media

75. E-mail message, 660
76. Text message, 660
77. Posting to an online discussion list, 660
78. Facebook post or comment, 661
79. Twitter post (tweet), 661

56b MLA list of works cited

The elements you will need for the works cited list will differ slightly for some sources, but the main principles apply to all sources, whether in print or from the Web: You should identify an author, a creator, or a producer whenever possible; give a title; and provide the date on which the source was produced. Some sources will require page numbers; some will require a publisher or sponsor; and some will require other identifying information.

Section 56b provides details for how to cite many of the sources you are likely to encounter. It also provides hints for what you can do when a source does not match one of the models exactly. When you cite sources, your goals are to show that your sources are reliable and relevant, to provide readers with enough information to find sources easily, and to provide that information consistently according to MLA conventions.

▶ Directory to MLA works cited models, page 611

▶ General guidelines for the works cited list, page 615

General guidelines for listing authors

The formatting of authors' names in items 1–12 applies to all sources—books, articles, Web sites—in print, on the Web, or in other media. For more models of specific source types, see items 13–79.

1. Single author

author: last name first — title (book) — publisher

Bowker, Gordon. *James Joyce: A New Biography*. Farrar, Straus and Giroux,

year

2012.

2. Two authors

first author: last name first — second author: in normal order — title (book)

Gourevitch, Philip, and Errol Morris. *Standard Operating Procedure*.

publisher — year

Penguin Books, 2008.

3. Three or more authors

Name the first author followed by "et al." (Latin for "and others"). In an in-text citation, use the same form for the authors' names as you use in the works cited entry. See item 7 on page 602.

first author: last name first — "et al." for other authors — title (book)

Zumeta, William, et al. *Financing American Higher Education in the Era of*

publisher — year

Globalization. Harvard Education Press, 2012.

General guidelines for the works cited list

In the list of works cited, include only sources that you have quoted, summarized, or paraphrased in your paper. MLA's guidelines are applicable to a wide variety of sources. At times you may find that you have to adapt the guidelines and models in this section to source types you encounter in your research.

Organization of the list

The elements, or pieces of information, needed for a works cited entry are the following:

- The author (if a work has one)
- The title
- The title of the larger work in which the source is located (MLA calls this a "container") — a collection, a journal, a magazine, a Web site, and so on
- As much of the following information as is available about the source and the container, listed in this order:

  Editor, translator, director, performer

  Version

  Volume and issue numbers

  Publisher or sponsor

  Date of publication

  Location of the source: page numbers, DOI, URL, and so on

Not all sources will require every element. See specific models in this section for more details.

Authors

- Arrange the list alphabetically by authors' last names or by titles for works with no authors.
- For the first author, place the last name first, a comma, and the first name. Put a second author's name in normal order (first name followed by last name). For three or more authors, use "et al." after the first author's name.
- Spell out "editor," "translator," "edited by," and so on. →

GENERAL GUIDELINES FOR THE WORKS CITED LIST (*cont.*)

Titles

- In titles of works, capitalize all words except articles (*a, an, the*), prepositions, coordinating conjunctions, and the *to* in infinitives—unless the word is first or last in the title or subtitle.
- Use quotation marks for titles of articles and other short works.
- Italicize titles of books and other long works.

Publication information

- MLA does not require the place of publication for a book publisher.
- Use the complete version of publishers' names. Omit terms such as "Inc." and "Co."; retain terms such as "Books" and "Press." For university publishers, use "U" and "P" for "University" and "Press."
- For a book, take the name of the publisher from the title page (or from the copyright page if it is not on the title page). For a Web site, the publisher might be at the bottom of a page or on the "About" page. If a work has two or more publishers, separate the names with slashes.
- If the title of a Web site and the publisher are the same or similar, use the title of the site but omit the publisher.

Dates

- For a book, give the most recent year on the title page or the copyright page. For a Web source, use the copyright date or the most recent update date. Use the complete date as listed in the source.
- Abbreviate all months except May, June, and July and give the date in inverted form: 13 Mar. 2016.
- If the source has no date, give your date of access at the end: Accessed 24 Feb. 2016.

Page numbers

- For most articles and other short works, give page numbers when they are available, preceded by "p." (or "pp." for more than one page).

- Do not use the page numbers from a printout of a Web source.

- If an article does not appear on consecutive pages, give the number of the first page followed by a plus sign: 35+.

URLs and DOIs

- Give a permalink or a DOI (digital object identifier) if a source has one. (See item 14c.)

- If a source does not have a permalink or a DOI, include a URL (omitting the protocol, such as http://).

- If a library's subscription database (such as Academic ASAP or JSTOR) does not give a permalink or a DOI, include only the basic URL for the database home page. (See item 15d.)

- For other sources from Web sites, give the complete URL for the source. (See item 30b.)

4. Organization or company as author

author: organization
name, not abbreviated · · · · · · title (book) · · · · · · publisher
Human Rights Watch. *World Report of 2015: Events of 2014.* Seven Stories

      date
Press, 2015.

Your in-text citation also should treat the organization as the author (see item 8 on p. 603).

5. No author listed

a. Article or other short work

                                    newspaper title
          article title   (city in brackets)   date
"Policing Ohio's Online Courses." *Plain Dealer* [Cleveland], 9 Oct. 2012,
    page(s)   label
    p. A5. Editorial.

5. No author listed (*cont.*)

| | title of
Web site | |
| title of short work | | publisher |

"Chapter 2: What Can Be Patented?" *Lemelson-MIT*, Massachusetts

                                                        URL

Institute of Technology, lemelson.mit.edu/resources/chapter

                                        date of access
for undated site

-2-what-can-be-patented. Accessed 4 Apr. 2016.

b. Television program

| | title of
TV show | |
| episode title | | producer |

"Fast Times at West Philly High." *Frontline*, produced by Debbie Morton,

network date

PBS, 2012.

c. Book, entire Web site, or other long work

title (Web site)

Women of Protest: Photographs from the Records of the National Woman's Party.

publisher/sponsor   URL

Library of Congress, www.loc.gov/collections/women-of-protest/.

date of access
for undated site

Accessed 1 May 2015.

6. Two or more works by the same author First alphabetize the works by title (ignoring the article *A*, *An*, or *The* at the beginning of a title). Use the author's name for the first entry; for subsequent entries, use three hyphens and a period. The three hyphens must stand for exactly the same name as in the first entry.

García, Cristina. *Dreams of Significant Girls*. Simon and Schuster, 2011.

---. *The Lady Matador's Hotel*. Scribner, 2010.

7. Two or more works by the same group of authors Alphabetize the works by title. Use the authors' names in the proper form for the first entry (see items 1–4). Begin subsequent entries with three hyphens and a period. The three hyphens must stand for the same names as in the first entry.

Agha, Hussein, and Robert Malley. "The Arab Counterrevolution." *The New York Review of Books*, 29 Sept. 2011, www.nybooks.com/articles/ 2011/09/29/arab-counterrevolution/.

---. "This Is Not a Revolution." *The New York Review of Books*, 8 Nov. 2012, www.nybooks.com/articles/2012/11/08/not-revolution/.

8. Editor or translator Begin with the editor's or translator's name. After the name(s), add "editor" (or "editors") or "translator" (or "translators").

first editor: second editor:
last name first in normal order   title (book)
Horner, Avril, and Anne Rowe, editors. *Living on Paper: Letters from Iris*

        publisher   year
    Murdoch. Princeton UP, 2016.

9. Author with editor or translator Begin with the name of the author. Place the editor's or translator's name after the title.

author: translator: in
last name first   title (book)   normal order
Ullmann, Regina. *The Country Road: Stories*. Translated by Kurt Beals,

        publisher   year
    New Directions Publishing, 2015.

10. Graphic narrative or other illustrated work If a work has both an author and an illustrator, the order in your citation will depend on which of those persons you emphasize in your paper.

a. Author first If you emphasize the author's work, begin with the author's name. After the title, add "Illustrated by," followed by the illustrator's name.

Gaiman, Neil. *The Sandman: Overture*. Illustrated by J. H. William, III, DC Comics, 2015.

Answer the basic question "Who is the author?"

Problem: Sometimes when you need to cite a source, it's not clear who the author is. This is especially true for sources on the Web or other nonprint sources, which may have been created by one person and uploaded by a different person or an organization. Whom do you cite as the author in such a case? How do you determine who *is* the author?

Example: The video "Surfing the Web on the Job" (see below) was uploaded to YouTube by CBSNewsOnline. Is the person or organization who uploads the video the author of the video? Not necessarily.

Surfing the Web on The Job

 CBSNewsOnline · 42,491 videos

▶ Subscribe 〈 85,736

Uploaded on Nov 12, 2009
As the Internet continues to emerge as a critical facet of everyday life, CBS News' Daniel Sieberg reports that companies are cracking down on employees' personal Web use.

Strategy: After you view or listen to the source a few times, ask yourself whether you can tell who is chiefly responsible for creating the content in the source. It could be an organization. It could be an identifiable individual. This video consists entirely of reporting by Daniel Sieberg, so in this case the author is Sieberg.

Citation: To cite the source, you would use the basic MLA guidelines for a video found on the Web (item 55).

| author: last name first | title of video | Web site title | update date |

Sieberg, Daniel. "Surfing the Web on the Job." *YouTube,* 12 Nov. 2009,

URL

www.youtube.com/watch?v=1wLhNwY-enY.

If you want to include the person or organization who uploaded the video, you can add it as supplementary information.

author:
last name first   title of video   Web site title   supplementary information

Sieberg, Daniel. "Surfing the Web on the Job." *YouTube*, uploaded by CBSNewsOnline,

update date   URL

12 Nov. 2009, www.youtube.com/watch?v=1wLhNwY-enY.

10. Graphic narrative or other illustrated work (*cont.*)

b. Illustrator first If you emphasize the illustrator, begin your citation with the illustrator's name and the label "illustrator." After the title of the work, put the author's name, preceded by "By."

Kerascoët, illustrator. *Beautiful Darkness*. By Fabien Vehlmann, Drawn and Quarterly, 2014.

c. Author and illustrator the same person If the illustrator and the author are the same person, cite the work as you would any other work with one author (not using any labels).

Ulinich, Anya. *Lena Finkle's Magic Barrel: A Graphic Novel*. Penguin Books, 2014.

11. Author using a pseudonym (pen name) or screen name
Give the author's name as it appears in the source (the pseudonym), followed by the author's real name, if available, in parentheses. (For screen names in social media, see items 78 and 79.)

Grammar Girl (Mignon Fogarty). "Lewis Carroll: He Loved to Play with Language." *QuickandDirtyTips.com*, 21 May 2015, www.quickanddirtytips.com/education/grammar/lewis-carroll-he-loved-to-play-with-language.

Pauline. Comment on "Is This the End?" by James Atlas. *The New York Times*, 25 Nov. 2012, nyti.ms/1BRUvqQ.

12. Author quoted by another author (indirect source) If one of your sources uses a quotation from another source and you'd like to use the quotation, provide a works cited entry for the source in which you found the quotation. In your in-text citation, indicate that the quoted words appear in the source (see item 23 on p. 608). In the following examples, Belmaker is the source in the works cited list; Townson is quoted in Belmaker.

SOURCE (BELMAKER) QUOTING ANOTHER SOURCE (TOWNSON)

Peter Townson, a journalist working with the DOHA Center for Press Freedom in Qatar, says there is one obvious reason that some countries in the Middle East have embraced social media so heartily. "It's kind of the preferred way for people to get news, because they know there's no self-censorship involved," Townson said in a phone interview.

WORKS CITED ENTRY

Belmaker, Genevieve. "Five Ways Journalists Can Use Social
    Media for On-the-Ground Reporting in the Middle East."
    Poynter, 19 Nov. 2012, www.poynter.org/2012/5-ways
    -journalists-can-use-social-media-for-on-the-ground
    -reporting-in-the-middle-east/195899/.

IN-TEXT CITATION

Peter Townson points out that social media in the Middle East are "kind of the preferred way for people to get news, because they know there's no self-censorship involved" (qtd. in Belmaker).

Articles and other short works

▶ Citation at a glance: Article in a journal, page 624

▶ Citation at a glance: Article from a database, page 626

13. Basic format for an article or other short work

a. Print

author:
last name first · · · · · · · · article title · · · · · · · · journal title · · · volume, issue

Tilman, David. "Food and Health of a Full Earth." *Daedalus*, vol. 144, no. 4,

date · · · page(s)

Fall 2015, pp. 5-7.

b. Web

author:
last name first · · · · · · · · · · · title of short work

Nelson, Libby. "How Schools Will Be Different without No Child Left

title of
Web site · · · date · · · · · · · · · · · URL

Behind." *Vox*, 11 Dec. 2015, www.vox.com/2015/12/11/9889350/

every-student-succeeds-act-schools.

c. Database

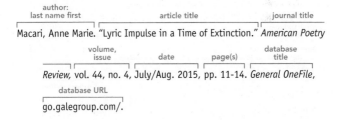

author:
last name first · · · · · · · · article title · · · · · · · · journal title

Macari, Anne Marie. "Lyric Impulse in a Time of Extinction." *American Poetry*

volume,
issue · · · date · · · page(s) · · · database title

Review, vol. 44, no. 4, July/Aug. 2015, pp. 11-14. *General OneFile,*

database URL

go.galegroup.com/.

14. Article in a journal

a. Print

author: last
name first · · · · · · · · article title · · · · · · · · journal title

Matchie, Thomas. "Law versus Love in *The Round House*." *Midwest*

volume,
issue · · · date · · · page(s)

Quarterly, vol. 56, no. 4, Summer 2015, pp. 353-64.

Citation at a glance
Article in a journal MLA

To cite an article in a print journal in MLA style, include the
following elements:

1 Author(s) of article
2 Title and subtitle of article
3 Title of journal
4 Volume and issue numbers
5 Date of publication (including month or season, if any)
6 Page number(s) of article

JOURNAL TABLE OF CONTENTS

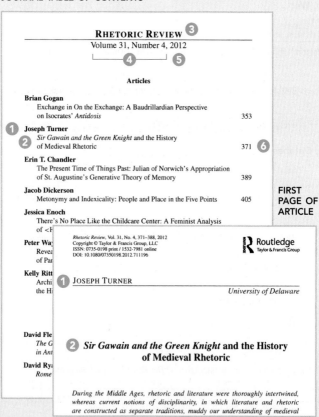

RHETORIC REVIEW 3

Volume 31, Number 4, 2012

4 — 5

Articles

Brian Gogan
 Exchange in On the Exchange: A Baudrillardian Perspective
 on Isocrates' *Antidosis* — 353

Joseph Turner
 Sir Gawain and the Green Knight and the History
 of Medieval Rhetoric — 371

Erin T. Chandler
 The Present Time of Things Past: Julian of Norwich's Appropriation
 of St. Augustine's Generative Theory of Memory — 389

Jacob Dickerson
 Metonymy and Indexicality: People and Place in the Five Points — 405

Jessica Enoch
 There's No Place Like the Childcare Center: A Feminist Analysis
 of <F

Peter Way
 Revea
 of Par

Kelly Ritt
 Archi
 the Hi

David Fle
 The G
 in Ant

David Rya
 Rome

FIRST
PAGE OF
ARTICLE

Rhetoric Review, Vol. 31, No. 4, 371–388, 2012
Copyright © Taylor & Francis Group, LLC
ISSN: 0735-0198 print / 1532-7981 online
DOI: 10.1080/07350198.2012.711196

R Routledge
Taylor & Francis Group

JOSEPH TURNER

University of Delaware

Sir Gawain and the Green Knight and the History of Medieval Rhetoric

*During the Middle Ages, rhetoric and literature were thoroughly intertwined,
whereas current notions of disciplinarity, in which literature and rhetoric
are constructed as separate traditions, muddy our understanding of medieval*

WORKS CITED ENTRY FOR AN ARTICLE IN A PRINT JOURNAL

     1   2

Turner, Joseph. *"Sir Gawain and the Green Knight* and the History of Medieval

                   3   4   5   6

    Rhetoric.*"* *Rhetoric Review*, vol. 31, no. 4, 2012, pp. 371-88.

For more on citing articles in MLA style, see items 13–16.

14. Article in a journal (*cont.*)

b. Online journal

    author:
    last name first   article title

Cáceres, Sigfrido Burgos. "Towards Concert in Africa: Seeking Progress and Power

                                 journal title   volume,
                                                     issue

    through Cohesion and Unity." *African Studies Quarterly*, vol. 12, no. 4,

    date   page(s)   URL

    Fall 2011, pp. 59-73, asq.africa.ufl.edu/files/Caceres-Vol12Is4.pdf.

c. Database

    author:
    last name first   article title

Maier, Jessica. "A 'True Likeness': The Renaissance City Portrait."

                              volume,
          journal title   issue   date   page(s)   database
                                                     title

    Renaissance Quarterly, vol. 65, no. 3, Fall 2012, pp. 711-52. *JSTOR*,

             DOI

    doi:10.1086/668300.

15. Article in a magazine

a. Print (*monthly*)

    author:
    last name first   article title   magazine title   date   page(s)

Bryan, Christy. "Ivory Worship." *National Geographic*, Oct. 2012, pp. 28-61.

Citation at a glance
Article from a database MLA

To cite an article from a database in MLA style, include the following elements:

1 Author(s) of article
2 Title and subtitle of article
3 Title of journal, magazine, or newspaper
4 Volume and issue numbers (for journal)
5 Date of publication (including month or season, if any)
6 Page number(s) of article
7 Name of database
8 DOI or permalink, if available; otherwise, shortened URL of database

DATABASE RECORD

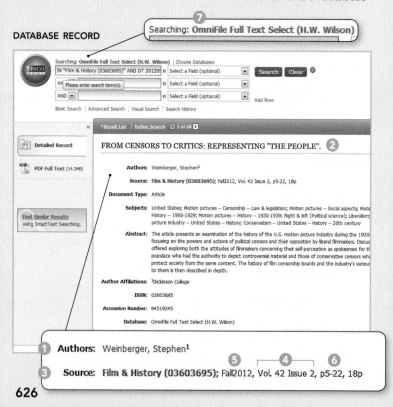

Searching: OmniFile Full Text Select (H.W. Wilson)

Searching: OmniFile Full Text Select (H.W. Wilson) | Choose Databases
JN "Film & History (03603695)" AND DT 20120 in Select a Field (optional) ▾ Search Clear
AN Please enter search term(s). in Select a Field (optional) ▾
AND ▾ in Select a Field (optional) ▾ Add Row
Basic Search | Advanced Search | Visual Search | Search History

◄ Result List | Refine Search ◄ 1 of 28 ►

Detailed Record

PDF Full Text (14.3MB)

FROM CENSORS TO CRITICS: REPRESENTING "THE PEOPLE".

Authors: Weinberger, Stephen[1]

Source: Film & History (03603695); Fall2012, Vol. 42 Issue 2, p5-22, 18p

Document Type: Article

Subjects: United States; Motion pictures -- Censorship -- Law & legislation; Motion pictures -- Social aspects; Motion History -- 1900-1929; Motion pictures -- History -- 1930-1939; Right & left (Political science); Liberalism; picture industry -- United States -- History; Conservatism -- United States -- History -- 20th century

Find Similar Results using SmartText Searching.

Abstract: The article presents an examination of the history of the U.S. motion picture industry during the 1920s focusing on the powers and actions of political censors and their opposition to liberal filmmakers. Discussion offered exploring both the attitudes of filmmakers concerning their self-perception as spokesmen for the populace who had the authority to depict controversial material and those of conservative censors who protect society from the same content. The history of film censorship boards and the industry's various to them is then described in depth.

Author Affiliations: [1]Dickinson College

ISSN: 03603695

Accession Number: 84519245

Database: OmniFile Full Text Select (H.W. Wilson)

Authors: Weinberger, Stephen[1]

Source: **Film & History (03603695);** Fall2012, Vol. 42 Issue 2, p5-22, 18p

WORKS CITED ENTRY FOR AN ARTICLE FROM A DATABASE

1   2

Weinberger, Stephen. "From Censors to Critics: Representing 'the People.'"

3   4   5   6   7

Film & History, vol. 42, no. 2, Fall 2012, pp. 5-22. *OmniFile Full Text*

                    8

Select, web.b.ebscohost.com.ezproxy.bpl.org.

For more on citing articles from a database in MLA style, see items 13–16.

15. Article in a magazine (*cont.*)

b. Print (weekly)

author:
last name first   article title   magazine title   date   page(s)

Vick, Karl. "The Stateless Statesman." *Time,* 15 Oct. 2012, pp. 32-37.

c. Web

author:
last name first   article title   Web site title   date

Leonard, Andrew. "The Surveillance State High School." *Salon,* 27 Nov. 2012,

URL

www.salon.com/2012/11/27/the_surveillance_state_high_school/.

d. Database

author:
last name first   article title   magazine title   date

Rosenbaum, Ron. "The Last Renaissance Man." *Smithsonian,* Nov. 2012,

page(s)   database title   database URL

pp. 39-44. *OmniFile Full Text Select,* web.b.ebscohost.com.ezproxy.bpl.org/.

16. Article in a newspaper If the city of publication is not obvious from the title of the newspaper, include the city in brackets after the newspaper title (see item 5a).

16. Article in a newspaper (*cont.*)

a. Print

author:
last name first · · · · · · · · · · · · · · · article title

Sherry, Allison. "Volunteers' Personal Touch Turns High-Tech Data into Votes."
newspaper title · · · date · · · page(s)
The Denver Post, 30 Oct. 2012, pp. 1A+.

b. Web

author: last
name first · · · · · · · · · · · · · article title

Crowell, Maddy. "How Computers Are Getting Better at Detecting Liars."
Web site
title · · · date · · · URL
The Christian Science Monitor, 12 Dec. 2015, www.csmonitor.com/Science/

Science-Notebook/2015/1212/How-computers-are-getting-better-at

-detecting-liars.

c. Database

article title · · · newspaper title · · · date · · · page(s) · · · label

"The Road toward Peace." *The New York Times,* 15 Feb. 1945, p. 18. Editorial.
database title · · · database URL
ProQuest Historical Newspapers: The New York Times, search.proquest

.com/hnpnewyorktimes.

17. Abstract or executive summary Include the label "Abstract" or "Executive summary," neither italicized nor in quotation marks, at the end of the entry (and before any database information).

a. Abstract of an article

Bottomore, Stephen. "The Romance of the Cinematograph." *Film History*,
vol. 24, no. 3, July 2012, pp. 341-44. Abstract. *JSTOR*, doi:10.2979/
filmhistory.24.3.341.

b. Abstract of a paper

Dixon, Rosemary, et al. "The Opportunities and Challenges of Virtual
Library Systems: A Case Study." Paper presented at the 2011 Chicago
Colloquium on Digital Humanities and Computer Science, U of Chicago,
20 Nov. 2011. Abstract.

c. Abstract of a dissertation

Moore, Courtney L. "Stress and Oppression: Identifying Possible Protective
Factors for African American Men." Dissertation, Chicago School of
Professional Psychology, 2016. Abstract. *ProQuest Dissertations and
Theses*, search.proquest.com/docview/1707351557.

d. Executive summary

Pintak, Lawrence. *The Murrow Rural Information Initiative: Final Report.*
Murrow College of Communication, Washington State U, 25 May 2012.
Executive summary.

18. Article with a title in its title Use single quotation marks
around a title of a short work or a quoted term that appears in an
article title. Italicize a title or term normally italicized.

Silber, Nina. "From 'Great Emancipator' to 'Vampire Hunter': The Many
Stovepipe Hats of Cinematic Lincoln." *Cognoscenti*, WBUR, 22 Nov.
2012, cognoscenti.wbur.org/2012/11/22/abraham-lincoln-nina-silber.

19. Editorial   Cite as a source with no author (see item 5) and use the label "Editorial" at the end (and before any database information).

"City's Blight Fight Making Difference." *The Columbus Dispatch*, 17 Nov. 2015,
www.dispatch.com/content/stories/editorials/2015/11/17/
1-citys-blight-fight-making-difference.html. Editorial.

20. Unsigned article   Cite as a source with no author (see item 5).

"Drought and Health." *Centers for Disease Control and Prevention*, 30 July
2012, www.cdc.gov/nceh/drought/default.htm.

21. Letter to the editor   Use the label "Letter" at the end of the entry (and before any database information). If the letter has no title, place the label after the author's name.

Fahey, John A. "Recalling the Cuban Missile Crisis." *The Washington Post*,
28 Oct. 2012, p. A16. Letter. *LexisNexis Library Express*, www.lexisnexis
.com/hottopics/Inpubliclibraryexpress/.

22. Comment on an online article   If the writer of the comment uses a screen name, see item 11. After the name, include "Comment on" followed by the title of the article and the author of the article (preceded by "by"). Continue with publication information for the article.

author:
screen name   article title

pablosharkman. Comment on "'We Are All Implicated': Wendell Berry Laments

                                                            author of
                                                            article

a Disconnection from Community and the Land," by Scott Carlson.
      Web site title   date   URL

The Chronicle of Higher Education, 23 Apr. 2012, chronicle.com/article/

In-Jefferson-Lecture-Wendell/131648.

23. Paper or presentation at a conference   If the paper or presentation is included in the proceedings of a conference, cite it as a selection in an anthology or a collection (see item 35; see also item 44 for proceedings of a conference). If you viewed the presentation live, cite it as a lecture or public address (see item 61).

first author: "et al." for
last name first others   presentation title

Zuckerman, Ethan, et al. "Big Data, Big Challenges, and Big Opportunities."

conference title

Presentation at Wired for Change: The Power and the Pitfalls of Big Data,

conference information   date   URL

Ford Foundation, New York, 15 Oct. 2012, www.fordfoundation.org/library/

multimedia/wired-for-change-big-data-big-challenges-and-big

-opportunities/.

24. Book review   Name the reviewer and the title of the review, if any, followed by "Review of" and the title and author of the work reviewed. Add the publication information for the publication in which the review appears. If the review has no author and no title, begin with "Review of" and alphabetize the entry by the first principal word in the title of the work reviewed.

a. Print

Flannery, Tim. "A Heroine in Defense of Nature." Review of *On a Farther Shore: The Life and Legacy of Rachel Carson*, by William Souder. *The New York Review of Books*, 22 Nov. 2012, pp. 21-23.

b. Web

Della Subin, Anna. "It Has Burned My Heart." Review of *The Lives of Muhammad*, by Kecia Ali. *London Review of Books*, 22 Oct. 2015, www.lrb.co.uk/v37/n20/anna-della-subin/it-has-burned-my-heart.

24. Book review (*cont.*)

c. Database

Spychalski, John C. Review of *American Railroads—Decline and Renaissance in the Twentieth Century*, by Robert E. Gallamore and John R. Meyer. *Transportation Journal*, vol. 54, no. 4, Fall 2015, pp. 535-38. *JSTOR*, doi:10.5325/transportationj.54.4.0535.

25. Film review or other review   Name the reviewer and the title of the review, if any, followed by "Review of" and the title and writer or director of the work reviewed. Add the publication information for the publication in which the review appears. If the review has no author and no title, begin with "Review of" and alphabetize the entry by the first principal word in the title of the work reviewed.

a. Print

Lane, Anthony. "Human Bondage." Review of *Spectre*, directed by Sam Mendes. *The New Yorker*, 16 Nov. 2015, pp. 96-97.

b. Web

Savage, Phil. "*Fallout 4* Review." Review of *Fallout 4*, by Bethesda Game Studios. *PC Gamer*, Future Publishing, 8 Nov. 2015, www.pcgamer .com/fallout-4-review/.

26. Performance review   Name the reviewer and the title of the review, if any, followed by "Review of" and the title and author of the work reviewed. Add publication information. If the review has no author and no title, begin with "Review of" and alphabetize the entry by the first principal word in the title of the work reviewed.

Stout, Gene. "The Ebullient Florence + the Machine Give KeyArena a Workout." Review of *How Big How Blue How Beautiful Odyssey*. *The Seattle Times*, 28 Oct. 2015, www.seattletimes.com/ entertainment/music/the-ebullient-florence-the-machine-give -keyarena-a-workout/.

27. Interview   Begin with the person interviewed, followed by the title of the interview (if there is one). If the interview does not have a title, include the word "Interview" after the interviewee's name. If you wish to include the name of the interviewer, put it after the title of the interview.

a. Print

Weddington, Sarah. "Sarah Weddington: Still Arguing for *Roe*." Interview by
    Michele Kort. *Ms.*, Winter 2013, pp. 32-35.

b. Web

Jaffrey, Madhur. "Madhur Jaffrey on How Indian Cuisine Won Western Taste
    Buds." Interview by Shadrach Kabango. *Q*, CBC Radio, 29 Oct. 2015,
    www.cbc.ca/1.3292918.

c. Television or radio

Putin, Vladimir. Interview by Charlie Rose. *Charlie Rose: The Week*, PBS,
    19 June 2015.

d. Personal   To cite an interview that you conducted, begin with the name of the person interviewed. Then write "Personal interview" or "Telephone interview," followed by the date of the interview.

Akufo, Dautey. Personal interview, 11 Apr. 2016.

Psoinos, Katherine. Telephone interview, 6 June 2016.

28. Article in a dictionary or an encyclopedia (including a wiki)   List the author of the entry (if there is one), the title of the entry, the title of the reference work, the edition number (if any), the publisher, and the date of the edition. Page numbers are not necessary because the entries in the source are arranged alphabetically and are therefore easy to locate.

28. Article in a dictionary or an encyclopedia (including a wiki) (*cont.*)

a. Print

Robinson, Lisa Clayton. "Harlem Writers Guild." *Africana: The Encyclopedia of the African and African American Experience*, 2nd ed., Oxford UP, 2005.

"Ball's in Your Court, The." *The American Heritage Dictionary of Idioms*, 2nd ed., Houghton Mifflin Harcourt, 2013.

b. Web

Durante, Amy M. "Finn Mac Cumhail." *Encyclopedia Mythica*, 17 Apr. 2011, www.pantheon.org/articles/f/finn_mac_cumhail.html.

"House Music." *Wikipedia*, 16 Nov. 2015, en.wikipedia.org/wiki/House_music.

29. Letter

a. Print Begin with the writer of the letter, the words "Letter to" and the recipient, and the date of the letter. Add the title of the collection, the editor, and publication information. Add the page range at the end.

Wharton, Edith. Letter to Henry James, 28 Feb. 1915. *Henry James and Edith Wharton: Letters, 1900-1915*, edited by Lyall H. Powers, Scribner, 1990, pp. 323-26.

b. Web After information about the letter writer, recipient, and date (if known), give the name of the Web site or archive, italicized; the publisher or sponsor of the site; and the URL.

Oblinger, Maggie. Letter to Charlie Thomas, 31 Mar. 1895. *Prairie Settlement: Nebraska Photographs and Family Letters, 1862-1912*, Library of Congress / American Memory, memory.loc.gov/cgi-bin/query/r?ammem/ ps:@field(DOCID+l306)#l3060001.

c. Personal To cite a letter that you received, begin with the writer's name and add the phrase "Letter to the author," followed by the date.

Primak, Shoshana. Letter to the author, 6 May 2016.

Books and other long works

▸ Citation at a glance: Book, page 636

30. Basic format for a book

a. Print book or e-book If you have used an e-book, give the e-reader type at the end of the entry.

author: last
name first | book title | publisher | year

Wolfe, Tom. *Back to Blood*. Little, Brown, 2012.

Beard, Mary. *SPQR: A History of Ancient Rome*. Liveright Publishing, 2015.

Tolstoy, Leo. *War and Peace*. 1869. Translated by Richard Pevear and
    Larissa Volokhonsky, Alfred A. Knopf, 2007. Nook.

b. Web Give whatever print publication information is available for the work, followed by the title of the Web site and the URL.

author: last
name first | book title

Piketty, Thomas. *Capital in the Twenty-First Century*. Translated by Arthur

translator: in
normal order | publisher | year | Web site title | URL

    Goldhammer, Harvard UP, 2014. *Google Books*, books.google.com/

    books?isbn=0674369556.

Saalman, Lora, editor and translator. *The China-India Nuclear Crossroads*.
    Carnegie Endowment for International Peace, 2012. *Scribd*, www.scribd
    .com/book/142083413/The-China-India-Nuclear-Crossroads.

Citation at a glance

Book MLA

To cite a print book in MLA style, include the following elements:

1 Author(s)
2 Title and subtitle
3 Publisher
4 Year of publication (latest year)

TITLE PAGE

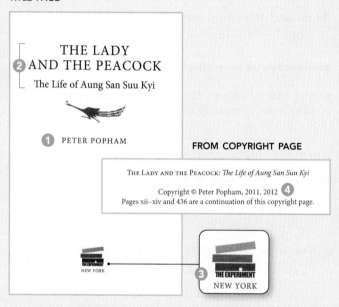

THE LADY
2 AND THE PEACOCK
The Life of Aung San Suu Kyi

1 PETER POPHAM

FROM COPYRIGHT PAGE

THE LADY AND THE PEACOCK: *The Life of Aung San Suu Kyi*

Copyright © Peter Popham, 2011, 2012 4
Pages xii–xiv and 436 are a continuation of this copyright page.

THE EXPERIMENT
NEW YORK

3 THE EXPERIMENT
NEW YORK

WORKS CITED ENTRY FOR A PRINT BOOK

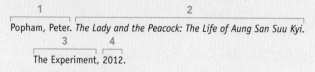

    1   2
Popham, Peter. *The Lady and the Peacock: The Life of Aung San Suu Kyi.*
       3   4
   The Experiment, 2012.

For more on citing books in MLA style, see items 30-41.

30. Basic format for a book (*cont.*)

c. Database

author: last
name first   book title   city and date
of original

Goldsmith, Oliver. *The Vicar of Wakefield: A Tale.* Philadelphia, 1801.

database title   URL

    America's Historical Imprints, infoweb.newsbank.com.ezproxy.bpl.org/.

31. Parts of a book

a. Foreword, introduction, preface, or afterword

author of foreword:
last name first   book part   book title

Bennett, Hal Zina. Foreword. *Shimmering Images: A Handy Little Guide to*

                  author of book:
                  in normal order   publisher   year   page(s)

    Writing Memoir, by Lisa Dale Norton, St. Martin's Griffin, 2008, pp. xiii-xvi.

Sullivan, John Jeremiah. "The Ill-Defined Plot." Introduction. *The Best*
     American Essays 2014, edited by Sullivan, Houghton Mifflin Harcourt,
     2014, pp. xvii-xxvi.

b. Chapter in a book

Rizga, Kristina. "Mr. Hsu." *Mission High: One School, How Experts Tried to Fail*
     It, and the Students and Teachers Who Made It Triumph, Nation Books,
     2015, pp. 89-114.

32. Book with a title in its title
If the book title contains a title normally italicized, neither italicize the internal title nor place it in quotation marks. If the title within the title is normally put in quotation marks, retain the quotation marks and italicize the entire book title.

Shanahan, Timothy. *Philosophy and* Blade Runner. Palgrave Macmillan, 2014.

Lethem, Jonathan. *"Lucky Alan" and Other Stories*. Doubleday, 2015.

33. Book in a language other than English   Capitalize the title according to the conventions of the book's language. If your readers are not familiar with the language, include a translation of the title in brackets.

Vargas Llosa, Mario. *El sueño del celta* [*The Dream of the Celt*]. Alfaguara,

    2010.

34. Entire anthology or collection   An anthology is a collection of works, often with various authors and an editor for the entire volume.

   editor: title of
last name first   anthology   publisher   year

Marcus, Ben, editor. *New American Stories*. Vintage Books, 2015.

35. One selection from an anthology or a collection

   ▶ Citation at a glance: Selection from an anthology or a
     collection, page 640

  author of   title of   editor(s)
  selection   selection   title of anthology   of anthology

Sayrafiezadeh, Saïd. "Paranoia." *New American Stories*, edited by Ben Marcus,

  publisher   year   page(s)

   Vintage Books, 2015, pp. 3-29.

36. Two or more selections from an anthology or a collection
Provide an entry for the entire anthology (see item 34) and a shortened entry for each selection. Alphabetize the entries by authors' or editors' last names.

  author of   title of   editor(s)
  selection   selection   of anthology page(s)

Eisenberg, Deborah. "Some Other, Better Otto." Marcus, pp. 94-136.

   editor: title of
last name first   anthology   publisher   year

Marcus, Ben, editor. *New American Stories*. Vintage Books, 2015.

                    title of   editor(s) of
 author of selection   selection   anthology page(s)

Sayrafiezadeh, Saïd. "Paranoia." Marcus, pp. 3-29.

37. Edition other than the first Include the number of the edition (2nd, 3rd, and so on). If the book has a translator or an editor in addition to the author, give the name of the translator or editor before the edition number (see item 9 for a book with an editor or translator).

Eagleton, Terry. *Literary Theory: An Introduction*. 3rd ed., U of
Minnesota P, 2008.

38. Multivolume work Include the total number of volumes at the end of the entry, using the abbreviation "vols." If the volumes were published over several years, give the inclusive dates of publication.

author: last   book   editor(s):   inclusive
name first   title   in normal order   publisher   dates

Stark, Freya. *Letters*. Edited by Lucy Moorehead, Compton Press, 1974-82.

total
volumes

8 vols.

If you cite only one volume in your paper, include the volume number before the publisher and give the date of publication for that volume. After the date, give the total number of volumes.

author: last   book   editor(s):   volume
name first   title   in normal order   cited   publisher

Stark, Freya. *Letters*. Edited by Lucy Moorehead, vol. 5, Compton Press,

date of   total
volume   volumes

1978. 8 vols.

39. Sacred text Give the title of the edition (taken from the title page), italicized; the editor's or translator's name (if any); and publication information. Add the name of the version, if there is one, before the publisher.

The Oxford Annotated Bible with the Apocrypha. Edited by Herbert G. May and
Bruce M. Metzger, Revised Standard Version, Oxford UP, 1965.

The Qur'an: Translation. Translated by Abdullah Yusuf Ali, Tahrike Tarsile Qur'an,
2001.

Citation at a glance

Selection from an anthology or a collection MLA

To cite a selection from an anthology in MLA style, include the following elements:

1   Author(s) of selection
2   Title and subtitle of selection
3   Title and subtitle of anthology
4   Editor(s) of anthology
5   Publisher
6   Year of publication
7   Page numbers of selection

TITLE PAGE OF ANTHOLOGY

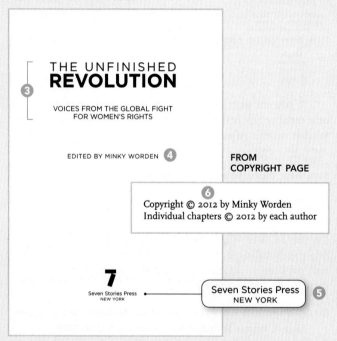

THE UNFINISHED
REVOLUTION

VOICES FROM THE GLOBAL FIGHT
FOR WOMEN'S RIGHTS

EDITED BY MINKY WORDEN **4**

**FROM
COPYRIGHT PAGE**

6
Copyright © 2012 by Minky Worden
Individual chapters © 2012 by each author

7
Seven Stories Press
NEW YORK

Seven Stories Press
NEW YORK **5**

FIRST PAGE OF SELECTION

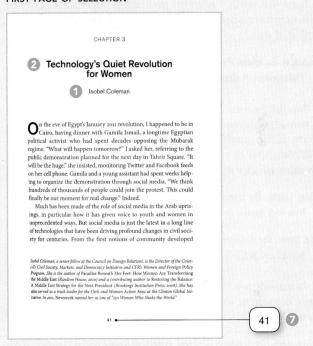

CHAPTER 3

  Technology's Quiet Revolution
for Women

Isobel Coleman

On the eve of Egypt's January 2011 revolution, I happened to be in Cairo, having dinner with Gamila Ismail, a longtime Egyptian political activist who had spent decades opposing the Mubarak regime. "What will happen tomorrow?" I asked her, referring to the public demonstration planned for the next day in Tahrir Square. "It will be the huge," she insisted, monitoring Twitter and Facebook feeds on her cell phone. Gamila and a young assistant had spent weeks helping to organize the demonstration through social media. "We think hundreds of thousands of people could join the protest. This could finally be our moment for real change." Indeed.

Much has been made of the role of social media in the Arab uprisings, in particular how it has given voice to youth and women in unprecedented ways. But social media is just the latest in a long line of technologies that have been driving profound changes in civil society for centuries. From the first notions of community developed

Isobel Coleman, a senior fellow at the Council on Foreign Relations, is the Director of the Council's Civil Society, Markets, and Democracy Initiative and CFR's Women and Foreign Policy Program. She is the author of Paradise Beneath Her Feet: How Women Are Transforming the Middle East (Random House, 2010) and a contributing author to Restoring the Balance: A Middle East Strategy for the Next President (Brookings Institution Press, 2008). She has also served as a track leader for the Girls and Women Action Area at the Clinton Global Initiative. In 2011, Newsweek named her as one of "150 Women Who Shake the World."

41 ●━━━━━━━━━━━━━━ **41** **7**

WORKS CITED ENTRY FOR A SELECTION FROM AN ANTHOLOGY

   1   2   3

Coleman, Isobel. "Technology's Quiet Revolution for Women." *The Unfinished*

                4   5   6   7
Minky Worden, Seven Stories Press, 2012, pp. 41-49.

For more on citing selections from anthologies in MLA style, see items 34–36.

40. Book in a series After the publication information, give the series name as it appears on the title page, followed by the series number, if any.

Denham, A. E., editor. *Plato on Art and Beauty*. Palgrave Macmillan, 2012.
Philosophers in Depth.

41. Republished book After the title of the book, give the original year of publication, followed by the current publication information. If the republished book contains new material, such as an introduction or an afterword, include information about the new material after the original date.

Trilling, Lionel. *The Liberal Imagination*. 1950. Introduction by Louis Menand,
New York Review Books, 2008.

Wilde, Oscar. *The Picture of Dorian Gray*. 1891. Barnes and Noble, 2012.
Barnes and Noble Signature Editions.

42. Pamphlet, brochure, or newsletter Cite a pamphlet, brochure, newsletter, or other small, self-contained publication as you would a book.

The Legendary Sleepy Hollow Cemetery. Friends of Sleepy Hollow Cemetery, 2008.

43. Dissertation

a. Published For dissertations that have been published in book form, italicize the title. After the title, give the label "Dissertation," the name of the institution, and the year the dissertation was accepted.

Kidd, Celeste. *Rational Approaches to Learning and Development*. Dissertation,
U of Rochester, 2013.

b. Unpublished Begin with the author's name, followed by the dissertation title in quotation marks. After the title, add the label

"Dissertation," the name of the institution, and the year the dissertation was accepted.

Abbas, Megan Brankley. "Knowing Islam: The Entangled History of Western
    Academia and Modern Islamic Thought." Dissertation, Princeton U, 2015.

44. Proceedings of a conference   Cite as you would a book, adding the name, date, and location of the conference after the title.

Sowards, Stacey K., et al., editors. *Across Borders and Environments:*
    Communication and Environmental Justice in International Contexts.
    Proceedings of Eleventh Biennial Conference on Communication
    and the Environment, 25-28 June 2011, U of Texas at El Paso.
    International Environmental Communication Association, 2012.

45. Manuscript   Give the author, a title or a description of the manuscript, and the date of composition (if known), followed by the location of the manuscript, including a URL if it is found on the Web.

Arendt, Hannah. *Between Past and Future.* 1st draft, Hannah Arendt Papers,
    Manuscript Division, Library of Congress, pp. 108-50, memory.loc.gov/
    cgi-bin/ampage?collId=mharendt&fileName=05/050030/050030page
    .db&recNum=0.

Web sites and parts of Web sites

46. An entire Web site

a. Web site with author or editor

author or editor: title of
last name first   Web site   publisher/sponsor

Railton, Stephen. *Mark Twain in His Times.* Stephen Railton / U of Virginia

            update
            date   URL

    Library, 2012, twain.lib.virginia.edu/.

46. An entire Web site (*cont.*)

Halsall, Paul, editor. *Internet Modern History Sourcebook*. Fordham U,
    4 Nov. 2011, legacy.fordham.edu/halsall/index.asp.

b. Web site with organization as author

organization   title of Web site

Transparency International. *Transparency International: The Global Coalition*

       date   URL

    against Corruption, 2015, www.transparency.org/.

c. Web site with no author   Begin with the title of the site. If the
site has no title, begin with a label such as "Home page."

The Newton Project. U of Sussex, 2016, www.newtonproject.sussex.ac.uk/
    prism.php?id=1.

d. Web site with no title   Use the label "Home page" or another
appropriate description in place of a title.

Bae, Rebecca. Home page. Iowa State U, 2015, www.engl.iastate.edu/
    rebecca-bae-directory-page/.

47. Short work from a Web site
▸ Citation at a glance: Short work from a Web site, page 646

a. Short work with author

author: last name first   title of short work   title of Web site

Gallagher, Sean. "The Last Nomads of the Tibetan Plateau." *Pulitzer Center*

        date   URL

   on Crisis Reporting, 25 Oct. 2012, pulitzercenter.org/reporting/china

   -glaciers-global-warming-climate-change-ecosystem-tibetan-plateau

   -grasslands-nomads.

b. Short work with no author

title of article   title of Web site

"Social and Historical Context: Vitality." *Arapesh Grammar and Digital Language*

publisher/sponsor

Archive Project, Institute for Advanced Technology in the Humanities,

URL

www.arapesh.org/socio_historical_context_vitality.php. Accessed

access date
for undated site

22 Mar. 2016.

48. Long work from a Web site

author: last   title of   title of   update
name first   long work   Web site   date

Milton, John. *Paradise Lost: Book I. Poetry Foundation*, 2014,

URL

www.poetryfoundation.org/poem/174987.

49. Entire blog   Cite a blog as you would an entire Web site (see item 46).

Ng, Amy. *Pikaland*. Pikaland Media, 2015, www.pikaland.com/.

50. Blog post or comment   Cite a blog post or comment as you would a short work from a Web site (see item 47). If the post or comment has no title, use the label "Blog post" or "Blog comment." Follow with the remaining information as for an entire blog (see item 49). (See item 11 for the use of screen names.)

author: last   title of   publisher/
name first   title of blog post   blog   sponsor

Eakin, Emily. "*Cloud Atlas*'s Theory of Everything." *NYR Daily*, NYREV,

date   URL

2 Nov. 2012, www.nybooks.com/daily/2012/11/02/ken-wilber-cloud-atlas/.

Citation at a glance

Short work from a Web site MLA

To cite a short work from a Web site in MLA style, include the following elements:

1. Author(s) of short work (if any)
2. Title and subtitle of short work
3. Title and subtitle of Web site
4. Publisher or sponsor of Web site (unless it is the same as the title of site)
5. Update date
6. URL of page (or of home page of site)
7. Date of access (if no update date on site)

INTERNAL PAGE OF WEB SITE

FOOTER ON PAGE

WORKS CITED ENTRY FOR A SHORT WORK FROM A WEB SITE

```
              2                      3              6
```

"Losing a Country, Finding a Home." *Amherst College,* www.amherst.edu/

```
                                                        7
```

academiclife/departments/russian/acrc/lcfh. Accessed 4 Jan. 2016.

For more on citing sources from Web sites in MLA style, see items 47 and 48.

50. Blog post or comment (*cont.*)

```
    author:
  screen name          label              title of blog post
```

mitchellfreedman. Comment on *"Cloud Atlas*'s Theory of Everything," by

```
    author of      title of   publisher/
    blog post        blog      sponsor      date              URL
```

Emily Eakin. *NYR Daily,* NYREV, 3 Nov. 2012, www.nybooks.com/daily/

2012/11/02/ken-wilber-cloud-atlas/.

51. Academic course or department home page Cite as a short work from a Web site (see item 47). For a course home page, begin with the name of the instructor and the title of the course or title of the page (use "Course home page" if there is no other title). For a department home page, begin with the name of the department and the label "Department home page." End with the URL.

Masiello, Regina. 355:101: Expository Writing. *Rutgers School of Arts and Sciences,* 2016, wp.rutgers.edu/courses/55-355101.

Film Studies. Department home page. *Wayne State University, College of Liberal Arts and Sciences,* 2016, clas.wayne.edu/FilmStudies/.

Audio, visual, and multimedia sources

52. Podcast

<u>author: last name first</u> <u>podcast title</u> <u>Web site title</u> <u>publisher/ sponsor</u>

Tanner, Laura. "Virtual Reality in 9/11 Fiction." *Literature Lab*, Department of

<u>URL</u>

English, Brandeis U, www.brandeis.edu/departments/english/literaturelab/

<u>access date for undated site</u>

tanner.html. Accessed 14 Feb. 2016.

McDougall, Christopher. "How Did Endurance Help Early Humans Survive?"
TED Radio Hour, National Public Radio, 20 Nov. 2015, www.npr.org/
2015/11/20/455904655/how-did-endurance-help-early-humans
-survive.

53. Film

Generally, begin the entry with the title, followed by the director and lead performers, as in the first example. If your paper emphasizes one or more people involved with the film, you may begin with those names, as in the second example.

<u>film title</u>

Birdman or (The Unexpected Virtue of Ignorance). Directed by

<u>director</u>

Alejandro González Iñárritu, performances by Michael Keaton,

<u>major performers</u>

Emma Stone, Zach Galifianakis, Edward Norton, and Naomi Watts,

<u>distributor</u> <u>release date</u>

Fox Searchlight, 2014.

<u>director: last name first</u> <u>film title</u> <u>major performers</u>

Scott, Ridley, director. *The Martian*. Performances by Matt Damon, Jessica

<u>distributor</u> <u>release date</u>

Chastain, Kristen Wiig, and Kate Mara, Twentieth Century Fox, 2015.

54. Supplementary material accompanying a film Begin with the title of the supplementary material, in quotation marks, and the names of any important contributors, as for a film. End with information about the film, as in item 53, and about the location of the supplementary material.

"Sweeney's London." Produced by Eric Young. *Sweeney Todd: The Demon Barber of Fleet Street*, directed by Tim Burton, DreamWorks, 2007, disc 2.

55. Video or audio from the Web Cite video or audio that you accessed on the Web as you would a short work from a Web site (see item 47), giving information about the author before other information about the video or audio.

author: last name first | title of video | Web site title | date | URL

Lewis, Paul. "Citizen Journalism." *YouTube*, 14 May 2011, www.youtube .com/watch?v=9APO9_yNbcg.

author: last name first | title of video | Web site title | narrator | publisher/sponsor | date | URL

Fletcher, Antoine. "The Ancient Art of the Atlatl." *Russell Cave National Monument*, narrated by Brenton Bellomy, National Park Service, 12 Feb. 2014, www.nps.gov/media/video/view.htm?id=C92CODOA -1DD8-B71C-07CBC6E8970CD73F.

author: last name first | title of video | Web site title | date | URL

Burstein, Julie. "Four Lessons in Creativity." *TED*, Feb. 2012, www.ted.com/talks/julie_burstein_4_lessons_in_creativity.

56. Video game List the developer or author of the game (if any); the title, italicized; the version, if there is one; and the distributor and date of publication. If the game can be played on the Web, add information as for a work from a Web site (see item 47).

56. Video game (cont.)

Firaxis Games. *Sid Meier's Civilization Revolution*. Take-Two Interactive, 2008.

Edgeworld. Atom Entertainment, 1 May 2012, www.kabam.com/games/
    edgeworld.

57. Computer software or app Cite as a video game (see item 56), giving whatever information is available about the version, distributor, and date.

Words with Friends. Version 5.84. Zynga, 2013.

58. Television or radio episode or program If you are citing an episode or a segment of a program, begin with the title of the episode or segment, in quotation marks. Then give the title of the program, italicized; relevant information about the program, such as the writer, director, performers, or narrator; the episode number (if any); the network; and the date of broadcast.

For a program you accessed on the Web, after the information about the program give the network, the original broadcast date, and the URL. If you are citing an entire program (not an episode or a segment), begin your entry with the title of the program, italicized.

a. Broadcast

"Federal Role in Support of Autism." *Washington Journal*, narrated by
    Robb Harleston, C-SPAN, 1 Dec. 2012.

The Daily Show with Trevor Noah. Comedy Central, 18 Nov. 2015.

b. Web

title of episode | program title | narrator | episode

"The Cathedral." *Reply All,* narrated by Sruthi Pinnamaneni, episode 50,

publisher/ sponsor | date of posting | URL

Gimlet Media, 7 Jan. 2016, gimletmedia.com/episode/50-the-cathedral/.

"Take a Giant Step." *Prairie Home Companion,* narrated by Garrison Keillor,
American Public Media, 27 Feb. 2016, prairiehome.publicradio.org/
listen/full/?name=phc/2016/02/27/phc_20160227_128.

59. Transcript You might find a transcript related to an interview or a program on a radio or television Web site or in a transcript database. Cite the source as you would an interview (see item 27) or a radio or television program (see item 58). Add the label "Transcript" at the end of the entry.

"How Long Can Florida's Citrus Industry Survive?" *All Things Considered,*
narrated by Greg Allen, National Public Radio, 27 Nov. 2015, www
.npr.org/templates/transcript/transcript.php?storyId=457424528.

"The Economics of Sleep, Part 1." *Freakonomics Radio,* narrated by Stephen J.
Dubner, 9 July 2015, freakonomics.com/2015/07/09/the-economics
-of-sleep-part-1-full-transcript/. Transcript.

60. Performance For a live performance of a concert, a play, a ballet, or an opera, begin with the title of the work performed, italicized (unless it is named by form, number, and key). Then give the author or composer of the work; relevant information such as the director, the choreographer, the conductor, or the major performers; the theater, ballet, or opera company, if any; the theater and location; and the date of the performance.

The Draft. By Peter Snoad, directed by Diego Arciniegas, Hibernian Hall,
Boston, 10 Sept. 2015.

Cite a source reposted from another source

Problem: Some sources that you find online, particularly on video-sharing sites, did not originate with the person who uploaded or published the source online. How do you give proper credit for such sources?

Example: Say you need to cite President John F. Kennedy's inaugural address. You have found a video on YouTube that provides footage of the address (see image). The video was uploaded by PaddyIrishMan2 on October 29, 2006. But clearly, PaddyIrishMan2 is not the author of the video or of the address.

JFK Inaugural Address 1 of 2

PaddyIrishMan2 · 12 videos

▶ Subscribe · 403

Uploaded on Oct 29, 2006
President John F. Kennedy's inaugural address, January 20th 1961.

Vice President Johnson, Mr. Speaker, Mr. Chief Justice, President Eisenhower, Vice President Nixon, President Truman, reverend clergy, fellow citizens, we observe today not a victory of party, but a celebration of freedom — symbolising an end, as well as a beginning — signifying renewal, as well as change. For I have sworn before you and Almighty God the same solemn oath our forebears prescribed nearly a century and three quarters ago.

Strategy: Start with what you know. The source is a video that you viewed on the Web. For this particular video, John F. Kennedy is the speaker and the author of the inaugural address. PaddyIrishMan2 is identified as the person who uploaded the source to YouTube.

Citation: To cite the source, you can combine the basic MLA guidelines for a lecture or public address (see item 61) and for a video found on the Web (see item 55).

Kennedy, John F. "JFK Inaugural Address: 1 of 2." *YouTube,*
29 Oct. 2006, www.youtube.com/watch?v=xE0iPY7XGBo.

Because Kennedy's inauguration is a well-known historical event, you can be fairly certain that this is not the only version of the inauguration video. It is a good idea, therefore, to include information about the version you viewed as supplementary information.

Kennedy, John F. "JFK Inaugural Address: 1 of 2." *YouTube,* uploaded by
PaddyIrishMan2, 29 Oct. 2006, www.youtube.com/watch?v=xE0iPY7XGBo.

NOTE: If your work calls for a primary source, you should try to find the original source of the video; a reference librarian can help.

60. Performance (*cont.*)

Symphony no. 4 in G. By Gustav Mahler, conducted by Mark Wigglesworth,
      performances by Juliane Banse and Boston Symphony Orchestra, Symphony
      Hall, Boston, 17 Apr. 2009.

61. Lecture or public address   Begin with the speaker's name, the title of the lecture, the sponsoring organization, location, and date. If you viewed the lecture on the Web, cite as you would a short work from a Web site (see item 47). Add the label "Address" or "Lecture" at the end if it is not clear from the title.

a. Live

Smith, Anna Deavere. "On the Road: A Search for American Character." National
      Endowment for the Humanities, John F. Kennedy Center for the Performing
      Arts, Washington, 6 Apr. 2015. Address.

61. Lecture or public address (*cont.*)

b. Web

Khosla, Raj. "Precision Agriculture and Global Food Security." *US Department of State: Diplomacy in Action,* 26 Mar. 2013, www.state.gov/e/stas/series/212172.htm. Address.

62. Musical score   For both print and online versions, begin with the composer's name; the title of the work, italicized (unless it is named by form, number, and key); and the date of composition. For a print source, give the publisher and date. For an online source, give the title of the Web site; the publisher or sponsor; the date; and the URL.

Beethoven, Ludwig van. Symphony no. 5 in C Minor, op. 67. 1807. *Center for Computer Assisted Research in the Humanities,* Stanford U, 2000, scores.ccarh.org/beethoven/sym/beethoven-sym5-1.pdf.

63. Sound recording   Begin with the name of the person you want to emphasize: the composer, conductor, or performer. For a long work, give the title, italicized (unless it is named by form, number, and key); the names of pertinent artists; and the orchestra and conductor. End with the manufacturer and the date.

Bizet, Georges. *Carmen*. Performances by Jennifer Larmore, Thomas Moser, Angela Gheorghiu, and Samuel Ramey, Bavarian State Orchestra and Chorus, conducted by Giuseppe Sinopoli, Warner, 1996.

Blige, Mary J. "Don't Mind." *Life II: The Journey Continues (Act 1),* Geffen, 2011.

64. Work of art   (a) For an original work of art, cite the artist's name; the title of the artwork, italicized; the date of composition; and the institution and city in which the artwork is located. (b) For artworks found on the Web, include the title of the Web site (unless it is the same as the institution) and the URL. (c) If you viewed the artwork as a reproduction in a print source, add publication information about the print source, including the page number or figure number for the artwork.

a. Original

Bradford, Mark. *Let's Walk to the Middle of the Ocean*. 2015, Museum of Modern Art, New York.

b. Web

Clough, Charles. *January Twenty-First*. 1988-89, Joslyn Art Museum, Omaha, www.joslyn.org/collections-and-exhibitions/permanent-collections/ modern-and-contemporary/charles-clough-january-twenty-first/.

c. Reproduction (print)

O'Keeffe, Georgia. *Black and Purple Petunias*. 1925, private collection. *Two Lives: A Conversation in Paintings and Photographs*, edited by Alexandra Arrowsmith and Thomas West, HarperCollins, 1992, p. 67.

65. Photograph (a) For an original photograph, cite the photographer's name; the title of the photograph, italicized; the date of composition; and the institution and city in which the photograph is located. (b) For photographs found on the Web, include the title of the Web site (unless it is the same as the institution) and the URL. (c) If you viewed the photograph as a reproduction in a print source, add publication information about the print source, including the page number or figure number for the artwork. Add the label "Photograph" at the end if it is not clear from the rest of the entry.

a. Original

Feinstein, Harold. *Hangin' Out, Sharing a Public Bench, NYC*. 1948, Panopticon Gallery, Boston. Photograph.

65. Photograph (*cont.*)

Finotti, Leonardo. *Edificio Girón, Havana, Cuba*. 2014, Museum of Modern Art, New York. Photograph.

b. Web

Hura, Sohrab. *Old Man Lighting a Fire*. 2015, *Magnum Photos*, www
.magnumphotos.com/C.aspx?VP3=SearchResult&ALID
=2K1HRG681B_Q.

c. Reproduction (print)

Kertész, André. *Meudon*. 1928. *Street Photography: From Atget to Cartier-Bresson*, by Clive Scott, Tauris, 2011, p. 61.

66. Cartoon   Give the cartoonist's name; the title of the cartoon, if it has one, in quotation marks; publication information; and the label "Cartoon" at the end. To cite an online cartoon, cite as a short work from a Web site (item 47).

Zyglis, Adam. "City of Light." *Buffalo News*, 8 Nov. 2015, adamzyglis
.buffalonews.com/2015/11/08/city-of-light/. Cartoon.

67. Advertisement   Name the product or company being advertised and publication information for the source in which the advertisement appears. Add the label "Advertisement" at the end.

AT&T. *National Geographic*, Dec. 2015, p. 14. Advertisement.

Toyota. *The Root*. Slate Group, 28 Nov. 2015, www.theroot.com. Advertisement.

68. Visual such as a table, a chart, or another graphic   Cite a visual as you would a short work within a longer work.

"Brazilian Waxing and Waning: The Economy." *The Economist*, 1 Dec. 2015, www
.economist.com/blogs/graphicdetail/2015/12/economic-backgrounder.

"Number of Measles Cases by Year since 2010." *Centers for Disease Control and Prevention*, 2 Jan. 2016, www.cdc.gov/measles/cases -outbreaks.html.

69. Map Cite a map as you would a short work within a longer work. Or, if the map is published on its own, cite it as a book or another long work. Use the label "Map" at the end if it is not clear from the title or source information.

"Map of Sudan." *Global Citizen*, Citizens for Global Solutions, 2011, globalsolutions.org/blog/bashir#.VthzNMfi_FI.

Government and legal documents

70. Government document Treat the government agency as the author, giving the name of the government followed by the name of the department and the agency, if any. For sources found on the Web, follow the model for an entire Web site (see item 46) or for short or long works from a Web site (see items 47 and 48).

government   department   agency (or agencies)

United States, Department of Agriculture, Food and Nutrition Service, Child

title (long work)

Nutrition Programs. *Eligibility Manual for School Meals: Determining*

Web site title

and Verifying Eligibility. National School Lunch Program,

date   URL

July 2015, www.fns.usda.gov/sites/default/files/cn/SP40_CACFP18

_SFSP20-2015a1.pdf.

Canada, Minister of Aboriginal Affairs and Northern Development. *2015-16 Report on Plans and Priorities*. Minister of Public Works and Government Services Canada, 2015.

Cite course materials

Problem: Sometimes you will be assigned to work with materials that an instructor has uploaded to a course site or has handed out in class. Complete publication information may not always be given for such sources. A PDF file or a hard copy article, for instance, may have a title and an author's name but give no other information. Or a video may not include information about the creator or the date the video was created. When you write a paper using such sources, how should you cite them in your own work?

THE IMAGE OF THE RAILROAD IN *ANNA KARENINA*

Gary R. Jahn, University of Minnesota

The motif of the railroad recurs so frequently in Lev Tolstoj's *Anna Karenina* that the conclusion that it is somehow integral to a full understanding of the novel is inescapable. According to a recent study the railroad is mentioned at least thirty-two times in the book,[1] and every reader will remember that Anna and Vronskij first meet at a railway station, that Levin intensely dislikes the railroad, and that Anna commits suicide by leaping under a train.[2]

M. S. Al'tman once asked why Anna, having decided to do away with herself, should have selected such a gruesome method. The question is flippant only in its formulation, and a great deal of scholarly effort has been devoted to answering it. A searching of the extensive biographical data on Tolstoj has amply attested his personal aversion for the railroad. He wrote Turgenev in 1857 that "the railroad is to travel as a whore is to love,"[3] and it is known that he was discomfited to the point of nausea by the swaying of railway carriages. These facts provide a credible physiological basis for the standard, although not unanimous,[4] Soviet view that Levin's dyspeptic attitude toward the railroad is the correlative of Tolstoj's, that the highly autobiographical Levin was expressing Tolstoj's belief that the railroad served only to pander to and further inflame the already monstrous appetite of the idle and privileged for foreign luxuries, and that this belief overlies their mutual resentment of the forces tending to displace the landholding nobility from its position of inherited privilege: forces which the railroad is said to symbolize. The railroad is present in the novel so that it can be attacked, and this is precisely what Levin does in the book which he writes about contemporary Russian life.[5] There is an indubitable measure of truth in this understanding of the railway motif. It does account for Levin's view of the railroad and it is also true that for him the railroad symbolizes forces harmful to the traditional style of life of

Example: Perhaps your instructor has included a PDF file of an article in a collection of readings on the course site (see image at right). You are writing a paper in which you use a passage from the work.

Strategy: Look through section 56b for a model that matches the type of source you're working with. Is it an article? A chapter from a book? A photograph? A video? The model or models you find will give you an idea of the information you need to gather about the source. The usual required information is (1) the author or creator, (2) the title, (3) the date the work was published or created, and (4) the URL for sources on the Web.

Citation: For your citation, you can give only as much of the required information as you can find in the source. In this example, you know the source is an article with an author and a title, so you can use item 13a (basic format for an article). Because you don't have much other information about the source, it is a good idea to include the description "Course materials" and supplementary information about the course (such as its title or number and the term).

author:
last name first   article title

Jahn, Gary R. "The Image of the Railroad in *Anna Karenina*."

supplementary information

Course materials, EN101, Fall 2013.

NOTE: When in doubt about how much information to include or where to find it, consult your instructor.

71. Testimony before a legislative body

Russel, Daniel R. "Burma's Challenge: Democracy, Human Rights, Peace, and the Plight of the Rohingya." Testimony before the US House Foreign Affairs Committee, Subcommittee on East Asian and Pacific Affairs. *US Department of State: Diplomacy in Action*, 21 Oct. 2015, www.state.gov/p/eap/rls/rm/2015/10/248420.htm.

72. Historical document The titles of most historical documents, such as the US Constitution and the Canadian Charter of Rights and Freedoms, are neither italicized nor put in quotation marks. For a print version, cite as a selection in an anthology (see item 35) or as a book (with the title not italicized). For an online version, cite as a short work from a Web site (see item 47).

Jefferson, Thomas. First Inaugural Address. 1801. *The American Reader: Words That Moved a Nation*, edited by Diane Ravitch, 2nd ed., William Morrow, 2000, pp. 79-82.

Constitution of the United States. 1787. *The Charters of Freedom*, US National Archives and Records Administration, www.archives.gov/exhibits/charters/.

73. Legislative act (law) Begin with the name of the act, neither italicized nor in quotation marks. Then provide the act's Public Law number; its Statutes at Large volume and page numbers; and its date of enactment.

73. Legislative act (law) (*cont.*)

Electronic Freedom of Information Act Amendments of 1996. Pub. L.
104-231. 110 Stat. 3048. 2 Oct. 1996.

74. Court case Name the first plaintiff and the first defendant. Then give the volume, name, and page number of the law report; the court name; the year of the decision; and publication information. Do not italicize the name of the case. (In the text of the paper, the name of the case is italicized; see item 19 on p. 607.)

Utah v. Evans. 536 US 452. Supreme Court of the US. 2002. *Legal Information
Institute,* Cornell U Law School, www.law.cornell.edu/supremecourt/
text/536/452.

Personal communication and social media

75. E-mail message Begin with the writer's name and the subject line. Then write "Received by," followed by the name of the recipient. End with the date of the message.

Lowe, Walter. "Review Questions." Received by Rita Anderson, 20 Oct. 2015.

76. Text message

Wiley, Joanna. Message to the author, 4 Apr. 2014.

77. Posting to an online discussion list When possible, cite archived versions of postings. Begin with the author's name, followed by the title or subject line, in quotation marks (use the label "Online posting" if the posting has no title). Then proceed as for a short work from a Web site (see item 47).

Robin, Griffith. "Write for the Reading Teacher." *Developing Digital
Literacies*, NCTE, 23 Oct. 2015, ncte.connectedcommunity.org/
communities/community-home/digestviewer/viewthread
?GroupId=1693&MID=24520&tab=digestviewer
&CommunityKey=628d2ad6-8277-4042-a376-2b370ddceabf.

78. Facebook post or comment   Cite as a short work from a Web site (see item 47), beginning with the writer's screen name followed by the real name in parentheses, if both are given. Otherwise use whatever name is given in the source. Follow with the title of the post, if any, in quotation marks. If there is no title, use the label "Post."

Bedford English. "Stacey Cochran explores Reflective Writing in the
    classroom and as a writer: http://ow.ly/YkjVB." *Facebook*, 15 Feb. 2016,
    www.facebook.com/BedfordEnglish/posts/10153415001259607.

79. Twitter post (tweet)   Begin with the writer's screen name followed by the real name in parentheses, if both are given. Otherwise use whatever name is given in the source. Give the text of the entire tweet in quotation marks, using the writer's capitalization and punctuation. Follow the text with the date and time noted on the tweet, and end with the URL.

Curiosity Rover. "Can you see me waving? How to spot #Mars in the night
    sky: https://youtu.be/hv8hVvJlcJQ." *Twitter*, 5 Nov. 2015, 11:00 a.m.,
    twitter.com/marscuriosity/status/672859022911889408.

@grammarphobia (Patricia T. O'Conner and Steward Kellerman). "Is 'if you
    will,' like, a verbal tic? #English #language #grammar #etymology
    #usage #linguistics #WOTD." *Twitter*, 14 Mar. 2016, 9:12 a.m., twitter
    .com/grammarphobia.

56c MLA information notes (optional)

Researchers who use the MLA system of parenthetical documentation may also use information notes for one of two purposes:

1. to provide additional material that is important but might interrupt the flow of the paper
2. to refer to several sources that support a single point or to provide comments on sources

Information notes may be either footnotes or endnotes. Footnotes appear at the foot of the page; endnotes appear on a separate page at the end of the paper, just before the list of works cited. For either style, the notes are numbered consecutively throughout the paper. The text of the paper contains a raised arabic numeral that corresponds to the number of the note.

TEXT

In the past several years, employees have filed a number of lawsuits against employers because of online monitoring practices.[1]

NOTE

1. For a discussion of federal law applicable to electronic surveillance in the workplace, see Kesan 293.

57 MLA manuscript format; sample research paper

The following guidelines are consistent with advice given in the *MLA Handbook*, 8th edition (MLA, 2016), and with typical requirements for student papers. For a sample MLA research paper, see pages 666–73.

57a MLA manuscript format

Formatting the paper

Papers written in MLA style should be formatted as follows.

Font   If your instructor does not require a specific font, choose one that is standard and easy to read (such as Times New Roman).

Title and identification   MLA does not require a title page. On the first page of your paper, place your name, your instructor's name, the course title, and the date on separate lines against the left margin. Then center your title. (See p. 666 for a sample first page.)

If your instructor requires a title page, ask for formatting guidelines.

Page numbers (running head)   Put the page number preceded by your last name in the upper right corner of each page, one-half inch below the top edge. Use arabic numerals (1, 2, 3, and so on).

Margins, line spacing, and paragraph indents   Leave margins of one inch on all sides of the page. Left-align the text.

Double-space throughout the paper. Do not add extra space above or below the title of the paper or between paragraphs.

Indent the first line of each paragraph one-half inch from the left margin.

Capitalization, italics, and quotation marks   In titles of works, capitalize all words except articles (*a, an, the*), prepositions (*to, from, between*, and so on), coordinating conjunctions (*and, but, or, nor, for, so, yet*), and the *to* in infinitives—unless the word is first or last in the title or subtitle. Follow these guidelines in your paper even if the title appears in all capital or all lowercase letters in the source.

In the text of an MLA paper, when a complete sentence follows a colon, lowercase the first word following the colon unless the sentence is a quotation or a well-known expression or principle.

Italicize the titles of books, journals, magazines, and other long works, such as Web sites. Use quotation marks around the titles of articles, short stories, poems, and other short works.

Long quotations   When a quotation is longer than four typed lines of prose or three lines of poetry, set it off from the text by indenting the entire quotation one-half inch from the left margin. Double-space the indented quotation and do not add extra space above or below it.

Do not use quotation marks when a quotation has been set off from the text by indenting. See page 671 for an example.

URLs　If you need to break a URL at the end of a line in the text of a paper, break it only after a slash or a double slash or before any other mark of punctuation. Do not add a hyphen. If you will post your project online or submit it electronically and you want your readers to click on your URLs, do not insert any line breaks. For MLA guidelines on dividing URLs in your list of works cited, see page 665.

Headings　MLA neither encourages nor discourages the use of headings and provides no guidelines for their use. If you would like to insert headings in a long essay or research paper, check first with your instructor.

Visuals　MLA classifies visuals as tables and figures (figures include graphs, charts, maps, photographs, and drawings). Label each table with an arabic numeral ("Table 1," "Table 2," and so on) and provide a clear title that identifies the subject. Capitalize as you would the title of an article (see 45c), but do not use italics or quotation marks. Place the number and title on separate lines above the table and at the left margin.

For a table that you have borrowed or adapted, give the source below the table in a note like the following:

Source: Boris Groysberg and Michael Slind, "Leadership Is a Conversation," *Harvard Business Review*, June 2012, p. 83.

For each figure, place the figure number (using the abbreviation "Fig.") and a title below the figure, aligned left. Capitalize the title as you would a sentence; include source information following the title. (When referring to the figure in your paper, use the abbreviation "fig." in parenthetical citations; otherwise spell out the word.) See page 668 for an example of a figure in a paper.

Place visuals in the text, as close as possible to the sentences that relate to them, unless your instructor prefers that visuals appear in an appendix.

Preparing the list of works cited

Begin the list of works cited on a new page at the end of the paper. Center the title "Works Cited" about one inch from the top of the page. Double-space throughout. See pages 190 and 672–73 for sample lists of works cited.

Alphabetizing the list   Alphabetize the list by the last names of the authors (or editors); if a work has no author or editor, alphabetize by the first word of the title other than *A, An,* or *The.*

If your list includes two or more works by the same author, use the author's name for the first entry only. For subsequent entries, use three hyphens followed by a period. List the titles in alphabetical order. (See items 6 and 7 on p. 618.)

Indenting   Do not indent the first line of each works cited entry, but indent any additional lines one-half inch. This technique highlights the names of the authors, making it easy for readers to scan the alphabetized list. See pages 672–73.

URLs   If you need to include a URL in a works cited entry and it must be divided across lines, break it only after a slash or a double slash or before any other mark of punctuation. Do not add a hyphen. If you will post your project online or submit it electronically and you want your readers to click on your URLs, do not insert any line breaks.

57b Sample MLA research paper

On the following pages is a research paper on the topic of the role of government in legislating food choices, written by Sophie Harba, a student in a composition class. Harba's paper is documented with in-text citations and a list of works cited in MLA style. Annotations in the margins of the paper draw your attention to Harba's use of MLA style and her effective writing.

Harba 1

Sophie Harba

Professor Baros-Moon

Engl 1101

30 April 2013

Title is centered.

What's for Dinner? Personal Choices vs. Public Health

Opening research question engages readers.

Should the government enact laws to regulate healthy eating choices? Many Americans would answer an emphatic "No," arguing that what and how much we eat should be left to individual choice rather than unreasonable laws. Others might argue that it would be unreasonable for the government not to enact legislation, given

Writer highlights the research conversation.

the rise of chronic diseases that result from harmful diets. In this debate, both the definition of reasonable regulations and the role of government to legislate food choices are at stake. In the name of

Thesis answers the research question and presents Harba's main point.

public health and safety, state governments have the responsibility to shape health policies and to regulate healthy eating choices, especially since doing so offers a potentially large social benefit for a relatively small cost.

Debates surrounding the government's role in regulating

Signal phrase names the author. The parenthetical citation includes a page number.

food have a long history in the United States. According to Lorine Goodwin, a food historian, nineteenth-century reformers who sought to purify the food supply were called "fanatics" and "radicals" by critics who argued that consumers should be free

Historical background provides context for debate.

to buy and eat what they want (77). Thanks to regulations, though, such as the 1906 federal Pure Food and Drug Act, food, beverages, and medicine are largely free from toxins. In addition, to prevent contamination and the spread of disease, meat and dairy products are now inspected by government agents to ensure that they meet health requirements. Such regulations

Harba explains her use of a key term, *reasonable*.

can be considered reasonable because they protect us from harm

Harba 2

with little, if any, noticeable consumer cost. It is not considered
an unreasonable infringement on personal choice that
contaminated meat or arsenic-laced cough drops are *un*available
at our local supermarket. Rather, it is an important government
function to stop such harmful items from entering the
marketplace.

Even though our food meets current safety standards, there
is a need for further regulation. Not all food dangers, for example,
arise from obvious toxins like arsenic and *E. coli*. A diet that is
low in nutritional value and high in sugars, fats, and refined grains—
grains that have been processed to increase shelf life but that contain
little fiber, iron, and B vitamins—can be damaging over time (United
States, Dept. of Agriculture and Dept. of Health and Human Services
36). A graph from the government's *Dietary Guidelines for Americans,
2010* provides a visual representation of the American diet and how
far off it is from the recommended nutritional standards (see fig. 1).

Michael Pollan, who has written extensively about Americans'
unhealthy eating habits, notes that "[t]he Centers for Disease
Control estimates that fully three quarters of US health care
spending goes to treat chronic diseases, most of which are
preventable and linked to diet: heart disease, stroke, type 2
diabetes, and at least a third of all cancers." In fact, the amount
of money the United States spends to treat chronic illnesses is
increasing so rapidly that the Centers for Disease Control has
labeled chronic disease "the public health challenge of the 21st
century" (United States, Dept. of Health and Human Services,
Centers for Disease Control and Prevention 1). In fighting this
epidemic, the primary challenge is not the need to find a cure; the
challenge is to prevent chronic diseases from striking in the first place.

Harba establishes
common ground
with the reader.

Transition helps
readers move from
one paragraph to
the next.

Harba provides a
text reference to
the figure on the
next page.

No page number
is available for this
Web source.

Harba sets forth
the urgency of her
argument.

Harba 3

Harba uses a graph to illustrate Americans' poor nutritional choices.

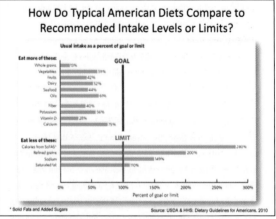

Fig. 1. This graph shows that Americans consume about three times more fats and sugars and twice as many refined grains as is recommended but only half of the recommended foods (United States, Dept. of Agriculture and Dept. of Health and Human Services, fig. 5-1).

The visual includes a figure number, descriptive caption, and source information.

Harba treats both sides fairly.

Legislation, however, is not a popular solution when it comes to most Americans and the food they eat. According to a nationwide poll, 75% of Americans are opposed to laws that restrict or put limitations on access to unhealthy foods (Neergaard and Agiesta). When New York mayor Michael Bloomberg proposed a regulation in 2012 banning the sale of soft drinks in servings greater than twelve ounces in restaurants and movie theaters, he was ridiculed as "Nanny Bloomberg." In California in 2011, legislators failed to pass a law that would impose a penny-per-ounce tax on soda, which would have funded obesity prevention programs. And in Mississippi, legislators passed "a ban on bans—a law that forbids . . . local restrictions on food or drink" (Conly A23).

Why is the public largely resistant to laws that would limit unhealthy choices or penalize those choices with so-called fat taxes? Many consumers and civil rights advocates find such laws to be an unreasonable restriction on individual freedom of choice. As health policy experts Mello et al. point out, opposition to food and beverage regulation is similar to the opposition to early tobacco legislation: the public views the issue as one of personal responsibility rather than one requiring government intervention (2602). In other words, if a person eats unhealthy food and becomes ill as a result, that is his or her choice. But those who favor legislation claim that freedom of choice is a myth because of the strong influence of food and beverage industry marketing on consumers' dietary habits. According to one nonprofit health advocacy group, food and beverage companies spend roughly two billion dollars per year marketing directly to children. As a result, kids see nearly four thousand ads per year encouraging them to consume unhealthy food and drinks ("Facts"). As was the case with antismoking laws passed in recent decades, taxes and legal restrictions on junk food sales could help to counter the strong marketing messages that promote unhealthy products.

The United States has a history of state and local public health laws that have successfully promoted a particular behavior by punishing an undesirable behavior. The decline in tobacco use as a result of antismoking taxes and laws is perhaps the most

Harba anticipates objections to her idea. She counters opposing views and provides support for her argument.

An analogy extends Harba's argument.

obvious example. Another example is legislation requiring the use of seat belts, which have significantly reduced fatalities in car crashes. One government agency reports that seat belt use saved an average of more than fourteen thousand lives per year in the United States between 2000 and 2010 (United States, Dept. of Transportation, Natl. Highway Traffic Safety Administration 231). Perhaps seat belt laws have public support because the cost of wearing a seat belt is small, especially when compared with the benefit of saving fourteen thousand lives per year.

Laws designed to prevent chronic disease by promoting healthier food and beverage consumption also have potentially enormous benefits. To give just one example, Marion Nestle, New York University professor of nutrition and public health, notes that "a 1% reduction in intake of saturated fat across the population would prevent more than 30,000 cases of coronary heart disease annually and save more than a billion dollars in health care costs" (7). Few would argue that saving lives and dollars is not an enormous benefit. But three-quarters of Americans say they would object to the costs needed to achieve this benefit—the regulations needed to reduce saturated fat intake.

Why do so many Americans believe there is a degree of personal choice lost when regulations such as taxes, bans, or portion limits on unhealthy foods are proposed? Some critics of anti-junk-food laws believe that even if state and local laws were successful in curbing chronic diseases, they would still be unacceptable. Bioethicist David Resnik emphasizes that such policies, despite their potential to make our society healthier, "open the door to excessive government control over food, which could restrict dietary choices, interfere with cultural, ethnic, and religious traditions, and exacerbate socioeconomic

Harba introduces a direct quotation with a signal phrase and follows with a comment that shows readers why she chose to use the source.

Harba acknowledges critics and counterarguments.

inequalities" (31). Resnik acknowledges that his argument relies on "slippery slope" thinking, but he insists that "social and political pressures" regarding food regulation make his concerns valid (31). Yet the social and political pressures that Resnik cites are really just the desire to improve public health, and limiting access to unhealthy, artificial ingredients seems a small price to pay. As legal scholars L. O. Gostin and K. G. Gostin explain, "[I]nterventions that do not pose a truly significant burden on individual liberty" are justified if they "go a long way towards safeguarding the health and well-being of the populace" (214).

> Including the source's credentials makes Harba more credible.

To improve public health, advocates such as Bowdoin College philosophy professor Sarah Conly contend that it is the government's duty to prevent people from making harmful choices whenever feasible and whenever public benefits outweigh the costs. In response to critics who claim that laws aimed at stopping us from eating whatever we want are an assault on our freedom of choice, Conly offers a persuasive counterargument:

> Long quotation is introduced with a signal phrase naming the author.

> [L]aws aren't designed for each one of us individually. Some of us can drive safely at 90 miles per hour, but we're bound by the same laws as the people who can't, because individual speeding laws aren't practical. Giving up a little liberty is something we agree to when we agree to live in a democratic society that is governed by laws. (A23)

> Long quotation is set off from the text. Quotation marks are omitted.

As Conly suggests, we need to change our either/or thinking (either we have complete freedom of choice *or* we have government regulations and lose our freedom) and instead need to see health as a matter of public good, not individual liberty. Proposals such as Mayor Bloomberg's that seek to limit portions of unhealthy beverages aren't about giving up liberty; they are about asking individuals to choose substantial public health benefits at a very small cost.

> Long quotation is followed with comments that connect the source to Harba's argument.

Harba 7

Conclusion sums up Harba's argument and provides closure.

Despite arguments in favor of regulating unhealthy food as a means to improve public health, public opposition has stood in the way of legislation. Americans freely eat as much unhealthy food as they want, and manufacturers and sellers of these foods have nearly unlimited freedom to promote such products and drive increased consumption, without any requirements to warn the public of potential hazards. Yet mounting scientific evidence points to unhealthy food as a significant contributing factor to chronic disease, which we know is straining our health care system, decreasing Americans' quality of life, and leading to unnecessary premature deaths. Americans must consider whether to allow the costly trend of rising chronic disease to continue in the name of personal choice or whether to support the regulatory changes and public health policies that will reverse that trend.

Harba 8

Heading is centered.

Works Cited

Conly, Sarah. "Three Cheers for the Nanny State." *The New York Times*, 25 Mar. 2013, p. A23.

"The Facts on Junk Food Marketing and Kids." *Prevention Institute*, www.preventioninstitute.org/focus-areas/supporting -healthy-food-a-activity/supporting-healthy-food-and-activity -environments-advocacy/get-involved-were-not-buying-it/735 -were-not-buying-it-the-facts-on-junk-food-marketing-and-kids .html. Accessed 21 Apr. 2013.

Goodwin, Lorine Swainston. *The Pure Food, Drink, and Drug Crusaders, 1879-1914*. McFarland, 2006.

Access date used for an online source that has no update date.

Gostin, L. O., and K. G. Gostin. "A Broader Liberty: J. S. Mill,
    Paternalism, and the Public's Health." *Public Health*, vol. 123,
    no. 3, 2009, pp. 214-21, doi:10.1016/j.puhe.2008.12.024.

Mello, Michelle M., et al. "Obesity—the New Frontier of Public
    Health Law." *New England Journal of Medicine*, vol. 354, no.
    24, 2006, pp. 2601-10, www.nejm.org/doi/pdf/10.1056/
    NEJMhpr060227.

Neergaard, Lauran, and Jennifer Agiesta. "Obesity's a Crisis but
    We Want Our Junk Food, Poll Shows." *The Huffington Post*,
    4 Jan. 2013, www.huffingtonpost.com/2013/01/04/obesity
    -junk-food-government-intervention-poll_n_2410376.html.

Nestle, Marion. *Food Politics: How the Food Industry Influences
    Nutrition and Health.* U of California P, 2013.

Pollan, Michael. "The Food Movement, Rising." *The New York Review of
    Books*, 10 June 2010, www.nybooks.com/articles/2010/06/10/
    food-movement-rising/.

Resnik, David. "Trans Fat Bans and Human Freedom." *American
    Journal of Bioethics*, vol. 10, no. 3, Mar. 2010, pp. 27-32.

United States, Department of Agriculture and Department of Health and
    Human Services. *Dietary Guidelines for Americans, 2010*, health
    .gov/dietaryguidelines/dga2010/dietaryguidelines2010.pdf.

United States, Department of Health and Human Services, Centers
    for Disease Control and Prevention. *The Power of Prevention*.
    National Center for Chronic Disease Prevention and Health
    Promotion, 2009, www.cdc.gov/chronicdisease/pdf/2009
    -Power-of-Prevention.pdf.

United States, Department of Transportation, National Highway Traffic
    Safety Administration. *Traffic Safety Facts 2010: A Compilation
    of Motor Vehicle Crash Data from the Fatality Analysis Reporting
    System and the General Estimates System.* 2010, www-nrd.nhtsa
    .dot.gov/Pubs/811659.pdf.

First line of each entry is at the left margin; extra lines are indented ½".

Double-spacing is used throughout.

List is alphabetized by authors' last names (or by title when a work has no author).

The government agency is used as the author of a government document.

Writing APA papers

BRIEF DIRECTORY

58 Supporting a thesis, 674
59 Citing sources; avoiding plagiarism, 678
60 Integrating sources, 683
61 Documenting sources, 693
Directory to APA in-text citation models, 694
Directory to APA reference list models, 702
62 Manuscript format; sample research paper, 735

Most instructors in the social sciences and some instructors in other disciplines will ask you to document your sources with the American Psychological Association (APA) system of in-text citations and references described in 61. When writing an APA-style paper that draws on sources, you face three main challenges: (1) supporting a thesis, (2) citing your sources and avoiding plagiarism, and (3) integrating source material effectively.

Examples in this section are drawn from one student's research for a review of the literature on technology's role in the shift to student-centered learning. April Wang's paper appears on pages 741–53.

NOTE: For advice on finding and evaluating sources and on managing information in all your college courses, see sections 50–52.

58 Supporting a thesis

Most research assignments ask you to form a thesis, or main idea, and to support that thesis with well-organized evidence. In a paper reviewing the literature on a topic, the thesis analyzes conclusions drawn by a variety of researchers.

58a Form a working thesis.

Once you have read a range of sources, considered your issue from different perspectives, and chosen an entry point in the research conversation (see 50b), you are ready to form a working thesis: a one-sentence (or occasionally a two-sentence) statement of your central idea. (See also 1c.) The working thesis expresses more than your opinion; it expresses your informed, reasoned answer to your research question—a question about which people might disagree. As you learn more about your subject, your ideas may change, and your working thesis will evolve, too. You can revise your thesis as you draft. Here, for example, is a research question posed by April Wang, a student in an education class, followed by her thesis in response.

RESEARCH QUESTION

Can educational technology improve student learning and solve the problem of teacher shortages?

WORKING THESIS

Educational technology can help solve teacher shortages by shifting the focus from teachers to students.

The thesis usually appears at the end of the introductory paragraph. To read April Wang's thesis in the context of her introduction, see page 743.

See page 571 for guidelines for testing your working thesis statement.

58b Organize your ideas.

The American Psychological Association encourages the use of headings to help readers follow the organization of a paper. For an original research report, the major headings often follow a standard model: Method, Results, Discussion. The introduction does not have a heading; it consists of the material between the title of the paper and the first heading.

For a literature review, headings will vary. Student writer April Wang used three questions to focus her research; the questions then became headings in her paper (see 62b).

58c Use sources to inform and support your argument.

The source materials you have gathered will help you develop your argument. Sources can play several different roles to support your thesis and develop your points.

Providing background information or context

You can use facts and statistics to support generalizations or to establish the importance of your topic, as student writer April Wang does in her introduction.

> In the United States, most public school systems are struggling with teacher shortages, which are projected to worsen as the number of applicants to education schools decreases (Donitsa-Schmidt & Zuzovsky, 2014, p. 420). Citing federal data, *The New York Times* reported a 30% drop in "people entering teacher preparation programs" between 2010 and 2014 (Rich, 2015).

Explaining terms or concepts

If readers are unfamiliar with a term or concept important to your topic, you will want to define or explain it; or if your argument depends on a term with multiple meanings, you will want to explain your use of the term. Quoting or paraphrasing a source can help you define terms and concepts in accessible language. April Wang uses a source to define a key concept, student-centered learning.

According to the International Society for Technology in Education (2016), "Student-centered learning moves students from passive receivers of information to active participants in their own discovery process."

Supporting your claims

As you draft, make sure to back up your assertions with facts, examples, and other evidence from your research (see also 6f). April Wang, for example, uses one source's findings to support her claim that a combination of teachers and educational technology can promote student-centered learning.

> Many schools have already effectively paired a reduced faculty with educational technology to support successful student-centered learning. For example, Watson (2008) offered a case study of the Cincinnati Public Schools Virtual High School, which brought students together in a physical school building to work with an assortment of online learning programs. Although there were only 10 certified teachers in the building, students were able to engage in highly individualized instruction according to their own needs, strengths, and learning styles, using the 10 teachers as support (p. 7).

Lending authority to your argument

Expert opinion can add credibility to your argument (see also 6h). But don't rely on experts to make your points for you. State your ideas in your own words and, when appropriate, cite the judgment of an authority in the field to support your position.

> Horn and Staker (2011) concluded that the chief benefit of technological learning was that it could adapt to the individual student in a way that whole-class delivery by a single teacher could not. Their study examined various schools where technology enabled student-centered learning.

Anticipating and countering alternative interpretations

Do not ignore sources that seem contrary to your position. Instead, use them to give voice to opposing points of view and to state potential objections to your argument before you counter them (see 6i). Readers often have objections in mind already, whether or not they agree with you. Wang uses a source to acknowledge that some teachers oppose student instruction driven by technology.

> Some researchers have expressed doubt that schools are ready for student-centered learning—or any type of instruction—that is driven by technology. In a recent survey conducted by the Nellie Mae Education Foundation, Moeller and Reitzes (2011) reported not only that many teachers lacked confidence in their ability to incorporate technology in the classroom but that 43% of polled high school students said that they lacked confidence in their technological proficiency going into college and careers.

59 Citing sources; avoiding plagiarism

In a research paper, you will draw on the work of other researchers and writers, and you must document their contributions by citing your sources. Sources are cited for two reasons:

1. to tell readers where your information comes from—so that they can assess its reliability and, if interested, find and read the original source

2. to give credit to the writers from whom you have borrowed words and ideas

You must cite anything you borrow from a source, including direct quotations; statistics and other facts; visuals such as tables and graphs; and summaries and paraphrases. Borrowing without proper acknowledgment is a form of dishonesty known as *plagiarism.* The only exception is common knowledge—information that your readers may know or could easily locate in any number of reference sources.

59a Understand how the APA system works.

The American Psychological Association recommends an author-date system of citation. The following describes that system.

1. The source is introduced by a signal phrase that includes the last name of the author followed by the date of publication in parentheses.

2. The material being cited is followed by a page number in parentheses (unless the source is unpaginated).

3. At the end of the paper, an alphabetized list of references gives complete publication information for the source.

IN-TEXT CITATION

Bell (2010) reported that students engaged in this kind of learning performed better on both project-based assessments and standardized tests (pp. 39-40).

ENTRY IN THE LIST OF REFERENCES

Bell, S. (2010). Project-based learning for the 21st century: Skills for the future. *The Clearing House, 83*(2), 39-43.

This basic APA format varies for different types of sources. For a detailed discussion and other models, see 61.

59b Understand what plagiarism is.

Your research paper represents your ideas in conversation with the ideas in your sources. To be fair and responsible, you must acknowledge your debt to the writers of those sources. When you acknowledge your sources, you avoid plagiarism, a form of academic dishonesty.

Three different acts are considered plagiarism: (1) failing to cite quotations and borrowed ideas, (2) failing to enclose borrowed language in quotation marks, and (3) failing to put summaries and paraphrases in your own words. Definitions of plagiarism may vary; it's a good idea to find out how your school defines and addresses academic dishonesty.

59c Use quotation marks around borrowed language.

To indicate that you are using a source's exact phrases or sentences, you must enclose them in quotation marks unless they have been set off from the text by indenting (see p. 687). To omit the quotation marks is to claim—falsely—that the language is your own. Such an omission is plagiarism even if you have cited the source.

> **MORE HELP**
>
> When you use exact language from a source, you need to show that it is a quotation.
>
> ▶ Quotation marks for direct quotations: 37a

ORIGINAL SOURCE

Student-centered learning, or student centeredness, is a model which puts the student in the center of the learning process.

—Z. Çubukçu, "Teachers' Evaluation of Student-
Centered Learning Environments" (2012), p. 50

PLAGIARISM

According to Çubukçu (2012), student-centered learning . . . is a
model which puts the student in the center of the learning process (p. 50).

The student writer has cited the source, Çubukçu; however,
the writer has not put quotation marks around the definition of
student-centered learning, which is taken word-for-word from
the source.

BORROWED LANGUAGE IN QUOTATION MARKS

According to Çubukçu (2012), "student-centered learning . . . is a
model which puts the student in the center of the learning process" (p. 50).

NOTE: Quotation marks are not used when quoted sentences are
set off from the text by indenting (see p. 687).

59d Put summaries and paraphrases in your own words.

Summaries and paraphrases are written in your own words.
A summary condenses information; a paraphrase conveys the
information using roughly the same number of words as in
the original source.

When you summarize or paraphrase, it is not enough to
name the source; you must restate the source's meaning using
your own language. (See also 51c.) You commit plagiarism if you
patchwrite—half-copy the author's sentences, either by mixing the
author's phrases with your own without using quotation marks or by
plugging your own synonyms into the author's sentence structure.

The following paraphrases are plagiarized—even though
the source is cited—because their language and sentence structure are too close to those of the source.

ORIGINAL SOURCE

Student-centered teaching focuses on the student. Decision-making, organization and content are determined for most by taking individual students' needs and interests into consideration. Student-centered teaching provides opportunities to develop students' skills of transferring knowledge to other situations, triggering retention, and adapting a high motivation for learning.

> —Z. Çubukçu, "Teachers' Evaluation of Student-Centered Learning Environments" (2012), p. 52

UNACCEPTABLE BORROWING OF PHRASES

According to Çubukçu (2012), student-centered teaching takes into account the needs and interests of each student, making it possible to foster students' skills of transferring knowledge to new situations and triggering retention (p. 52).

UNACCEPTABLE BORROWING OF STRUCTURE

According to Çubukçu (2012), this new model of teaching centers on the student. The material and flow of the course are chosen by considering the students' individual requirements. Student-centered teaching gives a chance for students to develop useful, transferable skills, ensuring they'll remember material and stay motivated (p. 52).

To avoid plagiarizing an author's language, resist the temptation to look at the source while you are summarizing or paraphrasing. After you have read the passage you want to paraphrase, set the source aside. Ask yourself, "What is the author's meaning?" In your own words, state your understanding of the author's basic point. Return to the source and check that you haven't used the author's language or sentence structure or misrepresented the author's ideas. When you fully understand another writer's meaning, you can more easily and accurately present those ideas in your own words.

ACCEPTABLE PARAPHRASE

Çubukçu's (2012) research has documented the numerous benefits
of student-centered teaching in putting the student at the center of
teaching and learning. When students are given the option of deciding
what they learn and how they learn, they are motivated to apply their
learning to new settings and to retain the content of their learning
(p. 52).

60 Integrating sources

Your research draws on and borrows from the work of others
to help you develop and support your ideas. As you conduct
research, you gather language and ideas from your sources that
you might want to use in your paper. Section 59 shows you how
to acknowledge sources to avoid plagiarism. This section will
help you integrate those sources into your paper so that readers understand how your use of quotation, summary, and paraphrase contributes to your argument.

As you integrate sources, you need to find a balance
between the words of your sources and your own voice. Readers
should always know who is speaking in your paper — you or your
source. You can use several strategies to integrate sources into
your paper while maintaining your own voice.

- Use sources as concisely as possible so that your own
  thinking and voice aren't lost (60a and 60b).

- Use signal phrases and avoid dropped quotations. Clearly
  indicate the boundary between your words and the
  source's words (60c).

- Discuss and analyze your sources to show readers how each source supports your points and how the sources relate to one another (60d).

60a Summarize and paraphrase effectively.

In your academic writing, keep the emphasis on your ideas and your language; use your own words to summarize and to paraphrase your sources and to explain your points. How you choose to use a source—as summary or paraphrase—depends on your purpose.

Summarizing

When you summarize a source, you express another writer's ideas in your own words, condensing the author's key points and using fewer words than the author. Even though a summary is in your own words, the original ideas remain the intellectual property of the author, so you must include a citation. Summarizing allows you to state the source's main idea simply before you respond to or counter it.

See "When to use a summary" (p. 586) for more advice.

Paraphrasing

When you paraphrase, you express an author's ideas in your own words, using approximately the same number of words and details as in the source. Even though the words are your own, the original ideas are the author's intellectual property, so you must give a citation. Paraphrasing allows you to capture a source's ideas but perhaps simplify or reorder them.

See "When to use a paraphrase" (p. 586) for more advice.

60b Use quotations appropriately.

In your academic writing, keep the emphasis on your ideas; use your own words to summarize and to paraphrase your sources and to explain your points. Sometimes, however, quotations can be the most effective way to integrate a source.

WHEN TO USE QUOTATIONS

- When language is especially vivid or expressive
- When exact wording is needed for technical accuracy
- When it is important to let the debaters of an issue explain their positions in their own words
- When the words of an authority lend weight to your argument
- When the language of a source is the topic of your discussion

Limiting your use of quotations

Although it is tempting to insert many quotations in your paper and to use your own words only for connecting passages, do not quote excessively. It is almost impossible to integrate numerous long quotations smoothly into your own text.

It is not always necessary to quote full sentences from a source. You can often integrate language from a source into your own sentence structure.

> Citing federal data, *The New York Times* reported a 30% drop in "people entering teacher preparation programs" between 2010 and 2014 (Rich, 2015).

> Bell (2010) has argued that the chief benefit of student-centered learning is that it can connect students with "real-world tasks," thus making learning more engaging as well as more comprehensive.

Using the ellipsis mark

To condense a quoted passage, you can use the ellipsis mark (three periods, with spaces between) to indicate that you have omitted words. What remains must be grammatically complete.

> Demski (2012) noted that "personalized learning . . . acknowledges and accommodates the range of abilities, prior experiences, needs and interests of each student" (p. 33).

The writer has omitted the phrase *a student-centered teaching and learning model that* from the source.

When you want to leave out one or more full sentences, use a period before the three ellipsis dots.

> According to Demski (2012), "In any personalized learning model, the student—not the teacher—is the central figure. . . . Personalized learning may finally allow individualization and differentiation to actually happen in the classroom" (p. 34).

Ordinarily, do not use an ellipsis mark at the beginning or at the end of a quotation. Readers will understand that you have taken the quoted material from a longer passage. The only exception occurs when you feel it is necessary, for clarity, to indicate that your quotation begins or ends in the middle of a sentence.

USING SOURCES RESPONSIBLY: Make sure that omissions and ellipsis marks do not distort the meaning of your source.

Using brackets

Brackets allow you to insert your own words into quoted material. You can insert words in brackets to clarify a confusing reference or to keep a sentence grammatical in the context of your own writing.

> Demski's (2012) research confirms that "implement[ing] a true personalized learning model on a national level" is difficult for a number of reasons (p. 36).

To indicate an error such as a misspelling in a quotation, insert [*sic*], italicized and with brackets around it, right after the error. (See 39c.)

Setting off long quotations

When you quote forty or more words from a source, set off the quotation by indenting it one-half inch from the left margin. Use the normal right margin and do not single-space the quotation.

Long quotations should be introduced by an informative sentence, usually followed by a colon. Quotation marks are unnecessary because the indented format tells readers that the passage is taken word-for-word from the source.

> According to Svokos (2015), College and Education Fellow for *The Huffington Post*, some educational technology resources entertain students while supporting student-centered learning:
>
>> GlassLab, a nonprofit that was launched with grants from the Bill & Melinda Gates and MacArthur Foundations, creates educational games that are now being used in more than 6,000 classrooms across the country. Some of the company's games are education versions of existing ones—for example, its first release was SimCity EDU—while others are originals. Teachers get real-time updates on students' progress as well as suggestions on what topics students need to spend more time on.

For a source with page numbers (unlike the example, which is a Web source), the parenthetical citation with a page number goes outside the final mark of punctuation. (When a quotation is run into your text, the opposite is true. See the sample citations on p. 686.)

60c Use signal phrases to integrate sources.

Whenever you include a paraphrase, summary, or direct quotation of another writer's work in your paper, prepare your readers for it with a signal phrase. A signal phrase usually names the author of the source, gives the publication year in parentheses, and often provides some context. It is generally acceptable in APA style to call authors by their last name only, even on a first mention. If your paper refers to two authors with the same last name, use initials as well.

When you write a signal phrase, choose a verb that is appropriate for the way you are using the source (see 58c). Are you providing background, explaining a concept, supporting a claim, lending authority, or refuting an argument? See the chart on page 691 for a list of verbs commonly used in signal phrases. Note that APA requires using verbs in the past tense or present perfect tense (*explained* or *has explained*) to introduce source material. Use the present tense only for discussing the applications or effects of your own results (*the data suggest*) or knowledge that has been clearly established (*researchers agree*).

Marking boundaries

Readers need to move from your words to the words of a source without feeling a jolt. Avoid dropping direct quotations into your text without warning. Instead, provide clear signal phrases, including at least the author's name and the year of publication. Signal phrases mark the boundaries between source material and your own words; they can also tell readers why a source is worth quoting. (The signal phrase is highlighted in the second example.)

DROPPED QUOTATION

Many educators have been intrigued by the concept of blended learning but have been unsure how to define it. "Blended learning is a formal education program in which a student learns at least in part through online delivery of content and instruction with some element of student control over time, place, and pace" (Horn & Staker, 2011, p. 4).

QUOTATION WITH SIGNAL PHRASE

Many educators have been intrigued by the concept of blended learning but have been unsure how to define it. As Horn and Staker (2011) have argued, "Blended learning is a formal education program in which a student learns at least in part through online delivery of content and instruction with some element of student control over time, place, and pace" (p. 4).

Using signal phrases with summaries and paraphrases

As with quotations, you should introduce most summaries and paraphrases with a signal phrase that mentions the author and the year and places the material in the context of your own writing. Readers will then understand where the summary or paraphrase begins.

Without the signal phrase (highlighted) in the following example, readers might think that only the last sentence is being cited, when in fact the whole paragraph is based on the source.

Watson (2008) reported that for American postsecondary students, technology is integral to their academic lives. Nearly three-quarters own their own laptops, and 83% have used a course management system for an online component of a class. Watson pointed out that online and blended learning models are even more widespread outside of the United States (p. 15).

There are times, however, when a summary or a paraphrase does not require a signal phrase naming the author. When the context makes clear where the cited material begins, you may omit the signal phrase and include the author's name and the year in parentheses.

Integrating statistics and other facts

When you are citing a statistic or another specific fact, a signal phrase is often not necessary. In most cases, readers will understand that the citation refers to the statistic or fact (not the whole paragraph).

> Of polled high school students, 43% said that they lacked
> confidence in their technological proficiency going into college and
> careers (Moeller & Reitzes, 2011).

There is nothing wrong, however, with using a signal phrase to introduce a statistic or another fact.

Putting source material in context

Readers should not have to guess why source material appears in your paper. If you use another writer's words, you must explain how they relate to your point. In other words, you must put the source in context. It's a good idea to embed a quotation between sentences of your own, introducing it with a signal phrase and following it up with interpretive comments that link the quotation to your paper's argument. (See also 60d.)

QUOTATION WITH EFFECTIVE CONTEXT

According to the International Society for Technology in Education (2016), "Student-centered learning moves students from passive receivers of information to active participants in their own discovery process. What students learn, how they learn it and how their learning is assessed are all driven by each individual student's needs and abilities." The results of student-centered learning have been positive, not only for academic achievement but also for student self-esteem. In this model of instruction, the teacher acts as a facilitator, and the students actively participate in the process of learning and teaching.

Using signal phrases in APA papers

To avoid monotony, try to vary both the language and the placement of your signal phrases.

Model signal phrases

In the words of Mitra (2013), ". . ."

As Bell (2010) has noted, ". . ."

Donitsa-Schmidt and Zuzovsky (2014), educational researchers,
pointed out that ". . ."

". . . ," claimed Çubukçu (2012).

". . . ," explained Demski (2012), ". . ."

Horn and Staker (2011) have offered a compelling argument for
this view: ". . ."

Moeller and Reitzes (2011) answered objections with the following
analysis: ". . ."

Verbs in signal phrases

admitted	contended	reasoned
agreed	declared	refuted
argued	denied	rejected
asserted	emphasized	reported
believed	insisted	responded
claimed	noted	suggested
compared	observed	thought
confirmed	pointed out	wrote

60d Synthesize sources.

When you synthesize multiple sources in a research paper, you
create a conversation about your research topic. You show readers how the ideas of one source relate to those of another by connecting and analyzing the ideas in the context of your argument.

Keep the emphasis on your own writing. The thread of your argument should be easy to identify and to understand, with or without your sources.

SAMPLE SYNTHESIS

Student writer April Wang begins with a claim that needs support.

A signal phrase indicates how the source contributes to Wang's paper and shows that the ideas that follow are not her own.

Wang extends the argument and sets up two additional sources.

Wang closes the paragraph by interpreting the source and connecting it to her claim.

It is clear that educational technology will continue to play a role in student and school performance. Horn and Staker (2011) acknowledged that they focused on programs in which integration of educational technology led to improved student performance. In other schools, technological learning is simply distance learning—watching a remote teacher—and not student-centered learning that allows students to partner with teachers to develop enriching learning experiences. That said, many educators seem convinced that educational technology has the potential to help them transition from traditional teacher-driven learning to student-centered learning. All four schools in the Stanford study heavily relied on technology (Friedlaender et al., 2014). And indeed, Demski (2012) argued that technology is not supplemental but instead is "central" to student-centered learning (p. 33). Rather than turning to a teacher as the source of information, students are sent to investigate solutions to problems by searching online, e-mailing experts, collaborating with one another in a wiki space, or completing online practice. Rather than turning to a teacher for the answer to a question, students are driven to perform—driven to use technology to find those answers themselves.

Student writer

Source 1

Student writer

Source 2

Source 3

Student writer

In this synthesis, Wang uses her own analyses to shape the conversation among her sources. She does not simply string quotations and statistics together or allow her sources to overwhelm her writing. The final sentence, written in her own voice, gives her an opportunity to explain to readers how her sources support and extend her argument.

When synthesizing sources, ask yourself these questions:

- How do your sources address your research question?

- How do your sources respond to each other's ideas?

- Have you varied the functions of sources—to provide background, explain concepts, lend authority, and anticipate counterarguments? Do your signal phrases indicate these functions?

- Do you explain how your sources support your argument?

- Do you connect and analyze sources in your own voice?

- Is your own argument easy to identify and to understand, with or without your sources?

61 APA documentation style

In most social science classes, you will be asked to use the APA system for documenting sources, which is set forth in the *Publication Manual of the American Psychological Association*, 6th ed. (Washington, DC: APA, 2010).

APA recommends in-text citations that refer readers to a list of references. An in-text citation gives the author of the source (often in a signal phrase), the year of publication, and often a page number in parentheses. At the end of the paper, a list of references provides publication

> **MORE HELP**
>
> A reference list includes all the sources cited in the text of a paper.
>
> ▸ APA reference list: 61b
> ▸ Preparing the reference list: 62a
> ▸ Sample reference list: page 752

Directory to APA in-text citation models

1. Basic format for a quotation, 695
2. Basic format for a summary or a paraphrase, 695
3. Work with two authors, 696
4. Work with three to five authors, 696
5. Work with six or more authors, 697
6. Work with unknown author, 697
7. Organization as author, 697
8. Authors with the same last name, 698
9. Two or more works by the same author in the same year, 698
10. Two or more works in the same parentheses, 698
11. Multiple citations to the same work in one paragraph, 698
12. Web source, 699
    a. No page numbers, 699
    b. Unknown author, 699
    c. Unknown date, 700
13. An entire Web site, 700
14. Multivolume work, 700
15. Personal communication, 700
16. Course materials, 701
17. Part of a source (chapter, figure), 701
18. Indirect source (source quoted in another source), 701
19. Sacred or classical text, 701

information about the source; the list is alphabetized by authors' last names (or by titles for works with no authors). The direct link between the in-text citation and the entry in the reference list is highlighted in the following example.

IN-TEXT CITATION

Bell (2010) reported that students engaged in this kind of learning performed better on both project-based assessments and standardized tests (pp. 39-40).

ENTRY IN THE LIST OF REFERENCES

Bell, S. (2010). Project-based learning for the 21st century: Skills for the future. *The Clearing House, 83*(2), 39-43.

For a reference list that includes this entry, see page 752.

61a APA in-text citations

APA's in-text citations provide the author's last name and the year of publication, usually before the cited material, and a page number in parentheses directly after the cited material. In the following models, the elements of the in-text citation are highlighted.

NOTE: APA style requires the use of the past tense or the present perfect tense in signal phrases introducing cited material: *Smith (2012) reported, Smith (2012) has argued.* (See also p. 688.)

1. Basic format for a quotation Ordinarily, introduce the quotation with a signal phrase that includes the author's last name followed by the year of publication in parentheses. Put the page number (preceded by "p.") in parentheses after the quotation. For sources from the Web without page numbers, see item 12a on page 699.

> Çubukçu (2012) argued that for a student-centered approach to work, students must maintain "ownership for their goals and activities" (p. 64).

If the author is not named in the signal phrase, place the author's name, the year, and the page number in parentheses after the quotation: (Çubukçu, 2012, p. 64). (See items 6 and 12 for citing sources that lack authors; item 12 also explains how to handle sources without dates or page numbers.)

NOTE: Do not include a month in an in-text citation, even if the entry in the reference list includes the month.

2. Basic format for a summary or a paraphrase As for a quotation (see item 1), include the author's last name and the year either in a signal phrase introducing the material or in parentheses following it. Use a page number, if one is available, following the cited material. For sources from the Web without page numbers, see item 12a on page 699.

Watson (2008) offered a case study of the Cincinnati Public Schools Virtual High School, which brought students together in a physical school building to work with an assortment of online learning programs. Although there were only 10 certified teachers in the building, students were able to engage in highly individualized instruction according to their own needs, strengths, and learning styles, using the 10 teachers as support (p. 7).

The Cincinnati Public Schools Virtual High School brought students together in a physical school building to work with an assortment of online learning programs. Although there were only 10 certified teachers in the building, students were able to engage in highly individualized instruction according to their own needs, strengths, and learning styles, using the 10 teachers as support (Watson, 2008, p. 7).

3. Work with two authors   Name both authors in the signal phrase or in parentheses each time you cite the work. In the parentheses, use "&" between the authors' names; in the signal phrase, use "and."

According to Donitsa-Schmidt and Zuzovsky (2014), "demographic growth in the school population" can lead to teacher shortages (p. 426).

In the United States, most public school systems are struggling with teacher shortages, which are projected to worsen as the number of applicants to education schools decreases (Donitsa-Schmidt & Zuzovsky, 2014, p. 420).

4. Work with three to five authors   Identify all authors in the signal phrase or in parentheses the first time you cite the source.

In 2013, Harper, Findlen, Ibori, and Wenz studied teachers' perceptions of project-based learning (PBL) before and after participating in a PBL pilot program.

In subsequent citations, use the first author's name followed by "et al." in either the signal phrase or the parentheses.

Surprisingly, Harper et al. (2013) advised school administrators "not to jump into project-based pedagogy without training and feedback."

5. Work with six or more authors Use the first author's name followed by "et al." in the signal phrase or in parentheses.

Hermann et al. (2012) tracked 42 students over a three-year period to look closely at the performance of students in the laptop program (p. 49).

6. Work with unknown author If the author is unknown, mention the work's title in the signal phrase or give the first word or two of the title in the parentheses. Titles of short works such as articles are put in quotation marks; titles of long works such as books and reports are italicized.

Collaboration increases significantly among students who own or have regular access to a laptop ("Tech Seeds," 2015).

NOTE: In the rare case when "Anonymous" is specified as the author, treat it as if it were a real name: (Anonymous, 2011). In the list of references, also use the name Anonymous as author.

7. Organization as author If the author is an organization or a government agency, name the organization in the signal phrase or in the parentheses the first time you cite the source.

According to the International Society for Technology in Education (2016), "Student-centered learning moves students from passive receivers of information to active participants in their own discovery process."

If the organization has a familiar abbreviation, you may include it in brackets the first time you cite the source and use the abbreviation alone in later citations.

FIRST CITATION	(Texas Higher Education Coordinating Board [THECB], 2012)
LATER CITATIONS	(THECB, 2012)

8. Authors with the same last name To avoid confusion if your reference list includes two or more authors with the same last name, use initials with the last names in your in-text citations.

> Research by E. Smith (1989) revealed that . . .

> One 2012 study contradicted . . . (R. Smith, p. 234).

9. Two or more works by the same author in the same year When your list of references includes more than one work by the same author in the same year, you will use lowercase letters ("a," "b," and so on) with the year to order the entries in the reference list. (See item 8 on p. 708.) Use those same letters with the year in the in-text citation.

> Research by Durgin (2013b) has yielded new findings about the role of smartphones in the classroom.

10. Two or more works in the same parentheses Put the works in the same order that they appear in the reference list, separated with semicolons.

> Researchers have indicated that studies of educational technology initiatives reveal the high cost of change (Nazer, 2015; Serrao et al., 2014).

11. Multiple citations to the same work in one paragraph If you give the author's name in the text of your paper (not in parentheses) and you mention that source again in the text of the same paragraph, give only the author's name, not the date, in the later citation. If any subsequent reference in the same paragraph is in parentheses, include both the author and the date in the parentheses.

> Principal Jean Patrice said, "You have to be able to reach students where they are instead of making them come to you. If you don't, you'll lose them" (personal communication, April 10, 2006). Patrice expressed her desire to

see all students get something out of their educational experience. This feeling is common among members of Waverly's faculty. With such a positive view of student potential, it is no wonder that 97% of Waverly High School graduates go on to a four-year university (Patrice, 2006).

12. Web source   Cite sources from the Web as you would cite any other source, giving the author and the year when they are available.

Atkinson (2011) found that children who spent at least four hours a day engaged in online activities in an academic environment were less likely to want to play video games or watch TV after school.

Usually a page number is not available; occasionally a Web source will lack an author or a date (see 12a, 12b, and 12c).

a. No page numbers   When a Web source lacks stable numbered pages, you may include paragraph numbers or headings to help readers locate the passage being cited.

If the source has numbered paragraphs, use the paragraph number preceded by the abbreviation "para.": (Hall, 2012, para. 5). If the source has no numbered paragraphs but contains headings, cite the appropriate heading in parentheses; you may also indicate which paragraph under the heading you are referring to, even if the paragraphs are not numbered.

Crush and Jayasingh (2015) pointed out that several other school districts in low-income areas had "jump-started their distance learning initiatives with available grant funds" ("Funding Change," para. 6).

NOTE: For PDF documents that have stable page numbers, give the page number in the parenthetical citation.

b. Unknown author   If no author is named in the source, mention the title of the source in a signal phrase or give the first word or two of the title in parentheses (see also item 6). (If an organization serves as the author, see item 7.)

12. Web source (*cont.*)

> A student's IEP may, in fact, recommend the use of mobile technology
> ("Considerations," 2012).

c. Unknown date   When the source does not give a date, use the abbreviation "n.d." (for "no date").

> Administrators believe 1-to-1 programs boost learner engagement
> (Magnus, n.d.).

13. An entire Web site   If you are citing an entire Web site, not an internal page or a section, give the URL in the text of your paper but do not include it in the reference list.

> The Berkeley Center for Teaching and Learning website (https://
> teaching.berkeley.edu/) shares ideas for using mobile technology in the
> classroom.

14. Multivolume work   If you have used more than one volume from a multivolume work, add the volume number in parentheses with the page number.

> Banford (2013) has demonstrated steady increases in performance since
> the program began a decade ago (Vol. 2, p. 135).

15. Personal communication   Interviews that you conduct, memos, letters, e-mail messages, social media posts, and similar communications that would be difficult for your readers to retrieve should be cited in the text only, not in the reference list. (Use the first initial with the last name in parentheses.)

> One of Yim's colleagues, who has studied the effect of social media
> on children's academic progress, has contended that the benefits of
> this technology for children under 12 years old are few (F. Johnson,
> personal communication, October 20, 2013).

16. Course materials Cite lecture notes from your instructor or your own class notes as personal communication (see item 15). If your instructor distributes or posts materials that contain publication information, cite as you would the appropriate source (for instance, an article, a section in a Web document, or a video). See also item 65 on page 733.

17. Part of a source (chapter, figure) To cite a specific part of a source, such as a whole chapter or a figure or table, identify the element in parentheses. Don't abbreviate terms such as "Figure," "Chapter," and "Section"; "page" is always abbreviated "p." (or "pp." for more than one page).

> The data support the finding that peer relationships are difficult to replicate in a completely online environment (Hanniman, 2010, Figure 8-3, p. 345).

18. Indirect source (source quoted in another source) When a writer's or a speaker's quoted words appear in a source written by someone else, begin the parenthetical citation with the words "as cited in." In the following example, Demski is the author of the source given in the reference list; that source contains a quotation by Cator.

> Karen Cator, director of the U.S. Department of Education's Office of Educational Technology, calls technology "the essence" of a personalized learning environment (as cited in Demski, 2012, p. 34).

19. Sacred or classical text Identify the text, the version or edition you used, and the relevant part (chapter, verse, line). It is not necessary to include the source in the reference list.

> Peace activists have long cited the biblical prophet's vision of a world without war: "And they shall beat their swords into plowshares, and their spears into pruning hooks; nation shall not lift up sword against nation, neither shall they learn war any more" (Isaiah 2:4, Revised Standard Version).

Directory to APA reference list models

General guidelines for listing authors

1. Single author, 706
2. Two to seven authors, 707
3. Eight or more authors, 707
4. Organization as author, 707
5. Unknown author, 708
6. Author using a pseudonym (pen name) or screen name, 708
7. Two or more works by the same author, 708
8. Two or more works by the same author in the same year, 708
9. Editor, 709
10. Author and editor, 709
11. Translator, 709
12. Editor and translator, 709

Articles and other short works

13. Article in a journal, 710
    a. Print, 710
    b. Web, 710
    c. Database, 711
14. Article in a magazine, 711
    a. Print, 711
    b. Web, 711
    c. Database, 711
15. Article in a newspaper, 715
    a. Print, 715
    b. Web, 715
16. Abstract, 715
    a. Abstract of a journal article, 715
    b. Abstract of a paper, 716
17. Supplemental material, 716
18. Article with a title in its title, 716
19. Letter to the editor, 716

20. Editorial or other unsigned article, 716
21. Newsletter article, 717
22. Review, 717
23. Published interview, 717
24. Article in a dictionary or an encyclopedia (including a wiki), 718
    a. Print, 718
    b. Web, 718
25. Comment on an online article, 718
26. Testimony before a legislative body, 718
27. Paper presented at a meeting or symposium (unpublished), 718
28. Poster session at a conference, 719

Books and other long works

29. Basic format for a book, 719
    a. Print, 719
    b. Web (or online library), 719
    c. E-book, 719
    d. Database, 721
30. Edition other than the first, 721
31. Selection in an anthology or a collection, 721
    a. Entire anthology, 721
    b. Selection in an anthology, 721
32. Multivolume work, 722
    a. All volumes, 722
    b. One volume, with title, 722
33. Introduction, preface, foreword, or afterword, 722
34. Dictionary or other reference work, 722
35. Republished book, 722
36. Book with a title in its title, 722
37. Book in a language other than English, 723

Directory to APA reference list models (cont.)

38. Dissertation, 723
   a. Published, 723
   b. Unpublished, 723
39. Conference proceedings, 723
40. Government document, 723
41. Report from a private organization, 724
42. Legal source, 724
43. Sacred or classical text, 724

Web sites and parts of Web sites

44. Entire Web site, 725
45. Document from a Web site, 725
46. Section in a Web document, 725
47. Blog post, 728
48. Blog comment, 728

Audio, visual, and multimedia sources

49. Podcast, 728
50. Video or audio on the Web, 728
51. Transcript of an audio or a video file, 729
52. Film (DVD, BD, or other format), 729
53. Television or radio program, 729
   a. Series, 729

   b. Episode on the air, 730
   c. Episode on the Web, 730
54. Music recording, 730
55. Lecture, speech, or address, 730
56. Data set or graphic representation of data (graph, chart, table), 731
57. Mobile application software (app), 731
58. Video game, 731
59. Map, 732
60. Advertisement, 732
61. Work of art or photograph, 732
62. Brochure or fact sheet, 732
63. Press release, 733
64. Presentation slides, 733
65. Lecture notes or other course materials, 733

Personal communication and social media

66. E-mail, 733
67. Online posting, 734
68. Twitter post (tweet), 734
69. Facebook post, 734

61b APA list of references

As you gather sources for an assignment, you will likely find sources in print, on the Web, and in other places. The information you will need for the reference list at the end of your paper will differ slightly for some sources, but the main principles apply to all sources: You should identify an author, a creator, or a producer whenever possible; give a title; and provide the date on which the source was produced.

Some sources will require page numbers; some will require a publisher; and some will require retrieval information.

Section 61b provides specific requirements for and examples of many of the sources you are likely to encounter. When you cite sources, your goals are to show that the sources you've used are reliable and relevant to your work, to provide your readers with enough information so that they can find your sources easily, and to provide that information in a consistent way according to APA conventions.

In the list of references, include only sources that you have quoted, summarized, or paraphrased in your paper.

General guidelines for listing authors

The formatting of authors' names in items 1–12 (beginning on p. 706) applies to all sources in print and on the Web — books, articles, Web sites, and so on. For more models of specific source types, see items 13–69.

General guidelines for the reference list

In APA style, the alphabetical list of works cited, which appears at the end of the paper, is titled "References."

Authors and dates

- Alphabetize entries in the list of references by authors' last names; if a work has no author, alphabetize it by its title.

- For all authors' names, put the last name first, followed by a comma; use initials for the first and middle names.

- With two or more authors, use an ampersand (&) before the last author's name. Separate the names with commas. Include names for the first seven authors; if there are eight or more authors, give the first six authors, three ellipsis dots, and the last author.

- If the author is a company or an organization, give the name in normal order.

GENERAL GUIDELINES FOR THE REFERENCE LIST (*cont.*)

- Put the date of publication immediately after the first element of the citation. Enclose the date in parentheses, followed by a period (outside the parentheses).

- For books, give the year of publication. For magazines, newspapers, and newsletters, give the exact date as in the publication (the year plus the month or the year plus the month and the day). For sources on the Web, give the date of posting, if it is available. Use the season if the publication gives only a season and not a month.

Titles

- Italicize the titles and subtitles of books, journals, and other long works.

- Use no italics or quotation marks for the titles of articles.

- For books and articles, capitalize only the first word of the title and subtitle and all proper nouns.

- For the titles of journals, magazines, and newspapers, capitalize all words of four letters or more (and all nouns, pronouns, verbs, adjectives, and adverbs of any length).

Place of publication and publisher (books)

- Take the information from the title page and copyright page. If more than one place of publication is listed, use only the first.

- Give the city and state for all US cities. Use postal abbreviations for all states.

- Give the city and country for all non-US cities; include the province for Canadian cities. Do not abbreviate the country and province.

- Do not give a state if the publisher's name includes it (Ann Arbor: University of Michigan Press, for example).

- In publishers' names, omit terms such as "Company" (or "Co.") and "Inc." but keep "Books" and "Press." Omit first names or initials (Norton, not W. W. Norton, for example).

- If the publisher is the same as the author, use the word "Author" in the publisher position.

GENERAL GUIDELINES FOR THE REFERENCE LIST (*cont.*)

Volume, issue, and page numbers (articles)

- For a journal or a magazine, give only the volume number if the publication is paginated continuously through each volume; give the volume and issue numbers if each issue begins on page 1.

- Italicize the volume number and put the issue number, not italicized, in parentheses.

- For monthly magazines, give the year and the month; for weekly magazines, add the day.

- For daily and weekly newspapers, give the month, day, and year; use "p." or "pp." before page numbers (if any). For journals and magazines, do not add "p." or "pp."

- When an article appears on consecutive pages, provide the range of pages. When an article does not appear on consecutive pages, give all page numbers: A1, A17.

URLs, DOIs, and other retrieval information

- For articles and books from the Web, use the DOI (digital object identifier) if the source has one, and do not give a URL. If a source does not have a DOI, give the URL.

- Use a retrieval date for a Web source only if the content is likely to change. Most of the examples in 61b do not show a retrieval date because the content of the sources is stable. If you are unsure about whether to use a retrieval date, include the date or consult your instructor.

1. Single author

author: last name + initial(s) — year (book) — title (book) — place of publication — publisher

Yanagihara, H. (2015). *A little life.* New York, NY: Doubleday.

2. Two to seven authors List up to seven authors by last names followed by initials. Use an ampersand (&) before the name of the last author. (See items 3–5 on pp. 696–97 for citing works with multiple authors in the text of your paper.)

all authors: year
last name + initial(s)   (book)   title (book)

Stanford, D. J., & Bradley, B. A. (2012). *Across the Atlantic ice: The origins of*

place of
publication   publisher

America's Clovis culture. Berkeley: University of California Press.

all authors: year
last name + initial(s)   (journal)

Hurtley, F., Roberts, L., Ray, L. B., Purnell, B. A., & Ash, C. (2014).

journal
title (article)   title   volume   page(s)

Putting off the inevitable. *Science, 350,* 1180-1181.

DOI

doi:10.1126/science.aad3267

3. Eight or more authors List the first six authors followed by three ellipsis dots and the last author's name.

Datta, S. J., Khumnoon, C., Lee, Z. H., Moon, W. K., Docao, S., Nguyen,

    T. H., . . . Yoon, K. B. (2015). CO_2 capture from humid flue gases and

    humid atmosphere using a microporous coppersilicate. *Science, 350,*

    302-306. doi:10.1126/science.aab1680

4. Organization as author

author:
organization name   year   title (book)

American Psychiatric Association. (2013). *Diagnostic and statistical manual of*

organization
place   as author
edition   of publication   and publisher

mental disorders (5th ed.). Washington, DC: Author.

5. Unknown author   Begin the entry with the work's title.

| | year + month + day | | volume, | |
| title (article) | (weekly publication) | journal title | issue | page(s) |

The rise of the sharing economy. (2013, March 9). *The Economist, 406*(8826), 14.

| | | | place of | |
| title (book) | edition | year | publication | publisher |

New concise world atlas (4th ed.). (2013). New York, NY: Oxford University Press.

6. Author using a pseudonym (pen name) or screen name   Use the author's real name, if known, and give the pseudonym or screen name in brackets exactly as it appears in the source. If only the screen name is known, begin with that name and do not use brackets. (See also items 47 and 68 on citing screen names in social media.)

| | year + month + day | |
| screen name | (daily publication) | title of original article |

BasicInstinct. (2015, December 4). Re: U.S. economy added 211,000 jobs in

| | label |
| | |

November; unemployment rate holds at 5 percent [Comment].

| title of publication | URL for Web publication |
| | |

The Washington Post. Retrieved from http://washingtonpost.com/

7. Two or more works by the same author   Use the author's name for all entries. List the entries by year, the earliest first.

Coates, T. (2008). *The beautiful struggle*. New York, NY: Spiegel & Grau.

Coates, T. (2015). *Between the world and me*. New York, NY: Spiegel & Grau.

8. Two or more works by the same author in the same year   List the works alphabetically by title. In the parentheses, following the year add "a," "b," and so on. Use these same letters when giving the year in the in-text citation. (See also p. 739 and item 9 on p. 698.)

Bower, B. (2012a, December 15). Families in flux. *Science News, 182*(12), 16.

Bower, B. (2012b, November 3). Human-Neandertal mating gets a new date.
   Science News, 182(9), 8.

9. Editor Begin with the name of the editor or editors; place the abbreviation "Ed." (or "Eds." for more than one editor) in parentheses following the name. (See item 10 for a work with both an author and an editor.)

<pre>
   all editors:
last name + initial(s)   year   title (book)
</pre>
Rohleder, P., & Lyons, A. (Eds.). (2014). *Qualitative research in clinical and*

<pre>
                    place of
                  publication   publisher
</pre>
health psychology. New York, NY: Palgrave.

10. Author and editor Begin with the name of the author, followed by the name of the editor and the abbreviation "Ed." For an author with two or more editors, use the abbreviation "Ed." after each editor's name: Gray, W., & Jones, P. (Ed.), & Smith, A. (Ed.).

<pre>
  author   editor   year   title (book)
</pre>
James, W., & Pelikan, J. (Ed.). (2009). *The varieties of religious experience.*

<pre>
    place of   original
  publication   publisher   publication information
</pre>
New York, NY: Library of America. (Original work published 1902)

11. Translator Begin with the name of the author. After the title, in parentheses place the name of the translator (in normal order) and the abbreviation "Trans." (for "Translator"). Add the original date of publication at the end of the entry.

<pre>
  author   year   title (book)
</pre>
Murakami, H. (2014). *Colorless Tsukuru Tazaki and his years of pilgrimage*

<pre>
                    place of   original
  translator   publication   publisher   publication information
</pre>
(P. Gabriel, Trans.). Cambridge, England: Knopf. (Original work published 2013)

12. Editor and translator If the editor and translator are the same person, the same name appears in both the editor position and the translator position.

Girard, R., & Williams, J. G. (Ed.). (2012). *Resurrection from the underground*
(J. G. Williams, Trans.). East Lansing: Michigan State University Press.
(Original work published 1996)

Articles and other short works

- ▶ Citation at a glance: Article in a journal or magazine, page 712
- ▶ Citation at a glance: Article from a database, page 714

13. Article in a journal If an article from the Web or a database has no DOI, include the URL for the journal's home page.

a. Print

authors: last name + initial(s) | year | article title

Terry, C. P., & Terry, D. L. (2015). Cell phone-related near accidents among

journal title

young drivers: Associations with mindfulness. *The Journal of Psychology,*

volume page(s)
149, 665-683.

b. Web

all authors:
last name + initial(s) | year | article title

Vargas, N., & Schafer, M. H. (2015). Cultural capital in context: Heterogeneous

journal title

returns to cultural capital across schooling environments. *Social Science*

volume,
issue page(s) | DOI

Research, 50(1), 177-188. doi:10.1016/j.ssresearch.2014.11.015

all authors:
last name + initial(s) | year | article title

Eavers, E. R., Berry, M. A., & Rodriguez, D. N. (2015). The effects of

counterfactual thinking on college students' intentions to quit smoking

journal title (no volume available)

cigarettes. *Current Research in Social Psychology.* Retrieved from

URL for journal home page

http://www.uiowa.edu/~grpproc/crisp/crisp.html

c. Database

author | year (journal) | | article title
Lyons, M. (2015). Writing up: How the weak wrote to the powerful. *Journal of*

journal title | volume, issue | page(s) | DOI
Social History, 49(2), 317-330. doi:10.1093/jsh/shv038

14. Article in a magazine If an article from the Web or a database has no DOI, include the URL for the magazine's home page.

a. Print

author | year + month (monthly magazine) | article title | magazine title
Paris, W. (2015, March/April). The new survivors. *Psychology Today,*

volume, issue | page(s)
48(2), 66-73, 82.

b. Web

author | date of posting (when available) | article title
Bensman, D. (2015, December 4). Security for a precarious workforce.

magazine title | URL for home page
The American Prospect. Retrieved from http://prospect.org/

c. Database

author | year + month + day (weekly magazine) | article title | magazine title | volume, issue
Thompson, M. (2015, December 3). Sending women to war. *Time, 186*(24),

page(s) | URL for magazine home page
52-55. Retrieved from http://time.com/

Citation at a glance

Article in a journal or magazine APA

To cite an article in a print journal or magazine in APA style, include the following elements:

1. Author(s)
2. Year of publication for journal; complete date for magazine
3. Title and subtitle of article
4. Name of journal or magazine
5. Volume number; issue number, if required (see p. 706)
6. Page number(s) of article

JOURNAL TABLE OF CONTENTS

FIRST PAGE OF ARTICLE

feature

School Choice Marches Forward

One year ago, the *Wall Street Journal* dubbed 2011 "the year of school choice," opining that "this year is shaping up as the best for reformers in a very long time." Such quotes were bound to circulate among education reformers and give traditional opponents of school choice, such as teachers unions, heartburn. Thirteen states enacted new programs that allow K–12 students to choose a public or private school instead of attending their assigned school, and similar bills were under consideration in more than two dozen states.

With so much activity, school choice moved from the margins of education reform debates and became the headline. In January 2012, *Washington Post* education reporter Michael Alison Chandler said school choice has become "a mantra of 21st-century education reform," citing policy across the country have traditional public schools competing for students alongside charter schools and private schools.

"It took us 20 years to pass 20 private school-choice programs in America and in the 21st year we passed 13 new programs," says Scott Jensen of the American Federation for Children,

2011
a year of
new laws
and
new lawsuits

By
JONATHAN BUTCHER

a school-choice advocacy group based in Washington, D.C. "So we went from passing, on average, one each year, to seven in one fell swoop."

Programs enacted in 2011 include
• a tax-credit scholarship program in North Carolina
• Arizona's education savings account system for K–12 students
• Maine's new charter school law, which brings the total number of states, along with the District of

WINTER 2013 / EDUCATION NEXT   **21**

REFERENCE LIST ENTRY FOR AN ARTICLE IN A PRINT JOURNAL OR MAGAZINE

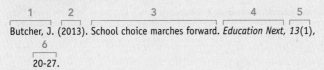

Butcher, J. (2013). School choice marches forward. *Education Next, 13*(1), 20-27.

For more on citing articles in APA style, see items 13–15.

713

Citation at a glance

Article from a database APA

To cite an article from a database in APA style, include the following elements:

1 Author(s)
2 Year of publication for journal; complete date for magazine or newspaper
3 Title and subtitle of article
4 Name of periodical
5 Volume number; issue number, if required (see p. 706)
6 Page number(s)
7 DOI (digital object identifier)
8 URL for periodical's home page (if there is no DOI)

DATABASE RECORD

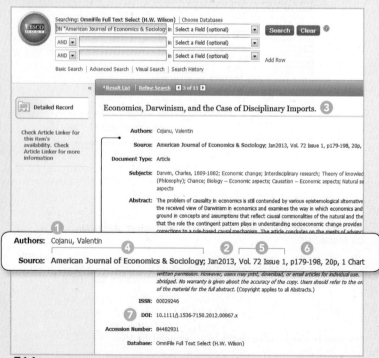

REFERENCE LIST ENTRY FOR AN ARTICLE FROM A DATABASE

<u>1</u> <u>2</u> <u>3</u>

Cojanu, V. (2013). Economics, Darwinism, and the case of disciplinary

<u>4</u> <u>5</u> <u>6</u>

imports. *American Journal of Economics & Sociology, 72*, 179-198.

<u>7</u>

doi:10.1111/j.1536-7150.2012.00867.x

For more on citing articles from a database in APA style, see items 13–15.

15. Article in a newspaper

a. Print

author year + month + day article title

Saul, S. (2015, December 6). Colleges pile renovation costs onto the

newspaper title page(s)

plates of students. *The New York Times*, pp. 1, 18.

b. Web

author year + month + day article title

Roberson, K. (2015, May 3). Innovation helps address nurse shortage.

newspaper title URL for home page

Des Moines Register. Retrieved from http://www.desmoinesregister.com/

16. Abstract   Add the label "Abstract," in brackets, after the title.

a. Abstract of a journal article

Heyman, G. D., Fu, G., Lin, J., Qian, M., & Lee, K. (2015). Eliciting promises
from children reduces cheating [Abstract]. *Journal of Experimental Child
Psychology, 139*, 242-248. Retrieved from http://www.sciencedirect.com/

16. Abstract (*cont.*)

b. Abstract of a paper

Chung, J. E. (2015). A smoking cessation campaign on Twitter: Understanding the use of Twitter and identifying major players in a health campaign [Abstract]. Paper presented at the AEJMC 2015 Conference, San Francisco, CA. Retrieved from http://www.aejmc.org/home/2015/06/2015-abstracts/

17. Supplemental material If an article on the Web contains supplemental material that is not part of the main article, cite the material as you would an article and add the label "Supplemental material" in brackets following the title.

Hansen, J. D., & Reich, J. (2015). Democratizing education? Examining access and usage patterns in massive open online courses [Supplemental material]. *Science, 350*(6265), 1245-1248. doi:10.1126/science.290.5494.1148

18. Article with a title in its title If an article title contains another article title or a term usually placed in quotation marks, use quotation marks around the internal title or the term.

Easterling, D., & Millesen, J. L. (2012, Summer). Diversifying civic leadership: What it takes to move from "new faces" to adaptive problem solving. *National Civic Review, 101*(2), 20-27. doi:10.1002/ncr.21073

19. Letter to the editor Insert the words "Letter to the editor" in brackets after the title of the letter. If the letter has no title, use the bracketed words as the title (as in the following example).

Lange, F. (2014, May-June). [Letter to the editor]. *Sierra*. Retrieved from http://www.sierraclub.org/sierra/

20. Editorial or other unsigned article

The business case for transit dollars [Editorial]. (2012, December 9). *Star Tribune*. Retrieved from http://www.startribune.com/

21. Newsletter article Cite as you would an article in a magazine, giving whatever publication information is available (volume, issue, page numbers, and so on).

Scrivener, L. (n.d.). Why is the minimum wage issue important for food
justice advocates? *Food Workers—Food Justice, 15.* Retrieved from
http://www.thedatabank.com/dpg/199/pm.asp?nav=1&ID=41429

22. Review Give the author and title of the review (if any) and, in brackets, the type of work, the title, and the author for a book or the year for a film. If the review has no author or title, use the material in brackets as the title.

author
of review | year
(journal) | book title

Chernus, L. A. (2014). [Review of the book *Therapist in mourning: From the*

book author(s) | journal title

faraway nearby, by A. J. Adelman & K. J. Malawista]. *Psychotherapy,*

volume,
issue | page(s) | DOI

51(3), 464-465. doi:10.1037/a0036509

author | year + month(s)
(magazine) | review title

Pinkerton, N. (2016, January/February). Review: *In the shadow of women*

film title | year
(film)

[Review of the motion picture *In the shadow of women*, 2015].

magazine title | volume,
issue | URL

Film Comment, 52(1). Retrieved from http://www.filmcomment.com/

23. Published interview Begin with the person interviewed, and put the interviewer in brackets following the title (if any).

Al-Jeraisy, H. (2016, January 8). An interview with a female Saudi councillor
[Interview by Z. M. Beddoes]. *The Economist.* Retrieved from http://
www.economist.com/

24. Article in a dictionary or an encyclopedia (including a wiki)

a. Print   See also item 32 on citing one volume in a multivolume work.

Konijn, E. A. (2015). Health communication. In W. Donsbach (Ed.), *The concise encyclopedia of communication* (Vol. 1, pp. 240-242). Malden, MA: Blackwell.

b. Web

Actor-network theory (ANT). (2011, February 22). In *STS wiki*. Retrieved December 10, 2015, from http://www.stswiki.org/index .php?title=Actor-network_theory_(ANT)

25. Comment on an online article   Begin with the writer's real name or screen name. If both are given, put the real name first, followed by the screen name in brackets. Before the title, use "Re" and a colon. Add "Comment" in brackets following the title.

MintDragon. (2015, December 9). Re: The very real pain of exclusion [Comment]. *The Atlantic*. Retrieved from http://www.theatlantic.com/

26. Testimony before a legislative body

Goodman, J. (2013, June 27). *Addressing the neglected diseases treatment gap*. Testimony before the Subcommittee on Africa, Global Health, Global Human Rights, and International Organizations of the U.S. House of Representatives Committee on Foreign Affairs. Retrieved from http://www.hhs.gov/asl/testify/2013/06/4484.html

27. Paper presented at a meeting or symposium (unpublished)

González-Nosti, M. (2015, July 3). *Creating visual representations in Alzheimer's disease*. Paper presented at the International Symposium of Psycholinguistics, Valencia, Spain.

28. Poster session at a conference

Kim, D., & Cho, M. (2015, July 2). *Orthographic processing in Korean-English bilinguals*. Poster session presented at the International Symposium of Psycholinguistics, Valencia, Spain.

Books and other long works

▸ Citation at a glance: Book, page 720

29. Basic format for a book

a. Print

author(s): last name + initial(s) | year | book title | place of publication

Southard, S. (2015). *Nagasaki: Life after nuclear war.* New York, NY:

publisher
Viking.

b. Web (or online library) Give the URL for the home page of the Web site or the online library.

author(s) or editor(s) | year | book title

Ansari, S., & Martin, V. (Eds.). (2014). *Women, religion, and culture in Iran.*

URL
Retrieved from http://books.google.com/

c. E-book Give the version in brackets after the title ("Kindle version," "Nook version," and so on). Include the DOI or, if a DOI is not available, the URL for the home page of the site from which you downloaded the book.

Wolf, D. A., & Folbre, N. (Eds.). (2012). *Universal coverage of long-term care in the United States* [Adobe Digital Editions version]. Retrieved from https://www.russellsage.org/

Citation at a glance
Book APA

To cite a print book in APA style, include the following elements:

1 Author(s)
2 Year of publication
3 Title and subtitle
4 Place of publication
5 Publisher

TITLE PAGE

CITY

A GUIDEBOOK FOR THE URBAN AGE

P. D. SMITH

FROM COPYRIGHT PAGE

First published in Great Britain and the USA in 2012

Bloomsbury Publishing Plc, 50 Bedford Square, London WC1B 3DP
Bloomsbury USA, 175 Fifth Avenue, New York, NY 10010

Copyright © 2012 by P. D. Smith

BLOOMSBURY
LONDON · BERLIN · NEW YORK · SYDNEY

5 BLOOMSBURY
4 LONDON · BERLIN · NEW YORK · SYDNEY

REFERENCE LIST ENTRY FOR A PRINT BOOK

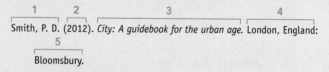

Smith, P. D. (2012). *City: A guidebook for the urban age.* London, England:
Bloomsbury.

For more on citing books in APA style, see items 29–37.

29. Basic format for a book (*cont.*)

d. Database   Give the URL for the database.

Bertz, N. (2015). *Diaspora and nation in the Indian Ocean: Transnational
histories of race and urban space in Tanzania.* Retrieved from http://
muse.jhu.edu/

30. Edition other than the first   Include the edition number
(abbreviated) in parentheses after the title.

Harvey, P. (2013). *An introduction to Buddhism: Teachings, history, and
practices* (2nd ed.). Cambridge, England: Cambridge University Press.

31. Selection in an anthology or a collection   An anthology is a
collection of works on a common theme, often with different authors
for the selections and usually with an editor for the entire volume.

a. Entire anthology

editor(s)   year

Amelina, A., Horvath, K., & Meeus, B. (Eds.). (2016). *An anthology of migration*

title of anthology   place of publication   publisher

and social transformation: European perspectives. Cham, Switzerland: Springer.

b. Selection in an anthology

author of selection   year   title of selection

Abdou, L. H. (2016). The Europeanization of immigration policies.

editors of anthology   title of anthology

In A. Amelina, K. Horvath, & B. Meeus (Eds.), *An anthology of migration*

page numbers of selection

and social transformation: European perspectives (pp. 105-119).

place of publication   publisher

Cham, Switzerland: Springer.

32. Multivolume work   If the volumes have been published over several years, give the span of years in parentheses. If you have used only one volume of a multivolume work, indicate the volume number after the title of the complete work; if the volume has its own title, add that title after the volume number.

a. All volumes

Khalakdina, M. (2008-2011). *Human development in the Indian context: A socio-cultural focus* (Vols. 1-2). New Delhi, India: Sage.

b. One volume, with title

Palmer, S., & Gyllensten, K. (Eds.). (2015). *Psychological stress, resilience, and wellbeing: Vol. 2. The measurement of stress.* London, England: Sage.

33. Introduction, preface, foreword, or afterword

Bloomberg, M. (2014). Foreword. In S. Goldsmith & S. Crawford, *The responsive city: Engaging communities through data-smart governing* (pp. v-vi). San Francisco, CA: Jossey-Bass.

34. Dictionary or other reference work

Leong, F. T. L. (Ed.). (2008). *Encyclopedia of counseling* (Vols. 1-4). Thousand Oaks, CA: Sage.

Nichols, J. D., & Nyholm, E. (2012). *A concise dictionary of Minnesota Ojibwe.* Minneapolis: University of Minnesota Press.

35. Republished book

Białoszewski, M. (2015). *Memoir of the Warsaw uprising* (M. G. Levine, Trans.). New York, NY: New York Review Books. (Original work published 1970)

36. Book with a title in its title   If the book title contains another book title or an article title, do not italicize the internal title and do not put quotation marks around it.

Marcus, L. (Ed.). (1999). *Sigmund Freud's* The interpretation of dreams: *New interdisciplinary essays*. Manchester, England: Manchester University Press.

37. Book in a language other than English Place the English translation, not italicized, in brackets.

Carminati, G. G., & Méndez, A. (2012). *Étapes de vie, étapes de soins* [Stages of life, stages of care]. Chêne-Bourg, Switzerland: Médecine & Hygiène.

38. Dissertation

a. Published

Moore, C. L. (2016). *Stress and oppression: Identifying possible protective factors for African American men* (Doctoral dissertation). Available from ProQuest Dissertations and Theses database. (AAT 3717844)

b. Unpublished

Morcos, S. M. (2015). *From Cairo to California: A journey through the lives and roles of Coptic women from Egypt to the diaspora* (Unpublished doctoral dissertation). Claremont Graduate University, Claremont, CA.

39. Conference proceedings

Liu, C.-C., Hiraoki, O., Kong, S. C., & Kasihara, A. (2014). *Proceedings of the 22nd International Conference on Computers in Education: ICCE 2014*. Retrieved from http://icce2014.jaist.ac.jp/icce2014/wp-content /uploads/2015/08/ICCE2014-Main-Proceedings-lite.pdf

40. Government document If the document has a number, place the number in parentheses after the title.

U.S. Transportation Department, Pipeline and Hazardous Materials Safety Administration. (2012). *Emergency response guidebook 2012*. Washington, DC: Author.

40. Government document (*cont.*)

U.S. Census Bureau, Bureau of Economic Analysis. (2015, December). *U.S. international trade in goods and services, October 2015* (Report No. CB15-197, BEA15-60, FT-900 [15-10]). Retrieved from http://www .census.gov/foreign-trade/Press-Release/current_press_release/ft900.pdf

41. Report from a private organization If the publisher and the author are the same, begin with the publisher. For a print source, use "Author" as the publisher at the end of the entry (see item 4 on p. 707); for an online source, give the URL. If the report has a number, put it in parentheses following the title.

Ford Foundation International Fellowships Program. (2014, September). *Linking higher education and social change*. Retrieved from http:// fordifp.net/portals/0/IFP%20PDF/IFP%20Final%20Publication.pdf

Atwood, B., Beam, M., Hindman, D. B., Hindman, E. B., Pintak, L., & Shors, B. (2012, May 25). *The Murrow Rural Information Initiative: Final report*. Pullman: Murrow College of Communication, Washington State University.

42. Legal source The title of a court case is italicized in an in-text citation, but it is not italicized in the reference list.

Sweatt v. Painter, 339 U.S. 629 (1950). Retrieved from Cornell University Law School, Legal Information Institute website: http://www.law.cornell .edu/supct/html/historics/USSC_CR_0339_0629_ZS.html

43. Sacred or classical text It is not necessary to list sacred works such as the Bible or the Qur'an or classical Greek and Roman works (such as the *Odyssey*) in your reference list. See item 19 on page 701 for how to cite these sources in the text of your paper.

Web sites and parts of Web sites

▶ Citation at a glance: Section in a Web document, page 726

NOTE: In an APA paper or an APA reference list entry, the word "website" is spelled as one word, all lowercase.

44. Entire Web site Do not include an entire Web site in the reference list. Give the URL in parentheses when you mention it in the text of your paper. (See item 13 on p. 700.)

45. Document from a Web site List as many of the following elements as are available: author's name, publication date (or "n.d." if there is no date), title (in italics), publisher (if any), and URL. If the publisher is known and is not named as the author, include the publisher in your retrieval statement.

Badrunnesha, M., & Kwauk, C. (2015, December). *Improving the quality of girls' education in madrasa in Bangladesh*. Retrieved from Brookings Institution website: http://www.brookings.edu/research /papers/2015/12/05-bangladesh-girls-education-madrasa-badrunnesha

Peters, M. (2015). *Open trade, closed borders: Immigration in the era of globalization*. Retrieved from Yale Institution for Social and Policy Studies website: http://isps.yale.edu/research/data/d131#.Vmkx47xll-U

Centers for Disease Control and Prevention. (2012, December 10). *Concussion in winter sports*. Retrieved from http://www.cdc.gov/Features /HockeyConcussions/index.html

46. Section in a Web document Cite as you would a chapter in a book or a selection in an anthology (see item 31b).

Pew Research Center. (2015, October 22). About the 2012 Current Population Survey. In *Self-employed workers and job creation*. Retrieved from http://www.pewsocialtrends.org/2015/10/22/three-in-ten-u-s-jobs-are -held-by-the-self-employed-and-the-workers-they-hire/

Chang, W.-Y., & Milan, L. M. (2012, October). Relationship between degree field and emigration. In *International mobility and employment characteristics among recent recipients of U.S. doctorates*. Retrieved from National Science Foundation website: http://www.nsf.gov/statistics /infbrief/nsf13300

Citation at a glance

Section in a Web document   APA

To cite a section in a Web document in APA style, include the following elements:

1   Author(s)
2   Date of publication or most recent update ("n.d." if there is no date)
3   Title of section
4   Title of document
5   URL of section

WEB DOCUMENT CONTENTS PAGE

5

http://www.health.state.mn.us/divs/chs/annsum/10annsum/Fertility2010.pdf

ON-SCREEN VIEW OF DOCUMENT

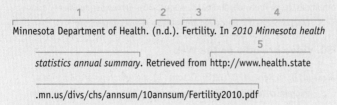

Fertility Table 1
Total Reported Pregnancies by Outcome and Rate
Minnesota Residents, 1981 - 2010

Year	Total Reported Pregnancies*	Live Births	Induced Abortions	Fetal Deaths	Female Population Ages 15-44	Pregnancy Rate**
1981	84,934	68,652	15,821	461	967,087	87.8
1982	84,500	68,512	15,559	429	977,905	86.4
1983	80,530	65,559	14,514	457	981,287	82.1
1984	82,736	66,715	15,556	465	985,608	83.9
1985	83,853	67,412	16,002	439	994,249	84.3
1986	81,882	65,766	15,716	400	997,501	82.1
1987	81,318	65,168	15,746	404	1,004,801	80.9
1988	83,335	66,745	16,124	466	1,020,209	81.7
1989	83,426	67,490	15,506	430	1,024,576	81.4
1990	83,714	67,985	15,280	449	1,025,919	81.6
1991	81,904	67,037	14,441	426	1,036,146	79.0
1992	79,844	65,591	13,846	407	1,049,175	76.1
1993	77,939	64,646	12,955	338	1,060,396	73.5
1994	78,344	64,277	13,702	365	1,073,649	73.0
1995	76,338	63,259	12,715	364	1,053,136	72.5
1996	76,909	63,681	12,876	352	1,066,220	72.1
1997	77,850	64,491	12,997	362	1,050,544	74.1
1998	78,646	65,207	13,050	389	1,054,458	74.6
1999	79,374	65,953	13,037	384	1,054,543	75.3
2000	81,039	67,451	13,200	388	1,082,642	74.9

REFERENCE LIST ENTRY FOR A SECTION IN A WEB DOCUMENT

1   2   3   4

Minnesota Department of Health. (n.d.). Fertility. In *2010 Minnesota health*

5

statistics annual summary. Retrieved from http://www.health.state

.mn.us/divs/chs/annsum/10annsum/Fertility2010.pdf

For more on citing documents from Web sites in APA style, see items 45 and 46.

47. Blog post Begin with the writer's real name or screen name. If both are given, put the real name first, followed by the screen name in brackets. Add the date of the post (or "n.d." if the post is undated). Place the label "Blog post" in brackets following the title of the post. If there is no title, use the bracketed material as the title. End with the URL for the post.

Costandi, M. (2015, April 9). Why brain scans aren't always what they seem [Blog post]. Retrieved from http://www.theguardian.com/science /neurophilosophy

48. Blog comment Cite as a blog post, but add "Re" and a colon before the title of the original post and the label "Blog comment" in brackets following the title.

mkt42. (2015, November 9). Re: Big data and the logic of consumerism [Blog comment]. Retrieved from https://www.insidehighered.com/blogs /library-babel-fish/big-data-and-logic-consumerism

Audio, visual, and multimedia sources

49. Podcast

Ekstrom, A. (2015, March). *The moral bias behind your search results* [Video podcast]. Retrieved from TED on http://itunes.apple.com/

Abumrad, J., & Krulwich, R. (2015, August 30). *Remembering Oliver Sacks* [Audio podcast]. Retrieved from http://www.radiolab.org

50. Video or audio on the Web

Renaud, B., & Renaud, C. (2015, October 8). *Between borders: America's migrant crisis* [Video file]. Retrieved from https://www.youtube.com /watch?v=rxF0t-SMEXA

Gershenfeld, N. (2015, January 23). *Digital reality* [Video file]. Retrieved from http://edge.org/conversation/collective-intelligence

Bever, T., Piattelli-Palmarini, M., Hammond, M., Barss, A., & Bergesen, A. (2012, February 2). *A basic introduction to Chomsky's linguistics* [Audio file]. Retrieved from University of Arizona, College of Social & Behavioral Sciences, Department of Linguistics website: http:// linguistics.arizona.edu/node/711

51. Transcript of an audio or a video file

Gershenfeld, N. (2015, January 23). *Digital reality* [Transcript of video file]. Retrieved from http://edge.org/conversation/collective-intelligence

Glass, I. (2015, April 24). *The incredible rarity of changing your mind* [Transcript of audio file No. 555]. In *This American life*. Retrieved from http://www.thisamericanlife.org/

52. Film (DVD, BD, or other format)   Give the director, producer, and other relevant contributors, followed by the year of the film's release and the title. In brackets, add a description of the medium. Use "Motion picture" if you viewed the film in a theater; "Video file" if you downloaded the film from the Web or through a streaming service such as Netflix; "DVD" or "BD" if you viewed the film on DVD or Blu-ray Disc. For a motion picture or a DVD or BD, add the location where the film was made and the studio. If you retrieved the film from the Web or used a streaming service, give the URL for the home page.

Cooper, S. (Director). (2015). *Black mass* [Motion picture]. Burbank, CA: Warner Bros.

Ross, G. (Director and Writer), & Collins, S. (Writer). (2012). *The hunger games* [Video file]. Retrieved from http://netflix.com/

53. Television or radio program

a. Series

Hager, M. (Executive producer), & Dickerson, J. (Moderator). (2015). *Face the nation* [Television series]. Washington, DC: CBS News.

53. Television or radio program (*cont.*)

b. Episode on the air

Oliver, J. (Host). (2015, October 4). Mental health [Television series
    episode]. In *Last week tonight*. New York, NY: HBO.

c. Episode on the Web

Hirsch, L. (Producer). (2015). ISIS in Afghanistan [Television series episode].
    In M. Smith (Executive producer), *Frontline*. Retrieved from http://www
    .wgbh.org/

Glass, I. (Host). (2015, November 27). Status update (No. 573) [Radio
    series episode]. In *This American life*. Retrieved from http://www
    .thisamericanlife.org/

54. Music recording

Chibalonza, A. Jubilee. (2012). On *African voices* [CD]. Merenberg, Germany:
    ZYX Music.

African voices [CD]. (2012). Merenberg, Germany: ZYX Music.

55. Lecture, speech, or address

Mills, A. (2015, April 21). *Primary healthcare and the private sector in
    low- and middle-income countries: Asia in comparative perspective*.
    Address at the Freeman Spogli Institute, Stanford University,
    Stanford, CA.

Furman, J. (2015, November 20). Jason Furman on housing finance
    [Video file]. *Data, demand, and demographics: A symposium on
    housing finance*. Urban Institute, Washington, DC. Retrieved from
    http://www.c-span.org/video/?401010-1/discussion-demographics
    -housing-finance

56. Data set or graphic representation of data (graph, chart, table)   Give information about the type of source in brackets following the title. If there is no title, give a brief description of the content of the source in brackets in place of the title. If the item is numbered in the source, indicate the number in parentheses after the title. If the graphic appears within a larger document, do not italicize the title of the graphic.

U.S. Department of Agriculture, Economic Research Service. (2015). *USDA expenditures for food and nutrition assistance, FY 1980-2014* [Chart]. Retrieved from http://www.ers.usda.gov/data-products/chart-gallery /detail.aspx?chartId=40105&ref=collection&embed=True

Gallup. (2015). *Gallup worldwide research data collected from 2005-2015* [Data set]. Retrieved from http://www.gallup.com/services/177797 /country-data-set-details.aspx

57. Mobile application software (app)   Begin with the developer of the app, if known (as in the second example). Add the label "Mobile application software" in brackets after the title of the program.

Instagram 7.12 [Mobile application software]. (2015). Retrieved from http:// itunes.apple.com/

Quora, Inc. (2015). Quora 2.2.6 [Mobile application software]. Retrieved from http://play.google.com

58. Video game   Begin with the creator of the video game, if known. Add the label "Video game" in brackets after the title of the program. If the game can be played on the Web or was downloaded from the Web, give the URL instead of publication information.

Firaxis Games. (2014). Sid Meier's civilization: Beyond earth [Video game]. New York, NY: Take-Two Interactive. PC.

58. Video game (*cont.*)

Atom Entertainment. (2012). Edgeworld [Video game]. Retrieved from http://www.addictinggames.com/

59. Map

Ukraine [Map]. (2015). Retrieved from the University of Texas at Austin Perry-Castañeda Library Map Collection website: https://www.lib.utexas.edu/maps/ukraine.html

Syria: Mapping the conflict [Map]. (2015, July). Retrieved from http://www.bbc.com/news/world-middle-east-22798391

60. Advertisement

VMware [Advertisement]. (2012, September). *Harvard Business Review, 90*(9), 27.

61. Work of art or photograph

Olson, A. (2011). *Short story* [Painting]. Museum of Contemporary Art, Chicago, IL.

Whitten, J. (2015). *Soul map* [Painting]. Retrieved from http://www.walkerart.org/

Sabogal, J. (2015). *Los hijos of the revolution* [Outdoor mural]. San Francisco, CA.

62. Brochure or fact sheet

National Council of State Boards of Nursing. (2014). *A nurse's guide to professional boundaries* [Brochure]. Retrieved from https://www.ncsbn.org/

World Health Organization. (2015, December). *Food safety* (No. 399) [Fact sheet]. Retrieved from http://www.who.int/mediacentre/factsheets/fs399/en/

63. Press release Generally, list the organization responsible for the press release. Give the exact date.

Urban Institute. (2012, October 11). Two studies address health policy on
campaign trail [Press release]. Retrieved from http://www.urban.org
/publications/901537.html

64. Presentation slides

Perry, M. (2015, September). *Eras in epidemiology* [Presentation slides].
Retrieved from http://acepidemiology.org/content/2015
-presentation-slides

65. Lecture notes or other course materials Cite materials that your instructor has posted on the Web as you would a Web document or a section in a Web document (see item 45 or 46). If the materials are handouts or printouts, cite whatever information is available in the source. Cite the instructor's personal notes or material that is not posted (such as slides) as personal communication in the text of your paper (see items 15 and 16 on pp. 700–01).

Blum, R. (2011). Neurodevelopment in the first decade of life [Lecture notes
and audio file]. In R. Blum & L. M. Blum, *Child health and development*.
Retrieved from http://ocw.jhsph.edu/index.cfm/go/viewCourse/course
/childhealth/coursePage/lectureNotes/

Personal communication and social media

66. E-mail E-mail messages, letters, and other personal communication are not included in the list of references. (See item 15 on p. 700 for citing these sources in the text of your paper.)

67. Online posting If an online posting is not archived, cite it as a personal communication in the text of your paper and do not include it in the list of references. If the posting is archived, give the URL and the name of the discussion list if it is not part of the URL.

McKinney, J. (2006, December 19). Adult education-healthcare partnerships
[Electronic mailing list message]. Retrieved from http://www.nifl.gov
/pipermail/healthliteracy/2006/000524.html

68. Twitter post (tweet) Use the author's real name, if it is given, and put the screen name in brackets exactly as it appears in the source (including capitalization and punctuation). If only the screen name is known, begin with that name and do not enclose it in brackets. Include the entire text of the tweet as the title, followed by the label "Tweet" in brackets; end with the URL.

National Science Foundation. (2015, December 8). Simulation shows key
to building powerful magnetic fields 1.usa.gov/1TZUiJ6 #supernovas
#supercomputers [Tweet]. Retrieved from https://twitter.com/NSF
/status/674352440582545413

69. Facebook post Use the author's name exactly as it appears in the post. In place of a title, give a few words of the post followed by the label "Facebook post" in brackets. Include the date you retrieved the source and the URL for the poster's Facebook page. If you are citing a personal Facebook page that will not be accessible to your readers, cite it as personal communication in your text, not in the reference list (see item 15 on p. 700).

U.S. Department of Education. (2015, December 10). We're watching
President Obama sign the Every Student Succeeds Act [Facebook
post]. Retrieved December 15, 2015, from http://www.facebook
.com/ED.gov

62 APA manuscript format; sample research paper

The guidelines in this section are consistent with advice given in the *Publication Manual of the American Psychological Association*, 6th ed. (Washington, DC: APA, 2010), and with typical requirements for undergraduate papers.

62a APA manuscript format

Formatting the paper

The guidelines on pages 735–38 describe APA's recommendations for formatting the text of your paper. For guidelines on preparing the reference list, see pages 739–40.

Font If your instructor does not require a specific font, use one that is standard and easy to read (such as Times New Roman).

Title page Begin at the top left, with the words "Running head," followed by a colon and the title of your paper (shortened to no more than fifty characters) in all capital letters. Put the page number 1 at the right margin.

About halfway down the page, on separate lines, center the full title of your paper, your name, and your school's name. At the bottom of the page, you may add the heading "Author Note," centered, followed by a brief paragraph that lists specific information about the course or department or provides acknowledgments or contact information. See page 741 for a sample title page.

Page numbers and running head Number all pages with arabic numerals (1, 2, 3, and so on) in the upper right corner one-half inch from the top of the page. At the left margin on the same line as the page number, type a running head consisting of the title of the paper (shortened to no more than fifty characters) in all capital letters. On the title page only, include the words "Running head" followed by a colon before the title. See pages 741–53.

Margins, line spacing, and paragraph indents   Use margins of one inch on all sides of the page. Left-align the text.

Double-space throughout the paper. Indent the first line of each paragraph one-half inch.

Capitalization, italics, and quotation marks   In headings and in titles of works that appear in the text of the paper, capitalize all words of four letters or more (and all nouns, pronouns, verbs, adjectives, and adverbs of any length). Capitalize the first word following a colon if the word begins a complete sentence.

In the body of your paper, italicize the titles of books, journals, magazines, and other long works, such as Web sites. Use quotation marks around the titles of articles, short stories, and other short works.

NOTE: APA has different requirements for titles in the reference list. See pages 739–40.

Long quotations   When a quotation is forty or more words, set it off from the text by indenting it one-half inch from the left margin. Double-space the quotation. Do not use quotation marks around it. (See p. 747 for an example. See also p. 687 for more information about integrating long quotations.)

Footnotes   If you insert a footnote number in the text of your paper, place the number, raised above the line, immediately following any mark of punctuation except a dash. At the bottom of the page, begin the note with a one-half-inch indent and the superscript number corresponding to the number in the text. Insert an extra double-spaced line between the last line of text on the page and the footnote. Double-space the footnote.

Abstract and keywords An abstract is a 150-to-250-word paragraph that provides readers with a quick overview of your essay. It should express your main idea and your key points; it might also briefly suggest any implications or applications of the research you discuss in the paper.

If your instructor requires one, include an abstract on a new page after the title page. Center the word "Abstract" (in regular font, not boldface) one inch from the top of the page. Double-space the abstract and do not indent the first line.

A list of keywords follows the abstract; the keywords help readers search for a published paper on the Web or in a data-base. On the line following the abstract, begin with the word "Keywords," italicized and indented one-half inch, followed by a colon. Then list important words related to your paper. Check with your instructor for requirements in your course. (See p. 742 for an example of an abstract.)

Headings Although headings are not always necessary, their use is encouraged in the social sciences. For most undergradu-ate papers, one level of heading is usually sufficient. (See pp. 743–51.)

First-level headings are centered and boldface. In research papers and laboratory reports, the major headings are "Method," "Results," and "Discussion." In other types of papers, the major headings should be informative and concise, conveying the structure of the paper.

Second-level headings are left-aligned and boldface. Third-level headings are indented and boldface, followed by a period and the text on the same line.

In first- and second-level headings, capitalize the first and last words and all words of four or more letters (and nouns, pronouns, verbs, adjectives, and adverbs of any length). In third-level head-ings, capitalize only the first word, any proper nouns, and the first word after a colon.

First-Level Heading Centered

Second-Level Heading Aligned Left

    Third-level heading indented. Text immediately follows.

Visuals (tables and figures) APA classifies visuals as tables and figures. Tables display complex data in an efficient, easily understood way. Figures include graphs, charts, drawings, and photographs.

Label each table with an arabic numeral (Table 1, Table 2, and so on) and provide a clear title. Place the label and title on separate lines above the table, left-aligned and double-spaced. Type the table number in regular font; italicize the table title.

If you have used data from an outside source or have taken or adapted the table from a source, give the source information in a note below the table. Begin with the word "Note," italicized and followed by a period. If any data in the table require an explanatory footnote, use a superscript lowercase letter in the table and in a footnote following the source note. Double-space source notes and footnotes; do not indent the first line of each note.

For each figure, place the figure number and a caption below the figure, left-aligned and double-spaced. Begin with the word "Figure" and an arabic numeral, both italicized, fol-lowed by a period. Place the caption, not italicized, on the same line. If you have taken or adapted the figure from an outside source, give the source information immediately following the caption. Use the term "From" or "Adapted from" before the source information.

In the text of your paper, discuss the most significant features of each visual. Place the visual as close as possible to the sentences that relate to it unless your instructor prefers that visuals appear in an appendix.

Preparing the list of references

Begin your list of references on a new page at the end of the paper. Center the title "References" one inch from the top of the page. Double-space throughout. For a sample reference list, see page 752.

Indenting entries Type the first line of each entry at the left margin and indent any additional lines one-half inch.

Alphabetizing the list Alphabetize the reference list by the last names of the authors (or editors) or by the first word of an organization name (if the author is an organization). When a work has no author or editor, alphabetize by the first word of the title other than *A*, *An*, or *The*.

If your list includes two or more works by the same author, arrange the entries by year, the earliest first. If your list includes two or more works by the same author in the same year, arrange the works alphabetically by title. Add the letters "a," "b," and so on within the parentheses after the year. For journal articles, use only the year and the letter: (2012a). For articles in magazines and newspapers, use the full date and the letter in the reference list: (2012a, July 7). Use only the year and the letter in the in-text citation.

Authors' names Invert all authors' names and use initials instead of first names. Separate the names with commas. For two to seven authors, use an ampersand (&) before the last author's name. For eight or more authors, give the first six authors, three ellipsis dots, and the last author (see item 3 on p. 707).

Titles of books and articles In the reference list, italicize the titles and subtitles of books. Do not italicize or use quotation marks around the titles of articles. For both books and articles, capitalize only the first word of the title and subtitle (and all proper nouns). Capitalize names of journals, magazines, and newspapers as you would capitalize them normally (see 45c).

Abbreviations for page numbers Abbreviations for "page" and "pages" ("p." and "pp.") are used before page numbers of newspaper articles and selections in anthologies (see item 15 on p. 715 and item 31 on p. 721). Do not use "p." or "pp." before page numbers of articles in journals and magazines (see items 13 and 14 on pp. 710–11).

Breaking a URL or DOI When a URL or a DOI (digital object identifier) must be divided, break it after a double slash or before any other mark of punctuation. Do not insert a hyphen; do not add a period at the end.

62b Sample APA research paper

On the following pages is a research paper on the use of educational technology in the shift to student-centered learning, written by April Wang, a student in an education class. Wang's assignment was to write a literature review paper documented with APA-style citations and references.

Running head: TECHNOLOGY AND STUDENT-CENTERED LEARNING

1 A running head consists of a title (shortened to no more than fifty characters) in all capital letters. On the title page, it is preceded by the label "Running head." Page numbers appear in the upper right corner.

Technology and the Shift From Teacher-Delivered

to Student-Centered Learning:

A Review of the Literature

April Bo Wang

Glen County Community College

Full title, writer's name, and school name are centered halfway down the page.

Author Note

This paper was prepared for Education 107, taught by Professor Gomez.

An author's note lists specific information about the course or department and can provide acknowledgments and contact information.

Marginal annotations indicate APA-style formatting and effective writing.

Abstract appears
on a separate page.
Heading is centered
and not boldface.

Keywords (optional)
help readers search
for a paper on
the Web or in a
database.

Abstract

In recent decades, instructors and administrators have viewed student-centered learning as a promising pedagogical practice that offers both the hope of increasing academic performance and a solution for teacher shortages. Differing from the traditional model of instruction in which a teacher delivers content from the front of a classroom, student-centered learning puts the students at the center of teaching and learning. Students set their own learning goals, select appropriate resources, and progress at their own pace. Student-centered learning has produced both positive results and increases in students' self-esteem. Given the recent proliferation of technology in classrooms, school districts are poised for success in making the shift to student-centered learning. The question for district leaders, however, is how to effectively balance existing teacher talent with educational technology.

Keywords: digital learning, student-centered learning, personalized learning, education technology, transmissive, blended

Technology and the Shift From Teacher-Delivered
to Student-Centered Learning:
A Review of the Literature

In the United States, most public school systems are struggling with teacher shortages, which are projected to worsen as the number of applicants to education schools decreases (Donitsa-Schmidt & Zuzovsky, 2014, p. 420). Citing federal data, *The New York Times* reported a 30% drop in "people entering teacher preparation programs" between 2010 and 2014 (Rich, 2015). Especially in science and math fields, the teacher shortage is projected to escalate in the next 10 years (Hutchison, 2012). In recent decades, instructors and administrators have viewed the practice of student-centered learning as one promising solution. Unlike traditional teacher-delivered (also called "transmissive") instruction, student-centered learning allows students to help direct their own education by setting their own goals and selecting appropriate resources for achieving those goals. Though student-centered learning might once have been viewed as an experimental solution in understaffed schools, it is gaining credibility as an effective pedagogical practice. What is also gaining momentum is the idea that technology might play a significant role in fostering student-centered learning. This literature review will examine three key questions:

1. In what ways is student-centered learning effective?
2. Can educational technology help students drive their own learning?
3. How can public schools effectively combine teacher talent and educational technology?

In the face of mounting teacher shortages, public schools should embrace educational technology that promotes student-centered learning in order to help all students become engaged and successful learners.

Source provides background information and context.

Wang sets up her organization by posing three questions.

Wang states her thesis.

TECHNOLOGY AND STUDENT-CENTERED LEARNING 4

In What Ways Is Student-Centered Learning Effective?

According to the International Society for Technology in Education (2016), "Student-centered learning moves students from passive receivers of information to active participants in their own discovery process. What students learn, how they learn it, and how their learning is assessed are all driven by each individual student's needs and abilities." The results of student-centered learning have been positive, not only for academic achievement but also for student self-esteem. In this model of instruction, the teacher acts as a facilitator, and the students actively participate in the process of learning and teaching. With guidance, students decide on the learning goals most pertinent to themselves, they devise a learning plan that will most likely help them achieve those goals, they direct themselves in carrying out that learning plan, and they assess how much they learned (Çubukçu, 2012). The major differences between student-centered learning and instructor-centered learning are summarized in Table 1.

Bell (2010) has argued that the chief benefit of student-centered learning is that it can connect students with "real-world tasks," thus making learning more engaging as well as more comprehensive. For example, Bell observed a group of middle-school students who wanted to build a social justice monument for their school. They researched social justice issues, selected several to focus on, and then designed a three-dimensional playground to represent those issues. In doing so, they achieved learning goals in the areas of social studies, physics, and mathematics and practiced research and teamwork. Bell reported that students engaged in this kind of learning performed better on both project-based assessments and standardized tests (pp. 39-40).

Headings, centered and boldface, help readers follow the organization.

Wang uses a source to define the key term *student-centered learning*.

Because the author (Çubukçu) is not named in the signal phrase, the name and the date appear in parentheses.

When the author's name and year of publication are given in a signal phrase, only the page number or numbers, if available, are needed in parentheses at the end of the source material.

Table 1

Comparison of Two Approaches to Teaching and Learning

Wang creates a table to compare and contrast two key concepts for her readers.

Teaching and learning period	Instructor-centered approach	Student-centered approach
Before class	• Instructor prepares lecture/instruction on new topic. • Students complete homework on previous topic.	• Students read and view new material, practice new concepts, and prepare questions ahead of class. • Instructor views student practice and questions, identifies learning opportunities.
During class	• Instructor delivers new material in a lecture or prepared discussion. • Students—unprepared—listen, watch, take notes, and try to follow along with the new material.	• Students lead discussions of the new material or practice applying the concepts or skills in an active environment. • Instructor answers student questions and provides immediate feedback.
After class	• Instructor grades homework and gives feedback about the previous lesson. • Students work independently to practice or apply the new concepts.	• Students apply concepts/skills to more complex tasks, some of their own choosing, individually and in groups. • Instructor posts additional resources to help students.

Note. Adapted from "The Flipped Class Demystified," n.d., retrieved from New York University website: https://www.nyu.edu/faculty /teaching-and-learning-resources/instructional-technology-support /instructional-design-assessment/flipped-classes/the-flipped-class -demystified.html.

TECHNOLOGY AND STUDENT-CENTERED LEARNING   6

Wang summarizes an important article, providing parenthetical citations even for a summary.

A Stanford study came to a similar conclusion; researchers examined four schools that had moved from teacher-driven instruction to student-centered learning (Friedlaender, Burns, Lewis-Charp, Cook-Harvey, & Darling-Hammond, 2014). The study focused on students from a mix of racial, cultural, and socioeconomic backgrounds, with varying levels of English-language proficiency. The researchers predicted that this mix of students, representing differing levels of academic ability, would benefit from a student-centered approach. Through interviews, surveys, and classroom observations, the researchers identified key characteristics of the new student-centered learning environments at the four schools:

- teachers who prioritized building relationships with students
- support structures for teachers to improve and collaborate on instruction
- a shift in classroom activity from lectures and tests to projects and performance-based assessments (pp. 5-7)

After the schools designed their curriculum to be personalized to individual students rather than standardized across a diverse student body and to be inclusive of skills such as persistence as well as traditional academic skills, students outperformed peers on state tests and increased their rates of high school and college graduation (Friedlaender et al., 2014, p. 3).

When this article was first cited, all authors were named. In subsequent citations of a work with three to five authors, "et al." is used after the first author's name.

Can Educational Technology Help Students Drive Their Own Learning?

When students engage in self-directed learning, they rely less on teachers to deliver information and require less face-to-face time with teachers. For content delivery, many school districts have begun to use educational technology resources that, in recent years, have become more available, more affordable, and easier to use. For the purposes of this paper, the term "educational technology resources" encompasses

the following: distance learning, by which students learn from a
remote instructor online; other online education programming such as
slide shows and video or audio lectures; interactive online activities,
such as quizzing or games; and the use of computers, tablets,
smartphones, SMART Boards, or other such devices for coursework.

Much like student-centered learning, the use of educational
technology began in many places as a temporary measure to keep
classes running despite teacher shortages. A Horn and Staker
study (2011) examined the major patterns over time for students
who subscribed to distance learning, for example. A decade ago,
students who enrolled in distance learning often fell into one of the
following categories: They lived in a rural community that had no
alternative for learning; they attended a school where there were not
enough qualified teachers to teach certain subjects; or they were
homeschooled or homebound. But faced with tighter budgets, teacher
shortages, increasingly diverse student populations, and rigorous state
standards, schools recognized the need and the potential for distance
learning across the board.

As the teacher shortage has intensified, educational technology
resources have become more tailored to student needs and more
affordable. Pens that convert handwritten notes to digital text and
organize them, backpacks that charge electronic devices, and apps
that create audiovisual flash cards are just a few of the more recent
innovations. According to Svokos (2015), College and Education
Fellow for *The Huffington Post*, some educational technology resources
entertain students while supporting student-centered learning:

> GlassLab, a nonprofit that was launched with grants from
> the Bill & Melinda Gates and MacArthur Foundations, creates
> educational games that are now being used in more than
> 6,000 classrooms across the country. Some of the company's

Wang develops her thesis.

In a signal phrase, the word "and" links the names of two authors; the date is given in parentheses.

A quotation longer than forty words is indented without quotation marks.

TECHNOLOGY AND STUDENT-CENTERED LEARNING   8

games are education versions of existing ones—for example,
its first release was SimCity EDU—while others are originals.
Teachers get real-time updates on students' progress as well as
suggestions on what topics students need to spend more time on.
Many of the companies behind these products offer institutional
discounts to schools where such devices are used widely by students
and teachers.

Horn and Staker (2011) concluded that the chief benefit of
technological learning was that it could adapt to the individual
student in a way that whole-class delivery by a single teacher could
not. Their study examined various schools where technology enabled
student-centered learning. For example, Carpe Diem High School in
Yuma, Arizona, hired only six certified subject teachers and then
outfitted its classrooms with 280 computers connected to online
learning programs. The programs included software that offered
"continual feedback, assessment, and incremental victory in a way
that a face-to-face teacher with a class of 30 students never could.
After each win, students continue to move forward at their own
pace" (p. 9). Students alternated between personalized 55-minute
courses online and 55-minute courses with one of the six teachers.
The academic outcomes were promising. Carpe Diem ranked first in
its county for student math and reading scores. Similarly, Rocketship
Education, a charter network that serves low-income, predominantly
Latino students, created a digital learning lab, reducing the need to
hire more teachers. Rocketship's academic scores ranked in the top 15
of all California low-income public schools.

It is clear that educational technology will continue to play
a role in student and school performance. Horn and Staker (2011)
acknowledged that they focused on programs in which integration of
educational technology led to improved student performance. In

Wang uses her own
analysis to shape
the conversation
among her sources
in this synthesis
paragraph.

other schools, technological learning is simply distance learning—watching a remote teacher—and not student-centered learning that allows students to partner with teachers to develop enriching learning experiences. That said, many educators seem convinced that educational technology has the potential to help them transition from traditional teacher-driven learning to student-centered learning. All four schools in the Stanford study heavily relied on technology (Friedlaender et al., 2014). And indeed, Demski (2012) argued that technology is not supplemental but instead is "central" to student-centered learning (p. 33). Rather than turning to a teacher as the source of information, students are sent to investigate solutions to problems by searching online, e-mailing experts, collaborating with one another in a wiki space, or completing online practice. Rather than turning to a teacher for the answer to a question, students are driven to perform—driven to use technology to find those answers themselves.

How Can Public Schools Effectively Combine Teacher Talent and Educational Technology?

Some researchers have expressed doubt that schools are ready for student-centered learning—or any type of instruction—that is driven by technology. In a recent survey conducted by the Nellie Mae Education Foundation, Moeller and Reitzes (2011) reported not only that many teachers lacked confidence in their ability to incorporate technology in the classroom but that 43% of polled high school students said that they lacked confidence in their technological proficiency going into college and careers. The study concluded that technology alone would not improve learning environments. Yet others argued that students adapt quickly to even unfamiliar technology and use it to further their own learning. For example, Mitra (2013) caught the attention of the education world with his study of how to educate

Wang uses a source to introduce a counterposition.

students in the slums of India. He installed an Internet-accessible computer in a wall in a New Delhi urban slum and left it there with no instructions. Over a few months, many of the children had learned how to use the computer, how to access information over the Internet, how to interpret information, and how to communicate this information to one another. Mitra's experiment was "not about making learning happen. [It was] about letting it happen." He concluded that in the absence of teachers, even in developing countries less inundated by technology, a tool that allowed access to an organized database of knowledge (such as a search engine) was sufficient to provide students with a rewarding learning experience.

According to the Stanford study, however, the presence of teachers is still crucial (Friedlaender et al., 2014). Their roles will simply change from distributors of knowledge to facilitators and supporters of self-directed student-centered learning. The researchers asserted that teacher education and professional development programs can no longer prepare their teachers in a single instructional mode, such as teacher-delivered learning; they must instead equip teachers with a wide repertoire of skills to support a wide variety of student learning experiences. The Stanford study argued that since teachers would be partnering with students to shape the learning experience, rather than designing and delivering a curriculum on their own, the main job of a teacher would become relationship building. The teacher would establish a relationship with each student so that the teacher could support whatever learning the student pursues.

Many schools have already effectively paired a reduced faculty with educational technology to support successful student-centered learning. For example, Watson (2008) offered a case study of the Cincinnati Public Schools Virtual High School, which brought students together in a physical school building to work with an

Brackets indicate Wang's change in the quoted material.

assortment of online learning programs. Although there were only 10 certified teachers in the building, students were able to engage in highly individualized instruction according to their own needs, strengths, and learning styles, using the 10 teachers as support (p. 7). Commonwealth Connections Academy (CCA), a public school in Pennsylvania, also brings students into a physical school building to engage in digital curriculum. However, rather than having students identify their own learning goals and design their own curriculum around those goals, CCA uses educational technology as an assessment tool to identify areas of student weakness. It then partners students with teachers to address those areas (pp. 8-9).

Conclusion

Public education faces the opportunity for a shift from the model of teacher-delivered instruction that has characterized American public schools since their foundation to a student-centered learning model. Not only has student-centered learning proved effective in improving student academic and developmental outcomes, but it can also synchronize with technological learning for widespread adaptability across schools. Because it relies on student direction rather than an established curriculum, student-centered learning supported by educational technology can adapt to the different needs of individual students and a variety of learning environments—urban and rural, well funded and underfunded. Similarly, when student-centered learning relies on technology rather than a corps of uniformly trained teachers, it holds promise for schools that would otherwise suffer from a lack of human or financial resources.

The tone of the conclusion is objective and presents answers to Wang's three organizational questions.

References

Bell, S. (2010). Project-based learning for the 21st century: Skills for the future. *The Clearing House, 83*(2), 39-43.

Çubukçu, Z. (2012). Teachers' evaluation of student-centered learning environments. *Education, 133*(1), 49-66.

Demski, J. (2012, January). This time it's personal. *THE Journal (Technological Horizons in Education), 39*(1), 32-36.

Donitsa-Schmidt, S., & Zuzovsky, R. (2014). Teacher supply and demand: The school level perspective. *American Journal of Educational Research, 2*(6), 420-429.

Friedlaender, D., Burns, D., Lewis-Charp, H., Cook-Harvey, C. M., & Darling-Hammond, L. (2014). Student-centered schools: Closing the opportunity gap [Research brief]. Retrieved from Stanford Center for Opportunity Policy in Education website: https:// edpolicy.stanford.edu/sites/default/files/scope-pub-student -centered-research-brief.pdf

Horn, M. B., & Staker, H. (2011). The rise of K-12 blended learning. Retrieved from Innosight Institute website: http://www .christenseninstitute.org/wp-content/uploads/2013/04/The -rise-of-K-12-blended-learning.pdf

Hutchison, L. F. (2012). Addressing the STEM teacher shortage in American schools: Ways to recruit and retain effective STEM teachers. *Action in Teacher Education, 34*(5/6), 541-550.

International Society for Technology in Education. (2016). *Student-centered learning*. Retrieved from http://www.iste.org /standards/essential-conditions/student-centered-learning

Mitra, S. (2013, February). *Build a school in the cloud* [Video file]. Retrieved from https://www.ted.com/talks/sugata_mitra _build_a_school_in_the_cloud?language=en

List of references begins on a new page. Heading is centered and not boldface.

List is alphabetized by authors' last names. All authors' names are inverted.

The first line of an entry is at the left margin; subsequent lines indent ½".

Double-spacing is used throughout.

Moeller, B., & Reitzes, T. (2011, July). Integrating technology
    with student-centered learning. Retrieved from Nellie Mae
    Education Foundation website: http://www.nmefoundation
    .org/research/personalization/integrating-technology-with
    -student-centered-learn

Rich, M. (2015, August 9). Teacher shortages spur a nationwide hiring
    scramble (credentials optional). *The New York Times*. Retrieved
    from http://www.nytimes.com

Svokos, A. (2015, May 7). 5 innovations from the past decade that
    aim to change the American classroom [Blog post]. Retrieved
    from http://www.huffingtonpost.com/2015/05/07/technology
    -changes-classrooms_n_7190910.html

Watson, J. (2008, January). *Blended learning: The convergence
    of online and face-to-face education*. Retrieved from North
    American Council for Online Learning website: http://
    www.inacol.org/wp-content/uploads/2015/02/NACOL
    _PP-BlendedLearning-lr.pdf

Writing *Chicago* papers

BRIEF DIRECTORY

63 *Chicago* papers, 754
63a Supporting a thesis, 755
63b Citing sources; avoiding plagiarism, 758
63c Integrating sources, 762
63d Documenting sources, 768
Directory to *Chicago*-style notes and
bibliography entries, 769
63e Manuscript format, 794
63f Sample pages from a *Chicago*-style research paper, 797

Most history instructors and some humanities instructors require
you to document sources with footnotes or endnotes based on
The Chicago Manual of Style, 16th ed. (Chicago: University of
Chicago Press, 2010). (See 63d for details about *Chicago* documentation style.)

63 *Chicago* papers

You face three main challenges when you write a paper that
draws on sources: (1) supporting a thesis, (2) citing your sources
and avoiding plagiarism, and (3) integrating quotations and
other source material.

Examples in this section are written in *Chicago* style and are
drawn from one student's research on the Fort Pillow massacre,
which occurred during the Civil War. Sample pages from Ned
Bishop's paper are on pages 798–804.

63a Supporting a thesis

Most assignments based on reading or research—such as those assigned in history or other humanities classes—ask you to form a thesis, or main idea, and to support that thesis with well-organized evidence.

Forming a working thesis

Once you have read a variety of sources, considered your issue from different perspectives, and chosen an entry point in the research conversation (see 50b), you are ready to form a working thesis: a one-sentence (or occasionally a two-sentence) statement of your central idea. (See also 1c and 53a.) Because it is a working, or tentative, thesis, you can remain flexible and revise it as your ideas develop. Ultimately, the thesis will express not just your opinion but your informed, reasoned answer to your research question (see 50b). Here, for example, are student writer Ned Bishop's research question and working thesis statement.

> **RESEARCH QUESTION**
>
> To what extent was Confederate Major General Nathan Bedford Forrest responsible for the massacre of Union troops at Fort Pillow?
>
> **WORKING THESIS**
>
> By encouraging racism among his troops, Nathan Bedford Forrest was directly responsible for the massacre of Union troops at Fort Pillow.

Notice that the thesis expresses a view on a debatable issue—an issue about which intelligent, well-meaning people might disagree. The writer's job is to convince such readers that this view is worth taking seriously.

To read Ned Bishop's thesis in the context of his introduction, see page 799.

Organizing your ideas

The body of your paper will consist of evidence in support of your thesis. It will be useful to sketch an informal plan that helps you begin to organize your ideas. Ned Bishop, for example, used a simple outline to structure his ideas. In the paper, the points in the outline became headings that helped readers follow his line of argument.

> What happened at Fort Pillow?
>
> Did Forrest order the massacre?
>
> Can Forrest be held responsible for the massacre?

Using sources to inform and support your argument

The source materials you have gathered will make your argument more complex and convincing for readers. Sources can play several different roles as you develop your points.

Providing background information or context   You can use facts and statistics to support generalizations or to establish the importance of your topic, as student writer Ned Bishop does early in his paper.

> Fort Pillow, Tennessee, which sat on a bluff overlooking the Mississippi River, had been held by the Union for two years. It was garrisoned by 580 men, 292 of them from United States Colored Heavy and Light Artillery regiments, 285 from the white Thirteenth Tennessee Cavalry. Nathan Bedford Forrest commanded about 1,500 troops.[1]

Explaining terms or concepts   If readers are unlikely to be familiar with a word or an idea important to your topic, you must explain it for them. Quoting or paraphrasing a source can help you define terms and concepts clearly and concisely.

The Civil War practice of giving no quarter to an enemy—in other words, "denying [an enemy] the right of survival"—defied Lincoln's mandate for humane and merciful treatment of prisoners.[9]

Supporting your claims As you draft, make sure to back up your assertions with facts, examples, and other evidence from your research. (See also 6h.) Ned Bishop, for example, uses an eyewitness report of the racially motivated violence perpetrated by Nathan Bedford Forrest's troops.

> The slaughter at Fort Pillow was no doubt driven in large part by racial hatred. . . . A Southern reporter traveling with Forrest makes clear that the discrimination was deliberate: "Our troops maddened by the excitement, shot down the ret[r]eating Yankees, and not until they had attained t[h]e water's edge and turned to beg for mercy, did any prisoners fall in[t]o our hands—Thus the whites received quarter, but the negroes were shown no mercy."[19]

Lending authority to your argument Expert opinion can give weight to your argument. (See also 6h.) But don't rely on experts to make your argument for you. Construct your argument in your own words and, when appropriate, cite the judgment of an authority in the field for support.

> Fort Pillow is not the only instance of a massacre or threatened massacre of black soldiers by troops under Forrest's command. Biographer Brian Steel Wills points out that at Brice's Cross Roads in June 1864, "black soldiers suffered inordinately" as Forrest looked the other way and Confederate soldiers deliberately sought out those they termed "the damned negroes."[21]

Anticipating and countering alternative interpretations Do not ignore sources that seem contrary to your position or that offer arguments different from your own. Instead, use them to give voice to opposing points of view and alternative interpretations before you counter them (see 6i). Readers often have opposing points of view in mind already, whether or not they agree with you. Ned Bishop, for example, presents conflicting evidence to acknowledge that some readers may credit Nathan Bedford Forrest with stopping the massacre. In doing so, Bishop creates an opportunity to counter that objection and persuade those readers that Forrest can be held accountable.

> Hurst suggests that the temperamental Forrest "may have ragingly ordered a massacre and even intended to carry it out—until he rode inside the fort and viewed the horrifying result" and ordered it stopped.[15] While this is an intriguing interpretation of events, even Hurst would probably admit that it is merely speculation.

63b Citing sources; avoiding plagiarism

In a research paper, you will draw on the work of other writers, and you must document their contributions by citing your sources. Sources are cited for two reasons:

1. to tell readers where your information comes from — so that they can assess its reliability and, if interested, find and read the original source

2. to give credit to the writers from whom you have borrowed words and ideas

You must cite anything you borrow from a source, including direct quotations; statistics and other specific facts; visuals such as tables, graphs, and diagrams; and any ideas you present in a summary or paraphrase. Borrowing another writer's language, sentence structures, or ideas without proper acknowledgment is a form of dishonesty known as *plagiarism*. The only exception is common knowledge — information that your readers may know or could easily locate in any number of reference sources.

Using the Chicago *system for citing sources*

Chicago citations consist of superscript numbers in the text of
the paper that refer readers to notes with corresponding numbers either at the foot of the page (footnotes) or at the end of the
paper (endnotes).

TEXT

Governor John Andrew was not allowed to recruit black soldiers from
out of state. "Ostensibly," writes Peter Burchard, "no recruiting was
done outside Massachusetts, but it was an open secret that Andrew's
agents were working far and wide."[1]

NOTE

    1. Peter Burchard, *One Gallant Rush: Robert Gould Shaw and His
Brave Black Regiment* (New York: St. Martin's, 1965), 85.

For detailed advice on using *Chicago*-style notes, see 63d.
When you use footnotes or endnotes, you will usually need to
provide a bibliography as well.

BIBLIOGRAPHY ENTRY

Burchard, Peter. *One Gallant Rush: Robert Gould Shaw and His Brave
    Black Regiment*. New York: St. Martin's, 1965.

*Avoiding plagiarism when quoting, summarizing,
and paraphrasing sources*

In a research paper, you draw on the work of other writers, and
you must document their contributions by citing your sources.
When you acknowledge your sources, you avoid plagiarism, a
serious academic offense.

    Three different acts are considered plagiarism: (1) failing
to cite quotations and borrowed ideas, (2) failing to enclose
borrowed language in quotation marks, or (3) failing to put
summaries and paraphrases in your own words. Definitions of

plagiarism may vary; it's a good idea to find out how your school defines and addresses academic dishonesty.

Using quotation marks around borrowed language   To indicate that you are using a source's exact phrases or sentences, you must enclose them in quotation marks unless they have been set off from the text by indenting (see pp. 764–65). To omit the quotation marks is to claim—falsely—that the language is your own. Such an omission is plagiarism even if you have cited the source.

ORIGINAL SOURCE

For many Southerners it was psychologically impossible to see a black man bearing arms as anything but an incipient slave uprising complete with arson, murder, pillage, and rapine.

— Dudley Taylor Cornish, *The Sable Arm*, p. 158

PLAGIARISM

According to Civil War historian Dudley Taylor Cornish, for many Southerners it was psychologically impossible to see a black man bearing arms as anything but an incipient slave uprising complete with arson, murder, pillage, and rapine.[2]

BORROWED LANGUAGE IN QUOTATION MARKS

According to Civil War historian Dudley Taylor Cornish, "For many Southerners it was psychologically impossible to see a black man bearing arms as anything but an incipient slave uprising complete with arson, murder, pillage, and rapine."[2]

NOTE: Long quotations are set off from the text by indenting and do not need quotation marks (see the example on p. 765).

Putting summaries and paraphrases in your own words   Summaries and paraphrases are written in your own words. A summary condenses information; a paraphrase uses roughly the same number of words as in the original source to convey the information. When you summarize or paraphrase, it is not enough to name the source; you must restate the source's meaning using your own language. (See also 51c.) You commit plagiarism if you patchwrite—half-copy the author's sentences, either by mixing the author's phrases with your own without using quotation marks or by plugging your own synonyms into the author's sentence structure.

The first paraphrase of the following source is plagiarized—even though the source is cited—because too much of its language is borrowed from the original. The highlighted strings of words have been copied exactly (without quotation marks). In addition, the writer has closely followed the sentence structure of the original source, merely making a few substitutions (such as *Fifty percent* for *Half* and *angered and perhaps frightened* for *enraged and perhaps terrified*).

ORIGINAL SOURCE

Half of the force holding Fort Pillow were Negroes, former slaves now enrolled in the Union Army. Toward them Forrest's troops had the fierce, bitter animosity of men who had been educated to regard the colored race as inferior and who for the first time had encountered that race armed and fighting against white men. The sight enraged and perhaps terrified many of the Confederates and aroused in them the ugly spirit of a lynching mob.

— Albert Castel, "The Fort Pillow Massacre," pp. 46–47

PLAGIARISM: UNACCEPTABLE BORROWING

Albert Castel suggests that much of the brutality at Fort Pillow can be traced to racial attitudes. Fifty percent of the troops holding Fort Pillow were Negroes, former slaves who had joined the Union Army. Toward them Forrest's soldiers displayed the savage hatred of men who had been taught the inferiority of blacks and who for the first time had confronted them armed and fighting against white men. The vision angered and perhaps frightened the Confederates and aroused in them the ugly spirit of a lynching mob.[3]

To avoid plagiarizing an author's language, resist the temptation to look at the source while you are summarizing or paraphrasing. After you have read the passage you want to paraphrase, set the source aside. Ask yourself, "What is the author's meaning?" In your own words, state your understanding of the author's basic point. Return to the source and check that you haven't used the author's language or sentence structure or misrepresented the author's ideas. Following these steps will help you avoid plagiarizing the source. When you fully understand another writer's meaning, you can more easily and accurately represent those ideas in your own words.

ACCEPTABLE PARAPHRASE

Albert Castel suggests that much of the brutality at Fort Pillow can be traced to racial attitudes. Fifty percent of the Union troops were blacks, men whom the Confederates had been raised to consider their inferiors. The shock and perhaps fear of facing armed ex-slaves in battle may well have unleashed the fury that led to the massacre.[3]

63c Integrating sources

Quotations, summaries, paraphrases, and facts will support your argument, but they cannot speak for you. You can use several strategies to integrate information from research sources into your paper while maintaining your own voice.

Using quotations appropriately

In your academic writing, keep the emphasis on your ideas and your language; use your own words to summarize and to paraphrase your sources and to explain your points. Sometimes, however, quotations can be the most effective way to integrate a source.

Limiting your use of quotations   Although it is tempting to insert many quotations in your paper and to use your own words only for connecting passages, do not quote excessively. It is almost impossible to integrate numerous quotations smoothly into your own text.

WHEN TO USE QUOTATIONS

- When language is especially vivid or expressive
- When exact wording is needed for technical accuracy
- When it is important to let the debaters of an issue explain their positions in their own words
- When the words of an authority lend weight to an argument
- When the language of a source is the topic of your discussion (as in an analysis or interpretation)

It is not always necessary to quote full sentences from a source. To reduce your reliance on the words of others, you can often integrate language from a source into your own sentence structure.

As Hurst has pointed out, until "an outcry erupted in the Northern press," even the Confederates did not deny that there had been a massacre at Fort Pillow.[4]

Union surgeon Dr. Charles Fitch testified that after he was in custody he "saw" Confederate soldiers "kill every negro that made his appearance dressed in Federal uniform."[20]

Using the ellipsis mark   To condense a quoted passage, you can use the ellipsis mark (three periods, with spaces between) to indicate that you have left words out. What remains must be grammatically complete.

> Union surgeon Fitch's testimony that all women and children had been evacuated from Fort Pillow before the attack conflicts with Forrest's report: "We captured . . . about 40 negro women and children."[6]

The writer has omitted several words not relevant to the issue at hand: *164 Federals, 75 negro troops, and.*

When you want to leave out one or more full sentences, use a period before the three ellipsis dots. For an example, see the long quotation on page 765.

Ordinarily, do not use the ellipsis mark at the beginning or at the end of a quotation. Readers will understand that you have taken the quoted material from a longer passage, so such marks are not necessary. The only exception occurs when you have dropped words at the end of the final quoted sentence. In such cases, put three ellipsis dots before the closing quotation mark.

USING SOURCES RESPONSIBLY: Make sure omissions and ellipsis marks do not distort the meaning of your source.

Using brackets   Brackets allow you to insert words of your own into quoted material to clarify a confusing reference or to keep a sentence grammatical in the context of your own writing.

> According to Albert Castel, "It can be reasonably argued that he [Forrest] was justified in believing that the approaching steamships intended to aid the garrison [at Fort Pillow]."[7]

NOTE: Use the word *sic,* italicized and in brackets, to indicate that an error in a quoted sentence appears in the original source. (An example appears on p. 765.) Do not overuse *sic* to call attention to errors in a source. Sometimes paraphrasing is a better option. (See 39c.)

Setting off long quotations   *Chicago* style allows you some flexibility in deciding whether to set off a long quotation or run it into your text. You may want to set off a quotation of more than four or five typed lines of text; almost certainly you should set off quotations of ten or more lines. To set off a quotation, indent it one-half inch from the left margin and use the normal right margin. Double-space the indented quotation.

Long quotations should be introduced by an informative sentence, usually followed by a colon. Quotation marks are unnecessary because the indented format tells readers that the passage is taken word-for-word from the source.

> In a letter home, Confederate officer Achilles V. Clark recounted what happened at Fort Pillow:
>> Words cannot describe the scene. The poor deluded negroes would run up to our men fall upon their knees and with uplifted hands scream for mercy but they were ordered to their feet and then shot down. The whitte [*sic*] men fared but little better. . . . I with several others tried to stop the butchery and at one time had partially succeeded[,] but Gen. Forrest ordered them shot down like dogs, and the carnage continued.[8]

Using signal phrases to integrate sources

Whenever you include a paraphrase, summary, or direct quotation of another writer's work in your paper, prepare your readers for it with introductory words called a *signal phrase*. A signal phrase names the author of the source, points out the author's credentials, and often provides some context for the source material.

When you write a signal phrase, choose a verb that is appropriate for the way you are using the source (see pp. 756–58). Are you providing background, explaining a concept, supporting a claim, lending authority, or refuting a belief? By choosing an appropriate verb, you can make your source's role clear. See the chart on page 766 for a list of verbs commonly used in signal phrases.

Note that *Chicago* style calls for verbs in the present tense or present perfect tense (*points out, has pointed out*) to introduce source material unless you include a date that specifies the time of the original author's writing.

Using signal phrases in *Chicago* papers

To avoid monotony, try to vary both the language and the placement of your signal phrases.

Model signal phrases

In the words of historian James M. McPherson, ". . ."[1]

As Dudley Taylor Cornish has argued, ". . ."[2]

In a letter to his wife, a Confederate soldier who witnessed the massacre wrote that ". . ."[3]

". . . ," claims Benjamin Quarles.[4]

". . . ," writes Albert Castel, ". . ."[5]

Shelby Foote offers an intriguing interpretation: ". . ."[6]

Verbs in signal phrases

admits	compares	insists	rejects
agrees	confirms	notes	reports
argues	contends	observes	responds
asserts	declares	points out	suggests
believes	denies	reasons	thinks
claims	emphasizes	refutes	writes

The first time you mention an author, use the full name: *Shelby Foote argues. . . .* When you refer to the author again, you may use the last name only: *Foote raises an important question.*

Marking boundaries Readers should be able to move from your own words to the words of a source without feeling a jolt. Avoid dropping quotations into the text without warning. Instead, provide clear signal phrases, usually including the author's name, to indicate the boundary between your words and the source's words. (The signal phrase is highlighted in the second example.)

DROPPED QUOTATION

Not surprisingly, those testifying on the Union and Confederate sides recalled events at Fort Pillow quite differently. Unionists claimed that their troops had abandoned their arms and were in full retreat. "The Confederates, however, all agreed that the Union troops retreated to the river with arms in their hands."[9]

QUOTATION WITH SIGNAL PHRASE

Not surprisingly, those testifying on the Union and Confederate sides recalled events at Fort Pillow quite differently. Unionists claimed that their troops had abandoned their arms and were in full retreat. "The Confederates, however," writes historian Albert Castel, "all agreed that the Union troops retreated to the river with arms in their hands."[9]

Using signal phrases with summaries and paraphrases As with quotations, introduce most summaries and paraphrases with a signal phrase that mentions the author and places the material in the context of your own writing. Readers will then understand where the summary or paraphrase begins.

Without the signal phrase (highlighted) in the following example, readers might think that only the last sentence is being cited, when in fact the whole paragraph is based on the source.

According to Jack Hurst, official Confederate policy was that black soldiers were to be treated as runaway slaves; in addition, the Confederate Congress decreed that white Union officers commanding black troops be killed. Confederate Lieutenant General Kirby Smith went one step further, declaring that he would kill all captured black troops. Smith's policy never met with strong opposition from the Richmond government.[10]

Integrating statistics and other facts When you are citing a statistic or another specific fact, a signal phrase is often not necessary. In most cases, readers will understand that the citation refers to the statistic or fact (not the whole paragraph).

> Of the 295 white troops garrisoned at Fort Pillow, 168 were taken
> prisoner. Black troops fared worse, with only 58 of 262 captured and
> most of the rest presumably killed or wounded.[12]

There is nothing wrong, however, with using a signal phrase to
introduce a statistic or another fact.

Putting source material in context   Readers should not have
to guess why source material appears in your paper. A signal
phrase can help you make the connection between your own
ideas and those of another writer by setting up how a source will
contribute to your paper (see 52a).

If you use another writer's words, you must explain how
they relate to your point. It's a good idea to embed a quotation
between sentences of your own. In addition to introducing it
with a signal phrase, follow the quotation with interpretive comments that link it to your paper's argument.

QUOTATION WITH EFFECTIVE CONTEXT

In a respected biography of Nathan Bedford Forrest, Hurst suggests
that the temperamental Forrest "may have ragingly ordered a massacre
and even intended to carry it out—until he rode inside the fort and
viewed the horrifying result" and ordered it stopped.[15] While this is an
intriguing interpretation of events, even Hurst would probably admit
that it is merely speculation.

NOTE: When you bring other sources into a conversation about
your research topic, you are synthesizing (see 55d).

63d Documenting sources

In history and some other humanities courses, you may be asked to
use the documentation system of *The Chicago Manual of Style*, 16th
ed. (Chicago: University of Chicago Press, 2010). In *Chicago* style,
superscript numbers (like this[1]) in the text of the paper refer readers

Directory to *Chicago*-style notes and bibliography entries

General guidelines for listing authors

1. One author, 772
2. Two or three authors, 772
3. Four or more authors, 772
4. Organization as author, 773
5. Unknown author, 773
6. Multiple works by the same author, 773
7. Editor, 773
8. Editor with author, 773
9. Translator with author, 773

Books and other long works

10. Basic format for a book, 774
    a. Print, 774
    b. E-book, 774
    c. Web (or online library), 774
11. Edition other than the first, 774
12. Volume in a multivolume work, 774
13. Work in an anthology, 775
14. Introduction, preface, foreword, or afterword, 775
15. Republished book, 775
16. Book with a title in its title, 775
17. Work in a series, 775
18. Sacred text, 777
19. Government document, 777
20. Unpublished dissertation, 778
21. Published proceedings of a conference, 778
22. Source quoted in another source (a secondary source), 778

Articles and other short works

23. Article in a journal, 779
    a. Print, 779
    b. Web, 779
    c. Database, 779
24. Article in a magazine, 781
    a. Print, 781
    b. Web, 783
    c. Database, 783
25. Article in a newspaper, 783
    a. Print, 784
    b. Web, 784
    c. Database, 784
26. Unsigned newspaper article, 784
27. Article with a title in its title, 785
28. Review, 785
29. Letter to the editor, 785
30. Article in a dictionary or an encyclopedia (including a wiki), 785
31. Letter in a published collection, 786

Web sources

32. An entire Web site, 786
33. Short work from a Web site, 787
34. Blog post, 787
35. Comment on a blog post, 787

Audio, visual, and multimedia sources

36. Podcast, 787
37. Online audio or video, 790

→

Directory to *Chicago*-style notes
and bibliography entries (*cont.*)

38. Published or broadcast
    interview, 790
39. Film (DVD, BD, or other format), 791
40. Sound recording, 791
41. Musical score or composition, 791
42. Work of art, 791
43. Performance, 791

**Personal communication
and social media**

44. Personal communication, 793
45. Online posting or e-mail, 793
46. Facebook post, 794
47. Twitter post (tweet), 794

to notes with corresponding numbers either at the foot of the page
(footnotes) or at the end of the paper (endnotes). A bibliography is
often required as well; it appears at the end of the paper and gives
publication information for all the works cited in the notes.

TEXT

A Union soldier, Jacob Thompson, claimed to have seen Forrest order
the killing, but when asked to describe the six-foot-two general, he
called him "a little bit of a man."[12]

FOOTNOTE OR ENDNOTE

12. Brian Steel Wills, *A Battle from the Start: The Life of Nathan
Bedford Forrest* (New York: HarperCollins, 1992), 187.

BIBLIOGRAPHY ENTRY

Wills, Brian Steel. *A Battle from the Start: The Life of Nathan Bedford
    Forrest*. New York: HarperCollins, 1992.

First and later notes for a source

The first time you cite a source, the note should include publication information for that work as well as the page number for the
passage you are citing.

1. Peter Burchard, *One Gallant Rush: Robert Gould Shaw and His
Brave Black Regiment* (New York: St. Martin's, 1965), 85.

For later references to a source you have already cited, you may simply give the author's last name, a short form of the title, and the page or pages cited. A short form of the title of a book or another long work is italicized; a short form of the title of an article or another short work is put in quotation marks.

    4. Burchard, *One Gallant Rush*, 31.

When you have two notes in a row from the same source, you may use "Ibid." (meaning "in the same place") and the page number for the second note. Use "Ibid." alone if the page number is the same.

    5. Jack Hurst, *Nathan Bedford Forrest: A Biography* (New York: Knopf, 1993), 8.

    6. Ibid., 174.

Chicago-style bibliography

A bibliography at the end of your paper lists the works you have cited in your notes; it may also include works you consulted but did not cite. See page 797 for how to construct the list; see page 804 for a sample bibliography.

NOTE: If you include a bibliography, *The Chicago Manual of Style* suggests that you shorten all notes, including the first reference to a source, as described at the top of this page. Check with your instructor, however, to see whether using an abbreviated note for a first reference to a source is acceptable.

Model notes and bibliography entries

The following models are consistent with guidelines in *The Chicago Manual of Style*, 16th ed. For each type of source, a model note appears first, followed by a model bibliography entry. The note shows the format you should use when citing a source for the first time. For subsequent, or later, citations of a source, use shortened notes (see pp. 770–71).

Some sources on the Web, typically periodical articles, use a permanent locator called a digital object identifier (DOI). Use the DOI, when it is available, in place of a URL in your citations of sources from the Web.

When a URL or a DOI must break across lines, do not insert a hyphen or break at a hyphen if the URL or DOI contains one. Instead, break after a colon or a double slash or before any other mark of punctuation.

General guidelines for listing authors

1. One author

1. Salman Rushdie, *Two Years Eight Months and Twenty-Eight Nights* (New York: Random House, 2015), 73.

Rushdie, Salman. *Two Years Eight Months and Twenty-Eight Nights.* New York: Random House, 2015.

2. Two or three authors
For a work with two or three authors, give all authors' names in both the note and the bibliography entry.

2. Bill O'Reilly and Martin Dugard, *Killing Reagan: The Violent Assault That Changed a Presidency* (New York: Holt, 2015), 44.

O'Reilly, Bill, and Martin Dugard. *Killing Reagan: The Violent Assault That Changed a Presidency.* New York: Holt, 2015.

3. Four or more authors
For a work with four or more authors, in the note give the first author's name followed by "et al." (for "and others"); in the bibliography entry, list all authors' names.

3. Lynn Hunt et al., *The Making of the West: Peoples and Cultures,* 5th ed. (Boston: Bedford/St. Martin's, 2015), 541.

Hunt, Lynn, Thomas R. Martin, Barbara H. Rosenwein, and Bonnie G. Smith. *The Making of the West: Peoples and Cultures.* 5th ed. Boston: Bedford/ St. Martin's, 2015.

4. Organization as author

4. The Big Horn Basin Foundation, *Wyoming's Dinosaur Discoveries* (Charleston, SC: Arcadia Publishing, 2015), 24.

The Big Horn Basin Foundation. *Wyoming's Dinosaur Discoveries*. Charleston, SC: Arcadia Publishing, 2015.

5. Unknown author

5. *The Men's League Handbook on Women's Suffrage* (London, 1912), 23.

The Men's League Handbook on Women's Suffrage. London, 1912.

6. Multiple works by the same author

In the bibliography, arrange the entries alphabetically by title. Use six hyphens in place of the author's name in the second and subsequent entries.

Kolbert, Elizabeth. *Field Notes from a Catastrophe: Man, Nature, and Climate Change*. New York: Bloomsbury USA, 2006.

------. *The Sixth Extinction: An Unnatural History*. New York: Holt, 2014.

7. Editor

7. Teresa Carpenter, ed., *New York Diaries: 1609-2009* (New York: Modern Library, 2012), 316.

Carpenter, Teresa, ed. *New York Diaries: 1609-2009*. New York: Modern Library, 2012.

8. Editor with author

8. Susan Sontag, *As Consciousness Is Harnessed to Flesh: Journals and Notebooks, 1964-1980*, ed. David Rieff (New York: Farrar, Straus and Giroux, 2012), 265.

Sontag, Susan. *As Consciousness Is Harnessed to Flesh: Journals and Notebooks, 1964-1980*. Edited by David Rieff. New York: Farrar, Straus and Giroux, 2012.

9. Translator with author

9. Karin Wieland, *Dietrich and Riefenstahl: Hollywood, Berlin, and a Century in Two Lives*, trans. Shelley Frisch (New York: Liveright, 2015), 52.

Wieland, Karin. *Dietrich and Riefenstahl: Hollywood, Berlin, and a Century in Two Lives*. Translated by Shelley Frisch. New York: Liveright, 2015.

Books and other long works

▸ Citation at a glance: Book, page 776

10. Basic format for a book

a. Print

10. David Leatherbarrow, *Topographical Studies in Landscape and Architecture* (Philadelphia: University of Pennsylvania Press, 2015), 45.

Leatherbarrow, David. *Topographical Studies in Landscape and Architecture*. Philadelphia: University of Pennsylvania Press, 2015.

b. E-book

10. Atul Gawande, *Being Mortal: Medicine and What Matters in the End* (New York: Metropolitan, 2014), Nook edition, chap. 3.

Gawande, Atul. *Being Mortal: Medicine and What Matters in the End*. New York: Metropolitan, 2014. Nook edition.

c. Web (or online library)

10. Charles Hursthouse, *New Zealand, or Zealandia, the Britain of the South* (1857; Hathi Trust Digital Library, n.d.), 2:356, http://catalog .hathitrust.org/Record/006536666.

Hursthouse, Charles. *New Zealand, or Zealandia, the Britain of the South*. 2 vols. 1857. Hathi Trust Digital Library, n.d. http://catalog.hathitrust .org /Record/006536666.

11. Edition other than the first

11. Judy Root Aulette and Judith Wittner, *Gendered Worlds*, 3rd ed. (Oxford: Oxford University Press, 2012), 86.

Aulette, Judy Root, and Judith Wittner. *Gendered Worlds*. 3rd ed. Oxford: Oxford University Press, 2015.

12. Volume in a multivolume work
If each volume has its own title, give the volume title first, followed by the volume number and the title of the entire work, as in the following examples. If the volumes do not have individual titles, give the volume and page number in the note (for example, 2:356) and the total number of volumes in the bibliography entry (see item 10c).

12. Robert A. Caro, *The Passage of Power*, vol. 4 of *The Years of Lyndon Johnson* (New York: Knopf, 2012), 198.

Caro, Robert A. *The Passage of Power*. Vol. 4 of *The Years of Lyndon Johnson*. New York: Knopf, 2012.

13. Work in an anthology

13. Ben Merriman, "Lessons of the Arkansas," in *City by City: Dispatches from the American Metropolis*, ed. Keith Gessen and Stephen Squibb (New York: n+1/Farrar, Straus and Giroux, 2015), 142.

Merriman, Ben. "Lessons of the Arkansas." In *City by City: Dispatches from the American Metropolis*, edited by Keith Gessen and Stephen Squibb, 142–56. New York: n+1/Farrar, Straus and Giroux, 2015.

14. Introduction, preface, foreword, or afterword

14. Alice Walker, afterword to *The Indispensable Zinn: The Essential Writings of the "People's Historian,"* by Howard Zinn, ed. Timothy Patrick McCarthy (New York: New Press, 2012), 373.

Walker, Alice. Afterword to *The Indispensable Zinn: The Essential Writings of the "People's Historian,"* by Howard Zinn, 371–76. Edited by Timothy Patrick McCarthy. New York: New Press, 2012.

15. Republished book

15. Arthur M. Okun, *Equality and Efficiency: The Big Tradeoff* (1975; repr., Washington, DC: Brookings Institution Press, 2015), 26.

Okun, Arthur M. *Equality and Efficiency: The Big Tradeoff*. 1975. Reprint, Washington, DC: Brookings Institution Press, 2015.

16. Book with a title in its title   Use quotation marks around any title, whether a long or a short work, within an italicized title.

16. Noel Merino, ed., *Wilderness Adventure in Jon Krakauer's "Into the Wild"* (Detroit, MI: Greenhaven Press, 2015), 47.

Merino, Noel, ed. *Wilderness Adventure in Jon Krakauer's "Into the Wild."* Detroit, MI: Greenhaven Press, 2015.

17. Work in a series   The series name follows the book title.

17. Omar H. Ali, *Islam in the Indian Ocean World: A Brief History with Documents*, Bedford Series in History and Culture (Boston: Bedford/St. Martin's, 2016), 35.

Citation at a glance

Book *Chicago*

To cite a print book in *Chicago* style, include the following elements:

1 Author(s)
2 Title and subtitle
3 City of publication
4 Publisher
5 Year of publication
6 Page number(s) cited (for notes)

TITLE PAGE

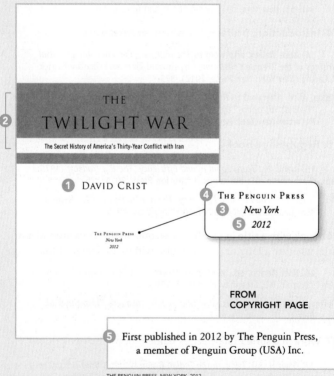

FROM COPYRIGHT PAGE

5 First published in 2012 by The Penguin Press, a member of Penguin Group (USA) Inc.

THE PENGUIN PRESS, NEW YORK, 2012.

NOTE

1. David Crist, *The Twilight War: The Secret History of America's Thirty-Year Conflict with Iran* (New York: Penguin, 2012), 354.

BIBLIOGRAPHY

Crist, David. *The Twilight War: The Secret History of America's Thirty-Year Conflict with Iran*. New York: Penguin, 2012.

For more on citing books in *Chicago* style, see items 10–18.

17. Work in a series (*cont.*)

Ali, Omar H. *Islam in the Indian Ocean World: A Brief History with Documents*. Bedford Series in History and Culture. Boston: Bedford/St. Martin's, 2016.

18. Sacred text   Sacred texts such as the Bible are usually not included in the bibliography.

18. Matt. 20:4-9 (Revised Standard Version).

18. Qur'an 18:1-3.

19. Government document

19. United States Senate, Committee on Foreign Relations, *The U.S. Role in the Middle East: Hearing before the Committee on Foreign Relations, United States Senate*, 114th Cong., 1st sess. (Washington, DC: GPO, 2015), 35.

United States Senate. Committee on Foreign Relations. *The U.S. Role in the Middle East: Hearing before the Committee on Foreign Relations, United States Senate*, 114th Cong., 1st sess. Washington, DC: GPO, 2015.

20. Unpublished dissertation

20. Courtney L. Moore, "Stress and Oppression: Identifying Possible Protective Factors for African American Men" (PhD diss., Chicago School of Professional Psychology, 2016), 110-11, ProQuest (AAT 3717844).

Moore, Courtney L. "Stress and Oppression: Identifying Possible Protective Factors for African American Men." PhD diss., Chicago School of Professional Psychology, 2015. ProQuest (AAT 3717844).

For a published dissertation, italicize the title and give publication information as for a book.

21. Published proceedings of a conference   Cite as a book, adding the location and dates of the conference after the title.

21. Stacey K. Sowards et al., eds., *Across Borders and Environments: Communication and Environmental Justice in International Contexts*, University of Texas at El Paso, June 25-28, 2011 (Cincinnati, OH: International Environmental Communication Association, 2012), 114.

Sowards, Stacey K., Kyle Alvarado, Diana Arrieta, and Jacob Barde, eds. *Across Borders and Environments: Communication and Environmental Justice in International Contexts*. University of Texas at El Paso, June 25-28, 2011. Cincinnati, OH: International Environmental Communication Association, 2012.

22. Source quoted in another source (a secondary source) Sometimes you will want to use a quotation from one source that you have found in another source. In your note and bibliography entry, cite whatever information is available about the original source of the quotation, including a page number. Then add the words "quoted in" and give publication information for the source in which you found the words. In the following examples, author John Matteson quotes the words of Thomas Wentworth Higginson. Matteson's book includes a note with information about the Higginson book.

22. Thomas Wentworth Higginson, *Margaret Fuller Ossoli* (Boston: Houghton Mifflin, 1890), 11, quoted in John Matteson, *The Lives of Margaret Fuller* (New York: Norton, 2012), 7.

Higginson, Thomas Wentworth. *Margaret Fuller Ossoli*. Boston: Houghton Mifflin, 1890, 11. Quoted in John Matteson, *The Lives of Margaret Fuller* (New York: Norton, 2012), 7.

Articles and other short works

▸ Citation at a glance: Article in a journal, page 780
▸ Citation at a glance: Article from a database, page 782

23. Article in a journal Include the volume and issue numbers (if the journal has them) and the date; end the bibliography entry with the page range of the article. If an article in a database or on the Web shows only a beginning page, use a plus sign after the page number instead of a page range: 212+.

a. Print

23. Bernard Dubbeld, "Capital and the Shifting Ground of Emancipatory Politics: The Limits of Radical Unionism in Durban Harbor, 1974-85," *Critical Historical Studies* 2, no. 1 (2015): 86.

Dubbeld, Bernard. "Capital and the Shifting Ground of Emancipatory Politics: The Limits of Radical Unionism in Durban Harbor, 1974-85." *Critical Historical Studies* 2, no. 1 (2015): 85-112.

b. Web
Give the DOI if the article has one; if there is no DOI, give the URL for the article. For unpaginated articles on the Web, you may include in your note a locator, such as a numbered paragraph or a heading from the article.

23. Anne-Lise François, "Flower Fisting," *Postmodern Culture* 22, no. 1 (2011), doi:10.1353/pmc.2012.0004.

François, Anne-Lise. "Flower Fisting." *Postmodern Culture* 22, no. 1 (2011). doi:10.1353/pmc.2012.0004.

c. Database
Give one of the following pieces of information from the database listing, in this order of preference: a DOI for the article; or the name of the database and the article number, if any; or a "stable" or "persistent" URL for the article.

23. Estelle Joubert, "Performing Sovereignty, Sounding Autonomy: Political Representation in the Operas of Maria Antonia of Saxony," *Music and Letters* 96, no. 3 (2015): 345, Project Muse.

Joubert, Estelle. "Performing Sovereignty, Sounding Autonomy: Political Representation in the Operas of Maria Antonia of Saxony." *Music and Letters* 96, no. 3 (2015): 344-89. Project Muse.

Citation at a glance

Article in a journal `Chicago`

To cite an article in a print journal in *Chicago* style, include the
following elements:

1 Author(s)
2 Title and subtitle of article
3 Title of journal
4 Volume and issue numbers
5 Year of publication
6 Page number(s) cited
   (for notes); page range of
   article (for bibliography)

FIRST PAGE OF ARTICLE

> Work, Family, and the Eighteenth-
> 2 Century History of a Middle Class
> in the American South

1 By Emma Hart

ON OCTOBER 15, 1800, WIDOW VIOLETTA WYATT APPEARED BEFORE
... Charleston District,
... er married life, which
... rlier, when she took
... hter of a blacksmith,
... eston from childhood,
... h century, her experi-
... record as those of so
... usband at the head of
... deral census not as an
... e sole records of her
... in her father's 1767
... e documents are now
... , in her lengthy testi-
... cery Court, the course
... inary detail. Violetta
... heir marriage through
... American Revolution,
... household.[1]

... Census of the United States
... , 39; Will of James Lingard,
... leston County Wills (South
... S.C.). The case of Mary
... ane, September 23, 1771, is
... under the royal government,
... ds of the Court of Chancery
... he case of Executors of the
... (hereinafter Richardsons v.
... older 20, Box 4, Charleston
... th Carolina Department of
... ecision in the case is cited as
... 1. 2, pp. 1–2, Series L10092,

**TITLE PAGE OF
JOURNAL**

The Journal of
3 **SOUTHERN HISTORY**

4 VOLUME LXXVIII 5 AUGUST 2012 NUMBER 3 4

Contents

2 Work, Family, and the Eighteenth-Century History of a
Middle Class in the American South
1 By Emma Hart 551 6

A Twice Sacred Circle: Women, Evangelicalism, and Honor
in the Deep South, 1784–1860
By Robert Elder 579

The Free Black Experience in Antebellum Wilmington,
North Carolina: Refining Generalizations about
Race Relations
By Richard C. Rohrs 615

Looking the Thing in the Face: Slavery, Race, and the
Commemorative Landscape in Charleston,
South Carolina, 1865–2010
By Blain Roberts and Ethan J. Kytle 639

Book Reviews 685

Historical News and Notices 794

1. Emma Hart, "Work, Family, and the Eighteenth-Century History of a Middle Class in the American South," *Journal of Southern History* 78, no. 3 (2012): 565.

BIBLIOGRAPHY

Hart, Emma. "Work, Family, and the Eighteenth-Century History of a Middle Class in the American South." *Journal of Southern History* 78, no. 3 (2012): 551-78.

For more on citing articles in *Chicago* style, see items 23–25.

24. Article in a magazine   Give the month and year for a monthly publication; give the month, day, and year for a weekly publication. End the bibliography entry with the page range of the article. If an article in a database or on the Web shows only a beginning page, use a plus sign after the page number instead of a page range: 212+.

a. Print

Alexandra Fuller, "Haiti on Its Own Terms," *National Geographic*, December 2015, 112.

Fuller, Alexandra. "Haiti on Its Own Terms." *National Geographic*, December 2015, 98-118.

Citation at a glance

Article from a database `Chicago`

To cite an article from a database in *Chicago* style, include the following elements:

1. Author(s)
2. Title and subtitle of article
3. Title of journal
4. Volume and issue numbers
5. Year of publication
6. Page number(s) cited (for notes); page range of article (for bibliography)
7. DOI; *or* database name and article number; *or* "stable" or "persistent" URL for article

ON-SCREEN VIEW OF DATABASE RECORD

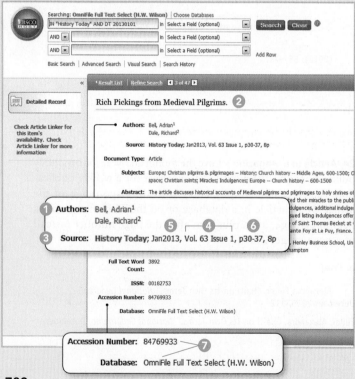

NOTE

1. Adrian Bell and Richard Dale, "Rich Pickings from Medieval Pilgrims,"

History Today 63, no. 1 (2013): 33. OmniFile Full Text Select (84769933).

BIBLIOGRAPHY

Bell, Adrian, and Richard Dale, "Rich Pickings from Medieval Pilgrims," *History*

Today 63, no. 1 (2013): 30-37. OmniFile Full Text Select (84769933).

For more on citing articles from databases in *Chicago* style, see items 23–25.

24. Article in a magazine (*cont.*)

b. Web If no DOI is available, include the URL for the article.

24. Alan Lightman, "What Came before the Big Bang?" *Harper's*, January 2016, http://harpers.org/archive/2016/01/what-came-before-the-big-bang.

Lightman, Alan. "What Came before the Big Bang?" *Harper's*, January 2016. http://harpers.org/archive/2016/01/what-came-before-the-big-bang.

c. Database Give one of the following from the database listing, in this order of preference: a DOI for the article; or the name of the database and the article number, if any; or a "stable" or "persistent" URL for the article.

24. Ron Rosenbaum, "The Last Renaissance Man," *Smithsonian*, November 2012, 40, OmniFile Full Text Select (83097302).

Rosenbaum, Ron. "The Last Renaissance Man." *Smithsonian*, November 2012, 39-44. OmniFile Full Text Select (83097302).

25. Article in a newspaper

Page numbers are not necessary; a section letter or number, if available, is sufficient.

25. Article in a newspaper (*cont.*)

a. Print

> 25. Neil Irwin, "Low Rates May Stay for Years After the Fed Reverses Course," *New York Times*, December 15, 2015, sec. A.

Irwin, Neil. "Low Rates May Stay for Years After the Fed Reverses Course." *New York Times*, December 15, 2015, sec. A.

b. Web Include the URL for the article; if the URL is very long, use the URL for the newspaper's home page. Omit page numbers, even if the source provides them.

> 25. Chris Mooney, "The World Just Adopted a Tough New Climate Goal. Here's How Hard It Will Be to Meet," *Washington Post*, December 15, 2015, http://www.washingtonpost.com/.

Mooney, Chris. "The World Just Adopted a Tough New Climate Goal. Here's How Hard It Will Be to Meet." *Washington Post*, December 15, 2015. http://www.washingtonpost.com/.

c. Database Give one of the following from the database listing, in this order of preference: a DOI for the article; or the name of the database and the number assigned by the database; or a "stable" or "persistent" URL for the article.

> 25. "Safe in Sioux City at Last: Union Pacific Succeeds in Securing Trackage from the St. Paul Road," *Omaha Daily Herald*, May 16, 1889, America's Historical Newspapers.

"Safe in Sioux City at Last: Union Pacific Succeeds in Securing Trackage from the St. Paul Road." *Omaha Daily Herald*, May 16, 1889. America's Historical Newspapers.

26. Unsigned newspaper article   In the note, begin with the title of the article. In the bibliography entry, begin with the title of the newspaper.

> 26. "Next President Better Be a Climate Change Believer," *Chicago Sun-Times*, December 14, 2015, http://www.suntimes.com/.

Chicago Sun-Times. "Next President Better Be a Climate Change Believer." December 14, 2015. http://www.suntimes.com/.

27. Article with a title in its title   Use italics for titles of long works such as books and for terms that are normally italicized. Use single quotation marks for titles of short works and terms that would otherwise be placed in double quotation marks.

27. Julia Hudson-Richards, "'Women Want to Work': Shifting Ideologies of Women's Work in Franco's Spain, 1939–1962," *Journal of Women's History* 27, no. 2 (2015): 91.

Hudson-Richards, Julia. "'Women Want to Work': Shifting Ideologies of Women's Work in Franco's Spain, 1939–1962." *Journal of Women's History* 27, no. 2 (2015): 87–109.

28. Review   If the review has a title, provide it immediately following the author of the review.

28. Anthony Lane, "Deep and Dark," review of *In the Heart of the Sea*, directed by Ron Howard, *New Yorker*, December 21/28, 2015, 86.

Lane, Anthony. "Deep and Dark." Review of *In the Heart of the Sea*, directed by Ron Howard. *New Yorker*, December 21/28, 2015, 86–87.

28. Richard Mandrachio, review of *The Beat Generation FAQ: All That's Left to Know about the Angelheaded Hipsters*, by Rich Weidman, *San Francisco Book Review*, December 10, 2015, http://www.sanfranciscobookreview.com.

Mandrachio, Richard. Review of *The Beat Generation FAQ: All That's Left to Know about the Angelheaded Hipsters*, by Rich Weidman. *San Francisco Book Review*, December 10, 2015. http://www.sanfranciscobookreview.com.

29. Letter to the editor   Do not use the letter's title, even if the publication gives one.

29. Fredric Rolando, letter to the editor, *Economist*, December 5, 2015, http://www.economist.com/.

Rolando, Fredric. Letter to the editor. *Economist*, December 5, 2015. http://www.economist.com/.

30. Article in a dictionary or an encyclopedia (including a wiki) Reference works such as encyclopedias do not require publication information and are usually not included in the bibliography. The abbreviation "s.v." is for the Latin *sub verbo* ("under the word").

30. Article in a dictionary or an encyclopedia (*cont.*)

> 30. *Encyclopaedia Britannica*, 15th ed., s.v. "Monroe Doctrine."

> 30. *Wikipedia*, s.v. "James Monroe," last modified December 19, 2012, http://en.wikipedia.org/wiki/James_Monroe.

> 30. Bryan A. Garner, *Garner's Modern American Usage*, 3rd ed. (Oxford: Oxford University Press, 2009), s.v. "brideprice."

Garner, Bryan A. *Garner's Modern American Usage*. 3rd ed. Oxford: Oxford University Press, 2009.

31. Letter in a published collection If the letter writer's name is part of the book title, begin the note with only the last name but begin the bibliography entry with the full name.

▸ Citation at a glance: Letter in a published collection, page 788

> 31. Hughes to James Nathaniel Hughes, 5 September 1921, in *Selected Letters of Langston Hughes*, ed. Arnold Rampersad, David Roessel, and Christa Fratantoro (New York: Knopf, 2015), 6-7.

Hughes, Langston. *Selected Letters of Langston Hughes*. Edited by Arnold Rampersad, David Roessel, and Christa Fratantoro. New York: Knopf, 2015.

Web sources

For most Web sites, include an author if a site has one, the title of the site, the sponsor, the date of publication or the modified (update) date, and the site's URL. Do not italicize a Web site title unless the site is an online book or periodical. Use quotation marks for the titles of sections or pages in a Web site. If a site does not have a date of publication or a modified date, give the date you accessed the site ("accessed January 3, 2013").

32. An entire Web site

> 32. Chesapeake and Ohio Canal National Historical Park, National Park Service, last modified November 25, 2015, http://www.nps.gov/choh/index.htm.

Chesapeake and Ohio Canal National Historical Park. National Park Service. Last modified November 25, 2015. http://www.nps.gov/choh/index.htm.

33. Short work from a Web site

▶ Citation at a glance: Primary source from a Web site, page 792

33. Alexios Mantzarlis, "How TV Fact-Checked Spain's Final Debate," Poynter, last modified December 15, 2015, http://www.poynter.org/.

Mantzarlis, Alexios. "How TV Fact-Checked Spain's Final Debate." Poynter, last modified December 15, 2015. http://www.poynter.org/.

34. Blog post Treat as a short work from a Web site (see item 33), but italicize the name of the blog. Insert "blog" in parentheses after the name if the word *blog* is not part of the name. If the blog is part of a larger site (such as a newspaper's or an organization's site), add the title of the site after the blog title. Do not list the blog post in the bibliography; but if you cite the blog frequently in your paper, you may give a bibliography entry for the entire blog.

34. Gregory LeFever, "Skull Fraud 'Created' the Brontosaurus," *Ancient Tides* (blog), December 16, 2012, http://ancient-tides.blogspot .com/2012/12/skull-fraud-created-brontosaurus.html.

LeFever, Gregory. *Ancient Tides* (blog). http://ancient-tides.blogspot.com/.

35. Comment on a blog post This bibliography entry gives the blog by title only because it has many contributors, not a single author.

35. OllyPye, comment on Graham Readfern, "Paris Agreement a Victory for Climate Science and Ultimate Defeat for Fossil Fuels," *Planet Oz* (blog), *Guardian*, December 12, 2015, http://www.theguardian.com/environment/ planet-oz/2015/dec/12/paris-agreement-a-victory-for-climate-science-and-ultimate-defeat-for-fossil-fuels#comments.

Planet Oz (blog). *Guardian*. http://www.theguardian.com/environment /planet-oz/.

Audio, visual, and multimedia sources

36. Podcast Treat as a short work from a Web site (see item 33), including the following, if available: the name of the author,

(*continued on p. 790*)

Citation at a glance

Letter in a published collection *Chicago*

To cite a letter in a published collection in *Chicago* style, include the following elements:

1. Author of letter
2. Recipient of letter
3. Date of letter
4. Title of collection
5. Editor of collection
6. City of publication
7. Publisher
8. Year of publication
9. Page number(s) cited (for notes); page range of letter (for bibliography)

TITLE PAGE

4

TO HIS EXCELLENCY THOMAS JEFFERSON

········ *Letters to a President* ········

5 JACK McLAUGHLIN

FROM COPYRIGHT PAGE

8

Copyright © 1991 by Jack McLaughlin
Cover painting by Giraudon/Art Resource, New York
Published by arrangement with W.W. Norton & Company, Inc.
Library of Congress Catalog Card Number: 90-27824
ISBN: 0-380-71964-9

AVON BOOKS ▲ NEW YORK

7 **6**

AVON BOOKS ▲ NEW YORK

Washington 30th. Oct 1805 ③

His Excellency Ths. Jefferson ②

SIR,

I have not the honor to be personally known to your Excellency therefore you will no doubt think it strange to receive t[...] smallest [...] in as few [...] a young [...] partly ed[...] had been [...] sequence [...] that unh[...] anything [...] few yea[...] [m]isfortu[...] [I] can at[...]

Patronage 6 1 ⑨

your Excellency this very prolix letter which should it please your Excellency to give me some little Office or appointment in that extensive Country of Louisiana It should be my constant endeavour to merit the same by fidelity and an indefatigable attention to whatever business I should be assigned. May I have the satisfaction in whatsoever Country or situation [I] may be in to hear of your Excellencies long continuence of your Natural powers unempaired to conduct the Helm of this Extensive Country which are the sincere wishes of your Excellencies Mo. Obt. Hum. Servt.

① JOHN O'NEILL

NOTE

    1   2   3   4
1. John O'Neill to Thomas Jefferson, 30 October 1805, in *To His*

                                     5
Excellency Thomas Jefferson: Letters to a President, ed. Jack McLaughlin
 6   7   8 9
(New York: Avon Books, 1991), 61.

BIBLIOGRAPHY

 1   1   2   3
O'Neill, John. John O'Neill to Thomas Jefferson, 30 October 1805. In

                      4
To His Excellency Thomas Jefferson: Letters to a President, edited by
    5   9   6   7   8
Jack McLaughlin, 59-61. New York: Avon Books, 1991.

For another citation of a letter in *Chicago* style, see item 31.

speaker, or host; the title of the podcast, in quotation marks; an identifying number, if any; the title of the site on which it appears; the sponsor of the site; and the URL. Identify the type of podcast or file format; before the URL, give the date of posting or your date of access.

36. Toyin Falola, "Creativity and Decolonization: Nigerian Cultures and African Epistemologies," Episode 96, Africa Past and Present, African Online Digital Library, podcast audio, November 17, 2015, http://afripod .aodl.org/.

Falola, Toyin. "Creativity and Decolonization: Nigerian Cultures and African Epistemologies." Episode 96. Africa Past and Present. African Online Digital Library. Podcast audio. November 17, 2015. http://afripod .aodl.org/.

37. Online audio or video   Cite as a short work from a Web site (see item 33). If the source is a downloadable file, identify the file format or medium before the URL.

37. Will Potter, "The Secret US Prisons You've Never Heard of Before," TED Talks, November 9, 2015, https://www.youtube.com /watch?v=xuAAPsiD768.

Potter, Will. "The Secret US Prisons You've Never Heard of Before." TED Talks, November 9, 2015. https://www.youtube.com/watch?v=xuAAPsiD768.

38. Published or broadcast interview

38. Ta-Nehisi Coates, interview by James Bennet, *Atlantic,* October 16, 2015, http://www.theatlantic.com/video/index/410815/in-conversation -with-ta-nehisi-coates/.

Coates, Ta-Nehisi. Interview by James Bennet. *Atlantic*, October 16, 2015. http://www.theatlantic.com/video/index/410815/in-conversation -with-ta-nehisi-coates/.

38. Vladimir Putin, interview by Charlie Rose, *Charlie Rose Show*, WGBH, Boston, June 19, 2015.

Putin, Vladimir. Interview by Charlie Rose. *Charlie Rose Show*. WGBH, Boston, June 19, 2015.

39. Film (DVD, BD, or other format)

39. *Brooklyn*, directed by John Crowley (Los Angeles, CA: Fox Searchlight Pictures, 2015).

Brooklyn. Directed by John Crowley. Los Angeles, CA: Fox Searchlight Pictures, 2015.

39. *The Roosevelts: An Intimate History*, directed by Ken Burns (Washington, DC: PBS, 2014), DVD.

The Roosevelts: An Intimate History. Directed by Ken Burns. Washington, DC: PBS, 2014. DVD.

40. Sound recording

40. Gustav Holst, *The Planets*, Royal Philharmonic Orchestra, conducted by André Previn, Telarc 80133, compact disc.

Holst, Gustav. *The Planets*. Royal Philharmonic Orchestra. Conducted by André Previn. Telarc 80133, compact disc.

41. Musical score or composition

41. Antonio Vivaldi, *L'Estro armonico*, op. 3, ed. Eleanor Selfridge-Field (Mineola, NY: Dover, 1999).

Vivaldi, Antonio. *L'Estro armonico*, op. 3. Edited by Eleanor Selfridge-Field. Mineola, NY: Dover, 1999.

42. Work of art

42. Hope Gangloff, *Vera*, acrylic on canvas, 2015, Kemper Museum of Contemporary Art, Kansas City, MO.

Gangloff, Hope. *Vera*. Acrylic on canvas, 2015. Kemper Museum of Contemporary Art, Kansas City, MO.

43. Performance

43. Wendy Wasserstein, *The Heidi Chronicles*, directed by Vivienne Benesch, Trinity Repertory Company, Providence, RI, December 3, 2015.

Wasserstein, Wendy. *The Heidi Chronicles*. Directed by Vivienne Benesch. Trinity Repertory Company, Providence, RI, December 3, 2015.

Citation at a glance

Primary source from a Web site `Chicago`

To cite a primary source (or any other document) from a Web site
in *Chicago* style, include as many of the following elements as are
available:

1 Author(s)
2 Title of document
3 Title of site
4 Sponsor of site

5 Publication date or
  modified date; date of
  access (if no publication
  date)
6 URL of document page

WEB SITE HOME PAGE

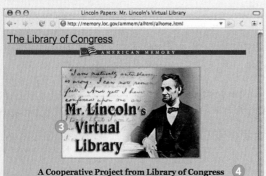

FIRST PAGE OF DOCUMENT

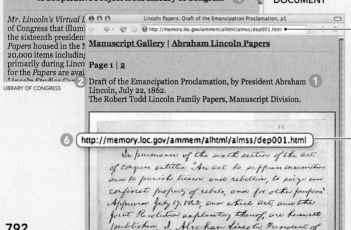

NOTE

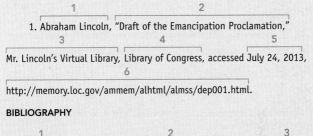

1. Abraham Lincoln, "Draft of the Emancipation Proclamation," Mr. Lincoln's Virtual Library, Library of Congress, accessed July 24, 2013, http://memory.loc.gov/ammem/alhtml/almss/dep001.html.

BIBLIOGRAPHY

Lincoln, Abraham. "Draft of the Emancipation Proclamation." Mr. Lincoln's Virtual Library. Library of Congress. Accessed July 24, 2013. http://memory.loc.gov/ammem/alhtml/almss/dep001.html.

For more on citing documents from Web sites in *Chicago* style, see item 33.

Personal communication and social media

44. Personal communication Personal communications are not included in the bibliography.

44. Sara Lehman, e-mail message to author, August 13, 2015.

45. Online posting or e-mail If an online posting has been archived, include a URL. E-mails that are not part of an online discussion are treated as personal communication (see item 44). Online postings and e-mails are not included in the bibliography.

45. Bart Dale to Historum General History Forums, December 15, 2015, http://historum.com/general-history/46089-country-made-best-science-technology-contribution-16.html.

46. Facebook post Facebook posts are not included in the bibliography.

46. US Department of Housing and Urban Development's Facebook page, accessed October 15, 2015, http://www.facebook.com/HUD.

47. Twitter post (tweet) Tweets are not included in the bibliography.

47. National Geographic's Twitter feed, accessed December 18, 2015, https://twitter.com/NatGeo.

63e Manuscript format

The following guidelines for formatting a *Chicago*-style paper and preparing its endnotes and bibliography are based on *The Chicago Manual of Style*, 16th ed. (Chicago: University of Chicago Press, 2010). For pages from a sample paper, see 63f.

Formatting the paper

The guidelines in this section describe recommendations for formatting the text of your paper. For guidelines on preparing the endnotes, see pages 796–97, and for preparing the bibliography, see page 797.

Font If your instructor does not require a specific font, choose one that is standard and easy to read (such as Times New Roman).

Title page Include the full title of your paper, your name, the course title, the instructor's name, and the date. See page 798 for a sample title page.

Pagination Using arabic numerals, number the pages in the upper right corner. Do not number the title page but count it in the manuscript numbering; that is, the first page of the text will be numbered 2. Depending on your instructor's preference, you may also use a short title or your last name before the page numbers to help identify pages.

Margins, line spacing, and paragraph indents   Leave margins of at least one inch at the top, bottom, and sides of the page. Double-space the body of the paper, including long quotations that have been set off from the text. (For line spacing in notes and the bibliography, see p. 797.) Left-align the text.

Indent the first line of each paragraph one-half inch from the left margin.

Capitalization, italics, and quotation marks   In titles of works, capitalize all words except articles (*a, an, the*), prepositions (*at, from, between,* and so on), coordinating conjunctions (*and, but, or, nor, for, so, yet*), and *to* and *as*—unless the word is first or last in the title or subtitle. Follow these guidelines in your paper even if the title is styled differently in the source.

Lowercase the first word following a colon even if the word begins a complete sentence. When the colon introduces a series of sentences or questions, capitalize the first word in all sentences in the series, including the first.

Italicize the titles of books and other long works. Use quotation marks around the titles of periodical articles, short stories, poems, and other short works.

Long quotations   You can choose to set off a long quotation of five to ten typed lines by indenting the entire quotation one-half inch from the left margin. (Always set off quotations of ten or more lines.) Double-space the quotation; do not use quotation marks and do not add extra space above or below it. (See p. 800 for a long quotation in the text of a paper; see also p. 765.)

Visuals   *Chicago* classifies visuals as tables and figures (graphs, drawings, photographs, maps, and charts). Keep visuals as simple as possible.

Label each table with an arabic numeral (Table 1, Table 2, and so on) and provide a clear title that identifies the table's subject. The label and the title should appear on separate lines above the table, flush left. For a table that you have borrowed or adapted, give its source in a note like this one, below the table:

Source: Edna Bonacich and Richard P. Appelbaum, *Behind the Label* (Berkeley: University of California Press, 2000), 145.

For each figure, place a label and a caption below the figure, flush left. The label and caption need not appear on separate lines. The word "Figure" may be abbreviated to "Fig."

In the text of your paper, discuss the most significant features of each visual. Place visuals as close as possible to the sentences that relate to them unless your instructor prefers that visuals appear in an appendix.

URLs and DOIs When a URL or a DOI (digital object identifier) must break across lines, do not insert a hyphen or break at a hyphen. Instead, break after a colon or a double slash or before any other mark of punctuation. If your word processing program automatically turns URLs into links (by underlining them and changing the color), turn off this feature.

Headings *Chicago* does not provide guidelines for the use of headings in student papers. If you would like to insert headings in a long essay or research paper, check first with your instructor. See pages 799–802 for typical placement and formatting of headings in a *Chicago*-style paper.

Preparing the endnotes

Begin the endnotes on a new page at the end of the paper. Center the title "Notes" about one inch from the top of the page, and number the pages consecutively with the rest of the paper. See page 803 for an example.

Indenting and numbering   Indent the first line of each note one-half inch from the left margin; do not indent additional lines in the note. Begin the note with the arabic numeral that corresponds to the number in the text. Put a period after the number.

Line spacing   Single-space each note and double-space between notes (unless your instructor prefers double-spacing throughout).

Preparing the bibliography

Typically, the notes in *Chicago*-style papers are followed by a bibliography, an alphabetically arranged list of all the works cited or consulted. Center the title "Bibliography" about one inch from the top of the page. Number bibliography pages consecutively with the rest of the paper. See page 804 for a sample bibliography.

Alphabetizing the list   Alphabetize the bibliography by the last names of the authors (or editors); when a work has no author or editor, alphabetize it by the first word of the title other than *A, An,* or *The.*

If your list includes two or more works by the same author, arrange the entries alphabetically by title. Then use six hyphens instead of the author's name in all entries after the first. (See item 6 on p. 773.)

Indenting and line spacing   Begin each entry at the left margin, and indent any additional lines one-half inch. Single-space each entry and double-space between entries (unless your instructor prefers double-spacing throughout).

63f Sample pages from a *Chicago*-style research paper

Following are pages from a research paper by Ned Bishop, a student in a history class. Bishop used *Chicago*-style endnotes, bibliography, and manuscript format.

Title of paper.

The Massacre at Fort Pillow:
Holding Nathan Bedford Forrest Accountable

Writer's name.

Ned Bishop

Title of course,
instructor's name,
and date.

History 214
Professor Citro
March 22, 2012

Marginal annotations indicate *Chicago*-style formatting and effective writing.

Bishop 2

Although Northern newspapers of the time no doubt exaggerated some of the Confederate atrocities at Fort Pillow, most modern sources agree that a massacre of Union troops took place there on April 12, 1864. It seems clear that Union soldiers, particularly black soldiers, were killed after they had stopped fighting or had surrendered or were being held prisoner. Less clear is the role played by Major General Nathan Bedford Forrest in leading his troops. Although we will never know whether Forrest directly ordered the massacre, evidence suggests that he was responsible for it.

Thesis asserts Bishop's main point.

What happened at Fort Pillow?

Headings, centered, help readers follow the organization.

Fort Pillow, Tennessee, which sat on a bluff overlooking the Mississippi River, had been held by the Union for two years. It was garrisoned by 580 men, 292 of them from United States Colored Heavy and Light Artillery regiments, 285 from the white Thirteenth Tennessee Cavalry. Nathan Bedford Forrest commanded about 1,500 troops.[1]

Statistics are cited with an endnote.

The Confederates attacked Fort Pillow on April 12, 1864, and had virtually surrounded the fort by the time Forrest arrived on the battlefield. At 3:30 p.m., Forrest demanded the surrender of the Union forces, sending in a message of the sort he had used before: "The conduct of the officers and men garrisoning Fort Pillow has been such as to entitle them to being treated as prisoners of war. . . . Should my demand be refused, I cannot be responsible for the fate of your command."[2] Union Major William Bradford, who had replaced Major Booth, killed earlier by sharpshooters, asked for an hour to consider the demand. Forrest, worried that vessels in the river were bringing in more troops, "shortened the time to twenty minutes."[3] Bradford refused to surrender, and Forrest quickly ordered the attack.

Quotation is cited with an endnote.

The Confederates charged to the fort, scaled the parapet, and fired on the forces within. Victory came quickly, with the Union forces

Bishop 3

running toward the river or surrendering. Shelby Foote describes the scene like this:

> Some kept going, right on into the river, where a number drowned and the swimmers became targets for marksmen on the bluff. Others, dropping their guns in terror, ran back toward the Confederates with their hands up, and of these some were spared as prisoners, while others were shot down in the act of surrender.[4]

In his own official report, Forrest makes no mention of the massacre. He does make much of the fact that the Union flag was not lowered by the Union forces, saying that if his own men had not taken down the flag, "few, if any, would have survived unhurt another volley."[5] However, as Jack Hurst points out and Forrest must have known, in this twenty-minute battle, "Federals running for their lives had little time to concern themselves with a flag."[6]

The federal congressional report on Fort Pillow, which charged the Confederates with appalling atrocities, was strongly criticized by Southerners. Respected writer Shelby Foote, while agreeing that the report was "largely" fabrication, points out that the "casualty figures . . . indicated strongly that unnecessary killing had occurred."[7] In an important article, John Cimprich and Robert C. Mainfort Jr. argue that the most trustworthy evidence is that written within about ten days of the battle, before word of the congressional hearings circulated and Southerners realized the extent of Northern outrage. The article reprints a group of letters and newspaper sources written before April 22 and thus "untainted by the political overtones the controversy later assumed."[8] Cimprich and Mainfort conclude that these sources "support the case for the occurrence of a massacre" but that Forrest's role remains "clouded" because of inconsistencies in testimony.[9]

Long quotation is set off from text by indenting. Quotation marks are omitted.

Bishop uses a primary source as well as secondary sources.

Quotation is introduced with a signal phrase.

Bishop draws attention to an article that reprints primary sources.

Bishop 4

Did Forrest order the massacre?

We will never really know whether Forrest directly ordered the massacre, but it seems unlikely. True, Confederate soldier Achilles Clark, who had no reason to lie, wrote to his sisters that "I with several others tried to stop the butchery . . . but Gen. Forrest ordered them [Negro and white Union troops] shot down like dogs, and the carnage continued."[10] But it is not clear whether Clark heard Forrest giving the orders or was just reporting hearsay. Many Confederates had been shouting "No quarter! No quarter!" and, as Shelby Foote points out, these shouts were "thought by some to be at Forrest's command."[11] A Union soldier, Jacob Thompson, claimed to have seen Forrest order the killing, but when asked to describe the six-foot-two general, he called him "a little bit of a man."[12]

Perhaps the most convincing evidence that Forrest did not order the massacre is that he tried to stop it once it had begun. Historian Albert Castel quotes several eyewitnesses on both the Union and Confederate sides as saying that Forrest ordered his men to stop firing.[13] In a letter to his wife three days after the battle, Confederate soldier Samuel Caldwell wrote that "if General Forrest had not run between our men & the Yanks with his pistol and sabre drawn not a man would have been spared."[14]

In a respected biography of Nathan Bedford Forrest, Hurst suggests that the temperamental Forrest "may have ragingly ordered a massacre and even intended to carry it out—until he rode inside the fort and viewed the horrifying result" and ordered it stopped.[15] While this is an intriguing interpretation of events, even Hurst would probably admit that it is merely speculation.

Topic sentence states the main idea for this section.

Writer presents a balanced view of the evidence.

Bishop 5

Can Forrest be held responsible for the massacre?

Topic sentence
for this section
reinforces the
thesis.

Even assuming that Forrest did not order the massacre, he can still be held accountable for it. That is because he created an atmosphere ripe for the possibility of atrocities and did nothing to ensure that it wouldn't happen. Throughout his career Forrest repeatedly threatened "no quarter," particularly with respect to black soldiers, so Confederate troops had good reason to think that in massacring the enemy they were carrying out his orders. As Hurst writes, "About all he had to do to produce a massacre was issue no order against one."[16] Dudley Taylor Cornish agrees:

> It has been asserted again and again that Forrest did not order a massacre. He did not need to. He had sought to terrify the Fort Pillow garrison by a threat of no quarter, as he had done at Union City and at Paducah in the days just before he turned on Pillow. If his men did enter the fort shouting "Give them no quarter; kill them; kill them; it is General Forrest's orders," he should not have been surprised.[17]

The slaughter at Fort Pillow was no doubt driven in large part by racial hatred. Numbers alone suggest this: of 295 white troops, 168 were taken prisoner, but of 262 black troops, only 58 were taken into custody, with the rest either dead or too badly wounded to walk.[18] A Southern reporter traveling with Forrest makes clear that the discrimination was deliberate: "Our troops maddened by the excitement, shot down the ret[r]eating Yankees, and not until they had attained t[h]e water's edge and turned to beg for mercy, did any prisoners fall in [t]o our hands—Thus the whites received quarter, but the negroes were shown no mercy."[19]

Notes begin on a
new page.

Notes

1. John Cimprich and Robert C. Mainfort Jr., eds., "Fort Pillow Revisited: New Evidence about an Old Controversy," *Civil War History* 28, no. 4 (1982): 293-94.

2. Quoted in Brian Steel Wills, *A Battle from the Start: The Life of Nathan Bedford Forrest* (New York: HarperCollins, 1992), 182.

3. Ibid., 183.

4. Shelby Foote, *The Civil War, a Narrative: Red River to Appomattox* (New York: Vintage, 1986), 110.

5. Nathan Bedford Forrest, "Report of Maj. Gen. Nathan B. Forrest, C.S. Army, Commanding Cavalry, of the Capture of Fort Pillow," Shotgun's Home of the American Civil War, accessed March 6, 2012, http://www.civilwarhome.com/forrest.htm.

6. Jack Hurst, *Nathan Bedford Forrest: A Biography* (New York: Knopf, 1993), 174.

7. Foote, *Civil War*, 111.

8. Cimprich and Mainfort, "Fort Pillow," 295.

9. Ibid., 305.

10. Ibid., 299.

11. Foote, *Civil War*, 110.

12. Quoted in Wills, *Battle from the Start*, 187.

13. Albert Castel, "The Fort Pillow Massacre: A Fresh Examination of the Evidence," *Civil War History* 4, no. 1 (1958): 44-45.

14. Cimprich and Mainfort, "Fort Pillow," 300.

15. Hurst, *Nathan Bedford Forrest*, 177.

16. Ibid.

17. Dudley Taylor Cornish, *The Sable Arm: Black Troops in the Union Army, 1861-1865* (Lawrence: University Press of Kansas, 1987), 175.

18. Foote, *Civil War*, 111.

19. Cimprich and Mainfort, "Fort Pillow," 304.

First line of each
note is indented ½".
Note number
is followed by a
period. Authors'
names are not
inverted.

Notes are single-
spaced, with
double-spacing
between notes.
(Some instructors
may prefer
double-spacing
throughout.)

Last names and title
refer to an earlier
note by the same
authors.

Writer cites an
indirect source:
words quoted in
another source.

Bibliography
begins on a new
page.

Bibliography

Entries are
alphabetized
by authors'
last names.

Castel, Albert. "The Fort Pillow Massacre: A Fresh Examination of the Evidence." *Civil War History* 4, no. 1 (1958): 37-50.

Cimprich, John, and Robert C. Mainfort Jr., eds. "Fort Pillow Revisited: New Evidence about an Old Controversy." *Civil War History* 28, no. 4 (1982): 293-306.

First line of entry
is at left margin;
additional lines are
indented ½".

Cornish, Dudley Taylor. *The Sable Arm: Black Troops in the Union Army, 1861-1865.* Lawrence: University Press of Kansas, 1987.

Foote, Shelby. *The Civil War, a Narrative: Red River to Appomattox.* New York: Vintage, 1986.

Forrest, Nathan Bedford. "Report of Maj. Gen. Nathan B. Forrest, C.S. Army, Commanding Cavalry, of the Capture of Fort Pillow." Shotgun's Home of the American Civil War. Accessed March 6, 2012. http://www.civilwarhome.com/forrest.htm.

Entries are single-
spaced, with
double-spacing
between entries.
(Some instructors
may prefer
double-spacing
throughout.)

Hurst, Jack. *Nathan Bedford Forrest: A Biography.* New York: Knopf, 1993.

McPherson, James M. *Battle Cry of Freedom: The Civil War Era.* New York: Oxford University Press, 1988.

Wills, Brian Steel. *A Battle from the Start: The Life of Nathan Bedford Forrest.* New York: HarperCollins, 1992.

PART XI

Writing in the Disciplines

64 Learning to write in a discipline 807

65 Approaching writing assignments in the disciplines 814

Writing in the Disciplines

ONLINE ACTIVITIES: **Writer's Help 2.0**
macmillan learning

writershelp.com/hacker

 LaunchPad Solo
macmillan learning

macmillanhighered.com/
launchpadsolo/hacker

Learning to write in a   1 Writing practice activity
discipline

Approaching writing   1 Writing practice activity
assignments in the disciplines

College courses expose you to the thinking of scholars in many disciplines, such as those within the humanities (literature, music, art), the social sciences (psychology, anthropology, sociology), and the sciences (biology, physics, chemistry). No matter what you study, you will be asked to write for a variety of audiences in a variety of formats. In a criminal justice course, for example, you may be asked to write a policy memo or a legal brief; in a nursing course, you may be asked to write a case study or a practice paper. To write in these courses is to think like a criminologist or a nurse and to engage in the debates of the discipline.

64 Learning to write in a discipline

Writing in any discipline provides the opportunity to practice the methods used by its scholars. Each field has its own questions, preferred types of evidence, language uses, and citation conventions, but all disciplines share certain expectations for good writing. Becoming a college writer means being able to reflect on earlier lessons learned about writing and to apply these lessons to the writing you are doing in any college course.

64a Find commonalities across disciplines.

If you understand the features that are common to writing in all disciplines, you will have an easier time sorting out the unique aspects of writing in a particular field.

In every discipline, scholars write about texts. For example, in the humanities scholars write about texts such as novels, poems, paintings, and music. In the social sciences, texts include journal articles, case studies, and reports on experiments. In the sciences, researchers write about data taken from reports that other researchers have published and about data drawn from site surveys and laboratory experiments.

A good paper in any field needs to communicate the writer's purpose to an audience and to explore an engaging question about a subject. Effective writers make an argument and support their claims with evidence. Writers in most fields show readers the thesis they're developing (or, in the sciences, the hypothesis they're testing) and how they counter the objections of other writers. In some fields, such as nursing and business, writers do not always state an explicit claim but still communicate a clear purpose and use evidence to support their ideas. All disciplines require writers to document where they found their evidence and from whom they borrowed ideas.

> **MORE HELP**
>
> When writing for any course, keep in mind the steps needed to write a strong academic paper.
>
> ▶ Communicating a purpose: 1a
> ▶ Determining your audience: 1a
> ▶ Asking an academic question: 64b
> ▶ Citing sources: 56 (MLA), 61 (APA), 63d (*Chicago*)

64b Recognize the questions that writers in a discipline ask.

Disciplines are characterized by the kinds of questions their scholars attempt to answer. Social scientists, who analyze human behavior, might ask about the factors that cause people to act in certain ways. Humanities scholars interpret texts within their cultural contexts; they ask questions about the society at the time a text was written or about the connections between an author's life and work. Historians, who seek an understanding of the past, ask questions about the causes and effects of events and about connections between current and past events. Scientists collect data and ask questions to help them interpret the data.

One way to understand how disciplines ask different questions is to look at assignments on the same topic in various fields. Many disciplines, for example, might be interested in the subject of disasters. The following are some questions that writers in different fields might ask about this subject.

EDUCATION	Should the elementary school curriculum teach students how to cope in disaster situations?
FILM	How has the disaster film genre changed since the advent of computer-generated imagery (CGI) in the early 1970s?
HISTORY	How did the formation of the American Red Cross change this country's approach to natural disasters?
ENGINEERING	What recent innovations in levee design are most promising and most likely to prevent disaster?
PSYCHOLOGY	What are the most effective ways to identify and treat post-traumatic stress disorder (PTSD) in disaster survivors?

The questions you ask in any discipline will form the basis of the thesis for your writing. The questions themselves don't communicate a central idea, but they may lead you to one. For an education paper, for example, you might begin with the question "Should the elementary school curriculum teach students how to cope in disaster situations?" After considering the issues involved, you might draft the following thesis.

School systems should adopt age-appropriate curriculum units that introduce children to the risks of natural and human-made disasters and that allow children to practice coping strategies.

Whenever you write for a college course, try to determine the kinds of questions scholars in the field might ask about a topic. You can find clues in assigned readings, lecture topics, discussion groups, and the paper assignment itself. When in doubt, ask your instructor for guidance.

64c Understand the kinds of evidence that writers in a discipline use.

Regardless of the discipline in which you are writing, you must support your claims with evidence—facts, statistics, examples and illustrations, and expert opinion. Familiarize yourself with the kinds of evidence writers use to support claims in your field.

- For an English paper that examines three types of parent-child relationships in Shakespeare's *King Lear*, you would look closely at lines from the play.

- For a psychology paper on the connection between certain medications and suicidal impulses, you might study the results of clinical trials.

- For a nursing practice paper about the medical condition of a particular patient, you would review the patient's chart as well as any relevant medical literature.

- For a history paper on Renaissance attitudes toward marriage, you might examine historical documents such as letters, diaries, and church records.

The kinds of evidence used in different disciplines may overlap. Students of geography, media studies, and political science, for example, might use census data to explore different topics. The evidence that one discipline values, however, might not be sufficient to support an interpretation or a conclusion in another field. You might use anecdotes or interviews in an anthropology paper, for example, but such evidence would be irrelevant in a biology lab report. The chart on the following page lists the kinds of evidence accepted in various disciplines.

Evidence typically used in various disciplines

Humanities: literature, art, film, music, philosophy

- Passages of text or lines of a poem
- Details from an image or a work of art
- Passages of a musical composition
- Critical essays that analyze original works

Humanities: history

- Primary sources such as photographs, letters, maps, and government documents
- Scholarly books and articles that interpret evidence

Social sciences: psychology, sociology, political science, anthropology

- Data from original experiments
- Results of field research such as interviews, observations, or surveys
- Statistics from government agencies
- Scholarly books and articles that interpret data from original experiments and from other researchers' studies
- Primary sources such as maps and government documents
- Primary sources such as artifacts

Sciences: biology, chemistry, physics

- Data from original experiments
- Scholarly articles that report findings from experiments
- Models, diagrams, or animations

64d Become familiar with a discipline's language conventions.

Every discipline has a specialized vocabulary. As you read the articles and books in a field, you'll notice certain words and phrases that come up repeatedly. Sociologists, for example, use terms such as *independent variables* and *dyads* to describe social phenomena; computer scientists might refer to *algorithm design* and *loop invariants* to describe programming methods. Practitioners in health fields such as nursing use terms like *treatment plan* and *systemic assessment* to describe patient care. Use discipline-specific terms only when you are certain that you and your readers fully understand their meaning.

In addition to vocabulary, many fields of study have developed specialized conventions for point of view and verb tense. See the chart on the following page.

64e Use a discipline's preferred citation style.

In any discipline, you must give credit to those whose ideas or words you have borrowed. Whenever you write, it is your responsibility to avoid plagiarism by citing sources honestly and accurately.

While all disciplines emphasize careful documentation, each follows a particular system of citation that its members have agreed on. Writers in the humanities usually use the system established by the Modern Language Association (MLA). Scholars in some social sciences, such as psychology and anthropology, follow the style guidelines of the American Psychological Association (APA). Scholars in history and other humanities typically follow *The Chicago Manual of Style*.

> **MORE HELP**
>
> You will need to document your sources in the style preferred by your discipline.
>
> ▶ Documenting sources:
> MLA (humanities), 56;
> APA (social sciences), 61;
> *Chicago* (history), 63d.

Point of view and verb tense in academic writing

Point of view

- Writers of analytical or research essays in the humanities usually use the third-person point of view: *Austen presents . . .* or *Castel describes the battle as. . . .*

- Scientists and most social scientists, who depend on quantitative research to present findings, tend to use the third-person point of view: *The results indicate. . . .*

- Writers in the humanities and in some social sciences occasionally use the first person in discussing their personal experience or in writing a personal narrative: *After spending two years interviewing families affected by the war, I began to understand that. . . .*

Present or past tense

- Literature scholars use the present tense to discuss a text: *Hughes effectively dramatizes different views of minority assertiveness.* (See 7e.)

- Science and social science writers use the past or present perfect tense to describe experiments from source materials and the present tense to discuss the writers' own findings: *In 2003, Berkowitz released the first double-blind placebo study. . . . Rogers and Chang have found that. . . . Our results paint a murky picture.* (See 60c.)

- Writers in history use the present tense or the present perfect tense to discuss a text: *Shelby Foote describes the scene like this . . .* or *Shelby Foote has described the scene like this. . . .* (See 63c.)

65 Approaching writing assignments in the disciplines

When you are asked to write in a specific discipline, or field of study, start by becoming familiar with the distinctive features of the writing in that discipline. Be curious about the discipline's conventions and expectations for asking and answering questions. Read the assignment carefully and try to identify the purpose of the assignment and the type of evidence you are expected to use. The following sections provide examples of assignments in four disciplines—psychology, business, biology, and nursing—along with excerpts from student papers that were written in response to the assignments.

65a Writing in psychology

Psychologists write with various purposes in mind—to publish research articles, to convince funding agencies to award grants for their research, or to influence the opinions held by the public or decision makers in government, for example. When you take courses in psychology, you may be asked to write reviews of the literature about a particular topic, research papers, theoretical papers, or poster presentations. On page 815 is a typical assignment for a review of the literature.

ASSIGNMENT: REVIEW OF THE LITERATURE

Write a literature review in which you report on and
evaluate the published research on a behavioral disorder.

1 Key terms
2 Purpose: to report on and evaluate a body of evidence
3 Evidence: research of other psychologists

ADHD IN BOYS VS. GIRLS   3

Always Out of Their Seats (and Fighting):

Why Are Boys Diagnosed With ADHD More Often Than Girls?

Attention deficit hyperactivity disorder (ADHD) is a commonly
diagnosed disorder in children that affects social, academic, or
occupational functioning. As the name suggests, its hallmark
characteristics are hyperactivity and lack of attention as well as
impulsive behavior. For decades, studies have focused on the causes,
expression, prevalence, and outcome of the disorder, but until recently
very little research investigated gender differences. In fact, until the
early 1990s most research focused exclusively on boys (Brown, Madan-
Swain, & Baldwin, 1991), perhaps because many more boys than
girls are diagnosed with ADHD. Researchers have speculated on the
possible explanations for the disparity, citing reasons such as true sex
differences in the manifestation of the disorder's symptoms, gender
biases in those who refer children to clinicians, and possibly even the
diagnostic procedures themselves (Gaub & Carlson, 1997). But the
most persuasive reason is that ADHD is often a comorbid condition—
that is, it coexists with other behavior disorders that are not
diagnosed properly and that do exhibit gender differences.

Background and
explanation of the
writer's purpose.

Evidence from
research the
writer has
reviewed.

APA citations
and specialized
language (*ADHD,
comorbid*).

Thesis: writer's
argument.

Marginal annotations indicate appropriate formatting and effective writing.

> It has been suggested that in the United States children are often misdiagnosed as having ADHD when they actually suffer from a behavior disorder such as conduct disorder (CD) or a combination of ADHD and another behavior disorder (Disney, Elkins, McGue, & Iancono, 1999; Lilienfeld & Waldman, 1990). Conduct disorder is characterized by negative and criminal behavior in children and is highly correlated with adult diagnoses of antisocial personality.

Two sources in one parenthetical citation are separated with a semicolon.

65b Writing in business

In business courses, you may be asked to create documents that mirror those written in professional settings. Assignments in business courses may include reports, proposals, executive summaries, memos, or newsletters.

Here, for example, is a typical proposal assignment.

ASSIGNMENT: PROPOSAL

Write a proposal, as a memo, for improving or adding a service at a company where you have worked. Address the pros and cons of your proposal; draw on relevant studies, research, and your knowledge of the company.

1 Key terms
2 Purpose: to analyze certain evidence and make a proposal based on that analysis
3 Appropriate evidence: relevant studies, research, personal experience

MEMORANDUM

To: Jay Crosson, Senior Vice President, Human Resources

From: Kelly Ratajczak, Intern, Purchasing Department

Subject: Proposal to Add a Wellness Program

Date: April 24, 2012

Health care costs are rising. In the long run, implementing a wellness program in our corporate culture will decrease the company's health care costs.

Research indicates that nearly 70% of health care costs are from common illnesses related to high blood pressure, overweight, lack of exercise, high cholesterol, stress, poor nutrition, and other preventable health issues (Hall, 2006). Health care costs are a major expense for most businesses, and they do not reflect costs due to the loss of productivity or absenteeism. A wellness program would address most, if not all, of these health care issues and related costs.

Benefits of Healthier Employees

Not only would a wellness program substantially reduce costs associated with employee health care, but our company would prosper through many other benefits. Businesses that have wellness programs show a lower cost in production, fewer sick days, and healthier employees ("Workplace Health," 2006). Our healthier employees will help to cut not only our production and absenteeism costs but also potential costs such as higher turnover because of low employee morale.

Implementing the Program

Implementing a good wellness program means making small changes to the work environment, starting with a series of information sessions.

Marginal annotations:

Writer's main idea.

Data from recent study as support for claim.

APA citation style, typical in business.

Headings define sections of proposal.

Business terms familiar to readers (*costs*, *productivity*, *absenteeism*).

Marginal annotations indicate appropriate formatting and effective writing.

65c Writing in biology

Biologists write reports analyzing the data they collect from their experiments, reviews of other scientists' research or proposed research, and proposals to convince funding agencies to award grants for their research. When you take courses in biology, you may be asked to write lab reports, research papers, literature reviews, or proposals.

Here, for example, is a typical lab report assignment.

ASSIGNMENT: LAB REPORT

Write a report on an experiment you conduct on the ⌐1⌐ ⌐1⌐

distribution pattern of a plant species indigenous to the ⌐1⌐ ⌐1⌐

Northeast. Describe your methods for collecting data and ⌐2⌐ ⌐3⌐

interpret your experiment's results. ⌐2⌐

1 Key terms
2 Purpose: to describe the methods and interpret the results of an experiment
3 Evidence: data collected during the experiment

Distribution Pattern of Dandelion 1

CSE style, typical in sciences.

Distribution Pattern of Dandelion (*Taraxacum officinale*)

on an Abandoned Golf Course

ABSTRACT

This paper reports our study of the distribution pattern of the common dandelion (*Taraxacum officinale*) on an abandoned golf course in Hilton, NY, on 10 July 2012. An area of 6 ha was sampled with 111 randomly placed 1×1 m^2 quadrats. The dandelion count from each quadrat was used to test observed frequencies against expected frequencies based on a hypothesized random distribution.

[Abstract continues.]

Abstract: an overview of hypothesis, experiment, and results.

INTRODUCTION

Theoretically, plants of a particular species may be aggregated, random, or uniformly distributed in space [1]. The distribution type may be determined by many factors, such as availability of nutrients, competition, distance of seed dispersal, and mode of reproduction [2].

The purpose of this study was to determine if the distribution pattern of the common dandelion (*Taraxacum officinale*) on an abandoned golf course was aggregated, random, or uniform.

Introduction: context and purpose of experiment. Instead of a thesis in the introduction, a lab report interprets the data in a later Discussion section.

METHODS

The study site was an abandoned golf course in Hilton, NY. The vegetation was predominantly grasses, along with dandelions, broad-leaf plantain (*Plantago major*), and bird's-eye speedwell (*Veronica chamaedrys*). We sampled an area of approximately 6 ha on 10 July 2012, approximately two weeks after the golf course had been mowed.

Scientific names for plant species.

To ensure random sampling, we threw a tennis ball high in the air over the study area. At the spot where the tennis ball came to rest, we placed one corner of a 1×1 m^2 metal frame (quadrat). We then counted the number of dandelion plants within this quadrat. We repeated this procedure for a total of 111 randomly placed quadrats.

Marginal annotations indicate appropriate formatting and effective writing.

65d Writing in nursing

For professional nurses, writing is an important means of communicating with colleagues in the health care profession. As a student in a nursing course, you may be asked to write practice papers, case studies, research papers, or reflective narratives.

Here, for example, is a typical assignment for a nursing practice paper.

ASSIGNMENT: NURSING PRACTICE PAPER

$$\overline{ 2 }$$

Write a client history, a nursing diagnosis, recommendations

$$\overline{ 2 }$$

for care, your rationales, and expected and actual outcomes.

Use interview notes, the client's health records, and relevant

research findings.

1 Key terms

2 Purpose: to provide client history, diagnosis, recommendations, and outcomes

3 Evidence: interviews, health records, and research findings

ALL AND HTN IN ONE CLIENT   1

Acute Lymphoblastic Leukemia and Hypertension in One Client:

A Nursing Practice Paper

Physical History

E.B. is a 16-year-old white male 5'10" tall weighing 190 lb.
He was admitted to the hospital on April 14, 2012, due to decreased
platelets and a need for a PRBC transfusion. He was diagnosed in
October 2011 with T-cell acute lymphoblastic leukemia (ALL), after
a 2-week period of decreased energy, decreased oral intake, easy
bruising, and petechia. The client had experienced a 20-lb weight
loss in the previous 6 months. At the time of diagnosis, his CBC
showed a WBC count of 32, an H & H of 13/38, and a platelet count
of 34,000. His initial chest X-ray showed an anterior mediastinal
mass. Echocardiogram showed a structurally normal heart. He began
induction chemotherapy on October 12, 2011, receiving vincristine,
6-mercaptopurine, doxorubicin, intrathecal methotrexate, and then
high-dose methotrexate per protocol. During his hospital stay, he
required packed red cells and platelets on two different occasions. He
was diagnosed with hypertension (HTN) due to systolic blood pressure
readings consistently ranging between 130s and 150s and was started
on nifedipine. E.B. has a history of mild ADHD, migraines, and deep
vein thrombosis (DVT). He has tolerated the induction and consolidation
phases of chemotherapy well and is now in the maintenance phase,
in which he receives a daily dose of mercaptopurine, weekly doses of
methotrexate, and intermittent doses of steroids.

Psychosocial History

There is a possibility of a depressive episode a year previously
when he would not attend school. He got into serious trouble and
was sent to a shelter for 1 month. He currently lives with his mother,
father, and 14-year old sister.

Writer uses APA
style, typical in
social sciences.

Evidence from
client's medical
chart for overall
assessment.

Specialized
nursing
language
(*echocardiogram,
chemotherapy,*
and so on).

Instead of a
thesis, or main
claim, the
writer gives
a diagnosis,
recom-
mendations
for care, and
expected
outcomes, all
supported by
evidence from
observations and
client records.

Marginal annotations indicate appropriate formatting and effective writing.

Appendix: A document design gallery

Good document design promotes readability and increases the chances that you will achieve your purpose for writing and reach your readers. How you design a document—how you format it for the printed page or for a computer screen, for example—affects your readers' response to it. Most readers have expectations about document design and format, usually depending on the context and the purpose of the piece of writing.

This gallery features pages from both academic and business documents. The annotations on the sides of the pages point out design choices as well as important features of the writing.

▶ Pages from an MLA-style research paper, 824–25
▶ Pages from an APA-style review of the literature, 826–28
▶ Page from a business report (showing a visual), 829
▶ Business letter, 830
▶ Résumé, 831
▶ Memo, 832
▶ E-mail message, 833

Standard academic formatting

Use the manuscript format that is recommended for your academic discipline. In most English and some other humanities classes, you will be asked to use MLA (Modern Language Association) format (see 57). In most social science, business, education, and health-related classes, you'll be asked to use APA (American Psychological Association) format (see 62).

Pages 824–28 show basic formatting in MLA and APA styles. For complete student papers in MLA and APA formats, see 57b and 62b.

Standard professional formatting

It helps to look at examples when you are preparing to write a professional document such as a letter, a memo, or a résumé. (See pp. 829–32 for examples.) In general, business and professional writing is direct, clear, and courteous, and documents are designed to be read easily and quickly. When writing less formal documents such as e-mail messages in academic contexts, it's just as important to craft the document for easy readability. (See p. 833 for a sample e-mail message.)

MLA essay format

Writer's name, instructor's name, course title, date flush left on first page; title centered.

Writer's last name and page number in upper right corner of each page.

1"

Dan Larson

Professor Duncan

English 102

19 April 2016

The Transformation of Mrs. Peters:

An Analysis of "A Jury of Her Peers"

½"
→ In Susan Glaspell's 1917 short story "A Jury of Her Peers,"
two women accompany their husbands and a county attorney to an

Double-spacing throughout.

isolated house where a farmer named John Wright has been choked
to death in his bed with a rope. The chief suspect is Wright's wife,
Minnie, who is in jail awaiting trial. The sheriff's wife, Mrs. Peters, has
come along to gather some personal items for Minnie, and Mrs. Hale

1"

has joined her. Early in the story, Mrs. Hale sympathizes with Minnie
and objects to the way the male investigators are "snoopin' round and

1"

Quotations from source cited with page numbers in parentheses.

criticizin'" her kitchen (249). In contrast, Mrs. Peters shows respect
for the law, saying that the men are doing "no more than their duty"
(249). By the end of the story, however, Mrs. Peters has joined Mrs.
Hale in a conspiracy of silence, lied to the men, and committed a crime—
hiding key evidence. What causes this dramatic change?

One critic, Leonard Mustazza, argues that Mrs. Hale recruits
Mrs. Peters "as a fellow 'juror' in the case, moving the sheriff's wife
away from her sympathy for her husband's position and towards
identification with the accused wom[a]n" (494). While this is true,
Mrs. Peters also reaches insights on her own. Her observations in the
kitchen lead her to understand Minnie's grim and lonely plight as the
wife of an abusive farmer, and her identification with both Minnie and
Mrs. Hale is strengthened as the men conducting the investigation
trivialize the lives of women.

1"

Larson 2

The first evidence that Mrs. Peters reaches understanding on her
own surfaces in the following passage:

> The sheriff's wife had looked from the stove to the sink—to the
> pail of water which had been carried in from outside. . . . That
> look of seeing into things, of seeing through a thing to something
> else, was in the eyes of the sheriff's wife now. (251-52)

Something about the stove, the sink, and the pail of water connects

A long quotation
is set off by
indenting; no
quotation marks
are needed;
ellipsis dots
indicate a
sentence omitted
from the source.

MLA works cited page

Larson 7

Works Cited

Ben-Zvi, Linda. "'Murder, She Wrote': The Genesis of Susan Glaspell's
Trifles." *Susan Glaspell: Essays on Her Theater and Fiction*,
edited by Ben-Zvi, U of Michigan P, 1995, pp. 19-48. Originally
published in *Theatre Journal*, vol. 44, no. 2, 1992, pp. 141-62.

Glaspell, Susan. "A Jury of Her Peers." *Literature and Its Writers: A
Compact Introduction to Fiction, Poetry, and Drama*, edited by
Ann Charters and Samuel Charters, 6th ed., Bedford/St. Martin's,
2013, pp. 243-58.

Hedges, Elaine. "Small Things Reconsidered: 'A Jury of Her Peers.'"
Susan Glaspell: Essays on Her Theater and Fiction, edited by Linda
Ben-Zvi, U of Michigan P, 1995, pp. 49-69.

Mustazza, Leonard. "Generic Translation and Thematic Shift in Susan
Glaspell's *Trifles* and 'A Jury of Her Peers.'" *Studies in Short
Fiction*, vol. 26, no. 4, 1989, pp. 489-96.

Heading
centered.

List alphabetized
by authors' last
names (or by title
for works with no
author).

First line of
each entry at left
margin; extra lines
indented ½".

Double-spacing
throughout;
no extra space
between entries.

APA title page

Header consists of shortened title (no more than 50 characters) in all capital letters at left margin and page number at right margin; on title page only, words "Running head" and colon precede shortened title.

Running head: REACTION TIMES IN VISUAL SEARCH TASKS   1

Full title, writer's name, and school centered halfway down page.

Reaction Times for Detection of Objects

in Two Visual Search Tasks

Allison Leigh Johnson

Carthage College

Author's note (optional) gives writer's affiliation, information about course, and possibly acknowledgments and contact information.

Author Note

Allison Leigh Johnson, Department of Psychology, Carthage College. This research was conducted for Psychology 2300, Cognition: Theories and Application, taught by Professor Leslie Cameron.

APA abstract

Abstract

Visual detection of an object can be automatic or can require attention. The reaction time varies depending on the type of search task being performed. In this visual search experiment, 3 independent variables were tested: type of search, number of distracters, and presence or absence of a target. A feature search contains distracters notably different from the target, while a conjunctive search contains distracters with features similar to the target. For this experiment, 14 Carthage College students participated in a setting of their choice. A green circle was the target. During the feature search, reaction times were similar regardless of the number of distracters and the presence or absence of the target. In the conjunctive search, the number of distracters and the presence or absence of the target affected reaction times. This visual search experiment supports the idea that feature searches are automatic and conjunctive searches require attention from the viewer.

Keywords: visual search, cognition, feature search, conjunctive search

Shortened title and page number on every page.

Abstract, a 150-to-250-word overview of paper, appears on separate page. Heading centered, not boldface.

Numerals for all numbers in abstract, even numbers under 10.

Keywords (optional) help readers search for paper on the Web or in a database.

APA essay format

½"

Full title,
repeated and
centered, not
boldface.

Reaction Times for Detection of Objects

in Two Visual Search Tasks

½"

→ Vision is one of the five senses, and it is the sense trusted most

by humans (Reisberg, 2010). We use our vision for everything. We are

always looking for things, whether it is where we are going or finding

→a friend at a party. Our vision detects the object(s) we are looking for. ←

1"   1"

Some objects are easier to detect than others. Spotting your sister

wearing a purple shirt in a crowd of boring white shirts is automatic

and can be done with ease. However, if your sister was also wearing a

white shirt, it would take much time and attention to spot her in that

same crowd.

Sources cited
in parentheses
with author's
last name and
date.

The "pop out effect" describes the quick identification of an

object being searched for because of its salient features (Reeves,

2007). When you look for your sister wearing a purple shirt, for

APA list of references

References

List of references
begins on new
page; heading
centered, not
boldface.

Reeves, R. (2007). *The Norton psychology labs workbook*. New York, NY:
Norton.

Reisberg, D. (2010). *Cognition: Exploring the science of the mind*. New
York, NY: Norton.

List alphabetized
by authors' last
names.

First line of each
entry flush left;
additional lines
indented ½".
Double-spacing
throughout.

Treisman, A. (1986). Features and objects in visual processing.
Scientific American, *255*, 114-125.

Wolfe, J. M. (1998). What do 1,000,000 trials tell us about visual
search? *Psychological Science*, *9*, 33-39.

ZAPS: The Norton psychology labs. (2004). Retrieved from http://
wwnorton.com/ZAPS/

Business report with a visual

Employee Motivation 5

Doug Ames, manager of operations for OAISYS, noted that some of these issues keep the company from outperforming expectations: "Communication is not timely or uniform, expectations are not clear and consistent, and some employees do not contribute significantly yet nothing is done" (personal communication, February 28, 2006).

Recommendations

It appears that a combination of steps can be used to unlock greater performance for OAISYS. Most important, steps can be taken to strengthen the corporate culture in key areas such as communication, accountability, and appreciation. Employee feedback indicates that these are areas of weakness or motivators that can be improved. This feedback is summarized in Figure 1.

A plan to use communication effectively to set expectations, share results in a timely fashion, and publicly offer appreciation to specific contributors will likely go a long way toward aligning individual motivation with corporate goals. Additionally, holding individuals

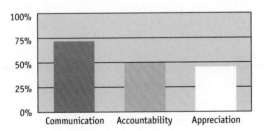

Figure 1. Areas of greatest need for improvements in motivation.

Report formatted in typical business style, with citations in APA style.

Visual referred to in body of report.

Figure, a bar graph, appears at bottom of page on which it is mentioned. Figure number and caption placed below figure.

Business letter in full block style

LatinoVoice⊚

Date ——— March 16, 2015

Jonathan Ross
Managing Editor
Latino World Today   — Inside
2971 East Oak Avenue   address
Baltimore, MD 21201

Salutation ——— Dear Mr. Ross:

Thank you very much for taking the time yesterday to speak to the University of
Maryland's Latino Club. A number of students have told me that they enjoyed
your presentation and found your job search suggestions to be extremely helpful.

Paragraphs   As I mentioned to you, the club publishes a monthly newsletter, *Latino Voice*. Our
single-spaced,   purpose is to share up-to-date information and expert advice with members of the
not indented;   university's Latino population. Considering how much students benefited from your   Body
double-spacing   talk, I would like to publish excerpts from it in our newsletter.
between
paragraphs.   I have transcribed parts of your presentation and organized them into a question-
                  and-answer format for our readers. Would you mind looking through the enclosed
                  article and letting me know if I may have your permission to print it? I'm hoping to
                  include this article in our next newsletter, so I would need your response by April 4.

                  Once again, Mr. Ross, thank you for sharing your experiences with us. I would love to
                  be able to share your thoughts with students who couldn't hear you in person.

Close ——— Sincerely,

Jeffrey Richardson ——— Signature

Jeffrey Richardson
Associate Editor

Indicates
something ——— Enc.
enclosed
with letter.

210 Student Center University of Maryland College Park MD 20742

Résumé

Alexis A. Smith

404 Ponce de Leon Avenue NE, #B7   404-231-1234
Atlanta, GA 30308   alexis_smith@smith.localhost

SKILLS SUMMARY
- Writing: competent communicating to different audiences, using a range of written forms (articles, reports, flyers, pamphlets, memos, letters)
- Design: capable of creating visually appealing, audience-appropriate documents; skilled at taking and editing photographs
- Technical: proficient in Microsoft Office; comfortable with Dreamweaver, Photoshop, InDesign
- Language: fluent in spoken and written Spanish

EDUCATION
Bachelor of Arts in English   expected May 2018
Georgia State University, Atlanta, GA
- Emphasis areas: journalism and communication
- Study Abroad, Ecuador (Fall 2016)
- Dean's List (Fall 2016, Fall 2017)

EXPERIENCE
Copyeditor   Jan. 2017-present
The Signal, Atlanta, GA
- copyedit articles for spelling, grammar, and style
- fact-check articles
- prepare copy for Web publication in Dreamweaver

Writing Tutor   Oct. 2015-present
Georgia State University Writing Studio, Atlanta, GA
- work with undergraduate and graduate students on writing projects in all subject areas
- provide technical support for multimedia projects

OUTREACH AND ACTIVITIES
- Publicity Director, English Department
  Student Organization   Aug. 2017-present
- Coordinator, Georgia State University
  Relay for Life Student Team   April 2017, 2018

Limit résumé to one page, if possible, two pages at most.

Information organized into clear categories— Skills Summary, Education, Experience, etc.—and formatted for easy scanning.

Information presented in reverse chronological order.

Bulleted lists organize information.

Present-tense verbs (*provide*) used for current activities.

Professional memo

COMMONWEALTH PRESS

MEMORANDUM

February 28, 2017

To: Editorial assistants, Advertising Department

cc: Stephen Chapman

From: Helen Brown

Subject: Training for new database software

The new database software will be installed on your computers next week. I have scheduled a training program to help you become familiar with the software and with our new procedures for data entry and retrieval.

Training program

A member of our IT staff will teach in-house workshops on how to use the new software. If you try the software before the workshop, please be prepared to discuss any problems you encounter.

We will keep the training groups small to encourage hands-on participation and to provide individual attention. The workshops will take place in the training room on the third floor from 10:00 a.m. to 2:00 p.m.

Lunch will be provided in the cafeteria.

Sign-up

Please sign up by March 1 for one of the following dates by adding your name in the department's online calendar:

- Wednesday, March 8
- Friday, March 10
- Monday, March 13

If you will not be in the office on any of those dates, please let me know by March 6.

Margin annotations:

Date, name of recipient, name of sender on separate lines.

Subject line describes topic clearly and concisely.

Introduction states point of memo.

Headings guide readers and promote quick scanning of document.

List calls attention to important information.

E-mail message

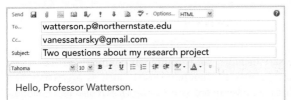

To... watterson.p@northernstate.edu

Cc... vanessatarsky@gmail.com

Subject: Two questions about my research project

Hello, Professor Watterson.

Thank you for taking the time to meet with me yesterday to talk about my research project. I am excited to start the project this week. As we discussed, I am planning to meet with a reference librarian to learn more about NSU's online resources. And I will also develop an online survey to gather my fellow nursing students' perspectives on the topic. In the meantime, I have two questions:

- Do I need approval from the college's institutional review board before I conduct my survey?

- Do I need students' approval to quote their responses in my paper?

I know this is a busy time of year, but if possible, please let me know the answers to these questions before the end of the week.

Thanks for all your help with my project.

Sincerely,

Vanessa Tarsky

Clear, specific subject line explains purpose of message.

Introduction explains reason for writing.

Formal tone and language appropriate for communicating with professor.

Message formatted to be read quickly. Bullets draw reader's eye to important details.

Desired outcome of message: request stated briefly.

Message ends with brief, friendly closing.

Glossary of Usage

This glossary includes words commonly confused (such as *accept* and *except*), words commonly misused (such as *aggravate*), and words that are nonstandard (such as *hisself*). It also lists colloquialisms and jargon. Colloquialisms are casual expressions that may be appropriate in informal speech but are inappropriate in formal writing. Jargon is needlessly technical or pretentious language that is inappropriate in most contexts. If an item is not listed here, consult the index. For irregular verbs (such as *sing, sang, sung*), see 27a. For idiomatic use of prepositions, see 18d.

a, an Use *an* before a vowel sound, *a* before a consonant sound: *an apple, a peach.* Problems sometimes arise with words beginning with *h* or *u*. If the *h* is silent, the word begins with a vowel sound, so use *an*: *an hour, an honorable deed.* If the *h* is pronounced, the word begins with a consonant sound, so use *a*: *a hospital, a historian, a hotel.* Words such as *university* and *union* begin with a consonant sound (a *y* sound), so use *a*: *a union.* Words such as *uncle* and *umbrella* begin with a vowel sound, so use *an*: *an underground well.* When an abbreviation or an acronym begins with a vowel sound, use *an*: *an EKG, an MRI, an AIDS prevention program.*

accept, except *Accept* is a verb meaning "to receive." *Except* is usually a preposition meaning "excluding." *I will accept all the packages except that one. Except* is also a verb meaning "to exclude." *Please except that item from the list.*

adapt, adopt *Adapt* means "to adjust or become accustomed"; it is usually followed by *to. Adopt* means "to take as one's own." *Our family adopted a Vietnamese child, who quickly adapted to his new life.*

adverse, averse *Adverse* means "unfavorable." *Averse* means "opposed" or "reluctant"; it is usually followed by *to. I am averse to your proposal because it could have an adverse impact on the economy.*

advice, advise *Advice* is a noun, *advise* a verb. *We advise you to follow John's advice.*

affect, effect *Affect* is usually a verb meaning "to influence." *Effect* is usually a noun meaning "result." *The drug did not affect the disease, and it had adverse side effects. Effect* can also be a verb meaning "to bring about." *Only the president can effect such a dramatic change.*

aggravate *Aggravate* means "to make worse or more troublesome." *Overgrazing aggravated the soil erosion.* In formal writing, avoid the use of *aggravate* meaning "to annoy or irritate." *Her babbling annoyed* (not *aggravated*) *me.*

agree to, agree with *Agree to* means "to give consent to." *Agree with* means "to be in accord with" or "to come to an understanding with." *He agrees with me about the need for change, but he won't agree to my plan.*

ain't *Ain't* is nonstandard. Use *am not, are not (aren't),* or *is not (isn't). I am not* (not *ain't*) *going home for spring break.*

all ready, already *All ready* means "completely prepared." *Already* means "previously." *Susan was all ready for the concert, but her friends had already left.*

all right *All right,* written as two words, is correct. *Alright* is nonstandard.

all together, altogether *All together* means "everyone or everything in one place." *Altogether* means "entirely." *We were not altogether certain that we could bring the family all together for the reunion.*

allude To *allude* to something is to make an indirect reference to it. Do not use *allude* to mean "to refer directly." *In his lecture, the professor referred* (not *alluded*) *to several pre-Socratic philosophers.*

allusion, illusion An *allusion* is an indirect reference. An *illusion* is a misconception or false impression. *Did you catch my allusion to Shakespeare? Mirrors give the room an illusion of depth.*

a lot *A lot* is two words. Do not write *alot. Sam lost a lot of weight.* See also *lots, lots of.*

among, between   See *between, among.*

amongst   In American English, *among* is preferred.

amoral, immoral   *Amoral* means "neither moral nor immoral"; it also means "not caring about moral judgments." *Immoral* means "morally wrong." *Until recently, most business courses were taught from an amoral perspective. Murder is immoral.*

amount, number   Use *amount* with quantities that cannot be counted; use *number* with those that can. *This recipe calls for a large amount of sugar. We have a large number of toads in our garden.*

an   See *a, an.*

and etc.   *Et cetera* (*etc.*) means "and so forth"; *and etc.* is redundant. See also *etc.*

and/or   Avoid the awkward construction *and/or* except in technical or legal documents.

angry at, angry with   Use *angry with,* not *angry at,* when referring to a person. *The coach was angry with the referee.*

ante-, anti-   The prefix *ante-* means "earlier" or "in front of"; the prefix *anti-* means "against" or "opposed to." *William Lloyd Garrison was a leader of the antislavery movement during the antebellum period. Anti-* should be used with a hyphen when it is followed by a capital letter or a word beginning with *i.*

anxious   *Anxious* means "worried" or "apprehensive." In formal writing, avoid using *anxious* to mean "eager." *We are eager (not anxious) to see your new house.*

anybody, anyone   *Anybody* and *anyone* are singular. (See 21e and 22a.)

anymore   Use the adverb *anymore* in a negative context to mean "any longer" or "now." *The factory isn't producing shoes anymore.* Using *anymore* in a positive context is colloquial; in formal writing, use *now* instead. *We order all our food online now* (not *anymore*).

anyone   See *anybody, anyone.*

anyone, any one *Anyone*, an indefinite pronoun, means "any person at all." *Any one*, the pronoun *one* preceded by the adjective *any*, refers to a particular person or thing in a group. *Anyone from the winning team may choose any one of the games on display.*

anyplace *Anyplace* is colloquial. In formal writing, use *anywhere*.

anyways, anywheres *Anyways* and *anywheres* are nonstandard. Use *anyway* and *anywhere*.

as Do not use *as* to mean "because" if there is any chance of ambiguity. *We canceled the picnic because* (not *as*) *it began raining. As* here could mean either "because" or "when."

as, like See *like, as*.

as to *As to* is jargon for *about*. *He inquired about* (not *as to*) *the job*.

averse See *adverse, averse*.

awful The adjective *awful* and the adverb *awfully* are not appropriate in formal writing.

awhile, a while *Awhile* is an adverb; it can modify a verb, but it cannot be the object of a preposition such as *for*. The two-word form *a while* is a noun preceded by an article and therefore can be the object of a preposition. *Stay awhile. Stay for a while.*

back up, backup *Back up* is a verb phrase. *Back up the car carefully. Be sure to back up your hard drive. Backup* is a noun meaning "a copy of electronically stored data." *Keep your backup in a safe place. Backup* can also be used as an adjective. *I regularly create backup files.*

bad, badly *Bad* is an adjective, *badly* an adverb. *They felt bad about ruining the surprise. Her arm hurt badly after she slid into second base.* (See 26a, 26b, and 26c.)

being as, being that *Being as* and *being that* are nonstandard expressions. Write *because* instead. *Because* (not *Being as*) *I slept late, I had to skip breakfast.*

beside, besides *Beside* is a preposition meaning "at the side of" or "next to." *Annie sleeps with a flashlight beside her bed. Besides* is a preposition meaning "except" or "in addition to." *No one besides Terrie can have that ice cream. Besides* is also an adverb meaning "in addition." *I'm not hungry; besides, I don't like ice cream.*

between, among Ordinarily, use *among* with three or more entities, *between* with two. *The prize was divided among several contestants. You have a choice between carrots and beans.*

bring, take Use *bring* when an object is being transported toward you, *take* when it is being moved away. *Please bring me a glass of water. Please take these forms to Mr. Scott.*

burst, bursted; bust, busted *Burst* is an irregular verb meaning "to come open or fly apart suddenly or violently." Its past tense is *burst*. The past-tense form *bursted* is nonstandard. *Bust* and *busted* are slang for *burst* and, along with *bursted*, should not be used in formal writing.

can, may The distinction between *can* and *may* is fading, but some writers still observe it in formal writing. *Can* is traditionally reserved for ability, *may* for permission. *Can you speak French? May I help you?*

capital, capitol *Capital* refers to a city, *capitol* to a building where lawmakers meet. *Capital* also refers to wealth or resources. *The residents of the state capital protested plans to close the streets surrounding the capitol.*

censor, censure *Censor* means "to remove or suppress material considered objectionable." *Censure* means "to criticize severely." *The administration's policy of censoring books has been censured by the media.*

cite, site *Cite* means "to quote as an authority or example." *Site* is usually a noun meaning "a particular place." *He cited the zoning law in his argument against the proposed site of the gas station.* Locations on the Internet are usually referred to as *sites. The library's Web site improves every week.*

climactic, climatic *Climactic* is derived from *climax*, the point of greatest intensity in a series or progression of events. *Climatic* is derived from *climate* and refers to meteorological conditions. *The climactic period in the dinosaurs' reign was reached just before severe climatic conditions brought on an ice age.*

coarse, course *Coarse* means "crude" or "rough in texture." *The coarse weave of the wall hanging gave it a three-dimensional quality. Course* usually refers to a path, a playing field, or a unit of study; the expression *of course* means "certainly." *I plan to take a course in car repair this summer. Of course, you are welcome to join me.*

compare to, compare with *Compare to* means "to represent as similar." *She compared him to a wild stallion. Compare with* means "to examine similarities and differences." *The study compared the language ability of apes with that of dolphins.*

complement, compliment *Complement* is a verb meaning "to go with or complete" or a noun meaning "something that completes." As a verb, *compliment* means "to flatter"; as a noun, it means "flattering remark." *Her skill at rushing the net complements his skill at volleying. Martha's flower arrangements receive many compliments.*

conscience, conscious *Conscience* is a noun meaning "moral principles." *Conscious* is an adjective meaning "aware or alert." *Let your conscience be your guide. Were you conscious of his love for you?*

continual, continuous *Continual* means "repeated regularly and frequently." *She grew weary of the continual telephone calls. Continuous* means "extended or prolonged without interruption." *The broken siren made a continuous wail.*

could care less *Could care less* is nonstandard. Write *couldn't care less* instead. *He couldn't* (not *could*) *care less about his psychology final.*

could of *Could of* is nonstandard for *could have. We could have* (not *could of*) *taken the train.*

council, counsel A *council* is a deliberative body, and a *councilor* is a member of such a body. *Counsel* usually means "advice" and can also mean "lawyer"; a *counselor* is one who gives advice or guidance. *The councilors met to draft the council's position paper. The pastor offered wise counsel to the troubled teenager.*

criteria *Criteria* is the plural of *criterion*, which means "a standard or rule or test on which a judgment or decision can be based." *The only criterion for the scholarship is achievement.*

data *Data* is a plural noun technically meaning "facts or propositions." But *data* is increasingly being accepted as a singular noun. *The new data suggest* (or *suggests*) *that our theory is correct.* (The singular *datum* is rarely used.)

different from, different than Ordinarily, write *different from*. *Your sense of style is different from Jim's.* However, *different than* is acceptable to avoid an awkward construction. *Please let me know if your plans are different than* (to avoid *from what*) *they were six weeks ago.*

differ from, differ with *Differ from* means "to be unlike"; *differ with* means "to disagree with." *My approach to the problem differed from hers. She differed with me about the wording of the agreement.*

disinterested, uninterested *Disinterested* means "impartial, objective"; *uninterested* means "not interested." *We sought the advice of a disinterested counselor to help us solve our problem. Mark was uninterested in anyone's opinion but his own.*

don't *Don't* is the contraction for *do not. I don't want any. Don't* should not be used as the contraction for *does not*, which is *doesn't. He doesn't* (not *don't*) *want any.*

due to *Due to* is an adjective phrase and should not be used as a preposition meaning "because of." *The trip was canceled because of* (not *due to*) *lack of interest. Due to* is acceptable as a subject complement and usually follows a form of the verb *be. His success was due to hard work.*

each *Each* is singular. (See 21e and 22a.)

effect See *affect, effect.*

e.g. In formal writing, replace the Latin abbreviation *e.g.* with its English equivalent: *for example* or *for instance.*

either *Either* is singular. (See 21e and 22a.) For *either . . . or* constructions, see 21d and 22a.

elicit, illicit *Elicit* is a verb meaning "to bring out" or "to evoke." *Illicit* is an adjective meaning "unlawful." *The reporter was unable to elicit any information from the police about illicit drug traffic.*

emigrate from, immigrate to *Emigrate* means "to leave one country or region to settle in another." *In 1903, my great-grandfather emigrated from Russia to escape the religious pogroms. Immigrate* means "to enter another country and reside there." *More than fifty thousand Bosnians immigrated to the United States in the 1990s.*

eminent, imminent *Eminent* means "outstanding" or "distinguished." *We met an eminent professor of Greek history. Imminent* means "about to happen." *The snowstorm is imminent.*

enthused Avoid using *enthused* as an adjective. Use *enthusiastic* instead. *The children were enthusiastic* (not *enthused*) *about baking.*

etc. Avoid ending a list with *etc.* It is more emphatic to end with an example, and in most contexts readers will understand that the list is not exhaustive. When you don't wish to end with an example, *and so on* is more graceful than *etc.* (See also *and etc.*)

eventually, ultimately Often used interchangeably, *eventually* is the better choice to mean "at an unspecified time in the future," and *ultimately* is better to mean "the furthest possible extent or greatest extreme." *He knew that eventually he would complete his degree. The existentialists considered suicide the ultimately rational act.*

everybody, everyone *Everybody* and *everyone* are singular. (See 21e and 22a.)

everyone, every one *Everyone* is an indefinite pronoun. *Every one,* the pronoun *one* preceded by the adjective *every,* means "each individual or thing in a particular group." *Every one* is usually followed by *of. Everyone wanted to go. Every one of the missing books was found.*

except See *accept, except.*

expect Avoid the informal use of *expect* meaning "to believe, think, or suppose." *I think* (not *expect*) *it will rain tonight.*

explicit, implicit *Explicit* means "expressed directly" or "clearly defined"; *implicit* means "implied, unstated." *I gave him explicit instructions not to go swimming. My mother's silence indicated her implicit approval.*

farther, further *Farther* usually describes distances. *Further* usually suggests quantity or degree. *Chicago is farther from Miami than I thought. I would be grateful for further suggestions.*

fewer, less Use *fewer* for items that can be counted; use *less* for items that cannot be counted. *Fewer people are living in the city. Please put less sugar in my tea.*

finalize *Finalize* is jargon meaning "to make final or complete." Use ordinary English instead. *The architect prepared final drawings* (not *finalized the drawings*).

firstly *Firstly* sounds pretentious, and it leads to the ungainly series *firstly, secondly, thirdly,* and so on. Write *first, second, third* instead.

further See *farther, further.*

get *Get* has many colloquial uses. In writing, avoid using *get* to mean the following: "to evoke an emotional response" (*That music always gets to me*); "to annoy" (*After a while, his sulking got to me*); "to take revenge on" (*I got back at her by leaving the room*); "to become" (*He got sick*); "to start or begin" (*Let's get going*). Avoid using *have got to* in place of *must. I must* (not *have got to*) *finish this paper tonight.*

good, well *Good* is an adjective, *well* an adverb. (See 26a, 26b, and 26c.) *He hasn't felt good about his game since he sprained his wrist last season. She performed well on the uneven parallel bars.*

graduate Both of the following uses of *graduate* are standard: *My sister was graduated from UCLA last year. My sister graduated from UCLA last year.* It is nonstandard, however, to drop the word *from*:

My sister graduated UCLA last year. Though this usage is common in informal English, many readers object to it.

grow Phrases such as *to grow the economy* and *to grow a business* are jargon. Usually the verb *grow* is intransitive (it does not take a direct object). *Our business has grown very quickly.* Use *grow* in a transitive sense, with a direct object, to mean "to cultivate" or "to allow to grow." *We plan to grow tomatoes this year. John is growing a beard.*

hanged, hung *Hanged* is the past-tense and past-participle form of the verb *hang* meaning "to execute." *The prisoner was hanged at dawn. Hung* is the past-tense and past-participle form of the verb *hang* meaning "to fasten or suspend." *The stockings were hung by the chimney with care.*

hardly Avoid expressions such as *can't hardly* and *not hardly*, which are considered double negatives. *I can* (not *can't*) *hardly describe my surprise at getting the job.* (See 26e.)

has got, have got *Got* is unnecessary and awkward in such constructions. It should be dropped. *We have* (not *have got*) *three days to prepare for the opening.*

he At one time *he* was commonly used to mean "he or she." Today such usage is inappropriate. (See 17f and 22a.)

he/she, his/her In formal writing, use *he or she* or *his or her*. For alternatives to these wordy constructions, see 17f and 22a.

hisself *Hisself* is nonstandard. Use *himself.*

hopefully *Hopefully* means "in a hopeful manner." *We looked hopefully to the future.* Some usage experts object to the use of *hopefully* as a sentence adverb, apparently on grounds of clarity. To be safe, avoid using *hopefully* in sentences such as the following: *Hopefully, your son will recover soon.* Instead, indicate who is doing the hoping: *I hope that your son will recover soon.*

however In the past, some writers objected to the conjunctive adverb *however* at the beginning of a sentence, but current experts allow placing the word according to the intended meaning and emphasis. All of the following sentences are correct. *Pam decided, however, to attend the lecture. However, Pam decided to attend the lecture.* (She had been considering other activities.) *Pam, however, decided to attend the lecture.* (Unlike someone else, Pam chose to attend the lecture.) (See 32f.)

hung See *hanged, hung*.

i.e. In formal writing, use "in other words" or "that is" rather than the Latin abbreviation *i.e.* to introduce a clarifying statement. *Exposure to borax usually causes only mild skin irritation; in other words* (not *i.e.*), *it's not especially toxic.*

if, whether Use *if* to express a condition and *whether* to express alternatives. *If you go on a trip, whether to Nebraska or Italy, remember to bring identification.*

illusion See *allusion, illusion*.

immigrate See *emigrate from, immigrate to*.

imminent See *eminent, imminent*.

immoral See *amoral, immoral*.

implement *Implement* is a pretentious way of saying "do," "carry out," or "accomplish." Use ordinary language instead. *We carried out* (not *implemented*) *the director's orders.*

implicit See *explicit, implicit*.

imply, infer *Imply* means "to suggest or state indirectly"; *infer* means "to draw a conclusion." *John implied that he knew all about databases, but the interviewer inferred that John was inexperienced.*

in, into *In* indicates location or condition; *into* indicates movement or a change in condition. *They found the lost letters in a box after moving into the house.*

in regards to *In regards to* confuses two different phrases: *in regard to* and *as regards*. Use one or the other. *In regard to* (or *As regards*) *the contract, ignore the first clause.*

irregardless *Irregardless* is nonstandard. Use *regardless*.

is when, is where These mixed constructions are often incorrectly used in definitions. *A runoff election is a second election held to break a tie* (not *is when a second election is held to break a tie*). (See 11c.)

its, it's *Its* is a possessive pronoun; *it's* is a contraction of *it is*. (See 36c and 36e.) *It's always fun to watch a dog chase its tail.*

kind(s) *Kind* is singular and should be treated as such. Don't write *These kind of chairs are rare.* Write instead *This kind of chair is rare. Kinds* is plural and should be used only when you mean more than one kind. *These kinds of chairs are rare.*

kind of, sort of Avoid using *kind of* or *sort of* to mean "somewhat." *The movie was somewhat* (not *sort of*) *boring.* Do not put *a* after either phrase. *That kind of* (not *kind of a*) *salesclerk annoys me.*

lay, lie See *lie, lay.*

lead, led *Lead* is a metallic element; it is a noun. *Led* is the past tense of the verb *lead. He led me to the treasure.*

learn, teach *Learn* means "to gain knowledge"; *teach* means "to impart knowledge." *I must teach* (not *learn*) *my sister to read.*

leave, let *Leave* means "to exit." Avoid using it with the nonstandard meaning "to permit." *Let* (not *Leave*) *me help you with the dishes.*

led See *lead, led.*

less See *fewer, less.*

let, leave See *leave, let.*

liable *Liable* means "obligated" or "responsible." Do not use it to mean "likely." *You're likely* (not *liable*) *to trip if you don't tie your shoelaces.*

lie, lay *Lie* is an intransitive verb meaning "to recline or rest on a surface." Its forms are *lie, lay, lain. Lay* is a transitive verb meaning "to put or place." Its forms are *lay, laid, laid.* (See 27b.)

like, as *Like* is a preposition, not a subordinating conjunction. It can be followed only by a noun or a noun phrase. *As* is a subordinating conjunction that introduces a subordinate clause. In casual speech, you may say *She looks like she hasn't slept* or *You don't know her like I do.* But in formal writing, use *as. She looks as if she hasn't slept. You don't know her as I do.* (See also 46f and 46g.)

loose, lose *Loose* is an adjective meaning "not securely fastened." *Lose* is a verb meaning "to misplace" or "to not win." *Did you lose your only loose pair of work pants?*

lots, lots of *Lots* and *lots of* are informal substitutes for *many, much,* or *a lot.* Avoid using them in formal writing.

mankind Avoid *mankind* whenever possible. It offends many readers because it excludes women. Use *humanity, humans, the human race,* or *humankind* instead. (See 17f.)

may See *can, may.*

maybe, may be *Maybe* is an adverb meaning "possibly." *Maybe the sun will shine tomorrow. May be* is a verb phrase. *Tomorrow may be brighter.*

may of, might of *May of* and *might of* are nonstandard for *may have* and *might have. We might have* (not *might of*) *had too many cookies.*

media, medium *Media* is the plural of *medium. Of all the media that cover the Olympics, television is the medium that best captures the spectacle of the events.*

might of See *may of, might of.*

most *Most* is informal when used to mean "almost" and should be avoided. *Almost* (not *Most*) *everyone went to the parade.*

must of See *may of, might of. Must of* is nonstandard for *must have.*

myself *Myself* is a reflexive or intensive pronoun. Reflexive: *I cut myself.* Intensive: *I will drive you myself.* Do not use *myself* in place of *I* or *me. He gave the pie to Ed and me* (not *myself*). (See also 24a and 24b.)

neither *Neither* is singular. For *neither . . . nor* constructions, see 21d, 22a, and 22d.

none *None* may be singular or plural. (See 21e.)

nowheres *Nowheres* is nonstandard. Use *nowhere* instead.

number See *amount, number*.

of Use the verb *have*, not the preposition *of*, after the verbs *could, should, would, may, might*, and *must*. *They must have* (not *must of*) *left early.*

off of *Off* is sufficient. Omit *of*. *The ball rolled off* (not *off of*) *the table.*

OK, O.K., okay All three spellings are acceptable, but avoid these expressions in formal speech and academic writing.

parameters *Parameter* is a mathematical term that has become jargon for "boundary" or "guideline." Use ordinary English instead. *The task force worked within certain guidelines* (not *parameters*).

passed, past *Passed* is the past tense of the verb *pass*. *Ann passed me another slice of cake. Past* usually means "belonging to a former time" or "beyond a time or place." *Our past president spoke until past midnight. The hotel is just past the next intersection.*

percent, per cent, percentage *Percent* (also spelled *per cent*) is always used with a specific number. *Percentage* is used with a descriptive term such as *large* or *small*, not with a specific number. *The candidate won 80 percent of the primary vote. A large percentage of registered voters turned out for the election.*

phenomena *Phenomena* is the plural of *phenomenon*, which means "an observable occurrence or fact." *Strange phenomena occur at all hours of the night in that house, but last night's phenomenon was the strangest of all.*

plus *Plus* should not be used to join independent clauses. *This raincoat is dirty; moreover* (not *plus*), *it has a hole in it.*

precede, proceed *Precede* means "to come before." *Proceed* means "to go forward." *As we proceeded up the mountain path, we noticed fresh tracks in the mud, evidence that a group of hikers had preceded us.*

principal, principle *Principal* is a noun meaning "the head of a school or an organization" or "a sum of money." It is also an adjective meaning "most important." *Principle* is a noun meaning "a basic truth or law." *The principal expelled her for three principal reasons. We believe in the principle of equal justice for all.*

proceed, precede See *precede, proceed.*

quote, quotation *Quote* is a verb; *quotation* is a noun. Avoid using *quote* as a shortened form of *quotation. Her quotations* (not *quotes*) *from current movies intrigued us.*

raise, rise *Raise* is a transitive verb meaning "to move or cause to move upward." It takes a direct object. *I raised the shades. Rise* is an intransitive verb meaning "to go up." *Heat rises.*

real, really *Real* is an adjective; *really* is an adverb. *Real* is sometimes used informally as an adverb, but avoid this use in formal writing. *She was really* (not *real*) *angry.* (See 26a and 26b.)

reason . . . is because Use *that* instead of *because. The reason she's cranky is that* (not *because*) *she didn't sleep last night.* (See 11c.)

reason why The expression *reason why* is redundant. *The reason* (not *The reason why*) *Jones lost the election is clear.*

relation, relationship *Relation* describes a connection between things. *Relationship* describes a connection between people. *There is a relation between poverty and infant mortality. Our business relationship has cooled over the years.*

respectfully, respectively *Respectfully* means "showing or marked by respect." *Respectively* means "each in the order given." *He respectfully submitted his opinion to the judge. John, Tom, and Larry were a butcher, a baker, and a lawyer, respectively.*

rise See *raise, rise.*

sensual, sensuous *Sensual* means "gratifying the physical senses," especially those associated with sexual pleasure. *Sensuous* means "pleasing to the senses," especially those involved in the experience of art, music, and nature. *The sensuous music and balmy air led the dancers to more sensual movements.*

set, sit *Set* is a transitive verb meaning "to put" or "to place." Its past tense is *set. She set the dough in a warm corner of the kitchen. Sit* is an intransitive verb meaning "to be seated." Its past tense is *sat. The cat sat in the doorway.*

shall, will *Shall* was once used in place of the helping verb *will* with *I* or *we: I shall, we shall.* Today, however, *will* is generally accepted even when the subject is *I* or *we.* The word *shall* occurs primarily in polite questions (*Shall I find you a pillow?*) and in legalistic sentences suggesting duty or obligation (*The applicant shall file form A by December 31*).

should of *Should of* is nonstandard for *should have. They should have* (not *should of*) *been home an hour ago.*

since Do not use *since* to mean "because" if there is any chance of ambiguity. *Because* (not *Since*) *we won the game, we have been celebrating with a pitcher of root beer. Since* here could mean "because" or "from the time that."

sit See *set, sit.*

site See *cite, site.*

somebody, someone *Somebody* and *someone* are singular. (See 21e and 22a.)

something *Something* is singular. (See 21e.)

sometime, some time, sometimes *Sometime* is an adverb meaning "at an indefinite time." *Some time* is the adjective *some* modifying the noun *time* and means "a period of time." *Sometimes* is an adverb meaning "at times, now and then." *I'll see you all sometime soon. I haven't lived there for some time. Sometimes I see him at work.*

suppose to *Suppose to* is nonstandard for *supposed to*. *I was supposed to* (not *suppose to*) *be there by noon.*

sure and Write *sure to*. *We were all taught to be sure to* (not *sure and*) *look both ways before crossing a street.*

take See *bring, take.*

than, then *Than* is a conjunction used in comparisons; *then* is an adverb denoting time. *That pizza is more than I can eat. Tom laughed, and then we recognized him.*

that See *who, which, that.*

that, which Many writers reserve *that* for restrictive clauses, *which* for nonrestrictive clauses. (See 32e.)

theirselves *Theirselves* is nonstandard for *themselves*. *The crash victims pushed the car out of the way themselves* (not *theirselves*).

them The use of *them* in place of *those* is nonstandard. *Please take those* (not *them*) *flowers to the patient in room 220.*

then, than See *than, then.*

there, their, they're *There* is an adverb specifying place; it is also an expletive (placeholder). Adverb: *Sylvia is sitting there patiently.* Expletive: *There are two plums left. Their* is a possessive pronoun: *Fred and Jane finally washed their car. They're* is a contraction of *they are: They're later than usual today.*

they The use of *they* to indicate possession is nonstandard. Use *their* instead. *Cindy and Sam decided to sell their* (not *they*) *1975 Corvette.*

they, their The use of the plural pronouns *they* and *their* to refer to singular nouns or pronouns is nonstandard. *No one handed in his or her* (not *their*) *draft on time.* (See 22a.)

this kind See *kind(s).*

to, too, two *To* is a preposition; *too* is an adverb; *two* is a number. *Too many of your shots slice to the left, but the last two were just right.*

toward, towards *Toward* and *towards* are generally interchangeable, although *toward* is preferred in American English.

try and *Try and* is nonstandard for *try to*. *The teacher asked us all to try to* (not *try and*) *write an original haiku.*

ultimately, eventually See *eventually, ultimately.*

unique Avoid expressions such as *most unique, more straight, less perfect, very round.* Either something is unique or it isn't. It is illogical to suggest degrees of uniqueness. (See 26d.)

usage The noun *usage* should not be substituted for *use* when the meaning is "employment of." *The use* (not *usage*) *of insulated shades has cut fuel costs dramatically.*

use to *Use to* is nonstandard for *used to*. *I used to* (not *use to*) *take the bus to work.*

utilize *Utilize* means "to make use of." It often sounds pretentious; in most cases, *use* is sufficient. *I used* (not *utilized*) *the 3-D printer.*

wait for, wait on *Wait for* means "to be in readiness for" or "to await." *Wait on* means "to serve." *We're waiting for* (not *waiting on*) *Ruth to take us to the museum.*

ways *Ways* is nonstandard when used to mean "distance." *The city is a long way* (not *ways*) *from here.*

weather, whether The noun *weather* refers to the state of the atmosphere. *Whether* is a conjunction referring to a choice between alternatives. *We wondered whether the weather would clear.*

well, good See *good, well.*

where Do not use *where* in place of *that*. *I heard that* (not *where*) *the crime rate is increasing.*

whether See *if, whether.*

which See *that, which* and *who, which, that.*

while Avoid using *while* to mean "although" or "whereas" if there is any chance of ambiguity. *Although* (not *While*) *Gloria lost money in the slot machine, Tom won it at roulette.* Here *While* could mean either "although" or "at the same time that."

who, which, that Do not use *which* to refer to persons. Use *who* instead. *That*, though generally used to refer to things, may be used to refer to a group or class of people. *The player who* (not *that* or *which*) *made the basket at the buzzer was named MVP. The team that scores the most points in this game will win the tournament.*

who, whom *Who* is used for subjects and subject complements; *whom* is used for objects. (See 25.)

who's, whose *Who's* is a contraction of *who is; whose* is a possessive pronoun. *Who's ready for more popcorn? Whose coat is this?* (See 36c and 36e.)

will See *shall, will.*

would of *Would of* is nonstandard for *would have. She would have* (not *would of*) *had a chance to play if she had arrived on time.*

you In formal writing, avoid *you* in an indefinite sense meaning "anyone." (See 23d.) *Any spectator* (not *You*) *could tell by the way John caught the ball that his throw would be too late.*

your, you're *Your* is a possessive pronoun; *you're* is a contraction of *you are. Is that your new bike? You're in the finals.* (See 36c and 46b.)

Answers to Exercises

NOTE: Possible revisions to paragraph-style exercises such as 9–2 and 13–1 appear in the Instructor's Annotated Edition only.

Exercise 6–2, page 145

a. hasty generalization; b. false analogy; c. *either . . . or* fallacy; d. biased language; e. faulty cause-and-effect reasoning

Exercise 8–1, page 197   *Possible revisions:*

a. The Prussians defeated the Saxons in 1745.
b. Ahmed, the producer, manages the entire operation.
c. The tour guides expertly paddled the sea kayaks.
d. Emphatic and active; no change
e. Protesters were shouting on the courthouse steps.

Exercise 8–2, page 197

a. passive; b. active; c. passive; d. active; e. active

Exercise 9–1, page 203   *Possible revisions:*

a. Police dogs are used for finding lost children, tracking criminals, and detecting bombs and illegal drugs.
b. Hannah told her rock-climbing partner that she bought a new harness and that she wanted to climb Otter Cliffs.
c. It is more difficult to sustain an exercise program than to start one.
d. During basic training, I was told not only what to do but also what to think.
e. Jan wanted to drive to the wine country or at least to Sausalito.

Exercise 10–1, page 208   *Possible revisions:*

a. A grapefruit or an orange is a good source of vitamin C.
b. The women entering the military academy can expect haircuts as short as those of the male cadets.
c. Looking out the family room window, Sarah saw that her favorite tree, which she had climbed as a child, was gone.
d. The graphic designers are interested in and knowledgeable about producing posters for the balloon race.
e. The Great Barrier Reef is larger than any other coral reef in the world.

Exercise 11–1, page 212   *Possible revisions:*

a. Using surgical gloves is a precaution now taken by dentists to prevent contact with patients' blood and saliva.

b. A career in medicine, which my brother is pursuing, requires at least ten years of challenging work.

c. The pharaohs had bad teeth because tiny particles of sand found their way into Egyptian bread.

d. Recurring bouts of flu caused the team to forfeit a record number of games.

e. This box contains the key to your future.

Exercise 12–1, page 216   *Possible revisions:*

a. More research is needed to evaluate effectively the risks posed by volcanoes in the Pacific Northwest.

b. Many students graduate from college with debt totaling more than fifty thousand dollars.

c. It is a myth that humans use only 10 percent of their brains.

d. A coolhunter is a person who can find the next wave of fashion in the unnoticed corners of modern society.

e. Not all geese fly beyond Narragansett for the winter.

Exercise 12–6, page 220   *Possible revisions:*

a. To complete an online purchase with a credit card, you must enter the expiration date and the security code.

b. Though Martha was only sixteen, UCLA accepted her application.

c. As I settled in the cockpit, the pounding of the engine was muffled only slightly by my helmet.

d. After studying polymer chemistry, Phuong found computer games less complex.

e. When I was a young man, my mother enrolled me in tap dance classes.

Exercise 13–5, page 227   *Possible revisions:*

a. An incredibly talented musician, Ray Charles mastered R&B, soul, and gospel styles. He even performed country music well.

b. Environmentalists point out that shrimp farming in Southeast Asia is polluting water and making farmlands useless. They warn that governments must act before it is too late.

c. We observed the samples for five days before we detected any growth. *Or* The samples were observed for five days before any growth was detected.

d. In his famous soliloquy, Hamlet contemplates whether death would be preferable to his difficult life and, if so, whether he is capable of committing suicide.

e. The lawyer told the judge that Miranda Hale was innocent and asked that she be allowed to prove the allegations false. *Or* The lawyer told the judge, "Miranda Hale is innocent. Please allow her to prove the allegations false."

Exercise 13–6, page 227 *Possible revisions:*

a. Courtroom lawyers need to have more than a touch of theater in their blood.

b. The interviewer asked whether we had brought our proof of citizenship and our passports.

c. Experienced reconnaissance scouts know how to make fast decisions and use sophisticated equipment to keep their teams from being detected.

d. After the animators finish their scenes, the production designer arranges the clips according to the storyboard and makes synchronization notes for the sound editor and the composer.

e. Madame Defarge is a sinister figure in Dickens's *A Tale of Two Cities*. On a symbolic level, she represents fate; like the Greek Fates, she knits the fabric of individual destiny.

Exercise 14–1, page 235 *Possible revisions:*

a. Williams played for the Boston Red Sox from 1939 to 1960, and he managed the Washington Senators and Texas Rangers for several years after retiring as a player.

b. In 1941, Williams finished the season with a batting average of .406; no player has hit over .400 for a season since then.

c. Although he acknowledged that Joe DiMaggio was a better all-around player, Williams felt that he was a better hitter than DiMaggio.

d. Williams was a stubborn man; for example, he always refused to tip his cap to the crowd after a home run because he claimed that fans were fickle.

e. Williams's relationship with the media was unfriendly at best; he sarcastically called baseball writers the "knights of the keyboard" in his memoir.

Exercise 14–2, page 236 *Possible revisions:*

a. The X-Men comic books and Japanese woodcuts of kabuki dancers, all part of Marlena's research project on popular culture, covered the tabletop and the chairs.

b. Our waitress, costumed in a kimono, had painted her face white and had arranged her hair in a beehive.

c. Students can apply for a spot in the leadership program, which teaches thinking and communication skills.

d. Shore houses were flooded, beaches were washed away, and Brant's Lighthouse was swallowed by the sea.

e. Laura Thackray, an engineer at Volvo, addressed women's safety needs by designing a pregnant crash-test dummy.

Exercise 14–8, page 237   *Possible revisions:*

a. These particles, known as "stealth liposomes," can hide in the body for a long time without detection.

b. Irena, a competitive gymnast majoring in biochemistry, intends to apply her athletic experience and her science degree to a career in sports medicine.

c. Because students, textile workers, and labor unions have loudly protested sweatshop abuses, apparel makers have been forced to examine their labor practices.

d. Developed in a European university, IRC (Internet relay chat) was created as a way for a group of graduate students to talk about projects from their dorm rooms.

e. The cafeteria's new menu, which has an international flavor, includes everything from enchiladas and pizza to pad thai and sauerbraten.

Exercise 14–10, page 239   *Possible revisions:*

a. Working as an aide for the relief agency, Gina distributed food and medical supplies.

b. Janbir, who spent every Saturday learning tabla drumming, noticed with each hour of practice that his memory for complex patterns was growing stronger.

c. When the rotor hit, it gouged a hole about an eighth of an inch deep in my helmet.

d. My grandfather, who was born eighty years ago in Puerto Rico, raised his daughters the old-fashioned way.

e. By reversing the depressive effect of the drug, the Narcan saved the patient's life.

Exercise 15–1, page 246   *Possible revisions:*

a. Across the hall from the fossils exhibit are the exhibits for insects and spiders.

b. After growing up desperately poor in Japan, Sayuri becomes a successful geisha.

c. Researchers who have been studying Mount St. Helens for years believe that a series of earthquakes in the area may have caused the 1980 eruption.

d. Ice cream typically contains 10 percent milk fat, but premium ice cream may contain up to 16 percent milk fat and has considerably less air in the product.

e. If home values climb, the economy may recover more quickly than expected.

Exercise 16–1, page 254   *Possible revisions:*

a. Martin Luther King Jr. set a high standard for future leaders.

b. Alice has loved cooking since she could first peek over a kitchen tabletop.

c. Bloom's race for the governorship is futile.

d. A successful graphic designer must have technical knowledge and an eye for color and balance.

e. You will set up e-mail for all employees.

Exercise 17–1, page 259   *Possible revisions:*

a. When I was young, my family was poor.

b. This conference will help me serve my clients better.

c. The meteorologist warned the public about the possible dangers of the coming storm.

d. Government studies show a need for after-school programs.

e. Passengers should try to complete the customs declaration form before leaving the plane.

Exercise 17–6, page 266   *Possible revisions:*

a. Dr. Geralyn Farmer is the chief surgeon at University Hospital. Dr. Paul Green is her assistant.

b. All applicants want to know how much they will earn.

c. Elementary school teachers should understand the concept of nurturing if they intend to be effective.

d. Obstetricians need to be available to their patients at all hours.

e. If we do not stop polluting our environment, we will perish.

Exercise 18–2, page 271   *Possible revisions:*

a. We regret this delay; thank you for your patience.

b. Ada's plan is to acquire education and experience to prepare herself for a position as property manager.

c. Serena Williams, the ultimate competitor, has earned millions of dollars just in endorsements.

d. Many people take for granted that public libraries have up-to-date computer systems.

e. The effect of Gao Xingjian's novels on other Chinese exiles is hard to gauge.

Exercise 18–5, page 273 *Possible revisions:*

a. Queen Anne was so angry with Sarah Churchill that she refused to see her again.

b. Correct

c. The parade moved off the street and onto the beach.

d. The frightened refugees intend to make the dangerous trek across the mountains.

e. What type of wedding are you planning?

Exercise 18–8, page 275 *Possible revisions:*

a. John stormed into the room like a hurricane.

b. Some people insist that they'll always be available to help, even when they haven't been before.

c. The Cubs easily beat the Mets, who were in trouble early in the game today at Wrigley Field.

d. We worked out the problems in our relationship.

e. My mother accused me of evading her questions when in fact I was just saying the first thing that came to mind.

Exercise 19–1, page 286 *Possible revisions:*

a. Listening to the CD her sister had sent, Mia was overcome with a mix of emotions: happiness, homesickness, and nostalgia.

b. Cortés and his soldiers were astonished when they looked down from the mountains and saw Tenochtitlán, the magnificent capital of the Aztecs.

c. Although my spoken Spanish is not very good, I can read the language with ease.

d. There are several reasons for not eating meat. One reason is that dangerous chemicals are used throughout the various stages of meat production.

e. To learn how to sculpt beauty from everyday life is my intention in studying art and archaeology.

Exercise 20–1, page 295   *Possible revisions:*

a. The city had one public swimming pool that stayed packed with children all summer long.

b. The building is being renovated, so at times we have no heat, water, or electricity.

c. The view was not what the travel agent had described. Where were the rolling hills and the shimmering rivers?

d. Walker's coming-of-age novel is set against a gloomy scientific backdrop; the Earth's rotation has begun to slow down.

e. City officials had good reason to fear a major earthquake: Most [*or* most] of the business district was built on landfill.

Exercise 20–2, page 295   *Possible revisions:*

a. Wind power for the home is a supplementary source of energy that can be combined with electricity, gas, or solar energy.

b. Correct

c. In the Middle Ages, when the streets of London were dangerous places, it was safer to travel by boat along the Thames.

d. "He's not drunk," I said. "He's in a state of diabetic shock."

e. Are you able to endure extreme angle turns, high speeds, frequent jumps, and occasional crashes? Then supermoto racing may be a sport for you.

Exercise 21–1, page 308

a. One of the main reasons for elephant poaching is the profits received from selling the ivory tusks.

b. Correct

c. A number of students in the seminar were aware of the importance of joining the discussion.

d. Batik cloth from Bali, blue and white ceramics from Delft, and a bocce ball from Turin have made Angelie's room the talk of the dorm.

e. Correct

Exercise 22–1, page 314   *Possible revisions:*

a. Every presidential candidate must appeal to a wide variety of ethnic and social groups to win the election.

b. David lent his motorcycle to someone who allowed a friend to use it.

c. The trainer motioned for all the students to move their arms in wide, slow circles.

d. Correct
e. Applicants should be bilingual if they want to qualify for this position.

Exercise 23–1, page 320 *Possible revisions:*

a. Some professors say that engineering students should have hands-on experience with dismantling and reassembling machines.
b. Because she had decorated her living room with posters from chamber music festivals, her date thought that she was interested in classical music. Actually she preferred rock.
c. In my high school, students didn't need to get all A's to be considered a success; they just needed to work to their ability.
d. Marianne told Jenny, "I am worried about your mother's illness." [*or* ". . . about my mother's illness."]
e. Though Lewis cried for several minutes after scraping his knee, eventually his crying subsided.

Exercise 24–1, page 326

a. Correct [But the writer could change the end of the sentence: . . . *than he was.*]
b. Correct [But the writer could change the end of the sentence: . . . *that she was the coach.*]
c. She appreciated his telling the truth in such a difficult situation.
d. The director has asked you and me to draft a proposal for a new recycling plan.
e. Five close friends and I rented an SUV, packed it with food, and drove two hundred miles to Mardi Gras.

Exercise 25–1, page 331

a. Correct
b. The environmental policy conference featured scholars whom I had never heard of. [*or* . . . scholars I had never heard of.]
c. Correct
d. Daniel always gives a holiday donation to whoever needs it.
e. So many singers came to the audition that Natalia had trouble deciding whom to select for the choir.

Exercise 26–1, page 338 *Possible revisions:*

a. Do you expect to perform well on the nursing board exam next week?
b. With the budget deadline approaching, our office has hardly had time to handle routine correspondence.

c. Correct
d. The customer complained that he hadn't been treated nicely by the agent on the phone.
e. Of all the smart people in my family, Uncle Roberto is the cleverest [*or* most clever].

Exercise 27–1, page 345

a. When I get the urge to exercise, I lie down until it passes.
b. Grandmother had driven our new hybrid to the sunrise church service, so we were left with the van.
c. A pile of dirty rags was lying at the bottom of the stairs.
d. How did the game know that the player had gone from the room with the blue ogre to the hall where the gold was heaped?
e. Abraham Lincoln took good care of his legal clients; the contracts he drew for the Illinois Central Railroad could never be broken.

Exercise 27–5, page 351

a. The glass sculptures of the Swan Boats were prominent in the brightly lit lobby.
b. Visitors to the glass museum were not supposed to touch the exhibits.
c. Our church has all the latest technology, even a closed-circuit television.
d. Christos didn't know about Marlo's promotion because he never listens. He is [*or* He's] always talking.
e. Correct

Exercise 27–9, page 358   *Possible revisions:*

a. Correct
b. Watson and Crick discovered the mechanism that controls inheritance in all life: the workings of the DNA molecule.
c. When city planners proposed rezoning the waterfront, did they know that the mayor had promised to curb development in that neighborhood?
d. Tonight's concert begins at 9:30. If it were earlier, I'd consider going.
e. Correct

Exercise 28–1, page 368

a. In the past, tobacco companies denied any connection between smoking and health problems.
b. The volunteer's compassion has touched many lives.

c. I want to register for a summer tutoring session.
d. By the end of the year, the state will have tested 139 birds for avian flu.
e. The golfers were prepared for all weather conditions.

Exercise 28–4, page 371

a. A major league pitcher can throw a baseball more than ninety-five miles per hour.
b. The writing center tutor will help you revise your essay.
c. A reptile must adjust its body temperature to its environment.
d. Correct
e. My uncle, a cartoonist, could sketch a face in less than a minute.

Exercise 28–7, page 374 *Possible revisions:*

a. The electrician might have discovered the broken circuit if she had gone through the modules one at a time.
b. If Verena wins a scholarship, she will go to graduate school.
c. Whenever a rainbow appears after a storm, everybody comes out to see it.
d. Sarah did not understand the terms of her internship.
e. If I lived in Budapest with my cousin Szusza, she would teach me Hungarian cooking.

Exercise 28–10, page 378 *Possible answers:*

a. I enjoy riding my motorcycle.
b. The tutor told Samantha to come to the writing center.
c. The team hopes to work hard and win the championship.
d. Ricardo and his brothers miss surfing during the winter.
e. Jon remembered to lock the door. *Or* Jon remembered seeing that movie years ago.

Exercise 29–1, page 388

a. Doing volunteer work often brings satisfaction.
b. As I looked out the window of the plane, I could see Cape Cod.
c. Melina likes to drink her coffee with lots of cream.
d. Correct
e. I completed my homework assignment quickly. *Or* I completed the homework assignment quickly.

Exercise 30–1, page 393

a. There are some cartons of ice cream in the freezer.

b. I don't use the subway because I am afraid.
c. The prime minister is the most popular leader in my country.
d. We tried to get in touch with the same manager whom we spoke to earlier.
e. Recently there have been a number of earthquakes in Turkey.

Exercise 30–4, page 395 *Possible revisions:*

a. Although freshwater freezes at 32 degrees Fahrenheit, ocean water freezes at 28 degrees Fahrenheit.
b. Because we switched cable packages, our channel lineup has changed.
c. The competitor confidently mounted his skateboard.
d. My sister performs the *legong*, a Balinese dance, well.
e. Correct

Exercise 30–7, page 397

a. Listening to everyone's complaints all day was irritating.
b. The long flight to Singapore was exhausting.
c. Correct
d. After a great deal of research, the scientist made a fascinating discovery.
e. Surviving that tornado was one of the most frightening experiences I've ever had.

Exercise 30–10, page 398

a. an intelligent young Vietnamese sculptor
b. a dedicated Catholic priest
c. her old blue wool sweater
d. Joe's delicious Scandinavian bread
e. many beautiful antique jewelry boxes

Exercise 31–1, page 399

a. Whenever we eat at the Centerville Café, we sit at a small table in the corner of the room.
b. Correct
c. On Thursday, Nancy will attend her first home repair class at the community center.
d. Correct
e. We decided to go to a restaurant because there was no fresh food in the refrigerator.

Exercise 32–1, page 409

a. Alisa brought the injured bird home and fashioned a splint out of Popsicle sticks for its wing.
b. Considered a classic of early animation, *The Adventures of Prince Achmed* used hand-cut silhouettes against colored backgrounds.
c. If you complete the evaluation form and return it within two weeks, you will receive a free breakfast during your next stay.
d. Correct
e. Roger had always wanted a handmade violin, but he couldn't afford one.

Exercise 32–2, page 410

a. J. R. R. Tolkien finished writing his draft of *The Lord of the Rings* trilogy in 1949, but the first book in the series wasn't published until 1954.
b. In the first two minutes of its ascent, the space shuttle had broken the sound barrier and reached a height of over twenty-five miles.
c. German shepherds can be gentle guide dogs, or they can be fierce attack dogs.
d. Some former professional cyclists admit that the use of performance-enhancing drugs is widespread in cycling, but they argue that no rider can be competitive without doping.
e. As an intern, I learned most aspects of the broadcasting industry, but I never learned about fundraising.

Exercise 32–5, page 412

a. The cold, impersonal atmosphere of the university was unbearable.
b. An ambulance threaded its way through police cars, fire trucks, and irate citizens.
c. Correct
d. After two broken arms, three cracked ribs, and one concussion, Ken quit the varsity football team.
e. Correct

Exercise 32–6, page 412

a. NASA's rovers on Mars are equipped with special cameras that can take close-up, high-resolution pictures of the terrain.
b. Correct
c. Correct
d. Love, vengeance, greed, and betrayal are common themes in Western literature.

e. Many experts believe that shark attacks on surfers are a result of the sharks' mistaking surfboards for small injured seals.

Exercise 32–9, page 416

a. Choreographer Alvin Ailey's best-known work, *Revelations*, is more than just a crowd-pleaser.
b. Correct
c. Correct
d. A member of an organization that provides job training for teens was also appointed to the education commission.
e. Brian Eno, who began his career as a rock musician, turned to meditative compositions in the late 1970s.

Exercise 32–11, page 421

a. Cricket, which originated in England, is also popular in Australia, South Africa, and India.
b. At the sound of the starting pistol, the horses surged forward toward the first obstacle, a sharp incline three feet high.
c. After seeing an exhibition of Western art, Gerhard Richter escaped from East Berlin and smuggled out many of his notebooks.
d. Corrie's new wet suit has an intricate blue pattern.
e. We replaced the rickety old spiral staircase with a sturdy new ladder.

Exercise 32–13, page 422

a. On January 15, 2012, our office moved to 29 Commonwealth Avenue, Mechanicsville, VA 23111.
b. Correct
c. Ms. Carlson, you are a valued customer whose satisfaction is very important to us.
d. Mr. Mundy was born on July 22, 1939, in Arkansas, where his family had lived for four generations.
e. Correct

Exercise 33–1, page 427

a. Correct
b. Tricia's first artwork was a bright blue clay dolphin.
c. Some modern musicians (trumpeter Jon Hassell is an example) blend several cultural traditions into a unique sound.
d. Myra liked hot, spicy foods such as chili, kung pao chicken, and buffalo wings.
e. On the display screen was a soothing pattern of light and shadow.

Exercise 34–1, page 431

a. "Do not ask me to be kind; just ask me to act as though I were."
b. "When men talk about defense, they always claim to be protecting women and children, but they never ask the women and children what they think."
c. "When I get a little money, I buy books; if any is left, I buy food and clothes."
d. Correct
e. "Wit has truth in it; wisecracking is simply calisthenics with words."

Exercise 34–2, page 431

a. Strong black coffee will not sober you up; the truth is that time is the only way to get alcohol out of your system.
b. Margaret was not surprised to see hail and vivid lightning; conditions had been right for violent weather all day.
c. There is often a fine line between right and wrong, good and bad, truth and deception.
d. Correct
e. Severe, unremitting pain is a ravaging force, especially when the patient tries to hide it from others.

Exercise 35–1, page 434

a. Correct [Either *It* or *it* is correct.]
b. If we have come to fight, we are far too few; if we have come to die, we are far too many.
c. The travel package includes a round-trip ticket to Athens, a cruise through the Cyclades, and all hotel accommodations.
d. The news article portrays the land use proposal as reckless, although 62 percent of the town's residents support it.
e. Psychologists Kindlon and Thompson (2000) offer parents a simple starting point for raising male children: "Teach boys that there are many ways to be a man" (p. 256).

Exercise 36–1, page 438

a. Correct
b. The innovative shoe fastener was inspired by the designer's young son.
c. Each day's menu features a different European country's dish.
d. Sue worked overtime to increase her family's earnings.

e. Ms. Jacobs is unwilling to listen to students' complaints about computer failures.

Exercise 37–1, page 445

a. As for the advertisement "Sailors have more fun," if you consider chipping paint and swabbing decks fun, then you will have plenty of it.
b. Correct
c. After winning the lottery, Juanita said that she would give half the money to charity.
d. After the movie, Vicki said, "The reviewer called this flick 'trash of the first order.' I guess you can't believe everything you read."
e. Correct

Exercise 39–1, page 453

a. A client left his or her [*or* a] cell phone in our conference room after the meeting.
b. The films we made of Kilauea on our trip to Hawaii Volcanoes National Park illustrate a typical spatter cone eruption.
c. Correct
d. Of three engineering fields — chemical, mechanical, and materials — Keegan chose materials engineering for its application to toy manufacturing.
e. Correct

Exercise 40–1, page 460

a. Correct
b. Some combat soldiers are trained by government diplomats to be sensitive to issues of culture, history, and religion.
c. Correct
d. A gluten-free diet is not always the best strategy for shedding pounds.
e. The work of Dr. Khan, a psychology professor and researcher, has helped practitioners better understand post-traumatic stress.

Exercise 41–1, page 462

a. *MLA style:* The carpenters located three maple timbers, twenty-one sheets of cherry, and ten oblongs of polished ebony for the theater set. *APA style:* The carpenters located three maple timbers, 21 sheets of cherry, and 10 oblongs of polished ebony for the theater set.
b. Correct

c. Correct

d. Eight students in the class had been labeled "learning disabled."

e. The Vietnam Veterans Memorial in Washington, DC, had 58,132 names inscribed on it when it was dedicated in 1982.

Exercise 42–1, page 465

a. Howard Hughes commissioned the *Spruce Goose*, a beautifully built but thoroughly impractical wooden aircraft.

b. The old man screamed his anger, shouting to all of us, "I will not leave my money to you worthless layabouts!"

c. I learned the Latin term *ad infinitum* from an old nursery rhyme about fleas: "Great fleas have little fleas upon their back to bite 'em, / Little fleas have lesser fleas and so on *ad infinitum*."

d. Correct

e. Neve Campbell's lifelong interest in ballet inspired her involvement in the film *The Company*, which portrays a season with the Joffrey Ballet.

Exercise 44–1, page 478

a. Correct

b. The swiftly moving tugboat pulled alongside the barge and directed it away from the oil spill in the harbor.

c. Correct

d. Your dog is well known in our neighborhood.

e. Roadblocks were set up along all the major highways leading out of the city.

Exercise 45–1, page 483

a. Assistant Dean Shirin Ahmadi recommended offering more world language courses.

b. Correct

c. Kalindi has an ambitious semester, studying differential calculus, classical Hebrew, brochure design, and Greek literature.

d. Lydia's aunt and uncle make modular houses as beautiful as modernist works of art.

e. We amused ourselves on the long flight by discussing how spring in Kyoto stacks up against summer in London.

Exercise 46–1, page 488

a. stage, confrontation, proportions; b. courage, mountain (noun/

adjective), climber, inspiration, rescuers; c. need, guest, honor, fog; d. defense (noun/adjective), attorney, appeal, jury; e. museum, women (noun/adjective), artists, 1987

Exercise 46–5, page 490

a. his; b. that, our (pronoun/adjective); c. he, himself, some, his (pronoun/adjective); d. I, my (pronoun/adjective), you, one; e. no one, her

Exercise 46–9, page 493

a. told; b. were, killed; c. brought down; d. Stay, 'll [will] arrive; e. struggled, was trapped

Exercise 46–13, page 495

a. Adjectives: weak, unfocused; b. Adjectives: The (article), Spanish, flexible; adverb: wonderfully; c. Adjectives: The (article), fragrant, the (article), steady; adverb: especially; d. Adjectives: hot, cold; adverbs: rather, slightly, bitterly; e. Adjectives: The (article), its (pronoun/adjective), wicker (noun/adjective); adverb: soundly

Exercise 47–1, page 502

a. Complete subjects: The hills and mountains, the snow atop them; simple subjects: hills, mountains, snow
b. Complete subject: points; simple subject: points
c. Complete subject: (You)
d. Complete subject: hundreds of fireflies; simple subject: hundreds
e. Complete subject: The evidence against the defendant; simple subject: evidence

Exercise 47–5, page 505

a. Subject complement: innovative; b. Direct object: death; c. Direct object: their players' efforts; d. Subject complement: the capital of the Russian Empire; e. Subject complement: bitter

Exercise 47–6, page 505

a. Direct objects: adults and children; object complement: weary
b. Indirect object: students; direct object: healthy meal choices
c. Direct object: the work; object complement: finished
d. Indirect objects: the agent, us; direct objects: our tickets, boarding passes
e. Direct object: community service; object complement: her priority

Exercise 48–1, page 510

a.   In northern Italy (adverb phrase modifying *met*); as their first language (adverb phrase modifying *speak*)
b.   through the thick forest (adjective phrase modifying *hike*); with ease (adverb phrase modifying *completed*)
c.   To my boss's dismay (adverb phrase modifying *was*); for work (adverb phrase modifying *late*)
d.   of Mayan artifacts (adjective phrase modifying *exhibit*); into pre-Columbian culture (adjective phrase modifying *insight*)
e.   In 2002, in twelve European countries (adverb phrases modifying *became*)

Exercise 48–6, page 513

a.   Updating your software (gerund phrase used as subject)
b.   decreasing the town budget (gerund phrase used as object of the preposition *in*); identifying nonessential services (gerund phrase used as subject complement)
c.   to help her mother by raking the lawn (infinitive phrase used as direct object); raking the lawn (gerund phrase used as object of the preposition *by*)
d.   Understanding little (participial phrase modifying *I*); passing my biology final (gerund phrase used as object of the preposition *of*)
e.   Working with animals (gerund phrase used as subject)

Exercise 48–10, page 519

a.   so that every vote would count (adverb clause modifying *adjusted*)
b.   that targets baby boomers (adjective clause modifying *campaign*)
c.   After the Tambora volcano erupted in the southern Pacific in 1815 (adverb clause modifying *realized*); that it would contribute to the "year without a summer" in Europe and North America (noun clause used as direct object of *realized*)
d.   that at a certain point there will be no more oil to extract from the earth (noun clause used as direct object of *implies*)
e.   when you are rushing (adverb clause modifying *are overlooked*)

Exercise 49–1, page 522

a. Complex; that are ignited in dry areas (adjective clause); b. Compound;
c. Simple; d. Complex; Before we leave for the station (adverb clause);
e. Compound-complex; when you want to leave (noun clause)

Acknowledgments

Index

A

a, an. See also the
  a vs. *an*, 380, 834
    choosing, with common nouns, 384–85
    defined, 378
    multilingual/ESL challenges with, 378–80, 384–85
    needed, 207
    omission of, 207, 384–85
Abbreviations, 457–61
  acronyms as, 458
  in APA in-text citations, 696–97
  in APA reference list, 740
  of company names, 457–58, 460, 603
  familiar, 457–58
  inappropriate, 460
  Latin, 459
  in MLA in-text citations, 601, 603, 607, 608, 610
  in MLA works cited list, 614, 615–16
  periods with, 447–48, 457–59
  plurals of, 437, 459
  for titles with proper names, 457
  for units of measurement, 458–59, 460
abide by (not *with*) *a decision*, 272
Absolute concepts (such as *unique*), 337
Absolute phrases
  commas with, 418–19
  defined, 514
Abstract nouns, 270
Abstracts
  in APA papers, 737, 742, 827
  in databases, 539, 557–58
  keywords in, 737, 827
Academic degrees, abbreviations for, 457–58

Academic habits, developing. *See* Becoming a college writer; Habits of mind
Academic reading and writing, 95–190. *See also* Sample student writing
  analysis papers, 95–130
  APA papers, 674–753
  argument papers, 130–66
  audience for, 10
  Chicago papers, 754–804
  e-mail, 13, 833
  literary analysis papers, 167–90
  manuscript formats, 822–28
    APA style, 735–40, 826–29
    Chicago style, 794–97
    MLA style, 59–61, 662–65, 824–25
  MLA papers, 569–673
  questions asked in the disciplines, 808–10
  research papers, 525–68
  writing in the disciplines, 807–21
accept, except, 834
according to (not *with*), 272
Acronyms, 458
Active reading. *See* Reading
Active verbs, 193–98. *See also* Active voice
Active voice
  avoiding shifts between passive and, 225
  vs. *be* verbs, 194, 196
  changing to passive, 503, 507–08
  choosing, 194, 195
  vs. passive, 193–98, 507–08
  and wordy sentences, 253
  writer's choice, 195
adapt, adopt, 834
AD, BC (*CE, BCE*), 458
Addresses. *See also* URLs
  commas with, 420

Addresses (*cont.*)
e-mail, 478
numbers in, 462
Ad hominem fallacy, 140
Adjective clauses
avoiding repetition in, 392–93
defined, 516
punctuation of, 414–15
words introducing, 516–17
Adjective phrases
infinitive, 512–13
introductory, with comma, 408–09
participial, 511–12
prepositional, 508–10
punctuation of, 415–16
restrictive (essential) vs.
nonrestrictive (nonessential),
415–16
Adjectives
and absolute concepts, 337
and adverbs, 332–39, 494–95
commas with coordinate, 411
comparative forms (with -*er* or
more), 336–37
cumulative, 411, 424
defined, 493–94
after direct objects (object
complements), 334, 504
hyphens with, 476
after linking verbs (subject
complements), 333, 503
order of, 397–98
with prepositions (idioms), 401–02
superlative forms (with -*est* or
most), 336–37
adopt. See *adapt, adopt*, 834
Adverb clauses
comma with, 408–09
defined, 517
no comma with, 425
punctuation of, 408, 425
words introducing, 517
Adverb phrases
infinitive, 512–13
prepositional, 508–10
Adverbs. *See also* Conjunctive
adverbs

and adjectives, 332–39
avoiding repetition of, 392–93
comparative forms (with -*er* or
more), 336–37
defined, 494–95
introducing clauses, 392–93,
516–17
no comma after, 424
placement of, 395
relative, 392–93, 516–17
superlative forms (with -*est* or
most), 336–37
adverse, averse, 834
Advertisements. *See* Multimodal
texts
advice, advise, 835
affect, effect, 835
aggravate, 835
Agreement of pronoun and
antecedent, 309–15
with antecedents joined by *and*,
312
with antecedents joined by
either . . . or or *neither . . . nor*,
314
with antecedents joined by *or* or
nor, 314
and avoiding sexist language,
310–11, 313
with collective nouns (*audience,
family, team*, etc.), 312
with generic nouns, 311
with indefinite pronouns (*anyone,
each*, etc.), 310–11
Agreement of subject and verb,
297–309
with collective nouns (*audience,
family, team*, etc.), 303–04
with company names, 307
with gerund phrases, 307
with indefinite pronouns, 302–03
with intervening words, 297, 300
with nouns of plural form, singular
meaning (*athletics, economics*,
etc.), 307
standard subject-verb
combinations, 297, 298–99

with subject, not subject
complement, 305
with subject after verb, 304–05
with subjects joined with *and*,
300–01
with subjects joined with *or* or *nor*,
301
with *the number, a number*, 304
with *there is, there are*, 304–05
with titles of works, 307
with units of measurement, 304
with *who, which, that*, 306
with words between subject and
verb, 297, 300
with words used as words, 307
agree to, agree with, 272, 835
ain't (nonstandard), 835
Aircraft, italics for names of, 464
Alignment of text (left, right,
centered, justified)
in APA papers, 736, 826–28
in *Chicago* papers, 795
in MLA papers, 663, 824–25
all (singular or plural), 302
all-, as prefix, with hyphen, 477
all ready, already, 835
all right (not *alright*), 835
all together, altogether, 835
allude, 835
allusion, illusion, 835
almost, placement of, 212–13
a lot (not *alot*), 835
already. See *all ready, already*, 835
alright (nonstandard). See *all right*,
835
although
avoiding with *but* or *however*,
394
introducing subordinate clause,
497–98, 516–19
no comma after, 426
altogether. See *all together, altogether*,
835
American Psychological Association.
See APA papers
among, between. See *between, among*,
838

amongst, 836
amoral, immoral, 836
amount, number, 836
a.m., p.m., AM, PM, 458
am vs. *is* or *are*. See Agreement of
subject and verb
an, a. See *a, an*
Analogy
as argument strategy, 134
false, 134
as paragraph pattern, 81
Analysis. *See also* Analysis papers
critical reading, 95–109, 115–20
defined, 108
in the disciplines, 108
evaluating sources, 131–45,
535–38, 552–68
of literature, 108, 168–72, 175–77
outlining for, 102–04, 120–21
rhetorical, 95–114
summarizing for, 104–05, 121–23
how-to guide, 123
synthesizing sources
APA style, 691–93
MLA style, 594–97
of multimodal texts, 115–26
of written texts, 95–114
Analysis papers, 95–130. *See also*
Literature, writing about
and critical thinking, 95–108,
115–26
drafting, 106–11
engagement with, 96
evidence for, 106–11, 124–26
interpretation in, 106–11, 124–26
judgment in, 107–11, 126
sample papers, 112–14, 126–30,
187–90
summaries in
balancing with analysis, 106–07,
110, 124–25
writing, 104–05, 121–23
thesis in, 107–11, 126
writing guide, 110–11
writing practice, 112
and
antecedents joined by, 312

and (cont.)
  comma with, 407–08
  as coordinating conjunction, 201, 497
  excessive use of, 236–37
  no comma with, 422–23, 426
  no semicolon with, 431
  parallelism and, 201
  subjects joined by, 300–01
and etc. (nonstandard), 836
and/or
  avoiding, 836
  slash with, 453
angry with (not *at*), 272, 836
Annotated bibliography, 565–68
  sample entry (MLA style), 566
  writing guide, 567–68
Annotating texts
  electronic texts, 104
  to generate ideas, 17–18, 97–99, 548
  guidelines for, 101
  literary texts, 168
  multimodal texts, 117–18, 119
    sample, 119
  written texts, 97–99, 101
    sample annotated written texts, 97–99, 548, 594
ante-, anti-, 836
Antecedent
  agreement of pronoun and, 309–15
  defined, 309, 315, 488
  pronoun reference, 315–21
  singular vs. plural, 309–15
  unclear or unstated, 317–18
  of *who, which, that*, 306
Anthology or collection, citing
  APA style, 721
  Chicago style, 775, 786
    citation at a glance, 788–89
  MLA style, 606, 638
    citation at a glance, 640–41
anti-, ante-. See *ante-, anti-*, 836
Antonyms (opposites), 471–72

a number (plural), *the number* (singular), 304
anxious, 836
any, 302
anybody (singular), 302, 310–11, 836
anymore, 836
anyone (singular), 302, 310–11, 836
anyone, any one, 837
anyplace, 837
anything (singular), 302, 310–11
anyways, anywheres (nonstandard), 837
APA papers, 674–753
  abstracts in, 737, 742, 827
  authority in, 539, 677
  author note in (optional), 735, 741, 826
  avoiding plagiarism in, 678–83
  citation at a glance
    article from a database, 714–15
    article in a journal or magazine, 712–13
    book, 720
    section in a Web document, 726–27
  citations, in-text
    directory to models for, 694
    models for, 695–701
  evidence for, 676–78
  footnotes in, 736–37
  format, 735–40, 826–28
  keywords in, 737, 742, 827
  numbers in, 461, 827
  organizing, 675–76
  reference list
    directory to models for, 702–03
    DOIs (digital object identifiers) in, 706
    formatting, 739–40, 828
    general guidelines for, 704–06
    models for, 703–34
    sample, 752–53, 828
  sample paper, 741–53
  signal phrases in, 687–91
  sources in
    citing, 678–83, 693–734

integrating, 683–93
synthesizing, 691–93
uses of, 676–78
supporting arguments in, 676–78, 691–93
tables and figures in
formatting, 738
sample, 745
tenses in, 355, 688, 695
thesis in, 674–78
title page
formatting, 735, 826
samples, 741, 826
URLs in, 706, 740
Apostrophes, 434–39
in contractions, 436
misuse of, 438
in plurals, 436–37
in possessives, 434–36
Appeals, in arguments. See *Ethos* (ethical appeals); *Logos* (logical appeals); *Pathos* (emotional appeals)
Apposition, faulty, 211
Appositive phrases, 514, 515
Appositives (nouns that rename other nouns)
building credibility with (writer's choice), 515
case of pronouns with, 323
colon with, 432
commas with, 416
dashes with, 450
defined, 323, 416, 514
no commas with, 424–25
as sentence fragments, 283
Appropriate language (avoiding jargon, slang, etc.), 256–68
Apps
citing in APA style, 731
citing in MLA style, 650
italics for titles of, 464
Archetypes, in literature, questions to ask about, 172
are vs. *is*. See Agreement of subject and verb

Argument papers, 130–66. *See also* Arguments, evaluating
appeals in, 148
audience for, 147–48
common ground in, 148, 149–50, 157, 164
context in, 146–47, 164
counterarguments in
addressing, 155–56, 164
reflecting on, 132, 143–45
revising for, 42
credibility in, 148, 149–50
evidence in, 148, 152–55, 164
introduction to, 149–50
lines of argument in, 150, 152
oral presentations of, 166
purpose in, 146–47
researching, 146–47
sample paper, 157–63
support for, 150, 152
thesis in, 149–50, 164
how-to guide, 151
writing guide, 164–65
Arguments, evaluating, 130–46. *See also* Argument papers
argumentative tactics, 131–43, 145
assumptions, 137–38
bias, 139–40, 559–61
checklist for, 145
claims, 137–38
deductive reasoning, 138–39
ethos (ethical appeals), 141–42, 148
fairness, 139–43
generalizations, hasty, 133
inductive reasoning, 133–34, 135
logical fallacies, 131–43
logos (logical appeals), 131–39, 141–42, 148
pathos (emotional appeals), 139–43, 148
writing practice, 146

Article from a database, citing. *See also* Articles in periodicals
  APA style, 710–15
    citation at a glance, 714–15
  Chicago style, 779–84
    citation at a glance, 782–83
  MLA style, 623–32
    citation at a glance, 626–27
Articles (*a, an, the*), 378–89. *See also a, an*; *the*
Articles in periodicals. *See also* Article from a database
  abstracts of, 539, 557–58
  capitalizing titles of, 481
    APA style, 705, 736, 739–40
    Chicago style, 795
    MLA style, 616, 663
  citation at a glance
    APA style, 712–15
    Chicago style, 780–81
    MLA style, 624–25
  citing
    APA style, 710–19
    Chicago style, 779–86
    MLA style, 622–35
  finding, 535, 536
  previewing, 554–55, 556
  quotation marks for titles of, 441
    APA style, 705, 736, 739–40
    Chicago style, 795
    MLA style, 616, 663
Artwork, italics for titles of, 464
as
  ambiguous use of, 837
  needed word, 206
  parallelism and, 202
  pronoun after, 324
as, like. See like, as, 846
Assessment, self-, 62, 65–71. *See also* Reflection
Assignments
  samples of, 814–21
  understanding, 11, 808–10, 814–21
Assumptions, in arguments, 137–38
as to, 837

at, in idioms (common expressions)
  with adjectives, 401–02
  vs. *in, on*, to show time and place, 399–403
  with verbs, 402–03
audience. See Collective nouns
Audience
  for argument paper, 147–48
  assessing, 6, 10, 12, 13
  and document design, 822
  for e-mail, 13
  and genre (type of writing), 12–15
  and global (big-picture) revision, 50–51
  and level of formality, 262–64
  and peer review, 39
  and thesis, 21–24
Audio texts. *See* Multimedia sources, citing; Multimodal texts
Authority, establishing, 539
  in APA papers, 677
  in *Chicago* papers, 757
  in MLA papers, 574, 591–92
Author note (optional), in APA papers, 735, 741, 826
Authors
  of literary works, 178–80
  of sources
    in APA reference list, 704–09
    in *Chicago* notes and bibliography, 772–73
    identifying, 562, 620–21
    in MLA works cited list, 614–22, 652–53
    in reposted files, 652–53
Auxiliary verbs. *See* Helping verbs
averse. See adverse, averse, 834
awful, 837
awhile, a while, 837
Awkward sentences, 208–12

B

back up, backup, 837
bad, badly, 335, 837
Bandwagon appeal fallacy, 140–41

Base form of verb, 340, 492
  modal (*can*, *should*, etc.) with, 350,
    368–71
  in negatives with *do*, 371–72
BC, *AD* (*BCE*, *CE*), 458
be, as irregular verb, 340–41, 348,
    362, 492
be, forms of, 298, 362, 491
  vs. active verbs, 194, 196
  and agreement with subject,
    297–309
  in conditional sentences, 374
  as helping verbs, 196, 363–64,
    365–67, 491
  as linking verbs, 194, 196, 350,
    390, 503
  in passive voice, 193–94, 365–67,
    507–08
  in progressive forms, 353, 363–64,
    366
  and subjunctive mood, 356–58
  in tenses, 342, 351–53
  as weak verbs, 194, 196
because
  avoiding after *reason . . . is*, 211,
    848
  avoiding with *so* or *therefore*, 394
  introducing subordinate clause,
    497–98
  not omitting, 202–03
Becoming a college writer, 1–2. *See
    also* Habits of mind
  counterarguments, 132
  curiosity, 1, 2, 526
  editing logs, 41, 57
  engagement, 1, 40, 96, 527
  reading, 96
  reflection, 1, 62, 65–71, 132, 527
  responsibility, 1, 527, 543–52,
    584
Beginning of essay. *See* Introduction
Beginning of sentences
  capitalizing words at, 481–82
  numbers at, 461
  varying, 242–44
  writer's choice, 244

being as, *being that* (nonstandard),
    837
beside, *besides*, 837–38
better, *best*, 336–37
between, *among*, 838
Bias, signs of, 139–40, 559–61
Biased language, avoiding, 140,
    267–68. *See also* Sexist
    language, avoiding
Bible. *See* Sacred texts (Bible,
    Qur'an)
Bibliography. *See also* Reference list
    (APA); Works cited list (MLA)
  annotated, 565–68
    sample entry (MLA style), 566
    writing guide, 567–68
  Chicago style
    directory to models for,
      769–70
    formatting, 797
    models for, 771–94
    sample, 804
  scholarly, 538, 539
  working, 543–44, 545–46
    information for, 37, 543–44,
      545–46
Block quotation. *See* Quotations,
    long
Blog
  citing
    APA style, 728
    Chicago style, 787
    MLA style, 645–47
  to explore ideas, 19
  to improve English-language skills,
    361
Body of essay, 31–35
Books
  capitalizing titles of, 481
    APA style, 705, 736, 739–40
    Chicago style, 795
    MLA style, 616, 663
  citation at a glance
    APA style, 720
    Chicago style, 776–77, 788–89
    MLA style, 636, 640–41

Books (*cont.*)
  citing
    APA style, 719–24
    Chicago style, 774–78
    MLA style, 635–43
  italics for titles of, 463
    APA style, 705, 736, 739–40
    Chicago style, 795
    MLA style, 616, 663
  library catalog for finding, 535, 555
  previewing, 539, 556–57
Borrowed language and ideas. *See* Citing sources; Plagiarism, avoiding
both . . . and, 201, 497
Brackets, 451–52
  APA style, 686–87
  Chicago style, 764–65
  in literary analysis papers, 180–81
  MLA style, 588–89
Brainstorming, 18
bring, take, 838
Broad reference of *this, that, which, it*, 316–17
Bullets, in document design, 831–33
burst, bursted; bust, busted, 838
Business writing
  audience for, 12
  e-mail, 13, 833
  formatting, 823
  letters, 830
  memos, 816–17, 832
  reports, 829
  résumés, 831
  sample assignment and proposal, 816–17, 829
but
  avoiding with *although* or *however*, 394
  comma with, 407–08
  as coordinating conjunction, 201, 497
  excessive use of, 236–37
  no comma with, 422–23, 426
  no semicolon with, 431
  parallelism and, 201

  as preposition, 496
by, not omitting, 202–03

C

can, as modal verb, 350, 368–69, 491–92
can, may, 838
capable of (not *to*), 272
capital, capitol, 838
Capitalization, 479–83
  after colon, 433, 482–83
    APA style, 736
    Chicago style, 795
    MLA style, 663
  of first word of sentence, 481–82
  of Internet terms, 480
  misuse of, 479–80
  of proper nouns, 479–80
  in quotations, 482
  of titles of persons, 480
  of titles of works, 481
    APA style, 705, 736, 739–40
    Chicago style, 795
    MLA style, 616, 663
capitol. See capital, capitol, 838
Captions, 32–33
  APA style, 738, 829
  Chicago style, 795–96
  MLA style, 664, 668
  responsibility and, 33
Case. *See* Pronoun case
Catalog, library, 535, 555
Cause and effect
  as paragraph pattern, 81–82
  reasoning, 134, 136
CE, BCE (AD, BC), 458
censor, censure, 838
Central idea. *See* Focus; Thesis
cf., 459
Characters, in literary analysis, 171, 178, 179–80
Charts, 32, 34. *See also* Visuals, in documents
Chicago Manual of Style, The, 754, 768, 771

Chicago papers, 754–804
  authority in, 539, 757
  authors in, 772–73
  avoiding plagiarism in, 758–62
  bibliography, 768–94
    directory to models for,
      769–70
    DOIs (digital object identifiers)
      in, 772, 796
    formatting, 797
    models for, 771–94
    sample, 804
  citation at a glance
    article from a database, 782–83
    article in a journal, 780–81
    book, 776–77
    letter in a published collection,
      788–89
    primary source from a Web site,
      792–93
  evidence for, 756–58
  footnotes or endnotes, 768–94
    directory to models for, 769–70
    formatting, 796–97
    models for, 771–94
    sample, 803–04
  manuscript format, 794–97
  organizing, 756
  sample pages, 798–804
  signal phrases in, 765–68
  sources in
    citing, 758–62, 768–94
    integrating, 762–68
    uses of, 756–58
  supporting arguments in, 756–58
  tenses in, 765
  thesis in, 755–58
  URLs in, 772, 782
Choppy sentences, 230, 232
Citation at a glance
  APA style
    article from a database, 714–15
    article in a journal or magazine,
      712–13
    book, 720
    section in a Web document,
      726–27
Chicago style
    article from a database, 782–83
    article in a journal, 780–81
    book, 776–77
    letter in a collection, 788–89
    primary source from a Web site,
      792–93
  MLA style
    article from a database, 626–27
    article in a journal, 624–25
    book, 636
    selection from an anthology or a
      collection, 640–41
    short work from a Web site,
      646–47
Citations. *See* Citation at a glance;
    Citing sources
cited in, for a source in another
    source, 701. *See also quoted in*
cite, site, 838
Citing sources. *See also* Integrating
    sources; Plagiarism, avoiding;
    Quotations
  APA style, 678–83, 693–734
  Chicago style, 758–62, 768–94
  choosing a citation style, 812
  common knowledge
    in APA papers, 679
    in *Chicago* papers, 758
    in MLA papers, 579
  how-to guide, 583
  in literary analysis papers, 181–87
  MLA style, 577–83, 598–661
  responsibility and, 583
  reviewer comments about, 43
Claims. *See* Arguments, evaluating;
    Thesis
class. See Collective nouns
Class (social), in literature, questions
    to ask about, 171
Classification, as paragraph pattern,
    82–83
Clauses. *See* Independent clauses;
    Subordinate clauses
Clichés, 272–74
climactic, climatic, 838–39
coarse, course, 839

Coherence, 84–91

Collaborative writing. *See* Peer review

Collection. *See* Anthology or collection, citing

Collective nouns (*audience, family, team*, etc.)
  agreement of pronouns with, 312
  agreement of verbs with, 303–04

Colloquial words, 263, 472

Colon, 432–34
  with appositives (nouns that rename other nouns), 432
  capitalization after, 433, 482–83
    APA style, 736
    Chicago style, 795
    MLA style, 663
  common uses, 433, 830
  for emphasis, 242
  to fix run-on sentences, 292–93
  introducing quotations, 432, 443–44
  with lists, 432
  misuse of, 433–34
  outside quotation marks, 443

Combining sentences (coordination and subordination), 228–36

Commands. *See* Imperative mood; Imperative sentences

Commas, 407–27. *See also* Commas, unnecessary
  with absolute phrases, 418–19
  in addresses, 420
  with *and, but*, etc., 407–08
  with contrasted elements, 419
  between coordinate adjectives, 411
  before coordinating conjunctions, 407–08
  in dates, 420
  with direct address, 419
  with interrogative tags (questions), 419
  with interruptions (*he writes* etc.), 419
  after introductory elements, 408–09, 444

  with items in a series, 410
  joining ideas with, 407–08
  with mild interjections, 419
  with modifiers, 411
  with nonrestrictive (nonessential) elements, 413–17
  in numbers, 420
  with parenthetical expressions, 418
  with quotation marks, 419, 442
  with semicolons, 429
  to set off words or phrases, 417–19
  with titles following names, 420
  with transitional expressions, 417–18
  before *which* or *who*, 414–15
  with *yes* and *no*, 419

Commas, unnecessary, 422–27
  between adjective and noun, 424
  between adverb and adjective, 424
  after *although*, 426
  after *and, but*, etc., 426
  between compound elements, 422–23
  before concluding adverb clauses, 425
  after a coordinating conjunction, 426
  between cumulative adjectives, 411, 424
  with indirect quotations, 426
  in an inverted sentence (verb before subject), 425–26
  before a parenthesis, 426
  with a question mark or an exclamation point, 427
  with restrictive (essential) elements, 424–25
  before or after a series, 423
  between subject and verb, 423
  after *such as* or *like*, 426
  between verb and object, 423

Comma splices. *See* Run-on sentences

Comments on a draft, understanding. *See* Revising with comments

Comments on online articles, citing
APA style, 718
MLA style, 630

committee. See Collective nouns

Common ground, establishing in an argument, 148, 149–50, 157, 164

Common knowledge
in APA papers, 679
in *Chicago* papers, 758
in MLA papers, 579

Common nouns, 379–87, 479–80

Common terms, abbreviations for, 457–58

Company names
abbreviations in, 457–58, 460, 603
agreement of verb with, 307
in MLA documentation, 603, 616

Comparative form of adjectives and adverbs (with *-er* or *more*), 336–37. *See also* Superlative form of adjectives and adverbs (with *-est* or *most*)

compare to, compare with, 839

Comparisons
with adjectives and adverbs, 336–37
needed words in, 206–07
as paragraph pattern, 79–80
parallel elements in, 202
with pronoun following *than* or *as,* 324

complement, compliment, 839

Complements, object, 504

Complements, subject
adjectives as, 333, 503
case of pronouns as, 322
defined, 502
and subject-verb agreement, 305

Complete subject, 499–500

Complex sentences, 521

compliment. See complement, compliment, 839

comply with (not *to*), 272

Compound antecedents, 312, 314

Compound-complex sentences, 521

Compound elements
case of pronoun in, 322–23
comma with, 407–08
needed words in, 204–05
no comma with, 422–23
parallelism and, 200–02

Compound nouns (*father-in-law* etc.)
plural of, 467
possessive of, 436

Compound numbers, hyphens with, 476

Compound predicates
fragmented, 289
no comma in, 408, 422–23

Compound sentences
comma in, 407–08
defined, 520–21
excessive use of, 236–37
semicolon in, 428

Compound subjects
agreement of pronoun with, 312, 314
agreement of verb with, 300–01
defined, 500

Compound verbs. *See* Compound predicates

Compound words
in dictionary entry, 471
hyphens with, 475–76
plural of, 467

Conciseness, 251–55

Conclusion
in deductive reasoning, 138–39
of essay, 33, 36–37
in inductive reasoning, 131, 133–34, 135
strategies for drafting, 36

Concrete nouns, 270

Conditional sentences, 372–74. *See also* Subjunctive mood

Confused words, 270–71. *See also* Glossary of usage

Conjunctions, 497–98. *See also*
Conjunctive adverbs
   in coordination and subordination,
    224–34
   to fix run-on sentences, 290, 292
Conjunctive adverbs (*therefore* etc.).
See also Conjunctions
   comma after, 417–18, 498
   and coordination, 229–30
   defined, 498
   and run-on sentences, 289–90,
    292
   semicolon with, 289, 290, 428–29,
    498
Connotation (implied meaning of
   word), 269–70
conscience, conscious, 839
Consistency
   in headings, 199–200
   in lists, 200
   in mood and voice, 225
   in paragraphs, 87
   in point of view, 220–23
   in questions and quotations, 226
   in verb tense, 223–24
Constructive criticism, 44
Context, establishing
   in APA papers, 690
   with appositives, 515
   in argument papers, 146–47, 164
   in *Chicago* papers, 768
   in literary analysis papers, 180
   in MLA papers, 584, 593
   when researching, 527–28, 539
Context, in literature, questions to
   ask about, 171
continual, continuous, 839
Contractions
   apostrophe in, 436
   in informal language, 263
   needed verbs and, 350
Contrary-to-fact clauses, 357–58,
   374
Contrast, as paragraph pattern,
   79–80
Contrasted elements, comma with,
   419

Conventions (standard practices)
   in business writing, 816–17
   in the disciplines, 807–13
   of genres (types of writing), 6–7,
    12–15
   in literary analysis papers, 178
   in nursing practice papers,
    820–21
   in science writing, 818–19
   in writing about psychology,
    814–16
Conversations, academic and
   research. *See* Synthesizing
   sources; Talking and listening
Conversing with a text, 99–101, 118,
   120
Coordinate adjectives, comma with,
   411
Coordinating conjunctions (*and, but,*
   etc.)
   comma before, 407–08
   coordination and, 229, 233
   defined, 497
   to fix run-on sentences, 290,
    292
   no comma after, 422–23, 426
   no semicolon with, 431
   parallelism and, 201
Coordination
   for combining ideas of equal
    importance, 229–30, 233
   comma and coordinating
    conjunction for, 407–08
   excessive use of, 236–37
   to fix choppy sentences, 232
   to fix run-on sentences, 290, 292
   and subordination, 236–37
Copies of drafts, saving, 37–38
Correlative conjunctions (*either . . . or*
   etc.), 201, 497
could, as modal verb, 350, 368–69,
   491–92
could care less (nonstandard), 839
could of (nonstandard), 839
council, counsel, 839–40
Counterarguments
   addressing, 132, 155–56, 164

in APA papers, 678
in *Chicago* papers, 757–58
evaluating, 143–45
in MLA papers, 574
reflecting on, 132, 143–45
revising for, 42
Count nouns, articles (*a, an, the*)
    with, 379–84
Country names, abbreviations for,
    457–58
couple. See Collective nouns
course. See coarse, course, 839
Course materials, citing
    APA style, 701, 733
    MLA style, 658–59
Cover letters, for portfolios, 62,
    65–71
CQ Researcher, 536
Credibility, establishing, 148,
    149–50. *See also* Authority
    with appositives (writer's choice),
    515
criteria, 840
Critical reading. *See* Reading
Critical thinking
    for analysis, 95–108, 115–26
    about arguments, 130–46
    and engagement with texts, 96
    evaluating sources, 535–38,
        552–68
    introduction to, 1
    about literature, 167–72
Criticism, constructive, 44
crowd. See Collective nouns
Culture and race, in literature,
    questions to ask about,
    172
Cumulative adjectives
    no comma with, 411, 424
    order of, 397–98
Curiosity. *See* Habits of mind

D

-d, -ed, verb ending, 340, 348–49,
    363
Dangling modifiers, 216–20

Dashes, 449–50
    for emphasis, 242
    to fix run-on sentences, 292–93
data, 840
Data. *See* Statistics
Database, article from. *See* Article
    from a database, citing
Databases, for finding sources, 535,
    536, 554–55
Dates
    abbreviations in, 458, 460
    in APA reference list, 704–05
    capitalization of, 480
    commas with, 420
    in MLA works cited list, 616
    numbers in, 462
Days of the week, 460, 480
Deadlines, planning and, 7, 525,
    527, 529
Debates, entering, 532. *See also*
    Argument papers; Arguments,
    evaluating
Declarative sentences, 522
Deductive reasoning, 138–39
Definite article. *See the*
Definition
    of key terms or concepts
        in APA papers, 676–77
        in MLA papers, 573
    as paragraph pattern, 84
    of words, 269–70, 471–72
Degree of adjectives and adverbs. *See*
    Comparative form of adjectives
    and adverbs; Superlative form
    of adjectives and adverbs
Degrees, academic, abbreviations for,
    457–58
Demonstrative pronouns, 489–90
Denotation (dictionary definition of
    word), 269–70
Dependent clauses. *See* Subordinate
    clauses
Description, as paragraph pattern,
    78–79
Descriptive word groups. *See*
    Adjective phrases; Adverb
    phrases

Design. *See* Document design; Visuals, in documents

desirous of (not *to*), 272

Detail, adequate, 75–76, 176. *See also* Development, of ideas; Evidence

Determiners, 378–89

Development, of ideas, 53–55, 75–76. *See also* Paragraph patterns

Diagrams, 32, 34. *See also* Visuals, in documents

Dialects, 261–62

Dialogue, 182–83, 440

Diction. *See* Words

Dictionaries
  guide to use of, 468–72
  sample entries, 469–70

different from, different than, 272, 840

differ from, differ with, 840

Digital object identifier. *See* DOI (digital object identifier)

Digital texts. *See* Electronic documents; Multimodal texts; Web sources

Direct address, commas with, 419

Direct language, 252–53

Direct objects
  case of pronouns as, 322–23
  defined, 503
  followed by adjective or noun (object complement), 504
  placement of adverbs and, 395
  transitive verbs and, 503

Directories to documentation models
  APA style, 694, 702–03
  Chicago style, 769–70
  MLA style, 599, 611–13

Direct questions. *See* Questions, direct and indirect

disinterested, uninterested, 840

Division, as paragraph pattern, 82–84

Division of words
  in dictionary entry, 471

  hyphen and, 477–78

do, as irregular verb, 342

do, forms of
  in forming negatives, 371–72
  as helping verbs, 491
  and subject-verb agreement, 298, 347

do vs. *does*. *See* Agreement of subject and verb

Document design, 822–33
  academic writing, 822–23, 824–28
    APA format, 735–40, 826–29
    Chicago format, 794–97
    MLA format, 662–65, 824–25
  business letters, 830
  and critical reading, 115–16, 118
  e-mail, 13, 833
  format options, 7, 16, 822–23
  genre (type of writing) and, 7, 12–15
  headings
    in APA papers, 675–76, 737–38, 827–28
    in *Chicago* papers, 796, 799–802
    in MLA papers, 664, 825
  lists in, 831–33
  memos, 832
  model documents, 822–33
  and multimodal texts, 117–18
  for purpose and audience, 32–33, 822–23
  reports, 829
  résumés, 831
  visuals, 32, 34–35
    in APA papers, 738, 745, 829
    in *Chicago* papers, 795–96
    in MLA papers, 664, 668

Documenting sources. *See* Citing sources

does vs. *do*. *See* Agreement of subject and verb

DOI (digital object identifier)
  in APA citations, 706
  in *Chicago* citations, 772, 796
  in MLA citations, 617

don't vs. *doesn't*, 840. *See also* Agreement of subject and verb

Dots, ellipsis. *See* Ellipsis mark
Double comparatives and
    superlatives, avoiding, 337
Double-entry notebook, 99–100,
    120
Double negatives, avoiding, 338,
    372
Doublespeak, avoiding, 258–59
Double subjects, avoiding, 391–92
Drafting
    analysis papers, 111
    annotated bibliographies, 568
    argument papers, 165
    body, 31–35
    conclusion, 33, 36–37
    essays, 1, 28–37
    introduction, 28–30
    literacy narratives, 64
    portfolio cover letters, 71
    sample rough draft, 47–48
    and saving files, 37–38, 65
    thesis, 19–25, 28–30
Drawing conclusions (deductive
    reasoning), 138–39
Dropped quotation, avoiding
    in APA papers, 688–89
    in *Chicago* papers, 767–68
    in MLA papers, 591
due to, 840

E

each (singular), 302, 310–11, 840
E-books, citing
    APA style, 719
    Chicago style, 774
    MLA style, 635
economics (singular), 307
-ed, verb ending, 340, 348–49, 363
Editing log, 41
    how-to guide, 57
Editing sentences, 38, 55–56, 57
effect. See *affect, effect*, 835
Effect. *See* Cause and effect
e.g. ("for example"), 459, 840
either (singular), 302, 310–11, 314,
    841

either . . . or, 497
    and parallel structure, 201
    and pronoun-antecedent
        agreement, 314
    and subject-verb agreement, 301
either . . . or fallacy, 136–37
-elect, hyphen with, 477
Electronic documents. *See also*
        Multimodal texts; Web sources
    annotated bibliographies, 567
    annotating, 104
    double-entry notebooks, 99–100,
        120
    e-mail messages, 13, 833
    managing, 37–38
    reading, 104
elicit, illicit, 841
Ellipsis mark
    in arguments, 144–45
    for omissions in quotations, 452
        APA style, 686
        Chicago style, 763–64
        MLA style, 587–88, 825
Elliptical clause, dangling, 217–18
Elliptical constructions, 518
E-mail
    addresses, division of, 478
    audience for, 13
    effective, 13, 833
    formatting, 833
    italics in, 463
emigrate from, immigrate to, 841
eminent, imminent, 841
Emotional appeals (*pathos*), in
        argument, 139–43, 148
Emphasis, 228–42
    active verbs for, 193–98
    avoiding italics for, 463
    choppy sentences and, 230, 232
    parallel structure and, 241
    punctuation for, 242, 448, 449
    sentence endings for, 240–41
    subordinating minor ideas for,
        231, 238–39
    writer's choice, 231, 291
Enc., used in business writing, 830
Ending. *See* Conclusion

Endnotes. *See* Footnotes or endnotes
End punctuation, 447–49
Engagement. *See* Habits of mind
English as a second language (ESL).
    See Multilingual writers
enough, with infinitive, 377–78
enthused, 841
-er ending (*faster, stronger*), 336–37
Errors
    identifying, 41, 57
    sic for, 451–52
    in APA papers, 687
    in *Chicago* papers, 764
    in MLA papers, 589
ESL (English as a second language).
    See Multilingual writers
especially, and sentence fragments,
    284–85
-es, -s
    spelling rules, for plurals, 459, 467
    as verb ending, 297, 298–99,
        345–46
Essays. *See also* Sample student
    writing
    drafting, 1, 28–37
    editing, 55–56, 57
    planning, 5–38
    researching, 525–68
    revising, 49–55
    saving drafts of, 37–38
-est ending (*fastest, strongest*), 336–37
et al. ("and others"), 459
    in APA papers, 696–97
    in *Chicago* papers, 772
    in MLA papers, 602–03, 617
etc., 459, 841
Ethos (ethical appeals), in arguments,
    141–42, 148
Etymology, 471–72
Euphemisms, avoiding, 258–59
Evaluating arguments. *See*
    Arguments, evaluating
Evaluating sources, 535–38, 552–68
    writing practice, 561
even, placement of, 212–13
eventually, ultimately, 841

everybody, everyone, everything
    (singular), 302, 310–11, 841
everyone, every one, 841
Evidence
    adding for support, 43
    in analysis papers, 106–11, 124–26
    in APA papers, 676–78
    in argument papers, 148, 152–55,
        164
    in *Chicago* papers, 756–58
    in literary analysis papers, 176
    in MLA papers, 572–74
    for papers in the disciplines,
        810–11
ex-, hyphen with, 477
Exact language, 268–76
Examples
    as evidence, 43, 153–54
    as paragraph pattern, 76–77
    as sentence fragments, 285
except. See *accept, except*, 834
Excerpts, of articles and books,
    online, 557–58
Exclamation points, 448
    no comma with, 427
    with in-text citiations (MLA style),
        443, 600
    with quotation marks, 443
Exclamations, 419, 448
Exclamatory sentence, 522
expect, 842
Expert opinion, using as support,
    154–55
Expletives *there, it*
    and subject following verb,
        390–91, 501, 507
    and subject-verb agreement,
        304–05
    and wordy sentences, 253
explicit, implicit, 842
Expressions
    idiomatic (common), 271–73
    regional, 261–62
    transitional, 417–18, 428–29
    trite or worn-out (clichés),
        272–74

F

Facebook. *See* Social media, citing
Facts
    in APA papers, 676–77, 689–90
    in argument papers, 153
    avoiding in thesis statements, 22
    in *Chicago* papers, 756, 767–68
    in MLA papers, 572–73, 593, 597
    scientific, and verb tense, 354
Fairness, in arguments
    assessing, 132, 139–45
    establishing, 132, 155–56
Fallacies, logical
    ad hominem, 140
    bandwagon appeal, 140–41
    biased language, 140
    either . . . or, 136–37
    false analogy, 134
    hasty generalization, 133
    non sequitur, 137–38
    post hoc, 136
    red herring, 141
    stereotype, 133–34
    straw man, 144
    transfer, 140
False analogy, 134
family. See Collective nouns
farther, further, 842
Faulty apposition, 211
Faulty predication, 210–11
Feedback. *See also* Peer review;
        Revising with comments
    giving to other writers, 41, 44
    seeking and using, 1, 38–44
fewer, less, 842
Field research, 540–41, 811
Figures. *See* Numbers; Visuals, in
        documents
Figures of speech, 274–75
Files, managing, 37–38, 65
finalize, 842
firstly, 842
First-person point of view
    appropriate uses, 221
    consistency with, 220–23

    in literacy narratives, 63
    in portfolio cover letters, 70
    revising for, 54
    writer's choice, 221
Flow (coherence), 84–91
Flowcharts, 32, 35. *See also* Visuals,
        in documents
Focus. *See also* Thesis
    of argument paper, 149–50
    of essay, 8, 19–25, 51–52, 54
    of introduction, 42
    of literary analysis paper, 170
    of paragraph, 72–75
    of research paper, 530–31
Fonts (typeface)
    in APA papers, 735, 737–38
    in *Chicago* papers, 794
    in MLA papers, 662
Footnotes or endnotes
    APA style, 736–37
    Chicago style, 768–94
        directory to models for, 769–70
        models for, 770–94
        sample, 803–04
    MLA style, 661–62
for
    comma before, 407–08
    as coordinating conjunction, 201,
        497
    parallelism and, 201
    as preposition, 496
Foreign words, italics for, 465
for example
    no colon after, 434
    and sentence fragments, 285
Formality, level of, 262–64
Formal outline, 26–28, 102–03. *See
        also* Informal outline
Formatting. *See* Document design;
        Manuscript formats
Fractions, 462, 476
Fragments, sentence
    acceptable, 285–86
    clauses as, 281–82
    for emphasis or effect, 285–86
    examples as, 285

Fragments, sentence (*cont.*)
  finding and recognizing, 279–81
  fixing, 281–85
  lists as, 284–85
  phrases as, 283
  predicates as, 284
  testing for, 280
Freewriting, 18
Full-block style, for business letters, 830
further. See *farther, further*, 842
Fused sentences. *See* Run-on sentences
Future perfect tense, 352, 367
Future progressive forms, 353, 367
Future tense, 352, 363, 366

G

Gender, and pronoun agreement, 310–11, 313
Gender, in literature, questions to ask about, 172
Gender-neutral language, 264–67, 310–11, 313
Generalization, hasty, 133
Generating ideas. *See* Planning an essay
Generic *he*, 265, 310–11, 313, 843
Generic nouns, 311
Genre (type of writing), 12–15. *See also* Writing guides; Writing in the disciplines
  and format, 6–7, 32–33
  of multimodal texts, 116
  purpose and, 6–7, 12–15, 30
  thesis and, 30
  and writer's choices
    active and passive voice, 195
    point of view, 221
  writing situation and, 6–7
Geographic names, *the* with, 387–88
Gerunds
  defined, 512
  following prepositions, 400–01
  following verbs, 375–76
  phrases, agreement of verb with, 307

  possessives as modifiers of, 325–26
get, 842
Global (big-picture) revisions, 49–55. *See also* Revising with comments
Glossary of usage, 834–52
good, well, 335, 842
Google Docs and Google Drive, and keeping track of files, 37–38
Google Scholar, 536
Government documents
  citing
    APA style, 723–24
    Chicago style, 777
    MLA style, 657–60
  as evidence, 811
graduate, 842–43
Graphic narrative, MLA citation of, 619, 621
Graphs, 32, 34, 829. *See also* Visuals, in documents
Greetings and salutations, colon with, 433, 830
grow, 843
Guides to writing. *See* How-to guides; Writing guides

H

Habits of mind, 1–2. *See also* Becoming a college writer
  curiosity, 1, 2, 526, 527
  engagement
    with arguments, 130–66
    with other writers, 40
    with readers, 42
    with research topics, 525, 527
    with written texts, 96, 167–68
  reflection, 1, 62, 65–71, 132, 527
  responsibility, 1, 527, 543–52, 584
Handouts (course materials), citing
  APA style, 701, 733
  MLA style, 658–59
hanged, hung, 843
hardly, 843
  avoiding double negative with, 338

placement of, 212–13

has got, have got, avoiding, 843

Hasty generalization, 133

has vs. *have*, 298, 347. *See also*
Agreement of subject and verb

have, as irregular verb, 343

have, forms of
as helping verbs, 364–65, 366–67,
491
and passive voice, 365–67
and perfect tenses, 364–65,
366–67
and subject-verb agreement, 298,
347

have got, has got, avoiding, 843

have vs. *has*, 298, 347. *See also*
Agreement of subject and verb

Headings
in APA papers, 675–76, 737–38,
827–28
in *Chicago* papers, 756, 796
in document design, 825, 832
in MLA papers, 664, 825
to organize ideas, 53, 675–76,
756
parallel phrasing of, 199–200
planning with, 28, 675–76, 756

he, him, his, sexist use of, 265,
310–11, 313, 843

Helping verbs
contractions with, 350
defined, 350, 491–92
and forming passive voice, 341,
365–67
and forming perfect tenses, 341,
352, 355, 364, 366–67
and forming verb tenses, 341,
352–53, 363–64
modals (*can, should*, etc.), 350,
368–70, 491–92
needed, 350
and progressive forms, 363–64,
365

here, not used as subject, 391

her vs. *she*, 321–27

he/she, his/her, 453, 843

he vs. *him*, 321–27

he writes, she writes, comma with,
419, 444

hisself (nonstandard), 843

Historical context, in literature,
questions to ask about, 171

Homophones (words that sound
alike), 472–73

Hook, in introduction, 29–30, 42,
575

hopefully, 843

however
avoiding with *but* or *although*, 394
at beginning of sentence, 843–44
comma with, 417–18
semicolon with, 428–29

How-to guides
analysis papers
drafting an analytical thesis
statement, 109
summarizing a multimodal text,
123
argument papers, 151
editing logs, 57
MLA papers
being a responsible research
writer, 583
citing a reposted source,
652–53
citing course materials, 658–59
identifying authors, 620–21
peer review, 44
research
avoiding plagiarism from the
Web, 550
being a responsible research
writer, 583
entering a research
conversation, 532
going beyond a Google search,
536
summary of multimodal texts, 123
thesis statements
drafting for analysis papers,
109
drafting for argument papers,
151
solving problems with, 22–23

Humanities, writing in, 807–13. *See also Chicago* papers; Literature, writing about; MLA papers
hung. See *hanged, hung,* 843
Hyphens, 475–78
    with adjectives, 476
    to avoid confusion, 477
    in compound words, 475–76
    and division of words, 477–78
    in e-mail addresses, 478
    to form dash, 449
    in fractions, 476
    in numbers, 476
    with prefixes and suffixes, 477
    in URLs, 478
        APA style, 740
        Chicago style, 772, 782
        MLA style, 664, 665

I

I
    avoiding shifts with *you, he,* or *she,* 220–23
    vs. *me,* 321–27
    point of view, 54, 220–23
Ibid. ("in the same place"), 771
Idioms (common expressions)
    adjective + preposition combinations, 401–02
    with prepositions showing time and place (*at, on, in,* etc.), 399–400
    standard, 271–73
    verb + preposition combinations, 402–03
i.e. ("that is"), 459, 844
-ie, -ei, spelling rule, 466
if clauses, 357, 372–74
if, whether, 844
illicit. See *elicit, illicit,* 841
illusion. See *allusion, illusion,* 835
Illustrated work, MLA citation of, 619, 621
Illustrations. *See* Examples; Visuals, in documents

Images. *See* Visuals, in documents
immigrate. See *emigrate from, immigrate to,* 841
imminent. See *eminent, imminent,* 841
immoral. See *amoral, immoral,* 836
Imperative mood, 356
Imperative sentences, 501, 522
    you understood in, 390, 501, 506
implement, 844
implicit. See *explicit, implicit,* 842
Implied meaning of word (connotation), 269–70
imply, infer, 844
in, in idioms (common expressions)
    with adjectives, 401–02
    vs. *at, on,* to show time and place, 399–403
    with verbs, 402–03
including, no colon after, 434
Inclusive language, 264–67, 310–11, 313
Incomplete comparison, 206–07
Incomplete construction, 204–08
Incomplete sentences. *See* Fragments, sentence
Indefinite articles. *See a, an*
Indefinite pronouns
    agreement of verb with, 302–03
    as antecedents, 310–11, 313
    apostrophe with, 436
    defined, 490
Indenting
    in APA reference list, 739
    in *Chicago* bibliography, 797
    in *Chicago* notes, 797
    of long quotations, 440–41
        APA style, 687, 736, 747–48
        Chicago style, 764–65, 800, 802
        in literary analysis papers, 181–82
        MLA style, 181–82, 589, 663–64, 671, 825
        no quotation marks with, 440–41
    in MLA works cited list, 665, 825
    in outlines, 26–28

Independent clauses
  colon between, 433
  combined with subordinate
    clauses, 521
  and comma with coordinating
    conjunction, 407–08
  defined, 520
  and run-on sentences, 287–96
  semicolon between, 428–29
Indexes to periodical articles. *See*
    Databases, for finding sources
Indicative mood, 356
Indirect objects
  case of pronouns as, 322–23
  defined, 503–04
Indirect questions
  avoiding shifts to direct questions,
    226
  no question mark after, 448
Indirect quotations
  avoiding shifts to direct
    quotations, 226
  no comma with, 426
  no quotation marks with, 440
Indirect source (source quoted in
    another source), citing
  APA style, 701
  Chicago style, 778
  MLA style, 608, 622
Inductive reasoning, 131, 133–34,
    135
infer. See *imply, infer*, 844
Infinitive phrases, 512–13
Infinitives
  case of pronouns with, 324–25
  dangling, 217–18
  following verbs, 375–78
  marked (with *to*), 375–78, 400–01
  and sequence of tenses, 355–56
  split, 215–16
  subject of, objective case for,
    324–25
  to, infinitive marker vs.
    preposition, 400–01
  with *too* and *enough*, 377–78
  unmarked (without *to*), 377

Inflated phrases, 252
Infographics, 32, 34–35. *See also*
    Visuals, in documents
Informal language, 262–64
Informal outline, 25–26, 120–21,
    174–75. *See also* Formal outline
Information, for essay
  finding, 525–68
  managing, 543–52
  sources of, 7, 15–16
  working bibliography, 37, 543–44,
    545
Information notes (MLA), 661–62
-ing verb ending. See Gerunds;
    Present participles
in, into, 844
in regards to, 844
Inserted material, in quotations. *See*
    Brackets
Institutional review board (IRB), for
    research subjects, 540
Instructor's comments, responding
    to. *See* Revising with comments
Integrating sources
  in APA papers, 683–93
  in *Chicago* papers, 762–68
  in literary analysis papers, 179–83
  in MLA papers, 585–97
intend to do (not *on doing*), 272
Intensive pronouns, 489
Interjections (exclamations), 419,
    448, 498
Internet. *See also* URLs; Web sources
  avoiding plagiarism from, 540,
    544, 550
  capitalization of terms for, 480
  reading on, 104
  scanning, 555
  searching, 535–38
    how-to guide, 536
Interpretation
  in analysis papers, 106–11,
    124–26
  different perspectives and, 101,
    132
  of literary texts, 168–72, 176

Interpretation (*cont.*)
  of multimodal texts, 115–26
  of written texts, 102–11
Interrogative pronouns
  defined, 489
  who, whom, 328–31, 852
Interrogative sentences, 522
Interrogative tags (questions),
    commas with, 419
Interruptions, commas with, 419
Interviews, as information source,
    15–16, 540–41, 811
In-text citations. *See also* Integrating
    sources
  APA style
    directory to models for, 694
    models for, 695–701
  Chicago style (notes), 768–94
    directory to models for, 769–70
    models for, 770–94
  choosing a documentation style
    for, 812
  exclamation points with, 443, 600
  in literary analysis papers, 181–87
  MLA style
    directory to models for, 599
    models for, 599–610
  periods with, 578
  question marks with, 443, 600
into. See in, into, 844
Intransitive verbs
  defined, 504–05
  not used in passive voice, 367
Introducing sources. *See* Signal
    phrases
Introduction. *See also* Thesis
  of argument paper, 149–50
  in business document, 832, 833
  of essay, 28–30
  hook in, 29–30, 42, 575
  of literary analysis paper, 175
  to portfolio, 62, 65–71
  of research paper, 575–76
  revising, 42, 51
  sample student writing, 575–76
  strategies for drafting, 30

Introductory word groups, comma
    with, 408–09
Invented words, 260–61
Inverted sentence order
  for emphasis, 240–41
  with expletives *there, it,* 304–05,
    390–91, 501, 507
  no comma with, 425–26
  and position of subject, 501, 507
  in questions, 501, 506
  and subject-verb agreement,
    304–05
  for variety, 245–46
IRB (institutional review board), for
    research subjects, 540
irregardless (nonstandard), 844
Irregular verbs, 340–45, 492
  be, am, is, are, was, were, 340–41
  do, does, 342, 347
  have, has, 343, 347
  lie, lay, 344–45, 845
  list of, 342–44
Issue and volume numbers,
  in APA reference list, 706
  in MLA works cited list, 615
is vs. *are. See* Agreement of subject
    and verb
is when, is where, avoiding, 211, 845
it
  broad reference of, 316–17
  as expletive (placeholder),
    390–91
  indefinite use of, 318
  as subject of sentence, 390–91
Italics, 463–65
  in e-mail, 463
  for foreign words, 465
  for names of ships, spacecraft, and
    aircraft, 465
  for titles of works, 463–64
    APA style, 705, 736, 739–40
    Chicago style, 771, 795
    in literary analysis papers, 178
    MLA style, 616, 663
  for words as words, 465
its, it's, 436, 438, 472, 845

J

Jargon, 256–58
  writer's choice, 257
Journal, keeping a, 18–19, 361
Journalist's questions, 18, 536
Journals. *See* Periodicals
Judgment, in analysis papers,
  107–11, 126
jury. See Collective nouns
just, placement of, 212–13

K

Key words
  and APA abstracts, 737, 742, 827
  defining for readers
    in APA papers, 676–77
    in MLA papers, 573
  repeating for coherence, 85–86
Keyword searching
  in databases, 535, 536
  in library catalog, 535
  scanning results of, 554–55
  in search engines, 535, 536, 538
    how-to guide, 536
kind(s), 845
kind of, sort of, 845

L

Labels for people, caution with,
  267–68
Labels for visuals. *See* Captions
Lab report, sample assignment and
  excerpt, 818–19
Language. *See also* Tone; Words
  appropriate, 256–68, 833
  biased, avoiding, 140, 267–68
  borrowed. *See* Citing sources;
    Plagiarism, avoiding
  clichés, avoiding, 273–74
  colloquial, 263, 472
  direct, 252–53
  doublespeak, avoiding, 258–59
  euphemisms, avoiding, 258–59

  exact, 268–76
  formality of, 262–64
  idioms (common expressions),
    271–73
  invented, 260–61
  jargon, 256–58, 812
  in literature, questions to ask
    about, 171
  nonstandard English, avoiding,
    261–62
  obsolete, 260–61
  offensive, avoiding, 267–68
  plain, 256–61
  pretentious, avoiding, 258–59
  regionalisms, avoiding, 261–62
  sexist, avoiding, 264–67
  slang, avoiding, 261–62
  specialized, 257, 812
  wordy, 251–55
Latin abbreviations, 459
lay, lie; laying, lying 344–45, 845
Layout of documents. *See* Document
  design
lead, led, 845
Learning community, 40
learn, teach, 845
leave, let, 845
Legal sources
  APA citation of, 724
  MLA citation of, 659–60
Length
  of paper, 7, 16
  of paragraph, 72, 91–92
less. See fewer, less, 842
let. See leave, let, 845
Letter in a published collection
  Chicago citation of, 786
  citation at a glance, 788–89
  MLA citation of, 634
Letters, writing
  for business, 830
  for a portfolio, 62, 65–71
  writing guide, 70–71
Letters of the alphabet
  capitalizing, 479–83
  italics for, 465

Letters of the alphabet (*cont.*)
plural of, 437
liable, 845
Library resources. *See also* Web
sources
articles in periodicals, 535
databases for, 535, 536, 554–55
bibliographies, 538, 539
books, 535, 539
catalog for, 535, 555
reference librarians, 535
scholarly citations, 538, 539
Web page, library, 535
lie, lay; lying, laying, 344–45, 845
like
no comma after, 426
and sentence fragments, 284–85
like, as, 846
Limiting modifiers (*only, almost,*
etc.), 212–13
Line spacing
in APA paper, 736, 828
in business letters, 830
in *Chicago* paper, 795
in MLA paper, 663, 824–25
Linking verbs
adjective after, 333, 502–03
defined, 502
omission of, 350, 390
pronoun after, 322
Listing ideas, 18
List of sources. *See* Bibliography,
Chicago style; Reference list
(APA); Works cited list (MLA)
Lists. *See also* Series
with colon, 432
with dash, 450
and document design, 831–33
as fragments, 284–85
for generating ideas, 18
parallelism and, 200
Literacy narrative
sample student writing, 47–48,
58–61
writing guide, 63–64
Literary present tense, 224, 354, 813
avoiding shifts and, 178, 180–81

Literature, writing about, 167–90
active reading for, 167–68
analysis and, 98, 108
avoiding excessive summary in,
177
avoiding plot summary in, 177
avoiding shifts in tense, 178,
180–81, 223–24
conventions (standard practices)
in, 178
details from the work in, 175–83
discussion for, 168–69
evidence in, 176
interpretation in, 168–72
introduction for, 175
MLA style for, 179, 183–84
outline for, 174–75
questions to ask for literary
analysis, 170–72, 173
quotations from the work
citing, 181–83
context for, 180
formatting, 181–83
integrating, 179–83
sample paper, 187–90
secondary sources in
avoiding plagiarism, 185–87
documenting, 183–84
thesis in, 172–75
verb tense and, 178, 180–81,
223–24, 354, 813
Literature review
sample assignment and excerpt,
814–16
sample paper (APA style),
741–53
Logic
analogies, 81, 134
cause-and-effect reasoning, 134,
136
deductive reasoning, 138–39
fallacies. *See* Fallacies, logical
inductive reasoning, 131, 133–34,
135
logos (logical appeals), 131–39,
141–42, 148
of sentences, 210–11

Logos (logical appeals), in arguments, 131–39, 141–42, 148. *See also* Logic

Logs
  editing, 41, 57
  research, 527, 543
  revision, 41
loose, lose, 846
lots, lots of, 846
-ly ending on adverbs, 332
lying vs. *laying,* 344–45

M

Magazines. *See* Periodicals
Main clauses. *See* Independent clauses
Main point. *See* Focus; Thesis; Topic sentence
Main verbs, 362, 492–93
  with modals (*can, should,* etc.), 350, 368–71
man, mankind, sexist use of, 265, 846
Manuscript formats. *See also* Document design
  academic formats, 822–23, 824–28
    APA style, 735–40, 826–29
    Chicago style, 794–97
    MLA style, 59–61, 662–65, 824–25
  business and professional formats, 823, 829–33
  writing situation and, 16
Mapping. *See* Outlines
Maps, 32, 34, 811. *See also* Visuals, in documents
Margins
  in APA papers, 736, 828
  in *Chicago* papers, 795
  in MLA papers, 663, 824–25
Mass (noncount) nouns, 380–81, 384–87
mathematics (singular), 307
may. See can, may, 838
may, as modal verb, 350, 368–69, 491–92

maybe, may be, 846
may of, might of (nonstandard), 846
Meaning, finding in a text, 106–11, 124–26
measles (singular), 307
Measurement, units of
  abbreviations for, 458–59, 460
  and agreement of subject and verb, 304
media, medium, 846
Memos, 832
Metaphor, 274–75
Metric measurements, abbreviations for, 458–59, 460
me vs. *I,* 321–27
might, as modal verb, 350, 368–69, 491–92
might of (nonstandard). See *may of, might of,* 846
Minor ideas. *See* Subordination
Misplaced modifiers, 212–20. *See also* Modifiers
Missing claims, in arguments, 137–38
Missing words. *See* Needed words
Misspelled words, common, 473–74
Misuse of words, 270–71
Mixed constructions
  illogical connections, 210–11
  is when, is where, 211, 845
  mixed grammar, 208–10
  reason . . . is because, 211
Mixed metaphors, 274–75
MLA Handbook, 598, 662
MLA papers, 569–673. *See also* Literature, writing about
  authority in, 539, 574, 591–92
  avoiding plagiarism in, 577–83
  citation at a glance
    article from a database, 626–27
    article in a journal, 624–25
    book, 636
    selection from an anthology or a collection, 640–41
    short work from a Web site, 646–47

MLA papers (*cont.*)
  citations, in-text
    directory to models for, 599
    models for, 599–610
  evidence for
    in literary analysis, 176
    in nonfiction analysis, 572–74
  how-to guides
    being a responsible research
      writer, 583
    citing a reposted source, 652–53
    citing course materials, 658–59
    identifying authors, 620–21
  information notes (optional),
    661–62
  literary analysis, 167–90
  manuscript format, 59–61,
    662–65, 824–25
  numbers in, 461
  organizing, 174–75, 572
  sample papers
    analysis, 112–14, 127–30
    argument, 157–63
    literary analysis, 187–90
    research, 666–73
  signal phrases in, 590–94
  sources in
    citing, 577–83, 598–661
    integrating, 585–97
    synthesizing, 584, 594–97
    uses of, 572–74
  supporting arguments in, 176,
    183–87, 572–74, 594–97
  tenses in, 178, 180–81, 223–24,
    354, 591, 811
  thesis in, 172–75, 570–77
  URLs in, 617, 664, 665
  voice (tone) in, 576–77
  works cited list, 611–61, 825
    directory to models for, 611–13
    DOIs (digital object identifiers)
      in, 617, 626
    formatting, 665, 825
    general guidelines for, 615–17
    models for, 613–61
    sample, 163, 190, 672–73, 825

Modal verbs (*can, should*, etc.), 350,
  368–70, 491–92. *See also*
  Helping verbs
Model documents, gallery of, 822–33
Modern Language Association. *See*
  MLA papers
Modes. *See* Multimodal texts;
  Paragraph patterns
Modifiers
  adjectives as, 332–39, 493–94
  adverbs as, 332–39, 494–95
  commas with, 411
  dangling, 216–20
  of gerunds, 325–26
  limiting, 212–13
  misplaced, 212–20
  redundant, 251
  restrictive (essential) and
    nonrestrictive
    (nonessential), 413–17
  split infinitives, 215–16
  squinting, 214
Money
  abbreviations for, 458
  numerals for, 462
Mood of verbs, 356–58. *See also*
  Conditional sentences
  avoiding shifts in, 225
more, most (comparative, superlative),
  336–37
moreover
  comma with, 417–18
  semicolon with, 428–29
most, 846
Motive. *See* Purpose in writing;
  Writing situation
Multilingual writers, 360–403
  adjectives, 396–98
  adjectives and adverbs, placement
    of, 397–98
  articles (*a, an, the*), 378–89
  and English-language skills,
    361
  idioms (common expressions),
    399–403
  nouns, types of, 379–80

omitted subjects or expletives, 390–91
omitted verbs, 390
participles, present vs. past, 396–97
prepositions, in idioms (common expressions)
  with adjectives, 401–02
  with nouns and *-ing* forms, 400–01
  to show time and place (*at, in, on*, etc.), 399–400
  with verbs, 402–03
repeated objects or adverbs, 232, 392–93
repeated subjects, 210, 391–92
sentence structure, 389–98
verbs, 361–78
  active voice, 363–65
  conditional, 372–74
  forms of, 362–65
  with gerunds or infinitives, 375–78
  modals (*can, should*, etc.), 350, 368–70
  negative forms, 371–72
  passive voice, 365–68
  tenses, 362–65, 372–74
Multimedia sources, citing. *See also* Web sources
  APA style, 728–33
  Chicago style, 790–94
  MLA style, 648–57
Multimodal texts. *See also* Genre (type of writing)
  analyzing, 124–26
  annotating, 104, 117–18, 119
  conversing with, 118, 119
  defined, 115
  evaluating, 564–65
  outlining, 120–21
  planning, 63, 70, 110, 164, 567
  purpose and, 12–15
  reading, 104, 115–20
  sample paper analyzing, 126–30

  summarizing, 121–22
    how-to guide, 123
  writing about, 121–26, 807–08
  writing practice, 120
Multitasking, avoiding, 104
must, as modal verb, 350, 368–69, 491–92
must of (nonstandard). See *may of, might of*, 846
myself, 323, 846–47

N

namely, and sentence fragments, 284–85
Narration, as paragraph pattern, 77–78
Narrative writing. *See* Literacy narrative
Narrowing a subject. *See* Topic
N.B. ("note well"), 459
n.d. ("no date"), in APA reference list, 700, 725, 726, 728
nearly, placement of, 212–13
Needed words, 204–08
  articles (*a, an, the*), 207, 378–89
  in comparisons, 206–07
  in compound structures, 204–05
  it, 390–91
  in parallel structures, 202–03
  subjects, 390–91
  that, 202–03, 205
  there, 390–91
  verbs, 350, 390
Negatives
  avoiding double, 338, 372
  forming, 371–72
  not and *never*, 495
neither (singular), 302, 310–11, 314, 847
neither . . . nor
  and parallel structure, 201
  and pronoun-antecedent agreement, 314
  and subject-verb agreement, 301

never
  as adverb, 495
  avoiding double negative with, 338
nevertheless
  comma with, 417–18
  semicolon with, 428–29
news (singular), 307
Newspapers. *See* Periodicals
no
  avoiding double negative with,
    338, 372
  comma with, 338, 419
nobody (singular), 302, 310–11
Noncount nouns, 380–81, 384–87
none, 302, 847
Nonrestrictive (nonessential)
    elements, commas with,
    413–17
Non sequitur, 137–38
Nonsexist language, 264–67, 310–11,
    313
Nonstandard English, avoiding,
    261–62
no one (singular), 302, 310–11
nor
  comma with, 407–08
  as coordinating conjunction, 201,
    497
  parallelism and, 201
  and pronoun-antecedent
    agreement, 314
  and subject-verb agreement, 301
not
  as adverb, 371–72, 495
  avoiding double negative with,
    338, 371–72
  in forming negatives, 371–72
  placement of, 212–13
Notes. *See* Footnotes or endnotes;
    Information notes (MLA)
Note taking
  for analysis, 97–101, 117–18, 119
  and avoiding plagiarism, 544–51
  double-entry notebook for,
    99–100, 120
  on drafts, 37
  on electronic documents, 104

  to generate ideas, 17–18
  for literary analysis papers, 168
  responsibility and, 544
  sample notes, 97–99, 119
nothing (singular), 302, 310–11
not only . . . but also, 497
  and parallel structure, 201
  and pronoun-antecedent
    agreement, 314
  and subject-verb agreement, 301
Noun/adjectives, 487, 499
Noun clauses, 518–19
  words introducing, 517
Noun markers, 378–89
Nouns. *See also* Nouns, types of
  adjectives with, 493–94
  articles with, 378–89
  avoiding shifts between singular
    and plural, 220–23
  capitalizing, 479–80
  defined, 487
  of direct address, comma with,
    419
  plural form, singular meaning
    (*athletics, economics,* etc.), 307
  plural of, 467–68
  after prepositions, 400–01
  renaming other nouns. *See*
    Appositives
Nouns, types of. *See also* Nouns
  abstract, 270–71
  collective (*audience, family, team,*
    etc.), 303–04, 312
  common, 379–87, 479–80
  count, 379–84
  defined, 487
  generic, 311
  noncount, 380–81, 384–87
  possessive, 434–36, 487
  proper, 379–80, 381–82, 387–88,
    479–80
  singular and plural, 380, 382
  specific, concrete, 270
  specific vs. general, 270, 380, 382
Novels, titles of
  capitalization of, 481
  italics for, 463

nowheres (nonstandard), 847
number. See *amount, number,* 836
number, agreement of verb with, 304
Number and person
  avoiding shifts in, 220–23
  and subject-verb agreement,
    297–309
Numbers
  commas in, 420
  consistency of, 461
  hyphens with, 476
  italics for, 465
  plural of, 436
  spelled out vs. numerals, 461–62
    APA style, 461, 827
    MLA style, 461
Nursing practice paper, sample
  assignment and excerpt,
    820–21

O

Object complements, 504
  adjectives as, following direct
    object, 334
Objections, to arguments. *See*
  Counterarguments
Objective case, of pronouns
  for objects, 322–23
  for subjects and objects of
    infinitives, 324–25
  whom, 328–31
Objectivity
  assessing, in sources, 143–45,
    559–61
  in writing a summary, 105,
    121–23
Objects
  avoiding repetition of, 392–93
  direct, 503
  indirect, 503–04
  of infinitives, 324–25
  no comma between verb and, 423
  objective case for, 322–23,
    328–31
  of prepositions, 508
  pronouns as, 322–23

Observation, as information source,
  15, 541, 811
Obsolete words, 260–61
of, after *could, would, may,* etc.
  (nonstandard), 847
Offensive language, avoiding, 267–68
off of (nonstandard), 272, 847
OK, O.K., okay, 847
Omission of needed words. *See*
  Needed words
Omissions of letters and words
  apostrophe for, 436
  ellipsis mark for, 452
on, in idioms (common expressions)
  with adjectives, 401–02
  vs. *at, in,* to show time and place,
    399–403
  with verbs, 402–03
one of the, agreement of verb with,
  306
Online sources. *See* Web sources
only, placement of, 212–13
only one of the, agreement of verb
  with, 306
Opening. *See* Introduction
Opinion, expert, using as support,
  154–55
Opposing arguments. *See*
  Counterarguments
Opposites (antonyms), 471–72
or
  comma with, 407–08
  as coordinating conjunction, 201,
    497
  excessive use of, 236–37
  parallelism and, 201
  and pronoun-antecedent
    agreement, 314
  and subject-verb agreement, 301
Oral presentations, 166
Organization. *See also* Outlines
  of APA papers, 675–76
  of *Chicago* papers, 756
  improving, 52–53, 54
  of literacy narratives, 63
  of literary analysis papers, 174–75
  of MLA papers, 572, 615

Organization (*cont.*)
    patterns of. *See* Paragraph patterns
    of résumés, 831
Organizations, abbreviations for,
    457–58
    in APA in-text citations, 697
    conventional uses, 457–58
    in MLA in-text citations, 603
ought to, as modal verb, 491–92
Outlines
    for essay, 25–28
    formal, 26–28, 102–03
    informal, 25–26, 120–21
    for literary analysis paper, 174–75
    for MLA paper, 572
    for summary or analysis, 102–03,
        120–21
Ownership. *See* Possessive case

P

Page numbers (of sources). *See also*
    Pagination (of paper)
    APA style, 706
    Chicago style, 770–71
    MLA style, 615, 616, 824
Page setup. *See* Document design;
    Manuscript formats
Pagination (of paper)
    APA style, 735–36, 826–28
    Chicago style, 794–95
    MLA style, 663, 824–25
Paired ideas, parallelism and, 200–02
Paragraph patterns. *See also*
    Paragraphs
    analogy, 81
    cause and effect, 81–82
    classification, 82–83
    comparison and contrast, 79–80
    definition, 84
    description, 78–79
    division, 82–84
    examples, 76–77
    illustrations, 76–77
    narration, 77–78
    process, 79

Paragraphs, 79–92. *See also*
    Paragraph patterns
    coherence in, 84–91
    concluding, 33, 36–37
    defined, 72
    details in, 75–76
    development of, 53–55, 75–76,
        176
    focus of, 72–75
    introductory, 28–30
    length of, 72, 91–92
    main point in, 74
    organizing, 52–53
    revising, 53–55
    sample student writing, 50–51,
        122, 166, 575–76
    topic sentences in, 52–53, 72–73
    transitions in, 87–91
    unity of, 74
Parallelism
    for emphasis, 241
    in headings, 199–200
    in lists, 200
    in paragraphs, 86–87
    in sentences, 198–203
parameters, 847
Paraphrases
    acceptable and unacceptable
        in APA papers, 681–83
        in *Chicago* papers, 760–62
        in MLA papers, 580–83
    integrating
        in APA papers, 684, 687–91
        in *Chicago* papers, 767
        in MLA papers, 585–86,
            590–94
    in literary analysis papers, 186–87
    no quotation marks for, 440
    and note taking, 549
Parentheses, 450–51
    capitalizing sentences in, 481
    no comma before, 426
Parenthetical citations. *See* In-text
    citations
Parenthetical elements
    commas with, 418

dashes with, 449
parentheses with, 450
Participial phrases. *See also* Past
    participles; Present participles
for combining sentences, 234
dangling, 217–18
defined, 511–12
Participles. *See* Past participles;
    Present participles
Particles, with verbs, 492–93
Parts of speech, 487–98
adjectives, 493–94
adverbs, 494–95
conjunctions, 497–98
in dictionary entry, 471
interjections (exclamations), 498
nouns, 487–88
prepositions, 496
pronouns, 488–91
verbs, 491–93
passed, past, 847
Passive voice
vs. active voice, 193–98, 507–08
appropriate uses of, 194, 195
forming, 365–68
shifts between active and,
    avoiding, 225
and wordy sentences, 253
writer's choice, 195
past. See *passed, past,* 847
Past participles
as adjectives, 396
defined, 341
of irregular verbs, 340–45
in participial phrases, 511
and passive voice, 365–67, 508
and perfect tenses, 352, 355, 364,
    366–67
vs. present participles, 396–97
of regular verbs, 340, 348–49
as verbals, 511–12
Past perfect tense, 352, 355, 364,
    367
Past progressive form, 353, 364, 366
Past tense
in APA papers, 355, 688, 695, 813

and *-d, -ed* endings, 340, 348–49
defined, 352, 363, 366
of irregular verbs, 340–45
vs. past perfect, 355
of regular verbs, 340, 348–49
Pathos (emotional appeals), 139–43,
    148
Patterns of organization. *See*
    Paragraph patterns
PDF documents, MLA citation of,
    658–59
Peer review. *See also* Revising with
    comments
acknowledging, 70
for an analytical essay, 111
for an annotated bibliography,
    568
for an argument paper, 165
comments
    giving, 41, 44, 45
    how-to guide, 44
    revising with, 39, 42–43
    samples of, 45, 47–48
community and, 40
engagement with, 1, 40
for a literacy narrative, 64
for a reflective letter, 71
responsibility and, 1
seeking feedback, 38–41
writing practice, 46, 62, 112
Percentages, numerals for, 462. *See*
    also Statistics
percent, per cent, percentage, 847
Perfect progressive forms, 353, 365,
    367
Perfect tenses, 352, 355, 364,
    366–67
Periodicals. *See also* Articles in
    periodicals
capitalizing titles of, 481
    APA style, 705, 736, 739–40
italics for titles of, 463
    APA style, 705, 736, 739–40
    Chicago style, 771, 795
    MLA style, 616, 663
Periodic sentences, 241

Periods, 447–48
with abbreviations, 447–48,
457–59
and ellipsis mark, 452
to end a sentence, 447
with in-text citations, 578
with quotation marks, 442–43
Permalinks, in MLA works cited, 617
Personal experience, writing about,
2, 8, 526
Personal pronouns
case of, 321–27
defined, 488
Personal titles. *See* Titles of persons
Person and number
avoiding shifts in, 220–23
and subject-verb agreement,
297–309
Persons, names of. *See* Nouns
Persuasive writing. *See* Argument
papers
phenomena, 847
Photographs, 32, 35, 811. *See also*
Visuals, in documents
Phrasal verbs. *See* Particles, with
verbs
Phrases. *See also* Phrases, types of
dangling, 216–20
empty or inflated, 252
fragmented, 283
introductory, comma after, 408–09
misplaced, 213–14
as modifiers, 511–12
nonrestrictive (nonessential), with
commas, 413–17
restrictive (essential), with no
commas, 413–17, 424–25
separating subject and verb,
214–15
Phrases, types of. *See also* Phrases
absolute, 514
appositive, 514, 515
gerund, 512
infinitive, 512–13
participial, 511–12
prepositional, 508–10
verbal, 510–14

physics (singular), 307
Pictures, 32, 35. *See also* Visuals, in
documents
Place of publication
in APA reference list, 705
not used in MLA works cited list,
616
Places, names of. *See* Nouns
Plagiarism, avoiding
in APA papers, 678–83
in *Chicago* papers, 758–62
and drafting, 32
how-to guides
avoiding plagiarism from the
Web, 550
being a responsible research
writer, 583
in literary analysis papers,
185–87
in MLA papers, 577–83
and note taking, 544–51
responsibility and, 544
reviewer comments about, 43
and Web sources, 33, 544, 550
working bibliography and, 543–44,
545–46
Planning an essay. *See also* Outlines
assessing the writing situation,
5–17
exploring ideas, 17–19
working thesis, 19–25
and writing about literature,
172–75
plan to do (not *on doing*), 272
Plays
quoting from, 182–83
titles of
capitalizing, 481
italics for, 463
Plot, in literature
avoiding summary of, 177
questions to ask about, 171
Plurals. *See also* Agreement of
pronoun and antecedent;
Agreement of subject and
verb; Singular vs. plural
of abbreviations, 437, 459

of compound nouns, 467
of letters, 437
of numbers, 436
spelling of, 467–68
of words used as words, 437
plus, 848
p.m., a.m., PM, AM, 458
Podcast, citing
APA style, 728
Chicago style, 787
MLA style, 648
Poems
quoting from, 182, 452–53, 811
slash to separate lines of, 182, 453
titles of
capitalizing, 481
quotation marks with, 441
Point of view
consistency in, 54, 87, 220–23
dominant, 54
in literature, questions to ask about, 171
opposing, in arguments. *See* Counterarguments
revising for, 54
writer's choice, 221
in writing for different disciplines, 813
politics (singular), 307
Portfolios, 62, 65–71
Position, stating. *See* Thesis
Possessive case
apostrophe for, 434–36
with gerund, 325–26
Possessive pronouns
defined, 489
no apostrophe in, 438
Post hoc fallacy, 136
precede, proceed, 848
Predicate, 284, 499
Predicate adjective. *See* Subject complements
Predicate noun. *See* Subject complements
Predication, faulty, 210–11
preferable to (not *than*), 272
Prefixes, hyphen after, 477

Premises, in deductive reasoning, 138–39
Prepositional phrases
defined, 508–10
fragmented, 283
restrictive (essential) vs. nonrestrictive (nonessential), 415–16
between subject and verb, 300
Prepositions
after adjectives, 401–02
at, in, on, to show time and place, 399–403
defined, 496
followed by nouns or *-ing* forms, not verbs, 400–01
in idioms (common expressions), 271–73, 399–403
list of, 496
objects of, 508
and parallel structure, 202–03
after verbs, 402–03, 492–93
Present participles
as adjectives, 396
in gerund phrases, 512
in participial phrases, 511
vs. past participles, 396–97
and progressive forms, 353, 364
and sequence of tenses, 355–56
Present perfect tense, 352, 355–56, 364, 366–67
in APA papers, 355, 688, 695, 813
in *Chicago* papers, 765, 813
Present progressive form, 353, 363, 366
Present tense, 351–52, 363, 366
in APA papers, 813
avoiding tense shifts with, 180–81, 223–24
in *Chicago* papers, 765, 813
in MLA papers, 591
in résumés, 831
subject-verb agreement in, 297–309
in summaries, 105, 121, 123
in writing about literature, 178, 180–81, 224, 354, 813

Present tense (*cont.*)
  in writing about science, 354
Presentations, oral, 166
Pretentious language, avoiding,
  258–59
Previewing
  multimodal texts, 116
  sources, 555–57
  written texts, 95–96, 101
Prewriting strategies, 17–19
Primary sources
  for authenticity, 539
  citation at a glance (*Chicago* style),
    792–93
  as evidence, 811
  in literary analysis papers, 175–83,
    811
  on the Web, 652–53, 792–93
  sample papers using, 187–90,
    798–804
  vs. secondary sources, 559
principal, principle, 848
prior to (not *than*), 272
Problem/solution approach, for
    revising a thesis, 22–23
proceed. See *precede, proceed*, 848
Process
  of evaluating sources, 552
  as paragraph pattern, 79
  of writing an essay
    drafting, 1, 28–37
    editing, 55–56, 57
    planning, 5–38
    reviewing, 38–49
    revising, 49–55
    as social activity, 1, 38–39
Professional documents. *See* Business
    writing
Progressive forms, 353, 363–64, 366
Pronoun/adjectives, 488
Pronoun-antecedent agreement. *See*
    Agreement of pronoun and
    antecedent
Pronoun case
  I vs. *me* etc., 321–27
  who vs. *whom*, 328–31
  you vs. *your*, 325–26

Pronoun reference, 315–21
  ambiguous, 316
  broad *this, that, which, it*, 316–17
  implied, 317–18
  indefinite *they, it, you*, 318
  remote, 316
  unstated antecedent, 317–18
  who (not *that, which*) for persons,
    319, 852
Pronouns. *See also* Pronouns, types of
  adjectives with, 493–94
  agreement of verbs with, 297–309
  agreement with antecedent,
    309–15
  as appositives, 323
  avoiding shifts in person and
    number, 220–23
  case (*I* vs. *me* etc.), 321–31
  defined, 488
  lists of, 488–90
  as objects, 322–23
  pronoun/adjectives, 488
  reference of, 315–21
  singular vs. plural, 309–15
  as subjects, 322
  who, whom, 328–31, 852
Pronouns, types of, 488–90. *See also*
    Pronouns
  demonstrative (*those, that*, etc.),
    489–90
  indefinite (*some, any*, etc.), 490
  intensive (*herself, themselves*, etc.),
    489
  interrogative (*who, which*, etc.),
    489
  personal (*you, they*, etc.), 488
  possessive (*your, his*, etc.), 325–26,
    489
  reciprocal (*each other* etc.), 490
  reflexive (*myself, yourselves*, etc.),
    489
  relative (*that, which*, etc.), 489,
    516, 517
Pronunciation, in dictionary entry,
    471
Proof. *See* Evidence
Proofreading, 56, 57

Proper nouns, 379–80, 381–82
  capitalizing, 479–80
  the with, 387–88
Proposals
  business, sample assignment and
    excerpt, 816–17
  research, 542
Psychology literature review, sample
    assignment and excerpt,
    814–16
*Publication Manual of the American
    Psychological Association*, 693,
    735. *See also* APA papers
Public speaking. *See* Presentations,
  oral
Public writing, audience for, 12
Publisher names
  in APA reference list, 705
  in MLA works cited list, 616
Punctuation, 406–54
  apostrophe, 434–39
  brackets, 451–52
  colon, 432–34
  comma, 407–27
  dash, 449–50
  ellipsis mark, 452
  for emphasis, 242
  exclamation point, 448
  parentheses, 450–51
  period, 447–48
  question mark, 448
  quotation marks, 439–46
  with quotation marks, 442–45
  semicolon, 428–32
  slash, 453
Purpose in writing, 8–10
  for argument papers, 146–47
  assignments and, 11
  for business proposals, 816–17
  curiosity and, 2
  and finding sources, 533–34
  and genre (type of writing),
    12–15
  for lab reports, 818–19
  for literary analysis papers, 170
  for nursing practice papers,
    820–21

  for psychology papers, 814–16
  for research papers, 528–34
  and writer's choices
    active and passive voice, 195
    emphasis, 231, 291
    point of view, 221
  and writing situation, 6, 8–10

Q

Quantifiers with noncount nouns,
    384–85
Question mark, 448
  and APA citations, 443
  and MLA citations, 443, 600
  no comma with, 427
  with quotation marks, 443
Questionnaires, as information
    source, 40, 541
Questions
  adding for variety, 246
  avoiding in thesis statements, 22
  commas with, 419
  direct and indirect, 226, 448
  pronouns for, 489
  punctuation of, 448
  recognizing in assignments, 11
  subject in, 501, 506
Questions to ask
  for an analysis paper, 111
  for an annotated bibliography,
    568
  about arguments, 53, 141–42,
    151, 165
  for assignments in the disciplines,
    808–10
  about audience, 10
  for drafting, 31
  about formatting, 32–33
  to generate ideas, 18
  about genre (type of writing),
    14–15
  for a literacy narrative, 64
  about literature, 170–72, 173
  of peer reviewers, 39
  about reading, 101
  for a reflective letter, 71

Questions to ask (*cont.*)
  about a research subject, 526,
    528–32, 542
    for APA papers, 675
    for *Chicago* papers, 755
    how-to guide, 532
    for MLA papers, 570
  to shape a thesis, 20–21, 151
Quotation marks, 439–46. *See also*
    Quotations
  to avoid plagiarism, 43, 551
  with direct quotations (exact
    language), 439–41, 551
  misuses of, 445
  not used with indented (long)
    quotations, 440–41
  not used with paraphrases and
    summaries, 440
  other punctuation with, 442–45
  single, 441
  with titles of works, 441
    APA style, 705, 736, 739–40
    Chicago style, 795
    MLA style, 178, 616, 663
  with words used as words, 442
quotation, quote. See quote, quotation,
    848
Quotations. *See also* Quotation marks
  adding for variety, 266
  in APA papers
    accuracy of, 686–87
    appropriate use of, 685–87
    avoiding dropped, 688–89
    avoiding plagiarism in, 579–80,
      680–81
    brackets with, 686–87
    citing, 680–81, 693–734
    context for, 690
    ellipsis mark with, 686
    embedding, 690
    indenting, 687, 736, 747–48
    integrating, 683–93
    long (indented), 687, 736,
      747–48
    quotation marks for, 680–81
    sic for errors in, 687

    signal phrase with, 687–91
    synthesizing, 691–93
  in argument papers, 144–45
  capitalization in, 482
  in *Chicago* papers
    accuracy of, 763–64
    appropriate use of, 762–65
    avoiding dropped, 766–67
    avoiding plagiarism in, 759–60
    brackets with, 764–65
    citing, 759–60, 768–94
    context for, 768
    ellipsis mark with, 763–64
    embedding, 768
    indenting, 764–65, 800, 802
    integrating, 762–68
    long (indented), 764–65, 800,
      802
    quotation marks for, 760
    sic for errors in, 764
    with signal phrase, 765–68
  colons introducing, 432
  commas with, 419
  direct and indirect, 226, 439–41
  ellipsis marks to indicate deletions
    in, 452
  integrating, 43, 73, 179–83
  from interviews, 541
  in literary analysis papers
    avoiding plagiarism in, 185–87
    and avoiding shifts in tense,
      178, 180–81
    citing, 181–87
    context for, 180
    formatting, 181–83
    indenting, 181–82
    integrating, 179–83
    long (indented), 181–82, 825
  long (indented), 440–41
  in MLA papers
    accuracy of, 587–88
    avoiding dropped, 591
    avoiding plagiarism in, 579–80
    brackets with, 588–89
    citing, 579, 598–661
    context for, 584, 593

effective use of, 587–89, 597
ellipsis mark with, 587–88, 825
embedding, 584, 593
indenting, 589, 663–64, 671,
    825
integrating, 585–97
long (indented), 181–82, 589,
    663–64, 671, 825
quotation marks for, 580
"sic" for errors in, 589
with signal phrase, 590–94
synthesizing, 594–97
in paraphrases, 549
punctuation of, 439–46
in quotations, 441
quoted in (qtd. in), for a source in
    another source, 608, 622. *See
    also cited in*
quote, quotation, 848
Quotes. *See* Quotations

R

Race and culture, in literature,
    questions to ask about, 172
raise, rise, 848
Ratios, colon with, 433
Readability, document design for,
    822
Readers, engaging, 29–30, 40, 42,
    50–51, 575
Reading
    active and critical
        for analysis, 95–102, 110,
            115–26
        of arguments, 130–46
        of literary works, 167–68
        of research sources, 558–65
        of multimodal texts, 115–26,
            564–65
        of written texts, 95–102
    annotating. *See* Annotating texts
    conversing with a text, 99–101,
        118, 119
    engagement with, 96, 167–68,
        527

evaluating arguments, 130–46
evaluating sources, 535–38,
    552–68
to explore a subject, 15, 17–18
to improve English-language skills,
    361
literary works and, 167–68
multimodal texts, 115–26, 564–65
previewing sources, 555–57
previewing texts, 95–96, 101, 116
responding to, 96. *See also* Analysis
    papers
on the Web, 104
writing practice, 120
real, really, 335, 848
Reasoning. *See also* Argument papers
    deductive, 138–39
    inductive, 131, 133–34, 135
    logical fallacies, 131–43
reason . . . is because (nonstandard),
    211, 848
reason why (nonstandard), 848
Reciprocal pronouns, 490
Red herring fallacy, 141
Redundancies, 251
Reference list (APA). *See also*
    Bibliography, *Chicago* style;
    Works cited list (MLA)
    directory to models for, 702–03
    formatting, 739–40, 828
    general guidelines for, 704–06
    models for, 703–34
    sample, 752–53, 828
Reference of pronouns. *See* Pronoun
    reference
Reflection. *See also* Habits of mind
    for an argument paper, 132
    developing habit of, 1
    letter of
        sample, 66–69
        writing guide, 70–71
    for a literacy narrative, 58–61,
        63–64
    for a portfolio, 62, 65–71
    for a research project, 527
Reflexive pronouns, 489

Regional expressions, 261–62
Regular verbs
   -d, *-ed* endings on, 340, 348–49
   defined, 340, 492
   -s forms of, 345–46
relation, *relationship*, 848
Relative adverbs
   defined, 516
   introducing adjective clauses,
      392–93, 516–17
Relative pronouns
   agreement with verb, 306
   defined, 489, 516
   introducing adjective clauses,
      392–93, 516–17
   in noun clauses, 517
   who, *whom*, 328–31, 852
Repetition
   of function words, for parallel
      structure, 202–03
   of key words, 85–86
   unnecessary, 251–52, 391–93
Reposted source, citing (MLA), 652–53
Requests, subjunctive mood for, 358
Researched writing. *See also*
      Literature, writing about;
      Researching a topic;
      Responsibility, with sources
   APA papers, 674–753
   Chicago papers, 754–804
   how-to guides
      avoiding plagiarism, 550
      being a responsible research
         writer, 583
      entering a research
         conversation, 532
   MLA papers, 569–673
   sample student writing
      APA style, 741–53
      Chicago style, 798–804
      MLA style, 112–14, 157–63,
         187–90, 666–73, 824–25
Researching a topic, 525–68. *See also*
      Researched writing;
      Synthesizing sources
   for argument papers, 146–47

bibliography
   annotated, 565–68
   sample annotated entry, 566
   scholarly, 538–39
   working, 543–44, 545
catalog, library, 535, 555
context and, 584
databases, 535, 536, 554–55
entry point for, finding, 525
evaluating sources, 535–38,
   552–68
field research, 540–41
getting started, 525–32
how-to guides
   entering a research
      conversation, 532
   going beyong a Google search,
      536
joining a research conversation,
   525, 527–28
keeping a research log, 527, 543
keeping records and copies of
   sources, 544
keyword searches, 535
library resources, 535
managing information, 525,
   527–29, 543–52
narrowing the focus, 530–31
note taking, 543, 544–51
planning, 525, 527–29, 553
purpose and, 528–34
questionnaires, 541
reading critically, 553, 558–65
reading selectively, 554–57
reference librarians, 535
research proposals, 542
research questions, 528–32, 542
schedule for, 525, 527, 529
search strategy, 533–34, 542, 553
shortcuts to related sources,
   534–39
surveys, 541
thinking like a researcher, 527
tips for smart searching, 536, 539
Web resources, 535–38
writing practice, 561

respectfully, respectively, 848
Response papers. *See* Analysis
    papers
Responsibility, with sources
    altering quotations, 541
        in APA papers, 686
        in *Chicago* papers, 764
        in MLA papers, 588
    copying from electronic files, 544
    crediting visuals, 33
    developing habit of, 1
    documenting evidence, 152
    how-to guide, 583
    keeping notes and records, 32,
        100, 543–52
    in literary analysis papers, 185–87
    and note taking, 100, 543–52
    providing context for sources,
        584
    reading critically, 559
    and thinking like a researcher,
        527
Restrictive (essential) elements, no
    commas with, 413–17, 424–25
Résumés, 831
Reviewers. *See* Peer review
Review of the literature, samples of
    (APA style), 741–53, 815–16
Revising with comments, 39–43. *See
    also* Peer review
    "Be specific," 43
    "Cite your sources," 43
    "Consider opposing viewpoints,"
        42
    giving comments, 44
    sample peer review process, 45–49
    strategies for, 42–43
    "Unfocused introduction," 42
Revision, 38–62. *See also* Revising
    with comments
    cyles of, 38–41, 49–55
    vs. editing, 38, 55
    engagement with, 40
    global (big-picture), 49–55
    readers and, 40
    reflection and, 62, 65–71

revision and editing log for, 41
    sample revised draft, 58–61
    sentence-level, 55–56, 57
    as social process, 1, 38–39
    strategies for, 42–43
    of thesis, 21–24
    writing practice, 62
Rhetorical analysis, 95–114. *See also*
    Analysis papers
rise. See raise, rise, 848
Running heads. *See also* Pagination
    (of paper)
    in APA papers, 735–36, 826–28
    in MLA papers, 663
Run-on sentences
    finding and recognizing, 287–88,
        289
    fixing, 288–94
        with colon or dash, 292–93
        with comma and coordinating
            conjunction, 290, 292
        by making two sentences,
            293–94
        by restructuring, 294
        with semicolon, 292
        writer's choice, 291
    testing for, 289

S

-s
    and apostrophe, 434–37
    and plurals of abbreviations, 459
    and spelling, 467
    as verb ending, 297, 298–99,
        345–46
Sacred texts (Bible, Qur'an)
    citing
        APA style, 701, 724
        Chicago style, 777
        MLA style, 610, 639
    no italics for, 464
    punctuation between chapter and
        verse, 433
Salutations and greetings, colon with,
    433, 830

Sample student writing
  analysis
    of a literary text, 187–90
    of a multimodal text, 126–30
    of a written text, 112–14
  argument, 157–63
  business letter, 830
  in the disciplines, excerpts
    business proposal, 817
    lab report, 819
    nursing practice paper, 821
    psychology literature review, 815–16
  introduction for a research paper, 575–76
  literacy narrative, 58–61
  oral presentation, 166
  paragraphs, 50–51, 122, 166, 575–76
  portfolio letter, 66–69
  in progress (multiple drafts), 47–48, 59–61
  research
    APA style, 741–53
    Chicago style, 798–804
    MLA style, 575–76, 666–73
  résumé, 831
  revised draft, 59–61
  rough draft with peer comments, 47–48
Scholarly sources, identifying, 539, 557
Sciences, writing in the, 108, 807–13, 818–19
Scientific facts, and verb tense, 354
Scores, numerals for, 462
Search engines, 535–36, 538
Search strategy, 533–34
Secondary sources, 559, 811
  in literary analysis paper, 183–87, 188–90
  vs. primary sources, 559
  sample paper using, 188–90
Second-person point of view, 54, 220–23

self-, hyphen with, 477
Self-assessment, in portfolio, 62, 65–71. *See also* Reflection
Semicolon, 428–32
  for combining sentences, 229–30, 233
  with commas, 429
  to fix run-on sentences, 292
  between independent clauses, 428–29
  misuse of, 430–31
  outside quotation marks, 443
  with series, 430
  transitional expressions with, 428–29
sensual, sensuous, 849
Sentence endings, for emphasis, 240–41
Sentence fragments. *See* Fragments, sentence
Sentence patterns, 499–506
Sentence purposes, 522
Sentences. *See also* Sentence types
  awkward, 208–12
  choppy, combining, 230, 232
  comma splices. *See* Run-on sentences
  conditional, 372–74
  fragments. *See* Fragments, sentence
  fused. *See* Run-on sentences
  incomplete. *See* Fragments, sentence
  inverted (verb before subject), 245–46, 304–05, 390–91, 501, 507
  logical, 210–11
  parts of, 499–506
  patterns of, 499–506
  purposes of, 522
  revising and editing, 38, 55–56, 57
  run-on. *See* Run-on sentences
  thesis. *See* Thesis
  topic, 72–73
  transitional, 87–91
  variety in, 242–47

wordy, 251–55
writer's choice, 244
Sentence structure
mixed constructions, 208–12
multilingual/ESL challenges with,
389–98
adjectives, placement of,
397–98
adverbs, placement of, 395
although, because, 394
avoiding repetition of object or
adverb, 392–93
avoiding repetition of subject,
391–92
linking verb between subject
and subject complement,
390
present participle vs. past
participle, 396–97
subject, needed, 390–91
there, it, 390–91
paraphrases and, 549
simplifying, 253
variety in, 242–47
writer's choice, 244
Sentence types, 519–22
complex, 521
compound, 520–21
compound-complex, 521
declarative, 522
exclamatory, 522
imperative, 522
interrogative, 522
inverted, 240–41
periodic, 241
simple, 520
Series. *See also* Lists
comma with, 410
parallelism and, 199
parentheses with, 451
semicolon with, 430
set, sit, 849
Setting, in literature, questions to ask
about, 171
Setup, page. *See* Document design;
Manuscript formats

Sexist language, avoiding, 264–67,
310–11, 313
shall, as modal verb, 350, 368, 370,
491–92
shall, will, 849
she, her, hers, sexist use of, 265,
310–11, 313
she vs. *her,* 321–27
she writes, he writes, comma with,
419, 444
Shifts, avoiding
from indirect to direct questions
or quotations, 226
in levels of formality, 263
in mood or voice, 225
in point of view (person and
number), 220–23
in verb tense, 178, 180–81,
223–24
Ships, italics for names of, 465
Short stories, titles of
capitalizing, 481
quotation marks for, 441
APA style, 736
Chicago style, 795
MLA style, 616, 663
should, as modal verb, 350, 368, 370,
491–92
should of (nonstandard), 849
sic, 451–52
in APA paper, 687
in *Chicago* paper, 764
in MLA paper, 589
Signal phrases
APA style, 687–91
building credibility with (writer's
choice), 515
Chicago style, 765–68
in literary analysis papers, 180,
184
MLA style, 590–94
Simile, 274–75
Simple sentences, 520
Simple subjects, 500
Simple tenses, 351–52, 363, 366
since, 849

Singular vs. plural
  antecedents, 309–15
  nouns, 297–309, 345–48, 380, 382
  pronouns, 309–15
  subjects, 297–309, 345–48
sit. See *set, sit,* 849
site. See *cite, site,* 838
Skimming. *See* Previewing
Slang, avoiding, 261–62
Slash
  with lines of poetry, 182, 453
  with paired terms, 453
so
  comma with, 407–08
  as coordinating conjunction, 497
Social class, in literature, questions to ask about, 171
Social media, citing
  APA style, 700, 733–34
  Chicago style, 793–94
  MLA style, 608, 660–61
Social sciences, writing in, 108, 807–13. *See also* APA papers
Software. *See* Word processing programs
some, 302
somebody, someone (singular), 302, 310–11, 849
something (singular), 849
sometime, some time, sometimes, 849
Songs, titles of, quotation marks for, 441
sort of. See *kind of, sort of,* 845
Sound-alike words (homophones), 472–73
Sources
  citing. *See* Citing sources
  documenting. *See* APA papers; *Chicago* papers; MLA papers
  evaluating, 535–38, 552–68
    writing practice, 561
  finding, 533–39
  integrating, 73
    in APA papers, 683–93
    in *Chicago* papers, 762–68

  in literary analysis papers, 179–83
  in MLA papers, 585–97
  introducing. *See* Signal phrases
  keeping records of, 544
  list of. *See* Bibliography, *Chicago* style; Reference list (APA); Works cited list (MLA)
  online. *See* Web sources
  primary, 539, 559, 811
  and purpose of research project, 528–34, 553–54
  quoted in another source
    in APA papers, 701
    in *Chicago* papers, 778
    in MLA papers, 608, 622
  responsible use of. *See* Responsibility, with sources
  reviewer comments about, 43
  scholarly, 536, 539, 557
  secondary, 559, 811
  selecting, 554–57
  synthesizing
    in APA papers, 691–93
    in MLA papers, 584, 594–97
  uses of, 553–54
    in APA papers, 676–78
    in *Chicago* papers, 756–58
    in MLA papers, 572–74
  visuals, crediting, 32, 33
    in APA papers, 728–33, 738
    in *Chicago* papers, 790–91, 795–96
    in MLA papers, 648–57, 664
"So what?" test
  critical reading and, 100–02
  revision and, 50, 54
  thesis and, 21–24, 109, 571
Spacecraft, italics for names of, 465
Spacing. *See* Line spacing
Specific nouns, 270
  the with, 380–83
Speeches, 166
Spelling, 466–75
Split infinitives, 215–16

Sponsor, of Web sources
in *Chicago* notes and bibliography, 786
evaluating, 562
identifying, 535, 537–38
in MLA works cited list, 616
Squinting modifiers, 214. *See also* Misplaced modifiers
Standard English, 261–62
Standard (US) units, abbreviations for, 458–59, 460
statistics (singular), 307
Statistics
in APA papers, 689–90
in argument papers, 153
in *Chicago* papers, 767–68
integrating, 73
in MLA papers, 593, 597
numerals for, 462
in social science papers, 811
Stereotypes, avoiding, 133–34, 267–68
Straw man fallacy, 144
Student essays. *See* Sample student writing
Style. *See* Writer's choice boxes
Subject, of paper. *See* Topic
Subject, of sentence
and agreement with verb, 297–309
case of, 322
complete, 499–500
compound, 500
following verb, 245–46, 304–05, 390–91, 501, 507
identifying, 305
of infinitive, 324–25
naming the actor (active voice), 193–98, 507
naming the receiver (passive voice), 193–98, 507–08
pronoun as, 322
in questions, 501, 506
repeated, 391–92
required in sentences, 390–91
separated from verb, 214–15
simple, 500

singular vs. plural, 297–309
understood (*you*), 390, 501, 506
Subject complements
adjectives as, 333, 503
case of pronouns as, 322
defined, 502
with linking verbs, 502–03
and subject-verb agreement, 305
Subjective case, of pronouns, 322
who vs. *whom*, 328–31, 852
Subjects, of field research, 540
Subject-verb agreement. *See* Agreement of subject and verb
Subjunctive mood, 356–58. *See also* Conditional sentences
Subordinate clauses, 514, 516–19
adjective (beginning with *who*, *that*, etc.), 516
adverb (beginning with *if*, *when*, *where*, etc.), 517–18
avoiding repeated elements in, 392–93
defined, 514, 520
fragmented, 281–82
with independent clauses, 521
minor ideas in, 231, 238–39
misplaced, 213–14
noun, 518–19
and sentence types, 521
words introducing, 497–98, 516–18
Subordinate word groups, 508–19
Subordinating conjunctions, 497–98, 517
Subordination
for combining ideas of unequal importance, 230, 234, 236–37
and coordination, 232, 236–37
for emphasis, 231
for fixing choppy sentences, 230, 232
for fixing run-on sentences, 294
for fixing sentence fragments, 281–85
of major ideas, avoiding, 238–39

Subordination (*cont.*)
    overuse of, 239
    writer's choice, 231
Subtitles of works
    capitalizing, 481
        APA style, 481, 705, 736,
            739–40
        Chicago style, 795
        MLA style, 616, 663
    colon between title and, 433
such as
    no colon after, 434
    no comma after, 426
    and sentence fragments, 284–85
Suffixes
    hyphen before, 477
    spelling rules for, 466
Summary
    acceptable and unacceptable
        in APA papers, 681–82
        in *Chicago* papers, 760–61
        in MLA papers, 580–83
    vs. analysis, 106–07, 110, 124–25
    in annotated bibliographies,
        567–68
    integrating
        in APA papers, 684, 687–91
        in *Chicago* papers, 765–68
        MLA papers, 585–86,
            590–94, 597
    in literary analysis papers, 177,
        186–87
    no quotation marks for, 440
    and note taking, 547–48, 549
    outlining a text for, 102–03,
        120–21
    writing, 104–05, 121–23
        how-to guide, 123
superior to (not *than*), 272
Superlative form of adjectives and
    adverbs (with *-est* or *most*),
    336–37. *See also* Comparative
    form of adjectives and adverbs
    (with *-er* or *more*)
Support. *See* Evidence
suppose to (nonstandard), 850

sure and (nonstandard), 272, 850
Surveys, as information source,
    15–16, 541
Syllables, division of words into
    in dictionary, 471
    hyphen for, 477–78
Synonyms, 269–70, 471–72
Synthesizing sources
    in APA papers, 691–93
    in argument papers, 132, 146–47
    engagement and, 1, 527
    how-to guide, 532
    in MLA papers, 584, 594–97
    in research proposals, 542
    responsibility and, 584

T

Tables, 32, 34. *See also* Visuals, in
        documents
    in APA papers, 731, 738, 745
    in *Chicago* papers, 795–96
    in MLA papers, 656–57, 664
take. See bring, take, 838
Taking notes. *See* Note taking
Talking and listening
    to generate ideas, 1, 17–18,
        168–69
    to improve English-language skills,
        361
    in oral presentations, 166
Talking back to a text, 99–102, 118,
    119
teach. See learn, teach, 845
Teacher's comments, responding to.
    See Revising with comments
team. See Collective nouns
Teamwork. *See* Peer review
Tenses, verb, 351–56
    in active voice, 363–65
    and agreement with subject,
        297–309
    in APA papers, 355, 688, 695
    avoiding shifts in, 178, 180–81,
        223–24
    in *Chicago* papers, 765

conditional, 372–74
in the disciplines, 813
in literary analysis papers, 178,
    180–81, 354, 813
in MLA papers, 223–24, 354, 591
multilingual/ESL challenges with,
    362–65, 372–74
in passive voice, 366–67
present
    in summaries, 105, 121, 123
    in writing about literature, 178,
        180–81, 224, 354, 813
    in writing about science, 354
sequence of, 355–56
Text messages, MLA citation of, 660
Texts. *See* Multimodal texts; Written
    texts
than
    in comparisons, 206–07
    parallelism with, 202
    pronoun after, 324
than, then, 850
that
    agreement of verb with, 306
    broad reference of, 316–17
    needed word, 202–03, 205
    vs. *which,* 415, 850, 852
    vs. *who,* 319. See also *who, which,
        that,* 852
the. See also a, an
    with geographic names, 387–88
    multilingual/ESL challenges with,
        378–89
    omission of, 207, 387–88
    with proper nouns, 387–88
their
    misuse of, with singular
        antecedent, 220–23, 310–11,
        313, 850
    vs. *there, they're,* 850
    vs. *they,* 850
theirselves (nonstandard), 850
Theme, in literature, questions to ask
    about, 171
them vs. *they,* 321–27
them vs. *those,* 850

then, than. See *than, then,* 850
the number, a number, 304
there, as expletive (placeholder)
    not used as subject, 391
    and sentence order (verb before
        subject), 390–91, 501, 507
    and subject-verb agreement,
        304–05
    with verb, 390–91
    and wordy sentences, 253
therefore
    comma with, 417–18
    semicolon with, 428–29
there, their, they're, 850
Thesis
    active reading for, 102–03
    in analysis papers, 107–11, 126
    in APA papers, 674–78
    in argument papers, 149–50, 164
    audience and, 20–24
    in *Chicago* papers, 755–58
    developing, 19–25
    drafting, 20–21
    effective, 19, 22–23, 107–09, 126
    in essays, 19–25, 28–30, 51, 54
    evaluating, 21–24
    how-to guides
        drafting an analytical thesis
            statement, 109
        drafting an argumentative thesis
            statement, 151
        solving common thesis
            problems, 22–23
    in literary analysis papers,
        172–75
    in MLA papers, 570–77
        writing practice, 571
    revising, 21–24, 54
        writing practice, 25
    testing, 21–24
        for argument papers, 151
        in critical reading, 101–02
        for MLA papers, 571
    working, 19–25
        in APA papers, 675
        in *Chicago* papers, 755–58

Thesis (*cont.*)
  working (*cont.*)
    in literary analysis papers,
      172–75
    in MLA papers, 570–71
  writing practice, 25, 571
they
  indefinite reference of, 318
  vs. *I* or *you*, 220–23
  misuse of, with singular
    antecedent, 220–23, 310–11,
    313, 850
  nonstandard for *their*, 850
  vs. *them*, 321–27
they're. See *there, their, they're,*
  850
think of, about (not *on*), 272
Third-person point of view, 54,
  220–23, 813
this, broad reference of, 316–17
this kind. See *kind(s)*, 845
Time
  abbreviations for, 458
  colon with, 433
  managing, 525, 527–29
  numerals for, 462
Title page
  for APA paper
    formatting, 735, 826
    sample, 741, 826
  for *Chicago* paper
    formatting, 794
    sample, 798
  for MLA paper (optional)
    formatting, 663
Titles of persons
  abbreviations with names, 457
  capitalizing, 480
  comma with, 420
Titles of works
  capitalizing, 481
    APA style, 481, 705, 736,
      739–40
    Chicago style, 795
    MLA style, 616, 663

  italics for, 463–64
    APA style, 705, 736, 739–40
    Chicago style, 795
    MLA style, 616, 663
  in literary analysis papers, 178
  quotation marks for, 441
    APA style, 705, 736, 739–40
    Chicago style, 795
    MLA style, 616, 663
  treated as singular, 307
to
  needed word, 202–03
  as preposition vs. infinitive marker,
    400–01
Tone (voice). *See also* Language
  in APA paper, 683
  in argument paper, 149
  in e-mail, 833
  in MLA paper, 576–77
  in portfolio cover letter, 70
  revising for, 50–51
too, with infinitive, 377–78
Topic
  big picture for, 527–28
  caring about, 2, 8, 526
  choosing, 2, 526
  curiosity and, 1, 2
  exploring, 2, 8, 17–19
  narrowing, 8, 527, 530–31
  of research paper, 527–32
  working thesis and, 20–21
  writing situation and, 6, 8
Topic sentence, 52–53, 72–73, 176
to, too, two, 850
toward, towards, 850
Transfer fallacy, 140
Transitional expressions, 429
  commas with, 417–18
  semicolon with, 428–29
Transitions, for coherence, 87–91
Transitive verbs, 367, 503, 507–08
Trite expressions. *See* Clichés
try and (nonstandard), 272, 851
Tutorials. *See* How-to guides; Writing
  guides

Tutors, working with. *See* Peer review
Twitter. *See* Social media, citing
two. See *to, too, two*, 850
type of (not *of a*), 272
Types of writing. *See* Genre (type of writing)
Typing. *See* Document design; Manuscript formats

U

ultimately. See *eventually, ultimately*, 841
Underlining. *See* Italics
Understood subject (*you*), 390, 501, 506
uninterested. See *disinterested, uninterested*, 840
unique, 337, 851
Units of measurement. *See* Measurement, units of
Unity. *See* Focus
Universal types (archetypes), in literature, questions to ask about, 172
Unmarked infinitives, 377
Uploaded materials, MLA citation of, 620–21, 652–53, 658–59
URLs
  in citations
    APA style, 706
    Chicago style, 772, 782
    MLA style, 617
  dividing, 478
    APA style, 740
    Chicago style, 772, 796
    MLA style, 664, 665
  evaluating, 535, 537–38
usage, 851
Usage
  glossary of, 834–52
  labels in dictionary, 472
use to (nonstandard), 851
US standard units, abbreviations for, 458–59, 460

us vs. *we*, 321–27
utilize, 851

V

Variety
  in sentences, 242–47
    writer's choice, 244
  in signal phrases
    APA style, 691
    Chicago style, 766
    MLA style, 590
Verbal phrases, 510–14
  fragmented, 283
  gerund, 512
  infinitive, 512–13
  participial, 511–12
Verbs. *See also* Verbs, types of
  active, 193–98, 363–65, 507–08
  adverbs with, 494–95
  agreement with subjects, 297–309
  avoiding shifts in tense, mood, voice, 223–24
  be, forms of, vs. active, 194, 196
  compound predicates, 284
  in conditional sentences, 372–74
  -d, -ed ending on, 340, 348–49
  defined, 491
  followed by gerunds or infinitives, 375–78
  forms of, 362–65, 371–72
  mood of, 356–58
  multilingual/ESL challenges with. *See* Multilingual writers, verbs
  needed, 350
  negative forms of, 371–72
  without objects, 504–05
  passive, 193–98, 365–68, 507–08
  with prepositions (idioms), 402–03
  separated from subjects, 214–15
  -s form of, 297, 299, 345–46
  in signal phrases
    APA style, 688, 691
    Chicago style, 765–66
    MLA style, 590

Verbs (*cont.*)
  with singular vs. plural subjects, 345–48
  standard forms of, 340–44
  strong, vs. *be* and passive verbs, 193–98, 253
  before subjects (inverted sentence), 245–46, 304–05, 390–91, 501
  tenses of. *See* Tenses, verb
  two-word, 492–93
  voice of (active, passive), 193–98, 363–67, 507–08
Verbs, types of. *See also* Verbs
  helping. *See* Helping verbs
  intransitive (no direct object), 504–05
  irregular, 340–45, 362, 492
  linking, 333, 390, 502–03
  main, 350, 351–58, 368, 492–93
  modal (*can, should*, etc.). *See* Modal verbs
  phrasal. *See* Particles, with verbs
  regular, 340, 348–49, 362, 492
  transitive (with direct object), 367, 503, 507–08
Video, online, citing. *See also* Multimodal texts
  APA style, 728–29
  Chicago style, 790
  MLA style, 620–21, 649, 652–53
Video game, citing
  APA style, 731–32
  MLA style, 649–50
Visuals, in documents. *See also* Multimodal texts
  choosing, 32, 34–35
  citing, 32–33
    APA style, 728–33
    Chicago style, 790–91
    MLA style, 648–57
  in document design, 829
  as evidence, 154, 811
  labeling
    APA style, 738, 829
    Chicago style, 795–96

  MLA style, 664, 668
  purposes for, 32, 34–35, 154
  types of (bar graph, flowchart, etc.), 32, 34–35
Visual sources. *See* Multimedia sources, citing; Visuals, in documents
Visual texts (photo, ad, etc.). *See* Multimodal texts; Visuals, in documents
Vocabulary, specialized, 257, 812
Voice. *See also* Tone (voice)
  active (preferred), 193–98, 503, 507–08
  avoiding shifts between active and passive, 225
  choosing active or passive, 194, 195
  passive, 194, 365–68
  transforming active to passive, 507–08
  writer's choice, 195
Volume and issue numbers,
  in APA reference list, 706
  in MLA works cited list, 615

W

wait for, wait on, 851
was vs. *were*
  in conditional sentences, 372–74
  and subject-verb agreement, 298, 348
  and subjunctive mood, 356–58
ways, 851
we
  vs. *us*, 321–27
  vs. *you* or *they*, 220–23
weather, whether, 851
Web sources. *See also* Electronic documents; Internet; Multimodal texts
  abstracts of, 539, 557–58
  authors of, identifying, 620–21
  avoiding plagiarism from, 540, 544, 550

citation at a glance
  APA style, 714–15, 726–27
  Chicago style, 782–83, 792–93
  MLA style, 626–27, 646–47
citing
  APA style, 710–15, 724–34
  Chicago style, 771–94
  MLA style, 622–35, 643–57
  course materials, 658–59
  databases for, 535, 536, 554–55
  evaluating, 535–38, 555, 561–65
    writing practice, 561
  finding, 535–38
  how-to guides
    avoiding plagiarism from the Web, 550
    citing course materials (MLA style), 658–59
    citing a reposted source (MLA style), 652–53
    going beyond a Google search, 536
    identifying authors, 620
    summarizing a multimodal text, 123
  keeping records of, 544
  library catalog for, 535, 555
  previewing, 527–28, 556
  reading, 104
  reposted sources, citing (MLA style), 652–53
  scanning, 555
  search engines for, 535–36, 538
  selecting appropriate versions of, 557–58
  writing practice, 561
well, good, 335. See also *good, well,* 842
were, in conditional sentences, 356–58, 372–74
were vs. *was.* See *was* vs. *were*
when clauses, 356–57, 372–74
where vs. *that,* 851
whether. See *if, whether,* 844; *weather, whether,* 851

whether . . . or, 201, 497
which
  agreement of verb with, 306
  broad reference of, 316–17
  vs. *that,* 415, 850, 852
  vs. *who,* 319. See also *who, which, that,* 852
while, 851
who
  agreement of verb with, 306
  omission of, 204–05
  vs. *which* or *that,* 319. See also *who, which, that,* 852
  vs. *whom,* 328–31, 852
who's, whose, 438, 472, 852
who, which, that, 852
will, as modal verb, 350, 368, 370, 491–92
will, shall. See *shall, will,* 849
Wishes, subjunctive mood for, 358
Word groups. *See* Independent clauses; Phrases; Subordinate clauses
Wordiness, 251–55
Word processing programs
  and automatic division of words, 477–78
  and double-entry notebooks, 99–100
  and keeping track of files, 37–38, 544
Words. *See also* Language; Spelling
  abstract vs. concrete, 270
  antonyms (opposites), 471–72
  colloquial, 263, 472
  compound, 471, 475–76
  confused, 270–71. *See also* Glossary of usage
  connotation and denotation of, 269–70
  division of, 471, 477–78
  foreign, italics for, 465
  general vs. specific, 270, 380, 382
  homophones (sound-alike), 472–73
  invented, 260–61

Words (*cont.*)
  jargon, 256–58
  meaning of, 269–70, 471–72
  misuse of, 270–71
  needed. *See* Needed words
  obsolete, 260–61
  origin of (etymology), 471–72
  prefixes (beginnings of), 477
  sound-alike (homophones),
    472–73
  spelling of, 466–75
  suffixes (endings of), 466, 477
  synonyms (words with similar
    meanings), 269–70, 471–72
  unnecessary repetition of,
    251–52
  using your own. *See* Paraphrases;
    Summary
  as words
    italics for, 465
    plural of, 437
    quotation marks for, 442
    treated as singular, 307
Work in an anthology. *See* Anthology
  or collection, citing
Working bibliography. *See also*
  Annotated bibliography
  information for, 37
  maintaining, 543–44, 545
  research log for, 543
Working thesis. *See* Thesis, working
Works cited list (MLA)
  directory to models for, 611–13
  formatting, 665, 825
  general guidelines for, 615–17
  models for, 613–61
  sample, 163, 190, 672–73, 825
would, as modal verb, 350, 368, 370,
    491–92
would of (nonstandard), 852
Writer's choice boxes
  appositives, for credibility, 515
  discipline-specific terms, 257
  emphasis, 231, 291
  jargon, 257

  point of view (*I*, *you*, *they*, etc.),
    221
  position of major and minor ideas,
    231
  run-on sentences, 291
  sentence variety, 244
  signal phrases, 515
  subordination, 231
  verbs, voice of, 195
  voice, active or passive, 195
writes, comma with, 419, 444
Writing guides
  analytical essay, 110–11
  annotated bibliography, 567–68
  argument essay, 164–65
  literacy narrative, 63–64
  reflective letter for a portfolio,
    70–71
Writing in the disciplines, 807–21.
    See also Academic reading and
    writing; Genre (types of writing)
  analysis and, 108
  asking questions, 808–10
  assignments and excerpts
    business proposal, 816–17
    lab report, 818–19
    nursing practice paper, 820–21
    psychology literature review,
      814–16
  choosing a citation style, 812
  evidence for, 810–11
  language conventions, 257, 812,
    813
  writer's choice, 257
Writing practice prompts
  active reading, 102, 120, 146
  analysis, 112
  arguments, evaluating, 146
  multimodal texts, 120
  peer review, 46, 62, 112
  revision, 62, 112
  sources, evaluating, 561
  sources, searching for, 538
  thesis, working, 25, 571
  transitions, 91

Writing process
  drafting, 28–37
  editing, 38, 55–56, 57
  planning, 5–38
  reviewing, 38–49
  revising, 49–55
  as social activity, 1, 38–39
Writing situation, 5–17
Writing tutors, working with. *See* Peer review
Written texts. *See also* Literature, writing about; Reading
  analyzing, 95–114
  annotating, 97–99, 101, 548
  conversing with, 99–101
  engagement with, 96, 98, 130–46, 167–68
  evaluating, 130–46, 535–38, 552–68
  outlining, 102–03
  sample papers analyzing, 112–14, 188–90

summarizing, 104–05
writing about, 104–11, 807–08

Y

yes, no, commas with, 419
yet
  comma before, 407–08
  as coordinating conjunction, 497
you
  appropriate use of, 220–22, 318
  avoiding shifts in point of view, 220–23
  inappropriate use of, 318–19, 852
  vs. *I* or *they*, 220–23
  understood, 390, 501, 506
  writer's choice, 221
your, you're, 852
YouTube. *See* Video, online, citing

Multilingual Menu

A complete section for multilingual writers:

Multilingual and Academic English notes in other sections:

VI Multilingual Writers and ESL Challenges

28 Verbs   361
a Form and tense   362
b Passive voice   365
c Base form after modal   368
d Negative forms   371
e Conditional sentences   372
f With gerunds or infinitives   375

29 Articles (*a, an, the*)   378
a Articles and other noun markers   378
b When to use *the*   380
c When to use *a* or *an*   384
d When not to use *a* or *an*   384
e Not with general nouns   386
f With proper nouns   387

30 Sentence structure   389
a Linking verb with subject and complement   390
b Omitted subjects   390
c Repeated nouns, pronouns   391
d Repeated subjects, objects, adverbs   392
e Mixed constructions   394
f Adverb placement   395
g Present and past participles   396
h Order of adjectives   397

31 Prepositions and idiomatic expressions   399
a *at, on, in*   399
b Noun (and *-ing* form) after preposition   400
c Adjective + preposition   401
d Verb + preposition   402

I The Writing Process
The writing situation   7
Using a direct approach   30
Choosing transitions   88

II Academic Reading and Writing
Avoiding hasty generalizations   133
Making an argument   149

III Clear Sentences
Passive voice   193
Missing words   204
Articles   207
Double subjects, repeated objects   210
Adverb placement   215
Repeated objects or adverbs   232

IV Word Choice
Idioms   272

V Grammatical Sentences
Omitted subjects, verbs   281
Pronoun-antecedent gender agreement   309
Adjective and adverb placement   332
No plural adjectives   332
Omitted verbs   350
Verb tenses   353

VIII Mechanics
American and British spelling   468

X Researched Writing
Recognizing intellectual property   547
Summarizing and paraphrasing   549

A List of Charts

I   The Writing Process

Checklist for assessing the writing situation	6–7
Understanding an assignment	11
Considering audience when writing e-mail messages	13
How to solve five common problems with thesis statements	22–23
Strategies for drafting an introduction	30
Choosing visuals to suit your purpose	34–35
Strategies for drafting a conclusion	36
Strategies for revising with comments	42–43
How to write helpful peer review comments	44
Checklist for global revision	54
How to improve your writing with an editing log	57
Writing guide: How to write a literacy narrative	63–64
Writing guide: How to write a reflective letter	70–71
Common transitions	89

II   Academic Reading and Writing

Guidelines for active reading	101
Reading online	104
Guidelines for writing a summary	105
How to draft an analytical thesis statement	109
Writing guide: How to write an analytical essay	110–11
How to write a summary of a multimodal text	123
Guidelines for analyzing a multimodal text	124
Testing inductive reasoning	135
Evaluating ethical, logical, and emotional appeals as a reader	141–42
Checklist for reading and evaluating arguments	145
Using ethical, logical, and emotional appeals as a writer	148
How to draft a thesis statement for an argument	151
Anticipating and countering objections	156
Writing guide: How to write an argument essay	164–65
Questions to ask about literature	171–72

III   Clear Sentences

Writer's choice: Using the active or the passive voice	195
Checking for dangling modifiers	218
Writer's choice: Choosing a point of view	221
Writer's choice: Positioning major and minor ideas	231
Using coordination to combine sentences of equal importance	233

A List of Charts, continued

Using subordination to combine sentences of unequal importance 234
Writer's choice: Strengthening with variety 244

IV Word Choice

Writer's choice: Using discipline-specific terms 257

V Grammatical Sentences

Test for fragments 280
Recognizing run-on sentences 289
Writer's choice: Clustering ideas in meaningful ways 291
Subject-verb agreement at a glance 298
When to use the -s (or -es) form of a present-tense verb 299
Choosing a revision strategy that avoids sexist language 313
Checking for problems with *who* and *whom* 331

VI Multilingual Writers and ESL Challenges

Basic verb forms 362
Verb tenses commonly used in the active voice 363–65
Verb tenses commonly used in the passive voice 366–67
Modals and their meanings 369–70
Types of nouns 381–82
Choosing articles for common nouns 385
Commonly used noncount nouns 386
Using *the* with geographic nouns 388
Order of cumulative adjectives 398
At, *on*, and *in* to show time and place 401
Adjective + preposition combinations 402
Verb + preposition combinations 403

IX Grammar Basics

Writer's choice: Building credibility with appositives 515
Words that introduce subordinate clauses 517

X Researched Writing

Thinking like a researcher 527
Testing a research question 531
How to enter a research conversation 532
How to go beyond a Google search 536
Tips for smart searching 539
Information to collect for a working bibliography 545–46

A List of Charts, continued

How to avoid plagiarizing from the Web 550
Viewing evaluation as a process 553
Determining if a source is scholarly 557
Evaluating all sources 560
Evaluating sources you find on the Web 562
Writing guide: How to write an annotated bibliography 567–68
Testing your thesis 571
How to be a responsible research writer 583

MLA

Using signal phrases in MLA papers 590
Reviewing an MLA paper: Use of sources 597
Directory to MLA in-text citation models 599
Directory to MLA works cited models 611–13
General guidelines for the works cited list 615–17
How to answer the basic question "Who is the author?" 620–21
MLA citation at a glance: Article in a journal 624–25
MLA citation at a glance: Article from a database 626–27
MLA citation at a glance: Book 636
MLA citation at a glance: Selection from an anthology or a collection 640–41
MLA citation at a glance: Short work from a Web site 646–47
How to cite a source reposted from another source 652–53
How to cite course materials 658–59

APA

Using signal phrases in APA papers 691
Directory to APA in-text citation models 694
Directory to APA reference list models 702–03
General guidelines for the reference list 704–06
APA citation at a glance: Article in a journal or magazine 712–13
APA citation at a glance: Article from a database 714–15
APA citation at a glance: Book 720
APA citation at a glance: Section in a Web document 726–27

Chicago

Using signal phrases in *Chicago* papers 766
Directory to *Chicago*-style notes and bibliography entries 769–70
Chicago citation at a glance: Book 776–77
Chicago citation at a glance: Article in a journal 780–81
Chicago citation at a glance: Article from a database 782–83
Chicago citation at a glance: Letter in a published collection 788–89
Chicago citation at a glance: Primary source from a Web site 792–93

XI Writing in the Disciplines

Evidence typically used in various disciplines 811
Point of view and verb tense in academic writing 813

Revision Symbols

Boldface numbers refer to sections of the handbook.

abbr	abbreviation	**40**
add	add needed word	**10**
adj	misuse of adjective	**26**
adv	misuse of adverb	**26**
agr	agreement	**21, 22**
appr	inappropriate language	**17**
art	article (*a, an, the*)	**29**
awk	awkward	
cap	capital letter	**45**
case	pronoun case	**24, 25**
cliché	cliché	**18e**
coh	coherence	**3d**
coord	coordination	**14**
cs	comma splice	**20**
dev	inadequate development	**3b**
dm	dangling modifier	**12e**
-ed	*-ed* ending	**27d**
emph	emphasis	**14**
ESL	English as a second language, multilingual	**28–31**
exact	inexact language	**18**
frag	sentence fragment	**19**
fs	fused sentence	**20**
gl/us	see glossary of usage	
hyph	hyphen	**44**
idiom	idioms	**18d, 31**
inc	incomplete construction	**10**
irreg	irregular verb	**27a**
ital	italics	**42**
jarg	jargon	**17a**
lc	lowercase	**45**
mix	mixed construction	**11**
mm	misplaced modifier	**12a–d**
mood	mood of verb	**27g**
nonst	nonstandard usage	**17d, 27**
num	use of numbers	**41**
om	omitted word	**10, 29, 30a–b**

p	punctuation	
^,	comma	**32**
no ,	no comma	**33**
;	semicolon	**34**
:	colon	**35**
’	apostrophe	**36**
“ ”	quotation marks	**37**
. ?	period, question mark	**38a–b**
!	exclamation point	**38c**
— ( )	dash, parentheses	**39a–b**
[ ] . . .	brackets, ellipsis mark	**39c–d**
/	slash	**39e**
¶	new paragraph	**3e**
pass	ineffective passive	**8**
pn agr	pronoun agreement	**22**
proof	proofreading problem	**2g**
ref	pronoun reference	**23**
run-on	run-on sentence	**20**
-s	*-s* ending	**21, 27c**
sexist	sexist language	**17f, 22a**
shift	distracting shift	**13**
sl	slang	**17d**
sp	misspelled word	**43**
sub	subordination	**14**
sv agr	subject-verb agreement	**21, 27c**
t	verb tense	**27f, 28a**
trans	transition needed	**3d**
usage	see glossary of usage	
v	voice	**8a, 28b**
var	lack of variety in sentence structure	**14, 15**
vb	verb problem	**27, 28**
w	wordy	**16**
//	parallelism	**9**
^	insert	
#	insert space	
⁐	close up space	

A List of Grammatical Terms

Boldface numbers refer to sections of the handbook.

absolute phrase **48d**

active voice **8a, 47c**

adjective **46d**

adjective clause **48e**

adverb **46e**

adverb clause **48e**

agreement **21, 22**

antecedent **22, 23, 46b**

appositive phrase **48c**

article (*a, an, the*) **29**

case **24, 25**

clause **48e, 49a**

comparative **26d**

complement **47b**

complete subject **47a**

complex sentence **49a**

compound-complex sentence **49a**

compound sentence **49a**

compound subject **47a**

conjunction **46g**

conjunctive adverb **46g**

coordinating conjunction **46g**

correlative conjunction **46g**

demonstrative pronoun **46b**

dependent clause (*See* subordinate clause.)

determiner **29**

direct object **47b**

expletive **47a, 47c**

future tense **27f**

gerund **48b**

gerund phrase **48b**

helping verb **46c**

indefinite pronoun **46b**

independent clause **49a**

indirect object **47b**

infinitive **48b**

infinitive phrase **48b**

intensive pronoun **46b**

interjection **46h**

interrogative pronoun **46b**

intransitive verb **47b**

inverted sentence pattern **47a**

irregular verb **27a**

linking verb **47b**

main clause (*See* independent clause.)

main verb **46c**

modal **28c, 46c**

mood **27g**

noun **46a**

noun/adjective **46a**

noun clause **48e**

object complement **47b**

object of a preposition **48a**

particle **46c**

participial phrase **48b**

participle, present and past **27a, 30g, 46c**

parts of speech **46**

passive voice **8a, 47c**

past tense **27f**

perfect tense **27f**

personal pronoun **46b**

possessive pronoun **46b**

predicate **47**

predicate adjective (*See* subject complement.)

predicate noun (*See* subject complement.)

preposition **46f**

prepositional phrase **46f, 48a**

present tense **27f**

progressive forms **27f**

pronoun **46b**

pronoun/adjective **46b**

reciprocal pronoun **46b**

reflexive pronoun **46b**

regular verb **27a, 46c**

relative adverb **48e**

relative pronoun **46b, 48e**

-s form of verb **21, 27c**

sentence patterns **47**

sentence types **49**

simple sentence **49a**

simple subject **47a**

subject **47a**

subject complement **47b**

subordinate clause **48e**

subordinate word group **48**

subordinating conjunction **46g, 48e**

superlative **26d**

tense **27f**

transitive verb **47b**

understood subject **47a**

verb **27, 28, 46c, 47b**

verbal phrase **48b**

Detailed Menu

I The Writing Process 3

1 Explore, plan, draft plan, draft 5

2 Revise, edit, reflect rev 38
SAMPLE LITERACY NARRATIVE 59
Writing guide: Literacy narrative 63
SAMPLE REFLECTIVE LETTER 66
Writing guide: Reflective letter 70

3 Paragraphs par 72

II Academic Reading and Writing 93

4 Reading and writing critically texts 95
Writing guide: Analytical essay 110
SAMPLE ANALYSIS (ARTICLE) 112

5 Reading and writing about multimodal texts texts 115
SAMPLE ANALYSIS (ADVERTISEMENT) 127

6 Reading and writing arguments arg 130
SAMPLE ARGUMENT 158
Writing guide: Argument essay 164

7 Reading and writing about literature lit 167
SAMPLE LITERARY ANALYSIS 188

III Clear Sentences 191

8 Active verbs active 193
a versus passive verbs
b versus be verbs
c actor as subject

9 Parallelism // 198
a series
b pairs
c repeated words

10 Needed words add 204
a compound structures
b that
c in comparisons
d a, an, and the

11 Mixed constructions mix 208
a mixed grammar
b illogical connections
c is when etc.

12 Misplaced and dangling modifiers mm/dm 212
a limiting modifiers
b misplaced modifiers
c awkward placement
d split infinitives
e dangling modifiers

13 Shifts shift 220
a person, number
b tense
c mood, voice
d indirect to direct discourse

14 Emphasis emph 228
a coordination and subordination
b choppy sentences
c ineffective coordination
d ineffective subordination
e excessive subordination
f other techniques

15 Variety var 242

IV Word Choice 249

16 Wordy sentences w 251

17 Appropriate language appr 256
a jargon
b pretentious style
c obsolete, invented words
d slang, nonstandard English
e levels of formality
f sexist language
g offensive language

18 Exact words exact 268
a connotations
b concrete nouns
c misused words
d standard idioms
e clichés
f figures of speech

V Grammatical Sentences 277

19 Sentence fragments frag 279
a subordinate clauses
b phrases
c other word groups
d acceptable fragments

20 Run-on sentences run-on 287
a correction with and, but, etc.
b with semicolon, colon, or dash
c by separating sentences
d by restructuring

21 Subject-verb agreement sv agr 297
a standard forms
b words between subject and verb
c subjects with and
d subjects with or, nor
e indefinite pronouns
f collective nouns
g subject after verb
h subject complement
i who, which, that
j plural form
k titles, words as words

22 Pronoun-antecedent agreement pn agr 309
a indefinite pronouns, generic nouns
b collective nouns
c with and
d with or, nor

23 Pronoun reference ref 315
a ambiguous, remote reference
b broad this, that, which, it
c implied antecedents
d indefinite they, it, you
e who for persons

24 Pronoun case case 321
a subjective case
b objective case
c appositives
d after than, as
e we, us before a noun